WORLD HISTORY
IN
DOCUMENTS

WORLD HISTORY
IN
DOCUMENTS

·

A COMPARATIVE READER

·

Edited by Peter N. Stearns

NEW YORK UNIVERSITY PRESS
New York and London

NEW YORK UNIVERSITY PRESS
New York and London

Library of Congress Cataloging-in-Publication Data
World history in documents : a comparative reader / edited by Peter N. Stearns.
p.   cm.
Includes index.
ISBN 0-8147-8106-3 (clothbound : alk. paper).—ISBN
0-8147-8107-1 (pbk. : alk. paper)
1. World history—Sources.   I. Stearns, Peter N.
D5.W67   1998   98-7693
909—dc21   CIP

New York University Press books are printed on acid-free paper,
and their binding materials are chosen for strength and durability.

Manufactured in the United States of America

10 9 8 7 6 5 4 3 2 1

CONTENTS

ACKNOWLEDGMENTS

Assistance from Steven Beaudoin and Carl Zimring, both experienced world history teachers, was invaluable. Karen Callas assured vital clerical support. Several colleagues, including Andrew Barnes, Erick Langer, Michael Adas, Donald Sutton and Abraham Marcus, provided very useful suggestions. I wish to thank also what is now several generations of world history students at Carnegie Mellon University, whose interest and good ideas continue to motivate and educate me.

INTRODUCTION

Comparative World History

This book compares different societies during the major periods of world history, from early river valley civilizations to the late twentieth century. Although it emphasizes various materials drawn from the relevant periods in the world's past, it differs from a regular textbook and may be used as a companion to a basic textbook. Like a good text, it aims for a global span, drawing on societies that developed on five continents. But in contrast to most texts, this volume emphasizes a number of key topics rather than broadly summing up historical developments.

In establishing a distinctive entrée to world history in conjunction with more standard fare, the book has three goals: first, to challenge the reader to interpret primary sources and build historical arguments from them; second, to emphasize comparisons, by which key features—both contrasts and commonalities—can be established and assessed; third, to deal with change over time. This classic goal is served first by defining key periods in world history, so that readers can use sources and comparisons to discuss changing world frameworks. Major societies initially operated in considerable isolation, which thus requires comparison around similar functions but separate origins. Traces of this separateness persist to this day. The reasons that twentieth-century China embraced Communism but the Middle East did not, go back, in part, to distinctions in cultures and political systems established 1,500–2,500 years ago, when these regions formed their own identities. With the passage of time—and particularly from about 500 C.E.* onward—major societies accelerated mutual contacts and exchanges. By the fifteenth and sixteenth centuries contacts intensified still further. Even in the twentieth century, however, reactions to global contacts varied in the major civilizations, making comparison a vital analytical method in ongoing world history.

*The designation C.E. means "of the common era"; B.C.E. means "before the common era." B.C.E. technically starts from the beginning of time and moves to the conventional date for the birth of Christ. Many world historians prefer this term to the Christian B.C. ("before Christ"), but it covers the same time period, as do C.E. and the Christian A.D. (*anno domini* or "in the year of the Lord"). The first century B.C.E. (100–1 B.C.E.) comes right before the first century C.E. (1–100); there was no year zero.

Primary Sources

This book's first emphasis is on primary sources, that is, documents written for the time, and not intended, like a textbook, to explicitly inform current college students of world history. These primary sources, drawn from religious treatises, government pronouncements, economic regulations, and the like, require careful interpretation in order to figure out what the historical significance of the material is. The sources must be not only read; they must be assessed and recombined, so that they can be used to answer historical questions that go beyond merely repeating what the document said. Thus, a religious passage intended to define morality might be asked questions about gender—basic views concerning men and women—that the author was not fully aware of. Or a company record listing the daily obligations of factory workers might be expected to reveal the fundamental definitions of the nature of work. Through sources of this sort, the volume deals with various facets of modern civilizations in Asia, Africa, Europe, and the Americas, ranging from the growth of governments and the impact of new science to the formation of novel work systems and the development of intense loyalties such as nationalism.

Reading a primary source requires some creative imagination, because the thinking behind it will almost never be just like your own. Words that appear to be the same as ours may have different meanings. It's useful to ask of each source, What are the key assumptions here, and which ones require the biggest stretch from current habits of thought? Different kinds of sources involve different interpretive tasks. Some are accounts of happenings; they need to be assessed for possible bias. Others are documents in action, such as a declaration of war or a treaty. These can be evaluated for assumptions, but a bias test is less relevant. In every case there is some subtlety of meaning to be discovered, with the aid of the contexts provided in the introductory notes to each chapter. The results can reach deeper into the notions of past societies than any other type of reading.

Grouping the materials in comparative settings actually helps focus the task of analyzing their meaning. Documents can be read to determine what two or more societies had in common, in an area such as religion or slave-holding, and what differentiated them. They also reveal how differently major societies can operate and still be "successful." The documents themselves do not do the task of comparing, for with rare exceptions they were not written with another society in mind. But comparison can guide the task of deriving meaning. Documents on Indian and African nationalism, for example, invite interpretations that will produce a sense of what some of the central features of nationalism were—the features conveyed by both sets of documents—and also a sense of how the two movements differed around the common nationalist dynamic.

Setting up documents for comparative analysis requires some understanding of why individual societies play such an important role in world history as a whole. Using the documents also demands an active awareness of what comparison itself involves. These two points must be addressed before we map some other features of this collection.

World History and Civilizations

Studying world history involves examining the evolution of major individual societies or civilizations. Major civilizations include those such as China or Western Europe that generated certain shared cultural values and political forms and that were usually organized around strong internal trading networks. Each civilization, in other words, established some coherence that gave its members a certain sense of identity—an ability to determine that other societies were different, that members of other civilizations were "outsiders"—and that created more intense internal than external contacts, for example in commercial exchanges. A major civilization did not necessarily have a single government—it might be composed of many separate kingdoms or nations—but its regions or nations, even when rivalrous, nevertheless shared certain values. Thus, Western Europe has almost always been politically divided, often convulsed in internal wars, yet it has gained some common features through its participation in Christianity and more modern shared cultures, plus mutual trade.

The evolution of major societies is not the only subject of world history. Important international developments, such as sweeping contagious diseases, migrations, missionary religions, and world trade, affect individual societies powerfully, and these developments demand careful attention in their own right. Yet international factors are usually handled through the institutions and beliefs of the individual civilizations. An epidemic disease thus may be interpreted quite differently by two separate societies, even though objectively it is the same disease, with approximately the same physical consequences. International trade opportunities may affect all societies, but some, because of prior culture, will attempt to limit the impact of such trade while others will embrace the opportunity to gain new contacts. China, historically, has been less open to international exchanges than has India, for both cultural and geographical reasons. Global factors, in other words, need to be understood as they filtered through partially separate civilizations—even when they reduced the distinctiveness and isolation of those civilizations.

Several obvious problems result from the need to approach much of world history from the standpoint of individual societies and their interaction. Not all societies can really be covered. People's ingenuity and diverse conditions have generated an immense array of human settlements. All contribute to our understanding of the possibilities of being human. Even very small groups—for example, the fifty-or-so people in the Utku group of Inuits, studied because they have a remarkable ability to avoid expressing or feeling anger—can be revealing. World history focuses, however, mainly on societies that managed to embrace fairly large populations. With the advent of agriculture and then civilization itself, it looks at civilizations precisely because they produced significant economic surpluses over sheer survival needs—which allowed greater differentiation of roles, including specialization in particular trades or in politics or religion, along with greater social inequality. With more formal government, economic specialization, and trade, the organization of civilizations helped increase population and embraced a larger agglomeration of people than almost all noncivilized societies. World history normally highlights these major civilizations, them, not because they held a monopoly on interesting forms of human activities, but simply because they were particularly powerful and supported unusually large numbers of people. Other societies do enter the picture at times. For example, groups of nomadic herders from Central Asia periodically formed into invading bands, disrupting neighboring civilizations but also helping to transmit technologies and ideas from one civilization to the next.

The list of major civilizations in world history, defined in terms of what a civilization is (a form of human organization having economic surplus, formal government, and so on) and in terms of special size and importance, contains some standard entries. China, India, and the Muslim Middle East/North Africa are on any list. So is Western Europe. Many centers of civilization formed in Africa south of the Sahara, a vast land; they had some features in common, and so references to sub-Saharan African civilization are standard in world history, even though the category embraces a great deal of diversity. The Asian, European, and African civilizations were established well before 1450, but their separate trajectories continued to exercise a powerful influence on world history thereafter. Latin American civilization, emerging from the mixture of Spanish/Portuguese, American Indian, and African slave elements, created a distinct identity, building in part on earlier American Indian civilizations such as the Mayans, the Aztecs, and the Incas. The basic list of major civilizations, by the sixteenth century, thus includes at least six entries, most of them already quite old, with one, Latin America, just taking shape.

Eastern Europe was also an area of civilization, dominated at one point by the great Byzantine Empire that survived the collapse of Rome. (Eastern Europe may be treated as a separate civilization, or it may be combined with Western Europe and referred to simply as the European civilization; strategies differ in various treatments of world history.) The Middle East, from the seventh century onward, was defined particularly by Islam and the Arabs, but it also included remnants of an earlier Persian culture and later experienced the immigration of Turkic peoples and in the fifteenth century the formation of a Turkish-dominated Ottoman

Empire; it is particularly important to allow for variety and change in this civilization area. Parts of East Asia close to China were strongly influenced by Chinese culture and politics; hence Japan, Korea, and Vietnam are sometimes counted as belonging to an East Asia civilization zone initially inspired by China. But these smaller regions have distinctive features, some of which have increased during the past hundred years. Southeast Asia reflects influences from India, China, and Islamic lands; clearly an area of well-established civilization, it did not form a fully distinctive profile of its own. North America (aside from Mexico), Australia, and New Zealand are puzzlers as well, because, beginning in the seventeenth or eighteenth century, these regions combined extensive European settlement with native hunting-and-gathering groups, which were to varying degrees mistreated. Should they be considered separate civilizations because of their frontier experience and their extensive cultural diversity, or can they be treated as outcroppings of Western Europe?

The list of major civilizations begins with six centers; eastern, southern, and western Asia; Europe; sub-Saharan Africa; and Central and South America. Exactly what to include along with these six, how to acknowledge some shared features, as between China and Japan or the United States and Western Europe, is a matter for some debate. The number of distinct major civilizations remains open to discussion as well. Comparison is a vital tool in this analytical task, as well as in relating the major civilizations to each other.

Comparing Societies

Comparison is a standard form of human thought. We often try to understand individual entities better by comparing them with something else we know. To take a very simple example, person X gains identity and recognizability when we see that she is taller than person Y. The same gains accrue from comparing societies. The United States, to take another fairly simple example, is often called a violent society. By itself, that statement is hard to assess. It acquires meaning only if we compare rates of violence—murders per capita, for example—with those of other societies. And in fact, compared to Western Europe, the United States is a violent society. But—and here comparison obviously becomes more complex, for it entails questions about what comparisons are most revealing and relevant—compared with Latin America the United States is fairly violent but not extremely so.

Virtually every characteristic we use to identify societies assumes some comparative standard. China is usually portrayed in world history as having a relatively centralized government and a tendency to scorn outside cultures. These features can be traced by charting the evolution of Chinese history all by itself, but they gain real meaning only if we compare Chinese politics and cultural receptivity to another case, such as that of India (which comparison reveals that the characterizations are quite accurate).

Without comparison, world history risks becoming a list of developments in one place, followed by a list of developments in another, and on and on without much meaning. Comparison, actively juxtaposing major civilizations, helps us know what particularly to look for and appreciate about each case. It also sets up other analytical tasks. Causation is one: if China is more centralized politically than India, in most periods of world history including today, then why—what other factors in the two societies help explain the initial difference and then explain why it was perpetuated? Impact is the second: what difference does it make, in family life or beliefs, for example, that China is usually more centralized politically than India? (One twentieth-century answer is birthrate: because China has frequently used government to regulate society in the past, its policies toward birthrate limitations have been far more rigorous and successful than those of India.) Comparing major civilizations stands at the core of making sense of world history, by relating the identities of the civilizations and clarifying questions of causation and impact.

Comparison even helps chart the real results of that other principal strand of world history: international crosscutting. Why does one civilization respond differently to the arrival of religious missionaries, or a new military technology, or a major epidemic, than does another? In modern history, comparing differences between African and Indian reactions to Western influences is an obvious way to deal with one of the major international forces of modern times, as soon as we realize (what is obviously the case) that although Western influence has some common components, its actual impact varies considerably from case to case across the world.

Comparison generates better understanding. But it is not always an easy analytical assignment. Using the readings in each section of this book requires some vital analytical habits, and questions in each chapter will apply these habits to the materials presented. The comparer faces several key issues:

1. Comparison must be active. There is sometimes an impulse to describe one society, and then describe another, and assume that the comparison has been made. Not so. Comparison requires that the two cases be brought together, so that the comparer makes direct statements about how Muslim family structure, for example, compares to Christian. If a facet of one society is discussed, it must be discussed for the other as well, for otherwise comparison is impossible. Comparison may require some separate descriptions of each case by way of background, but ultimately, at the heart of the presentation, direct juxtaposition is essential. In comparing documentary sources of the sort presented in this book, this means that it is not enough simply to summarize one document and then another; they must be explicitly brought together.

2. Comparison must allow for similarities as well as differences. This is obvious, but sometimes it is tempting to stress differences above all. Major civilizations often had a lot in common, in part because they experienced similar international influences. The trick in comparison is to figure out what the balance between similarity and difference is, and not to overdraw contrasts.

3. Comparison involves a sensible choice of cases. Comparing the importance of palm trees in Jamaica and in northern Ontario is possible but silly—the contexts are too different to provide any useful meaning. Comparing Russian and American concerns about dieting in the twentieth century is also silly, beyond an initial finding that Russians, worried mainly about finding enough food, did not develop a systematic diet culture during the decades in which Americans worried about the subject incessantly. The most revealing comparisons involve societies that have enough in common that exploring differences really gets to the heart of some major distinctions between the two cases.

In the chapters of this book, that test has been imposed: total disparities are not presented, because they are not very informative. This is one reason that, with rare exceptions, societies are compared in the same time period. Comparing industrial Japan with early Mesopotamian civilizations would quickly reveal huge differences, starting with technology, but it would not be as useful as comparing Mesopotamia with its early civilization neighbor Egypt, or the Japanese version of industrial society with that of Germany. Even with relatively precise comparative choices, there is always room for debate. In the violence example presented above, which comparison is more useful if the goal is to understand the United States? Europe is Americans' standard historical reference, because a (shrinking) majority of Americans are of European origin and because many Americans think of Europe as the measure of all things civilized. But perhaps choosing Latin America, another society with a strong and recent frontier tradition, is actually more revealing. Here, selection of the cases is complex and invites open discussion. It will be well to keep in mind, while studying the chapters of this book, what other comparative sets might have been useful in dealing with the phenomenon in question.

4. Comparison involves a decision about how many cases to compare. Comparing two cases, Christianity and Islam, is easier than adding a third, Buddhism. Sometimes a three-way comparison may be helpful, for example in showing that two cases, which look rather different when compared with each other, actually have some striking similarities when an even more distinctive case is brought into the picture. Christianity and Islam, for example, are quite similar religions (and for good historical reason) compared with Buddhism, even though Christians and Muslims often like to emphasize their mutual differences and dislikes. (Disliking another society is not proof of difference; often the societies that are most similar particularly dislike each other because they need to establish separate identities.)

5. Comparison involves flexibility and imagination. Even the most devoted comparative analysis faces limits in the time and attention available, particularly since good comparison requires adequate information and some subtle thinking. This said, it is important to be alert to unexpected comparative possibilities. Compared to all other societies in the world today, the United States has more people in jail per capita. How and why has the nation generated this distinctive feature? The answer, even though the category is not a very standard component of our assessment of American history, could be very revealing. Another comparative topic: France has a rich history of fascination with fancy cooking and foods. Butter-based cooking entered French dining as early as the seventeenth century. The United States historically has been much more conscious of nutritional aspects of food (reformers were discussing this as early as the 1830s, hence new products like the graham cracker and Kellogg's cereals). So which society produces the lower percentage of overweight people? The answer: France, hands down. The average French person has lost an average of about two pounds since 1940, while the average American has gained eight, height held constant. This is on the surface an unexpected comparative finding, which should then dictate a search for the reasons, given a comparative food history that perhaps ought to have produced the opposite results. Moral: in comparing, be alert for revealing, if unfamiliar, subjects, and don't be surprised when comparisons don't produce the results that a preliminary comparative sense might lead one to anticipate. Take an unexpected comparative finding as a challenge to explore further.

Choosing Comparative Topics in World History

The chapters that follow, supplying documents for comparative analysis, obviously merely scratch the surface among the possibilities in world history. Comparative analysis is not as well developed among historians as its importance suggests, because it demands extensive training in at least two societies at a time when most historians devote their lives to exploring a single society in depth. Nevertheless, some intriguing comparative work is available on the history of slavery and emancipations, on modern labor history, on revolutions, on some aspects of family structure and demography, and on religion; the selections used here take advantage of these established areas while staking out some additional areas as well.

Three principles underlie the selections, in addition to the obvious requirement that they must lead to revealing and valid comparisons, suggesting important similarities and differences in the societies involved. *First, all major civilizations are recurrently represented.* It is not possible to bring all civilizations into each comparison; the result would be too demanding, and in some cases comparable materials are simply not available. But in the book as a whole, each society is explored recurrently.

Second, the comparisons invite consideration of the major facets of human societies and human activity. Those major facets include political structures and ideas, but also other aspects of cultures: religions, attitudes toward science, and other beliefs and expressions. Economic activities and organizations have to do with the ways goods are produced and exchanged, including relevant technologies and merchant ventures. Social history involves attention to the organization and justification of social inequalities—classes, castes, and the like—and also to family life and gender relations.

Finally, the book covers the major time periods of world history. Here, world historians operate amid considerable agreement, despite important differences of detail. The first section of these readings covers the formation of civilization and the first three phases of world history. A long period of prehistory extends from the emergence of a recognizable human species to the advent of agriculture, beginning first about 9000 B.C.E. The first civilizations appeared from 3500 B.C.E. onward. From this point until about 1000 B.C.E., most civilizations were small, clustering along river valleys used for irrigation. By 1000 B.C.E. several river valley centers had been disrupted, and then by 500 B.C.E. a series of larger, classical civilizations formed; these flourished and then finally collapsed or were transformed by 450 C.E. The first phases of world history thus embrace a river-valley, formative period (for which documentation is scant, despite the important developments involved) followed by a classical period. The third major period, the *postclassical,* opened with the decline of the great classical empires and extended until the mid–fifteenth century C.E. It was characterized by the rise of major world religions, by the centrality of Islamic society, and at the end by a few other ventures in intercivilizational contact, including the great Mongol empires. Intensifications in international contact were visible particularly from about 1000 C.E. onward, providing an internal dynamic within the postclassical period itself.

By 1450 Western Europe was beginning to emerge as the world's leading commercial society. Around the same time new weaponry became available, and the Americas began to be included in world exchange. This ushered in the early modern period of world history. The formation of important new Asian and Eurasian empires related in part to the advent of new weapons, whereas the intensification and redirection of African slave trade was a vital component of the new levels of world commerce. Together, these developments defined the *early modern period* of world history (1450–1750). This was followed by a further increase in Europe's world power thanks to the industrial revolution, which began the *industrial age,* the fifth major period in world history since the advent of civilization. This modern period of world history—sometimes simply called the long nineteenth century—began about 1750 and closed with the bloodbath of World War I. From 1914–1918 onward, a *contemporary world history period* has seen the relative decline of the West's political and economic power along with its ongoing worldwide cultural influence, the emergence of many new nations, a dramatic intensification of international cultural and economic contacts arising out of revolutionary new communications technologies, and a host of revolutions and cultural upheavals in societies around the world. As in the previous major periods in world history, comparative issues and insights abound.

Using the Book

Each section of this book opens with an introduction to the main characteristics of the time period in world history. The introductions explain how the ensuing chapter topics relate to basic patterns and why the comparative selections make sense in terms of the activities emphasized—trade, or religion, or gender—and in terms of the specific civilizations included.

Each chapter also has an introduction, identifying the comparative topic and the societies involved and placing both in world history context. This introduction also explains how the civilizations selected are significant for the topic—why classical China and Greece, for example, should be compared politically, or why Indian religions should be compared with religions that arose in the Middle East.

After the introduction to each chapter, a set of questions raises some of the specific comparative issues that can be found in the documents that follow. A final set of questions, "For Further Discussion," presents wider comparative issues that can be handled partially from the documents but that need further comparative information—from textbooks or other historical studies or, sometimes, from other chapters in this book.

Questions in the first segment, before "For Further Discussion," can be answered from the documents. Looking at the questions first can help guide the reading of the documents, and then the questions should be reexamined after the documents have been read. The questions apply to a particular topic—the conditions of women in Africa and Latin America, for example, using the comparative approaches discussed above. They thus ask about similarities as well as differences and about causes and impacts of comparative features (calling for imaginative extensions). And they promote direct comparison rather than a mere sequencing of data from one civilization to the next.

Finally, each document or document set has a brief heading that gives details about the time, the place, and the authorship of the document or documents. The context supplied by this information should be included in assessing the document's meanings and in preparing for the comparisons.

PART I

River Valley Civilizations, 3500–1000 B.C.E., and the Classical Period, 1000 B.C.E.–450 C.E.

THE EARLY RIVER VALLEY civilizations formed in the Middle East, and later the expansive classical civilizations developed both in that region and elsewhere. Early civilizations and their classical successors set up important cultural and institutional characteristics that had enduring influence, providing vital topics for comparative analysis.

Early Cultures and the Early Civilization Period

The early civilization period began around 3500 B.C.E. in the Tigris-Euphrates valleys in the northern Middle East. Early civilization periods in other regions, also for the most part based in river valleys exploited for irrigation as well as transportation, had somewhat different dates. Egypt developed from about 3000 B.C.E. onward, China from 1500, the first civilizations in Central America (the Olmecs) from about 800 B.C.E. No civilization could emerge without the prior development of agriculture.

For historians studying early cultures and civilizations, a key problem is the lack of abundant sources. Many important cultures, with well-defined belief systems and elaborate rules for behavior, never generated writing. We know something about them from artistic expressions—paintings and statuary—and something from oral accounts preserved in group memory. (People without writing rely heavily on stories passed from generation to generation, and they have marvelous memories.) Oral legends do change, however, even when the goal is to preserve tradition; many people argue about what the right story is, and this is one source of change. Hence, our knowledge of early beliefs is limited. Civilizations usually had writing, as well as more elaborate monuments; for those civilizations, historical knowledge is better. But much writing has been destroyed over time, and writing on stone tablets or bones was so laborious that it was not very widespread in any event.

The first chapter, as a result, deals with only a few topics, but those are fundamental to early societies. The writings of early civilizations must be asked questions that they were not explicitly designed to answer. Law codes, for example, provide our only real evidence about family patterns and social structures, even though these topics were not formally laid out. Only after the nature of the evidence is assessed, can comparison among belief systems or civilization forms be attempted.

The early civilization period ran from 3500 to about 1000 B.C.E. in Asia, Africa, and southern Europe. Long before 3500 B.C.E. human beings had set up separate societies in most inhabitable parts of the world. Although these societies had some links with neighboring areas through trade and periodic migration and invasion, and although many reflected common origins in language and myths, their considerable isolation created many opportunities for distinctive patterns to arise. Issues of comparison, to tease out both similarities and differences, can be well established at this point.

From about 9000 B.C.E. onward, well before the time civilization as a form of human organization first took shape in the northern Middle East (the region known as Mesopotamia, centered in present-day Iran), agriculture had been gaining ground as a system of food production, over the more traditional hunting and gathering. Agriculture provided the opportunity for some surplus production, that is, in excess of basic needs, and thereby made it possible for civilizations to expand trade and cities (though the majority of the population remained rural). They established more formal governments; they created new specializations, so that some people became priests and craft producers, for example; they also instituted new levels of social and economic inequality; and most of them developed or took over a system of writing. With writing and the creation of more elaborate material artifacts, including temples and monuments, records of human activity became more abundant, giving historians more to work with in attempting to understand the past, though important limitations persist. Opportunities to compare records are not massive, and they sometimes depend on writing that occurred later but captured (we think) some ideas that were being circulated less formally during this early period.

The early civilizations centered in fertile river valleys. From the origins in the Tigris-Euphrates area, civilizations in the Middle East developed the greatest number of centers. Egypt was a second civilization cradle, with connections to some other parts of Africa. River valley civilizations in India and China had important ramifications, though a wave of invasions snuffed out the cities along the Indus river after two millennia of development. This seedtime for major civilizations inevitably created a host of fundamental features, ranging from broadly similar efforts to establish religious priests and government officials to very different ideas about nature and beauty.

Civilizations grappled with some of the same issues. One common impulse, for example, was to reduce the status of women, in order to divide labor in farming households and enhance male power now that hunting prowess had become less significant. Thus, all early civilizations established substantial male control in the family, in a system called patriarchalism. Yet differences existed as well: patriarchalism varied in specifics, including the degree of harshness in the treatment of women. To determine the similarities and differences, comparing the early cultures and civilizations is vital.

Chapter 1 deals explicitly with the early civilization period (extending, however, slightly beyond 1000 B.C.E.). It highlights two of the leading developments of the period, the rise of writing and the development of formal states. As states made new claims to power, many rulers sought to extend the hold of their laws, to enhance order and manifest their power or that of the divine forces they felt they served. Two of the earliest systems of law emerged in the Middle East, sharing a number of impulses in the regulation of society (including a belief in slavery) but also differing in crucial ways. Pinpointing the differences furthers an exploration, in turn, of differences in religious ideas and family conditions.

The Classical Period, 1000 B.C.E.–450 C.E.

Between 1000 and 500 B.C.E., several civilization centers began to transcend the patterns of river valley societies. Using iron tools and weapons, governments conquered new territories and economies generated new opportunities for regional trade and specialization. The twin themes in this period were civilization expansion, from river valley origins to much larger regions, and territorial integration. As societies grew geographically, they had to find ways to form a region into a coherent trade area, into a roughly common cultural zone where elites, at least, would share some basic ideas and art forms, and—at times—into a single political unit. Major classical civilizations arose in India, China, and the Mediterranean, with a fourth center in Persia. All of these regions created political empires that sought considerable political unity as part of the integration—though the durability of the empires varied considerably. Everywhere, a series of new invasions, occurring between the third and the sixth centuries C.E., introduced disruptions that ended the classical period.

There were important developments in other parts of the world as well. Major kingdoms in northeastern Africa south of the Sahara maintained vital contacts with the Middle East and the Mediterranean area. Agriculture spread, and with it somewhat more organized political forms in places such as northern Europe and Japan. An early civilization emerged in Central America. Connections among key civilization areas also developed; silk trade, for example, linked China with India, the Middle East, and even the Mediterranean, and religious missionaries fanned out from India to other parts of Asia.

On balance, however, it was the emergence of the large regional centers and the new economic, political, and cultural forms that helped integrate these centers internally that set the tone for this long period in world history. Opportunities for comparison increase, to determine commonalities and contrasts among the civilizations. Developments in this period—the emergence of Confucianism in China and the religious emphases of classical India, for example—set an enduring framework for the areas involved, which makes comparison all the more significant. Some of the differences between India and China today go back to contrasts that first became apparent in the classical centuries.

The major classical civilizations built on the precedents of the river valley centers, but their territories were larger and their cultural systems were more formal. They used some earlier ideas, including the polytheistic religions, but they shaped more systematic statements. Thus, in India a priestly, polytheistic religion evolved into Hinduism. China produced Confucianism as a unifying cultural approach at least for much of the upper class. Political institutions expanded. All the major centers formed huge empires, at least during key portions of the classical period. In China the imperial form became the standard political framework. Commercial exchange increased. Social structures perpetuated inequalities that had undoubtedly started earlier but were now more formalized, more fully integrated with beliefs and political practices. Thus, India developed its caste system, and the Mediterranean region relied considerably on slavery. The same formalization applies to gender relations, where the assumptions of patriarchy were spelled out more fully.

Examination of the classical civilizations in Asia, Africa, and Europe focuses on the various facets of their operations. Political values and institutions were central to the classical achievement. Political traditions established in this period continued to mark China, India, and the Mediterranean for a long time to come, enduring in some ways into our own age. Value systems, expressed in literature and religion but also in science, helped articulate and perpetuate widely shared cultures. Although some literary forms, like the epic, were links to the early civilization period, the advance of characteristic forms of science and philosophical outlooks on nature represented an important extension of cultural operations. The development of major religions, particularly in India and the Middle East, shows another side of the flourishing cultures of the classical era; except for Islam, all the major religions of the world today were created during these centuries (though Judaism had slightly earlier roots). Social structures also express the distinctiveness of the classical period, particularly in the confident emphasis on inequalities. But some ideas, that were first systematically stated in the classical centuries, including patriarchal formulas concerning women, have left traces into modern times.

In politics, diverse cultural expressions, and social forms, the classical civilizations shared important characteristics. They were all rooted in agricultural economies in which trade was expanding. They all faced the task of integrating larger territories into a common civilization orbit, and this required innovation in political institutions and ideas and in cultural forms. The classical civilizations even had some mutual contacts—more, on the whole, than the more isolated river valley civilizations had maintained. Greek and Indian civilizations encountered each other in the fourth century B.C.E. through the conquests of Alexander the Great; the result was some mutual imitation of ethical ideas, artistic forms, and mathematics. Later in the classical period Chinese trade with India brought knowledge of Buddhism, and Chinese pilgrims journeyed to India to learn more. Trade routes took Chinese silk as far west as the Roman Empire.

On the whole, however, the key developments of the classical period took place separately, with each civilization putting a distinctive stamp on its social, political, and cultural forms. Rome received Chinese silk, but it knew absolutely nothing about China, and the converse was true as well. Separateness was compounded by a heightened sense of identity. As the Greeks or the Chinese developed their societies, they became proudly aware of how different (and usually, inferior) other peoples were. Separate historical patterns and a concern for identity add up to an obvious comparative challenge. As in the early civilization period, comparison most obviously focuses on how key civilizations differed, even as they addressed common themes such as the presumed inferiority of women. Explaining why the differences arose and what impact they had extends this comparative analysis. Comparison highlights the distinctive traditions and identities that were taking shape in the classical period and that would have a prolonged echo later on. But comparison can also tease out some of the common features, even when the leaders of the principal civilizations were unaware of them.

CHAPTER 1

COMPARING LAWS

The Importance of the State

Codes of law were a common product of relatively early civilizations. The following two selections reflect the development of written laws, associated with the operations of organized government. The first selection, the earliest law code on record, comes from the early civilization period in Mesopotamia. The second, the Jewish code, originated a bit later from a society in the same region. Jewish law was undoubtedly influenced by Mesopotamian precedent—an early case of formal cultural contact. But it also reflected some different ideas, some developed before Hebrew writing itself emerged and others originating at a later stage of social organization. Societies without formal states had all sorts of regulations, but they were not written down, and sometimes they had very personal aspects relating to birth relationships and kinship groups. Civilizations generated somewhat more systematic statements, though they reflected deep divisions in legal status between different social groups and between the genders. The first known code is that of the Babylonian emperor Hammurabi, issued around 1700 B.C.E. Jewish law, ultimately written as part of the Bible, particularly in the book of Deuteronomy, developed later, beginning about 950 B.C.E.

Law codes provide evidence well beyond simply defining crimes and punishments. They reveal beliefs about religion and the nature of the state, and they provide definitions of the family and society. Comparing codes can indicate deep-seated contrasts and commonalities between societies, though they must be interpreted beyond literal meanings.

Law codes in early civilizations shared many features—indeed, in defining crimes such as murder, they share features with modern codes as well. Codes worked toward replacing private feuds and violence with government-sponsored justice, for example—though early states often failed to enforce such edicts. Mesopotamian law surely influenced Jewish codes, for the Jewish state was often under Mesopotamian control. A surprising array of laws dealing with gender and regulating sexual behavior, particularly for women, characterized both systems, though in Judaism the rules were slightly harsher and the concern for limited protective rights slightly less well developed. Law in both societies reflected small bureaucracies in early states—hence a concern for punishing false testimony, in the absence of extensive investigatory police forces, and an emphasis on harsh punishments designed to deter crime. Provisions in both societies also expressed some interest in protecting general social welfare, for example in trying to assure wages for work or (in the Mesopotamian case) reimbursing for loss in crime—a notion still being debated in the United States.

The two codes displayed crucial differences as well, reflecting different religious cultures and political institutions. Mesopotamian law was more bent on defining social hierarchy and assuring the property rights of slave owners; Jewish law emphasized charity more heavily. What wider differences between the two societies might account for these distinctions? What caused the differences that also existed concerning the treatment of women? On a possibly related point: Mesopotamian law stressed the power of the state, though sanctioned by gods such as the creator Marduk and a polytheistic religion. In contrast, Jewish law was seen as emanating from Jehovah, in the world's first real monotheistic religion. Did this difference in framework show up in the laws themselves and in efforts to assure obedience? How much change was involved?

Questions

1. How did Babylonian law try to reconcile the needs of the state with the fact that it could not afford a large, professional bureaucracy? How did the state use "volunteers"? How did it arrange for public works?
2. What protections did women have in Babylonian law? How do these compare with the stipulations for women in Jewish law? How can we tell that both societies were patriarchal?
3. How many social classes did Babylonian have? Was Jewish law different in its approach to the poorer classes?
4. What were the key differences between Babylonian and Jewish religions?
5. What are the sources claimed for the law in the two societies? How did the differences in these claims relate to differences in the roles of priests and government officials?
6. What are the main similarities between the two law codes?

For Further Discussion

1. How did both law codes differ from modern ideas of law?
2. What might have caused the key differences between Jewish and Babylonian law?

MESOPOTAMIA: HAMMURABI'S CODE

The Babylonians were an invading people who reunited the city states of Mesopotamia by conquest. The victorious king, Hammurabi, reigned for forty-three
years, earning a reputation for justice and efficiency. His law code, from around
1700 B.C.E., consisted of 282 case laws written on a stone slab; it was discovered
in 1901 in Iran. The code does not represent a carefully articulated philosophy of
law or the state, but rather highlights selected decisions the king and his officials
rendered for the purpose of providing precedents for just rulings. It is not clear
that the code had great influence on the law itself, but it does provide a window
into various aspects of Babylonian society.

• • •

When the lofty Anu, king of the Anunnaki, and Bel, lord of heaven and earth, he
who determines the destiny of the land, committed the rule of all mankind to
Marduk, the chief son of Ea; when they pronounced the lofty name of Babylon:
when they made it famous among the quarters of the world and in its midst established an everlasting kingdom whose foundations were firm as heaven and earth—
at that time, Ann and Bel called me, Hummurabi, the exalted prince, the worshiper
of the gods, to cause justice to prevail in the land, to destroy the wicked and the
evil, to prevent the strong from oppressing the weak . . . to enlighten the land and
to further the welfare of the people. Hammurabi, the governor named by Bel, am I,
who brought about plenty and abundance; . . .

. . . the ancient seed of royalty, the powerful king, the Sun of Babylon, who
caused light to go forth over the lands of Sumer and Akkad; the king, who caused
the four quarters of the world to render obedience; the favorite of Nana, am I.
When Marduk sent me to rule the people and to bring help to the country, I
established law and justice in the land and promoted the welfare of the people.

§1.

¶ If a man bring an accusation against a man, and charge him with a (capital) crime,
but cannot prove it, he, the accuser, shall be put to death.

§2.

¶ If a man charge a man with sorcery, and cannot prove it, he who is charged with
sorcery shall go to the river, into the river he shall throw himself and if the river
overcome him, his accuser shall take to himself his house (estate). If the river show
that man to be innocent and he come forth unharmed, he who charged him with

From *The Code of Hammurabi, King of Babylon,* trans. Robert Francis Harper (Chicago: University of
Chicago Press, 1904), 3, 9, 11, 17, 19, 29, 45, 51, 73, 75, 89, 99, 101, 103, 105.

sorcery shall be put to death. He who threw himself into the river shall take to himself the house of his accuser.

❡ If a man has come forward to bear witness to a felony and then has not proved the statement he has made, if that case (is) a capital one, that man shall be put to death.

❡ If a man aid a male or female slave of the palace, or a male or female slave of a freeman to escape from the city gate, he shall be put to death.

❡ If a man seize a male or female slave, a fugitive, in the field and bring that (slave) back to his owner, the owner of the slave shall pay him two shekels of silver.

§23.

❡ If the brigand be not captured, the man who has been robbed, shall, in the presence of god, make an itemized statement of his loss, and the city and the governor, in whose province and jurisdiction the robbery was committed, shall compensate him for whatever was lost.

§24.

❡ If it be a life (that is lost), the city and governor shall pay one mana of silver to his heirs.

§26.

❡ If either an officer or a constable, who is ordered to go on an errand of the king, do not go but hire a substitute and despatch him in his stead, that officer or constable shall be put to death; his hired substitute shall take to himself his (the officer's) house.

§53.

❡ If a man neglect to strengthen his dyke and do not strengthen it, and a break be made in his dyke and the water carry away the farm-land, the man in whose dyke the break has been made shall restore the grain which he has damaged.

§127.

❡ If a man point the finger at a priestess or the wife of another and cannot justify it, they shall drag that man before the judges and they shall brand his forehead.

§128.

❡ If a man take a wife and do not arrange with her the (proper) contracts, that woman is not a (legal) wife.

§129.

❡ If the wife of a man be taken in lying with another man, they shall bind them and throw them into the water. If the husband of the woman would save his wife, or if the king would save his male servant (he may).

§130.

¶ If a man force the (betrothed) wife of another who has not known a male and is living in her father's house, and he lie in her bosom and they take him, that man shall be put to death and that woman shall go free.

§131.

¶ If a man accuse his wife and she has not been taken in lying with another man, she shall take an oath in the name of god and she shall return to her house.

§132.

¶ If the finger have been pointed at the wife of a man because of another man, and she have not been taken in lying with another man, for her husband's sake she shall throw herself into the river.

§142.

¶ If a woman hate her husband, and say: "Thou shalt not have me," they shall inquire into her antecedents for her defects; and if she have been a careful mistress and be without reproach and her husband have been going about and greatly belittling her, that woman has no blame. She shall receive her dowry and shall go to her father's house.

§143.

¶ If she have not been a careful mistress, have gadded about, have neglected her house and have belittled her husband, they shall throw that woman into the water.

§144.

¶ If a man take a wife and that wife give a maid servant to her husband and she bear children; if that man set his face to take a concubine, they shall not countenance him. He may not take a concubine.

§145.

¶ If a man take a wife and she do not present him with children and he set his face to take a concubine, that man may take a concubine and bring her into his house. That concubine shall not rank with his wife.

§146.

¶ If a man take a wife and she give a maid servant to her husband, and that maid servant bear children and afterwards would take rank with her mistress; because she has borne children, her mistress may not sell her for money, but she may reduce her to bondage and count her among the maid servants.

§196.

❡ If a man destroy the eye of another freeman [i.e., a man in the upper class], they shall destroy his eye.

§197.

❡ If one break a man's bone, they shall break his bone.

§198.

❡ If one destroy the eye of a villein [a dependent laborer] or break the bone of a freeman, he shall pay one mana of silver.

§199.

❡ If one destroy the eye of a man's slave or break a bone of a man's slave he shall pay one-half his price.

§200.

❡ If a man knock out a tooth of a man of his own rank, they shall knock out his tooth.

§201.

❡ If one knock out a tooth of a villein, he shall pay one-third mana of silver.

§203.

❡ If a man strike another man of his own rank, he shall pay one mana of silver.

§204.

❡ If a villein strike a villein, he shall pay ten shekels of silver.

§205.

❡ If a man's slave strike a man's son, they shall cut off his ear.

§253.

❡ If a man hire a man to oversee his farm and furnish him the seed-grain and intrust him with oxen and contract with him to cultivate the field, and that man steal either the seed or the crop and it be found in his possession, they shall cut off his fingers.

§254.

❡ If he take the seed-grain and overwork the oxen, he shall restore the quantity of grain which he has hoed.

§257.

❡ If a man hire a field-laborer, he shall pay him 8 GUR of grain per year.

§258.

❡ If a man hire a herdsman, he shall pay him 6 GUR of grain per year.

The righteous laws, which Hammurabi, the wise king, established and (by which) he gave the land stable support and pure government. Hammurabi, the *perfect king, am I. . . .*

The great gods proclaimed me and I am the guardian governor, whose scepter is righteous and whose beneficent protection is spread over my city. . . .

The king, who is pre-eminent among city kings, am I. My words are precious, my wisdom is unrivaled. By the command of Shamash, the great judge of heaven and earth, may I make righteousness to shine forth on the land. By the order of [the god] Marduk, my lord, may no one efface my statues. . . .

. . . Let any oppressed man, who has a cause, come before my image as king of righteousness! . . .

. . . Let him read the code and pray with a full heart before Marduk, my lord, and Zarpanit, my lady, and may the protecting deities. . . . look with favor on his wishes (plans) in the presence of Marduk, my lord, and Zarpanit, my lady! . . .

If that man pay attention to my words which I have written upon my monument, do not efface my judgments, do not overrule my words, and do not alter my statues, then will Shamash prolong that man's reign, as he has mine, who am king of righteousness, that he may rule his people in righteousness.

If that man do not pay attention to my words which I have written upon my monument: if he forget my curse and do not fear the curse of god: if he abolish the judgments which I have formulated, overrule my words, alter my statues, efface my name written thereon and write his own name: on account of these curses, commission another to do so—as for that man, be he king or lord, or priest-king or commoner, whoever he may be, may the great god, the father of the gods, who has ordained my reign, take from him the glory of his sovereignty, may be break his scepter, and curse his fate!

May Ea, the great prince, whose decrees take precedence, the leader of the gods, who knows everything, who prolongs the days of my life, deprive him of knowledge and wisdom! May he bring him to oblivion, and dam up his rivers at their sources! May he not permit corn, which is the life of the people, to grow in his land!

JEWISH LAW

Jewish settlers established a small kingdom along the eastern Mediterranean between 1200 and 1100 B.C.E. The people may have developed elements of their

religion and culture earlier—this is what is claimed in the initial stories of the Old Testament, particularly the book of Exodus. The definite emergence of a Jewish state occurred at a time when the greater empires of the region had weakened, at the end of the river valley civilization period. Jewish culture was marked by its elaborate, intense religion, which featured the first durable articulation of monotheistic beliefs. Laws, dealing with various social issues as well as with religious rules, were combined with the religion, and that is why they began to be written down, from the eighth century onward, in the books that were later collected into the Old Testament. Most of the book of Deuteronomy, from which the following passages come, was written in the seventh century B.C.E., though elements of the laws themselves had undoubtedly developed earlier.

• • •

You must be entirely faithful to Yahweh your God. For these nations whom you are dispossessing may listen to soothsayers and diviners, but this is not the gift that Yahweh your God gives to you: Yahweh your God will raise up for you a prophet like myself, from among yourselves, from your own brothers; to him you must listen. This is what you yourselves asked of Yahweh your God at Horeb on the day of the Assembly. "Do not let me hear again" you said "the voice of Yahweh my God, nor look any longer on this great fire, or I shall die"; and Yahweh said to me, "All they have spoken is well said. I will raise up a prophet like yourself for them from their own brothers; I will put my words into his mouth and he shall tell them all I command him. The man who does not listen to my words that he speaks in my name, shall be held answerable to me for it. But the prophet who presumes to say in my name a thing I have not commanded him to say, or who speaks in the name of other gods, that prophet shall die."

You may say in your heart, "How are we to know what word was not spoken by Yahweh?" When a prophet speaks in the name of Yahweh and the thing does not happen and the word is not fulfilled, then it has not been spoken by Yahweh. The prophet has spoken with presumption. You have nothing to fear from him. . . .

If anyone has struck his fellow accidentally, not having any previous feud with him (for example, he goes with his fellow into the forest to cut wood; his arm swings the axe to fell a tree; the head slips off the handle and strikes his companion dead), that man may take refuge in one of these cities and save his life. It must not be allowed that the avenger of blood, in the heat of his anger, should pursue the killer and that the length of the road should help him to overtake and fatally wound him; for the man has not deserved to die, having had no previous feud with his companion. . . .

From *The Jerusalem Bible* (Garden City, N.Y.: Doubleday, 1966) 241–48, 252–53. Copyright © 1966 by Darton, Longman & Todd, Ltd. and Doubleday, a division of Bantam Doubleday Dell Publishing Group, Inc. Reprinted by permission.

But if it happens that a man has a feud with his fellow and lies in wait for him and falls on him and wounds him fatally and he dies, and the man takes refuge in one of these cities, the elders of his own town shall send to have him seized and hand him over to the avenger of blood to die. You are to show him no pity. You must banish the shedding of innocent blood from Israel, and then you will prosper.

Boundaries

You must not displace your neighbour's boundary mark, set by your forbears, in the inheritance you receive in the land Yahweh is giving into your possession.

Witnesses

A single witness cannot suffice to convict a man of a crime or offence of any kind; whatever the misdemeanour, the evidence of two witnesses or three is required to sustain the charge.

If a malicious witness appears against a man to accuse him of rebellion, both parties to this dispute before Yahweh must be brought before the priests and judges then in office. •The judges must make a careful inquiry, and if it turns out that the witness who accused his brother is a lying witness, •you must deal with him as he would have dealt with his brother. You must banish this evil from your midst. •Others will hear of it and be afraid and never again do such an evil thing among you. •You are to show no pity.

The 'Lex Talionis'

Life for life, eye for eye, tooth for tooth, hand for hand, foot for foot.

War and Combatants

When you go to war against your enemies and see horses and chariots and an army greater than your own, you must not be afraid of them; Yahweh your God is with you, who brought you out of the land of Egypt. •When you are about to join battle the priest is to come forward and address the people. He is to say to them, "Listen, Israel; now that you are about to join battle against your enemies, do not be faint-hearted. Let there be no fear or trembling or alarm as you face them. •Yahweh your God goes with you to fight for you against your enemies and to save you."

Then the scribes are to address the people in words like these:

"Is there any man here who has built a new house and not yet dedicated it? Let him go home lest he die in battle and another perform the dedication.

"Is there any man here who has planted a vineyard and not yet enjoyed its fruit? Let him go home lest he die in battle and another enjoy its fruit.

Is there any man here who has betrothed a wife and not yet taken her? Let him go home lest he die in battle and another take her."

The scribes shall also address the people like this:

"Is there any man here who is fearful and faint of heart? Let him go home lest he make his fellows lose heart too."

And when the scribes have finished speaking to the people, commanders will be appointed to lead them.

Captured Towns

When you advance to the attack on any town, first offer it terms of peace. If it accepts these and opens its gates to you, all the people to be found in it shall do forced labour for you and be subject to you. . . .

When you go to war against your enemies and Yahweh your God delivers them into your power and you take prisoners, •if you see a beautiful woman among the prisoners and find her desirable, you may make her your wife •and bring her to your home. She is to shave her head and cut her nails •and take off her prisoner's garb; she is to stay inside your house and must mourn her father and mother for a full month. Then you may go to her and be a husband to her, and she shall be your wife. •Should she cease to please you, you will let her go where she wishes, not selling her for money: you are not to make any profit out of her, since you have had the use of her.

If a man has two wives, one loved and the other unloved, and the loved one and the unloved both bear him children, and if the first-born son is of the unloved wife, •then when the man comes to bequeath his goods to his sons, he may not treat the son of the wife whom he loves as the first-born at the expense of the son of the wife he does not love, the true first-born. •He must acknowledge as first-born the son of the wife he does not love and give to him a double share of his estate, for this son is the first-fruit of his strength, and the right of the first-born is his.

If a man has a stubborn and rebellious son who will not listen to the voice of his father or the voice of his mother, and even when they punish him still will not pay attention to them, •his father and mother shall take hold of him and bring him out to the elders of the town at the gate of that place. •And they shall say to the elders of his town, "This son of ours is stubborn and rebellious and will not listen to us; he is a wastrel and a drunkard." •Then all his fellow citizens shall stone him to death. You must banish this evil from your midst. All Israel will hear of it and be afraid. . . .

If a man marries a wife, and sleeps with her and then turns against her, and taxes her with misconduct and publicly defames her by saying, "I married this woman and when I slept with her I did not find the evidence of her virginity," the girl's father and mother must take her and produce the evidence of her virginity before the elders of the town at the gate. •The girl's father shall then declare to the elders, "I gave this man my daughter for a wife and he has turned against her, •and now he taxes her with misconduct: I found no evidence of virginity in your daughter, he says. But the evidence of my daughter's virginity is here." And they shall spread the cloth out before the elders of the town. •Then the elders of the town shall take the man and flog him •and fine him one hundred silver shekels for publicly defaming a virgin of Israel, and give this money to the girl's father. She shall remain his wife and as long as he lives he may not repudiate her

But if the accusation that the girl cannot show the evidence of virginity is substantiated, •they shall take her to the door of her father's house and her fellow citizens shall stone her to death for having committed an infamy in Israel by disgracing her father's House. You must banish this evil from your midst. . . .

You must not allow a master to imprison a slave who has escaped from him and come to you. •He shall live with you, among you, wherever he pleases in any one of your towns he chooses; you are not to molest him. . . .

You are not to exploit the hired servant who is poor and destitute, whether he is one of your brothers or a stranger who lives in your towns. •You must pay him his wage each day, not allowing the sun to set before you do, for he is poor and is anxious for it; otherwise he may appeal to Yahweh against you, and it would be a sin for you. . . .

You must not pervert justice in dealing with a stranger or an orphan, nor take a widow's garment in pledge. •Remember that you were a slave in Egypt and that Yahweh your God redeemed you from there. That is why I lay this charge on you.

When reaping the harvest in your field, if you have overlooked a sheaf in that field, do not go back for it. Leave it for the stranger, the orphan and the widow, so that Yahweh your God may bless you in all your undertakings.

When you beat your olive trees you must not go over the branches twice. Let anything left be for the stranger, the orphan and the widow.

When you harvest your vineyard you must not pick it over a second time. Let anything left be for the stranger, the orphan and the widow. . . .

When two men are fighting together, if the wife of one intervenes to protect her husband from the other's blows by putting out her hand and seizing the other by the private parts, •you shall cut her hand off and show no pity. . . .

If you do not keep and observe all the words of this Law that are written in this book, in the fear of this name of glory and awe: Yahweh your God, •Yahweh will strike you down with monstrous plagues, you and your descendants: with plagues grievous and lasting, diseases pernicious and enduring. •Once more he will bring on you the diseases of Egypt that you dreaded, and they will infect you. Further, Yahweh will bring on you every sickness, every plague, not mentioned in the Book of this Law, until you perish. •There will be only a handful of you left, you who were as many as the stars of heaven.

CHAPTER 2

THE EPIC TRADITION

Greece and India

Epic stories were one of the early cultural products in many civilizations. Conceived in verse for easier memorization and retelling, early epics were originally delivered orally and only later written down. Because they served some similar purposes, epics of different societies had some common qualities. They usually stressed stories of adventure; they sought to establish a common history for a people, often focused on the great deeds of early kings; and they usually had religious content, portraying the activities and qualities of gods and goddesses. They were also, frequently, quite long. The first written work of literature, the Mesopotamian *Gilgamesh,* was an epic. Sections of the Jewish Bible, what Christians call the Old Testament, had epic qualities. Epics played a role in Roman history, though here they were copied from Greek models, and later in Western Europe, where, for example, the first formal written work in French, the *Song of Roland,* had epic features.

Epic stories obviously served as something of a transition between characteristics of the long oral accounts early civilizations (though the process of writing down some of the most central stories had begun during that period) and the more diverse expressions of classical civilizations. Yet the epic itself was not a transitory phenomenon. It expressed crucial values in many societies, including religious ideas as in the creation stories. Because epics continued to be recited and read, they set themes for other kinds of writers, such as the Athenian dramatists who used some of the conflicts among the gods that Homer described, to frame their plays. The epics served as a challenge to later writers as well, for example the poet Virgil, who felt it was important to have a Roman epic to match the Greek and so wrote the *Aeneid* to connect Rome to the Homeric stories of the Trojan War. And the epics lived in public memory. In India, they not only served as sources of religious contemplation for Hinduism, but also continue today to provide themes and settings for the nation's culture and socialization.

Epics held a particularly important place in Greek and Indian civilizations. In India a series of epics, gradually committed to writing as Indo-European invaders settled down, provided the central stories and, through them, the values for the priestly religion that ultimately became Hinduism. Traditional Indian epics loom large in the culture even today, supplying the basis for popular films. The epic tradition in Greece was less influential, as other literary forms superseded it, but the two great Homeric epics, the *Iliad* and the *Odyssey,* unquestionably served as a vital expression of Greek culture, establishing patterns of a rich literary language and also setting out many features of the dominant religion. The two passages in this section, both dealing with stories of war and the roles of gods and goddesses, are taken from the *Bhagavad Gita* and from Homer's *Iliad,* written by one or more Greek poets around 800 B.C.E. Both epics probably refer to real battles; certainly the Greek war with Troy (located in present-day Turkey) really occurred; it took place in an earlier phase of Greek civilization, around 1200 B.C.E.

The two epics display many similar qualities (the sharp contrasts visible in the creation myths of various societies are not present). The epic form itself, with its focus on military stories, accounts for some similarities. It is also important to remember that both Greeks and Indians by this time had been profoundly affected by Indo-European invasions from Central Asia, which brought a common fund of ideas about gods and their roles in human affairs including battles. Similar warlike traditions produced common ideas of masculine valor and honor. But Greek and Indian cultures also differed, even in the early phases of the classical period. The specific roles of the gods—how much they interfered and how much they urged clear patterns of morality—vary greatly in these two passages. The Gita offers a definite illustration of the Indian (Hindu) concept of dharma, or moral duty, as well as a distinctive view of the basic nature of life and death. Greek religious beliefs were more traditionally polytheistic; unlike the Indians, the Greeks did not create a major religion. The Gita suggests an ultimate spiritual purpose, as well as the moral duty to live up to the obligations of one's social caste, that were not present in classical Greece. The epic traditions thus offer a clear comparative challenge, to sort out the mixture of common features and durably distinctive values.

Epic stories in the classical period, like Hollywood extravaganzas, had a host of characters, with lots of different gods and people interacting and with considerable attention to the lineage of the characters to help a kinship-minded society keep them straight. But the plot lines were not too complicated, and the values implied in the epics, about how heroes should be defined and how people should behave, came through clearly—which is why epics were used not just to entertain and to provide a common fund of stories for a particular culture, but to instruct.

Questions

1. What is an epic? Can you define it in terms of features shared by the *Iliad* and the Gita?

2. What other similarities existed between the epic values in classical Greece and India? Were there common military ideals?

3. What is the central moral dilemma in the passage from the Gita, and how is it resolved? How does the resolution relate to India's caste system, in which groups such as warriors were born to their roles in life? Did Greek epics pose moral dilemmas of this sort? How would Homer have dealt with a problem of the sort raised in the Gita? What does this suggest about the ethical content of Greek and Indian religions?

4. Can you compare the roles of the gods in Greek and Indian epic stories? What do the roles imply about the nature of the religions in the two societies and the obligations of people to the gods?

For Further Discussion

1. Do the contrasts between the two epics help explain why classical India became one of the key religious centers in world history, whereas classical Greek culture failed to produce a vigorous, unifying religion, but rather emphasized art and secular philosophy?

2. Can you think of some reasons that Greeks and Indians would share a fondness for epics?

THE GREEK EPIC TRADITION: THE *ILIAD*

The *Iliad,* composed in the ninth century B.C.E. and attributed to the blind poet Homer, deals with the Trojan War. Whether Homer was a single author or whether a number of authors collaborated is not known. The war, a real war, occurred between the Greek kingdom of Mycenae, which flourished briefly before the rise of classical Greece, and a city-state across the Aegean Sea in present-day Turkey. The war probably occurred around 1200 B.C.E. and resulted from Greek invasion. In Homer's epic, the war becomes a battleground for Greeks and Trojans and for quarrels among the gods. The epic focuses on the war's tenth year and ultimately includes the famous ploy in which the Greeks gave the Trojans a huge wooden horse that concealed Greek warriors who burst forth when the horse was moved inside the city walls. Homer's epic helped solidify Greek literary language and the attributes ascribed to major gods and goddesses in Greek polytheism.

• • •

Thus beside the beaked ships and all around you,
O war-starved Achilles, Achaeans [Greeks] armed for the fight,
And up the plain from them the Trojans did likewise.
But powerful Zeus, from the many-ridged peak of Olympus,
Bade Themis call the gods to a meeting, and quickly
She went to them all and summoned them to the assembly
At Zeus's palace. Not one river-god was absent
Except Oceanus, nor any nymph, of all those
Who haunt the lovely groves, the springs where rivers
Rise, and the grassy fields. Once there at the house
Of the cloud-gathering god, all the immortals took seats
Within the rows of bright columns which skillful Hephaestus
Had made for Zeus their Father.
    Nor did earth-shaking
Poseidon ignore Themis' call, but emerged from the brine
To join them. And now he sat in their midst and inquired
About Zeus's purpose: "Why, O lord of the lightning,
Have you called this meeting of gods? Are you worried about
The Achaeans and Trojans, between whom battle is almost
Ready to blaze?"
    Then Zeus of the gathering gale
Answered him thus: "You're right, great shaker of shores,
I have indeed called this gathering of the immortals
Because of my deep concern for those warriors, doomed
Though they are. I myself, of course, will stay on a ridge
Of Olympus, from which I may watch the war as I please.
But all of you other immortals go down and help
The Achaeans and Trojans, aiding whichever side
You prefer. For if fast-fighting Achilles attacks
The unaided Trojans, they won't be able to hold out
A moment. They've never been able to so much as see him
Without fear and trembling, and now that flaming rage
For the death of his friend is eating his heart, I'm afraid
He will outstrip his fate by leveling the walls of the city."
    These words of Cronos' son Zeus awoke stubborn war,
And the gods went down to join their differing favorites.
Hera and Pallas Athena went to the ships

From *The Iliad of Homer,* trans. Ennis Rees (New York: Oxford University Press, 1963), 406–11, 413–16, 418–22. Reprinted by permission of Ennis Rees.

Of the Argives, and with them Poseidon and luck-bringing
    Hermes,
The wiliest god of all. And with these went Hephaestus,
Exulting in might, for though he limped, his thin legs
Were nimble enough. But huge bright-helmeted Ares
And Apollo with hair unshorn went down to the Trojans,
Along with arrow-showering Artemis, Leto,
The river-god Xanthus, and Aphrodite, adorer
Of smiles.

    So long as the gods were not there, the Achaeans
Won glorious victory, since now Achilles, who had
For so long stayed out of the painful fighting, had come forth
Again, and there was no Trojan whose legs did not tremble
At sight of quick-footed Achilles, flaming in arms
Like the man-maiming War-god himself. But when the
    Olympians
Entered the tumult, host-harrying Hatred arose
With a vengeance. Athena screamed her great war-cry, now
From beside the deep trench outside the wall, now
From the surf-beaten shore of the sea, and opposite her
Dread Ares, ominous as a dark whirlwind, screamed
From the citadel heights, and again as he charged down the
    slope
Of Callicolone beside the banks of Simoeis.
Thus the happy gods greatly augmented the clash
Of battle and made bitter strife break out everywhere
Between the two armies fighting in horrible uproar.
Then from on high the Father of gods and men
Awesomely thundered, while down below Poseidon
Caused the limitless earth to rumble and quake
From plain to sheer mountain peaks. Well-watered Ida
Was shaken from bottom to top, as were the city
Of Troy and ships of Achaea. Hades, god
Of ghosts in the world under ground, was filled with panic
And sprang from his throne with a scream, lest Poseidon,
    shaker
Of earth, should split the ground open above him and thus
Reveal to men and immortals the ghastly abodes
Of death, the moldering horrors that even the gods
Would look on with loathing.

    Such was the mighty uproar

When god clashed with god in strife. For against lord Poseidon
Stood Phoebus Apollo, god of the winged shafts,
And opposite Ares stood bright-eyed Athena. Opposing
Hera was Phoebus' sister, the archer Artemis,
Goddess of golden shafts and the echoing shouts
Of the chase, while coming forth against Leto was powerful
Luck-bringing Hermes, and there opposing Hephaestus
Came the god of the great deep-swirling river,
Called Xanthus by the immortals, Scamander by men.

    So gods advanced to meet gods. But Achilles had interest
In none but Priam's son Hector, with whose blood
He most lusted to glut the battling Ares, him
Of the tough hide shield. Host-urging Apollo, however,
Inspired great strength in Aeneas and sent him to face
The raging son of Peleus. Assuming the form
And voice of Priam's son Lycaon, Apollo,
Son of Zeus, spoke thus to the counselor of Trojans:

    "Aeneas, where now are the brags you made to the princes
Of Troy when you, over wine, declared yourself ready
To fight man to man with Peleus' son Achilles?"

    To which Aeneas: "Lycaon, why would you tell me
This way to fight face to face, against my will,
With haughty Achilles? Not that it would be
My first encounter with him, since once already
He put me to flight with his spear, driving me down
From Mount Ida where he had come for our cattle the time
He sacked and laid waste Lyrnessus and Pedasus both.
That time Zeus saved me by giving me strength and putting
Great speed in my legs. Else I would surely have died
At the hands of Achilles and those of Athena, who went
Before him bearing the light of victory and bidding him
Kill with his bronze-headed spear both Trojans and Leleges.
May no man, then, fight face to face with Achilles,
For always beside him a god goes, warding off death.
And even unaided his spear flies very straight,
Not does it stop save deep in the flesh of some mortal.
Still, were God to give us an equal chance
In man-to-man combat, he would not easily beat me,
Not though he claims to be made of solid bronze!"

    Then lord Apollo, son of Zeus, replied:
"Heroic Aeneas, why don't you also invoke

The gods everlasting? After all, men say Aphrodite,
Daughter of Zeus, is your mother, while surely Achilles
Was born of a lesser goddess. Remember, your mother
Is Zeus's own daughter, his the sea-ancient's child.
But on! Charge with your unyielding bronze straight at him,
And don't be turned aside by any insults
Or threats from him."
   So saying, he breathed great power
Into Aeneas, and he, the people's shepherd,
     Strode out through the front line of fighters, his bronze
      helmet flashing. . . .

[The goddess Hera speaks:]

"Here we have come from Olympus to mix in this melee
And keep Achilles safe all this day long,
Though afterward he shall suffer whatever Fate spun
For him with the thread of his life on the day his mother
Bore him. But if he fails to learn all this
From heaven itself, he may be unduly afraid
When some god confronts him in battle. For hard indeed
Are the gods to look upon when they appear
In their own true forms." . . .
   Meanwhile, the whole plain was aflame
With bronze-flashing men and horses, and earth resounded
And rang beneath the tumultuous beat of their feet
As they charged toward each other. But now their two greatest
     champions
Came out in the space between the two armies, spoiling
To battle each other, Aeneas, son of Anchises,
And noble Achilles. First came Aeneas, defiantly
Tossing his heavy-helmeted head, gripping
His gallant shield close in front of his chest, and brandishing
Fiercely his bronze-headed spear. Against him Achilles,
Son of Peleus, came charging on like a lion,
A ravenous beast that all the men of a village
Have come out anxious to kill. At first he pays them
No heed, but goes his way till one of the fast
And lusty young spearmen sinks a lance in his flesh.
Then with a jaw-splitting roar he gathers himself
To charge, and foam forms all round his fangs, while in him
His great heart groans. Lashing his ribs and flanks

With his tail, he works himself up for the fight, then charges
Straight on in his fiery-eyed fury, careless of whether
He kill or be killed there in the front line of spearmen.
So now Achilles was driven on by his fury
And warrior's pride to go out and face great Aeneas. . . .

[Aeneas answers:]

"But as for prowess
In battle, Zeus gives it or takes it away as he,
The almighty, sees fit. So come, let us no longer
Stand here in the midst of battle prating like two
Little boys. There is surely no lack of insults for either
Of us to mouth, vile things so many they'd sink
A ship of two hundred oars. For the tongue of man
Is a glib and versatile organ, and from it come many
And various words, whose range of expression is wide
In every direction. And the sort of words a man says
Is the sort he hears in return. But what makes the two of us
Wrangle and nag like a couple of spiteful women,
Who having aroused in each other heart-eating hatred
Go out in the street and spit harsh words back and forth,
As many false as true, since hateful rage
Does the talking? For since I am eager for combat, you'll not
Turn me back with mere words before we have battled with
bronze
Man to man. Come then, let us at once have a taste
Of each other's spear-points!"
He spoke, and drove his huge lance
Into Achilles' dread and marvelous shield,
Which loudly cried out about the bronze point of the weapon.
Achilles, gripped with quick terror, shoved the shield out
With his powerful hand, away from his flesh, for he thought
The long-shadowing spear of great-hearted Aeneas would easily
Pierce it—childish fool that he was not to know
In his mind and heart that the glorious gifts of the gods
Will not easily break or give way before the onslaught
Of mortals. Nor did the huge lance of fiery Aeneas
Tear through the shield, for the gold, the god's gift, held it back.
Though he drove it clean through the first two layers, there
remained
Three other folds, for the great limping god had hammered

Together five layers in all, two bronze, two tin,
And between them a gold one, in which the ashen spear stopped.
   Then great Achilles let fly his long-shadowing spear
And struck the round shield of Aeneas not far from the rim
Where the bronze and backing of bull's-hide were thinnest. And
    the shield
Gave out a strident shriek as through it tore
The shaft of Pelian ash. Then Aeneas was gripped
With panic, and cringing he held the shield up, away
From his flesh, as the spear shot over his back and stilled
Its force in the ground, though it split apart two circles
Of the Trojan's man-guarding shield. Having thus escaped
The long lance, Aeneas stood up, and the sight of that shaft
So close to his flesh filled his bright eyes with measureless
Panic and pain. But Achilles whipped out his keen blade
And charged down upon him, ferociously screaming his war-cry,
And mighty Aeneas picked up a huge stone, one
That no two men of today could even lift
But that he picked up with one hand and easily threw.
Then Aeneas would surely have struck with the stone the helmet
Or life-saving shield of charging Achilles, who then
Would have closed with him and taken his life with the sword,
If Poseidon had not been keeping sharp watch. At once
He spoke thus mid the gods everlasting: . . .
So come, let us save him from death, for Zeus himself
Will be angry if now Achilles cuts the man down.
It is surely already decreed that Aeneas shall outlive
The war, so that Dardanus' seed may not die and his line
Disappear, since Zeus adored Dardanus more than he did
Any other child he had by a mortal woman.
For now Cronos' son has come to despise the house
Of Priam, and surely the mighty Aeneas shall soon rule
The Trojans, and after him the sons of his sons,
Great princes yet to be born."
   Then heifer-eyed Hera,
Queen of the gods, replied: "O shaker of shores,
You must decide for yourself concerning Aeneas,
Whether you wish to save him or let him be killed,
Despite his great prowess, by Peleus' son Achilles.
For we two, Pallas Athena and I, have sworn
Very numerous oaths in the presence of all the immortals

That we would never keep from the Trojans the hard day
Of doom, not even when Troy shall burn with furious
Fire lit by the warlike sons of Achaeans."
   When Poseidon heard this, he went alone through the fight
Mid a tumult of hurtling spears till he came to Aeneas
And famous Achilles. Quickly he covered the eyes
Of Peleus' son with mist, then drew from the shield
Of Aeneas the sharp ashen spear. This he laid down
At the feet of Achilles, but Aeneas he swept from the ground
And sent him vaulting high over the heads of numerous
Heroes and horses . . .
Then Alastor's son Tros—he reached for the knees of Achilles,
Pleading with him to take him alive, to pity
A man the same age as himself and not cut him off
So young, fool that he was not to know that with him
There would be no heeding, that there was nothing sweet-
    tempered
Or mild in Achilles, but only ferocious heart—
Tros tried to hug the man's knees, jabbering a prayer
To be spared, but Achilles thrust his sword in at the liver,
Which slipped from the wound as the dark blood quickly welled
    out
And slithered down to drip from his chest. . . .
Horses of great-souled Achilles trampled on corpses
And shields. And the axle below and handrails above
Were all splashed and bespattered with blood from the battering
    hooves
Of the horses and metal rims of the wheels, as onward
Achilles pressed in pursuit of glory, soiling
His unconquered hands with the filth of horrible slaughter.

THE INDIAN EPIC TRADITION: THE BHAGAVAD GITA

The title of this poem, written in the classical language Sanskrit, means "song of god." Inserted into the longer epic Mahabharata, the Gita served as a popular and scholarly religious source and devotional book. It was framed as a long debate between the god Krishna and Arjuna, son of Pandu, as they anticipated a great human battle. The debate allowed discussion of the goals of human life and the nature of death, as well as the ethical obligations of military warriors. The Gita was undoubtedly originally an oral tradition that took on increasing abstraction as early Hinduism developed in India. The present form of the epic dates from the second century B.C.E.

• • •

Producing joy in his heart,
  The aged grandsire of the Kurus
Roared a lion's roar on high,
  And blew his conch-shell, full of valor.

Then conch-shells and drums,
  Kettle-drums, cymbals, and trumpets,
All at once were sounded;
  The sound was tremendous.

Then on the white-horse-yoked
  Mighty car standing,
Mādhava (Kṛṣṇa) and the son of Pāṇḍu (Arjuna)
  Blew their wondrous conch-shells: . . .

And the king of Benares, supreme archer,
  And Śikhaṇḍin, of the great car,
And Dhṛṣṭadyumna and Virāṭa,
  And the unconquered Sātyaki,

Drupada and the sons of Draupadī,
  All together, O king,
And the great-armed son of Subhadrā,
  Blew their conch-shells severally.

That sound Dhṛtarāṣṭra's men's
  Hearts did rend;
And both sky and earth
  It made to resound, swelling aloft.

Then seeing arrayed
  Dhṛtarāṣṭra's sons, the ape-bannered (Arjuna),
When the clash of arms had already begun,
  Lifted up his bow, the son of Pāṇḍu,

And to Hṛṣīkeśa then words
  Like these spoke, O king.
Between the two armies
  Halt my chariot, O unshaken one,

From *The Bhagavad Gītā*, trans. Franklin Edgerton (New York: Harper, 1944), 4–13.

Until I espy these
   That are drawn up eager to fight,
(And see) with whom I must fight
   In this warlike enterprise. . . .

There the son of Pṛthā [Arjuna] saw stationed
   Fathers and grandsires,
Teachers, uncles, brothers,
   Sons, grandsons, and comrades too,

Fathers-in-law and friends as well,
   In both the two armies.
The son of Kuntī, seeing them,
   All his kinsmen arrayed,

Filled with utmost compassion,
   Despondent, spoke these words:
Seeing my own kinsfolk here, Kṛṣṇa,
   That have drawn near eager to fight,

My limbs sink down,
   And my mouth becomes parched,
And there is trembling in my body,
   And my hair stands on end.

(The bow) Gāṇḍīva falls from my hand,
   And my skin, too, is burning,
And I cannot stand still,
   And my mind seems to wander.

And I see portents
   That are adverse, Keśava;
And I foresee no welfare,
   Having slain my kinsfolk in battle.

I wish no victory, Kṛṣṇa,
   Nor kingdom nor joys;
Of what use to us were kingdom, Govinda,
   Of what use enjoyments or life?

For whose sake we desire
   Kingdom, enjoyments, and happiness,
They are drawn up here in battle,
   Giving up life and wealth:

Teachers, fathers, sons,
    Grandsires as well,
Uncles, fathers-in-law, grandsons,
    Brothers-in-law, and (other) kinsfolk.

Then I do not wish to slay,
    Even tho they slay (me), O slayer of Madhu,
Even for three world-rulership's
    Sake; how much less for the sake of the earth!

Having slain Dhṛtarāṣṭra's men, to us
    What joy would ensue, Janīdana?
Evil alone would light upon us,
    Did we slay these (our would-be) murderers.

Therefore we should not slay
    Dhṛtarāṣṭra's men, our own kinsfolk.
For how, having slain our kinsfolk,
    Could we be happy, Mādhava?

Even if they do not see,
    Because their intelligence is destroyed by greed,
The sin caused by destruction of family,
    And the crime involved in injury to a friend,

How should we not know enough
    To turn back from this wickedness,
The sin caused by destruction of family
    Perceiving, O Janārdana?

Upon the destruction of the family, perish
    The immemorial holy laws of the family;
When the laws have perished, the whole family
    Lawlessness overwhelms also.

Because of the prevalence of lawlessness, Kṛṣṇa,
    The women of the family are corrupted;
When the women are corrupted, O Vṛṣṇi-clansman,
    Mixture of caste ensues.

Mixture (of caste) leads to naught but hell
    For the destroyers of the family and for the family;
For their ancestors fall (to hell),
    Because the rites of (giving) food and water are interrupted.

By these sins of family-destroyers,
    (Sins) which produce caste-mixture,
The caste laws are destroyed,
    And the eternal family laws.

When the family laws are destroyed,
    Janārdana, then for men
Dwelling in hell certainly
    Ensues: so we have heard (from the Holy Word).

Ah woe! 'Twas a great wickedness
    That we had resolved to commit,
In that, thru greed for the joys of kingship,
    We undertook to slay our kinsfolk.

If me unresisting,
    Weaponless, with weapons in their hands
Dhṛtarāṣṭra's men should slay in battle,
    That would be a safer course for me.

Thus speaking Arjuna in the battle
    Sat down in the box of the car,
Letting fall his bow and arrows,
    His heart smitten with grief.

    The Blessed One said:
Whence to thee this faintheartedness
    In peril has come,
Offensive to the noble, not leading to heaven,
    Inglorious, O Arjuna?

Yield not to unmanliness, son of Pṛthā;
    It is not meet for thee.
Petty weakness of heart
    Rejecting, arise, scorcher of the foe!

    Arjuna said: . . .
And we know not which of the two were better for us,
    Whether we should conquer, or they should conquer us;
What very ones having slain we wish not to live,
    They are arrayed in front of us, Dhṛtarāṣṭra's men.

My very being afflicted with the taint of weak compassion,
    I ask Thee, my mind bewildered as to the right:
Which were better, that tell me definitely;
    I am Thy pupil, teach me that have come to Thee (for instruction).

For I see not what would dispel my
    Grief, the witherer of the senses,
If I attained on earth rivalless, prosperous
    Kingship, and even overlordship of the gods.

    As he was despondent, these words:
      The Blessed One said:
Thou hast mourned those who should not be mourned,
    And (yet) thou speakest words about wisdom!
Dead and living men
    The (truly) learned do not mourn.

But not in any respect was I (ever) not,
    Nor thou, nor these kings;
And not at all shall we ever come not to be,
    All of us, henceforward.

As to the embodied (soul) in this body
    Come childhood, youth, old age,
So the coming to another body;
    The wise man is not confused herein.

But contacts with matter, son of Kuntī,
    Cause cold and heat, pleasure and pain;
They come and go, and are impermanent;
    Put up with them, son of Bharata! . . .

But know that that is indestructible,
    By which this all is pervaded;
Destruction of this imperishable one
    No one can cause.

These bodies come to an end,
    It is declared, of the eternal embodied (soul),
Which is indestructible and unfathomable.
    Therefore fight, son of Bharata!

Who believes him a slayer,
    And who thinks him slain,
Both these understand not:
    He slays not, is not slain.

He is not born, nor does he ever die;
    Nor, having come to be, will he ever more come not to be.
Unborn, eternal, everlasting, this ancient one
    Is not slain when the body is slain.

Who knows as indestructible and eternal
   This unborn, imperishable one,
That man, son of Pṛthā, how
   Can he slay or cause to slay—whom?

As leaving aside worn-out garments
   A man takes other, new ones,
So leaving aside worn-out bodies
   To other, new ones goes the embodied (soul).

Swords cut him not,
   Fire burns him not,
Water wets him not,
   Wind dries him not.

Not to be cut is he, not to be burnt is he,
   Not to be wet nor yet dried;
Eternal, omnipresent, fixed,
   Immovable, everlasting is he.

Unmanifest he, unthinkable he,
   Unchangeable he is declared to be;
Therefore knowing him thus
   Thou shouldst not mourn him.

Moreover, even if constantly born
   Or constantly dying thou considerest him,
Even so, great-armed one, thou
   Shouldst not mourn him.

For to one that is born death is certain,
   And birth is certain for one that has died;
Therefore, the thing being unavoidable,
   Thou shouldst not mourn. . . .

   (But) even having heard (of) him, no one whatsoever knows him.

This embodied (soul) is eternally unslayable
   In the body of every one, son of Bharata;
Therefore all beings
   Thou shouldst not mourn.

Likewise having regard for thine own (caste) duty
   Thou shouldst not tremble;

For another, better thing than a fight required of duty
    Exists not for a warrior.

Presented by mere luck,
    An open door of heaven—
Happy the warriors, son of Pṛthā,
    That get such fight!

Now, if thou this duty-required
    Conflict wilt not perform,
Then thine own duty and glory
    Abandoning, thou shalt get thee evil.

Disgrace, too, will creatures
    Speak of thee, without end;
And for one that has been esteemed, disgrace
    Is worse than death.

That thou hast abstained from battle thru fear
    The (warriors) of great chariots will think of thee;
And of whom thou wast highly regarded,
    Thou shalt come to be held lightly.

And many sayings that should not be said
    Thy ill-wishers will say of thee,
Speaking ill of thy capacity:
    What, pray, is more grievous than that?

Either slain thou shalt gain heaven,
    Or conquering thou shalt enjoy the earth.
Therefore arise, son of Kuntī,
    Unto battle, making a firm resolve.

Holding pleasure and pain alike,
    Gain and loss, victory and defeat,
Then gird thyself for battle:
    Thus thou shalt not get evil.

This has been declared to thee (that is found) in Reason-method,
    This mental attitude: but hear this in Discipline-method,
Disciplined with which mental attitude, son of Pṛthā,
    Thou shalt get rid of the bondage of action.

CHAPTER 3

POLITICAL IDEALS IN CHINA AND GREECE

Political life and the state were basic features of both Chinese and Mediterranean civilization. Both civilizations had a strong secular emphasis, with provision of appropriate political order a vital component of successful societies and with appropriate service to the state a vital component of the good life. But the forms of government and the specific political ideals differed greatly.

Confucianism was the most important single political philosophy developed in classical China; it has enduring influence on Chinese thought and politics even to the present day. There were other, conflicting value systems in China, which could modify the Confucian approach, but an emphasis on Confucianism is not unjustified.

Confucius (551–476 B.C.E.) developed his emphases on the state, stable social hierarchy, and social and personal order at a time of disunity and strife in China. He claimed to be restoring traditional Chinese values, and a concept of balance may well have permeated Chinese culture from an earlier period, supporting the Confucian emphasis on personal restraint. Confucian ideas were not immediately adopted. After continued regional warfare, the first solution to China's political problems came in the form of an authoritarian emperor (of the Qin dynasty) who unified the country but attacked books and learning. By the time of the Han dynasty (202 B.C.E.–220 C.E.), however, emperors understood the importance of Confucian thinking in supporting the government and providing guidelines for the training of a growing bureaucracy. Confucian values were actively taught to government servants in China and, later, in other parts of East Asia, into the twentieth century.

In contrast to classical China under the Han dynasty, Athens was not a great empire, though it gained colonies. Rather, it was a Greek city-state. Like other city-states in the divided, mountainous peninsula, Athens generated an aristocratic government early on, after 800 B.C.E. But then it went through other political phases, some of which entailed greater involvement of ordinary citizens. To be sure, Athenian citizenry excluded women, slaves, and foreigners—well over two-thirds of the adult population. By the fifth century, Athens had developed an extensive participatory democracy for those who did have full rights. It also became a leading commercial center and was the site of one of the most vibrant outpourings of art, literature, and philosophy the world has ever known. Pericles, the principal leader of Athens after the mid–fifth century, was an aristocrat who usually operated behind the scenes of the bustling democracy. He was well aware of his city's diverse strengths.

Pericles' Funeral Oration, issued by Athens's main democratic leader (though of aristocratic origin) during the early stages of the Peloponnesian War (between Athens and Sparta, 431–404 B.C.E.), sought to lay out the chief qualities of Athenian democracy. (The speech is conveyed by the contemporary historian Thucydides, who probably sums up its spirit accurately, though he, not Pericles, may be responsible for the actual words written down.) Here it is even more important to remember that Athenian democracy was not the only political style in the classical Mediterranean—not even the most typical one, because most systems had a stronger aristocratic element. But Pericles captures some wider features of Mediterranean politics, including the plea for a great devotion to the state. Pericles' ideas form part of the mixture of political thinking available in the Mediterranean, and they were revived and often cited in Western Europe and the United States in recent centuries when modern democratic systems were being constructed. Pericles' beliefs in the political value of the citizenry and in wide cultural tolerance have inspired many contemporary theorists.

Confucianism and Athenian democracy demonstrate the great diversity possible in the development of classical societies. Confucianism served a strong, durable empire, with the world's first explicitly educated, centralizing bureaucracy. Not surprisingly, Confucian values and China's government forms were repeatedly revived and, in East Asia, widely imitated, for they provided the most successful political formula devised by any civilization until modern times. Periclean Athens, in contrast, failed after exhaustion and defeat in the war with Sparta. Later societies in the Mediterranean retained a democratic element and certainly a high esteem for cultural achievements, but aristocratic or authoritarian rule became more common. Yet the Periclean ideal, because it was so vividly stated in Thucydides' history and because it was associated with such unusual achievements in art and philosophy, did not die. It became part of a complex Greek legacy to later societies, including those of Western Europe and North America, when conditions ripened for a different kind of political democracy.

Questions

1. What political values do Pericles and Confucius share? Would they agree at all on the features of a good government, a good family, or a good servant of the state?
2. What are their main differences, and how would these show up in the way the

two societies organized their governments and in what individuals expected from the state? How would Confucius react to the idea of a democracy? What kind of personality training does each passage suggest?

3. Both Pericles and Confucius discuss social inequality, directly or indirectly, along with gender and the role and use of wealth. What are the main differences in social views, and how do these relate to the larger political styles? How would Pericles and Confucius debate the role of merchants in a well-arranged society? How would they defend social and economic inequality?

For Further Discussion

1. Does the comparison between these two great classical leaders suggest any reason that Confucianism had much greater importance in Chinese history than Pericles and his ideas gained in the larger history of the classical Mediterranean civilization and its successors?
2. How did Confucian and Greek ideas about proper human behavior and the importance of political goals compare with the emerging ideas of Hinduism, as expressed in epics such as the Gita (chapter 2)?
3. How did Pericles' ideals compare with the Homeric values in the *Iliad* (chapter 2)?
4. What changes had occurred in Greek politics by Pericles' time? What were the continuities in political and social values?

CONFUCIANISM: CHINESE POLITICAL VALUES

The following Confucian passage is entitled "The Great Learning." Its origin is uncertain. It may have been written by Confucius himself, but possibly some early followers devised it in the Confucian spirit—like all great systems of thought, Confucianism depended greatly on a steady stream of intellectual supporters who added to the legacy. The passage was certainly completed by 200 B.C.E. It gained further importance from the attention given to it by a later, neo-Confucian philosopher, Chu Hsi (1120–1200 C.E.), and by the fourteenth century C.E. it had become a standard part of China's civil service examination. Regardless of precise authorship, it is a characteristic presentation of Confucian thought.

• • •

The Way of learning to be great (or adult education) consists in manifesting the clear character, loving the people, and abiding (*chih*) in the highest good.

From Wing-Tsit Chan, ed., *A Source Book in Chinese Philosophy* (Princeton, N.J.: Princeton University Press, 1963), 86–92, 94. Reprinted by permission of the publisher.

Only after knowing what to abide in can one be calm. Only after having been calm can one be tranquil. Only after having achieved tranquillity can one have peaceful repose. Only after having peaceful repose can one begin to deliberate. Only after deliberation can the end be attained. Things have their roots and branches. Affairs have their beginnings and their ends. To know what is first and what is last will lead one near the Way.

The ancients who wished to manifest their clear character to the world would first regulate their families. Those who wished to bring order to their states would first regulate their families. Those who wished to regulate their families would first cultivate their personal lives. Those who wished to rectify their minds would first make their wills sincere. Those who wished to make their wills sincere would first extend their knowledge. The extension of knowledge consists in the investigation of things. When things are investigated, knowledge is extended; when knowledge is extended, the will becomes sincere; when the will is sincere, the mind is rectified; when the mind is rectified, the personal life is cultivated; when the personal life is cultivated, the family will be regulated; when the family is regulated, the state will be in order; and when the state is in order, there will be peace throughout the world. From the Son of Heaven [the Emperor] down to the common people, all must regard cultivation of the personal life as the root or foundation. There is never a case when the root is in disorder and yet the branches are in order. There has never been a case when what is treated with great importance becomes a matter of slight importance or what is treated with slight importance becomes a matter of great importance. . . .

The *Book of Odes* says . . . "The twittering yellow bird rests (chih) on a thickly wooded mount." Confucius said, "When the bird rests, it knows where to rest. Should a human being be unequal to a bird?" The *Book of Odes* says, "How profound was King Wen! How he maintained his brilliant virtue without interruption and regarded with reverence that which he abided (chih)." As a ruler, he abided in humanity. As a minister, he abided in reverence. As a son, he abided in filial piety. As a father, he abided in deep love. And in dealing with the people of the country, he abided in faithfulness.

The *Book of Odes* says, "Look at that curve in the Ch'i River. How luxuriant and green are the bamboo trees there! Here is our elegant and accomplished prince. [His personal life is cultivated] as a thing is cut and filed and as a thing is carved and polished. How grave and dignified! How majestic and distinguished! Here is our elegant and accomplished prince. We can never forget him!" "As a thing is cut and filed" refers to the pursuit of learning. "As a thing is carved and polished" refers to self-cultivation. "How grave and how dignified" indicates precaution. "How majestic and distinguished" expresses awe-inspiring appearance. "Here is our elegant and accomplished prince. We can never forget him" means that the people cannot forget his eminent character and perfect virtue. The *Book of Odes* says, "Ah! the ancient kings are not forgotten." [Future] rulers deemed worthy what they deemed worthy and loved what they loved, while the common people enjoyed what they enjoyed and benefited from their beneficial arrangements. That was why they are not forgotten even after they passed away. . . .

Confucius said, "In hearing litigations, I am as good as anyone. What is necessary is to enable people not to have litigations at all." Those who would not tell the truth will not dare to finish their words, and a great awe would be struck into people's minds. This is called knowing the root. . . .

What is meant by "making the will sincere" is allowing no self-deception, as when we hate a bad smell or love a beautiful color. This is called satisfying oneself. Therefore the superior man will always be watchful over himself when alone. When the inferior man is alone and leisurely, there is no limit to which he does not go in his evil deeds. Only when he sees a superior man does he then try to disguise himself, concealing the evil and showing off the good in him. But what is the use? For other people see him as if they see his very heart. That is what is meant by saying that what is true in a man's heart will be shown in his outward appearance. Therefore the superior man will always be watchful over himself when alone. Tseng Tzu said, "What ten eyes are beholding and what ten hands are pointing to—isn't it frightening?" Wealth makes a house shining and virtue makes a person shining. When one's mind is broad and his heart generous, his body becomes big and is at ease. Therefore the superior man always makes his will sincere. . . .

What is meant by saying that in order to govern the state it is necessary first to regulate the family is this: There is no one who cannot teach his own family and yet can teach others. Therefore the superior man (ruler) without going beyond his family, can bring education into completion in the whole state. Filial piety is that with which one serves his ruler. Brotherly respect is that with which one serves his elders, and deep love is that with which one treats the multitude. The "Announcement of K'ang" says, "Act as if you were watching over an infant." If a mother sincerely and earnestly looks for what the infant wants, she may not hit the mark but she will not be far from it. A young woman has never had to learn about nursing a baby before she marries. When the individual families have become humane, then the whole country will be aroused toward humanity. When the individual families have become compliant, then the whole country will be aroused toward compliance. When one man is greedy or avaricious, the whole country will be plunged into disorder. Such is the subtle, incipient activating force of things. This is what is meant by saying that a single word may spoil an affair and a single man may put the country in order. (Sage-emperors) Yao and Shun led the world with humanity and the people followed them. (Wicked kings) Chieh and Chou led the world with violence and the people followed them. The people did not follow their orders which were contrary to what they themselves liked. Therefore the superior man must have the good qualities in himself before he may require them in other people. He must not have the bad qualities in himself before he may require others not to have them.

There has never been a man who does not cherish altruism (*shu*) in himself and yet can teach other people. Therefore the order of the state depends on the regulation of the family.

The *Book of Odes* says, "How young and pretty is that peach tree! How luxuriant is its foliage! This girl is going to her husband's house. She will rightly order her household." Only when one has rightly ordered his household can he teach the people of the country. The *Book of Odes* says, "They were correct and good to their elder brothers. They were correct and good to their younger brothers." Only when one is good and correct to one's elder and younger brothers can one teach the people of the country. The *Book of Odes* says, "His deportment is all correct, and he rectifies all the people of the country." Because he served as a worthy example as a father, son, elder brother, and younger brother, therefore the people imitated him. This is what is meant by saying that the order of the state depends on the regulation of the family. . . .

What is meant by saying that peace of the world depends on the order of the state is this: When the ruler treats the elders with respect, then the people will be aroused toward filial piety. When the ruler treats the aged with respect, then the people will be aroused toward brotherly respect. When the ruler treats compassionately the young and the helpless, then the common people will not follow the opposite course. Therefore the ruler has a principle with which, as with a measuring square, he may regulate his conduct . . .

Therefore the ruler will first be watchful over his own virtue. If he has virtue, he will have the people with him. If he has the people with him, he will have the territory. If he has the territory, he will have wealth. And if he has wealth, he will have its use. Virtue is the root, while wealth is the branch. . . .

There is a great principle for the production of wealth. If there are many producers and few consumers, and if people who produce wealth do so quickly and those who spend it do so slowly, then wealth will always be sufficient. A man of humanity develops his personality by means of his wealth, while the inhumane person develops wealth at the sacrifice of his personality. There has never been a case of a ruler who loved humanity and whose people did not love righteousness. There has never been a case where the people loved righteousness and yet the affairs of the state have not been carried to completion. And there has never been a case where in such a state the wealth collected in the national treasury did not continue in the possession of the ruler.

ATHENIAN DEMOCRACY: PERICLES' FUNERAL ORATION

Pericles was born about 495 B.C.E. An aristocrat who lived a polished life, his oratory could stir the masses of Athenian citizens. He led the city, with few

interruptions, from 461 until his death in 429 and was active in advancing its empire as a source of funds. His Funeral Oration was delivered in the winter of 431–430 to honor early Athenian victims of the war with Sparta. A version of the speech was featured in the *History of the Peloponnesian War* by the historian Thucydides, who admired Pericles but who preferred outright aristocratic rule to what he saw as the whims of the masses in democracy. He began writing his history while the war still raged, during an exile that started in 423. Thucydides is widely regarded as the first great critical historian in the Mediterranean tradition, though his practice of inventing word-for-word speeches, instead of admitting he had to paraphrase, is not recommended today. Pericles died in 429, soon after his speech, of a plague that decimated the city and weakened its war effort.

• • •

I shall speak first of our ancestors, for it is right and at the same time fitting, on an occasion like this, to give them this place of honour in recalling what they did. For this land of ours, in which the same people have never ceased to dwell in an unbroken line of successive generations, they by their valour transmitted to our times a free state. And not only are they worthy of our praise, but our fathers still more; for they, adding to the inheritance which they received, acquired the empire we now possess and bequeathed it, not without toil, to us who are alive to-day. And we ourselves here assembled, who are now for the most part still in the prime of life, have further strengthened the empire in most respects, and have provided our city with all resources, so that it is sufficient for itself both in peace and in war. The military exploits whereby our several possessions were acquired, whether in any case it were we ourselves or our fathers that valiantly repelled the onset of war, Barbarian or Hellenic, I will not recall, for I have no desire to speak at length among those who know. But I shall first set forth by what sort of training we have come to our present position, and with what political institutions and as the result of what manner of life our empire became great, and afterwards proceed to the praise of these men; for I think that on the present occasion such a recital will be not inappropriate and that the whole throng, both of citizens and of strangers, may with advantage listen to it.

We live under a form of government which does not emulate the institutions of our neighbours; on the contrary, we are ourselves a model which some follow, rather than the imitators of other peoples. It is true that our government is called a democracy, because its administration is in the hands, not of the few, but of the many; yet while as regards the law all men are on an equality for the settlement of their private

From Thucydides, *History of the Peloponnesian War,* trans. Charles Smith (Cambridge, Mass.: Harvard University Press, 1919–1923), 321, 323, 325, 327, 329, 335, 337, 339, 341. Reprinted by permission of the publisher and the Loeb Classical Library.

disputes, as regards the value set on them it is as each man is in any way distinguished that he is preferred to public honours, not because he belongs to a particular class, but because of personal merits; nor, again, on the ground of poverty is a man barred from a public career by obscurity of rank if he but has it in him to do the state a service. And not only in our public life are we liberal, but also as regards our freedom from suspicion of one another in the pursuits of every-day life; for we do not feel resentment at our neighbour if he does as he likes, nor yet do we put on sour looks which, though harmless, are painful to behold. But while we thus avoid giving offence in our private intercourse, in our public life we are restrained from lawlessness chiefly through reverent fear, for we render obedience to those in authority and to the laws, and especially to those laws which are ordained for the succour of the oppressed and those which, though unwritten, bring upon the transgressor a disgrace which all men recognize.

Moreover, we have provided for the spirit many relaxations from toil: we have games and sacrifices regularly throughout the year and homes fitted out with good taste and elegance; and the delight we each day find in these things drives away sadness. And our city is so great that all the products of all the earth flow in upon us, and ours is the happy lot to gather in the good fruits of our own soil with no more home-felt security of enjoyment than we do those of other lands. . . .

For we are lovers of beauty yet with no extravagance and lovers of wisdom yet without weakness. Wealth we employ rather as an opportunity for action than as a subject for boasting; and with us it is not a shame for a man to acknowledge poverty, but the greater shame is for him not to do his best to avoid it. And you will find united in the same persons an interest at once in private and in public affairs, and in others of us who give attention chiefly to business, you will find no lack of insight into political matters. For we alone regard the man who takes no part in public affairs, not as one who minds his own business, but as good for nothing; and we Athenians decide public questions for ourselves or at least endeavour to arrive at a sound understanding of them, in the belief that it is not debate that is a hindrance to action, but rather not to be instructed by debate before the time comes for action. For in truth we have this point also of superiority over other men, to be most daring in action and yet at the same time most given to reflection upon the ventures we mean to undertake; with other men, on the contrary, boldness means ignorance and reflection brings hesitation. And they would rightly be adjudged most courageous who, realizing most clearly the pains no less than the pleasures involved, do not on that account turn away from danger. Again, in nobility of spirit, we stand in sharp contrast to most men; for it is not by receiving kindness, but by conferring it, that we acquire our friends. . . .

And so these men then bore themselves after a manner that befits our city; but you who survive, though you may pray that it be with less hazard, should resolve that you will have a spirit to meet the foe which is no whit less courageous; and you must estimate the advantage of such a spirit not alone by a speaker's words, for the could make a long story in telling you—what you yourselves know as well as he— all the advantages that are to be gained by warding off the foe. Nay rather you must daily fix your gaze upon the power of Athens and become lovers of her, and when the vision of her greatness has inspired you, reflect that all this has been acquired by men of courage who knew their duty and in the hour of conflict were moved by a high sense of honour, who, if ever they failed in any enterprise, were resolved that at least their country should not find herself deserted by their valour, but freely sacrificed to her the fairest offering it was in their power to give. For they gave their lives for the common weal, and in so doing won for themselves the praise which grows not old and the most distinguished of all sepulchres—not that in which they lie buried, but that in which their glory survives in everlasting remembrance, celebrated on every occasion which gives rise to word of eulogy or deed of emulation. For the whole world is the sepulchre of famous men, and it is not the epitaph upon monuments set up in their own land that alone commemorates them, but also in lands not their own there abides in each breast an unwritten memorial of them, planted in the heart rather than graven on stone. Do you, therefore, now make these men your examples, and judging freedom to be happiness and courage to be freedom, be not too anxious about the dangers of war. For it is not those that are in evil plight who have the best excuse for being unsparing of their lives, for they have no hope of better days, but rather those who run the risk, if they continue to live, of the opposite reversal of fortune, and those to whom it makes the greatest difference if they suffer a disaster. For to a manly spirit more bitter is humiliation associated with cowardice than death when it comes unperceived in close company with stalwart deeds and public hopes. . . .

But for such of you here present as are sons and brothers of these men, I see the greatness of the conflict that awaits you—for the dead are always praised—and even were you to attain to surpassing virtue, hardly would you be judged, I will not say their equals, but even a little inferior. For there is envy of the living on account of rivalry, but that which has been removed from our path is honoured with a good-will that knows no antagonism.

If I am to speak also of womanly virtues, referring to those of you who will henceforth be in widowhood, I will sum up all in a brief admonition: Great is your glory if you fall not below the standard which nature has set for your sex, and great also is hers of whom there is least talk among men whether in praise or in blame.

CHAPTER 4

SOCIAL INEQUALITY

All the classical civilizations paid considerable attention to organizing and justifying extensive social inequality. But the systems of hierarchy, and the thinking behind them, varied greatly. The two passages below discuss India's caste system and Roman slavery. Both documents lay out some of the fundamental features of the two systems (in the case of the Roman legal document, the key statement comes at the end). But both also grapple with gray areas in the systems. In the Roman case, lawyers focused on cases in which slaves might be freed (manumitted) and what their status would be as a result. In India, the caste system invited consideration of what would happen if people in a given caste did work outside normal caste boundaries, or even intermarried with another caste. Neither of these situations was normal. That is, although manumission was common in Rome, most slaves were never freed; and most people in India stayed within their caste boundaries. But unusual problems can bring out underlying assumptions. How did Roman and Indian jurists compare in their views of what social inequality was all about, how rigid it should be, how people came to be in the lower orders (slaves or servants or untouchables), and how inequality could be enforced?

There is much omitted from the documents. Roman law, most obviously, said nothing about the tasks slaves did. These in fact could vary widely, from dreadful labor in mines to household service or even tutoring upper-class children. Indian law shows how different kinds of jobs were associated with key castes. Neither document uncovers trends: slavery spread in Rome, undermining free labor and reducing the motivation to improve production technology; India's caste system, though it became more complex and moved into additional parts of the subcontinent, was fairly stable in essence. An omission in the Roman document even suggests one of the tricky features of using the existence of a law as evidence of how it affected people's lives: the document talks about an improvement in the legal protection of slaves, which did occur as far as the law itself was concerned; what the document does not reveal is that the treatment of slaves deteriorated as the Roman economy came to depend more heavily on slave labor. After all, few slaves could easily invoke the law on their own behalf.

Yet what the documents do convey is significant. India's laws linked the caste system to divine appointment. On what basis did Romans find slavery justified? Neither system emphasized individual change within the social system, or what in modern times we call social mobility, but the two systems obviously differed in their positions on this topic. How did birth affect social position in the two systems, and how great were the differences in this regard?

One other complication: Roman thinking about slavery influenced later Western slave systems, but Roman slave law obviously differed from laws in the subsequent slaveholding societies in the Americas. Notably, there was no particular racial element in Rome, though foreignness was a factor.

India's castes seem to have originated when the Indo-Europeans overran previous inhabitants of the subcontinent. Various epics refer to the formation of castes. The caste system was unusual in slotting people to certain social levels by birth and regulating contact among castes as well as jobs. People could move within castes, acquiring more or less money; but the system was fundamentally static, justified by a religion that argued that living up to caste duties in one life prepared a person for advancement, through reincarnation, in the next existence. The caste system solidified over time, gradually spreading through more of India and becoming more intricate, with scores of specific castes. The process continued in the next, postclassical world history period. The caste system persisted in India into the twentieth century. Now outlawed, the system has left its mark: caste origins still define considerable social barriers in Indian society. This system, in sum, is a basic feature of Indian history.

Slavery is a more common institution in the ancient world. Most early civilizations held some slaves, usually war captives. Extensive slavery existed in Greece, and it expanded in Rome as the empire grew, providing more prisoners. Ironically, dependence on slaves for labor in mines and on agricultural estates weakened Rome in the long run, by discouraging efforts to improve production technology and by forcing an effort to continue territorial expansion as a means of labor supply. Roman slavery and the ideas behind it declined in Western Europe after the empire collapsed, though some slavery persisted and the ideas, including legal concepts, were revived when the West sponsored slavery in the Americas. Slavery was a vital labor system in the Byzantine Empire, which took over the eastern part of Rome's holdings, and in the Islamic world. Here, Roman precedent had more immediate consequences.

Questions

1. What was manumission in the Roman slave system; why would it have no applicability in India's caste system?
2. What kind of religious arguments supported the caste system? How did Roman law argue that slavery was compatible with justice? How is it clear, from Roman law, that slaves did not constitute a caste?

3. Were lower castes in India freer or less free than Roman slaves? How might an Indian apologist argue that the caste system was a relatively beneficent form of social inequality?

For Further Discussion

1. Why did classical societies uniformly develop radical social inequality, and why were almost all major religious and political leaders comfortable in justifying it?
2. How do the Roman and Indian systems of inequality compare with systems of inequality (and their justifications) in modern industrial societies?
3. Which would be better, in terms of quality of life: to be a Roman slave or a lower-caste Indian?

INDIA'S CASTE SYSTEM: THE *LAWS OF MANU*

The *Laws of Manu* was written between the first century B.C.E. and the second or third century C.E., constituting the first systematic compilation of Indian law. Early legal statements had been extracted from the Indian epics. The *Laws of Manu* maintained a close relationship with Hinduism, and indeed Manu, the creator god, gave divine sanction to the social system. Other religious elements, such as the idea of pollution inherent in farming because of the need to kill even small creatures, were used to justify the laws' social prescriptions. Indian law was also closely related to the ethical concept of dharma, or caste duty (see chapter 2). It touched base with earlier Indian history (real or imagined) in positing a racial element associated with Indo-European (Aryan) invasions. Despite the apparent effort to segregate pre-Aryan residents into the lower castes, scholars now doubt that the racial aspects of the caste system were ever so clear-cut. The *Laws of Manu* provided the basic classification of the caste system, though the original four castes later expanded greatly. Note the relationship also to views of gender and the inferiority of women, and the low valuation of manual labor.

• • •

[*87*] But to protect this whole creation, the lustrous one made separate innate activities for those born of his mouth, arms, thighs, and feet. [88] For priests, he ordained teaching and learning, sacrificing for themselves and sacrificing for others, giving, and receiving. [*89*] Protecting his subjects, giving, having sacrifices performed, study-

From *The Laws of Manu*, trans. Wendy Doniger (Harmondsworth, Eng.: Penguin Books, 1991), 12–33, 242–50.

ing, and remaining unaddicted to the sensory objects are, in summary, for a ruler. [*90*] Protecting his livestock, giving, having sacrifices performed, studying, trading, lending money, and farming the land are for a commoner. [*91*] The Lord assigned only one activity to a servant: serving these (other) classes without resentment. . . .

[*50*] These (castes) should live near mounds, trees, and cremation-grounds, in mountains and in groves, recognizable and making a living by their own innate activities. [*51*] But the dwellings of 'Fierce' Untouchables and 'Dog-cookers' should be outside the village; they must use discarded bowls, and dogs and donkeys should be their wealth. [*52*] Their clothing should be the clothes of the dead, and their food should be in broken dishes; their ornaments should be made of black iron, and they should wander constantly. [*53*] A man who carries out his duties should not seek contact with them; they should do business with one another and marry with those who are like them. [*54*] Their food, dependent upon others, should be given to them in a broken dish, and they should not walk about in villages and cities at night. [*55*] They may move about by day to do their work, recognizable by distinctive marks in accordance with the king's decrees; and they should carry out the corpses of people who have no relatives; this is a fixed rule. [*56*] By the king's command, they should execute those condemned to death, always in accordance with the teachings, and they should take for themselves the clothing, beds, and ornaments of those condemned to death.

[*57*] An unknown man, of no (visible) class but born of a defiled womb and no Aryan [Ind.-European], may seem to have the form of an Aryan, but he can be discovered by his own innate activities. [*58*] Un-Aryan behaviour, harshness, cruelty, and habitual failure to perform the rituals are the manifestations in this world indicating that a man is born of a defiled womb. [*59*] A man born of a bad womb shares his father's character, or his mother's, or both; but he can never suppress his own nature. [*60*] A man born of the confusion of wombs, even if he comes from a leading family, will inherit that very character, to a greater or lesser degree. [*61*] But the kingdom in which these degraded bastards are born, defiling the classes, quickly perishes, together with the people who live there.

[*62*] Giving up the body instinctively for the sake of a priest or cow or in the defence of women and children is the way for even the excluded (castes) to achieve success. [*63*] Manu has said that non-violence, truth, not stealing, purification, and the suppression of the sensory powers is the duty of the four classes, in a nutshell. [*64*] If someone born from a priest in a servant woman produces a child with someone of the higher (caste), the lower (caste) reaches the status of birth of the higher caste after the seventh generation. [*65*] (Thus) a servant attains the rank of priest, and a priest sinks to the rank of servant; and you should know that this can happen to someone born of a ruler, too, or of a commoner. [*66*] But if this (question) should arise: 'Which is higher, someone born by chance from a priest father in a non-Aryan mother, or from a non-Aryan father in a mother of the priestly

class?', [*67*] this is the decision: 'Someone born from an Aryan father in a non-Aryan woman may become an Aryan in his qualities; but someone born from a non-Aryan father in an Aryan mother is a non-Aryan.' [*68*] The law has been established: neither of these may undergo the transformative rituals, because the birth of the former is deficient in (Aryan) characteristics, and the latter is born 'against the grain.' . . .

[*74*] Priests who remain within the womb of the Veda and are steadfast in carrying out their own innate activities should make a living properly by six innate activities, in order, [*75*] the six innate activities of a high-born priest: teaching (the Veda social writing, the Hindu epics), reciting (the Veda), sacrificing for themselves, sacrificing for others, giving, and receiving. [*76*] But of the six innate activities, three innate activities are his means of livelihood: sacrificing for others, teaching, and receiving gifts from a pure man. [*77*] Three duties of a priest are denied to a ruler: teaching, sacrificing for others, and, third, receiving gifts. [*78*] And these are also denied to a commoner; this is a fixed rule. For Manu the Lord of Creatures has said that these duties are not for those two (classes). [*79*] As a means of livelihood, bearing weapons and missiles is for a ruler, while trade, (tending) livestock, and farming are for a commoner. But their duty is giving, reciting (the Veda), and sacrificing. [*80*] Teaching the Veda, for a priest, protecting, for a ruler, and trading, for a commoner, are pre-eminent among their own innate activities.

[*81*] But a priest who cannot make a living by his own innate activity just described may make his living by fulfilling the duty of a ruler, for he is the very next lower class. [*82*] And if (this question) should arise: 'What if he cannot make a living by either of these two (livelihoods)?', he may make his living by farming and tending livestock, the livelihood of the commoner. [*83*] But a priest or ruler who makes a living by the livelihood of a commoner should try hard to avoid farming, which generally causes violence and is dependent on others. [*84*] Some people think, 'Farming is a virtuous trade,' but as a livelihood it is despised by good people, for the wooden (plough) with the iron mouth injures the earth and the creatures that live in the earth.

[*85*] But if, for insufficient means of livelihood, a man gives up the duty in which he is skilled, to increase his wealth he may sell the merchandise that commoners sell, with the following exceptions: [*86*] he should avoid (selling) all spices, cooked food with sesame oil, stones, salt, livestock, and human beings; [*87*] all dyed cloth, as well as cloth made of hemp, linen, or wool, even if they are not dyed; fruit, roots, and medicinal herbs; [*88*] water, weapons, poison, meat, Soma, all sorts of perfumes, milk, ordinary and special honey, yogurt, clarified butter, oil, sugar, and sacrificial grass; [*89*] all of the animals that live in the wilderness, animals with fangs, and birds; wine, indigo, lac, and all animals that have a whole hoof. . . .

[*92*] By (selling) meat, lac, or salt, a priest immediately falls; by selling milk, he becomes a servant in three days. [*93*] But by willingly selling other (forbidden) merchandise, a priest assumes the nature of a commoner here on earth in seven

nights. [*94*] Spices may be weighed in exchange for spices in equal quantities, but not salt for spices; cooked food (may be weighed in exchange) for uncooked food, and sesame seeds for equal (quantities of) grain.

[*95*] A ruler in adversity may also make a living by all of these (means); but he should never be so proud as to assume the livelihood of his betters. [*96*] If a man of the lowest caste should, through greed, make his living by the innate activities of his superiors, the king should confiscate his wealth and banish him immediately. [*97*] One's own duty, (even) without any good qualities, is better than someone else's duty well done; for a man who makes his living by someone else's duty immediately falls from (his own) caste. [*98*] A commoner who cannot make a living by his own duty may also subsist by the livelihood of a servant; but he must not commit actions that (he) should not do, and he should stop when he can. [*99*] If a servant is unable to engage in the service of the twice-born and is on the brink of losing his sons and wife, he may make a living by the innate activities of a manual labourer, [*100*] practising those activities of a manual labourer and those various handicrafts by which the twice-born are served.

[*101*] A priest who remains on his own path and does not engage in the commoner's livelihood, even when he is fainting and starving for lack of a livelihood, should act in keeping with the following law: [*102*] a priest in adversity may accept gifts from anyone, for the assertion that 'What is purifying can be defiled' is not established by law. [*103*] Accepting gifts from despicable people or teaching them or sacrificing for them is not a fault in priests, for they are the equals of fire or water. [*104*] A man who eats the food of anyone, no matter who, when he is on the brink of losing his life is not smeared with evil, just as the sky is not smeared with mud. . . .

[*109*] Among accepting gifts (from despicable men), sacrificing for them, or teaching them, accepting gifts is the worst and most despised for a priest (even) after his death. [*110*] Sacrificing and teaching are always done for men who have undergone the transformative rituals, but gifts are accepted even from a servant of the lowest birth. [*111*] The error of sacrificing or teaching (despicable men) is dispelled by chanting (the Veda) and making offerings into the fire, but the one that arises from accepting gifts (from them is dispelled) by discarding (the gift) and by inner heat.

[*112*] A priest who cannot make a living should even glean (ears of corn) and gather (single grains) from any (field) whatsoever; gleaning is better than accepting gifts, and gathering is preferable even to that. . . .

[*117*] Neither a priest nor a ruler should lend money at interest, but (either) may, if he really wishes, and for religious purposes, lend at very low interest to a very evil man.

[*118*] A ruler in extremity who takes even a quarter (of the crop) is free from offence if he protects his subjects to his utmost ability. [*119*] His own duty is conquest, and he must not turn his back on a challenge; when he has protected the

commoner with his sword, he may collect the just tax from him: [*120*] the tax on grain from the commoners is one eighth, (or) one twentieth, (or) at least one 'scratch-penny.' Servants, artisans, and craftsmen should give him the service of their innate activities . . .

[*123*] Serving priests alone is recommended as the best innate activity of a servant; for whatever he does other than this bears no fruit for him. [*124*] They should assign him a livelihood out of their own family property according to his deserts, taking into account his ability, his skill, and the number of his dependants. [*125*] They should give him the leftovers of their food, their old clothes, the spoiled parts of their grain, and their worn-out household utensils.

[*126*] A servant cannot commit any crime that causes him to fall, nor does he deserve any transformative ritual; he has no authority to carry out duties, nor is he forbidden to carry out duties. [*127*] But servants who want to carry out duties, who know duty, and who emulate the duties of good men, without reciting Vedic verses, are not defiled but praised. [*128*] For the more a servant undertakes the behavior of good men, without resentment, the more he gains this world and the next, blameless. [*129*] A servant should not amass wealth, even if he has the ability, for a servant who has amassed wealth annoys priests.

ROMAN SLAVERY

The Roman slave law evolved gradually, from the republic onward. The passage below is from a textbook written in the second century C.E. by a jurist named Gaius. It pulled together a great deal of prior legislation, particularly the *Lex* [law] *Aelia Sentia* of 4 C.E., early in the empire. The text claims, of course, that wise emperors had steadily improved the treatment of slaves. The law also reflects Roman belief in natural laws—laws that follow from the inherent order of nature—from which manmade law derived. This was a powerful concept, which to some extent substituted for a belief that the gods directly set up the social order, and it was used by societies that inherited cultural ingredients from Rome (including Western Europe and the United States as late as the eighteenth century). In this case how does the law-of-nature ideal seem to the author to make slavery absolutely normal? Finally, the code reflected the importance, and the limits, of the status of citizen an area in which Rome was like Athens in imposing strict definitions. Along with the belief that slaves were property, citizenship status helped mark off the boundaries of slave life—though, in contrast to the caste system of India, the boundaries were not impenetrable.

• • •

(1) Every community that is governed by laws and customs uses partly its own particular law and partly the law common to all mankind. For whatever system of

justice each community establishes for itself, that is its own particular law and is called 'civil law' as the law particular to that community (*civitas*), while that which natural reason has established among all human beings is observed equally by all peoples, and is called 'law of nations' (*ius gentium*) since it is the standard of justice which all mankind observes. Thus the Roman People in part follows its own particular system of justice and in part the common law of all mankind. We shall note what this distinction implies in particular instances at the relevant point. . . .

(8) The system of justice which we use can be divided according to how it relates to persons, to things and to actions. Let us first see how it relates to persons.

(9) The principal distinction made by the law of persons is this, that all human beings are either free men or slaves.

(10) Next, some free men are free-born (*ingenui*), others freedmen (*libertini*).

(11) The free-born are those who were free when they were born; freedmen are those who have been released from a state of slavery.

(12) Freedmen belong to one of three status groups: they are either Roman citizens, or Latins, or subjects (*dediticii*). Let us examine each status group separately, beginning with subjects.

Dediticii

(13) The *Lex Aelia Sentia* requires that any slaves who had been put in chains as a punishment by their masters or had been branded or interrogated under torture about some crime of which they were found to be guilty; and any who had been handed over to fight as gladiators or with wild beasts, or had belonged to a troupe of gladiators or had been imprisoned; should, if the same owner or any subsequent owner manumits them, become free men of the same status as subject foreigners (*peregrini dediticii*).

(14) 'Subject foreigners' is the name given to those who had once fought a regular war against the Roman People, were defeated, and gave themselves up.

(15) We will never accept that slaves who have suffered a disgrace of this kind can become either Roman citizens or Latins (whatever the procedure of manumission and whatever their age at the time, even if they were in their masters' full ownership); we consider that they should always be held to have the status of subjects.

Citizens

(16) But if a slave has suffered no such disgrace, he sometimes becomes a Roman citizen when he is manumitted, and sometimes a Latin.

(17) A slave becomes a Roman citizen if he fulfils the following three conditions. He

From Thomas Wiedemann, *Greek and Roman Slavery* (Baltimore: Johns Hopkins University Press, 1981), 23–29. Reprinted by permission of the publisher.

must be over thirty years of age; his master must own him by Quiritary right; and he must be set free by a just and legitimate manumission, i.e. by the rod (*vindicta*) or by census or by Will. If any of these conditions is not met, he will become a Latin.

(18) The condition about the age of the slave first appeared in the *Lex Aelia Sentia*. That law does not allow slaves below thirty to become Roman citizens on manumission unless they have been freed by the rod after a council (*consilium*) accepted there was just reason for the manumission.

(19) A just reason for manumission exists when, for example, a man manumits in the presence of a council a natural son, daughter, brother or sister; or a child he has brought up [*alumnus* = foundling], or his *paedagogus* [the slave whose job it had been to look after him as a child], or a slave whom he wants to employ as his manager (*procurator*), or a slave girl whom he intends to marry.

(20) In the city of Rome, the council comprises five Roman senators and five equestrians; in the provinces it consists of twenty local justices (*recuperatores*) who must be Roman citizens, and meets on the last day of the provincial assizes; at Rome there are certain fixed days for manumissions before a council. Slaves over thirty can in fact be manumitted at any time; so that manumissions can even take place when the Praetor or Proconsul is passing by on his way to the baths or theatre, for instance.

(21) Furthermore, a slave under thirty can become a Roman citizen by manumission if he has been declared free in the Will of an insolvent master and appointed as his heir [i.e. to take over the liabilities: the *heres necessarius*], provided that he is not excluded by another heir.

Junian Latins

(22) ... [persons who do not fulfil the conditions for full citizenship] are called 'Junian Latins': Latins because they are assimilated to the status of those Latins who lived in the ancient colonies; Junian because they received their freedom through the *Lex Junia*, since they were previously considered to have the status of slaves.

(23) But the *Lex Junia* does not give them the right to make a Will themselves, or to inherit or be appointed as guardians under someone else's Will.

(24) When we said that they cannot inherit under a Will, we meant that they cannot receive anything directly as an inheritance or legacy; but they can receive things by way of a trust (*fideicommissum*).

Digression—Dediticii

(25) But those who have the status of subjects cannot receive anything at all by Will, no more than any foreigner can, and according to the general opinion, they cannot make a Will themselves.

(26) The lowest kind of freedom is therefore that of those whose status is that of subjects; and no statute, Senate Recommendation or Imperial Constitution gives them access to Roman citizenship.

(27) They are even banned from the city of Rome or anywhere within the hundredth milestone from Rome, and any who break this law have to be sold publicly together with their property, subject to the condition that they must never serve as slaves in the city of Rome or within a hundred miles of Rome, and that they must never be manumitted; if they are manumitted, the law stipulates that they become slaves of the Roman People. All these provisions are laid down by the *Lex Aelia Sentia* . . .

(36) Not everyone who wishes to manumit is legally permitted to do so.

(37) A manumission made with a view to defraud creditors or a patron is void; the liberation is prevented by the *Lex Aelia Sentia.*

(38) The same *Lex* also prevents an owner under twenty from manumitting, except by the rod and after a council has accepted that there is a just reason.

(39) Just reasons for manumission exist where, for instance, someone manumits his father or mother, or his *paedagogus,* or someone who has been brought up with him. But the reasons instanced above for the case of slaves manumitted when under thirty can be put forward here too; and conversely, those mentioned in the case of an owner under twenty may also apply for a slave under thirty.

(40) The result of this restriction on the freeing of slaves by owners aged under twenty imposed by the *Lex Aelia Sentia* is that, although an owner who has reached the age of fourteen can make a Will and institute an heir and leave legacies, if he is still under twenty he cannot give a slave his freedom.

(41) And even if an owner under twenty wants to make his slave a Latin, he still has to prove before a council that there is a just reason, and only afterwards may he manumit the slave informally in the presence of his friends.

(42) The *Lex Fufia Caninia* [2 BCE] set an additional restriction on the manumission of slaves by Will.

(43) Those who own more than two and not more than ten slaves are allowed to manumit up to half the number; those who own more than ten and not more than thirty are allowed to manumit up to a third; but those who own more than thirty and not more than a hundred have the right to manumit up to a quarter; and finally, those who own more than a hundred and not more than five hundred are allowed to manumit not more than a fifth; those who own more than five hundred are not given the right to manumit any more—the law forbids anyone to manumit more than a hundred. But if you only own one or two slaves, you are not covered by this law, and there are no restrictions upon your freedom to manumit.

(44) Nor does this law apply to those who free their slaves by some other procedure than by Will. Thus a master manumitting by the rod or by census or informally in the presence of his friends, may set free his whole household, so long as there is no other impediment to giving them their freedom. . . .

(48) We now come to a second distinction made by the law of persons. Some persons are independent agents (*sui iuris*) and some are dependent on the rights of another (*alieni iruis*).

(49) Furthermore, some of those who are in a condition of dependence are in another's power (*potestas*), some in their hands (*manus*) and some in their ownership (*mancipium*).

(50) Let us now look at persons who are in a position of dependence; for when we have established what sort of people these are, we shall be able to see who are independent agents.

(51) And first let us consider those who are in another's power.

(52) Slaves are in the power of their owners. This power is derived from the common law of nations, for we can see that among all nations alike owners have the power of life and death over their slaves, and whatever is acquired by a slave is acquired on behalf of his owner.

(53) But nowadays neither Roman citizens nor any other people who are subject to the sovereignty of the Roman People have the right to treat their slaves with excessive and unreasonable brutality. For a Constitution of the Divine Emperor Antoninus orders anyone who kills his own slave without due reason to be brought to justice in exactly the same way as one who kills another's slave. Excessively harsh treatment on the part of owners is also limited by a Constitution of the same Emperor; for when certain provincial governors asked him for a ruling regarding slaves who had taken refuge at the temples of gods or statues of emperors, he declared that owners were to be forced to sell their slaves if the cruelty of their behaviour appeared to be unbearable.

CHAPTER 5

CONDITIONS OF WOMEN IN THE CLASSICAL CIVILIZATIONS

China, India, and Rome

Like the early civilizations, all the classical centers of civilization were patriarchal societies, in which women were treated as inferiors to men and, in some respects, as their property. Materials from China, India, and Rome abundantly illustrate women's inferiority. They also obviously contrast with predominant modern values, where inequality is at least more contested. Yet, it is important not to oversimplify classical patriarchy. Women were not absolutely powerless. By observing certain behaviors and by using various private or even public recourses available to them, they might gain partial control over their condition. This important complexity in patriarchy also emerges from presentations of women in the laws and literature of classical societies. Of course, these materials offer only partial insight into women's real lives; they suggest standards for women more then real behaviors, and they have more bearing on upper-class women than on women in general, who, as fellow workers, might be less unequal with men than their more privileged sisters were. Even the cultural discussions of women, however, suggest how some women might use existing standards to their benefit or, by force of personality, might even defy the standards to some degree. The discussions also demonstrate important disagreements within classical societies, even among dominant men, over exactly how women should be treated. Here, it is particularly important to assess the extent to which defenders of women really offered different evaluations of women's rights and qualities—a particularly interesting issue in Rome.

Each of the classical societies offered a somewhat different version of patriarchal inequality. Chinese materials reflect the Confucian emphasis on hierarchy and on order, while also illustrating certain opportunities for informal expression for women within this system. In India women's conditions were more commonly portrayed in terms of religion and intense emotion, with an emphasis on moral duty (dharma, applied to gender) but also more frequent reference to attachments through love and beauty. Rome may have offered more legal protections for women than most patriarchal societies did, particularly in the late republic and empire when the earlier laws were modified to provide greater fairness. Here, some of the more general features of Roman political life, including ideas of natural law, were brought to bear, without ever approaching equality. Are the differences among these three societies significant, compared to basic assumptions about inequality?

The selections that follow constitute cultural evidence—beliefs held by men and at least some women—of women's inferiority and separate roles. Culture is very powerful, and that helps explain why women, taught ideas of these sorts from girlhood, might accept their distinct conditions. But culture is not the only story of women and gender relations. Societies also have birthrates, specific work assignments, and educational systems, all of which may be influenced by beliefs but which also may vary or change for other reasons. These parts of the picture also affect women powerfully. We lack details in many of these areas for the classical period, which is one reason for relying on cultural documentation. Furthermore, cultures not only helped shape actual conditions but also tended to persist, which explains why ideas formed in classical civilizations lasted so long. One of the Chinese documents cited below, from a manual by the upper-class woman author Ban Zhao, was still being used to educate women in China as late as the nineteenth century. Nevertheless, there are limitations. Cultural statements probably affected upper-class women more than lower-class, for wealth allowed men to treat women more as ornaments. Most historians believe that, in agricultural societies, where women as well as men had to do necessary physical labor on farms and in craft manufacturing, relations between men and women were more flexible. How good a measurement do you think culture provides for gender relations overall? What other information would you like to have before venturing a full assessment?

One point is certain, if unsurprising: cultural approaches concerning women reflected larger cultural systems. In the documents that follow, the role of Confucianism is easily traced. It led to firmer statements of gender hierarchy and of the need for women to control themselves than were made in India or Rome. Even the form of the material varies among these societies. Confucianism contributed to relatively precise prescriptions about women. India's ideas about gender—as about other aspects of this epic, religious culture—must be gleaned from stories. Greece and Rome produced prescriptive statements, but Rome, particularly, also generated laws that tried to deal carefully with what women deserved. Clearly, ideas about women provide a good means of testing how larger cultural systems applied to specific social topics. And the differences among the systems show up in the variations among the patriarchal statements—an obvious place for comparative analysis.

Questions

1. Did any of the classical cultures encourage men to think they could treat women any way they saw fit?

2. How do Chinese ideas about women reflect larger Confucian values? How do Indian ideas mirror larger religious and social beliefs? (Note: Indian thinkers disagreed about whether women would need to be reincarnated as men to reach a higher spiritual plane).

3. What would Chinese and Indian thinkers agree about, where women are concerned? Where would they disagree? Did their ideal women embody the same characteristics? Which society produced greater emphasis on factors such as emotion and love in describing relations between men and otherwise inferior women?

4. Standards for women produced measurements of inadequacy. How do the Indian and Chinese materials differ in defining why a husband might want to reject a wife?

5. How did Rome compare with China and India in the rights husbands had over their wives?

6. What hints do the following materials give about how women could survive in classical, patriarchal societies? What kinds of women had the most power? (Answering this question provides an important clue to the lives of many real women in patriarchal families.) Could women make any claims to fair treatment in any of the societies? How could a Chinese woman make a case, within the cultural system, that she was not getting what she needed to fulfill her obligations as a woman? Could Roman or Indian women make such a case, and would it resemble China's?

For Further Discussion

1. Why did patriarchal conditions develop so widely? Why didn't women rebel against them?

2. Judging by the cultural standards, which of the three main classical societies worked best for women?

CHINA: "MOTHER OF MENCIUS," A LETTER, AND BAN ZHAO

Chinese authors paid considerable attention to women during the Han dynasty. The following three selections show various facets of patriarchal beliefs: the devoted mother, a bad wife, and a standard statement of women's characteristics and duties. Do they fit together consistently? The first selection is from *Biographies of Heroic Women* written by the eminent scholar Liu Xiang in about 79–78 B.C.E. Mencius was a Confucian philosopher who lived from about 372–289 B.C.E. and who was widely revered. Because he was left fatherless, his mother played a great role in raising him, and the stories about her provided standard examples of maternal ideals. The second selection comes from a letter from a husband, Feng Yan, to his wife's younger brother explaining his reasons for divorcing her. The third selection is from the most famous Han text on women's virtue, by Ban Zhao (ca. 45–116 C.E.); she was a prominent woman scholar whose own life would seem to contradict the values she preached. Ban Zhao's booklet continued to be reproduced in China into the nineteenth century, the longest-enduring statement about gender in world history.

• • •

THE MOTHER OF MENCIUS

The mother of Mencius lived in Zou in a house near a cemetery. When Mencius was a little boy he liked to play burial rituals in the cemetery, happily building tombs and grave mounds. His mother said to herself, "This is no place to bring up my son."

She moved near the marketplace in town. Mencius then played merchant games of buying and selling. His mother again said, "This is no place to bring up my son."

So once again she moved, this time next to a school house. Mencius then played games of ancestor sacrifices and practiced the common courtesies between students and teachers. His mother said, "At last, this is the right place for my son!" There they remained.

When Mencius grew up he studied the six arts of propriety, music, archery, charioteering, writing, and mathematics. Later he became a famous Confucian scholar. Superior men commented that Mencius's mother knew the right influences for her sons. The *Book of Songs* says, "That admirable lady, what will she do for them!"

When Mencius was young, he came home from school one day and found his mother was weaving at the loom. She asked him, "Is school out already?"

He replied, "I left because I felt like it."

His mother took her knife and cut the finished cloth on her loom. Mencius was startled and asked why. She replied, "Your neglecting your studies is very much like my cutting the cloth. The superior person studies to establish a reputation and gain wide knowledge. He is calm and poised and tries to do no wrong. If you do not study now, you will surely end up as a menial servant and will never be free from troubles. It would be just like a woman who supports herself by weaving to give it up. How long could such a person depend on her husband and son to stave off hunger? If a woman neglects her work or a man gives up the cultivation of his character, they may end up as common thieves if not slaves!"

From Patricia Buckley Ebrey, ed., *Chinese Civilization: A Sourcebook* (New York: Free Press, 1981), 72–76. Reprinted by permission of The Free Press, a Division of Simon & Schuster.

Shaken, from then on Mencius studied hard from morning to night. He studied the philosophy of the master and eventually became a famous Confucian scholar. Superior men observed that Mencius's mother understood the way of motherhood. The *Book of Songs* says, "That admirable lady, what will she tell them!"

After Mencius was married, one day as he was going into his private quarters, he encountered his wife not fully dressed. Displeased, Mencius stopped going into his wife's room. She then went to his mother, begged to be sent home, and said, "I have heard that the etiquette between a man and a woman does not apply in their private room. But lately I have been too casual, and when my husband saw me improperly dressed, he was displeased. He is treating me like a stranger. It is not right for a woman to live as a guest; therefore, please send me back to my parents."

Mencius's mother called him to her and said, "It is polite to inquire before you enter a room. You should make some loud noise to warn anyone inside, and as you enter, you should keep your eyes low so that you will not embarrass anyone. Now, you have not behaved properly, yet you are quick to blame others for their impropriety. Isn't that going a little too far?"

Mencius apologized and took back his wife. Superior men said that his mother understood the way to be a mother-in-law.

When Mencius was living in Qi, he was feeling very depressed. His mother saw this and asked him, "Why are you looking so low?"

"It's nothing," he replied.

On another occasion when Mencius was not working, he leaned against the door and sighed. His mother saw him and said, "The other day I saw that you were troubled, but you answered that it was nothing. But why are you leaning against the door sighing?"

Mencius answered, "I have heard that the superior man judges his capabilities and then accepts a position. He neither seeks illicit gains nor covets glory or high salary. If the dukes and princes do not listen to his advice, then he does not talk to them. If they listen to him but do not use his ideas, then he no longer frequents their courts. Today my ideas are not being used in Qi, so I wish to go somewhere else. But I am worried because you are getting too old to travel about the country."

His mother answered, "A woman's duties are to cook the five grains, heat the wine, look after her parents-in-law, make clothes, and that is all! Therefore, she cultivates the skills required in the women's quarters and has no ambition to manage affairs outside of the house. The *Book of Changes* says, 'In her central place, she attends to the preparation of the food.' The *Book of Songs* says, 'It will be theirs neither to do wrong nor to do good, / Only about the spirits and the food will they have to think.' This means that a woman's duty is not to control or to take charge. Instead she must follow the 'three submissions.' When she is young, she must submit to her parents. After her marriage, she must submit to her husband. When she is widowed, she must submit to her son. These are the rules of propriety. Now you are an adult and I am old; therefore, whether you go depends on what you consider right, whether I follow depends on the rules of propriety."

Superior men observed that Mencius's mother knew the proper course for women. The *Book of Songs* says, "Serenely she looks and smiles, / Without any impatience she delivers her instructions."

LETTER FROM FENG YAN TO HIS BROTHER-IN-LAW

Man is a creature of emotion. Yet it is according to reason that husband and wife are joined together or put asunder. According to the rules of propriety which have been set down by the sage, a gentleman should have both a primary wife and concubines as well. Even men from poor and humble families long to possess concubines. I am old and approaching the end of my life, but I have never had a concubine. I will carry regret for this into my grave.

My wife is jealous and has destroyed the Way of a good family. Yet this mother of five children is still in my house. For the past five years her conduct has become worse and worse day after day. She sees white as black and wrong as right. I never err in the slightest, yet she lies about me and nags me without end. It is like falling among bandits on the road, for I constantly encounter unpredictable disasters through this woman. Those who slander us good officials seem to have no regard for the deleterious effects this has on the welfare of the country. Likewise, those who indulge their jealousy seem to have no concern for the unjust strain this puts on other people's lives.

Since antiquity it has always been considered a great disaster to have one's household be dominated by a woman. Now this disaster has befallen me. If I eat too much or too little or if I drink too much or too little, she jumps all over me like the tyrant Xia Jie. If I play some affectionate joke on her, she will gossip about it to everyone. She glowers with her eyes and clenches her fists tightly in anger over things which are purely the product of her imagination. I feel a severe pang in my heart, as though something is poisoning my five viscera. Anxiety cuts so deeply that I can hardly bear to go on living. My rage is so great that I often forget the calamities I might cause.

When she is at home, she is always lounging in bed. After she gave birth to my principal heir, she refused to have any more children. We have no female servants at our home who can do the work of weaving clothes and rugs. Our family is of modest means and we cannot afford a man-servant, so I have to work myself like a humble commoner. My old friends see my situation and feel very sorry for me, but this woman has not the slightest twinge of sympathy or pity.

Wu Da, you have seen our one and only female servant. She has no hairpins or hair ornaments. She has no make-up for her face, looks haggard, and is in bad shape. My wife does not extend the slightest pity to her, nor does she try to understand her. The woman flies into a rage, jumps around, and yells at her. Her screaming is so shrill that even a sugar peddler's concubine would be ashamed to behave in such a manner.

I should have sent this woman back long ago, but I was concerned by the fact that the children were still young and that there was no one else to do the work in our house. I feared that my children, Jiang and Bao, would end up doing servants' work. Therefore I retained her. But worry and anxiety plunge like a dagger into my heart and cause me great pain. The woman is always screaming fiercely. One can hardly bear to listen to it.

Since the servant was so mistreated, within half a year her body was covered with scabs and scars. Ever since the servant became ill, my daughter Jiang has had to hull the grain and do the cooking, and my son Bao has had to do all sorts of dirty work. Watching my children struggle under such labor gives me distress.

Food and clothing are scattered all over the house. Winter clothes which have become frayed are not patched. Even though the rest of us are very careful to be neat, she turns the house into a mess. She does not have the manner of a good wife, nor does she posses the virtue of a good mother. I despise her overbearing aggressiveness, and I hate to see our home turned into a sty.

She relies on the power of Magistrate Zheng to get what she wants. She is always threatening people, and her barbs are numerous. It seems as if she carries a sword and lance to the door. Never will she make a concession, and it feels as if there were a hundred bows around our house. How can we ever return to a happy family life?

When the respectable members of our family try to reason with her, she flings insults at them and makes sharp retorts. She never regrets her scandalous behavior and never allows her heart to be moved. I realize that I have placed myself in a difficult position, and so I have started to plan ahead. I write you this letter lest I be remiss in keeping you informed of what is happening. I believe that I have just cause, and I am not afraid of criticism. Unless I send this wife back, my family will have no peace. Unless I send this wife back, my house will never be clean. Unless I send this wife back, good fortune will not come to my family. Unless I send this wife back, I will never again get anything accomplished. I hate myself for not having made this decision while I was still young. The decision is now made, but I am old, humiliated, and poor. I hate myself for having allowed this ulcer to grow and spread its poison. I brought a great deal of trouble on myself.

Having suffered total ruin as a result of this family catastrophe, I am abandoning the gentry life to live as a recluse. I will sever relationships with my friends and give up my career as an official. I will stay at home all the time and concentrate on working my land to supply myself with food and clothing. How can I think of success and fame?

BAN ZHAO'S *ADMONITIONS FOR WOMEN*

Humility

In ancient times, on the third day after a girl was born, people placed her at the base of the bed, gave her a pot shard to play with, and made a sacrifice to announce her birth. She was put below the bed to show that she was lowly and weak and should concentrate on humbling herself before others. Playing with a shard showed that she should get accustomed to hard work and concentrate on being diligent. Announcing her birth to the ancestors showed that she should focus on continuing the sacrifices. These three customs convey the unchanging path for women and the ritual traditions.

Humility means yielding and acting respectful, putting others first and oneself last, never mentioning one's own good deeds or denying one's own faults, enduring insults and bearing with mistreatment, all with due trepidation. Industriousness means going to bed late, getting up early, never shirking work morning or night, never refusing to take on domestic work, and completing everything that needs to be done neatly and carefully. Continuing the sacrifices means serving one's husband-master with appropriate demeanor, keeping oneself clean and pure, never joking or laughing, and preparing pure wine and food to offer to the ancestors.

There has never been a woman who had these three traits and yet ruined her reputation or fell into disgrace. If a woman loses these three traits, she will have no name to preserve and will not be able to avoid shame.

Devotion

According to the rites, a man is obligated to take a second wife but nothing is written about a woman marrying twice. Hence the saying, "A husband is one's Heaven: one cannot flee Heaven; one cannot leave a husband." Heaven punishes those whose actions offend the spirits; a husband looks down on a wife who violates the rites and proprieties. Thus the *Model for Women* says, "To please one man is her goal; to displease one man ends her goal." It follows from this that a woman must seek her husband's love—not through such means as flattery, flirting, or false intimacy, but rather through devotion. . . .

If a husband be unworthy then he possesses nothing by which to control his wife. If a wife be unworthy, then she possesses nothing with which to serve her husband. If a husband does not control his wife, then the rules of conduct manifesting his authority are abandoned and broken. If a wife does not serve her husband, then the proper relationship (between men and women) and the natural order of things are neglected and destroyed. As a matter of fact the purpose of these two (the controlling of women by men, and the serving of men by women) is the same.

Now examine the gentlemen of the present age. They only know that wives must be controlled, and that the husband's rules of conduct manifesting his authority must be established. They therefore teach their boys to read books and (study) histories. But they do not in the least understand that husbands and masters must (also) be served, and that the proper relationship and the rites should be maintained.

Yet only to teach men and not to teach women,—is that not ignoring the essential relation between them? According to the "Rites," it is the rule to begin to teach children to read at the age of eight years, and by the age of fifteen years they ought then to be ready for cultural training. Only why should it not be (that girls' education as well as boys' be) according to this principle? . . . As Yin and Yang are not of the same nature, so man and woman have different characteristics. The distinctive quality of the Yang is rigidity; the function of the Yin is yielding. Man is honored for strength; a woman is beautiful on account of her gentleness. Hence there arose the common saying: "A man though born like a wolf may, it is feared, become a weak monstrosity; a woman though born like a mouse may, it is feared, become a tiger."

Now for self-culture nothing equals respect for others. To counteract firmness nothing equals compliance. Consequently it can be said that the Way of respect and acquiescence is woman's most important principle of conduct. So respect may be defined as nothing other than holding on to that which is permanent; and acquiescence nothing other than being liberal and generous. Those who are steadfast in devotion know that they should stay in their proper places; those who are liberal and generous esteem others, and honor and serve (them).

If husband and wife have the habit of staying together, never leaving one another, and following each other around within the limited space of their own rooms, then they will lust after and take liberties with one another. From such action improper language will arise between the two. This kind of discussion may lead to licentiousness. Out of licentiousness will be born a heart of disrespect to the husband. Such a result comes from not knowing that one should stay in one's proper place.

Furthermore, affairs may be either crooked or straight; words may be either right or wrong. Straightforwardness cannot but lead to quarreling; crookedness cannot but lead to accusation. If there are really accusations and quarrels, then undoubtedly there will be angry affairs. Such a result comes from not esteeming others, and not honoring and serving (them).

(If wives) suppress not contempt for husbands, then it follows (that such wives) rebuke and scold (their husbands). (If husbands) stop not short of anger, then they are certain to beat (their wives). The correct relationship between husband and wife is based upon harmony and intimacy, and (conjugal) love is grounded in proper union. Should actual blows be dealt, how could matrimonial relationship be preserved? Should sharp words be spoken, how could (conjugal) love exist? If love and proper relationship both be destroyed, then husband and wife are divided.

INDIA: THE *RAMAYANA*

The following excerpts are from another great Indian epic, the *Ramayana,* attributed to an author named Valmiki. It was written in Sanskrit during the third century B.C.E., but a more definitive version was complied around 200 C.E. The story deals with the turbulent life of a god-king, Rama, and his wife Sita. Rama is driven into exile, and his wife insists on accompanying him (would this kind of assertiveness have been valued in China?). Sita is abducted and Rama battles successfully to win her back. The story provides a host of complex clues about marriage ideals in India's version of a patriarchal society. One reference, to an ordeal by burning, foreshadows a custom (suttee) introduced in a later period of Indian history, according to which some women were expected to throw themselves on their husbands' funeral pyres, based on the assumption that with her husband dead, a woman's life was over.

• • •

The sweet-speaking Sita, worthy of Rama's love, thus being instructed to remain in Ayodhya, though filled with affection, indignantly replied: "O Offspring of a great king, O Rama, how canst thou speak in such wise? O Prince, thy words evoke laughter. O Chief of Men, father, mother, son and daughter-in-law live according to their merit and are dependent on it, but a wife enjoys the fortune of her husband since she is a part of himself. I am therefore entitled to share they father's command and also go into exile.

"The happiness of a woman depends on her husband, neither father, mother, son, relative or companion avail her at death; in this world and in the other world, the husband alone is her all-in-all. If thou to-day depart for the forest, I will precede thee on foot, clearing the thorns and kusha grass from thy path. O Hero, relinquishing anger and pride, take me with thee without hesitation. There is no fault in me that merits my remaining here, without thee. The joy experienced by lords of men whether dwelling in a palace or transported in an aerial chariot through the heavens or possessing the eightfold psychic powers, is far inferior to the joy of the wife in the service of her lord. My royal father has instructed me fully in the duties of a wife and, therefore, I have no need of further instruction in the matter. Assuredly I shall accompany thee to the forest, uninhabited by men, filled with savage beasts, such as bears and bulls. O My Hero, I will dwell in the forest as happily as in the palace of my father, having no anxiety in the three worlds save the service of my spouse. O Hero, I will wander with thee in the forest according to the ancient spiritual ordinance, free from desire for pleasure, traversing the honey-scented wood-

From Valmiki, *The Ramayana,* trans. Hari Prasad Shastri (London, 1957), 1: 221, 227; 3: 103–4, 287–89, 310–16, 334–38, 341–42.

land. O Lord of my Life, since thou canst protect and support innumerable people, canst thou not more easily protect me? Without doubt to-day I shall enter the forest with thee, O Fortunate Prince, none can break my resolve. . . .

Thus Sita, lamenting and embracing . . . Rama, wept aloud. From her eyes, like a she elephant wounded by poisoned arrows, long-restrained tears issued, as fire is kindled by the friction of wood. Crystal drops fell from her eyes as water slips from the petals of the lotus flowers. The face of the princess resembling the full moon, withered by the fire of intense grief, looked like a lotus withdrawn from water.

Shri Ramachandra, taking Sita, afflicted and fainting, in his arms, spoke to her in the following wise: "O goddess I do not desire even to enter heaven if it causes thee pain! Nought do I fear! Like Brahma [the creator God], I am wholly fearless! Though able to protect thee in every way, yet not fully knowing thy mind, I declined to let thee share my exile. Seeing thou art destined to share my exile, I do not desire to abandon thee, as a man of virtuous conduct determines not to sacrifice his good name. . . .

This is eternal righteousness—to obey the command of thy parents, fixed in the practice of truth. O Sita, not knowing thy mind, I advised thee not to accompany me, but now seeing thy fixed resolve I desire to take thee with me. . . . [During the exile Sita is seized by a king, Ravana, aided by a demon. Rama ultimately defeats Ravana.]

Rama Repudiates Sita

Beholding Sita standing humbly beside him, Rama gave expression to the feelings he had concealed in his heart, saying:—

"O Illustrious Princess, I have re-won thee and mine enemy has been defeated on the battlefield; I have accomplished all that fortitude could do; my wrath is appeased; the insult and the one who offered it have both been obliterated by me. To-day my prowess has been manifested, to-day mine exertions have been crowned with success, to-day I have fulfilled my vow and am free. As ordained by destiny the stain of thy separation and thine abduction by that fickle-minded titan has been expunged by me, a mortal. Of what use is great strength to the vacillating, who do not with resolution avenge the insult offered to them? . . .

When Sita heard Rama speak in this wise, her large doe-like eyes filled with tears and, beholding the beloved of his heart standing close to him, Rama, who was apprehensive of public rumour, was torn within himself. Then, in the presence of the monkeys and the titans, he said to Sita, whose eyes were as large as lotus petals, her dark hair plaited, and who was endowed with faultless limbs:—

"What a man should do in order to wipe out an insult, I have done by slaying Ravana for I guard mine honour jealously! . . . Be happy and let it be known that this arduous campaign, so gloriously terminated through the support of my friends, was not undertaken wholly for thy sake. I was careful to wipe out the affront paid to me completely and to avenge the insult offered to mine illustrious House.

"A suspicion has arisen, however, with regard to thy conduct, and thy presence is as painful to me as a lamp to one whose eye is diseased! Henceforth go where it best pleaseth thee, I give thee leave, O Daughter of Janaka. O Lovely One, the ten regions are at thy disposal; I can have nothing more to do with thee! What man of honour would give rein to his passion so far as to permit himself to take back a woman who has dwelt in the house of another? Thou hast been taken into Ravana's lap and he has cast lustful glances on thee; how can I reclaim thee, I who boast of belonging to an illustrious House? The end which I sought in re-conquering thee has been gained; I no longer have any attachment for thee; go where thou desirest! This is the outcome of my reflections, O Lovely One Turn to [a man such as] Lakshmana or Bharata, Shatrughna, Sugriva or the Titan Bibishana, make thy choice, O Sita, as please thee best. Assuredly Ravana, beholding thy ravishing and celestial beauty, will not have respected thy person during the time that thou didst dwell in his abode."

On this, that noble lady, worthy of being addressed in sweet words, hearing that harsh speech from her beloved lord, who for long had surrounded her with every homage, wept bitterly, and she resembled a creeper that has been torn away by the trunk of a great elephant.

"Why dost thou address such words to me, O Hero, as a common man addresses an ordinary woman? I swear to thee, O Long-armed Warrior, that my conduct is worthy of thy respect! It is the behavior of other women that has filled thee with distrust! Relinquish thy doubts since I am known to thee! If my limbs came in contact with another's, it was against my will, O Lord, and not through any inclination on my part; it was brought about by fate. [Sita enters a burning pyre to demonstrate her innocence.] Thereafter the Witness of the whole world, the god of fire, addressed Rama, saying:—

"Here is Vaidehi, O Rama, there is no sin in her! Neither by word, feeling or glance has thy lovely consort shown herself to be unworthy of thy noble qualities. Separated from thee, that unfortunate one was borne away against her will in the lonely forest by Ravana, who had grown proud on account of his power. Though imprisoned and closely guarded by titan women in the inner apartments, thou wast ever the focus of her thoughts and her supreme hope. Surrounded by hideous and sinister women, though tempted and threatened, Maithili never gave place in her heart to a single thought for that titan and was solely absorbed in thee. She is pure and without taint, do thou receive Maithili; it is my command that she should not suffer reproach in any way."

These words filled Rama's heart with delight and he, the most eloquent of men, that loyal soul, reflected an instant within himself, his glance full of joy. Then the illustrious, steadfast and exceedingly valiant Rama, the first of virtuous men, hearing those words addressed to him, said to the Chief of the Gods:—

"On account of the people, it was imperative that Sita should pass through this trial by fire; this lovely woman had dwelt in Ravana's inner apartments for a long time. Had I not put the innocence of Janaki to the test, the people would have said: —'Rama, the son of Dasaratha is governed by lust!' It was well known to me that Sita had never given her heart to another and that [she], was ever devoted to me. . . . That virtuous woman could never belong to any other than myself for she is to me what the light is to the sun. [A later chapter was added, responding to the belief that even innocent cohabitation with another man is unacceptable and detailing Rama's renewed exile of Sita and her death.]

ROME: LEGAL DEBATES

The first selection here details the treatment of women in early Roman law, as reported in Valerius Maximus, *Memorable Deeds and Sayings,* written in the first century C.E. The second selection deals with a legal debate in the later republic, over the repeal of the Oppian law (which limited women's finery and was passed in 215 B.C.E. after a disastrous defeat in war). The law was seen as an emergency measure to limit women's use of expensive goods. But it stayed on the books for twenty years, and many conservatives, headed by Marcus Porcius Cato, argued that it should remain. Reform leaders, obviously, had different ethical ideas. This debate was reported in Livy's *History of Rome,* also produced in the first century C.E. At that time, during the reign of Augustus, debate over women's conditions resumed, as Augustus tried both to protect women from cruelty and to shore up family unity. These documents suggest some disagreement over women's treatment (though not over their inferiority) and some change over time; it is generally agreed that legal protections improved still further during the empire, making Rome one of the few agricultural civilizations in which deterioration did not occur as prosperity increased.

• • •

A. Punishment of Wives in Early Rome

Egnatius Metellus . . . took a cudgel and beat his wife to death because she had drunk some wine. Not only did no one charge him with a crime, but no one even blamed him. Everyone considered this an excellent example of one who had justly paid the penalty for violating the laws of sobriety. Indeed, any woman who immoderately seeks the use of wine closes the door on all virtues and opens it to vices.

From Mary R. Lefkowitz and Maureen B. Fant, eds., *Women's Life in Greece and Rome* (Baltimore: Johns Hopkins University Press, 1982), 176–80. Reprinted by permission of the publisher.

There was also the harsh marital severity of Gaius Sulpicius Gallus. He divorced his wife because he had caught her outdoors with her head uncovered: a stiff penalty, but not without a certain logic. 'The law,' he said, 'prescribes for you my eyes alone to which you may prove your beauty. For these eyes you should provide the ornaments of beauty, for these be lovely: entrust yourself to their more certain knowledge. If you, with needless provocation, invite the look of anyone else, you must be suspected of wrongdoing.'

Quintus Antistius Vetus felt no differently when he divorced his wife because he had seen her in public having a private conversation with a common freedwoman. For, moved not by an actual crime but, so to speak, by the birth and nourishment of one, he punished her before the sin could be committed, so that he might prevent the deed's being done at all, rather than punish it afterwards.

To these we should add the case of Publius Sempronius Sophus who disgraced his wife with divorce merely because she dared attend the games without his knowledge. And so, long ago, when the misdeeds of women were thus forestalled, their minds stayed far from wrongdoing.

B. Repeal of the Oppian Law. Rome, 195 B.C.E.

Among the troubles of great wars, either scarcely over or yet to come, something intervened which, while it can be told briefly, stirred up enough excitement to become a great battle. Marcus Fundanius and Lucius Valerius, the tribunes of the people, brought a motion to repeal the Oppian law before the people. Gaius Oppius had carried this law as tribune at the height of the Punic War, during the consulship of Quintus Fabius and Tiberius Sempronius. The law said that no woman might own more than half an ounce of gold nor wear a multicoloured dress nor ride in a carriage in the city or in a town within a mile of it, unless there was a religious festival. The tribunes, Marcus and Publius Junius Brutus, were in favour of the Oppian law and said that they would not allow its repeal. Many noble men came forward hoping to persuade or dissuade them; a crowd of men, both supporters and opponents, filled the Capitoline Hill. The matrons, whom neither counsel nor shame nor their husbands' orders could keep at home, blockaded every street in the city and every entrance to the Forum. As the men came down to the Forum, the matrons besought them to let them, too, have back the luxuries they had enjoyed before, giving as their reason that the republic was thriving and that everyone's private wealth was increasing with every day. This crowd of women was growing daily, for now they were even gathering from the towns and villages. Before long they dared go up and solicit the consuls, praetors, and other magistrates; but one of the consuls could not be moved in the least, Marcus Porcius Cato, who spoke in favour of the law:

'If each man of us, fellow citizens, had established that the right and authority of the husband should be held over the mother of his own family, we should have less difficulty with women in general; now, at home our freedom is conquered by female fury, here in the Forum it is bruised and trampled upon, and, because we have not contained the individuals, we fear the lot . . .

'Indeed, I blushed when, a short while ago, I walked through the midst of a band of women. Had not respect for the dignity and modesty of certain ones (not them all!) restrained me (so they would not be seen being scolded by a consul), I should have said, "What kind of behaviour is this? Running around in public, blocking streets, and speaking to other women's husbands! Could you not have asked your own husbands the same thing at home? Are you more charming in public with others' husbands than at home with your own? And yet, it is not fitting even at home (if modesty were to keep married women within the bounds of their rights) for you to concern yourselves with what laws are passed or repealed here." Our ancestors did not want women to conduct any—not even private—business without a guardian; they wanted them to be under the authority of parents, brothers, or husbands; we (the gods help us!) even now let them snatch at the government and meddle in the Forum and our assemblies. What are they doing now on the streets and crossroads, if they are not persuading the tribunes to vote for repeal? Give the reins to their unbridled nature and this unmastered creature, and hope that they will put limits on their own freedom; unless you do something yourselves, this is the least of the things imposed upon them either by custom or by law which they endure with hurt feelings. They want freedom, nay licence (if we are to speak the truth), in all things.

'If they are victorious now, what will they not attempt? . . . As soon as they begin to be your equals, they will have become your superiors . . .'

Lucius Valerius spoke on behalf of the motion which he himself had brought. ' . . . why should we wonder that they [the women] have taken action in a case which concerns themselves? What, after all, have they done? We have proud ears indeed, if, while masters do not scorn the appeals of slaves, we are angry when honourable women ask something of us . . .'

'Who then does not know that this is a recent law, passed twenty years ago? Since our matrons lived for so long by the highest standards of behaviour without any law, what risk is there that, once it is repealed, they will yield to luxury? . . .' 'Shall it be our wives alone to whom the fruits of peace and tranquillity of the state do not come? . . . Shall we forbid only women to wear purple? When you, a man, may use purple on your clothes, will you not allow the mother of your family to have a purple cloak, and will your horse be more beautifully saddled than your wife is garbed? . . . [Women] cannot partake of magistracies, priesthoods, triumphs, badges of office, gifts, or spoils of war; elegance, finery, and beautiful clothes are women's badges, in these they find joy and take pride, this our forebears called the women's world. . . . ' [The law was repealed.]

CHAPTER 6

BUDDHISM AND CHRISTIANITY

The origin and early development of two of the great world religions lie in the classical period. Both Buddhism and Christianity arose where important religious developments had already occurred, but partially in protest against established formulas. Both sought to dispense with what their leaders viewed as excessive ceremonies and religious officialdom, in favor of a focus on spiritual values. Both, unquestionably, spurred new interest in otherworldly goals.

Buddhism originated in India, with Prince Gautama (563–483 B.C.E.), who later took the name Buddha, or "Enlightened One." Protesting key features of Hinduism, including the great role of priests and ritual and the caste system, Buddhism maintained and extended Hindu disdain for earthly life, looking to an ultimate union with the divine essence, which the new religion called nirvana. Buddha transmitted his thoughts to disciples orally, and they were only gradually written down. From a small movement around its holy founder, Buddhism spread widely in India during the classical period, rivaling but also coexisting with Hinduism. Some governments, and particularly that of the great emperor Ashoka (269–232 B.C.E.), backed Buddhism solidly, helping develop missionary movements that began to spread the religion more widely. By the end of the classical period, Buddhism was shrinking in India itself, as Hinduism consolidated its majority hold. But it was gaining new converts in Sri Lanka, in other parts of southeastern Asia, and in China.

Christianity originated later, in the other great center of religious origins in world history, the Middle East. Inspired by Jesus Christ, who was crucified in 30 C.E., Christianity developed quickly as various disciples and early converts spelled out their story of Jesus' life and doctrines and began to form religious communities. For a brief time, Christian leaders emphasized reform within the Jewish religion, but soon other converts were sought. Paul of Tarsus (d. 67 C.E.) was a crucial figure in the development of the new religion; after his own conversion, he tirelessly preached to groups of Jews and non-Jews alike. Paul's writings emphasized Christianity as a religion for all peoples, in contrast to Judaism. Paul also introduced key Greco-Roman ideas into the religion—including a Roman-like emphasis on law. This also enhanced modern Christianity's appeal in the classical Mediterranean world.

Christianity began to spread widely in the Roman Empire and beyond, despite occasional persecution from the Roman government, which worried about a religion that placed devotion to God ahead of loyalty to the state. By 300 C.E. probably about 10 percent of all the people in the empire were Christian, drawn to the message of hope for the poor and an intellectual and spiritual structure that added important elements to existing Greco-Roman culture. A strong church organization, with religious officials such as priests and bishops, arose in many regions, paralleling the organization of the empire itself. Then in 313 C.E., the emperor Constantine essentially adopted Christianity as the religion of the empire. Official support greatly increased the religion's appeal, but it added some new problems, including the appropriate relations between church and state. Eventually the religion also had to grapple with disagreements about doctrine; methods were needed to deal with religious error, given an insistence that God intended a single truth.

Christianity and Buddhism shared many features, which helps explain their similar success in converting masses of people in various regions and of various cultural backgrounds. They both offered hope for religious advancement, mainly after this life but to a limited extent during it. They both expressed suspicion of worldly things and offered an ethic designed to help religious people avoid giving in to snares and temptations. Both, not surprisingly, sponsored monastic movements where small groups of people could seek holiness apart from normal worldly cares.

The two religions also differed greatly. Their attitude toward the world and its doings diverged; a careful comparison might being by trying to define this difference. Buddhists emphasized miseries, whereas Christian leaders such as Paul stressed sin. How would Christian and Buddhist attitudes toward government or human achievement compare? A second difference lies in the teachings about how to deal with misery or sin: what is the good religious life, and how much control does an individual have over it? Buddhists and Christians differed greatly in their views on how to lead a holy life and also on the intervention of divine forces. This difference relates to the strong organizational contrast between the two religions, with Christianity far more focused on church institutions as the embodiment of faith.

Both religions sent out active missionaries at various points in their histories. Both had their greatest success after the classical period, when Buddhism spread to much of eastern and southeastern Asia and Christianity went beyond the boundaries of the Roman Empire into the heart of Europe, as well as to a few parts of Asia and Africa. The dissemination of these two religions reflected growing potential disorder as the classical period closed; people in places like China and Europe turned anew to religion for solace and guidance. The same ideas set in motion important new cultural forces for the next period in world history.

Questions

1. What aspects of Christianity and Buddhism—whether similar or different—help explain their great appeal?
2. How did Buddhist and Christian leaders define the main goals of life? What are the concepts of nirvana and Christian salvation? How did the two religions view the human body and its needs?
3. How did Buddhist and Christian leaders define divinity? What were the roles of Buddha and of Christ in religious life?
4. In what respects did Buddhist and Christian leaders agree, and in what respects did they disagree, about how to lead a holy life? How would the two religions view the state? How would they view acts of charity in relation to a holy life?
5. Why did Buddhism develop less of a formal church structure than Christianity? Does the difference relate to differences in the ideals of the two religions? How would the two religions, as they matured, approach problems of truth and error? What was the Christian approach, by the fourth century, to what it called heresy? Which religion would be more tolerant, and why?

For Further Discussion

1. How did Buddhism and Christianity reflect the earlier traditions of their cultures—Hinduism and the Indian epics, for Buddhism; Greek philosophy and Roman law, for Christianity?
2. How did Buddhism resemble Hinduism? How did it differ (see Indian documents in chapters 2 and 4)?
3. How would Buddhist monasticism compare with Christian, in institutions devoted to the holiest possible life?
4. Why did Christianity and Buddhism both have such wide appeal during the late classical centuries and beyond?

BUDDHISM

The first Buddhist selection, below, entitled "The Four Noble Truths," lies at the core of Buddha's quest for understanding after he had renounced worldly things. It suggests a central definition of Buddhist goals. The second passage, which talks more explicitly about what an individual should do to live a holy life, comes from the Dhammapada, or Footsteps of the Law. This was probably written down toward the end of the period, when Buddhist doctrines had been fully established, at about 70 B.C.E. Although devout Buddhists often claimed that each sentence was preserved exactly as it came from the lips of the Master, some scholars believe that it is clearly a later, more polished work. Later Buddhism also reflected some belief in the holiness of Buddha himself, which had not been part of Gautama's original vision but which helped spread the religion as people sought to attach their otherworldly aspirations to the merits of saintly leaders.

• • •

THE FOUR NOBLE TRUTHS

1. The Truth Concerning Misery

And how, O priests, does a priest live, as respects the elements of being, observant of the elements of being in the four noble truths?

Whenever, O priest, a priest knows the truth concerning misery, knows the truth concerning the origin of misery, knows the truth concerning the cessation of misery, knows the truth concerning the path leading to the cessation of misery.

And what, O priests, is the noble truth of misery?

Birth is misery; old age is misery; disease is misery; death is misery; sorrow, lamentation, misery, grief, and despair are misery; to wish for what one cannot have is misery; in short, all the five attachment-groups are misery.

This, O priests, is called the noble truth of misery.

2. The Truth of the Origin of Misery

And what, O priests, is the noble truth of the origin of misery?

It is desire leading to rebirth, joining itself to pleasure and passion, and finding delight in every existence,—desire, namely, for sensual pleasure, desire for permanent existence, desire for transitory existence.

But where, O priests, does this desire spring up and grow? where does it settle and take root?

Where anything is delightful and agreeable to men, there desire springs up and grows, there it settles and takes root.

And what is delightful and agreeable to men, where desire springs up and grows, where it settles and takes root?

The eye is delightful and agreeable to men; there desire springs up and grows, there it settles and takes root.

The ear . . . the nose . . . the tongue . . . the body . . . the mind is delightful and agreeable to men; there desire springs up and grows, there it settles and takes root.

The Six Organs of Sense.

Forms . . . sounds . . . odors . . . tastes . . . things tangible . . . ideas are delightful and agreeable to men; there desire springs up and grows, there it settles and takes root.

The Six Objects of Sense.

Eye-consciousness . . . ear-consciousness . . . nose-consciousness . . . tongue-consciousness . . . body-consciousness . . . mind-consciousness is delightful and agreeable to men; there desire springs up and grows, there it settles and takes root.

The Six Consciousnesses.

Contact of the eye . . . ear . . . nose . . . tongue . . . body . . . mind is delightful and agreeable to men; there desire springs up and grows, there it settles and takes root.

The Six Contacts.

Sensation produced by contact of the eye . . . ear . . . nose . . . tongue . . . body . . . mind is delightful and agreeable to men; there desire springs up and grows, there it settles and takes root.

The Six Sensations.

Perception of forms . . . sounds . . . odors . . . tastes . . . things tangible . . . ideas is delightful and agreeable to men; there desire springs up and grows, there it settles and takes root.

The Six Perceptions.

Thinking on forms . . . sounds . . . odors . . . tastes . . . things tangible . . . ideas is delightful and agreeable to men; there desire springs up and grows, there it settles and takes root.

The Six Thinkings.

Desire for forms . . . sounds . . . odors . . . tastes . . . things tangible . . . ideas is delightful and agreeable to men; there desire springs up and grows, there it settles and takes root.

The Six Desires.

Reasoning on forms . . . sounds . . . odors . . . tastes . . . things tangible . . . ideas is delightful and agreeable to men; there desire springs up and grows, there it settles and takes root.

The Six Reasonings.

Reflection on forms . . . sounds . . . odors . . . tastes . . . things tangible . . . ideas is delightful and agreeable to men; there desire springs up and grows, there it settles and takes root.

The Six Reflections.

This, O priests, is called the noble truth of the origin of misery.

3. The Truth of the Cessation of Misery

And what, O priests, is the noble truth of the cessation of misery?

It is the complete fading out and cessation of this desire, a giving up, a losing hold, a relinquishment, and a nonadhesion.

But where, O priests, does this desire wane and disappear? where is it broken up and destroyed?

Where anything is delightful and agreeable to men; there desire wanes and disappears, there it is broken up and destroyed.

And what is delightful and agreeable to men, where desire wanes and disappears, where it is broken up and destroyed?

The eye is delightful and agreeable to men; there desire wanes and disappears, there it is broken up and destroyed.

[Similarly respecting the other organs of sense, the six objects of sense, the six consciousnesses, the six contacts, the six sensations, the six perceptions, the six thinkings, the six desires, the six reasonings, and the six reflections.]

This, O priests, is called the noble truth of the cessation of misery.

4. The Truth of the Path Leading to the Cessation of Misery

And what, O priests, is the noble truth of the path leading to the cessation of misery?

It is this noble eightfold path, to wit, right belief, right resolve, right speech, right behavior, right occupation, right effort, right contemplation, right concentration.

And what, O priests, is right belief?

The knowledge of misery, O priests, the knowledge of the origin of misery, the knowledge of the cessation of misery, and the knowledge of the path leading to the cessation of misery, this, O priests, is called "right belief."

And what, O priests, is right resolve?

The resolve to renounce sensual pleasures, the resolve to have malice towards none, and the resolve to harm no living creature, this, O priests, is called "right resolve."

And what, O priests, is right speech?

To abstain from falsehood, to abstain from backbiting, to abstain from harsh language, and to abstain from frivolous talk, this, O priests, is called "right speech."

And what, O priests, is right behavior?

To abstain from destroying life, to abstain from taking that which is not given one, and to abstain from immorality, this, O priests, is called "right behavior."

And what, O priests, is right occupation?

Whenever, O priests, a noble disciple, quitting a wrong occupation, gets his livelihood by a right occupation, this, O priests, is called "right occupation."

And what, O priests, is right effort?

Whenever, O priests, a priest purposes, makes an effort, heroically endeavors, applies his mind, and exerts himself that evil and demeritorious qualities not yet arisen may not arise; purposes, makes an effort, heroically endeavors, applies his mind, and exerts himself that evil and demeritorious qualities already arisen may be abandoned; purposes, makes an effort, heroically endeavors, applies his mind, and exerts himself that meritorious qualities not yet arisen may arise; purposes, makes an effort, heroically endeavors, applies his mind, and exerts himself for the preservation, retention, growth, increase, development, and perfection of meritorious qualities already arisen, this, O priest, is called "right effort."

And what, O priests, is right contemplation?

Whenever, O priests, a priest lives, as respects the body, observant of the body, strenuous, conscious, contemplative, and has rid himself of lust and grief; as respects sensations, observant of sensations, strenuous, conscious, contemplative, and has rid himself of lust and grief; as respects the mind, observant of the mind, strenuous, conscious, contemplative, and has rid himself of lust and grief; as respects the elements of being, observant of the elements of being, strenuous, conscious, contemplative, and has rid himself of lust and grief, this, O priests, is called "right contemplation."

And what, O priests, is right concentration?

Whenever, O priests, a priest, having isolated himself from sensual pleasures, having isolated himself from demeritorious traits, and still exercising reasoning, still exercising reflection, enters upon the first trance which is produced by isolation and characterized by joy and happiness; when, through the subsidence of reasoning and reflection, and still retaining joy and happiness, he enters upon the second trance, which is an interior tranquilization and intentness of the thoughts, and is produced by concentration; when, through the paling of joy, indifferent, contemplative, conscious, and in the experience of bodily happiness—that state which eminent men describe when they say, "Indifferent, contemplative, and living happily"—he enters upon the third trance; when, through the abandonment of happiness, through the abandonment of misery, through the disappearance of all antecedent gladness and grief, he enters upon the fourth trance, which has neither misery nor happiness, but is contemplation as refined by indifference, this, O priests, is called "right concentration."

This, O priests, is called the noble truth of the path leading to the cessation of misery.

THE WAY, FROM THE DHAMMAPADA

The best of ways is the eightfold; the best of truths the four words; the best of virtues passionlessness; the best of men he who has eyes to see.

From *The Sacred Books of the East*, trans. Epiphanus Wilson (New York: Colonial Press, 1900), 138–39.

This is the way, there is no other that leads to the purifying of intelligence. Go on this path! This is the confusion of Mâra, the tempter.

If you go on this way, you will make an end of pain! The way preached by me, when I had understood the removal of the thorns in the flesh.

You yourself must make an effort. The Tathâgatas (Buddhas) are only preachers. The thoughtful who enter the way are freed from the bondage of Mâra.

"All created things perish," he who knows and sees this becomes passive in pain; this is the way to purity.

"All created things are grief and pain," he who knows and sees this becomes passive in pain; this is the way that leads to purity.

"All forms are unreal," he who knows and sees this becomes passive in pain; this is the way that leads to purity.

He who does not rouse himself when it is time to rise, who, though young and strong, is full of sloth, whose will and thought are weak, that lazy and idle man never finds the way to knowledge.

Watching his speech, well restrained in mind, let a man never commit any wrong with his body! Let a man but keep these three roads of action clear, and he will achieve the way which is taught by the wise.

Through zeal knowledge is gained, through lack of zeal knowledge is lost; let a man who knows this double path of gain and loss thus place himself that knowledge may grow.

Cut down the whole forest of desires, not a tree only! Danger comes out of the forest of desires. When you have cut down both the forest of desires and its undergrowth, then, Bhikshus, you will be rid of the forest and of desires!

So long as the desire of man towards women, even the smallest, is not destroyed, so long is his mind in bondage, as the calf that drinks milk is to its mother.

Cut out the love of self, like an autumn lotus, with thy hand! Cherish the road of peace. Nirvâna has been shown by Sugata (Buddha).

"Here I shall dwell in the rain, here in winter and summer," thus the fool meditates, and does not think of death.

Death comes and carries off that man, honored for his children and flocks, his mind distracted, as a flood carries off a sleeping village.

Sons are no help, nor a father, nor relations; there is no help from kinsfolk for one whom death has seized.

A wise and well-behaved man who knows the meaning of this should quickly clear the way that leads to Nirvâna.

CHRISTIANITY

The two Christian passages below come from different stages of the religion's development. Paul's Letter to the Romans was written at the height of his career

as Christian missionary and formulator of doctrine, between 54 and 58 C.E. It became part of the New Testament of the Christian Bible. The letter reflects an effort to appeal to all peoples with the message of Christian truth, Christ's redemption from sin, and potential salvation. The second document was written by a monk, Vincent of Lerins, in 434, as Christianity became established and began to deal systematically with quarrels over doctrine. Vincent grappled with the problem of knowing religious truth from falsehood, in a work that became known as the Vincentian Canon. His approach obviously reflected the role the institutional church had gained in defining Christian beliefs.

• • •

LETTER FROM PAUL TO THE ROMANS

So sin must no longer reign in your mortal body, exacting obedience to the body's desires. You must no longer put its several parts at sin's disposal, as implements for doing wrong. No: put yourselves at the disposal of God, as dead men raised to life; yield your bodies to him as implements for doing right; for sin shall no longer be your master, because you are no longer under law, but under the grace of God.

What then? Are we to sin, because we are not under law but under grace? Of course not. You know well enough that if you put yourselves at the disposal of a master, to obey him, you are slaves of the master whom you obey; and this is true whether you serve sin, with death as its result; or obedience, with righteousness as its result. But God be thanked, you, who once were slaves of sin, have yielded whole-hearted obedience to the pattern of teaching to which you were made subject, and, emancipated from sin, have become slaves of righteousness (to use words that suit your human weakness)—I mean, as you once yielded your bodies to the service of impurity and lawlessness, making for moral anarchy, so now you must yield them to the service of righteousness, making for a holy life.

When you were slaves of sin, you were free from the control of righteousness; and what was the gain? Nothing but what now makes you ashamed, for the end of that is death. But now, freed from the commands of sin, and bound to the service of God, your gains are such as make for holiness, and the end is eternal life. For sin pays a wage, and the wage is death, but God gives freely, and his gift is eternal life, in union with Christ Jesus our Lord.

You cannot be unaware, my friends—I am speaking to those who have some knowledge of law—that a person is subject to the law so long as he is alive, and no longer. For example, a married woman is by law bound to her husband while he lives; but if her husband dies, she is discharged from the obligations of the marriage-law. If, therefore, in her husband's lifetime she consorts with another man, she will incur the charge of adultery; but if her husband dies she is free of the law, and she

From *The New English Bible* (New York: Cambridge University Press, 1922), 182–85, 189–91.

does not commit adultery by consorting with another man. So you, my friends, have died to the law by becoming identified with the body of Christ, and accordingly you have found another husband in him who rose from the dead, so that we may bear fruit for God. While we lived on the level of our lower nature, the sinful passions evoked by the law worked in our bodies, to bear fruit for death. But now, having died to that which held us bound, we are discharged from the law, to serve God in a new way, the way of the spirit, in contrast to the old way, the way of a written code.

What follows? Is the law identical with sin? Of course not. But except through law I should never have become acquainted with sin. For example, I should never have known what it was to covet, if the law had not said, 'Thou shalt not covet.' Through that commandment sin found its opportunity, and produced in me all kinds of wrong desires. In the absence of law, sin is a dead thing. There was a time when, in the absence of law, I was fully alive; but when the commandment came, sin sprang to life and I died. The commandment which should have led to life proved in my experience to lead to death, because sin found its opportunity in the commandment, seduced me, and through the commandment killed me.

Therefore the law is in itself holy, and the commandment is holy and just and good. Are we to say then that this good thing was the death of me? By no means. It was sin that killed me, and thereby sin exposed its true character: it used a good thing to bring about my death, and so, through the commandment, sin became more sinful than ever.

We know that the law is spiritual; but I am not: I am unspiritual, the purchased slave of sin. I do not even acknowledge my own actions as mine, for what I do is not what I want to do, but what I detest. But if what I do is against my will, it means that I agree with the law and hold it to be admirable. But as things are, it is no longer I who perform the action, but sin that lodges in me. For I know that nothing good lodges in me—in my unspiritual nature, I mean—for though the will to do good is there, the deed is not. The good which I want to do, I fail to do; but what I do is the wrong which is against my will; and if what I do is against my will, clearly it is no longer I who am the agent, but sin that has its lodging in me.

I discover this principle, then: that when I want to do the right, only the wrong is within my reach. In my inmost self I delight in the law of God, but I perceive that there is in my bodily members a different law, fighting against the law that my reason approves and making me a prisoner under the law that is in my members, the law of sin. Miserable creature that I am, who is there to rescue me out of this body doomed to death? God alone, through Jesus Christ our Lord! Thanks be to God! In a word then, I myself, subject to God's law as a rational being, am yet, in my unspiritual nature, a slave to the law of sin.

The conclusion of the matter is this: there is no condemnation for those who are united with Christ Jesus, because in Christ Jesus the life-giving law of the Spirit has set you free from the law of sin and death. What the law could never do, because our lower nature robbed it of all potency, God has done: by sending his own Son in a form like that of our own sinful nature, and as a sacrifice for sin, he has passed judgement against sin within that very nature, so that the commandment of the law may find fulfilment in us, whose conduct, no longer under the control of our lower nature, is directed by the Spirit.

Those who live on the level of our lower nature have their outlook formed by it, and that spells death; but those who live on the level of the spirit have the spiritual outlook, and that is life and peace. For the outlook of the lower nature is enmity with God; it is not subject to the law of God; indeed it cannot be: those who live on such a level cannot possibly please God.

But that is not how you live. You are on the spiritual level, if only God's Spirit dwells within you; and if a man does not possess the Spirit of Christ, he is no Christian. But if Christ is dwelling within you, then although the body is a dead thing because you sinned, yet the spirit is life itself because you have been justified. Moreover, if the Spirit of him who raised Jesus from the dead dwells within you, then the God who raised Christ Jesus from the dead will also give new life to your mortal bodies through his indwelling Spirit.

It follows, my friends, that our lower nature has no claim upon us; we are not obliged to live on that level. If you do so, you must die. But if by the Spirit you put to death all the base pursuits of the body, then you will live.

For all who are moved by the Spirit of God are sons of God. The Spirit you have received is not a spirit of slavery leading you back into a life of fear, but a Spirit that makes us sons, enabling us to cry 'Abba! Father!' In that cry the Spirit of God joins with our spirit in testifying that we are God's children; and if children, then heirs. We are God's heirs and Christ's fellow-heirs, if we share his sufferings now in order to share his splendour hereafter.

For I reckon that the sufferings we now endure bear no comparison with the splendour, as yet unrevealed, which is in store for us. . . .

Therefore, my brothers, I implore you by God's mercy to offer your very selves to him: a living sacrifice, dedicated and fit for his acceptance, the worship offered by mind and heart. Adapt yourselves no longer to the pattern of this present world, but let your minds be remade and your whole nature thus transformed. Then you will be able to discern the will of God, and to know what is good, acceptable, and perfect.

In virtue of the gift that God in his grace has given me I say to everyone among you: do not be conceited or think too highly of yourself; but think your way to a sober estimate based on the measure of faith that God has dealt to each of you. For just as in a single human body there are many limbs and organs, all with different functions, so all of us, united with Christ, form one body, serving individually as limbs and organs to one another.

The gifts we possess differ as they are allotted to us by God's grace, and must be exercised accordingly: the gift of inspired utterance, for example, in proportion to a man's faith; or the gift of administration, in administration. A teacher should employ his gift in teaching, and one who has the gift of stirring speech should use it to stir his hearers. If you give to charity, give with all your heart; if you are a leader, exert yourself to lead; if you are helping others in distress, do it cheerfully.

Love in all sincerity, loathing evil and clinging to the good. Let love for our brotherhood breed warmth of mutual affection. Give pride of place to one another in esteem.

With unflagging energy, in ardour of spirit, serve the Lord.

Let hope keep you joyful; in trouble stand firm; persist in prayer.

Contribute to the needs of God's people, and practise hospitality.

Call down blessings on your persecutors—blessings, not curses.

With the joyful be joyful, and mourn with the mourners.

Care as much about each other as about yourselves. Do not be haughty, but go about with humble folk. Do not keep thinking how wise you are.

Never pay back evil for evil. Let your aims be such as all men count honourable. If possible, so far as it lies with you, live at peace with all men. My dear friends, do not seek revenge, but leave a place for divine retribution; for there is a text which reads, 'Justice is mine, says the Lord, I will repay.' But there is another text: 'If your enemy is hungry, feed him; if he is thirsty, give him a drink; by doing this you will heap live coals on his head.' Do not let evil conquer you, but use good to defeat evil.

Every person must submit to the supreme authorities. There is no authority but by act of God, and the existing authorities are instituted by him; consequently anyone who rebels against authority is resisting a divine institution, and those who so resist have themselves to thank for the punishment they will receive. For government, a terror to crime, has no terrors for good behaviour. You wish to have no fear of the authorities? Then continue to do right and you will have their approval, for they are God's agents working for your good. But if you are doing wrong, then you will have cause to fear them; it is not for nothing that they hold the power of the sword, for they are God's agents of punishment, for retribution on the offender. That is why you are obliged to submit. It is an obligation imposed not merely by fear of retribution but by conscience. That is also why you pay taxes. The authorities are in God's service and to these duties they devote their energies.

Discharge your obligations to all men; pay tax and toll, reverence and respect, to those to whom they are due. Leave no claim outstanding against you, except that of mutual love. He who loves his neighbour has satisfied every claim of the law. For the commandments, 'Thou shalt not commit adultery, thou shalt not kill, thou shalt not steal, thou shalt not covet', and any other commandment there may be, are all summed up in the one rule, 'Love your neighbour as yourself.' Love cannot wrong a neighbour; therefore the whole law is summed up in love.

In all this, remember how critical the moment is. It is time for you to wake out of sleep, for deliverance is nearer to us now than it was when first we believed. It is far on in the night; day is near. Let us therefore throw off the deeds of darkness and put on our armour as soldiers of the light. Let us behave with decency as befits the day: no revelling or drunkenness, no debauchery or vice, no quarrels or jealousies! Let Christ Jesus himself be the armour that you wear; give no more thought to satisfying the bodily appetites.

If a man is weak in his faith you must accept him without attempting to settle doubtful points. For instance, one man will have faith enough to eat all kinds of food, while a weaker man eats only vegetables. The man who eats must not hold in contempt the man who does not, and he who does not eat must not pass judgement on the one who does; for God has accepted him. Who are you to pass judgement on someone else's servant? Whether he stands or falls is his own Master's business; and stand he will, because his Master has power to enable him to stand.

Again, this man regards one day more highly than another, while that man regards all days alike. On such a point everyone should have reached conviction in his own mind. He who respects the day has the Lord in mind in doing so, and he who eats meat has the Lord in mind when he eats, since he gives thanks to God; and he who abstains has the Lord in mind no less, since he too gives thanks to God.

For no one of us lives, and equally no one of us dies, for himself alone. If we live, we live for the Lord; and if we die, we die for the Lord. Whether therefore we live or die, we belong to the Lord. This is why Christ died and came to life again, to establish his lordship over dead and living. You, sir, why do you pass judgement on your brother? And you, sir, why do you hold your brother in contempt? We shall all stand before God's tribunal. For Scripture says, 'As I live, says the Lord, to me every knee shall bow and every tongue acknowledge God.' So, you see, each of us will have to answer for himself.

Let us therefore cease judging one another, but rather make this simple judgement: that no obstacle or stumbling-block be placed in a brother's way. I am absolutely convinced, as a Christian, that nothing is impure in itself; only, if a man considers a particular thing impure, then to him it is impure. If your brother is outraged by what you eat, then your conduct is no longer guided by love. Do not by your eating bring disaster to a man for whom Christ died! What for you is a good thing must not become an occasion for slanderous talk; for the kingdom of God is not eating and drinking, but justice, peace, and joy, inspired by the Holy Spirit. He who thus shows himself a servant of Christ is acceptable to God and approved by men.

Let us then pursue the things that make for peace and build up the common life.

VINCENT OF LERINS

I have therefore continually given the greatest pains and diligence to enquiring, from the greatest possible number of men outstanding in holiness and in doctrine, how I can secure a kind of fixed and, as it were, general and guiding principle for distinguishing the true Catholic Faith from the degraded falsehoods of heresy. And the answer that I receive is always to this effect; that if I wish, or indeed if any one wishes, to detect the deceits of heretics that arise and to avoid their snares and to keep healthy and sound in a healthy faith, we ought, with the Lord's help, to fortify our faith in a twofold manner, firstly, that is, by the authority of God's Law, then by the tradition of the Catholic Church.

(2) Here, it may be, some one will ask, Since the canon of Scripture is complete, and is in itself abundantly sufficient, what need is there to join to it the interpretation of the Church? The answer is that because of the very depth of Scripture all men do not place one identical interpretation upon it. The statements of the same writer are explained by different men in different ways, so much so that it seems almost possible to extract from it as many opinions as there are men. . . .

. . . Therefore, because of the intricacies of error, which is so multiform, there is great need for the laying down of a rule for the exposition of Prophets and Apostles in accordance with the standard of the interpretation of the Church Catholic.

(3) Now in the Catholic Church itself we take the greatest care to hold THAT WHICH HAS BEEN BELIEVED EVERYWHERE, ALWAYS, AND BY ALL.

That is truly and properly 'Catholic,' as is shown by the very force and meaning of the word, which comprehends everything almost universally. We shall hold to this rule if we follow universality [i.e. œcumenicity], antiquity, and consent. We shall follow universality if we acknowledge that one Faith to be true which the whole Church throughout the world confesses; antiquity, if we in no wise depart from those interpretations which it is clear that our ancestors and fathers proclaimed; consent, if in antiquity itself we keep following the definitions and opinions of all, or certainly nearly all, bishops and doctors alike.

From Henry Bettenson, ed., *Documents of the Christian Church*, 2d ed. (New York: Oxford University Press, 1963), 83–84. Reprinted by permission of Oxford University Press.

PART II

The Postclassical Period, 450–1450

A MAJOR PHASE OF world history opened with the decline or collapse of the great empires of Rome, Han China, and Gupta India by the fifth and sixth centuries C.E. New forces were set in motion that persisted until the thirteenth century, followed by a two-century transition lasting until about 1450.

During the classical period, the key developments in world history had been the construction of large regional civilizations and their integration. This theme did not disappear. Chinese history, for example, resumed many of its earlier patterns after three centuries of real confusion. Indian civilization retained its basic integrity also, though without the capacity to generate large, internally directed empires. The Mediterranean was hopelessly divided, however, with Greco-Roman traditions persisting only in the Byzantine Empire in the northeastern corner of the region. This empire combined the use of the Greek language and culture with Roman imperial institutions, Orthodox Christianity, and a lively trade. But overall, the formation of empires loomed less large in this new period; other, looser political structures were emphasized.

Several new trends emerged. First, major world religions, defined in terms of their ability to convert peoples in various civilization areas, began to gain a greater hold. The collapse of the classical empires prompted many people to turn to more otherworldly goals; in some cases, such as Western Europe, the new religions also provided the clearest shared beliefs and even institutional structures. Buddhism was not new, but during this period it spread far more widely in eastern and southeastern Asia. Christianity had already gained strength in the Mediterranean and in a few parts of the Middle East and sub-Saharan Africa. Now it spread vigorously northward, in two main strands (Catholic and Orthodox), ultimately reaching Scandinavia in the west and Russia in the east. The third religion was new and by far the most dynamic of all. Islam arose in the Middle East early in the seventh century. It spread rapidly with Arab conquests in the Middle East and North Africa and soon also won massive conversions in Central Asia, India (as a minority religion), parts of sub-Saharan Africa, Spain, and Southeast Asia.

The rise of Islam forms a second theme, beyond the missionary power of the new religion. A loose Arab empire, the caliphate, stretched from the borders of India to the western Mediterranean. Arab trade dominated the Indian Ocean and much of the Mediterranean, also crossing the Sahara Desert. It linked with Byzantine trade through Russia, and it extended to Western Europe and down Africa's Indian Ocean coast. Muslim art forms, mathematics, and medicine had wide influence. This was the first "world-class" civilization, for several centuries putting important pressure on much of the Afro-Eurasian world.

The sheer spread of civilization was the third major development of the postclassical period, in some cases related to the impact of Arab influence or the consequences of the various missionary religions. Although the most sophisticated cities and trade still were in the Middle East and North Africa, the Byzantine Empire, India, and China, civilization also developed in parts of sub-Saharan Africa (particularly a series of great kingdoms in present-day West Africa, known as the Sudanic kingdoms); in Western Europe, under the influence of Catholic Christianity; in additional parts of eastern Asia, including Japan, and in Southeast Asia; and in Russia and eastern Europe. These new civilization areas traded with the leading centers and were able to imitate important aspects of culture (often including writing itself) and some political forms. Finally, though quite separately, larger civilization zones spread in Central America, culminating in the great Aztec Empire, and in the Andes region, with the Inca Empire taking shape toward the end of the postclassical period.

By 1000 C.E. the major societies of Afro-Eurasia were in regular contact. Here was the fourth main theme of the postclassical centuries. Trade levels, cultural exchanges, and some military clashes created a new international network. Inventions developed in one center, such as China's introduction of paper, began to spread more rapidly to other areas. Not only religious ideas but also some artistic forms began to affect numerous different civilizations. Heightened international contact also sped the dissemination of diseases, for example, the great bubonic plague (Black Death) of the fourteenth century, which began in China and within decades reached both the Arab world and Europe, with deadly effects. An increasingly important component of world history is to understand the different reactions by the major civilizations to their international contacts.

The world network, intensifying the impact of international currents of various sorts, initially operated under Arab sponsorship above all. Here were the most active traders, the farthest-flung missionaries. But Arab power began to decline by the twelfth century, and other international systems developed. Mongol invasions from Central Asia, conquering China and Russia and reaching into other areas such as the Middle East, for a time created a huge interlocking empire that facilitated travel and exchange between Asia and Europe. As the Mongols declined, China briefly undertook a series of great trade expeditions early in the fifteenth century. Even before this, Chinese influence had radiated to surrounding regions: Japan, Korea, and Vietnam. Clearly, a variety of civilizations had come to depend on international contacts, creating a system that expanded even as individual civilizations reduced their leadership role. By the fifteenth century, various inventions from China and the Middle East, including explosive powder, the compass, and swifter sailing vessels, had created a technological basis for international contacts. European additions such as guns and improved ships, plus European acquisition of the Asian innovations, provided the setting for the next period in world history, from 1450 onward.

Two kinds of comparison focus attention on the major developments of the postclassical period: comparison of separate patterns and comparison of reactions to common forces.

First, the distinct characteristics of individual civilizations continue to command attention. Particular world religions provided new contrasts among regions, though also some religious issues that affected various regions became more important than they had been in the classical period, outside of India. Thus, the impacts of religion on government forms created some new differentiation but also some common themes, between the Middle East and Christian Europe. Conditions of women were affected by the different cultures of Islam and the major strands of Christianity, whereas China, less affected by new cultural influences, displayed more continuity. New civilization areas added to the comparative mix. Comparison is vital to determine the characteristics of the new centers and their relationship to the older civilizations. Japan and Western Europe, with no mutual contact, developed somewhat similar political patterns that had enduring implications for social organization in these regions. Both areas differed in this respect from places like China or Byzantium, which had more centralized bureaucracies. Civilization centers in the Americas, isolated from broader world currents, provide contrasts, though records of these civilizations are limited, partly as a result of later destruction by the invading Spaniards. Comparison of leading facets of separate societies, as in earlier periods of world history, reveals the diversity of human responses to common problems. But the comparative range was altered by the new impact of world religion and the expansion of civilization forms.

The second type of comparison is possible because of the intensification of interactions among civilizations in Asia, Africa, and Europe. Still distinctive, many civilizations had to respond to common influences and events. Increasing interaction thus organizes a new set of comparative issues, which had not existed in the previous world history periods: comparison around a common development or contact. Europeans and Muslims encountered each other in Christian crusades to conquer the Holy Land. These conflicts provided important new influences on Europe but also allow analysis of differences and hostilities between the two societies that were sharpened by contact. Merchant activity increased in the postclassical centuries, through both internal and external trade. Despite new commercial contacts, different societies maintained different ideas about merchants and their contributions. Near the end of the period, the Mongol conquests in China, Russia, and elsewhere created new channels of international exchange—but again, reactions to this episode varied, showing how civilizations could change as a result of common impacts but retain their distinctive patterns.

The chapters of part 2 deal with the comparative scenarios of the postclassical period including the emergence of a network connecting key civilizations—a new development in world history. The initial chapters update comparisons of political institutions and women's conditions under the impact of new religions and expanding civilizations. Then a set of chapters deals with contacts in war and in trade, involving major centers in Asia and in Europe, plus the significant Mongol interlude. Chapter 13 then returns to comparisons of separate centers, juxtaposing Europe, Africa, and the civilizations of the Americas, but in relation to their varied patterns of international contact.

CHAPTER 7

RELIGION AND STATE IN ISLAM AND CHRISTIANITY

Relationship with secular government is a problem for any religion and its priests or leaders (and vice versa). Governments normally concentrate at least in part on issues of war and earthly justice, and perhaps some economic issues such as provisioning cities or helping the poor. What connection do these functions and the people responsible for them have with the real, religious purposes of life? What if a government does not attend properly to religion or even is hostile to it? Or, from a government standpoint, what if religious officials seem to be falling down on the job or interfering with obviously secular concerns? The Chinese government ultimately turned against Buddhism in the ninth century, because it felt it must protect the primacy of loyalties to the state. Issues of this sort were different from leading political ideals in the classical period (see chapter 3). One change was clear: no Christian or Muslim ruler could claim he was god, unlike some Romans or the Chinese Son of Heaven concept.

Christian leaders had faced the issue of what to do about the state early on. One of Paul's emphases, as he tried to spread the new religion to a wide audience, was the importance of obeying government authorities even though the chief interests of the good Christian centered on divine power (see chapter 6). As the Christian church developed in Western Europe, with officials and institutions independent of the state, questions of mutual relations became more pressing. The adoption of Christianity by the Roman Empire, and then later by governments in Western Europe, complicated the issue still further: Christian political leaders thought they had a religious role to play (and might want to use religion to bolster their power); church leaders might welcome political support but would often fear secular control.

The rapid rise of Islam, following Muhammad's formulation of the religion early in the seventh century, raised broadly similar concerns. Here was another religion devoted to the power and glory of God; purely political purposes would pale by comparison. Yet, even more than Christianity, Islam developed a highly legalistic impulse. The Koran, which Muhammad presented as the word of Allah, contained a host of rules for family and business behavior. Further religious codes developed, particularly in the Hadith. But if religion regulated so many aspects of human affairs, was there a separate place for government? The situation was further complicated by the fact that although Islam had religious officials—including scholars who interpreted Muslim law—there was no institutional church of the sort that developed in Western Europe, with a clear leadership hierarchy. And Muhammad, like Paul, had explicitly urged the faithful to obey even a bad ruler—religious people should not be distracted by political concerns.

Despite important differences in context, Islam and Christianity had to work out arrangements with governments. No religion can seek wide adherence if it constantly does battle with military and judicial leaders. (Some sects define themselves by opposing the state, which may lead to important developments but will usually keep the religious groups small.) As major religions, Islam and Christianity certainly shared some specific problems in defining the proper relations between religion and the state during the postclassical period. Among other things, they could both be inconsistent in some similar ways. Islamic leaders could defend both the idea that a true state was united with religion, backed by Allah, and the idea that state and religion had somewhat separate functions. Similarly, Islam could support the notion that good Muslims should be obedient even to bad rulers (Muhammad said this explicitly) and that good Muslims might call a ruler to account if he was harming religion (a view current in some parts of Islam today). Catholic Christians most commonly defended a certain separation between church and state, with the church being superior but different; but they could also prefer a situation in which the church used the state to help defend religion, blurring the distinctions between the two institutions. Christian leaders, following Paul's lead, usually urged obedience to the state—after all, the real meaning of life did not depend on secular well-being—but they could rise against an unjust or irreligious state in God's name, too.

The following passages present some of the Christian and Muslim views as they took shape in the postclassical period, and suggest on balance that they are different. The Muslim document, from the eleventh century, emphasizes how Islam can be used to provide divine support and key religious functions to the state. Its author was a bureaucrat who undoubtedly sought to please his ruler. Certainly, with this approach, there was no clear independence for religious leaders, no basis for opposing the state. Yet the treatise is subtle: it also lays important responsibilities on the ruler, investing even secular functions like bridge repair with religious significance and sanctions, and it urges that religious figures be consulted and heeded.

The Christian approach is developed in documents debating the relations between popes and German emperors in the twelfth century. Both parties to the debate agree that the church, as the religious institution, is the superior body, but they argue over whether rulers have independent divine support. Is the ruler merely an inferior, carrying out some separate functions but always open to religious control? Or does he have a vital, independent sphere of operation? And what if the pope himself errs? Here, too, there is disagreement between the debaters. One wants a strong emperor and a controlled pope, while the other asserts the primacy of the pope—though both disputants admit that keeping an errant leader of the church in control is a tough issue. The jurists present their views in a style very characteristic of Western Europe at the time, with rationalistic arguments based on data from the Bible and earlier church authorities. This is a logical quarrel, far different in tone from the more familiar advice mode of the Persian bureaucrat.

Both Christianity and Islam could and did produce important mergers between religious and political arguments for the state. Many rulers in both religions sincerely believed that defending the true faith was one of their chief functions; many other rulers in both religions believed that claiming religious authority, however insincerely, was one of the best ways to bolster their own power. Certainly, the rise of these two religions greatly changed the nature of government in both Europe and the Middle East, compared to the classical period. But the power of each of the two religions was also great enough to constrain the state at certain key points. Ordinary people might use religious beliefs to attack an impious or immoral ruler; religion could support protest and its ethics could modify the behaviors of particular kings or caliphs.

The impact of new or newly important religions on the government was a key development in the postclassical era, in several parts of the world. Characteristic new tensions developed. At the same time, though major religions shared certain dilemmas and ambiguities, there were differences in approach. Most historians would agree that religion contributed to a more limited idea of the state in the West than in Islamic regions. There is a comparative difference to explore.

Questions

1. What were the main differences in the ways Christian and Muslim thinkers defined the state in its relationship to religion? What state functions would both religions agree on? How does the existence of a separate church differentiate the Christian from the Muslim approach?

2. Might Muslims disagree about the state's relation to religion in ways at all similar to the postclassical Christian debate? Did Islam impose any limits on a good ruler?

3. What would a Muslim think of the Christian debate about papal versus imperial power?

4. In the final analysis, are there major differences between Christian and Muslim definitions of a good ruler? Do the religions differ in their beliefs about what to do if a ruler is bad?

For Further Discussion

1. Why did both Christian and Muslim leaders urge obedience to the state in almost all circumstances?

2. Which approach, the Christian or the Muslim, would produce more responsible government?

3. Are differences between Christian and Muslim political traditions—complex as both traditions were—still visible in the world today? Do you agree that Christian ideas help explain a limited state concept in the West? What state concept most logically follows from Muslim ideals?

A Muslim View: Nizam al-Mulk

Nizam al-Mulk was a Persian bureaucrat who served sultans for the Seljuk Turks for thirty years during the eleventh century, at a time when the Seljuks controlled much of the Middle East (it was the Seljuks who a bit later opposed the Christians in the Crusades). This treatise in some ways resembles a host of works throughout history that were designed to please kings. Chinese legalists wrote such books in the classical period, as did an Indian bureaucrat named Kautilya; the Italian Machiavelli did the same in his book *The Prince,* during the European Renaissance. King-pleaser treatises flattered rulers by telling them how to get and keep power and generally insisting on their importance to their people. But this was a Muslim statement, and religion is very much present in the kinds of responsibilities and restraints Nizam al-Mulk insists upon in the name of God. The document refers to the title caliph, taken by the prophet Muhammad's Arab successors, who claimed wide religious powers and duties. It frequently invokes the holy book the Quran (Koran).

• • •

1. In every age and time God (be He exalted) chooses one member of the human race and, having adorned and endowed him with kingly virtues, entrusts him with the interests of the world and the well-being of His servants; He charges that person to close the doors of corruption, confusion and discord, and He imparts to him such dignity and majesty in the eyes and hearts of men, that under his just rule they may live their lives in constant security and ever wish for his reign to continue.

2. Whenever—Allah be our refuge!—there occurs any disobedience or disregard of divine laws on the part of His servants, or any failure in devotion and

From Nizam al-Mulk, *The Book of Government on Rules for Kings,* trans. Hubert Darke (London: Routledge and Kegan Paul, 1960), 9–13, 62–65. Reprinted by permission of the publisher.

attention to the commands of The Truth (be He exalted), and He wishes to chasten them and make them taste the retribution for their deeds—may God not deal us such a fate, and keep us far from such a calamity!—verily the wrath of The Truth overtakes those people and He forsakes them for the vileness of their disobedience; anarchy rears its head in their midst, opposing swords are drawn, blood is shed, and whoever has the stronger hand does whatever he wishes, until those sinners are all destroyed in tumults and bloodshed, and the world becomes free and clear of them; and through the wickedness of such sinners many innocent persons too perish in the tumults; just as, by analogy, when a reed-bed catches fire every dry particle is consumed and much wet stuff is burnt also, because it is near to that which is dry.

3. Then by divine decree one human being acquires some prosperity and power, and according to his deserts The Truth bestows good fortune upon him and gives him wit and wisdom, wherewith he may employ his subordinates every one according to his merits and confer upon each a dignity and a station proportionate to his powers. He selects ministers and their functionaries from among the people, and giving a rank and post to each, he relies upon them for the efficient conduct of affairs spiritual and temporal. If his subjects tread the path of obedience and busy themselves with their tasks he will keep them untroubled by hardships, so that they may pass their time at ease in the shadow of his justice. If one of his officers or ministers commits any impropriety or oppression, he will only keep him at his post provided that he responds to correction, advice or punishment, and wakes up from the sleep of negligence; if he fails to mend his ways, he will retain him no longer, but change him for someone who is deserving; and when his subjects are ungrateful for benefits and do not appreciate security and ease, but ponder treachery in their hearts, shewing unruliness and overstepping their bounds, he will admonish them for their misdeeds, and punish them in proportion to their crimes. Having done that he will cover their sins with the skirt of pardon and oblivion. Further he will bring to pass that which concerns the advance of civilization, such as constructing underground channels, digging main canals, building bridges across great waters, rehabilitating villages and farms, raising fortifications, building new towns, and erecting lofty buildings and magnificent dwellings; he will have inns built on the highways and schools for those who seek knowledge; for which things he will be renowned for ever; he will gather the fruit of his good works in the next world and blessings will be showered upon him.

4. Since the decree of God was such that this should be the era by which bygone ages are to be dated and that it should crown the achievements of former kings, whereby He might bestow on His creatures a felicity granted to none before them, He caused The Master of the World, the mightiest king of kings to come forth from two nobles' lines whose houses were cradles of royalty and nobility. . . . He furnished him with powers and merits such as had been lacking in the princes of the world before him, and endowed him with all that is needful for a king—such as a comely

appearance, a kindly disposition, integrity, manliness, bravery, horsemanship, knowl-edge, [skill in] the use of various kinds of arms and accomplishment in several arts, pity and mercy upon the creatures of God, [strictness in] the performance of vows and promises, sound faith and true belief, devotion to the worship of God and the practice of such virtuous deeds as praying in the night, supererogatory fasting, re-spect for religious authorities, honouring devout and pious men, winning the society of men of learning and wisdom, giving regular alms, doing good to the poor, being kind to subordinates and servants, and relieving the people of oppressors. Following all this God gave him power and dominion as befitted his worthiness and good faith, and made all the world subject to him, causing his dignity and authority to reach all climes; all the dwellers on earth are his tributaries, and as long as they seek his favour they are protected by his sword.

5. Now in the days of some of the caliphs, if ever their empire became extended it was never free from unrest and the insurrections of rebels; but in this blessed age (praise and thanks be to Allah) there is nobody in all the world who in his heart meditates opposition to our lord and master, or ventures his head outside the collar of obedience to him—may God perpetuate this empire until the resurrection and keep the evil eye far from the perfectness of this kingdom, so that His creatures may pass their days under the equity and authority of The Master of the World and be ever intent on blessing him.

6. Such is the happy state of this great empire; and in proportion to its greatness it is blessed with an abundance of wise and good institutions. The wisdom of The Master of the World is like a taper from which many lamps have been lighted; by its light men find their way and emerge from the darkness. He has no need of any counsellor or guide; nevertheless he is not without cares, and perhaps he wishes to test his servants, and assess their intelligence and wisdom. So when he commanded his humble servant to write down some of those good qualities that are indispensable to a king, indicating every principle which kings have followed in the past but now do not observe, whether praiseworthy or unpraiseworthy, whatever came to the mind of his humble servant that he had seen, learnt, read or heard, was written down, and The Sublime Command was fulfilled; these few chapters were composed in the manner of an epitome, and what was proper to each chapter was mentioned in that chapter in a simple style, by the grace of Allah.

On Recognizing the Extent of God's Grace towards Kings

1. It is for kings to observe His pleasure (His name be glorified) and the pleasure of The Truth is in the charity which is done to His creatures and in the justice which is spread among them. A kingdom which is blessed by its people will endure and increase from day to day, while its king will enjoy power and prosperity; in this world he will acquire good fame, in the next world salvation, and his reckoning will

be the easier. Great men have said [in Arabic], 'A kingdom may last while there is irreligion, but it will not endure when there is oppression.'

2. Tradition tells that when Joseph the prophet (the prayers of Allah and His peace be upon him) went out from this world, they were carrying him to Abraham's tomb (upon him be peace) to bury him near his forefathers, when Gabriel (upon him be peace) came and said, 'Stop where you are; this is not his place; for at the resurrection he will have to answer for the sovereignty which he has exercised.' Now if the case of Joseph the prophet was such, consider what the position of others will be.

3. It has come down in a tradition from The Prophet (may Allah bless him and save him) that on the day of the resurrection, when anyone is brought forward who [in his life] wielded power and command over God's creatures, his hands will be bound; if he has been just, his justice will loose his hands and send him to paradise; but if he has been unjust, his injustice will cast him into hell as he is, with his hands bound in chains.

4. There is also a tradition that on resurrection day whoever had any command in this world over God's creatures, even over the inhabitants of his own house or over his own underlings, will be questioned about it; likewise the shepherd who tended his sheep will be required to answer for that too.

5. They say that at the time of his father's leaving this world [caliph] 'Abd Allah ibn 'Umar ibn al Khattab (may Allah be pleased with them both) asked, 'O father, where and when shall I see you again?' 'Umar said, 'In the next world.' 'Abd Allah said, 'I would it were sooner.' He said, 'You will see me in a dream tonight, tomorrow night, or the next night.' Twelve years passed by without his appearing in a dream. Then one night he saw him in a dream and said, 'O father, did you not say that within three nights I should see you?' He said, 'O son, I was occupied, because in the country around Baghdad a bridge had become dilapidated and officials had not attended to repairing it. One day a sheep's forefoot fell into a hole on that bridge and was broken. Till now I have been answering for that.'

6. Of a certainty The Master of the World (may Allah perpetuate his reign) should know that on that great day he will be asked to answer for all those of God's creatures who are under his command, and if he tries to transfer [his responsibility] to someone else he will not be listened to. Since this is so it behoves the king not to leave this important matter to anyone else, and not to disregard the state of God's creatures. To the best of his ability let him ever acquaint himself, secretly and openly, with their conditions; let him protect them from extortionate hands, and preserve them from cruel tyrants, so that the blessings resulting from those actions may come about in the time of his rule, if Allah wills. . . .

1. It is incumbent upon the king to enquire into religious matters, to be acquainted with the divine precepts and prohibitions and put them into practice, and to obey the commands of God (be He exalted); it is his duty to respect doctors of religion and pay their salaries out of the treasury, and he should honour pious and

abstemious men. Furthermore it is fitting that once or twice a week he should invite religious elders to his presence and hear from them the commands of The Truth; he should listen to interpretations of the Quran and traditions of The Prophet (may Allah pray for him and give him peace); and he should hear stories about just kings and tales of the prophets (upon them be peace). During that time he should free his mind from worldly cares and give his ears and attention [wholly] to them. Let him bid them take sides and hold a debate, and let him ask questions about what he does not understand; when he has learnt the answers let him commit them to memory. After this has gone on for some time it will become a habit, and it will not be long before he has learnt and memorized most of the precepts of divine law, the meanings of the Quran and the traditions of The Prophet (upon him be peace). Then the way of prudence and rectitude in both spiritual and temporal affairs will be open to him; no heretic or innovator will be able to turn him from that path. His judgment will be strengthened and he will increase in justice and equity; vanity and heresy will vanish from his kingdom and great works will spring from his hands. The roots of wickedness, corruption and discord will be cut out in the time of his empire. The hand of the righteous shall become strong and the wicked shall be no more. In this world he shall have fame, and in the next world he shall find salvation, high degree and inestimable reward. In his age men will more than ever delight in gaining knowledge.

2. ['Abd Allah] ibn 'Umar (may Allah be pleased with him) says that The Prophet (peace be upon him) said, 'The righteous shall dwell in paradise in palaces [full] of the light of their justice towards their underlings.'

3. The most important thing which a king needs is sound faith, because kingship and religion are like two brothers; whenever disturbance breaks out in the country religion suffers too; heretics and evil-doers appear; and whenever religious affairs are in disorder, there is confusion in the country; evil-doers gain power and render the king impotent and despondent; heresy grows rife and rebels make themselves felt. . . .

5. Ardashir says, 'Any ruler who has not the power to check his courtiers will never be able to control his commoners and peasants.' There is a passage in the Quran [26. 214] to this effect, 'And warn thy relatives of near kin.'

6. The Commander of the Faithful 'Umar (may Allah be pleased with him) says 'There is nothing more detrimental to the country and more ruinous to the peasantry than difficulty of access to the king: conversely there is nothing more profitable to the people than ease of access to the king—or more impressive, especially to officers and tax-collectors, for when they know that the king is accessible they will not dare to practise oppression and extortion on the peasants.'

7. Luqman The Wise said, 'Man has no better friend in this world than knowledge, and knowledge is better than wealth, because you must take care of wealth but knowledge takes care of you.' . . .

9. But when a king possesses divine splendour and sovereignty, and knowledge withal is wedded to these, he finds happiness in both worlds, because everything he does is informed with knowledge and he does not allow himself to be ignorant. Consider how great is the fame of kings who were wise, and what great works they did; names such as these will be blessed until the resurrection—Afridun, Alexander, Ardashir, Nushirwan The Just, The Commander of the Faithful ʿUmar (may Allah be pleased with him), ʿUmar ibn ʿAbd al ʿAziz (may Allah illumine his resting place), Harun, al Maʾmun, al Muʿtasim, Ismaʿil ibn Ahmad the Samanid, and Sultan Mahmud (Allah's mercy be upon them all). The deeds and ways of them all are well known for they are recorded in histories and other books; men never cease reading about them and singing their praises and blessings.

The Story of ʿUmar ibn ʿAbd al ʿAziz and the Famine

10. They say that in the days of ʿUmar ibn ʿAbd al ʿAziz (Allah's mercy be upon him) there was a famine and the people were in distress. A party of Arabs approached him and complained saying, 'O Commander of the Faithful, we have consumed our own flesh and blood in the famine (that is, we have become thin), and our cheeks have turned yellow because we have not enough to eat. We need what is in your treasury; and as for that treasure, it belongs either to you or to God or to the servants of God. If it belongs to God's servants it is ours; if it belongs to God, He has no need of it; if it is yours, then [as the Quran 12. 88 says] "be charitable unto us, for Allah will requite the charitable" . . . ; and if it is ours let us have it that we may escape from these straits, for the skin is withered on our bodies.' ʿUmar ibn ʿAbd al ʿAziz was moved to sympathy for them, and tears came into his eyes; he said, 'I will do as you have said,' and in the same hour he gave orders for their requests to be attended to and their wants to be supplied. When they were about to get up and go, ʿUmar ibn ʿAbd al ʿAziz (Allah's mercy be upon him) said, 'O men where are you going? As you presented your case and that of the rest of God's servants to me, so do you present my case to God' (meaning: remember me in your prayers). Then those Arab tribesmen lifted their eyes to heaven and said, 'O Lord, by Thy glory [we pray] that Thou wilt do unto ʿUmar ibn ʿAbd al ʿAziz as he did unto Thy servants.'

11. When they had done praying, immediately a cloud came up and it began to rain heavily; a hailstone fell upon the bricks of ʿUmar's palace; it broke in two and a piece of paper fell from inside it. They looked at it and there was written upon it [in Arabic], 'This is a grace from Allah The Mighty to ʿUmar ibn ʿAbd al ʿAziz [exempting him] from the fire.'

A CHRISTIAN DEBATE: CANON LAWYERS IN THE TWELFTH CENTURY

The growth of state power, including the claims of the emperor of Germany, raised new church-state issues in Europe by the eleventh and twelfth centuries. A famous controversy in the eleventh century had pitted Pope Gregory VII against the emperor Henry IV over the issue of whether secular rulers had any right to appoint bishops. Gregory insisted on the supremacy of the church in religious matters and, by absolving Germans of religious obligations to obey their ruler, got the emperor to back down. But the issue would not go away. The church was itself a political institution, with rich lands and many officials, and governments often came into conflict with it. The following debate, from the end of the twelfth century, is between two eminent jurists. Church (canon) law was becoming more elaborate, and the revival of Roman law provided different arguments about the state. Law was a key interest in the expanding European culture, and law schools were components of some of the earliest Western universities. In this debate Huguccio favors the emperor's side. Alanus uses interpretations of the Bible, including the idea that Christ conveyed his authority to Peter, who became the first pope, plus claims about the power Constantine gave the church, to support papal supremacy. Disputes over history as well as characteristic efforts to use logic pepper this debate.

• • •

HUGUCCIO: *After the coming of the Truth.* Up until the coming of Christ the imperial and pontifical rights were not separated, for the same man was emperor and pontiff. . . . But the offices and rights of the emperor and the pontiff were separated by Christ and some things, namely temporal affairs, were assigned to the emperor, others, namely spiritual affairs, to the pontiff, and this was done for the sake of preserving humility and avoiding pride. If the emperor or the pontiff held all offices he would easily grow proud but now since each needs the other and sees that he is not fully self-sufficient he is made humble. . . . Here it can clearly be gathered that each power, the apostolic and imperial, was instituted by God and that neither is derived from the other and that the emperor does not have the sword from the apostle. . . . All these contrary arguments seem to imply that the emperor receives the power of the sword and the imperial authority from the apostle and that the pope makes him emperor and can depose him. I believe however, that the emperor has the power of the sword and the imperial dignity from election by the princes

From Brian Tierney, *The Crisis of Church and State, 1050–1300* (Englewood Cliffs, N.J.: Prentice-Hall, 1964), 122–126.

and people, . . . for there was an emperor before there was a pope, an empire before a papacy. Again the words, "Behold, here are two swords" (Luke 22:38), were spoken to symbolize the fact that the two powers, namely the apostolic and imperial, are distinct and separate. If, therefore, it is anywhere stated or implied that the emperor has the power of the sword from the pope, I understand it as meaning the unction and confirmation which he has from the pope when he swears fidelity to him; for before this, although he is not called emperor, he is an emperor as regards dignity though not as regards unction, and before this he has the power of the sword and exercises it. When it is said that the pope can depose him I believe this to be true, but by the will and consent of the princes if he is convicted before them. Then I take it, in the last resort, if he has been convicted and admonished and will not desist or give satisfaction, he should be excommunicated and all should be removed from fealty to him. . . . If still he is not corrected then finally he is justly smitten with a sentence and rightly expelled by armed force, and another legitimately elected. But by whom is the sentence pronounced? By the lord pope before whom he was convicted or by his princes if the Roman pontiff has approved this.

ALANUS: This indeed is certain according to everyone, that the pope has jurisdiction over the emperor in spiritual matters so that he can bind and loose him . . . but, according to Huguccio, by no means in temporal matters though the pope can judge him in temporal matters and depose him by the wish of the princes who elect him according to customary law. According to Huguccio the emperor has the sword from God alone and not from the pope except as regards coronation and confirmation, and he has full imperial jurisdiction beforehand although he is not called emperor.

But in truth, and according to the Catholic faith, he is subject to the pope in spiritual matters and also receives his sword from him, for the right of both swords belongs to the pope. This is proved by the fact that the Lord had both swords on earth and used both as is mentioned here, and he established Peter as his vicar on earth and all Peter's successors. Therefore today Innocent has by right the material sword. If you deny this you are saying that Christ established a secular prince as his vicar in this regard. Again Peter said to the Lord, "Behold, here are two swords" (Luke 22:38), so the material sword too was with Peter. Again if the emperor was not subject to the pope in temporalities he could not sin against the church in temporalities. Again the church is one body and so it shall have only one head or it will be a monster.

This opinion is not invalidated by the fact that there were emperors before there were popes, because they were only *de facto* emperors, and none except those who believed in the true God had a right to the sword; nor do infidel rulers have it nowadays. Likewise it is not invalidated by the fact that Constantine conferred temporal jurisdiction on Sylvester as is said at *Dist.* 63 c.30 . . . the Donation of Constantine at *Dist.* 63 c.30 Alanus commented,

From his plenitude of right the pope could take away the City and other possessions even if the emperor was unwilling.

The emperor then has the sword from the pope. The electors indeed confer it on him, not the pope, but every bishop has his bishopric from the pope and yet the pope does not confer it but rather canonical election of the clergy does. The pope therefore is the ordinary judge of the emperor in both temporal and spiritual affairs and can depose him. . . . But can he depose him for any crime? I answer, rather for none, unless he is determined to persist in it, and even then perhaps not for any offence but only for those which harm the people, as for instance the continued discord of heresy. But could the pope keep the material sword for himself if he wished? I answer no, because the Lord divided the swords as is said here, and the church would be gravely disturbed by this.

What has been said of the emperor may be held true of any prince who has no superior lord. Each one has as much jurisdiction in his kingdom as the emperor has in the empire, for the division of kingdoms that has been introduced nowadays by the law of nations is approved by the pope although the ancient law of nations held that there should be one emperor in the world.

Huguccio and Alanus also discussed the possibility of deposing a pope who fell into heresy in their commentaries on Distinctio *40 c.6 of the* Decretum.

HUGUCCIO: Behold, a pope can be condemned for heresy by his subjects! *Dist.* 21 c.7 above states the contrary. There it is said that Marcellinus was guilty of heresy but none the less his subjects did not condemn him. Some say that they did not wish to do so, but I say that they could not and should not have condemned him because he freely and humbly confessed his error, for the pope can be condemned for heresy only in the last resort when he contumaciously and persistently resists and strives to defend and uphold his error. . . . But behold, a pope invents a new heresy; some one wishes to prove that it is a heresy; the pope says it is not a heresy but the Catholic faith; is the proof against him to be accepted? I believe not. Again, he secretly adheres to a heresy already condemned. Some persons, however, know of this and wish to prove that the pope follows such a heresy. But he denies it. Ought they to be heard? I believe not; for the pope can be accused of heresy only in the last resort when there is agreement concerning the fact of heresy and the pope does not deny the fact and being admonished, refuses to come to his senses but contumaciously defends his error. . . .

Can the pope be accused of simony or any other crime? Some say no, whether it is notorious or not, because we ought not to stipulate what the canon does not stipulate. They say that the reason for the difference—why he can be accused of heresy more readily than of any other crime—is that if a pope were a heretic he would not harm only himself but the whole world, especially since the simple and foolish would easily accept that heresy, not believing it to be a heresy. But if the pope commits simony or fornication or theft or anything of the sort he seems to harm only himself, for everyone knows that no one is permitted to steal or commit fornication or simony or anything of the sort. But I believe that it is the same in any notorious crime, that the pope can be accused and condemned if, being admonished, he is not willing to desist. What then? Behold, he steals publicly, he fornicates publicly, he keeps a concubine publicly, he has intercourse with her publicly in the church, near the altar or on it, and being admonished will not desist. Shall he not be accused? Shall he not be condemned? Is it not like heresy to scandalize the church in such a fashion? Moreover contumacy is the crime of idolatry and like to heresy. . . . And so it is the same with any notorious crime as with heresy.

ALANUS: If he was a public usurer might he not be accused? He can be accused of any notorious crime according to some who accept "to sin in faith" in a broad sense as meaning to sin against the teaching of the faith, just as anyone committing mortal sin is said to deny Christ. . . . But, according to this view, the privilege of the pope would amount to nothing. Therefore it is to be said that, since he has no superior judge, he cannot be judged against his will except for the crime of heresy, in which case it was so decreed because of the enormity of the crime and the common danger to the church. But can anyone lay down a law for the pope, when the pope is not bound by the canons and can change them? Perhaps it is so in the case of that crime because there, as a consequence of it, a question arises whether he really is pope; for it seems that if he is a heretic he is not the head of the church. If he is suspected of any other crime and some one wishes to accuse him, lest he bring scandal on the church, although he cannot be compelled, nevertheless, having been admonished, he ought to select a judge and go to trial under him, for although he is not bound by the laws nevertheless he ought to live according to them.

CHAPTER 8

FEUDALISM IN WESTERN EUROPE AND JAPAN

Along with the impact of the world religions on the state (see chapter 7), a key development in the postclassical period was the formation of governments in areas where the forms of civilization were expanding for the first time. This chapter focuses on distinctive features of that process in Western Europe and Japan.

The general issue was this: societies that arose on the fringes of the classical world—including Russia and parts of sub-Saharan Africa, as well as Japan and northwestern Europe—often were forming governments with no particular historical precedent. At most, very loose, essentially tribal kingships had emerged before (save in parts of Africa, where more elaborate states preceded this period). Lacking highly developed economies, well-established political legitimacy, or even many trained officials, it was difficult to form elaborate states. Western Europe tried briefly to revive the Roman Empire (under the emperor Charlemagne, around 800 C.E.) but did not succeed. Japan made an attempt to imitate the Chinese Empire in the seventh century but could not. Russia was influenced by the powerful Byzantine Empire but was not able to match it. A looser, less demanding government was the only option in these new-civilization regions.

In Japan and Western Europe, the political relationships known as feudalism served this purpose. Feudalism linked local and regional military leaders—the lords—with some other military personnel. This was a system for elites: it did not directly involve the masses of ordinary people. A lord would form ties with other people who had the equipment (horses, some armor, and weaponry) necessary to fight. He would offer them protection and often his support or some land, or both, in return for their loyalty and their service in war. This was the essence of the feudal system. It could provide some orderliness in individual regions, as opposed to endemic local fighting; when it was extended to larger units, through feudal ties among great lords themselves, it could even support a monarchy.

Both Japan and Western Europe established this system in the postclassical period, out of similar needs. They were not in contacts with each other, so it is not surprising that the two feudalisms, though remarkably similar, had some differences—differences that would affect the two areas long after feudalism itself had perished. Here, then, is another comparison of societies without contact, developing separately but resembling each other to an intriguing degree.

Feudalism was an unusual political institution, based on decentralized power structures; for example, a variety of lords, and not the central ruler alone, had significant military forces under their command. But the feudal network of reciprocal benefits also encouraged warriors to cooperate with each other and form a lord-vassal hierarchy, cemented by oaths of loyalty. This was a system of relationships among members of the upper class, fighting men who usually claimed inherited rank.

Western Europe, after the fall of the Roman Empire and the decline of Charlemagne's effort to establish an empire in the ninth century, was politically chaotic. The only way rulers could obtain any service from other lords was to offer them feudal benefits, including grants of land. In addition, though, feudalism could provide relationships that generated greater stability and larger political units. By the eleventh century, rulers in places like England were using feudalism to command larger military forces and revenue bases, but without developing a central bureaucracy of any significance.

Feudalism in Japan arose by the ninth century, after the failure of efforts to set up a Chinese-style imperial, Confucian system. As in Western Europe, widespread disorder led to regional networks of lords and vassals. The central government attempted to regulate the system, but without great effect for several centuries. During the twelfth century, though, a central lord, Yorimoto, from the Minamoto family, set up the Kamakura shogunate, which imposed more effective control over regional vassals without dismantling the feudal system. (Regional wars later revived in Japan, and feudalism was not fully abolished until 1868.) As in Europe, feudalism in Japan involved a set of beliefs and values, not simply political rules and regulations.

The selections in this chapter describe various feudal situations in France, England, and Japan. Early documents in both the European and the Japanese sections show the kinds of disorder that made feudalism necessary and possible. For example, a king of France grants a whole province, Normandy, to a Scandinavian leader in return for his accepting vassalage and (after a fashion) swearing loyalty. Japanese sources show how regional lords were taking over. In both regions, rulers had to use grants of land (fiefs) and other promises in order to persuade regional warlords to accept any control. Documents from later in the postclassical period show how English rulers and the Minamoto shoguns, while confirming the feudal system, were able to command greater loyalty, to grant fiefs to more faithful officials, and even to manipulate fiefs to obtain payment from lords and ladies seeking to marry or to avoid marriage.

European feudal documents also describe oaths of loyalty and mutual obligations. But they express a certain tension as well: it was possible for a lord to fail in his obligations and for vassals to use this as an occasion to withdraw. Furthermore, vassals might come to have several different lords, as they inherited different fiefs, which was another way that loyalties might be qualified. European feudalism, in other words, though based strongly on hierarchy and devotion, developed a contractual quality that could allow vassals to claim some rights to monitor the actions of their lords. How did this feature relate to the political implications of Christianity (see chapter 7)?

Japanese feudalism was full of plots and counterplots, but it tended to emphasize a higher ideal of service and complete devotion. Confucian elements entered into this ideal of mutual respect, and a more specifically military commitment to honor arose as well. Comparing the later Japanese materials to the discussion by Bishop Fulbert of the European plan shows different kinds of idealizations of the feudal system.

Feudalism in these two societies, at opposite ends of Eurasia, though remarkably similar in origins and structure, had somewhat different consequences in the long run. European feudalism developed into efforts to institutionalize contractual relationships between rulers and vassals; it led in turn to early versions of parliaments set up to try to make sure that rulers would stay within agreed-upon bounds. Japanese feudalism's greater stress on loyalty led not to parliaments—which would arrive only through much later imitation of the West—but to a sense of group cohesiveness that still describes aspects of Japanese management style and political life.

Questions

1. What basic characteristics of feudalism emerge from the European and Japanese materials? What did lords and vassals gain from a feudal tie? What were their respective obligations?
2. How was the Magna Carta a feudal document? How had the king violated feudalism, and what remedies were proposed?
3. In what ways is it clear that vassals, though required to be loyal to their lords, were basically in the same social class and not to be treated as social inferiors?
4. How much difference was there between the loyalty emphases in Japanese feudalism and those in the European version? Would European vassals have agreed with the extent of devotion displayed in the Japanese *Tale of the Heike*? Would Japanese vassals have agreed with the approach taken in the Magna Carta?

For Further Discussion

1. What conditions account for the emergence of such similar political systems in Western Europe and Japan?

2. What would a Confucian bureaucrat think of feudalism? On what grounds would he criticize it? Would he prefer the Western or the Japanese version?

3. Are there any remnants of feudal ideas and institutions in the Western world today? Why might some observers argue that the special qualities of Japanese feudalism, removed from specific feudal institutions, are still useful in Japan today?

4. What aspects of Western feudalism generated the idea that if a lord misbehaved, his vassals could act as if a contract had been broken? How could feudal elites move from this idea to the idea of parliaments, composed of these and other elites who advised the king as feudal lord? Why would this particular evolution of feudalism be more difficult in Japan?

5. What are the differences between feudal and modern ideas of limited government?

EUROPEAN FEUDALISM

Feudal documents were legal records for the most part, and often short. What follows are various documents dating from the seventh to the twelfth centuries that treat different aspects of French and English feudalism.

In the first document, a pagan, that is non-Christian, Viking duke whose people had conquered Normandy is induced to enter a feudal relationship with the king of France, along with marriage to one of the king's daughters. What would each party get out of this relationship? Two documents then describe common feudal property grants and a standard oath of loyalty in what was a very ritual relationship. Then a well-known French bishop offers a more general description—obviously somewhat idealized—of what feudalism involved. Two documents describe potential complexities in European feudalism: conditions of separation and the quite common case—since feudal lands were inherited and also passed to husbands on marriage—in which a vassal had several lords (would this have been as likely in Japanese feudalism? what does it say about trends in the European system?) Two additional documents highlight standard vassal obligations.

The final document offers excerpts from the English Magna Carta, or great charter, which the feudal barons imposed by force of arms on King John in 1215 in defense of feudal rights. The passages suggest how John had been trying to extend government powers, mainly to gain resources for wars with France, and how feudalism allowed resistance to be framed. The passages also suggest how new institutions might emerge from feudalism. The Magna Carta itself had little direct effect, but its principles were revived fifty years later when the first English parliament was called; and the whole document was enshrined in the seventeenth century, when the parliamentary tradition moved toward more modern forms.

• • •

EUROPEAN FEUDAL DOCUMENTS

1. Granting Normandy (Tenth Century)

Immediately Charles [French king], having consulted with them, sent Franco, Archbishop of Rouen, to Rollo, Duke of the Pagans. Coming to him he began to speak with mild words. "Most exalted and distinguished of dukes, will you quarrel with the Franks as long as you live? Will you always wage war on them? What will become of you when you are seized by death? Whose creature are you? Do you think you are God? Are you not a man formed from filth? Are you not dust and ashes and food for worms? Remember what you are and will be and by whose judgment you will be condemned. You will experience Hell I think, and no longer injure anyone by your wars. If you are willing to become a Christian you will be able to enjoy peace in the present and the future and to dwell in this world with great riches. Charles, a long-suffering king, persuaded by the counsel of his men, is willing to give you this coastal province that you and Halstigno have grievously ravaged. He will also give you his daughter, Gisela, for a wife in order that peace and concord and a firm, stable and continuous friendship may endure for all time between you and him. . . ."

At the agreed time Charles and Rollo came together at the place that had been decided on. . . . Looking on Rollo, the invader of France, the Franks said to one another, "This duke who has fought such battles against the warriors of this realm is a man of great power and great courage and prowess and good counsel and of great energy too." Then, persuaded by the words of the Franks, Rollo put his hands between the hands of the king, a thing which his father and grandfather and great-grandfather had never done; and so the king gave his daughter Gisela in marriage to the duke and conferred on him the agreed lands from the River Epte to the sea as his property in hereditary right, together with all Brittany from which he could live.

Rollo was not willing to kiss the foot of the king. The bishops said, "Anyone who receives such a gift ought to be eager to kiss the king's foot." He replied, "I have never bent my knees at anyone's knees, nor will I kiss anyone's foot." But, urged by the entreaties of the Franks, he commanded one of his warriors to kiss the foot of the king. The warrior promptly seized the king's foot, carried it to his mouth and kissed it standing up while the king was thrown flat on his back. At that there was a great outburst of laughter and great excitement among the people. Nevertheless King Charles, Duke Robert, the counts and nobles, the bishops and abbots swore by the Catholic faith and by their lives, limbs and the honor of the whole

From Brian Tierney, *Sources of Medieval History*, (New York: Alfred A. Knopf, 1978), 1: 126–29, 131, 133–35.

kingdom to the noble Rollo that he should hold and possess the land described above and pass it on to his heirs.

2. Granting Fiefs (Landed Estates) (Seventh Century)

Those who from their early youth have served us or our parents faithfully are justly rewarded by the gifts of our munificence. Know therefore that we have granted to that illustrious man (name), with greatest good will, the villa called (name), situated in the county of (name), with all its possessions and extent, in full as it was formerly held by him *or* by our treasury. Therefore by the present charter which we command to be observed forever, we decree that the said (name) shall possess the villa of (name), as has been said, in its entirety, with lands, houses, buildings, inhabitants, slaves, woods, pastures, meadows, streams, mills, and all its appurtenances and belongings, and with all the subjects of the royal treasury who dwell on the lands, and he shall hold it forever with full immunity from the entrance of any public official for the purpose of exacting the royal portion of the fines from cases arising there: to the extent finally that he shall have, hold, and possess it in full ownership, no one having the right to expect its transfer, and with the right of leaving it to his successors or to anyone whom he desires, and to do with it whatever else he wishes.

3. Oaths of Loyalty

Thus shall one take the oath of fidelity:

By the Lord before whom this sanctuary is holy, I will to N. be true and faithful, and love all which he loves and shun all which he shuns, according to the laws of God and the order of the world. Nor will I ever with will or action, through word or deed, do anything which is unpleasing to him, on condition that he will hold to me as I shall deserve it, and that he will perform everything as it was in our agreement when I submitted myself to him and chose his will.

It is right that those who offer to us unbroken fidelity should be protected by our aid. And since *such and such* a faithful one of ours, by the favor of God, coming here in our palace with his arms, has seen fit to swear trust and fidelity to us in our hand, therefore we decree and command by the present precept that for the future *such and such* above mentioned be counted with the number of [followers]. And if anyone perchance should presume to kill him, let him know that he will be judged guilty of his wergild of 600 shillings.

4. Fulbert, Bishop of Chartres, on Feudal Obligations (1020)

To William most glorious duke of the Aquitanians, bishop Fulbert the favor of his prayers.

Asked to write something concerning the form of fealty, I have noted briefly for you on the authority of the books the things which follow. He who swears fealty to his lord ought always to have these six things in memory; what is harmless, safe, honorable, useful, easy, practicable. Harmless, that is to say that he should not be injurious to his lord in his body: safe, that he should not be injurious to him in his secrets or in the defenses through which he is able to be secure; honorable, that he should not be injurious to him in his justice or in other matters that pertain to his honor; useful, that he should not be injurious to him in his possessions; easy or practicable, that that good which his lord is able to do easily, he make not difficult, nor that which is practicable he make impossible to him.

However, that the faithful vassal should avoid these injuries is proper, but not for this does he deserve his holding: for it is not sufficient to abstain from evil, unless what is good is done also. It remains, therefore, that in the same six things mentioned above he should faithfully counsel and aid his lord, if he wishes to be looked upon as worthy of his benefice and to be safe concerning the fealty which he has sworn.

The lord also ought to act toward his faithful vassal reciprocally in all these things. And if he does not do this he will be justly considered guilty of bad faith, just as the former, if he should be detected in the avoidance of or the doing of or the consenting to them, would be perfidious and perjured.

I would have written to you at greater length, if I had not been occupied with many other things, including the rebuilding of our city and church which was lately entirely consumed in a great fire; from which loss though we could not for a while be diverted, yet by the hope of the comfort of God and of you we breathe again.

5. Lords and Vassals (816)

If anyone shall wish to leave his lord (*seniorem*), and is able to prove against him one of these crimes, that is, in the first place, if the lord has wished to reduce him unjustly into servitude; in the second place, if he has taken counsel against his life; in the third place, if the lord has committed adultery with the wife of his vassal; in the fourth place, if he has wilfully attacked him with a drawn sword; in the fifth place, if the lord has been able to bring defence to his vassal after he has commended his hands to him, and has not done so; it is allowed to the vassal to leave him. If the lord has perpetrated anything against the vassal in these five points it is allowed the vassal to leave him.

6. Vassals with Several Lords (1200)

I. Thiebault, count palatine of Troyes, make known to those present and to come that I have given in fee to Jocelyn d'Avalon and his heirs the manor which is called

Gillencourt, which is of the castellanerie of La Ferté sur Aube; and whatever the same Jocelyn shall be able to acquire in the same manor I have granted to him and his heirs in augmentation of that fief. I have granted, moreover, to him that in no free manor of mine will I retain men who are of this gift. The same Jocelyn, moreover, on account of this has become my liege man, saving however, his allegiance to Gerard d'Arcy, and to the lord duke of Burgundy, and to Peter, count of Auxerre. Done at Chouaude, by my own witness, in the year of the Incarnation of our Lord 1200 in the month of January. Given by the hand of Walter, my chancellor; note of Milo.

7. *Military Service (1072)*

William, king of the English, to Aethelwig, abbot of Evesham, greeting. I command you to summon all those who are under your charge and administration that they shall have ready before me at Clarendon on the octave of Pentecost all the knights that they owe me. Come to me likewise yourself on that day, and bring ready with you those five knights that you owe me from your abbey.

8. *Payments*

Alice, countess of Warwick, renders account of £1000 and 10 palfreys to be allowed to remain a widow as long as she pleases, and not to be forced to marry by the king. And if perchance she should wish to marry, she shall not marry except with the assent and on the grant of the king, where the king shall be satisfied; and to have the custody of her sons whom she has from the earl of Warwick her late husband.

Hawisa, who was wife of William Fitz Robert renders account of 130 marks and 4 palfreys that she may have peace from Peter of Borough to whom the king has given permission to marry her; and that she may not be compelled to marry.

Geoffrey de Mandeville owes 20,000 marks to have as his wife Isabella, countess of Gloucester, with all the lands and tenements and fiefs which fall to her.

Thomas de Colville renders an account of 100 marks for having the custody of the sons of Roger Torpel and their land until they come of age.

William, bishop of Ely, owes 220 marks for having the custody of Stephen de Beauchamp with his inheritance and for marrying him where he wishes.

William of St. Mary's church, renders an account of 500 marks for having the custody of the heir of Robert Young, son of Robert Fitzharding, with all his inheritance and all its appurtenances and franchises; that is to say with the services of knights and gifts of churches and marriages of women, and to be allowed to marry him to whatever one of his relatives he wishes; and that all his land is to revert to him freely when he comes of age.

THE MAGNA CARTA

John, by the grace of God, king of England, lord of Ireland, duke of Normandy and Aquitaine, and count of Anjou, to the archbishops, bishops, abbots, earls, barons, justiciars, foresters, sheriffs, stewards, servants, and to all his bailiffs and loyal persons, greeting. Know that, having regard to God and for the salvation of our souls, and those of all our predecessors and heirs, and unto the honour of God and the advancement of Holy Church, and for the reform of our realm, by the counsel of our venerable fathers . . . we have granted:

XII. No scutage [tax] or aid shall be imposed on our kingdom, unless by common counsel of our kingdom, except for ransoming our person, for making our eldest son a knight, and for marrying our eldest daughter once; and for them there shall not be levied more than a reasonable aid. In like manner it shall be done concerning aids from the city of London.

XXIX. No constable shall compel any knight to give money in stead of castle guard, when he is willing to perform it in his own person, or (if he himself cannot do it from any reasonable cause) then by another reliable man; and if we have led him or sent him upon military service, he shall be quit of guard, in proportion to the time during which he has been on service because of us.

XXXIX. No freeman shall be taken or imprisoned or disseised or exiled or in anyway destroyed, nor will we go upon him nor send upon him, except by the lawful judgement of his peers or by the law of the land.

LV. All fines made by us unjustly and against the law of the land, shall be entirely remitted, or else it shall be done concerning them according to the decision of the five-and-twenty barons of whom mention is made below in (the clause for) securing the peace, or according to the judgement of the majority of the same, along with the aforesaid Stephen, archbishop of Canterbury, if he can be present, and such others as he may wish to bring with him for this purpose; and if he cannot be present the business shall nevertheless proceed without him, provided always that if any one or more of the aforesaid five-and-twenty barons are in a similar suit, they shall be removed as far as shall concern this particular judgement, others being substituted in their places after having been selected by the rest of the five-and-twenty for this purpose only, and after having been sworn.

LXI. Since, moreover, for God and the amendment of our kingdom and for the better allaying of our quarrel that has arisen between us and our barons, we have granted all these concessions, desirous that they should enjoy them in complete and firm stability for ever, we give and grant to them the underwritten security, namely, that the barons choose five-and-twenty barons of the kingdom, whomsoever they will, who shall be obliged, to observe and hold, and cause to be observed, with all

From *Statutes of the Realm* (London, 1810), 1: 5ff.

their might, the peace and liberties which we have granted and confirmed to them by this our present Charter, so that if we, or our justiciar, or our bailiffs or any one of our officers, shall in anything be at fault towards anyone, or shall have broken any one of the articles of the peace or of this security, and the offence be notified to four barons of the aforesaid five-and-twenty, the said four barons shall come to us (or to our justiciar, if we are out of the realm) and, laying the transgression before us, petition to have that transgression redressed without delay. And if we shall not have corrected the transgression (or, in event of our being out of the kingdom, if our justiciar shall not have corrected it) within forty days, reckoning from the time it has been notified to us (or to our justiciar, if we should be out of the kingdom), the four barons aforesaid shall refer the matter to the rest of the five-and-twenty barons, and those five-and-twenty barons shall, together with the community of the whole land, distrain and distress us in all possible ways, namely, by seizing our castles, lands, possessions, and in any other way they can, until redress has been obtained as they deem fit, saving our own person and the persons of our queen and children; and when redress has been obtained, they shall resume their former relations toward us.

JAPANESE FEUDALISM

Japanese feudalism and its origins can be tracked in part through government decrees. Japan had an emperor from the sixth century onward. But several decrees between the ninth and the twelfth centuries make it clear that the government encountered increasing difficulties in maintaining order or even disciplining its own officials. In the late twelfth and thirteenth centuries, a leading family, the Kamakura (Minamoto), gained central authority (separate from the emperor, now a largely religious figurehead). The government, called a shogunate, established feudal ties with other lords, treating them as vassals with mutual obligations. Documents 3 and 4 suggest some of the characteristics, advantages, and limitations of this feudal monarchy system. The final two documents describe Japanese feudal ideals. The *Tale of the Heike* was a well-known story of the wars that led up to the Kamakura shogunate, written shortly thereafter; it is followed by a letter from a samurai—the characteristic vassal-warrior—to his son.

• • •

David John Lu, ed., *Japan: A Documentary History.* Copyright © 1997, M. E. Sharpe (Armonk, N.Y.), 1:103–110. Reprinted by permission of the editor.

JAPANESE FEUDAL DOCUMENTS

1. On Prohibiting People from Kyoto to Reside Outside of the Capital Region (Kinai) (871)

Lately, those people whose domiciles are in the capital city [of Heian], and who are children and heirs of princes and of important court officials, reside outside the capital region. Some intermarry [with people from outer provinces], and others engage in agriculture or commerce and are no different from the people in the provinces. There are also reports that vagabonds form gangs and treat villages as if they were their own possessions. They oppose provincial governors and local officials and make threats on poor people. They not only hinder the normal functioning of the provincial affairs, but also create a climate detrimental to public morality. The Minister of the Right [Minamoto Tooru] therefore declares: "In obedience to the Imperial command, an order must be given to supervise strictly [their activities]. They must withdraw from the outer provinces before the seventh month of the coming year. If they persist in their disobedience and do not mend their ways, regardless of any connection they may have, they must be banished to distant places. There shall be no exception made to our previous order that no governmental official be permitted to remain in his post after expiration of his present term. If the governmental officials in charge of this matter do not indict those who commit this offense, they must also be dealt with as if committing the similar offense."

2. On Matters Relating to the Business of a Province (1114)

1. Preventing riotous behavior.

When a newly appointed governor travels to the province to which he is assigned, some of his *rōtō* [entourage] and other followers either rob things from other persons or engage in quarrels among themselves. It is therefore ordered that a newly appointed governor must select from among his *rōtō*, pure and strong persons who can engage in the task of stopping this kind of behavior.

2. Do not permit members of your household (*ienoko*) to speak ill of others, and prevent unruly actions of your high ranking *rōtō*.

If on reflection one does not stop those conditions which lead to the use of foul language, and permit one's *rōtō* to engage freely in slandering or heaping abuse on others . . . as these things continue to multiply, people will start ridiculing you. When you take the responsibility of serving the public, you are really performing something good for yourself too. But if you do not put a stop to the abuse that some of your followers—whether they be your own most beloved children or *rōtō*—heap on others, and let this continue [those who are the object of abuse will not serve you]. In this way, you may not be able to collect taxes and send them to the central government. You will then gain the reputation of being an ineffectual governor. If your children and *rōtō* cannot uphold one another and also help you, your term of office will be one of emptiness. If all your followers will pursue their own follies, you will be left with no followers day and night. Then what benefit is there [of becoming a governor]?

3. Establishment of Relationship between Lord and Vassals (1184)

Following the destruction of the Ichinotani fortification in Settsu Province in the Second Month, members of the Heike have been plundering the various provinces in the west, and Genji troops have been sent into the region to check the Heike. One of the means employed has been the sending of Tachibana Kiminari and his men as an advance column into Sanuki Province to secure the support of the local lords. They have since submitted to the Minamoto, and a roster containing their names has been transmitted to Kamakura [central government]. Today, His Lordship has sent instructions to the local lords of Sanuki to take their orders from Kiminari.

[Yoritomo's monogram]

"Ordered to: Immediate vassals of Sanuki Province

"To submit forthwith to the command of Tachibana Kiminari and to join in the Kyushu campaign.

"At this time when the Heike are plundering your lands, you have indicated your submission to me. A roster of your names has been submitted to me. It is indeed a most loyal act on your part. Submit forthwith to the command of Kiminari and conduct yourselves in a loyal and meritorious manner. Thus ordered."

4. The Kamakura Shogunate (1232)

Of the duties devolving on Protectors (*shugō*) in the provinces. In the time of the august Right General [Yoritomo's] House, it was settled that those duties should be the calling out and despatching of the Grand Guard for service at the capital, the suppression of conspiracies and rebellion and the punishment of murder and violence (which included night attacks on houses, gang robbery and piracy). Of late years, however, deputies (*daikan*) have been taken on and distributed over the districts (*Kōri* or *gun*) and counties (*gō*) and these have been imposing public burdens (*kuji* or all forms of taxation) on the villages. Not being Governors of the provinces. (*kum no tsukasa* or *kokushi*), they yet hinder the work of the province: not being Stewards (*jitō*) they are yet greedy of the profits of the land. Such proceedings and schemes are utterly unprincipled.

Be it noted that no person, even if his family were for generations vassals (*gokenin*) of the august House of Minamoto is competent to impress [people] for military service unless he has an investiture [to the land] of the present date.

5. Tale of the Heike

Recognizing each other, master and retainer spurred their horses to join each other. Seizing Kanehira's hands, Yoshinaka said: "I would have fought to the death on the banks of the Kamo at Rokujō. Simply because of you, however, I have galloped here through the enemy swarms."

"It was very kind of you, my lord," replied Kanehira. "I too would have fought to the death at Seta. But in fear of your uncertain fate, I have come this way."

"We are still tied by karma," said Yoshinaka. "There must be more of my men around here, for I have seen them scattered among the hills. Unroll the banner and raise it high!"

As soon as Kanehira unfurled the banner, many men who had been in flight from the capital and Seta saw it and rallied. They soon numbered more than three hundred.

"Since we still have so many men, let us try one last fight!" shouted Yoshinaka jubilantly. "Look! That band of soldiers over there! Whose army is that?"

"I hear," replied one of Yoshinaka's men, "that is Tadayori's army, my lord."

"How many men are there in his army?"

"About six thousand, my lord."

"Just right!" cried out Yoshinaka. "Since we are determined to fight to the death, let us ride neck and neck with our valiant foes and die gallantly in their midst. Forward!"

Shouting, Yoshinaka dashed ahead. That day he wore armor laced with twilled silk cords over a red battle robe. His helmet was decorated with long golden horns. At his side hung a great sword studded with gold. He carried his quiver a little higher than usual on his back. Some eagle-feathered arrows still remained. Gripping his rattan-bound bow, he rode his famous horse, Oniashige [Gray Demon].

Rising high in his stirrups, he roared at the enemy: "You have often heard of me. Now take a good look at the captain of the Imperial Stables of the Left and governor of Iyo Province—Rising-Sun General Minamoto no Yoshinaka, that is who I am! I know that among you is Kai no Ichijōjirō Tadayori. We are fit opponents for each other. Cut off my head and show it to Yoritomo!"

At this challenge, Tadayori shouted to his men: "Now, hear this! He is the commander of our enemy. Let him not escape! All men—to the attack!" . . . When Yoshinaka found himself alone with Kanehira, he sighed: "My armor has never weighed upon me before, but today it is heavy."

From Hiroshi Kitagawa and Bruce T. Tsuchida, trans., *The Tale of the Heike* (Tokyo: University of Tokyo Press, 1975), 520–23.

"You do not look tired at all, my lord," replied Kanehira, "and your horse is still fresh. What makes it feel so heavy? If it is because you are discouraged at having none of your retainers but me, please remember that I, Kanehira, am a match for a thousand. Since I still have seven or eight arrows left in my quiver, let me hold back the foe while you withdraw to the Awazu pine wood. Now I pray you to put a peaceful end to yourself."

No sooner had he spoken to his master than another band of soldiers confronted them. "Please go to the pine wood, my lord," said Kanehira again. "Let me fight here to keep them away from you."

"I would have died in the capital!" replied Yoshinaka. "I have come this far with no other hope but to share your fate. How can I die apart from you? Let us fight until we die together!"

With these words, Yoshinaka tried to ride neck and neck with Kanehira. Now Kanehira alighted from his horse, seized the bridle of his master's mount, and pleaded in tears: "Whatever fame a warrior may win, a worthless death is a lasting shame for him. You are worn out, my lord. Your horse is also exhausted. If you are surrounded by the enemy and slain at the hand of a low, worthless retainer of some unknown warrior, it will be a great shame for you and me in the days to come. How disgraceful it would be if such a nameless fellow could declare, 'I cut off the head of Yoshinaka, renowned throughout the land of Japan!'"

Yoshinaka finally gave in to Kanehira's entreaty and rode off toward the pine wood of Awazu. Kanehira, riding alone, charged into the band of some fifty horsemen. Rising high in his stirrups, he cried out in a thunderous voice: "You have often heard of me. Now take a good look. I am Imai no Shirō Kanehira, aged thirty-three, a foster brother of Lord Yoshinaka. As I am a valiant warrior among the men of Lord Yoshinaka, your master, Yoritomo, at Kamakura must know my name well. Take my head and show it to him!"

Kanehira had hardly uttered these words when he let fly his remaining eight arrows one after another without pause. Eight men were shot from their horses, either dead or wounded. He then drew his sword and brandished it as he galloped to and fro. None of his opponents could challenge him face to face, though they cried out: "Shoot him down! Shoot him down!"

Sanehira's soldiers let fly a shower of arrows at Kanehira, but his armor was so strong that none of them pierced it. Unless they aimed at the joints of his armor, he could never be wounded.

Yoshinaka was now all alone in the pine wood of Awazu. It was the twenty-first day of the first month. Dusk had begun to fall. Thin ice covered the rice fields and the marsh, so that it was hard to distinguish one from the other. Thus it was that Yoshinaka had not gone far before his horse plunged deep into the muddy slime. Whipping and spurring no longer did any good. The horse could not stir. Despite his predicament, he still thought of Kanehira. As Yoshinaka was turning around to see how he fared, Tamehisa, catching up with him, shot an arrow under his helmet.

It was a mortal wound. Yoshinaka pitched forward onto the neck of his horse. Then two of Tamehisa's retainers fell upon Yoshinaka and struck off his head. Raising it high on the point of his sword, Tamehisa shouted: "Kiso no Yoshinaka, renowned throughout the land of Japan as a valiant warrior, has been killed by Miura no Ishida Jirō Tamehisa!"

Kanehira was fighting desperately as these words rang in his ears. At that moment he ceased fighting and cried out: "For whom do I have to fight now? You, warriors of the east, see how the mightiest warrior in Japan puts an end to himself!" Thrusting the point of his sword into his mouth, he flung himself headlong from his horse so that the sword pierced his head.

Yoshinaka and Kanehira died valiant deaths at Awazu. Could there have been a more heroic battle?

6. A Samurai Instructs His Son

The men under your command . . . must be carefully chosen for your service. Do not take "difficult" fellows. If men under your orders, however loyal, are wanting in intelligence, you must not trust them with important duties, but rely upon experienced older men. If you are in doubt refer to me, Shigetoki.

In dealing with subordinates do not make an obvious distinction between good and not-good. Use the same kind of language, give the same kind of treatment to all, and thus you will get the best out of the worst. But you yourself must not lose sight of the distinction between good character and bad character, between capable and incapable. You must be fair, but in practice you must not forget the difference between men who are useful and men who are not. Remember that the key to discipline is fair treatment in rewards and in punishments. But make allowance for minor misdeeds in young soldiers and others, if their conduct is usually good.

Do not be careless or negligent in the presence of subordinates, especially of older men. Thus do not spit or snuffle or lounge about on a chest with your legs dangling. This only gives men the impression that you do not care for their good opinion. Preserve your dignity. If you behave rudely, they will tell their families and gossip will spread. You must treat all servants with proper consideration and generosity, not only your own people but also those of your parents and other superiors. If you do not, they will scorn you and say to one another: "He thinks he is very important, but he doesn't amount to much."

Remember, however, that there are times when a commander must exercise his power of deciding questions of life or death. In those circumstances since human

Excerpted from George Sanson, *A History of Japan to 1334* (Stanford: Stanford University Press, 1958), 336,© 1958 by the Board of Trustees of the Leland Stanford Junior University. Reprinted by permission of the publisher.

life is at stake you must give most careful thought to your action. Never kill or wound a man in anger, however great the provocation. Better get somebody else to administer the proper punishment. Decisions made in haste before your feelings are calm can only lead to remorse. Close your eyes and reflect carefully when you have a difficult decision to make.

When accusations are brought to you, always remember that there must be another side to the question. Do not merely indulge in anger. To give fair decisions is the most important thing not only in commanding soldiers but also in governing a country.

CONDITIONS OF WOMEN IN ISLAM, BYZANTINE CHRISTIANITY, AND WESTERN CHRISTIANITY

The major world religions were at pains to deal with conditions for women, through their treatments of family law and in more general discussions of women's role in human society. Both Christianity and Islam faced a major tension in principle: they granted women souls and the chance of salvation, but they regarded women as inferior, more prone to evil (both relied on the same biblical account of Adam and Eve and God's creation). Neither religion undermined patriarchy: by emphasizing the story of Eve as the first sinner, they enhanced it culturally, and leading religious roles were reserved for men. But both religions granted women opportunities for religious expression: they could go on pilgrimages, for example. Both Muhammad and some early Christian leaders believed they were giving women important new opportunities through family law and religious prescriptions.

Elements of this tension between inferiority and equality clearly played out in rules concerning both families and public testimony. Women were given some rights in families—they could not be treated as mere property—but their rights were inferior to those of men. In the public sphere, women's rights were far more circumscribed, though ironically, favored upper-class women (in Byzantium, for example) might individually enjoy great opportunities. On what, besides upper-class birth, did these opportunities depend?

The following selections come from laws and commentary in the Byzantine Empire, the center of Orthodox Christianity; from Catholic Western Europe; and from Islam. There are many similarities in the complex statements of patriarchy in all three religions, and these should be the first points to identify. Are there also differences?

More than purely religious factors were involved. Of the three societies compared here, Western Europe was for a long time the most disorderly. Many historians believe that women's power vis-à-vis men's is greatest (at least until very recent times) when governments are weak, because then the informal authority they can wield in families counts for more. Germanic tribal traditions, arising among a hunting-and-gathering people, may also have affected women's conditions in Western Europe. But it is generally agreed also that, with time and as

Western Europe became better organized, women's position deteriorated some-what, and cultural scorn increased. The religious tension definitely existed in this civilization. Women's sinfulness was often emphasized; men alone could be priests; obedience was urged on women in religious marriage. But female figures, includ-ing Mary, the mother of Jesus, and many women saints, were often greatly venerated, because they seemed more accessible, milder, than the male religious figures. And holy women, including women in convents, often wielded real reli-gious influence through their ideas and their piety.

The Byzantine Empire obviously shared Christianity with Western Europe, though its Orthodox institutions were separate. Orthodox Christianity continued to allow priests to marry, which may have signaled less fear about sexuality and contamination through contact with women than arose in the West. Because the Byzantine Empire preserved Roman laws and political institutions, it might also have offered some extra protections for women—Rome had been rather careful to combine patriarchy with legal conditions (see chapter 5).

Islam poses some obvious problems for interpretation, both in the postclassical period and today. Arab peoples before Islam had a strongly patriarchal society in which women's family rights were not well established. Muhammad believed he added important protections for women—allowing them to divorce, for example, which was simply not possible in Christianity. On the other hand, Islam did not make women equal; they even prayed separately from men. Furthermore, traditions in the Middle East that were not officially part of Islam added to the complexity. The practice of veiling women in public, so that they would be kept separate from the freer interactions available to men, predated Islam, but it spread increasingly during the postclassical period save for some peasant women. Historians debate whether Islamic women were clearly more disadvantaged than their Christian sisters in the postclassical period. They seem to have been freer from male control in cer-tain circumstances, such as religious pilgrimages. Individual women, if well placed, could possess political power as in most patriarchal societies—an important com-plexity. On the other hand, Muhammad countenanced polygamy, in regulated cir-cumstances that restricted earlier Arab practices; is this a definite sign that Islam downplayed women's considerations (even though the majority of Muslim men could afford only one wife)? Some Muslims continue the debate today, arguing that feminism is less necessary in Islam than in Christian cultures, because women's rights were more carefully protected in the religion itself. Are there bases for this ar-gument in the materials derived from religious history?

Questions

1. How does the distinctive power of a particular woman, such as Anna Comnena, the mother of a Byzantine emperor, affect interpretations of women's condi-

tions more generally? Does it suggest that the patriarchal system had been modified?

2. Why did canon law punish men for adultery more than women (at least in principle)? How does this relate to patriarchal views about women?

3. How did the Koran and Christian church (canon) law reflect beliefs in the spiritual equality of both genders?

4. What were the crucial tensions in Islam concerning women's spiritual status, rights, and treatment?

5. In what ways is it clear that Byzantium, Western Europe, and the Islamic Middle East were all patriarchal societies, with women held to be distinctly inferior?

6. Did different religions (along with other factors) make a difference for women? What are the most important differences suggested in the documents that follow?

7. Why were Byzantium and Islam both at pains to distinguish between women's private roles and rights and their public roles? Did religion have anything to do with this distinction?

8. In which society were women's property rights better protected, Islam or Western Christianity? Can you think of factors besides religion that might contribute to the difference? Was the Muslim provision of divorce, compared to Christian family law, a distinct advantage for women (even though their divorce rights were far inferior to those of men)?

For Further Discussion

1. Compared to the patriarchal systems of classical civilizations (see chapter 5), were women's conditions improved by the impact of world religions such as Islam and Christianity? In which cultural system, Confucianism or Islam, would a woman be most protected? Which system would be most hostile to female infanticide, and why? How and why did the cultures differ about divorce?

2. Assuming you were an upper-class woman, in which of the three societies would you prefer to have lived during the postclassical period, and why—or do you regard them all as equally confining?

3. Why do some women in the contemporary Middle East argue that Western-style feminism is not necessary because women's rights can be maintained through Islam?

WOMEN IN ISLAM

The prophet Muhammad devoted considerable attention to women in the Koran, the holy book of Islam held to be inspired by Allah. The strong Islamic tendency to offer rules for various human affairs is demonstrated in detailed family laws, which in turn reveal both key principles applied to women and practical features of women's lives in Islamic societies. The second selection is from the Hadith, which consists of collections of traditions attributed to Muhammad and other early leaders; the Hadith set forth further rules and guidelines for Muslims. It began to be written down in the seventh century and was later codified by Muslim scholars. A short third selection, from Islamic law in the eleventh century, deals with public issues. The passage cites the Koran—does it suggest a tension with the Koranic principles of family law? Other Muslim legal authorities are also cited, for Islamic law built up elaborate precedent, becoming more and more complex during the postclassical period.

• • •

THE KORAN

O people, observe your Lord; the One who created you from one being and created from it its mate, then spread from the two many men and women. . . .

You shall not covet the qualities bestowed on each other by God; the men enjoy certain qualities, and women enjoy certain qualities. . . .

The men are made responsible for the women, since God endowed them with certain qualities, and made them the bread earners. The righteous women will cheerfully accept this arrangement, and observe God's commandments, even when alone in their privacy. If you experience opposition from the women, you shall first talk to them, then [you may use such negative incentives as] deserting them in bed, then you may beat them. If they obey you, you are not permitted to transgress against them. . . .

The Muslim men, the Muslim women, the believing men, the believing women, the obedient men, the obedient women, the truthful men, the truthful women, the steadfast men, the steadfast women, the reverent men, the reverent women, the charitable men, the charitable women, the fasting men, the fasting women, the chaste men, the chaste women, and the men who commemorate God frequently, and the commemorating women; God has prepared for them forgiveness and a great recompense. . . .

Inheritance

The men get a share of what the parents and the relatives leave behind. The women too shall get a share of what the parents and relatives leave behind. Whether it is a small or a large inheritance, [the women must get] a definite share. . . .

From *Quran, The Final Testament: Authorized English Version, with the Arabic Text*, trans. Rashad Khalifa (Tucson: Islamic Productions, 1989). Selections are from the following suras and verses: 2:221–23, 226–31, 233–37, 240–41, 282; 4:1, 3, 7, 11–12, 15–16, 19–25, 32, 34–35; 24:32–33, 60; 33:35–59. Reprinted by permission of the publisher.

God decrees a will for the benefit of your children; the male gets twice the share of the female. If the inheritors are only women, more than two, they get two-thirds of what is bequeathed. If only one daughter is left, she gets one-half. . . .

O you who believe, it is not lawful for you to inherit what the women leave behind, against their will. You shall not force them to give up anything you had given them, unless they commit a proven adultery. You shall treat them nicely. If you dislike them, you may dislike something wherein God has placed a lot of good.

Divorce

Those who intend to estrange their wives shall wait four months [for cooling off]; if they reconcile, then God is Forgiver, Most Merciful. If they go through with the divorce, then God is Hearer, Knower. The divorced women shall wait three menstruations [before marrying another man]. It is not lawful for them to conceal what God has created in their wombs, if they believe in God and the Last Day. [In case of pregnancy,] the husband's wishes shall supersede the wife's wishes if he wants to remarry her. The women have rights, as well as obligations, equitably. Thus, the men's wishes prevail [in case of pregnancy]. God is Almighty, Most Wise.

Divorce may be retracted twice. . . . If he divorces her for the third time, it is not lawful for him to remarry her, unless she marries another man, and he divorces her. The first husband can then remarry her, so long as they observe God's laws. . . .

You commit no error if you divorce the women before touching them, or before setting the dowry for them. In that case, you shall compensate them—the rich as he can afford and the poor as he can afford—an equitable compensation. This is a duty upon the righteous. If you divorce them before touching them, but after you had set the dowry for them, the compensation shall be half the dowry, unless they voluntarily forfeit their right, or the responsible party chooses to forfeit the whole dowry. To forfeit is closer to righteousness. Do not abandon amicable relations among you. . . .

The divorcees also shall be provided for, equitably. This is a duty upon the righteous. . . .

If you wish to marry another wife, in place of your present wife, and you had given the latter a great deal, you shall not take back anything you had given her. Would you take it fraudulently, maliciously, and sinfully? How could you take it back, after you have been intimate with each other, and after they have taken from you a solemn pledge? . . .

If a couple fears separation, you shall appoint an arbitrator from his family and an arbitrator from her family; if they decide to reconcile, God will help them get together. . . .

If a woman senses oppression or desertion from her husband, the couple will do better by reconciling their differences; conciliation is good. Since selfishness is a human trait, if you do good and lead a righteous life, then GOD is fully Cognizant of everything you do. . . .

They consult you; say, "GOD decrees for you the inheritance statutes concerning the loner. If one dies and leaves no children, and he had a sister, she gets half the inheritance. If there were two sisters, they get two-thirds of the inheritance. If the siblings are men and women, the male gets a share equal to that of two females." God thus clarifies for you, lest you go astray. God is fully aware of all things. . . .

The thief, male or female, you shall mark their hands as a punishment for their crime, and to serve as a deterrent from GOD. GOD is Almighty, Most Wise. . . .

Anyone who works righteousness, male or female, while believing, we will surely grant them a happy life in this world, and we will surely pay them their full recompense (*on the Day of Judgment*) for their righteous works.

THE HADITH

He who shows concern for the widows and the unfortunate [ranks as high] as one who goes on Jihād in the way of Allah, or one who fasts by day and who rises at night [for prayer].

To look at a woman is forbidden, even if it is a look without desire, so how much the more is touching her.

Said he—upon whom be Allah's blessing and peace—: "Avoid seven pernicious things." [His Companions] said: "And what are they, O Apostle of Allah?" He answered: "Associating anything with Allah, sorcery, depriving anyone of life where Allah has forbidden that save for just cause, taking usury, devouring the property of orphans, turning the back on the day of battle, and slandering chaste believing women even though they may be acting carelessly."

Said the Prophet—upon whom be Allah's blessing and peace—: "I had a look into Paradise and I saw that the poor made up most of its inhabitants, and I had a look into Hell and saw that most of its inhabitants were women."

Treat women-folk kindly for woman was created of a rib. The crookedest part of a rib is its upper part. If you go to straighten it out you will break it, and if you leave it alone it will continue crooked. So treat women in kindly fashion.

From Arthur Jeffery, ed., *A Reader on Islam* (New York: Books for Libraries. Division of Arno Press, 1980). Reprinted by permission of Ayer Company Publishers, Inc., North Stratford, NH 03590.

RULES FOR MUSLIM GOVERNMENT, ELEVENTH CENTURY

Exclusion of Women

Nobody may be appointed to the office of qadi [judge] who does not comply fully with the conditions required to make his appointment valid and his decisions effective. . . . The first condition is that he must be a man. This condition consists of two qualities, puberty and masculinity. As for the child below puberty, he cannot be held accountable, nor can his utterances have effect against himself; how much less so against others. As for women, they are unsuited to positions of authority, although judicial verdicts may be based on what they say. Abu Hanifa said that a woman can act as qadi in matters on which it would be lawful for her to testify, but she may not act as qadi in matters on which it would not be lawful for her to testify. Ibn Jarir al-Tabari, giving a divergent view, allows a woman to act as qadi in all cases, but no account should be taken of an opinion which is refuted by both the consensus of the community and the word of God. "Men have authority over women because of what God has conferred on the one in preference to the other" [Koran 4:38], meaning by this, intelligence and discernment. He does not, therefore, permit women to hold authority over men.

THE BYZANTINE EMPIRE

Byzantine family law, not surprisingly, reflected Roman principles, particularly early in the empire. The most important early Byzantine emperor, Justinian (483–565), had codified Roman law. A marriage contract of the eighth century reflects careful concern for legal equity. The Byzantine Empire also produced some extraordinary individual women. Justinian's wife, the empress Theodora, probably made key policy decisions. During the eleventh and twelfth centuries the Comnenus family dominated the imperial line, producing a period of stable, enlightened rule. The princess Anna was a noteworthy historian, and in the second selection below she describes the role of her grandmother, an empress, in affairs of state. Finally, another law code, from about 900 in the reign of Leo VI, suggests another facet of gender relations in the empire. Does it represent a change from the principles expressed in the earlier marriage contract?

• • •

From Bernard Lewis, ed. and trans. *Islam: From the Prophet Muhammed to the Capture of Constantinople*, vol. 2, *Religion and Society* (New York: Oxford University Press, 1974), 40. Reprinted by permission of Oxford University Press.

A MARRIAGE CONTRACT, 726

The marriage of Christians, man and woman, who have reached years of discretion, that is for a man at fifteen and for a woman at thirteen years of age, both being desirous and having obtained the consent of their parents, shall be contracted either by deed or by parol.

A written marriage contract shall be based upon a written agreement providing the wife's marriage portion; and it shall be made before three credible witnesses according to the new decrees auspiciously prescribed by us. The man on his part agreeing by it continually to protect and preserve undiminished the wife's marriage portion, and also such additions as he may naturally make thereto in augmentation thereof; and it shall be recorded in the agreement made on that behalf by him, that in case there are no children, one-fourth part thereof shall be secured in settlement.

If the wife happens to predecease the husband and there are no children of the marriage, the husband shall receive only one-fourth part of the wife's portion for himself, and the remainder thereof shall be given to the beneficiaries named in the wife's will or, if she be intestate, to the next of kin. If the husband predeceases the wife, and there are no children of the marriage, then all the wife's portion shall revert to her, and so much of all her husband's estate as shall be equal to a fourth part of his portion shall also inure to her as her own, and the remainder of his estate shall revert either to his beneficiaries or, if he be intestate, to his next of kin.

If the husband predecease the wife and there are children of the marriage, the wife being their mother, she shall control her marriage portion and all her husband's property as becomes the head of the family and household.

A HISTORY OF ANNA COMNENA (TWELFTH CENTURY, GRANDDAUGHTER OF EMPEROR ALEXIUS I)

One might be amazed that my father accorded his mother such high honor in these matters and that he deferred to her in all respects, as if he were turning over the reins of the empire to her and running alongside her while she drove the imperial chariot, contenting himself simply with the title of emperor. Indeed, he had already passed beyond the period of boyhood, an age especially when lust for power grows in men of such nature [as Alexius]. He took upon himself the wars against the barbarians and whatever battles and combats pertained to them, while he entrusted to his mother the complete management of [civil] affairs: the selection of civil magistrates, the collection of incoming revenues and the expenses of the govern-

From E. Freslfield, trans. *A Manual of Roman Law* (Cambridge: Bowes and Bowes, 1926), 72–74.
From Anna Comnena, *Alexiade* (London 1928), I: 123–25.

ment. A person who has reached this point in my text may blame my father for entrusting management of the empire to the *gynaiconites* [women's section of the palace]. But if he had known this woman's spirit, how great she was in virtue and intellect and how extremely vigorous, he would cease his reproach and his criticism would be changed into admiration. For my grandmother was so dextrous in handling affairs of state and so highly skilled in controlling and running the government, that she was not only able to manage the Roman empire but could have handled every empire under the sun. She had a vast amount of experience and understood the internal workings of many things: she knew how each affair began and to what result it might lead, which actions were destructive and which rather were beneficial. She was exceedingly acute in discerning whatever course of action was necessary and in carrying it out safely. She was not only acute in her thought, but was no less proficient in her manner of speech. Indeed, she was a persuasive orator, neither verbose nor stretching her phrases out at great length; nor did she quickly lose the sense of her argument. What she began felicitously she would finish even more so. . . .

But, as I was saying, my father, after he had assumed power, managed by himself the strains and labors of war, while making his mother a spectator to these actions, but in other affairs he set her up as ruler, and as if he were her servant he used to say and do whatever she ordered. The emperor loved her deeply and was dependent upon her advice (so much affection had he for his mother), and he made his right hand the executor of her orders, his ears paid heed to her words, and everything which she accepted or rejected the emperor likewise accepted or rejected. In a word, the situation was thus: Alexius possessed the external formalities of imperial power, but she held the power itself. She used to promulgate laws, to manage and administer everything while he confirmed her arrangements, both written and unwritten, either through his signature or by oral commands, so that he seemed the instrument of her imperial authority and not himself the emperor. Everything which she decided or ordered he found satisfactory. Not only was he very obedient to her as is fitting for a son to his mother, but even more he submitted his spirit to her as to a master in the science [*episteme*] of ruling. For he felt that she had attained perfection in everything and far surpassed all men of that time in prudence and in comprehension of affairs.

LEGAL STATUS

I do not know why the ancient authorities, without having thoroughly considered the subject, conferred upon women the right of acting as witnesses. It was, indeed, well known, and they themselves could not fail to be aware that it was dishonorable

From S. P. Scott, ed., *The Civil Law*, vol. 17, *The Novels of Emperor Leo VI* (Cincinnati: Central Trust Co., 1932), 249.

for them to appear frequently before the eyes of men, and that those who were modest and virtuous should avoid doing so. For this reason, as I have previously stated, I do not understand why they permitted them to be called as witnesses, a privilege which resulted in their frequently being associated with great crowds of men, and holding conversation with them of a character very unbecoming to the sex. . . .

And, indeed, the power to act as witnesses in the numerous assemblies of men with which they mingle, as well as taking part in public affairs, gives them the habit of speaking more freely than they ought, and, depriving them of the morality and reserve of their sex, encourages them in the exercise of boldness and wickedness which, to some extent, is even insulting to men. For is it not an insult, and a very serious one, for women to be authorized to do something which is especially within the province of the male sex?

Wherefore, with a view to reforming not only the errors of custom, but also of law, We hereby deprive them of the power of acting as witnesses, and by this constitution forbid them to be called to witness contracts under any circumstances. But, so far as matters in which they are exclusively interested are concerned, and when men cannot act as witnesses, as, for instance, in confinements, and other things where only women are allowed to be present, they can give testimony as to what is exclusively their own, and which should be concealed from the eyes of men.

WESTERN EUROPE: CITY AND CANON LAW

The following two documents outline both secular and religious laws concerning women and their rights in marriage. The city of Magdeburg, in northern Germany, was a prosperous center by the thirteenth century, and many merchant families would have had considerable disposable wealth. The codification of canon law on marriage was part of the general systematization of church law—and the rise of lawyers—as European society became more elaborate with economic advance, the growth of cities, and cultural change. An obvious question: were the provisions of the two types of law, city and church, essentially compatible, even as they focused on different sets of details?

• • •

A GERMAN CITY'S LAWS, 1261

1. When Magdeburg was founded the inhabitants were given such a charter as they wished. They determined that they would choose aldermen every year, who, on their

From Oliver J. Thatcher and Edgar H. McNeal, eds., *A Source Book for Mediæval History* (New York: Charles Scribner's, 1907), 592, 594–95, 600–601.

election, should swear that they would guard the law, honor, and interests of the city to the best of their ability and with the advice of the wisest people of the city. . . .

14. If a man dies leaving a wife, she shall have no share in his property except what he has given her in court, or has appointed for her dower. She must have six witnesses, male or female, to prove her dower. If the man made no provision for her, her children must support her as long as she does not remarry. If her husband had sheep, the widow shall take them.

15. If a man and woman have children, some of whom are married and have received their marriage portion, and the man dies, the children who are still at home shall receive the inheritance. Those who have received their marriage portion shall have no part of [the inheritance]. Children who have received an inheritance shall not sell it without the consent of the heirs. . . .

18. No one, whether man or woman, shall, on his sick-bed, give away more than three shillings' worth of his property without the consent of his heirs, and the woman must have the consent of her husband. . . .

55. When a man dies his wife shall give [to his heirs] his sword, his horse and saddle, and his best coat of mail. She shall also give a bed, a pillow, a sheet, a table-cloth, two dishes and a towel. Some say that she should give other things also, but that is not necessary. If she does not have these things, she shall not give them, but she shall give proof for each article that she does not have it.

56. If two or more children inherit these things, the oldest shall take the sword and they shall share the other things equally.

57. If the children are minors, the oldest male relative on the father's side, if he is of the same rank by birth, shall receive all these things and preserve them for the children. When they become of age, he shall give them to them, and in addition, all their property, unless he can prove that he has used it to their profit, or that it has been stolen or destroyed by some accident without any fault of his. He shall also be the guardian of the widow until she remarries, if he is of the same rank as she is.

58. After giving the above articles the widow shall take her dower and all that belongs to her; that is, all the sheep, geese, chests, yarn, beds, pillows, cushions, table linen, bed linen, towels, cups, candlesticks, linen, women's clothing, finger rings, bracelets, headdress, psalters, and all prayer-books, chairs, drawers, bureaus, carpets, curtains, etc., and there are many other trinkets which belong to her, such as brushes, scissors, and mirrors, but I do not mention them. But uncut cloth, and unworked gold and silver do not belong to her.

CHURCH (CANON) LAW ON MARRIAGE, TWELFTH CENTURY

1. [According to John Chrysostom, a leading early theologian:] "Coitus does not make a marriage; consent does; and therefore the separation of the body does not dissolve it, but the separation of the will. Therefore he who forsakes his wife, and does not take another, is still a married man. For even if he is now separated in his body, yet he is still joined in his will. When therefore he takes another woman, then he forsakes fully. Therefore he who forsakes is not the adulterer, but he who takes another woman."

2. . . . When therefore there is consent, which alone makes a marriage, between those persons, it is clear that they have been married.

20. A woman who has been sent to a monastery without the consent of her husband is not prohibited from returning to live with him. . . .

21. He who has become a monk without his wife's consent must return to her. . . .

22. A man may not make a monastic vow without his wife's consent. . . .

If any married man wishes to join a monastery, he is not to be accepted, unless he has first been released by his wife, and she makes a vow of chastity. For if she, through incontinence, marries another man while he is still living, without a doubt she will be an adulteress. . . .

24. A husband is not permitted to be celibate without his wife's consent. . . .

26. A wife is not permitted to take a vow of celibacy, unless her husband chooses the same way of life. . . .

29. If a woman proves that her husband has never known her carnally, there may be a separation. . . .

51. If a man plights his troth to any woman, he is not permitted to marry another. . . .

Betrothals may not be contracted before the age of seven. For only the consent is contracted, which cannot happen unless it is understood by each party what is being done between them. Therefore it is shown that betrothals cannot be contracted between children, whose weakness of age does not admit consent. This same is attested by Pope Nicholas: before the time of consent a marriage cannot be contracted. He says, "Where there is no consent from either party, there is no marriage. Therefore those who give girls to boys while they are still in the cradle, and vice versa, achieve nothing, even if the father and mother are willing and do this, unless both of the children consent after they have reached the age of understanding."

From Emilie Amt, ed., *Women's Lives in Medieval Europe: A Sourcebook* (New York: Routledge, 1993), 79.

1. A girl whose own agreement has never been shown is not required by the oath of her father to marry. . . .

3. Those who are to be of one body ought also to be of one spirit, and therefore no woman who is unwilling ought ever to be joined to anyone. . . .

Many authorities and arguments show that an immoral woman should not be taken to wife. For she who is found guilty of adultery is not supposed to be kept in marital fellowship except after the completion of penance. John Chrysostom said this:

1. He who does not wish to forsake his adulterous wife is a protector of vice. "Just as the man who forsakes a chaste woman is cruel and unjust, so he who keeps an immoral woman is foolish and unfair. For he who conceals the crime of his wife is a protector of vice."

2. A man may forsake his wife because of her fornication, but he may not marry another. . . .

14. It is no sin to marry an immoral woman. . . .

1. Childbirth is the sole purpose of marriage for women. . . .

3. Immoderate conjugal union is not an evil of marriage, but a venial sin, because of the good of marriage. . . .

7. Those who obtain drugs of sterility are fornicators, not spouses. . . .

19. A man is not permitted to forsake his wife except because of fornication. . . .

21. Let a man who forsakes his wife for a cause short of fornication be deprived of communion. . . .

23. Adultery in either sex is punished in the same way. . . .

1. A fornicator cannot forsake his wife for fornication. . . .

4. Men are to be punished more severely for adultery than women.

CHAPTER 10

THE CRUSADES

Muslim and European Reactions

Increasing interactions among civilizations can work in many different ways. They can promote mutual influence and imitation. But contact can also heighten mutual hostilities or establish new enmities. This chapter deals with the clash between Christians and Muslims during the Crusades. Enduring tension between Christian and Muslim was not the only product of this episode (nor was the tension new; the Crusades merely highlighted it, particularly for Christians), for the sources suggest other consequences as well. But the tension was there, and it persists in the present day.

Islam and Christianity were very similar religions, compared, for example, to Buddhism. They both emanated from the Middle East, and both had Jewish antecedents, including the Old Testament of the Bible, which both regarded as a holy (though preliminary) statement. Both were monotheistic, missionary religions, and both believed that religion should provide a host of rules for daily life. Their very resemblances may have heightened mutual hostility, for similar movements often use criticisms and attacks to sharpen their special identities.

During the postclassical period, both religions spread widely. Islam was clearly more successful, however, partly because it took root in a dynamic, politically and commercially successful region. Technically and often genuinely tolerant of Christians, whom Muhammad had regarded as partially enlightened, Muslims nevertheless looked down on Western Europe in this period as a backward, boorish place. Muslim wealth, cities, science, and learning easily surpassed European levels, and Muslim leaders were well aware of this fact. Muslims had not been able to conquer much of Europe beyond Spain—they were defeated by the Franks after they crossed the Pyrenees; references to Franks instead of Europeans reflect this early contact. But they encountered Europeans in Spain itself, and also in Mediterranean trade, where Muslims held the upper hand.

For their part, Christians viewed Islam as an infidel, false religion, all the more galling given Muslim success. There was far less tolerance in principle, and tension was exacerbated by European awareness that Muslims surpassed them, during this period, in economic and political achievements. As conditions improved in Europe, with economic advance and the establishment of somewhat more stable feudal monarchies, Christian leaders were able to act on their resentments and fears by calling for war. Although far weaker than their Muslim rivals and ultimately defeated, they were aided at first by growing political disunity in the Middle East. The Arab caliphate was in decline. Turkish bands had seized control of considerable territory and political power, though it was one of their generals who mounted the most successful opposition to the crusaders.

Christian crusades against Muslim control of the Holy Land (Jerusalem and its environs) were first called for at the end of the eleventh century. Feudal warriors from Western Europe volunteered to fight in the Middle East, for a time carving out a Christian kingdom of Jerusalem. The Third Crusade, 1188–1192, involving kings of England, France, and the Holy Roman Empire, responded to successful Muslim attacks on Jerusalem, under the leadership of the great Turkish warrior Saladin. This crusade led to negotiations that established temporary Christian access to, though not control of, Jerusalem.

The Crusades provided unusual contacts between people, mainly warriors, of two different cultures. Europeans learned much about the economically more advanced Middle East, despite their deep hatred of Islam as a false religion and their frequent attempt to portray Muslims as idol-worshipers. Muslims formed or confirmed a variety of opinions about Europeans. How much lasting impact did impressions of this sort have?

Both Muslim and Christian cultures supported the idea of military activity in defense of religion. Muslim accounts often referred to Muhammad's belief in a jihad, or holy war against attackers, in which Muslims would earn direct passage to heaven if they died in battle. Catholic popes promised the crusaders similar salvation if they died seeking the Holy Land. Accounts of battles and heroism might reflect shared values, despite emanating from opposite sides. They even harked back to epic accounts (see chapter 2). At the same time, battle accounts notoriously create possibilities for differing interpretations of the same event, such as an attack on hostages by King Richard of England. Can the use of different interpretations help establish what actually happened in a situation of this sort?

Treatments of the same event—such as the Crusades—by people from opposite sides have some fairly standard features. The other side commits atrocities, which contrast with the purity and high aims of our side. Individual participants may develop a grudging respect for the heroism or the simple humanity of opponents, a respect that sometimes contradicts expressions of hatred. Some of these elements clearly show up in the Christian and Muslim Crusade accounts. They reveal some of the specific religious terms and issues that translated the standard features into the tenor of the time: the worst mutual insults are those against the other religion, which is portrayed in the most degrading terms possible. They also reflect the specific disputes over access to holy places—still a factor in Jerusalem and its region today.

But the accounts offer more than the "you're another" type of mutual hostility. The economic gap between the two sides is evident in comments about Muslim luxury and European awe. Indeed, a key result of the Crusades (which in their own terms, after a short time, were miserable failures) was to increase European knowledge of and thirst for Asian luxury goods—stimulating new trading efforts and ultimately a different kind of European expansion to facilitate these efforts despite a backward economy. Another ingredient of the accounts, from the Muslim side, is scorn for European crudeness, which is seen in insults (by Muslim standards, and indeed by those of the Europeans themselves) to European manhood and claims of odd European magic. To the extent that the Crusades confirmed not only some dislike of European Christians but also a sense of their backwardness, they contributed to a Muslim reluctance to pay attention to changes in Europe in succeeding centuries that might have warranted greater openness.

The Crusades were an interesting episode in the postclassical period, not an earthshaking event. They stemmed from significant cultural and other tensions, and they unintentionally provided materials by which two important civilizations can be compared. They also had some lasting, if largely unexpected, side effects in world history later on.

Questions

1. In what ways were Christian and Muslim accounts of the Crusades similar? In what terms might each side praise the other?
2. How did the Christian account try to arouse sentiment against Muslim treatment of the Christian religion? How did Muslim accounts try to arouse sentiment against Christian mistreatment or scorn for Islam?
3. What elements of Islam prompt Ibn-Mundiqh, in the final passage, to simultaneously praise Christ and express shock at the idea of showing God as a child? What clearly inaccurate reference to Islam is included in the Christian account—and why would it have been included?
4. What references in the Muslim accounts particularly suggest a disdain for European backwardness? What is the jealousy passage all about: given Muslim (and Christian) views about men's rights concerning women, why was this probably a backhanded insult, designed to stimulate further disdain against Christians?
5. As expressed in these accounts, were the reasons for Christian and Muslim dislike of each other similar?

For Further Discussion

1. Which of the three accounts—all clearly partisan—strikes you as most accurate, and why? (Or do they all seem equally biased?) Which reference, in any of the accounts, seems most clearly distorted? What criteria help sort out accuracy when the historical sources are clearly tainted?

2. How do the Crusades and Muslim and Christian accounts of them demonstrate how these two religions resembled each other more than either one resembled Buddhism, during the postclassical period?

A CHRISTIAN ACCOUNT

This account was written by Richard of the Holy Trinity, probably Richard de Templo, who was later selected as Prior of the Holy Trinity but who served King Richard as knight or chaplain during the Crusade. His account suggests not only Christian views of Muslims, but also key feudal military values (see chapter 8). The subject of his biography, King Richard, known as the Lion-Hearted, won a huge reputation in England as a noble warrior, even though (or because) he spent little time at home (but he did spend considerable English revenues). King Richard fought against his brothers and father and then in 1190 departed for the Third Crusade. His attack on the city of Acre, in alliance with the King of France, failed, but he was able to negotiate access to the holy places in Jerusalem with the Muslim leader Saladin. He was captured and held for ransom on the way home and was later killed in a war with France. Richard's reputation as a brave and good king, enhanced by accounts such as this, entered into other English legends such as Robin Hood, and it contrasted with the image of his brother, later King John.

• • •

THE CRUSADE OF RICHARD I

King Richard was not yet quite recovered from his illness; yet, anxious to be doing something, he turned his thoughts to the capture of the city, and had it attacked by his men in the hopes of gaining some success with God's assistance. Accordingly he had a kind of hurdle-shed (commonly called a *circleia*) made and brought up to the ditch outside the city wall. Under its shelter were placed his most skilful crossbowmen; whilst, to hearten his own men for the combat and to dispirit the Saracens [Muslims] by his presence, he had himself carried there on silken cushions. From this position he worked a crossbow, in the management of which he was very skilful,

From T. A. Archer, ed., *The Crusade of Richard I* (New York: G. P. Putnam's, 1885), 92–95, 97–98, 99, 101–2, 103, 126–27.

how to break into a castle

and slew many of the foes by the bolts and quarrels he discharged. His miners also, approaching the tower against which his stone-casters were being levelled, by an underground passage dug down towards the foundations, filling the gaps they made with logs of wood, to which they would set fire, thus causing the walls, which had already been shaken by the stone-casters, to fall down with sudden crash.

Thereupon the king, seeing how difficult the work was and how valiant were the enemies, knowing also how needful it was to kindle men's valour at critical moments, thought it more fitting to encourage the young [warriors] on by promises of reward than to urge them on by harsh words. For who is there whom the prospect of gain will not entice? Accordingly he proclaimed that he would give two gold pieces to any one who would detach a stone from the wall near the before-mentioned tower. Later he promised three and even four gold-pieces for each stone. Then might you see the young men with their followers leap forth and rush against the wall and set themselves zealously to lugging out the stones—and this as much for the sake of praise as of pay. . . . The height of the wall was very great and it was of no slight thickness; yet, dispelling danger, by courage, they extracted many a stone. The Turks rushing against [the assailants] in bands strove to cast them down from the walls; and, while thus engaged in driving back their enemies, unwarily exposed themselves to darts; for in their haste they rashly neglected to put on their armour. One of the Turks who to his cost was glorying in the arms of Alberic Clements, with which he had girded himself, did king Richard wound to death, piercing him through the breast, with a dart from his cross-bow. Grieving over the death of this warrior the Turks recklessly rushed forward for vengeance, and, just as though energetic action were a cure for pain, showed themselves so bold that it seemed as if they feared neither darts nor any other missile. Never were our men engaged by warriors—of any creed whatever—more valorous or apter at defence. Memory staggers at the recollection of their deeds. In the press of this conflict neither armour of strongest proof nor two-fold coat of mail nor quilted work was strong enough to resist the missiles hurled from the stone-casters. Yet, for all this, the Turks kept countermining from within till they compelled our men to retreat; and then they began to raise a furious cry as though their object had been attained. . . . At last the Pisans [Italians], eager for fame and vengeance, scrambled up the tower itself with a mighty effort; but, bravely as they comported themselves, they too had to retreat before the onset of the Turks, who rushed on as if mad. Never has there been such a people as these Turks for prowess in war. And yet, for all the enemies' valour, the city would on that day have been taken and the whole siege finished if the entire army had displayed an equal valour. For, you must know, by far the larger part of the army was at that hour breakfasting; and, as the attack was made at an unsuitable time, it did not succeed.

Though its walls were partly fallen and partly shaken, though a great part of the inhabitants were slain or weakened by wounds, there still remained in the city 6,000 Turks. . . .

[Then leaders] imagined the Christian army had been very keenly touched at the death of Alberic Clements and at the loss of sons and kinsmen who had fallen in the war; and had determined to die or master the Turks—holding that no other course was consistent with honour. So, by common consent and counsel, the besieged begged a truce while they sent notice of their plight to Saladin, hoping that, in accordance with their Pagan ways, he would ensure their safety—as he ought to do—by sending them speedy aid or procuring leave for them to quit the city without disgrace. To obtain this favour, these two noble Saracens, the most renowned [warriors] in all Paganism, Mestoc and Caracois, came to our kings, promising to surrender the city, if Saladin did not send them speedy aid. They stipulated, however, that all the besieged Turks should have free leave to go wherever they wished with their arms and all their goods. The king of France and almost all the French agreed to this; but king Richard utterly refused to hear of entering an empty city after so long and toilsome a siege. . . .

Meanwhile, the Christians' stone-casters never ceased battering the walls night and day. Seeing this a panic seized the inhabitants and some, in utter despair, giving way to fear, threw themselves headlong from the walls by night. Many of them humbly begged to be baptized and made Christians. There is considerable doubt as to the real merits of these [converts], and not without due reason, since it is to be presumed that it was terror rather than divine grace that caused them to make this request. But the ways of salvation are many. . . .

Thus, on the Friday after the translation of the Blessed Benedict [*i.e.* July 12], the wealthier and nobler emirs were proffered and accepted as hostages, one month being allowed for the restoration of the Holy Cross and the collection of the captive Christians. When the news of this surrender became known, the unthinking crowd was moved with wrath; but the wiser folk were much rejoiced at getting so quickly and without danger what previously they had not been able to obtain in so long a time. Then the heralds made proclamation forbidding any one to insult the Turks by word or deed. No missiles were to be hurled against the walls or against the Turks if they chanced to appear on the battlements. On that day, when these famous Turks, of such wonderful valour and warlike excellence, began strolling about on the city walls in all their splendid apparel, previous to their departure [our men] gazed on them with the utmost curiosity. They were wonder-struck at the cheerful features of men who were leaving their city almost penniless and whom only the very sternest necessity had driven to beg for mercy: men whom loss did not deject, and whose visage betrayed no timidity, but even wore the look of victory. It was only their superstitious rites and their pitiful idolatry that had robbed such warriors of their strength. . . .

On the day of its surrender the city had been in the hands of the Saracens four years. It was surrendered, as has been already said, on the morrow of the translation of St. Benedict. But not without horror could the conquerors see the condition of the churches within the city; nor can they even now remember the shameful sights they witnessed there unmoved. What faithful Christian could, with tearless eyes, see the holy features of the crucified Son of God, or even of the saints, dishonoured and defiled? Who would not shudder when he actually saw the insulting way in which the accursed Turks had overthrown the altars, torn down and battered the holy crosses? Ay, and they had even set up their own images of Mahomet in the holy places, introducing foul Mahommedan superstitions, after casting out all the symbols of human redemption and the Christian religion.

MUSLIM ACCOUNTS

The first selection below was written by Bohadin or Beha-ed-Din, born at Mosul in 1145, a Muslim official of Jerusalem and later of Aleppo. He writes of the same Crusade as did Richard of the Holy Trinity, referring to the kings of England and France. The second account, dealing with a period earlier in the twelfth century, comes from the memoirs of Usamah ibn-Munqidh as an Arab-Syrian warrior. He writes of a time when the Christian crusaders controlled the city of Jerusalem; European reactions to Muslim ways (and ibn-Munqidh's reactions to the Europeans) obviously varied from case to case, as often happens when war and occupation combine with a certain familiarity.

• • •

BEH-ED-DIN

The same day Hossâm ad-Din Ibn Barîc . . . brought news that the king of France had set out for Tyre, and that they had come to talk over the matter of the prisoners and to see the true cross of the Crucifixion if it were still in the Musulman [Muslim] camp, or to ascertain if it really had been sent to Bagdad. It was shewn to them, and on beholding it they shewed the profoundest reverence, throwing themselves on the ground till they were covered with dust, and humbling themselves in token of devotion. These envoys told us that the French princes had accepted the Sultan's proposition, viz., to deliver all that was specified in the treaty by three instalments at intervals of a month. The Sultan then sent an envoy to Tyre with rich presents, quantities of perfumes, and fine raiment—all of which were for the king of the French.

. . . Ibn Barîc and his comrades returned to the king of England while the Sultan went off with his bodyguard and his closest friends to the hill that abuts on Shefa'Amr. . . . Envoys did not cease to pass from one side to the other in the hope

From T. A. Archer, ed., *The Crusade of Richard I* (New York: G. P. Putnams, 1885), 127–31.

of laying the foundation of a firm peace. These negotiations continued till our men had procured the money and the tale of the prisoners that they were to deliver to the French at the end of the first period in accordance with the treaty. The first instalment was to consist of the Holy Cross, 100,000 dinars and 1,600 prisoners. Trustworthy men sent by the Franks [French, or Europeans] to conduct the examination found it all complete saving only the prisoners who had been demanded by name, all of whom had not yet been gathered together. And thus the negotiations continued to drag on till the end of the first term. . . .

This proposition the Sultan rejected, knowing full well that if he were to deliver the money, the cross, and the prisoners, while our men were still kept captive by the Franks, he would have no security against treachery on the part of the enemy, and this would be a great disaster to Islam.

Then the king of England, seeing all the delays interposed by the Sultan to the execution of the treaty, acted perfidiously as regards his Musulman prisoners. On their yielding the town he had engaged to grant them life, adding that if the Sultan carried out the bargain he would give them freedom and suffer them to carry off their children and wives; if the Sultan did not fulfil his engagements they were to be made slaves. Now the king broke his promises to them and made open display of what he had till now kept hidden in his heart, by carrying out what he had intended to do after he had received the money and the Frank prisoners. It is thus that people of his nation ultimately admitted.

In the afternoon of Tuesday . . . about four o'clock, he came out on horseback with all the Frankish army; knights, footmen, Turcoples, and advanced to the pits at the foot of the hill of Al 'Ayâdîyeh, to which place he had already sent on his tents. The Franks, on reaching the middle of the plain that stretches between this hill and that of Keisân, close to which place the sultan's advanced guard had drawn back, ordered all the Musulman prisoners, whose martyrdom God had decreed for this day, to be brought before him. They numbered more than three thousand and were all bound with ropes. The Franks then flung themselves upon them all at once and massacred them with sword and lance in cold blood. Our advanced guard had already told the Sultan of the enemy's movements and he sent it some reinforcements, but only after the massacre. The Musulmans, seeing what was being done to the prisoners, rushed against the Franks and in the combat, which lasted till nightfall, several were slain and wounded on either side. On the morrow morning our people gathered at the spot and found the Musulmans stretched out upon the ground as martyrs for the faith. They even recognised some of the dead, and the sight was a great affliction to them. The enemy had only spared the prisoners of note and such as were strong enough to work.

The motives of this massacre are differently told; according to some, the captives were slain by way of reprisal for the death of those Christians whom the Musulmans had slain. Others again say that the king of England, on deciding to attempt the conquest of Ascalon, thought it unwise to leave so many prisoners in the town after his departure. God alone knows what the real reason was.

USAMAH IBN-MUNQIDH

A few days after the departure of my uncle, the public announcer called us to arms, and I started at the head of a small band, hardly amounting to twenty horsemen, with full conviction that Afaiyah had no cavalry in it. Accompanying me was a great body of pillagers and Bedouins. As soon as we arrived in the Valley of Bohemond, and while the pillagers and the Arabs were scattered all over the planted fields, a large army of the Franks set out against us. They had been reinforced that very night by sixty horsemen and sixty footmen. They repulsed us from the valley, and we retreated before them until we joined those of our number who were already in the fields, pillaging them. Seeing us, the Franks raised a violent uproar. Death seemed an easy thing to me in comparison with the loss of that crowd [24] in my charge. So I turned against a horseman in their vanguard, who had taken off his coat of mail in order to be light enough to pass before us, and thrust my lance into his chest. He instantly flew off his saddle, dead. I then faced their horsemen as they followed, and they all took to flight. Though a tyro in warfare, and having never before that day taken part in a battle, I, with a mare under me as swift as a bird, went on, now pursuing them and plying them with my lance, now taking cover from them.

In the rear guard of the Franks was a cavalier on a black horse, large as a camel, wearing a coat of mail and the full armor of war. I was afraid of this horseman, lest he should be drawing me further ahead in order to get an opportunity to turn back and attack me. All of a sudden I saw him spur his horse, and as the horse began to wave its tail, I knew that it was already exhausted. So I rushed on the horseman and smote him with my lance, which pierced him through and projected about a cubit in front of him. The lightness of my body, the force of the thrust and the swiftness of my horse made me lose my seat on the saddle. Moving backward a little, I pulled out my lance, fully assuming that I had killed him . . .

I once witnessed in an encounter between us and the Franks one of our cavaliers, named Badi ibn-Talil al-Qushayri, who was one of our brave men, receive in his chest, while clothed with only two pieces of garment, a lance thrust from a Frankish knight. The lance cut the vein in his chest and issued from his side. He turned back right away, but we never thought he would make his home alive. But as Allah (worthy of admiration is he!) had predestined, he survived and his wound was healed. But for one year after that, he could not sit up in case he was lying on his back unless somebody held him by the shoulders and helped him. At last what he suffered from entirely disappeared and he reverted to his old ways of living and riding. My only comment is: How mysterious are the works of him whose will is always executed among his creatures! He giveth life and he causeth death, but he is living and dieth not. In his hand is all good, and he is over all things potent. . . .

A case illustrating their [the Europeans] curious medicine is the following:

The lord of al-Munaytirah wrote to my uncle asking him to dispatch a physician to treat certain sick persons among his people. My uncle sent him a Christian physician named Thābit. Thābit was absent but ten days when he returned. So we said to him, "How quickly hast thou healed thy patients!" He said:

> They brought before me a knight in whose leg an abscess had grown; and a woman afflicted with imbecility. To the knight I applied a small poultice until the abscess opened and became well; and the woman I put on diet and made her humor wet. Then a Frankish physician came to them and said, "This man knows nothing about treating them." He then said to the knight, "Which wouldst thou prefer, living with one leg or dying with two?" The latter replied, "Living with one leg." The physician said, "Bring me a strong knight and a sharp ax." A knight came with the ax. And I was standing by. Then the physician laid the leg of the patient on a block of wood and bade the knight strike his leg with the ax and chop it off at one blow. Accordingly he struck it— while I was looking on—one blow, but the leg was not severed. He dealt another blow, upon which the marrow of the leg flowed out and the patient died on the spot. He then examined the woman and said, "This is a woman in whose head there is a devil which has possessed her. Shave off her hair." Accordingly they shaved it off and the woman began once more to eat their ordinary diet—garlic and mustard. Her imbecility took a turn for the worse. The physician then said, "The devil has penetrated through her head." He therefore took a razor, made a deep cruciform incision on it, peeled off the skin at the middle of the incision until the bone of the skull was exposed and rubbed it with salt. The woman also expired instantly. Thereupon I asked them whether my services were needed any longer, and when they replied in the negative I returned home, having learned of their medicine what I knew not before.

I have, however, witnessed a case of their medicine which was quite different from that.

The king of the Franks had for treasurer a knight named Bernard [barnād], who (may Allah's curse be upon him!) was one of the most accursed and wicked among the Franks. A horse kicked him in the leg, which was subsequently infected and which opened in fourteen different places. Every time one of these cuts would close in one place, another would open in another place. All this happened while I was praying for his perdition. Then came to him a Frankish physician and removed from the leg all the ointments which were on it and began to wash it with very strong vinegar. By this treatment all the cuts were healed and the man became well again. He was up again like a devil. . . .

Newly arrived Franks are especially rough: One insists that Usāmah should pray eastward.—Everyone who is a fresh emigrant from the Frankish lands is ruder in character than those who have become acclimatized and have held long association with the Moslems. Here is an illustration of their rude character.

Whenever I visited Jerusalem I always entered the Aqsa Mosque, beside which stood a small mosque which the Franks had converted into a church. When I used to enter the Aqsa Mosque, which was occupied by the Templars [*al-dāwiyyah*], who were my friends, the Templars would evacuate the little adjoining mosque so that I might pray in it. One day I entered this mosque, repeated the first formula, "Allah is great," and stood up in the act of praying, upon which one of the Franks rushed on me, got hold of me and turned my face eastward saying, "This is the way thou shouldst pray!" A group of Templars hastened to him, seized him and repelled him from me. I resumed my prayer. The same man, while the others were otherwise busy, rushed once more on me and turned my face eastward, saying, "This is the way thou shouldst pray!" The Templars again came in to him and expelled him. They apologized to me, saying, "This is a stranger who has only recently arrived from the land of the Franks and he has never before seen anyone praying except eastward." Thereupon I said to myself, "I have had enough prayer." So I went out and have ever been surprised at the conduct of this devil of a man, at the change in the color of his face, his trembling and his sentiment at the sight of one praying towards the *qiblah* [direction of Mecca].

Another wants to show to a Moslem God as a child.—I saw one of the Franks come to al-Amīr Mu'īn-al-Dī (may Allah's mercy rest upon his soul!) when he was in the Dome of the Rock and say to him, "Dost thou want to see God as a child?" Mu'īn-al-Dīn said, "Yes." The Frank walked ahead of us until he showed us the picture of Mary with Christ (may peace be upon him!) as an infant in her lap. He then said, "This is God as a child." But Allah is exalted far above what the infidels say about him!

The Franks are void of all zeal and jealousy. One of them may be walking along with his wife. He meets another man who takes the wife by the hand and steps aside to converse with her while the husband is standing on one side waiting for his wife to conclude the conversation. If she lingers too long for him, he leaves her alone with the conversant and goes away.

Here is an illustration which I myself witnessed:

When I used to visit Nāblus, I always took lodging with a man named Mu'izz, whose home was a lodging house for the Moslems. The house had windows which opened to the road, and there stood opposite to it on the other side of the road a house belonging to a Frank who sold wine for the merchants. He would take some wine in a bottle and go around announcing it by shouting, "So and so, the merchant, has just opened a cask full of this wine. He who wants to buy some of it will find it in such and such a place." The Frank's pay for the announcement made would be the wine in that bottle. One day this Frank went home and found a man with his wife in the same bed. He asked him, "What could have made thee enter into my wife's room?" The man replied, "I was tired, so I went in to rest." "But how," asked he, "didst thou get into my bed?" The other replied, "I found a bed that was spread, so I slept in it." "But," said he, "my wife was sleeping together with thee!" The other replied, "Well, the bed is hers. How could I therefore have prevented her from using her own bed?" "By the truth of my religion," said the husband, "if thou shouldst do it again, thou and I would have a quarrel." Such was for the Frank the entire expression of his disapproval and the limit of his jealousy.

CHAPTER 11

MERCHANTS AND TRADE

The postclassical period witnessed an important expansion of trade, within many civilizations and across their fluid boundaries. Merchants gained a growing role in West Africa, throughout the Islamic world, in Europe (both east and west), and in East Asia. Many traded locally, though international merchants made the biggest impression. Chinese commercial centers grew rapidly, supporting a more urban environment. The search for wealth had never been so extensive, the willingness to take risks had never been so great, and the desire to promote commercial interests in government circles had never been so strong. At the same time, many societies had reservations about merchants. Aristocrats worried about their social claims, rulers might envy their wealth, priests and philosophers questioned their motives. The clash of cultures, between religion and materialism, was particularly intense because of the complex new forces at work in these centuries. A genuine ambivalence about merchants was common throughout the postclassical world—and it could affect merchants themselves, as well as how they were treated.

Different civilizations had different levels of concern, though, and these could shift. Comparison and assessment of change over time are both essential analytical approaches to the issue of the merchant role. Christian tradition was uneasy with merchants' motives, fearing that they diverted people from religion; as trade increased, Christian concern relaxed somewhat. But efforts to find ways to accommodate the very different goals of capitalist trade and the holy life continued. Islam was initially more favorable to merchants, whose activities seemed compatible with religious obligations so long as they obeyed basic rules of fairness and gave to charity. It was no accident that Islam had up to about 1200 sponsored the most intense merchant activity known in world history. The region had long been a center of trade, even in the classical period. Muhammad, originally a merchant, praised the life of commerce, so long as it did not violate the primacy of religious goals, and so long as it was accompanied by active charity. But experience introduced greater caution, and toward the end of the postclassical period, as Muslim trade continued, though with slightly less dynamism, ambivalence became more obvious. What value did Muslim thinkers see in trade? What were the danger signals? How do Christian and Muslim views compare at this point?

Of all the major belief systems, Confucianism was the most suspicious of traders, who did not fit clearly into a stable social hierarchy and whose motives were suspect on philosophical, rather than religious, grounds. Yet China depended heavily on trade, and individual merchants did well. Trade between the grain-growing north and the rice-growing south helped sustain the world's most concentrated population, along with a relatively advanced technology. In the comment by a Confucian official, traditional anxieties about motives are obvious at first. Later parts of the passage show a more pragmatic stance, along with government regulations designed to control and exploit merchants more than to encourage them and with a clearly uncertain view, overall, about foreign traders.

Given the attitudes and policies suggested for the three societies—Western Europe, the Middle East, and China—which society in your judgment was becoming most favorable for merchant activity, and why?

The values tensions surrounding merchant activity were very real in the postclassical period in all three civilizations. They translated into individual ambiguities. Many European merchants—even some less holy than Godric—repented of their goals later in life and gave money away or entered a monastery. Chinese merchants often used their earnings to buy education and entry into the scholar gentry class for themselves or their sons, which amounted to an admission that Confucian goals were best.

The tensions also reflected a fascinating interaction between economic opportunities and cultural norms. None of the civilizations yielded entirely to one extreme or the other—which is why comparison must be subtle; a search for stark contrasts would be overly simple. The fact that some civilizations changed their balance over time adds another complexity. Nevertheless, certain of the differences were real, and they mattered in world history. China, to take the most obvious example, could have played a far larger trade role than it did, but it deliberately held back because of its own internal success—it did not need the outside world—and because of its cultural hostility to trade. Europe's growing commercial role required an adjustment of religious concerns, which did prove possible but caused wide anxiety about moral directions.

The description of the twelfth-century British merchant Godric was written by a biographer attracted to his saintly life (most merchants did not, it should be emphasized, become saints). It suggests both actual activities and cultural values. The Muslim description of merchants' vices and merits comes from the great historian and philosopher Ibn Khaldun, a North African who wrote in the fourteenth century. The Chinese essay on merchants was written by Chang Han, early in the sixteenth century (right after the postclassical period and more than a half century after the Ming dynasty had ended its most vigorous international trade). Chang Han was a Ming official whose family had made a fortune in the textile industry, which helps explain the combination of Confucian and reformist remarks.

Questions

1. What kinds of uneasiness did Muslim observers have about trade?
2. How did Chinese concerns about merchant motives differ from those of Christianity?
3. How did Islam offer a third combination of trade and cultural goals—this one more favorable to trade without slighting religion? In what ways did Islam and Christianity, such similar religions in many respects, differ over the validity of trade; would a Godric story have been probable in Islam?
4. What exceptions do the sources suggest, even as they emphasize high ideals? What kinds of activities in Europe clearly represented crasser motives than those of a holy merchant like Godric? Why, in fact, did Godric not enter a holy calling initially—what kinds of motives drew him to trade?
5. How could merchant activity increase within China—as it did in the postclassical period, as cities and business houses prospered—within an official Confucian framework? How did the Confucian bureaucracy collaborate?
6. Do the sources demonstrate that Europe was becoming wealthier than China by the late postclassical period?

For Further Discussion

1. In light of the postclassical sources and comparisons, how would you rate the following argument: No matter what their professed values, most people and societies are motivated by a desire for profit and will expand commercially whenever they can? Is a desire for economic gain an inherent part of human nature?
2. Which came first in world history: concern about trade or economic limitations? Did Christianity cause Western Europe's initial commercial lag in the postclassical period, or did economic decline encourage Christian concerns? How did Confucianism affect actual Chinese economic patterns in the postclassical period?

A MUSLIM VIEW: IBN KHALDUN

Ibn Khaldun was one of the greatest historians and geographers of all time. Born in Tunis, North Africa, he lived from 1332 to 1406. He served as an official in Tunis, Morocco, and Spain and traveled widely, finally settling, as a scholar, in Egypt. His great work was the *Kitab al-Ibar* (universal history). The first part, the Prolegomena, offered various observations on the principles of human conduct as well as on Muslim life. This provided a context for comments on the active trade that he saw around him, at the time when Muslim commercial success was still near its height.

• • •

CHARACTERISTICS OF TRADERS

Commerce, as we have said before, is the increasing of capital by buying goods and attempting to sell them at a price higher than their cost. This is done either by waiting for a rise in the market price; or by transporting the goods to another place where they are more keenly demanded and therefore fetch a higher price; or, lastly, by selling them on a long-term credit basis. Commercial profit is small, relatively to the capital invested, but if the capital is large, even a low rate of profit will produce a large total gain.

In order to achieve this increase in capital, it is necessary to have enough initial capital to pay in cash the sellers from whom one buys goods; it is also necessary to sell for cash, as honesty is not widespread among people. This dishonesty leads on the one hand to fraud and the adulteration of goods, and on the other to delays in payment which diminish profits because capital remains idle during the interval. It also induces buyers to repudiate their debts, a practice which is very injurious to the merchant's capital unless he can produce documentary evidence or the testimony of eyewitness. Nor are magistrates of much help in such cases, because they necessarily judge on evident proofs.

As a result of all this, the trader can only secure his meagre profits by dint of much effort and toil, or indeed he may well lose not only profits but capital as well. Hence, if he is known to be bold in entering law suits, careful in keeping accounts, stubborn in defending his point of view, firm in his attitude towards magistrates, he stands a good chance of getting his due. Should he not have these qualities, his only chance is to secure the support of a highly placed protector who will awe his debtors into paying him and the magistrates into meting justice out to him. Thus he gets justice spontaneously in the first case, and by compulsion in the second. Should a person, however, be lacking in boldness and the spirit of enterprise and at the same time have no protector to back him up, he had better avoid trade altogether, as he risks losing his capital and becoming the prey of other merchants. The fact of the matter is that most people, especially the mob and the trading classes, covet the goods of others; and but for the restraint imposed by the magistrates all goods would have been taken away from their owners. . . .

The manners of tradesmen are inferior to those of rulers, and far removed from manliness and uprightness. We have already stated that traders must buy and sell and

From Charles Issawi, ed. and trans. *An Arab Philosophy of History: Selections from the Prolegomena of Ibn Khaldun* (London: John Murray, 1950), 68–70, 78, 80, 81. Reprinted by permission of the publisher.

seek profits. This necessitates flattery, and evasiveness, litigation and disputation, all of which are characteristic of this profession. And these qualities lead to a decrease and weakening in virtue and manliness. For acts inevitably affect the soul; thus good acts produce good and virtuous effects in the soul while evil or mean acts produce the opposite. Hence the effects of evil acts will strike root and strengthen themselves, if they should come early in life and repeat themselves; while if they come later they will efface the virtues by imprinting their evil effects on the soul; as is the case with all habits resulting from actions.

These effects will differ according to the conditions of the traders. For those of them who are of mean condition and in direct contact with the cheating and extortion of sellers will be more affected by these evils and further removed from manliness. . . . The other kind of traders are those who are protected by prestige and do not have to undertake directly such operations. Such persons are very rare indeed and consist of those who have acquired wealth suddenly, by inheritance or by other, unusual means. This wealth enables them to get in touch with the rulers and thus to gain prestige and protection so that they are released from practising these things [viz. buying and selling] themselves; instead, they entrust such business to their agents. Moreover the rulers, who are not indifferent to the wealth and liberality of such traders, protect them in their right and thus free them from certain unpleasant actions and their resulting evil effects. Hence they will be more manly and honourable than the other kind of trader; yet certain effects will still make themselves felt behind the veil, inasmuch as they still have to supervise their agents and employees in their doings—but this only takes place to a limited extent and its effects are hardly visible. . . .

. . . Consider, as an example, the lands of the East, such as Egypt, Syria, Persia, India, or China; or the lands lying North of the Mediterranean. Because social life is flourishing there, notice how wealth has increased, the state has grown stronger, towns have multiplied, trade has prospected prospered, conditions have improved. . . .

As for Trade, although it be a natural means of livelihood, yet most of the methods it employs are tricks aimed at making a profit by securing the difference between the buying and selling prices, and by appropriating the surplus. This is why [religious] Law allows the use of such methods, which, although they come under the heading of gambling, yet do not constitute the taking without return of other people's goods. . . .

Should their standard of living, however, rise, so that they begin to enjoy more than the bare necessities, the effect will be to breed in them a desire for repose and tranquillity. They will therefore co-operate to secure superfluities; their food and clothing will increase in quantity and refinement; they will enlarge their houses and plan their towns for defence. A further improvement in their conditions will lead to habits of luxury, resulting in extreme refinement in cooking and the preparation of food; in choosing rich clothing of the finest silk; in raising lofty mansions and castles and furnishing them luxuriously, and so on. At this stage the crafts develop and reach their height. Lofty castles and mansions are built and decorated sumptuously, water is drawn to them and a great diversity takes place in the way of dress, furniture, vessels, and household equipment.

Such are the townsmen, who earn their living in industry or trade. Their gains are greater then those working in agriculture or animal husbandry and their standard of living higher, being in line with their wealth. We have shown, then, that both the nomadic and the urban stages are natural and necessary.

A Christian View: Reginald of Durham on Saint Godric

This excerpt from a biography of Godric, an English merchant who later became a saint, both describes actual merchant activities in Europe and provides an example of an established literary-religious form of writing in Christian Europe in which the main point was to stress the saint's virtues and use biography as an inspiration to others. There may be some distortion of reality here; certainly, some aspects of the merchant condition have to be discovered by reading between the lines.

• • •

This holy man's father was named Ailward, and his mother Edwenna; both of slender rank and wealth, but abundant in righteousness and virtue. They were born in Norfolk, and had long lived in the township called Walpole. . . . When the boy had passed his childish years quietly at home; then, as he began to grow to manhood, he began to follow more prudent ways of life, and to learn carefully and persistently the teachings of worldly forethought. Wherefore he chose not to follow the life of a husbandman, but rather to study, learn and exercise the rudiment of more subtle conceptions. For this reason, aspiring to the merchant's trade, he began to follow the chapman's [peddler's] way of life, first learning how to gain in small bargains and things of insignificant price; and thence, while yet a youth, his mind advanced little by little to buy and sell and gain from things of greater expense. For, in his beginnings, he was wont to wander with small wares around the villages and farmsteads of his own neighborhood; but, in process of time, he gradually associated himself by compact with city merchants. Hence, within a brief space of time, the youth who had trudged for many weary hours from village to village, from farm to

From Reginald of Durham, "Life of St. Godric," in G. G. Coulton, ed., *Social Life in Britain from the Conquest to the Reformation* (Cambridge: Cambridge University Press, 1918), 415–20.

farm, did so profit by his increase of age and wisdom as to travel with associates of his own age through towns and boroughs, fortresses and cities, to fairs and to all the various booths of the market-place, in pursuit of his public chaffer. He went along the high-way, neither puffed up by the good testimony of his conscience nor downcast in the nobler part of his soul by the reproach of poverty. . . .

Yet in all things he walked with simplicity; and, in so far as he yet knew how, it was ever his pleasure to follow in the footsteps of the truth. For, having learned the Lord's Prayer and the Creed from his very cradle, he oftentimes turned them over in his mind, even as he went alone on his longer journeys; and, in so far as the truth was revealed to his mind, he clung thereunto most devoutly in all his thoughts concerning God. At first, he lived as a chapman for four years in Lincolnshire, going on foot and carrying the smallest wares; then he travelled abroad, first to St Andrews in Scotland and then for the first time to Rome. On his return, having formed a familiar friendship with certain other young men who were eager for merchandise, he began to launch upon bolder courses, and to coast frequently by sea to the foreign lands that lay around him. Thus, sailing often to and fro between Scotland and Britain, he traded in many divers wares and, amid these occupations, learned much worldly wisdom. . . . He fell into many perils of the sea, yet by God's mercy he was never wrecked; for He who had upheld St Peter as he walked upon the waves, by that same strong right arm kept this His chosen vessel from all misfortune amid these perils. Thus, having learned by frequent experience his wretchedness amid such dangers, he began to worship certain of the Saints with more ardent zeal, venerating and calling upon their shrines, and giving himself up by wholehearted service to those holy names. In such invocations his prayers were oftentimes answered by prompt consolation; some of which prayers he learned from his fellows with whom he shared these frequent perils; others he collected from faithful hearsay; others again from the custom of the place, for he saw and visited such holy places with frequent assiduity. Thus aspiring ever higher and higher, and yearning upward with his whole heart, at length his great labours and cares bore much fruit of worldly gain. For he laboured not only as a merchant but also as a shipman . . . to Denmark and Flanders and Scotland; in all which lands he found certain rare, and therefore more precious, wares, which he carried to other parts wherein he knew them to be least familiar, and coveted by the inhabitants beyond the price of gold itself; wherefore he exchanged these wares for others coveted by men of other lands; and thus he chaffered most freely and assiduously. Hence he made great profit in all his bargains, and gathered much wealth in the sweat of his brow; for he sold dear in one place the wares which he had bought elsewhere at a small price.

Then he purchased the half of a merchant-ship with certain of his partners in the trade; and again by his prudence he bought the fourth part of another ship. At length, by his skill in navigation, wherein he excelled all his fellows, he earned promotion to the post of steersman. . . .

For he was vigorous and strenuous in mind, whole of limb and strong in body. He was of middle stature, broad-shouldered and deep-chested, with a long face, grey eyes most clear and piercing, bushy brows, a broad forehead, long and open nostrils, a nose of comely curve, and a pointed chin. His beard was thick, and longer than the ordinary, his mouth well-shaped, with lips of moderate thickness; in youth his hair was black, in age as white as snow; his neck was short and thick, knotted with veins and sinews; his legs were somewhat slender, his instep high, his knees hardened and horny with frequent kneeling; his whole skin rough beyond the ordinary, until all this roughness was softened by old age. . . . In labour he was strenuous, assiduous above all men: and, when by chance his bodily strength proved insufficient, he compassed his ends with great ease by the skill which his daily labours had given, and by a prudence born of long experience. . . . He knew, from the aspect of sea and stars, how to foretell fair or foul weather. In his various voyages he visited many saints' shrines, to whose protection he was wont most devoutly to commend himself; more especially the church of St Andrew in Scotland, where he most frequently made and paid his vows. On the way thither, he oftentimes touched at the island of Lindisfarne, wherein St Cuthbert had been bishop, and at the isle of Farne, where that Saint had lived as an anchoret, and where St Godric (as he himself would tell afterwards) would meditate on the Saint's life with abundant tears. Thence he began to yearn for solitude, and to hold his merchandise in less esteem than heretofore. . . .

And now he had lived sixteen years as a merchant, and began to think of spending on charity, to God's honour and service, the goods which he had so laboriously acquired. He therefore took the cross as a pilgrim to Jerusalem, and, having visited the Holy Sepulchre, came back to England by way of St James [of Compostella]. Not long afterwards he became steward to a certain rich man of his own country, with the care of his whole house and household. But certain of the younger household were men of iniquity, who stole their neighbours' cattle and thus held luxurious feasts, whereat Godric, in his ignorance, was sometimes present. Afterwards, discovering the truth, he rebuked and admonished them to cease; but they made no account of his warnings; wherefore he concealed not their iniquity, but disclosed it to the lord of the household, who, however, slighted his advice. Wherefore he begged to be dismissed and went on a pilgrimage, first to St Gilles and thence to Rome the abode of the Apostles, that thus he might knowingly pay the penalty for those misdeeds wherein he had ignorantly partaken. I have often seen him, even in his old age, weeping for this unknowing transgression. . . .

On his return from Rome, he abode awhile in his father's house; until, inflamed again with holy zeal, he purposed to revisit the abode of the Apostles and made his desire known unto his parents. Not only did they approve his purpose, but his mother besought his leave to bear him company on this pilgrimage; which he gladly granted, and willingly paid her every filial service that was her due. They came therefore to London; and they had scarcely departed from thence when his mother took off her shoes, going thus barefooted to Rome and back to London. Godric, humbly serving his parent, was wont to bear her on his shoulders. . . .

Godric, when he had restored his mother safe to his father's arms, abode but a brief while at home; for he was now already firmly purposed to give himself entirely to God's service. Wherefore, that he might follow Christ the more freely, he sold all his possessions and distributed them among the poor. Then, telling his parents of this purpose and receiving their blessing, he went forth to no certain abode, but whithersoever the Lord should deign to lead him; for above all things he coveted the life of a hermit.

A CHINESE VIEW: CHANG HAN

This passage was written early in the sixteenth century, right after the postclassical period and more than a half century after the Ming dynasty had stopped its international trade expeditions. Of the three authors in this chapter, Chang Han came the closest to having merchant experience of his own. He came from a family that had made a fortune in the textile industry, but he himself was sent to Confucian schools and became an official in the Ming dynasty. His background helps explain the combination of Confucian and reformist remarks.

• • •

ESSAY ON MERCHANTS

Money and profit are of great importance to men. They seek profit, then suffer by it, yet they cannot forget it. They exhaust their bodies and spirits, run day and night, yet they still regard what they have gained as insufficient. . . .

Those who become merchants eat fine food and wear elegant clothes. They ride on beautifully caparisoned, double-harnessed horses—dust flying as they race through the streets and the horses' precious sweat falling like rain. Opportunistic persons attracted by their wealth offer to serve them. Pretty girls in beautiful long-sleeved dresses and delicate slippers play string and wind instruments for them and compete to please them.

Merchants boast that their wisdom and ability are such as to give them a free hand in affairs. They believe that they know all the possible transformations in the universe and therefore can calculate all the changes in the human world, and that the rise and fall of prices are under their command. They are confident that they will not make one mistake in a hundred in their calculations. These merchants do not know how insignificant their wisdom and ability really are. As the *Chuang Tzu* says: "Great understanding is broad and unhurried; little understanding is cramped and busy."

Because I have traveled to many places during my career as an official, I am familiar with commercial activities and business conditions in various places. The capital is located in an area with mountains at its back and a great plain stretching in front. The region is rich in millet, grain, donkeys, horses, fruit, and vegetables, and has become a center where goods from distant places are brought. Those who engage in commerce, including the foot peddler, the cart peddler, and the shop-keeper, display not only clothing and fresh foods from the fields but also numerous luxury items such as priceless jade from K'un-lun, pearls from the island of Hai-nan, gold from Yunnan, and coral from Vietnam. These precious items, coming from the mountains or the sea, are not found in central China. But people in remote areas and in other countries, unafraid of the dangers and difficulties of travel, transport these items step by step to the capital, making it the most prosperous place in the empire. . . .

The profits from the tea and salt trades are especially great but only large-scale merchants can undertake these businesses. Furthermore, there are government reg-ulations on their distribution, which prohibit the sale of tea in the Northwest and salt in the Southeast. Since tea is produced primarily in the Southeast, prohibiting its sale to the non-Chinese on the northern border is wise and can be enforced. Selling privately produced salt where it is manufactured is also prohibited. This law is rigidly applied to all areas where salt was produced during the Ming dynasty. Yet there are so many private salt producers there now that the regulation seems too rigid and is hard to enforce.

Profits from selling tea and the officials' income from the tea tax are usually ten to twenty percent of the original investment. By contrast, merchants' profits from selling salt and the officials' income from the salt tax can reach seventy to eighty percent of the original invested capital. In either case, the more the invested capital, the greater the profit; the less the invested capital, the less the profit. The profits from selling tea and salt enrich the nation as well as the merchants. Skillful mer-chants can make great profits for themselves while the inept ones suffer losses. This is the present state of the tea and salt business.

In our Chekiang province it appears that most of the rich gain their wealth from engaging in salt trade. But the Chia family in Wu-ling became rich from selling tea and have sustained their prosperity for generations. The "Book of Chou" [one of the oldest classics] says: "If farmers do not work, there will be an insuffi-ciency of food; if craftsmen do not work, there will be an insufficiency of tools; if merchants do not work, circulation of the three necessities will be cut off, which will cause food and materials to be insufficient."

Foreigners [in the Northwest] are recalcitrant and their greed knows no bounds.

At the present time our nation spends over one million cash yearly from our treasury on these foreigners, still we cannot rid ourselves of their demands. What is more, the greedy heart is unpredictable. If one day they break the treaties and invade our frontiers, who will be able to defend us against them? I do not think our present trade with them will ensure us a century of peace.

As to the foreigners in the Southeast, their goods are useful to us just as ours are to them. To use what one has to exchange for what one does not have is what trade is all about. Moreover, these foreigners trade with China under the name of tributary contributions. That means China's authority is established and the foreigners are submissive. Even if the gifts we grant them are great and the tribute they send us is small, our expense is still less than one ten-thousandth of the benefit we gain from trading with them. Moreover, the Southeast sea foreigners are more concerned with trading with China than with gaining gifts from China. Even if they send a large tribute offering only to receive small gifts in return, they will still be content. In addition, trading with them can enrich our people. So why do we refrain from the trade?

Some people may say that the Southeast sea foreigners have invaded us several times so they are not the kind of people with whom we should trade. But they should realize that the Southeast sea foreigners need Chinese goods and the Chinese need their goods. If we prohibit the natural flow of this merchandise, how can we prevent them from invading us? I believe that if the sea trade were opened, the trouble with foreign pirates would cease. These Southeast sea foreigners are simple people, not to be compared to the unpredictable Northeast sea foreigners. Moreover, China's exports in the Northwest trade come from the national treasury. Whereas the Northwest foreign trade ensures only harm, the sea trade provides us with only gain. How could those in charge of the government fail to realize this?

Turning to the taxes levied on Chinese merchants, though these taxes are needed to fill the national treasury, excessive exploitation should be prohibited. Merchants from all areas are ordered to stop their carts and boats and have their bags and cases examined whenever they pass through a road or river checkpoint. Often the cargoes are overestimated and thus a falsely high duty is demanded. Usually merchants are taxed when they enter the checkpoint and are taxed again at the marketplace. When a piece of goods is taxed once, the merchant can still make some profit while complying with the state's regulations. But today's merchants often are stopped on the road for additional payments and also suffer extortions from the clerks. Such exploitation is hard and bitter enough but, in addition, the merchants are taxed twice. How can they avoid becoming more and more impoverished?

When I was Vice-President of the Board of Public Works in Nanking, I was also in charge of the customs duties on the upper and lower streams of the Black Dragon River. At that time I was working with Imperial Censor Fang K'o-yung. I told him: "In antiquity, taxes on merchants were in the form of voluntary contributions based on official hints, not through levies. Levying taxes on merchants is a bad policy. We should tax people according to their degree of wealth or poverty. Who says we cannot have good government!" Fang agreed with me, so we lowered the taxes on the merchants some twenty percent. After the taxes were lowered, merchants became willing to stop at the checkpoints. All boats stop when they should and the total tax income received from merchants increased fifty percent. From this example one can see that the people can be moved by benevolent policies.

CHAPTER 12

THE MONGOL ERA

Conquests and Connections

This chapter compares the experiences of China, Russia, and Western Europe during the period of the Mongol conquests in the thirteenth and fourteenth centuries. The development of interlocking Mongol empires, called khanates, produced significant but diverse consequences in world history. Coming on the heels of the decline of Arab world power, the Mongol episode facilitated vital exchanges among previously separate civilizations while producing new tensions in large parts of Asia and Eastern Europe.

The Mongols, a herding people from Central Asia, gained important leadership structure and culture values from interacting with more formal civilizations such as China. Contacts along China's northern border increased for several centuries. New leadership, and possibly some population pressure, inspired a wave of military ventures in the thirteenth century under the aegis of Genghis Khan. The Mongols swept through the empire of China from 1206 onward and controlled the society for over a century. They pushed into the Middle East, toppling the Arab caliphate and challenging Turkish forces, and into Southeast Asia. They also conquered Russia (1236), which they loosely controlled for almost two centuries. Mongol victories in Poland and Hungary did not lead to durable conquests in the rest of Europe. Two efforts to conquer Japan also failed, leading to a growing sense of confidence and isolation there. Even the consequences of failure, however, reveal the awesome sweep of Mongol power.

Overall, the Mongol era in world history had two results: it caused disruption and resentment, and it provided unusual, stimulating international contacts.

Mongol overlords were resented in most of their holdings, despite efforts by individual rulers, such as the famous Kublai Khan in China, to adapt to established political and cultural traditions. Although some Chinese officials assisted the Mongols in return for specific gains such as the preservation of Chinese unity, there were many points of discord. Confucianists believed that the Mongols scorned their commitment to bureaucracy and hierarchy. Kublai Khan praised Confucianism on occasion, but he utilized non-Confucian officials and, along with other leaders, increasingly inclined to the Buddhist religion, which Chinese officialdom had previously rejected. Other rifts included the greater independence of Mongol women and the eating and dress habits of a herding people, offensive to the punctilious Chinese upper classes. In general, the belief of the Chinese in their own established values contributed to their hostility toward outside rule, and the Mongol experience increased China's sense of separation and superiority.

The Russian situation was somewhat different. The resentment was strong here, too, in part because Mongol leaders concentrated on military coercion and demands for taxes and tribute, rather than the more systematic government developed in China. The cultural clash was different but severe, for Russia was committed to Orthodox Christianity, and its religious leaders condemned the Mongols as pagans, possibly a punitive visitation from God. Unlike China, however, with its history of strong government, Russia had been more loosely administered in the postclassical era. Kings, based in Kiev, claimed great power (the state is called Kievan Rus, reflecting its western concentration compared to later Muscovite rule); but in fact local princes and the aristocracy (called *boyars*) wielded much authority. Russia benefited from growing trade with the opulent Byzantine Empire. But by the twelfth century the Byzantines were declining, so trade resources were diminished; political effectiveness also decreased amid local wars, invasions, and bickering. Russia, then, was easy pickings for the Mongol invaders, who swept through without great resistance, and economic and cultural levels deteriorated further once the Mongols seized control. Russia, like China, would recover, but it faced a longer struggle to regain previous vigor. Indeed, Russia's trading role never really attained its postclassical prominence again.

If the Mongol period meant resentment and disruption in key civilizations, it meant new opportunity for other peoples. Many Muslims appreciated trade opportunities with Mongol China and reported their awe at the wealth of the leading cities. Western Europeans responded even more eagerly, despite criticism of the Mongol commitment to "pagan" religions. Since Europe was spared any direct Mongol invasions, European religious and commercial leaders took advantage of Mongol tolerance of foreign travelers and trading activities. Direct European contacts with China were established for the first time in world history, and as a result the Europeans gained access to China's superior technology. European appetite for trade with Asia, already encouraged by the Crusades (see chapter 10), increased as well.

The Western European contact with Mongol Asia was furthered by the khans' use of Christians in their own administrations, particularly in China, where various minorities substituted for reluctant Confucian bureaucrats. Kublai Khan not only welcomed several European emissaries, including the famous Polo family from Venice, but also sent an expedition of Chinese Christians to Europe.

The benefits of contact with China helped push European technology beyond the levels of otherwise similar societies, such as those in Africa, that had no interaction with the Mongol world (see chapter 13). Acquisition of new navigation devices and explosive powder were two key results.

The two strands of the Mongol Empire set up several obvious comparative issues. The reactions of Christian Russia and Christian Europe differed, despite common religious objections to Mongol beliefs, and those different experiences affected the later history of the two regions. A similar comparison pairs Russia and China, both resentful of Mongol control but for different reasons and with different consequences. What enabled China to surmount the Mongol period with less fundamental change than Russia required?

In the selections that follow, Russian resentment is clear, whereas the Chinese response reflects distinctive arguments and adjustments. Two primary sources convey some of the Russian and Chinese reactions, and they are supplemented by a historian's discussion of Mongol China. Treatment of the Western interaction returns to a primary source, but of a rather different sort. This account, based on travelers' impressions rather than the experience of conquest, conveys a much different sense of contacts and potential benefits.

The Mongol era, decisive in Eurasian history toward the end of the postclassical millennium, was also brief. China regained independence, with its new Ming dynasty, in 1328. Russia won increasing autonomy by the late fourteenth century, spearheaded by the dukes of the Moscow region, and then attained full autonomy around 1450, pushing the Mongol overlords farther and farther back into central Asia. With these changes, the period of easy Western contact with East Asia ended as well. But after the Mongol period the Eurasian civilizations did not return to the previous status quo. The diverse results of the Mongol experience continued to affect policies of expansion and isolation, and the heady period of technological exchange continued to be exploited.

Questions

1. What characteristics did even sympathetic Chinese observers assign to the Mongols? Why was it easy to look down on Mongol habits despite the Mongols' success in conquest?

2. What was the clash between Chinese bureaucrats and Mongol demands? Why did Chinese leaders generally resolve to adjust as little as possible to Mongol control?

3. What does the *Novgorod Chronicle* suggest about Russia's cultural levels and social unity as it encountered Mongol pressures?

4. What was Novgorod's reaction to the Tartars (Mongols)? How did Russian religious authorities describe Tartar characteristics? How did their reactions compare with those of the Chinese? What did the different bases for scorn

and fear imply about the nature of Russian and Chinese societies in a time of crisis?

5. How did Novgorod actually deal with the Tartars? Judging by this city's experience, what were the major impacts of the Mongol invasion on postclassical Russia? Did the Mongols cause or rather reflect the Russian disarray?

6. How did the Mongol approach to Russia differ from Kublai Khan's efforts in China? What did the Mongols want in each case? What might explain the differences in goals?

7. How did the Russian experience with the Mongols compare with that of China? Which society was more disrupted, and why?

8. Why did Russian attitudes toward the Mongols differ from the reactions of Western European Christians?

9. How did Marco Polo try to appeal both to critical and to envious impressions of Mongol rulers? Why would both reactions seem appropriate?

10. What were the main impressions of Western visitors to the Mongol realm? To what extent did these impressions reflect Christian values similar to those of the chroniclers in Novgorod? How did the Western travelers rate the relative economic and political strength of Mongol China, compared to their own society?

11. How did Western reactions explain why Western Europe was ready to gain from the new contacts with East Asia? Why did Russia not develop a similar set of contacts?

12. What was the relative weight of religion and of commercial assessment in Marco Polo's description of Mongol China? What kinds of trade interests might Polo's account strengthen in Europe? What unfamiliar products did he mention?

For Further Discussion

1. How did the Mongol experience affect later Russian policies: what might be predicted about later interests in expansion and about later attitudes toward Asia?

2. What were the long-term consequences of the Mongol experience in China? How and why did Russia's and China's "post-Mongol" policies diverge?

3. Why was the Mongol era important for Western Europe? How did Marco Polo's account compare with earlier European reactions to cultural contact, as suggested by previous travelers and by the tales of the Crusades? What kinds of misperceptions still accompanied Western beliefs about societies such as China, and why?

MONGOLS IN CHINA: LI CHIH-CH'ANG AND
JOHN K. FAIRBANK

The first of the following selections is a Taoist emissary's impressions of the Mongols under Genghis Khan, as the Mongol invasion of China began. The second is an eminent American historian's summary of actual Mongol policy in China during what the Chinese called the Yuan regime. Li Chih-Ch'ang, accompanying a Taoist master summoned by the khan into central Asia, had favorable discussions with the khan, who professed interest in the religion. Li's view, correspondingly, was less jaded than that of Confucian officials later on. But even these Chinese certainly saw the Mongols as very different: how did their reactions predict wider Chinese distaste for Mongol rule? What other problems, according to the wider-reaching historical account by Fairbank, did the Mongols have in consolidating power in China? Could they have adopted more durably successful policies?

• • •

LI CHIH-CH'ANG

The people live in black waggons and white tents; they are all herdsmen and hunters. Their clothes are made of hides and fur; they live on meat and curdled milk. The men wear their hair in two plaits that hang behind the ears. The married women wear a head-dress of birch-bark, some two feet high. This they generally cover with a black woollen stuff; but some of the richer women use red silk. The end (of this head-dress) is like a duck; they call it *ku-ku*. They are in constant fear of people knocking against it, and are obliged to go backwards and crouching through the doorways of their tents.

They have no writing. Contracts are either verbal or recorded by tokens carved out of wood. Whatever food they get is shared among them, and if any one is in trouble the others hasten to his assistance. They are obedient to orders and unfailing in their performance of a promise. They have indeed preserved the simplicity of primeval times. . . .

Both men and women plait their hair. The men's hats are often like *yüan-shan-mao* [theatrical caps], trimmed with all kinds of coloured stuffs, which are embroidered with cloud-patterns, and from the hats hang tasseled pendants. They are worn by all holders of official rank, from the notables downwards. The common people merely wear round their heads a piece of white muslin about six feet long. The wives

From Li Chih-Ch'ang, *The Travels of an Alchemist*, trans. Arthur Weley (Westport, Conn.: Greenwood Press, 1976), 67–68, 106–7. Reprinted by permission of Routledge UK.

of rich or important people wind round their heads a piece of black or purple gauze some six or seven feet long. This sometimes has flowers embroidered on it or woven patterns. The hair is always worn hanging down. Some cover it in a bag of floss-silk which may be either plain or coloured; others wear a bag of cloth or plain silk. Those who cover their heads with cotton or silk look just like Buddhist nuns. It is the women of the common people who do so. Their clothes are generally made of cotton, sewn like a straining-bag, narrow at the top and wide at the bottom, with sleeves sewn on. This is called the under robe and is worn by men and women alike. Their carriages, boats and agricultural implements are made very differently from ours. Their vessels are usually of brass or copper; sometimes of porcelain. They have a kind of porcelain that is very like our Ting [delicate] ware. For holding wire they use only glass. Their weapons are made of steel. In their markets they use gold coins without a hole in the middle. There are native written characters on both sides. The people are often very tall and strong; so much so that they can carry the heaviest load without a carrying-beam. If a woman marries and the husband becomes poor, she may go to another husband. If he goes on a journey and does not come back for three months, his wife is allowed to marry again. Oddly enough some of the women have beards and moustaches. There are certain persons called *dashman* who understand the writing of the country and are in charge of records and documents.

CHINA UNDER MONGOL RULE: JOHN K. FAIRBANK

Only gradually did the Mongols face the fact that conquered Chinese villagers, merchants, and city artisans could not be incorporated into the Mongol tribal society. Yeh-lü Ch'u-ts'ai, as chief minister in the conquered parts of North China after 1230, set up schools and held examinations to recruit Chinese into a bureaucracy. But the Mongols . . . found they could not use the rather simple dual type of divided Sino-"barbarian" administration. . . . The Yüan therefore continued the administrative structure of the Tang and Sung [dynasties], particularly the sixfold division under the Six Ministries at the capital. During the thirteen hundred years from the early Tang to 1906, this basic structure remained the same. The Yüan also continued a threefold division of central government among civil administrative, military, and supervisory (censorial) branches. Innovation was greater in provincial administration, where they followed the Chin example and made provincial governments into direct extensions of the central chancellery, an important step in perfecting the Chinese imperial structure.

The Mongol conquerors faced the age-old problem of how to rule in a Chinese fashion and still retain power. The Chinese populace had to be persuaded to acqui-

From John K. Fairbank, Edwin O. Reischauer, and Albert A. Craig, *East Asia: Tradition and Transformation*, rev. ed. 167–70. Copyright © 1989 by Houghton Mifflin Company. Reprinted by permission.

esce in foreign rule. To accomplish this, an alien dynasty had to maintain local order, give Chinese talent the opportunity to rise in bureaucratic political life, and lead the scholar-official class by fostering Confucian ideology and culture. For this exacting task the rank and file of Mongols were unprepared. Much of their success in the early Yüan era must therefore be ascribed to the commanding personality of Khubilai and his use of Confucian principles and collaborators.

The Mongols differed from their subjects in very striking ways, not only in language and status. For costume, they preferred the leather and furs of steppe horsemen. For food they liked mare's milk and cheese, and for liquor the fermented drink made of mare's milk. Bred on the almost waterless grasslands, the Mongols were unaccustomed to washing. They lacked even surnames. Their different moral code gave greater (and in Chinese eyes, immoral) freedom to women. Moreover, the Mongols' non-Chinese traits were constantly reinforced by their contact with a vast area outside China. They were the only *full* nomads to achieve a dynasty of conquest. The gap between them and the Chinese was thus greater culturally to begin with and was more strongly perpetuated politically. To make the division between conquerors and conquered even more complete, the recruiting of Southern Chinese talent for the Yüan bureaucracy was impeded by the heritage of Sung hatred for the plundering "barbarian." Later Chinese chroniclers, who have always had the last word on their conquerors, depicted the Mongols as primitive savages capable only of destruction and orgiastic excess. One later Chinese account states, "They smell so heavily that one cannot approach them. They wash themselves in urine."

In the face of native hostility, the Mongols in China as elsewhere employed many foreigners, particularly Muslims from Central and Western Asia. As Marco Polo recorded, "You see the Great Khan had not succeeded to the dominion of Cathay by hereditary right, but held it by conquest; and thus, having no confidence in the natives, he put all authority into the hands of Tartars, Saracens, or Christians, who were attached to his household and devoted to his service, and were foreigners in Cathay." The Mongols set up a hierarchy of social classes: they were the top class, and their non-Chinese collaborators second, followed by the Chinese of the North who had capitulated earlier, and, at the bottom, by those of the South, who of course outnumbered all the rest. Meanwhile the Mongol ruling class remained separate from Chinese life with separate systems of law for Chinese and for Mongols. The Great Khan kept his summer residence north of the Wall at Shang-tu (Coleridge's "Xanadu," meaning "Superior Capital"). His alien rule injected a heightened degree of centralized and ruthless despotism into the traditional Chinese Empire.

Life under the Yüan Dynasty

Khubilai on his accession had protected the Confucian temples, and he soon revived the state cult of Confucius. Later he exempted Confucian scholars from taxation.

But on the more fundamental issue of recruitment for government service, Khubilai did not seek out the talent of South China. The examination system had ceased to function in the North after 1237 and in the South after 1274. Its revival was delayed until 1315. Chinese clerks of course staffed the bureaucracy, but Confucian scholars did not often rise to the top.

The scholar class was antagonized also by the Mongols' patronage of foreign religions. In Persia many had embraced Islam, and in Central Asia, Nestorian Christianity. In China religious establishments of the Buddhist, Taoist, Nestorian, and Islamic faiths, like the Confucian temples, were all exempted from taxation. The Chin and Yüan periods saw many new Taoist monasteries built in North China. This multiple religious growth was a distinct setback for the Neo-Confucian doctrines of the Chu Hsi school.

The superstitious Mongols, with their background of shamanism, tended to accept the debased form of Buddhism that had developed in Tibet. . . . In the thirteenth century it spread rapidly into Mongolia and also China, with imperial support.

Khubilai was hailed by the Buddhist clergy in China as an ideal Buddhist monarch. Under his patronage the number of Buddhist establishments, including the great mountain retreats at Mount Wu-t'ai in Shansi, rose to 42,000 with 213,000 monks and nuns. . . . All this patronage of a religious cult could not be offset, in the eyes of the Confucian scholar class, by the emperor's performance of Confucian ritual. He lacked the personnel and the policies to patronize Chinese accomplishments in literature, the arts, and thought. Instead of performing this function of upper-class leadership in China, the Mongols maintained a cosmopolitan regime, under which the Chinese bureaucratic class was given little scope.

In fostering the people's livelihood, on the other hand, Khubilai had some temporary success. The landholding element of the Southern Sung was not dispossessed, taxation of land and labor and the usual government monopolies were developed, and trade was facilitated by the far-flung contact with the rest of Asia. Arab and Persian seafarers and merchants frequented the great port cities like Canton and Ch'üan-chou (Zayton). Foreign trade by land was chiefly conducted by Muslim merchants of Central Asian origin. Their corporate groups not only served as trading associations but also became tax-farmers for their Mongol patrons. These merchant "companies," whose members guaranteed one another, played a key role in collecting the agrarian surplus of the Yüan Empire and channeling some of this accumulated capital into an expanded commerce. They also shared in the inordinate graft and corruption which accompanied Mongol rule. Commerce was aided eventually by a unified nation-wide system of paper currency. Marco Polo, coming from a much less economically advanced Europe, was amazed at this use of paper for money.

Khubilai moved the Great Khan's capital from Karakorum in Outer Mongolia to Peking, where the main entrance through the Great Wall leads down to the North China Plain. There he built a new city called Khanbaligh (Marco Polo's "Cambaluc"), meaning in Turkish, "city of the Khan." Within it was a palace enclosed by double walls and complete with parks, treasuries, a lake and a big hill dredged from it. To feed the new capital, grain was transported from the lower Yangtze by extending the Grand Canal north to Peking from the Yellow River. On the stone embankments of this second Grand Canal system ran a paved highroad from Hangehow to Peking, a distance of eleven hundred miles, which took forty days to traverse.

Khubilai's grandson Temur, who succeeded him in 1294, maintained a strong central administration, but after his death in 1307 the Mongols' hold on China rapidly weakened. In the next twenty-six years, seven rulers occupied the throne. Open civil war began after 1328. Meanwhile paper money, which had earlier stimulated trade, was now issued in increasing quantities without backing, and so paper notes were no longer accepted for tax payments and steadily depreciated. In addition, the Yellow River was causing recurrent floods which ruined the well-watered productive areas of northern Anhwei and Kiangsu and southern Shantung. Financial, moral, and political bankruptcy thus came hand in hand.

RUSSIAN REACTIONS: THE *NOVGOROD CHRONICLE*

The *Novgorod Chronicle* is one of the most vital documents from postclassical Russia—or what is more properly called Kievan Russia, the first development of a Russian civilization centered in what is now western Russia, Ukraine, and Belarus. Maintained by Orthodox monks and reflecting their fervent religion, the *Chronicle* detailed major events, without much interpretation save that inspired by religious and local loyalties. Novgorod was a trading city of 250,000 people on the route between Scandinavia and Byzantium. As Kievan Rus fell apart in the twelfth century, Novgorod developed an increasingly independent regional government and army. During the mid–thirteenth century (from 1240 to 1263) the city was ruled by Prince Alexander Nevsky, who won important victories over Germans and Swedes but submitted to Mongol—called Tartar in the *Chronicle*—tax gatherers in order to buy his city's independence. Alexander also visited Mongol leaders to negotiate for his city. Mongols incursions occurred, but Novgorod remained the only Russian state to escape full Mongol (Tartar) control. Only in the late fourteenth century did the city begin to lose more of its independence, to the expanding Russian government now based in Moscow.

• • •

A.D. 1224. The same year for our sins, unknown tribes came, whom no one exactly knows, who they are, nor whence they came out, nor what their language is, nor of what race they are, nor what their faith is; but they call them Tartars. . . . God alone knows who they are and whence they came out. Very wise men know them exactly, who understand books; but we do not know who they are, but have written of them here for the sake of the memory of the Russian Princes and of the misfortune which came to them from them. For we have heard that they have captured many countries. . . .

A.D. 1238. And the accursed ones having come thence took Moscow, Pereyaslavl, Yurev, Dmitrov, *Volok*, and Tver; there also they killed the son of [King] Yaroslav. And thence the lawless ones came and invested [the city of] Torzhok on the festival of the first Sunday in Lent. They fenced it all round with a fence as they had taken other towns, and here the accursed ones fought with battering rams for two weeks. And the people in the town were exhausted and from Novgorod there was no help for them; but already every man began to be in perplexity and terror. And so the pagans took the town, and slew all from the male sex even to the female, all the priests and the monks, and all stripped and reviled gave up their souls to the Lord in a bitter and a wretched death, on March 5, the day of the commemoration of the holy Martyr Nikon, on Wednesday in Easter week. And there, too, were killed Ivanko the Posadnik of Novi-torg, Yakin Vlunkovich, Gleb Borisovich and Mikhailo Moiseivich. And the accursed godless ones then pushed on from Torzhok by the road of Seregeri right up to Ignati's cross, cutting down everybody like grass, to within 100 *versts* of Novgorod. God, however, and the great and sacred apostolic cathedral Church of St. Sophia, and St. Kyuril, and the prayers of the holy and orthodox archbishop, of the faithful Princess, and of the very reverend monks finally ended the attack. . . .

The same winter the accursed raw-eating Tartars, Berkai and Kasachik, came with their wives, and many others, and there was a great tumult in Novgorod, and they did much evil in the provinces, taking contribution for the accursed Tartars. And the accursed ones began to fear death; they said to [Prince] Alexander: "Give us guards, lest they kill us." And the Prince ordered . . . all the sons of the *Boyars* to protect them by night. The Tartars said: "Give us your numbers for tribute or we will run away." And the common people would not give their numbers for tribute but said: "Let us die honourably for St. Sophia and for the angelic houses." Then the people were divided: who was good stood by St. Sophia and by the True Faith; and they made opposition; the greater men bade the lesser be counted for tribute. And the accursed ones wanted to escape, driven by the Holy Spirit, and they devised an evil counsel how to strike at the town at the other side, and the others at this

From Robert Mitchell and Nevill Forbes, eds., The *Chronicle of Novgorod (1076–1471)* (London: Royal Historical Society, 1914), 186–88.

side by the lake; and Christ's power evidently forbade them, and they durst not. And becoming frightened they began to crowd to one point to St. Sophia, saying: "Let us lay our heads by St. Sophia." And it was on the morrow, the Prince rode down . . . and the accursed Tartars with him, and by the counsel of the evil they numbered themselves for tribute; for the *Boyars* thought it would be easy for themselves, but fall hard on the lesser men. And the accursed ones began to ride through the streets, writing down the Christian houses; because for our sins God has brought wild beasts out of the desert to eat the flesh of the strong, and to drink the blood of the *Boyars*. And having numbered them for tribute and taken it, the accursed ones went away, and Alexander followed them, having set his son Dmitri on the throne.

THE WEST AND THE MONGOLS: MARCO POLO

Marco Polo was one of the last, and certainly the most famous, Western travelers to Mongol China. It is important to remember that a substantial series of travelers visited in the thirteenth and fourteenth centuries, and many of them wrote accounts. Early emissaries, sent by the Pope, usually saw China and the Mongols in disapproving religious terms, their censure heightened by fear of military prowess. Later travelers, including Marco Polo, took a somewhat more accepting view, though hints of the earlier approach remained. Increasingly, their reports contained wondrous elements mixed with a fairly realistic, if awed, appraisal of China. Marco Polo repeated a number of legends about fabulous wealth and mythical kings, along with some solid data that increased European knowledge of Asia and of the benefits of contact. Marco Polo (1254–1324) came from a Venetian merchant family; his uncle and his father had gone to China in 1266. The family included Marco on a later visit, and he apparently became a favorite of Kublai Khan, who made use of him on business matters and in administering a city. Marco Polo returned to Italy and was later imprisoned during a war with Genoa; it was here that he wrote his account, which long served as the principal source of European information on China. Recent historical scholarship has cast some doubt on his trip; he may not have actually gone to China, but rather repeated his father's and uncle's account, as well as available Persian guide books, while glorifying himself in the best Italian Renaissance fashion. Nevertheless, his account reflected and promoted European ideas about the Mongols and about China.

• • •

In the middle of the hall, where the grand khan sits at table, there is a magnificent piece of furniture, made in the form of a square coffer, each side of which is three

From *The Travels of Marco Polo the Venetian*, ed. and trans. William Marsden (New York: Doubleday, 1948), 134–35, 152–53, 178, 211, 216, 218, 221–22, 243–45.

paces in length, exquisitely carved in figures of animals, and gilt. It is hollow within, for the purpose of receiving a capacious vase, shaped like a jar, and of precious materials, calculated to hold about a tun, and filled with wine. On each of its four sides stands a smaller vessel, containing about a hogshead, one of which is filled with mare's milk, another with that of the camel, and so of the others, according to the kinds of beverage in use. Within this buffet are also the cups or flagons belonging to his majesty, for serving the liquors. Some of them are of beautiful gilt plate. Their size is such that, when filled with wine or other liquor, the quantity would be sufficient for eight or ten men. Before every two persons who have seats at the tables, one of these flagons is placed, together with a kind of ladle, in the form of a cup with a handle, also of plate; to be used not only for taking the wine out of the flagon, but for lifting it to the head. This is observed as well with respect to the women as the men. The quantity and richness of the plate belonging to his majesty [are] quite incredible. Officers of rank are likewise appointed, whose duty it is to see that all strangers who happen to arrive at the time of the festival, and are unacquainted with the etiquette of the court, are suitably accommodated with places; and these stewards are continually visiting every part of the hall, inquiring of the guests if there is anything with which they are unprovided, or whether any of them wish for wine, milk, meat, or other articles, in which case it is immediately brought to them by the attendants. . . .

. . . From the city of Kanbalu there are many roads leading to the different provinces, and upon each of these, that is to say, upon every great high road, at the distance of twenty-five or thirty miles, accordingly as the towns happen to be situated, there are stations, with houses of accommodation for travellers, called *yamb* or post-houses. These are large and handsome buildings, having several well-furnished apartments, hung with silk, and provided with everything suitable to persons of rank. Even kings may be lodged at these stations in a becoming manner, as every article required may be obtained from the towns and strong places in the vicinity; and for some of them the court makes regular provision. At each station four hundred good horses are kept in constant readiness, in order that all messengers going and coming upon the business of the grand khan, and all ambassadors, may have relays, and, leaving their jaded horses, be supplied with fresh ones. Even in mountainous districts, remote from the great roads, where there are no villages, and the towns are far distant from each other, his majesty has equally caused buildings of the same kind to be erected, furnished with everything necessary, and provided with the usual establishment of horses. He sends people to dwell upon the spot, in order to cultivate the land, and attend to the service of the post; by which means large villages are formed. In consequence of these regulations, ambassadors to the court, and the royal messengers, go and return through every province and kingdom of the empire with the greatest convenience and facility; in all of which the grand khan exhibits a superiority over every other emperor, king, or human being. In his dominions no fewer than two hundred thousand horses are thus employed in the department of the post, and ten thousand buildings, with suitable furniture, are kept up. It is indeed so wonderful a system, and so effective in its operation, as it is scarcely possible to describe. If it be questioned how the population of the country can supply sufficient numbers of these duties, and by what means they can be victualled, we may answer, that all the idolaters [Chinese], and like-wise the Saracens [Turks], keep six, eight, or ten women, according to their circumstances, by whom they have a prodigious number of children; some of them as many as thirty sons capable of following their fathers in arms; whereas with us a man has only one wife, and even although she should prove barren, he is obliged to pass his life with her, and is by that means deprived of the chance of raising a family. Hence it is that our population is so much inferior to theirs. . . .

A scandalous custom, which could only proceed from the blindness of idolatry, prevails amongst the people of these parts [Western China], who are disinclined to marry young women so long as they are in their virgin state, but require, on the contrary, that they should have had previous commerce with many of the other sex; and this, they assert, is pleasing to their deities, and that a woman who has not had the company of men is worthless. Accordingly, upon the arrival of a caravan of merchants, and as soon as they have set up their tents for the night, those mothers who have marriageable daughters conduct them to the place, and each, contending for a preference, entreats the strangers to accept of her daughter and enjoy her society so long as they remain in the neighbourhood. Such as have most beauty to recommend them are of course chosen, and the others return home disappointed and chagrined, whilst the former continue with the travellers until the period of their departure. They then restore them to their mothers, and never attempt to carry them away. It is expected, however, that the merchants should make them presents of trinkets, rings, or other complimentary tokens of regard, which the young women take home with them. When, afterwards, they are designed for marriage, they wear all these ornaments about the neck or other part of the body, and she who exhibits the greatest number of them is considered to have attracted the attention of the greatest number of men, and is on that account in the higher estimation with the young men who are looking out for wives; nor can she bring to her husband a more acceptable portion than a quantity of such gifts. At the solemnization of her nuptials, she accordingly makes a display of them to the assembly, and he regards them as a proof that their idols have rendered her lovely in the eyes of men. From thenceforward no person can dare to meddle with her who has become the wife of another, and this rule is never infringed. These idolatrous people are treacherous and cruel, and holding it no crime or turpitude to rob, are the greatest thieves in the world. They subsist by the chase and by fowling, as well as upon the fruits of the earth.

Here are found the animals that produce the musk, and such is the quantity, that the scent of it is diffused over the whole country. . . . In the rivers gold-dust is found in very large quantities. . . .

Very different were [the habits] of Kublai-khan, emperor of the Tartars, whose whole delight consisted in thoughts of a warlike nature, of the conquest of countries, and of extending his renown. . . .

Of the province of Nan-ghin. Nan-ghin is the name of a large and distinguished province of Manji, situated towards the west. The people are idolaters, use paper money in currency, are subjects of the grand khan, and are largely engaged in commerce. They have raw silk, and weave tissues of silver and gold in great quantities, and of various patterns. The country produces abundance of corn [grain], and is stored as well with domestic cattle as with beasts and birds that are the objects of the chase, and plenty of tigers. It supplies the sovereign with an ample revenue, and chiefly from the imposts levied upon the rich articles in which the merchants trade. . . .

Leaving the city of Sa-yan-fu, and proceeding fifteen days' journey towards the south-east, you reach the city of Sin-gui, which, although not large, is a place of great commerce. The number of vessels that belong to it is prodigious, in consequence of its being situated near the Kiang, which is the largest river in the world, its width being in some places ten, in others eight, and in others six miles. Its length, to the place where it discharges itself into the sea, is upwards of one hundred days' journey. It is indebted for its great size to the vast number of other navigable rivers that empty their waters into it, which have their sources in distant countries. A great number of cities and large towns are situated upon its banks, and more than two hundred, with sixteen provinces, partake of the advantages of its navigation, by which the transport of merchandise is to an extent that might appear incredible to those who have not had an opportunity of witnessing it. When we consider, indeed, the length of its course, and the multitude of rivers that communicate with it (as has been observed), it is not surprising that the quantity and value of articles for the supply of so many places, lying in all directions, should be incalculable. . . . On one occasion, when Marco Polo was at the city of Sin-gui, he saw there not fewer than fifteen thousand vessels; and yet there are other towns along the river where the number is still more considerable. . . .

Sin-gui is a large and magnificent city, the circumference of which is twenty miles. The inhabitants are idolaters, subjects of the grand khan, and use his paper money. They have vast quantities of raw silk, and manufacture it, not only for their own consumption, all of them being clothed in dresses of silk, but also for other markets. There are amongst them some very rich merchants, and the number of inhabitants is so great as to be a subject of astonishment. . . . They have amongst them many physicians of eminent skill, who can ascertain the nature of the disorder, and know how to apply the proper remedies. There are also persons distinguished as professors of learning, or, as we should term them, philosophers, and others who may be called magicians or enchanters. On the mountains near the city, rhubarb grows in the highest perfection, and is from thence distributed throughout the province. Ginger is likewise produced in large quantities, and is sold at so cheap a rate, that forty pounds weight of the fresh root may be had for the value, in their money, of a Venetian silver groat. . . .

The city of Kue-lin-fu [is] of considerable size, and contains three very handsome bridges, upwards of a hundred paces in length, and eight paces in width. The women of the place are very handsome, and live in a state of luxurious ease. There is much raw silk produced here, and it is manufactured into silk pieces of various sorts. Cottons are also woven, of coloured threads, which are carried for sale to every part of the province of Manji. The people employ themselves extensively in commerce, and export quantities of ginger and galengal. I have been told, but did not myself see the animal, that there are found at this place a species of domestic fowls which have no feathers, their skins being clothed with black hair, resembling the fur of cats. Such a sight must be extraordinary. They lay eggs like other fowls, and they are good to eat. The multitude of tigers renders travelling through the country dangerous, unless a number of persons go in company. . . .

Upon leaving the city of Kue-lin-fu, and travelling three days, during which you are continually passing towns and castles, of which the inhabitants are idolaters, have silk in abundance, and export it in considerable quantities, you reach the city of Unguen. This place is remarkable for a great manufacture of sugar, which is sent from thence to the city of Kanbalu for the supply of the court. Previously to its being brought under the dominion of the grand khan, the natives were unacquainted with the art of manufacturing sugar of a fine quality, and boiled it in such an imperfect manner, that when left to cool it remained in the state of a dark-brown paste. But at the time this city became subject to his majesty's government, there happened to be at the court some persons from Babylon who were skilled in the process, and who, being sent thither, instructed the inhabitants in the mode of refining the sugar by means of the ashes of certain woods. . . .

Travelling fifteen miles further in the same direction, you come to the city of Kan-giu, which belongs to the kingdom or viceroyalty of Koncha, one of the nine divisions of Manji. In this place is stationed a large army for the protection of the country, and to be always in readiness to act, in the event of any city manifesting a disposition to rebel. Through the midst of it passes a river, a mile in breadth, upon the banks of which, on either side, are extensive and handsome buildings. In front of these, great numbers of ships are seen lying, having merchandise on board, and especially sugar, of which large quantities are manufactured here also. Many vessels arrive at this port from India, freighted by merchants who bring with them rich assortments of jewels and pearls, upon the sale of which they obtain a considerable profit. This river discharges itself into the sea, at no great distance from the port named Zai-tun. The ships coming from India ascend the river as high up as the city, which abounds with every sort of provision, and has delightful gardens, producing exquisite fruits. . . .

. . . At the end of five days' journey, you arrive at the noble and handsome city of Zai-tun, which has a port on the sea-coast celebrated for the resort of shipping, loaded with merchandise, that is afterwards distributed through every part of the province of Manji. The quantity of pepper imported there is so considerable, that what is carried to Alexandria, to supply the demand of the western parts of the world, is trifling in comparison, perhaps not more than the hundredth part.

CHAPTER 13

AFRICA, AMERICAN INDIAN CIVILIZATIONS, AND EUROPE

At the end of the postclassical period, civilization had for many centuries embraced large areas in sub-Saharan Africa, northwestern Europe, and the Americas. Civilization had begun earlier in all three cases: with the Olmecs in Central America during the classical period, with Greece and Rome in Mediterranean Europe, and with the great kingdom of Kush and its successors in northeastern Africa. But the expansion of civilization during the postclassical period included far larger territories. This meant, among other things, the development of formal states in places like England, West Africa, and the Andes.

Increasingly, for example, the center of gravity in postclassical Western Europe shifted northward to France, Germany, and the Low Countries. Here were the key locations of Catholic learning, of a burgeoning merchant network, and of some of the most characteristic examples of feudal government. Two new expansion areas arose in Africa: along the eastern coast, thanks to the stimulus of Arab traders but with new indigenous empires such as Zimbabwe, and in what the Arabs called the Sudanic kingdoms of West Africa—Ghana, Mali, Songhai, and others. Major civilizations expanded in central America in this period, including the Mayans and their intermixture with the Toltecs and capped by the Aztec Empire, which was established in the final centuries of the period. Also in these late postclassical centuries, the Incas set up their large empire stretching along the Pacific coast of South America.

This chapter offers some comparative insights into these three "partially new" civilization areas in the fifteenth and sixteenth centuries, going slightly beyond the postclassical period itself. The challenge is to recognize some unexpected commonalities, in terms of levels of trade and political experience, among three regions that were very different and on the verge of becoming more different still.

Analysis is complicated by the fact that neither Africa nor the Americas generated elaborate written sources available to later historians; Europe was far more verbose. Some African elites used Arabic for writing, but most historical information for this period must come from travelers or oral traditions. Central America offered elaborate writing systems (though the Inca Empire in the Andes had none), but most of its products were systematically destroyed by the Spaniards as part of an effort to extirpate native cultures and replace them with Catholicism. Hence comparison must rely on outsider accounts as well as a few surviving recollections and material artifacts. But the differences in sources must not obscure the fruitful comparisons that are possible among the three civilization centers.

Two kinds of pairings can be made in this comparative assessment, and they point in quite different directions. First, both Africa and Europe had active contact with the world network. Western Europe imitated aspects of Byzantine and Arab civilizations, whereas Africa gained greatly from its contacts with Islam. Africa was much larger than Europe, and its initial civilizations went back farther in time. But the two regions shared the process of developing regional kingdoms, advancing iron technology, and expanding trade and merchants' roles from the early postclassical period onward. The Americas, in contrast, were completely isolated, which meant that they lacked connections with any of the world religions, with key technologies such as iron or the wheel, and with commonly shared diseases. American civilizations were highly developed, nevertheless, which is why many European observers were so greatly impressed with the similarities between their achievements—their agriculture and cities, for example—and those back home, when the Europeans arrived and began commenting in the sixteenth century. In key respects, though, the Americas stood apart and would have a very different history as a result, from European contact onward. Africa, which would also be massively affected by Europe, was long able to preserve basic political and technological structures, in ways that Native Americans could not.

The other pairing couples Africa and the American civilization centers, despite their huge differences. Neither region, by the fifteenth century, was innovating as rapidly as Western Europe was. Western Europe was beginning to gain superiorities in sea trade and related weaponry that would allow it to explore Africa and the Americas, rather than the reverse. The European pattern resulted from fortunate contacts with Asian technology (which Africa, despite its connections, largely ignored); from distinctive problems, notably a trade deficit with Asia, which it hoped to remedy by establishing direct commercial links (which Africa did not need); and from strong military rivalries and religious zeal. By the sixteenth century, when Europe was conquering the Americas and spearheading an unprecedented transatlantic slave trade from Africa, these differences would loom large indeed.

The key comparative questions are thus deliberately complex. In what ways were these societies, at the end of the postclassical period, still similar—such that visitors to Africa or to the Americas were readily impressed by the achievements around them? And in what ways were the crucial differences already becoming visible?

Three selections allow exploration of these issues, crucial to the assessment not only of the later postclassical period but also of the new world history period that would open up during the fifteenth century. First, an Arab traveler discusses his impressions of Africa during the fourteenth century, when the Arab world and Islam were the only external points of reference for African states and traders. Ibn Battuta's comments allow some specific comparisons between the Arab and the African regions (compare also with other travelers' accounts, chapter 12). They also establish how African states looked to a sophisticated outsider—what seemed normal, what seemed more distinctively African.

The second selection is not a primary source; rather, it offers a current historian's treatment of African history in the period. Basil Davidson deliberately compares Africa and Europe, seeing them similar in many respects while noting some crucial differences that would become steadily more important with time.

Finally, two selections deal with American civilizations as they were viewed by early European commentators. Again, there is strong emphasis on what such observers considered normal and what they found impressive by the standards of their own society. Europeans looked down on American Indians in many ways, most often because of religious differences, less commonly because of the technology gap (see chapter 14); but they did not find key American Indian civilizations unrecognizable. As travelers, their impressions can be compared with those Ibn Battuta offered on Africa. They suggest biases and gaps, but also revealing insights.

Questions

1. How is it clear that Ibn Battuta assumes the presence of standard institutions of civilization in sub-Saharan Africa?
2. What does he find strange? Are his observations likely to have been accurate, and if not, what might explain his exaggerations?
3. How do Ibn Battuta's views of African government compare with those of the historian Davidson?
4. Are Ibn Battuta's observations consistent with Davidson's claims that Africa and Europe had many similarities as civilizations in the postclassical period?
5. What are the differences between Europe and Africa by the fifteenth century that Davidson finds most important?
6. What aspects of American Indian civilizations did Spanish observers find equal to their European standards? What did they most criticize? How do their criteria for a "proper" civilization compare with those of Ibn Battuta?
7. Were Europeans more or less amazed by American civilization than Ibn Battuta was by African civilizations? What might account for differences?

For Further Discussion

1. Given the many achievements of American Indian civilizations, why were they more vulnerable to European conquest than the civilizations of Africa?

2. Using also the readings in chapters 7 and 8, discuss the main features of government in postclassical Europe, Africa, and the American Indian civilizations: was any system better organized than the others? Were there major differences?

AFRICA: IBN BATTUTA

Ibn Battuta (1304–1369) was born in Morocco. He traveled for almost thirty years in Asia, Europe, and Africa. His accounts of Africa are extremely valuable; no really comparable sources exist for the period. Ibn Battuta visited several parts of Africa, mainly through contacts with existing Arab communities—the whites—in what was an established part of the Muslim world and its trading zone. This was a brave traveler, with some biases and a definite love of comfort, but also with an eager curiosity about the places he visited.

• • •

I went to the house of ibn Baddā', an excellent man of the people of Salā. I had written to him to rent a house for me and he had done that. Then the Overseer of Īwālātan, whose name was Manshā Jū, invited those who had come in the caravan to his hospitality. I refused to attend that affair, but my friends insisted very much; so I went with the rest. Then the meal was brought out: a concoction of *anlī* mixed with a drop of honey and milk, which they placed in a half calabash like a deep wooden bowl. Those present drank and went away. I said to them, 'Was it for this the black invited us?' They said, 'Yes, this is great entertainment in their country.' I became sure then that there was no good to be expected from them. I wanted to travel back with the pilgrims of Īwālātan. Then it seemed good to me to go to see the capital [or: residence, presence] of their King. My residence in Īwālātan was about fifty days. Its people were generous to me and entertained me. Among my hosts was its *qādī*, Muhammad ibn 'Abd Allāh ibn Yanümar and his brother, the *faqïh* [qādī and faqïh were Muslim legal authorities] and teacher Yahyä. The town of Īwālātan is very hot and there are in it a few small date palms in whose shade they plant melons. They obtain water from the ground which exudes it. Mutton is obtainable in quantity there. The clothes of its people are of fine Egyptian material. Most of the inhabitants belong to the Massūfa, and as for their women—they are extremely beautiful and are more important than the men.

From Said Hamdum and Noel King, eds., *Ibn Battuta in Black Africa* (London: Rex Collings, 1975), 27–29, 36–39, 47–48. Reprinted by permission of Markus Wiener Publishers, Inc.

Anecdote concerning the Massūfa Who Inhabit Īwālātan

The condition of these people is strange and their manners outlandish. As for their men, there is no sexual jealousy in them. And none of them derives his genealogy from his father but, on the contrary, from his maternal uncle. A man does not pass on inheritance except to the sons of his sister to the exclusion of his own sons. Now that is a thing I never saw in any part of the world except in the country of the unbelievers of the land of Mulaībār [Malabar] among the Indians. As to the former [the Massūfa], they are Muslims keeping to the prayers, studying *fiqh* [Islamic jurisprudence], and learning the Qur'ān by heart. With regard to their women, they are not modest in the presence of men, they do not veil themselves in spite of their perseverance in the prayers. He who wishes to marry among them can marry, but the women do not travel with the husband, and if one of them wanted to do that, she would be prevented by her family. The women there have friends and companions amongst men outside the prohibited degrees of marriage [i.e., other than brothers, fathers, etc.]. Likewise for the men, there are companions from amongst women outside the prohibited degrees. One of them would enter his house to find his wife with her companion and would not disapprove of that conduct. . . .

The sultan [emperor of Mali] has a raised cupola which is entered from inside his house. He sits in it a great part of the time. It has on the audience side a chamber with three wooden arches, the woodwork is covered with sheets of beaten silver and beneath these, three more covered with beaten gold, or, rather, it is silver covered with gilt. The windows have woollen curtains which are raised on a day when the sultan will be in session in his cupola: thus it is known that he is holding a session. When he sits, a silken cord is put out from the grill of one of the arches with a scarf of Egyptian embroidery tied to it. When the people see the scarf, drums are beaten and bugles sounded. Then from the door of the palace come out about three hundred slaves. Some have bows in their hands and some small spears and shields. Some of the spearmen stand on the right and some on the left, the bowmen sit likewise. Then they bring two mares saddled and bridled, and with them two rams. They say that these are effective against the evil eye. When the sultan has sat down three of his slaves go out quickly to call his deputy, Qanjā Mūsā. The *farāriyya* [commanders] arrive, and they are the *amīrs* [officers], and among them are the preacher and the men of *fiqh*, who sit in front of the armed men on the right and left of the place of audience. The interpreter Dūghā stands at the door of the audience chamber wearing splendid robes of *zardkhuāna* [official] and others. On his head is a turban which has fringes, they have a superb way of tying a turban. He is girt with a sword whose sheath is of gold, on his feet are light boots and spurs. And nobody wears boots that day except he. In his hands there are two small spears, one of gold and one of silver with points of iron. The soldiers, the district governors, the pages and the Massūfa and others are seated outside the place of audience in a broad street which has trees in it. Each *farārī* [commander] has his followers before him with their spears, bows, drums and bugles made of elephant tusks. Their instruments of music are made of reeds and calabashes, and they beat them with sticks and produce a wonderful sound. Each *farārī* has a quiver which he places between his shoulders. He holds his bow in his hand and is mounted on a mare. Some of his men are on foot and some on mounts.

Inside the audience chamber under the arches a man is standing; he who wants to speak to the sultan speaks to Dūg̱ẖā, Dūg̱ẖā speaks to the man who is standing, and he speaks to the sultan.

An Account of the Sessions in the Place of Audience

The sultan sits on certain days in the palace yard to give audience. There is a platform under a tree with three steps which they call *banbī*. It is covered with silk and has pillows placed on it. The *shatr* [umbrella] is raised, this is a shelter made of silk with a golden bird like a sparrowhawk above it. The sultan comes out from a gate in the corner of the palace, bow in hand, his quiver between his shoulders, and on his head a cap of gold tied with a golden band which has fringes like thin-bladed knives more than a span long. He often wears a robe which is soft and red, made from Roman cloth called *muṭanfas*. The singers go out before him carrying gold and silver *qanābir* [guitars] and behind him come three hundred armed slaves. The sultan walks slowly and pauses often and sometimes he stops completely. When he comes to the *banbī* he stops and looks at the people. Then he mounts the steps with dignity in the manner of a preacher getting into the pulpit. When he sits down they beat the drums, blow the bugles and the horns, and three of the slaves go out in haste and call the deputy and the *farāriyya* [commanders]. They enter and sit down. The two mares are brought in with the two rams. Damug̱ẖā stands at the door while the rest of the people are in the street under the tree. The blacks are the most humble of men before their king and the most extreme in their self-abasement before him. They swear by his name, saying, 'Mansā Sulaimānkī' [the law of Mansā Sulaimān]. When he calls one of them while he is in session in his cupola which we described above, the man invited takes off his clothes and wears patched clothes, takes off his turban, puts on a dirty cap, and goes in raising his clothes and trousers up his legs half-way to his knees. He advances with humility looking like a beggar. He hits the ground with his elbows, he hits it hard. He stands bowed, like one in the *ruku'* position in prayer, listening to what the king says. When one of them speaks to the sultan and he gives him an answer, he removes his clothes from his back and throws dust on his head and back, as a person does when bathing with water. I used to wonder how they do not blind their eyes. When the sultan speaks in his council, at his word those present take their turbans off their heads and listen to the speech. . . .

Amongst their good qualities is the small amount of injustice amongst them, for of all people they are the furthest from it. Their sultan does not forgive anyone in any matter to do with injustice. Among these qualities there is also the prevalence of peace in their country, the traveller is not afraid in it nor is he who lives there in fear of the thief or of the robber by violence. They do not interfere with the property of the white man who dies in their country even though it may consist of great wealth, but rather they entrust it to the hand of someone dependable among the white men until it is taken by the rightful claimant.

Another of the good habits amongst them is the way they meticulously observe the times of the prayers and attendance at them, so also it is with regard to their congregational services and their beating of their children to instill these things in them.

When it is Friday, if a man does not come early to the mosque he will not find a place to pray because of the numbers of the crowd. It is their custom for every man to send his boy with his prayer mat. He spreads it for him in a place commensurate with his position and keeps the place until he comes to the mosque. Their prayer-mats are made of the leaves of a tree like a date palm but it bears no fruit.

Among their good qualities is their putting on of good white clothes on Friday. If a man among them has nothing except a tattered shirt, he washes and cleans it and attends the Friday prayer in it. Another of their good qualities is their concern for learning the sublime Qur'ān by heart. They make fetters for their children when they appear on their part to be falling short in their learning of it by heart, and they are not taken off from them till they do learn by heart. I went in to visit the *qāḍī* on an 'Id day and his children were tied up. I said to him, 'Why do you not release them?' He said, 'I shall not do so until they learn the Qur'ān by heart.' One day I passed by a handsome youth from them dressed in fine clothes and on his feet was a heavy chain. I said to the man who was with me, 'What has this youth done— has he killed someone?' The youth heard my remark and laughed. It was told me, 'He has been chained so that he will learn the Qur'ān by heart.'

Among the bad things which they do—their serving women, slave women and little daughters appear before people naked, exposing their private parts. I used to see many of them in this state in Ramadān, for it was the custom of the *farāriyya* [commanders] to break the fast in the sultan's house. Everyone of them has his food carried in to him by twenty or more of his slave girls and they are naked, every one. Also among their bad customs is the way women will go into the presence of the sultan naked, without any covering; and the nakedness of the sultan's daughters— on the night of the twenty-seventh of Ramadān, I saw about a hundred slave girls coming out of his palace with food, with them were two of his daughters, they had full breasts and no clothes on. Another of their bad customs is their putting of dust and ashes on their heads as a sign of respect. And another is the laughing matter I mentioned of their poetic recitals. And another is that many of them eat animals not ritually slaughtered, and dogs and donkeys.

AFRICA AND EUROPE: A HISTORIAN'S VIEW

Basil Davidson, a British historian, has written one of the standard surveys of African history. Like most Africanists, he is at pains to emphasize the vitality, variety, and importance of developments in sub-Saharan Africa long before the arrival of Europeans. The old Western view of African history, that it was essentially defined by primitive conditions, a true "dark continent" before European contact, has long since been discarded. The postclassical period, as Davidson establishes, saw the emergence of large African states and the important Bantu migration, which spread agricultural societies steadily southward in the vast continent.

• • •

AFRICA AROUND 1300–1600

These few examples may serve to show how the subtle yet persistent pressures of Iron Age transformation carried many peoples of the Sudanese grasslands from simple systems of political organization to more complex systems, and how this ripening process continued over a long period more or less contemporary with the European Middle Ages and Renaissance. This is the period, taking shape roughly between AD 1000 and 1300, and displaying its full potential between AD 1300 and 1600, of what I shall call the Mature Iron Age in Africa.

Throughout this period, one may note in passing, there are several interesting parallels with Europe. Although Sudanese peoples never evolved systems based on the effective private ownership of land, such as in feudal Europe, they undoubtedly built systems based on taxation and tribute, on lord-and-vassal relations, on forms of slavery akin to European serfdom, that were not unlike some of the contemporary social structures of Europe. Here and there these African systems have been directly compared with European feudalism. But while this comparison can be useful as a stimulus to thought and argument, it will be misleading if made without serious reservation. These African societies never developed the autocracy of feudal rule that reposed on the alienation of land from those who used it. There occurred here no such decisive stratification of society.

Built on the collective ownership of land with market-cities playing no *dominant* general part in their economy, these kingdoms remained much more broadly dem-

From Basil Davidson, *Africa in History* (New York: Collier Books, 1991), 107–8, 111–13, 156–59, 205–6, 309–10, 314–15.

ocratic, even when allowing for the steady growth of royal power after the middle of the fifteenth century, than their contemporaries in Europe. Yet the parallel between the position of the towns in western Africa and western Europe remains interesting. For if it is true, to glance at another comparison, that the Western Sudan produced no parliamentary forms of a kind that were structurally close to those of western Europe, it is also true that the question of political representation was always present, often arduously and urgently present, and was certainly among the knottiest of problems ever laid before the rulers of states such as Mali or Songhay. As between the men and merchants of the towns and the chiefs and spokesmen of the country-side, there developed an increasingly acute rivalry for power in councils of state, at least from the time of Sundiata Keita in the thirteenth century. The triumph of the townsmen of feudal England in winning at that very time their first right of representation with the calling of Simon de Montfort's Parliament, in 1265, would have been well appreciated in the cities of the Western Sudan. With a deeper understanding of this long period there will be more parallels and comparisons of this kind. . . .

Thus we may take it as certain that the vast majority of the inhabitants of fourteenth-century Ife, Benin or other strong states of the forest country were descended from ancestors who had lived in those countries since remote Stone Age times. If they modified their culture with the arrival of migrants from the north, the migrants will have changed their own much more. So the resultant cultural patterns were neither exotic nor entirely local. On the contrary, they were the creative product of a marriage between local conditions and new social and political solutions whose origins may have lain elsewhere, but whose forms had become peculiar to the city-states of Bono, Ife, Benin and their like. Hence the southward diffusion of such institutions as spiritually sanctioned kingship, if this diffusion really did happen, must be regarded as anything but a simple transfer of ideas and structures.

If one probes a little further into this intriguing problem as to why states emerged in this or that part of Africa, one is constantly faced with the need to isolate and explain those crucial changes which called for a shift from older and much looser forms of community life to new and more structured forms. It was not the appearance of 'divine kings,' after all, that led to the formation of states, but the formation of states that led to the appearance of such kings. Expressing this another way, the need for more centrally organized forms of rule arose not merely or mainly from the habits of dominant cultures that moved southward across Africa. Far more important, in fixing the change to new forms of organization, were local changes in social and economic need. Behind the 'divine kings,' in short, lay the pressures of Iron Age transformation.

But what were these pressures? When trying to answer this question, one comes repeatedly across an apparently quite central factor: the growth of trade and production for trade. Here, of course, there is also need for caution. To reduce these intricate processes of transformation to the growth of trade and production for trade might be not much less of an over-simplification, perhaps, than to suppose that the transformation was the mere work of southward diffusion from Egypt and the Sudan. But there is no doubt that the factor of trade and production for trade, wherever it can be traced, is often illuminating and instructive.

If one applies this explanation to Bono, for example, the results are immediately helpful. One of the traditions of Bono has it that gold began to be exploited in that country during the founding reigns of Asaman and Ameyaa, traditionally in the thirteenth century but probably in about 1400, and that this discovery brought wealth and progress in its train. As so often, the traditions manifestly turn things upside down. They make the exploitation of gold, or of the gold trade, a product of the reigns of Asaman and Ameyaa, the founding rulers, whereas the truth is likely to have been just the reverse. Gold must have long been known in the Akan forest-lands, and sporadically mined as well. These lands were already several hundred years into their Iron Age. But the rise of Bono followed the rise of Mali, and the rise of Mali had promoted a rapid expansion of southward trade through the Mandinka agents whose professional name was Dyula. With increasing demands for gold the peoples of the gold-producing country must have been faced with many new and difficult problems. Who was to mine the gold, for instance, and who was to trade in it, and how were they to be protected from competing neighbours? There came the need for tighter political organization, and the state of Bono was founded. . . . A few other examples may be useful in illustrating the socio-political evolution that was nearly everywhere present in these central-southern regions.

The origins of the kingdom of Kongo, 'great and powerful, full of people, having many vassals', as the Portuguese described it four and a half centuries ago, are told in many traditions. Some of them say that the founders of this well-knit political system near the mouth of the Congo River had moved from the inland country beyond the river Kwango. Another and more likely version is that they came from the northern bank of the Congo estuary late in the fourteenth or early in the fifteenth century. This was again the pattern of a small but powerful intrusive group which imposed its superior organization on indigenous people. They conquered, inter-married and gradually gained the upper hand of recalcitrant neighbours until by 1483, when the Portuguese captain Diogo Cão first anchored in the waters of the Congo, these Kongo people (or BaKongo, *Ba* being a prefix indicating the plural) had built a large and closely articulated state in the northern region of modern Angola. Their king in Cão's time entered willingly into trade with the Portuguese, exchanged ambassadors with Lisbon, and received Christian missionaries with curiosity if not conviction. In this way they opened with Portugal a brief but friendly period of partnership.

From his capital at Mbanza, which the Portuguese later baptized São Salvador, the strong king of the Kongo (also Christian in more than name after about 1506) ruled the metropolitan lands of his empire, the country between the Kwilu and

Congo rivers. North of the Congo River were several small tributary states; south-wards lay several others. The Portuguese misinterpreted this lord-and-vassal hierarchy in terms of their own feudalism, and in 1512 presented the Mani-Kongo, the lord of these lands, with a list of noble titles which they thought he would do well to copy and which, nominally at least, he did adopt. A Portuguese report of 1595 can thus describe the organization of metropolitan government as including the authority of 'six Christian dukes, who may even be called little kings . . . and as well as these there are Catholic counts and marquises who obey the king's orders with very strict obedience. He dismisses any of them who do not carry out their responsibilities, and replaces them by other men.'

At the beginning the Portuguese found it necessary and even desirable to respect the sovereignty of this Kongo kingdom and its neighbours. They presented themselves as friends and allies, just as they had done along the coast of Senegal, at the mouth of the Gambia, at Elmina and at Benin. They remained for some time content with this state of affairs, while extracting from Kongo the greatest possible number of captives for enslavement elsewhere. Yet almost from the beginning the overseas slave trade had its grim effect in violence and deepening despair. As early as 1526 the baptized King Affonso of Kongo is writing to his 'royal brother' in Lisbon that 'we cannot reckon how great the damage is . . . and so great, Sire, is the corruption and licentiousness that our country is being completely depopulated . . . ' It made no difference. Slaving continued.

Events took a somewhat different course further south. Here, in the coastal country of the powerful Mbundu kingdom of Ndongo (whose king's title was *ngola*: hence the Angola of later times), the Portuguese ran into opposition and rejection. The reasons were not far to seek. It was by raids on Mbundu country that the Kongo rulers had obtained many of the captives whom they sold into Portuguese slavery. From the first, then, the Portuguese appeared along the coast of Ndongo as obvious enemies, and were treated as such. Yet the Portuguese, whether as royal agents or private adventurers, were not to be put off. Inspired partly by a fixed illusion that the mountains of Ndongo possessed rich silver mines, they at first attempted the same tactics of peaceful penetration by which they had acquired their influence in Kongo. Failing with these, they turned to outright invasion. From 1575 the wars went on for a weary century and more. Their little armies were repeatedly thrown back and scattered. Portuguese gangs roved the countryside, seizing captives wherever they could. Ndongo was steadily and disastrously depopulated. Shifting inland, its leaders set up a new state in Matamba, associated with the heroic name of Queen Nzinga, who fought the Portuguese for many years before coming to terms with them. By the 1680s the Kongo kingdom, like Ndongo, was far gone in ruin.

East of these Congo-Angola states were others of the same type, though varying in local structure and having no direct contact with Europeans. Many of their peoples, like those of the riverain populations of western Africa, were highly gifted in the plastic arts, while they shared with other tropical Africans their love of dancing and versatility in the use of rhythm. The Bushongo of the Kasai were among several who developed a fine art in raffia-weaving, a skill that still partially survives. Their state appears to have entered its mature form, with spiritually sanctioned kingship, a hierarchy of chiefs, some division of labour and a complex ideology of moral and political behaviour, some four centuries ago. . . .

Passing through Cairo in the 1320s on his way to Mecca, the great Mansa Musa of Mali had told a dramatic tale of maritime adventure. He said that his predecessor had sent two big expeditions, one of four hundred ships and the other of two thousand, across the ocean in order to discover what lay on the other side, but only one of these ships and its crew had ever returned. Even if these expeditions really took place, it is clear they were altogether exceptional. The coastal peoples of West Africa were skillful in building large canoes for inshore fishing and at handling these across thundering surf; but this was the obvious limit of their need. Until the coming of the Europeans, they faced an empty ocean. In this respect, of course, they were very differently placed from the Swahili peoples of the East Coast, who had long since learned ship-building and sailing skills from the Arab and Indian sailors of the Indian Ocean.

During the sixteenth century, however, there evolved in the Atlantic a trading community that was parallel to the much older and in many ways vastly different system of the Indian Ocean. From 1500 onwards the western seas were increasingly traced by sailing ship routes linking western Africa to western Europe, and soon afterwards to the eastern seaboard of the Americas and the islands of the Caribbean. In this new trading community West African played almost from the first an indispensable part. This was not as ship-builders or ship-masters, for they had none of the necessary skills, experience or incentive to impel them in that direction; and the carrying trade remained a European monopoly of skill and ownership. With rising European technological supremacy, this was the period in which the foundations for Africa's future dependence on Europe, whether economic or political, began to be laid. . . . When Affonso of Kongo, back at the beginning of the sixteenth century, had vainly pressed the king of Portugal to send him shipwrights, or at least to sell him a ship for ocean-going travel, he was only expressing the inability of African society to adapt itself to the needs of building ships and sailing them. When Kalonga Mzura, a hundred years later, had invited 'his' Portuguese to send in carpenters who could build sailing boats for Lake Malawi, he was really saying that his own people neither possessed the requisite skills nor were even interested in winning them. The further self-defence and self-realization of Africa required, in brief, a closing of the technological power gap in ways that could only result from new social attitudes and structures. . . .

Pre-colonial Africa lived within a multitude of petty frontiers; exceptions such as the wide empires of the Sudan, Guinea, Central Africa, only prove the rule. Underlying unities of culture there might certainly be; seldom or never did they lead to unities of action. This was the political weakness of Africa in face of the slave trade, and afterwards of the slave trade's natural successor, colonial invasion. Individual kings and merchants might perceive the damage of the slave trade. They could never prevent it, or turn it to more than local or immediate profit, because they could never achieve unity with rivals and competitors; and the same was to be true of the European imperialist challenge. Africans, in sum, did not build their own ships and sail the ocean seas (except for the Swahili of the East Coast, who sometimes did), or otherwise embark on revolutionary technical experiment, because they saw no sufficient reason and interest in doing so, or, when European pressure taught them differently, because they lacked the social power to command or invent the necessary means. They needed a structural revolution in the content as well as in the form of their societies; and the circumstances in which this could take place were not yet present.

AMERICAN CIVILIZATIONS: CORTÉS AND CIEZA DE LEÓN

Hernando Cortés took command of an expedition that arrived in Mexico in 1519; he conquered the country and destroyed the Aztec Empire by 1521. In the meantime he wrote regular reports to the Spanish government. The passages that follow describe his visit to a Toltec city near the sacred pyramid of Cholula, in east-central Mexico, and then his impressions of the Aztec king Montezuma (here called Muteczuma) and his capital city, Tenochtitlán.

The second selection records the impressions of a Spanish traveler to the Inca empire of Peru, also in the sixteenth century. Here, Spanish conquest came slightly later, under Pisarro, but it was just as decisive in destroying a well-established American Indian state. Pedro Cieza de León (1518?–1560) was an explorer associated with the conquest. His book on Peru is one of the most richly illustrated accounts of the whole period.

• • •

HERNANDO CORTÉS

The city is indeed so great and marvellous that though I abstain from describing many things about it, yet the little that I shall recount is, I think, almost incredible.

From Hernando Cortés, *Five Letters of Cortes to the Emperor* trans. J. Bayard Morris (New York: Norton, 1991), 3–5, 6–7, 8, 9–14. Translation copyright © 1969 by J. Bayard Morris. Reprinted by permission of W. W. Norton & Company, Inc.

It is much larger than Granada [Spain] and much better fortified. Its houses are as fine and its inhabitants far more numerous than those of Granada when that city was captured. Its provisions and food are likewise very superior—including such things as bread, fowl, game, fish and other excellent vegetables and produce which they eat. There is a market in this city in which more than thirty thousand people daily are occupied in buying and selling, and this in addition to other similar shops which there are in all parts of the city. Nothing is lacking in this market of what they are wont to use, whether utensils, garments, footwear or the like. There are gold, silver and precious stones, and jewellers' shops selling other ornaments made of feathers, as well arranged as in any market in the world. There is earthenware of many kinds and excellent quality, as fine as any in Spain. Wood, charcoal, medicinal and sweet smelling herbs are sold, in large quantities. There are booths for washing your hair and barbers to shave you: there are also public baths. Finally, good order and an efficient police system are maintained among them, and they behave as people of sense and reason: the foremost city of Africa cannot rival them.

The province contains many wide-spreading fertile valleys all tilled and sown, no part of it being left wild, and measures some ninety leagues in circumference. The order of government so far observed among the people resembles very much the republics of Venice, Genoa and Pisa for there is no supreme overlord. There are many chieftains all of whom reside in the capital city, the common people being tillers of the land and vassals of these chieftains, each of whom possesses certain land of his own. It is to be supposed that they have some system of justice for punishing wrongdoers, . . . They . . . took the thief, and after a public announcement of his crime led him through the great market and there placed him at the foot of a sort of stage which is in the middle of it: the crier ascended the stage and in a loud voice again rehearsed his crime, which being perceived by all they struck him a few blows with great clubs on the head and so killed him. Moreover we have seen many other criminals in prisons for theft and other evil doing. . . .

The city contains many large and fine houses, and for this reason. All the nobles of the land owing allegiance to Muteczuma have their houses in the city and reside there for a certain portion of the year; and in addition there are a large number of rich citizens who likewise have very fine houses. All possess in addition to large elegant apartments very delightful flower gardens of every kind, both on the ground level as on the upper storeys.

Along one of the causeways connecting this great city with the mainland two pipes are constructed of masonry, each two paces broad and about as high as a man, one of which conveys a stream of water very clear and fresh and about the thickness of a man's body right to the centre of the city, which all can use for drinking and other purposes. The other pipe which is empty is used when it is desired to clean the former. Moreover, on coming to the breaks in the causeway spanned by bridges under which the salt water flows through, the fresh water flows into a kind of trough as thick as an ox which occupies the whole width of the bridge, and thus the whole city is served. The water is sold from canoes in all the streets, the manner of their taking it from the pipes being in this wise: the canoes place themselves under the bridges where the troughs are to be found, and from above the canoes are filled by men who are especially paid for this work.

At all the entrances to the city and at those parts where canoes are unloaded, which is where the greatest amount of provisions enters the city, certain huts have been built, where there are official guards to exact so much on everything that enters. I know not whether this goes to the lord or to the city itself, and have not yet been able to ascertain, but I think that it is to the ruler, since in the markets of several other towns we have seen such a tax exacted on behalf of the ruler. Every day in all the markets and public places of the city there are a number of workmen and masters of all manner of crafts waiting to be hired by the day. The people of this city are nicer in their dress and manners than those of any other city or province, for since Muteczuma always holds his residence here and his vassals visit the city for lengthy periods, greater culture and politeness of manners in all things [have] been encouraged.

Finally, to avoid prolixity in telling all the wonders of this city, I will simply say that the manner of living among the people is very similar to that in Spain, and considering that this is a barbarous nation shut off from a knowledge of the true God or communication with enlightened nations, one may well marvel at the orderliness and good government which is everywhere maintained.

The actual service of Muteczuma and those things which call for admiration by their greatness and state would take so long to describe that I assure your Majesty I do not know where to begin with any hope of ending. For as I have already said, what could there be more astonishing than that a barbarous monarch such as he should have reproductions made in gold, silver, precious stones, and feathers of all things to be found in his land, and so perfectly reproduced that there is no goldsmith or silversmith in the world who could better them, nor can one understand what instrument could have been used for fashioning the jewels; as for the featherwork its like is not to be seen in either wax or embroidery, it is so marvellously delicate.

I was unable to find out exactly the extent of Muteczuma's kingdom, for in no part where he sent his messengers (even as much as two hundred leagues in either direction from this city) were his orders disobeyed; although it is true there were certain provinces in the middle of this region with whom he was at war. But so far as I could understand his kingdom was almost as large as Spain.

CIEZA DE LEÓN

Which Deals with Who These Lord-Incas Were and Their Dominions in Peru

As in this part I shall have to make frequent reference to the Incas and give an account of their many lodgings and other noteworthy things, it seems fitting to say something of them at this point, so that the reader will know who these lords were, and not be unaware of their importance nor confuse them.

On many occasions I asked the inhabitants of these provinces what they knew of what went on before the Incas ruled them, and in reply they said that they all lived without order, and that many of them went naked, like savages, without having houses or other dwellings except caves, of which we see many in the mountains and on the hillsides, from which they came out to eat what they could find in the fields. Others built fortresses, which they call *pucarás*, in the hills, from which they sallied forth, howling in strange tongues, to fight one another over the lands they planted, or for other reasons, and many were killed, and the victors carried off such booty as they could find and the women of the vanquished, with all of which they returned to the hilltops where they had their strongholds, and there made sacrifices to the gods they worshiped, pouring out before the stones and idols quantities of human blood and [the blood] of llamas. They were all uncivilized, recognizing no overlord except the captains who led them to war. If any of them went clothed, it was in scant attire, and not like the garments they now wear. The fillets or bands they wear on their head to identify themselves were like those they now use, they say.

From what I gathered from the accounts of the Indians of Cuzco, it would seem that in olden times there was great disorder in this kingdom we call Peru, and that the natives were stupid and brutish beyond belief. They say they were like animals, and that many ate human flesh, and others took their daughters and mothers to wife and committed other even graver sins, and had great traffic with the devil, whom they served and held in great esteem. Aside from this they had strongholds and fortresses in the mountains and hills, and on the least pretext, they sallied forth from them to make war on one another, and killed and took prisoner as many as they could. In spite of the fact that they were given over to these sins and worked these evils, they also say that some of them were religiously inclined, and for that reason in many parts of this kingdom they built great temples, where they prayed, performing their rites and superstitions before big idols, and the devil appeared to them and was worshiped. And while the people of this kingdom were living in this way, great tyrants arose in the provinces of the Colla and in the valleys of the Yungas and

From Victor Wolfgang Von Hagen, ed., *The Incas of Pedro de Cieza de León*, trans. Harriet de Onis (Norman: University of Oklahoma Press, 1959), 25–27. Reprinted by permission of University of Oklahoma Press.

elsewhere, who carried on war against one another, and committed many killings and thefts, and they all suffered great calamities. Many fortresses and castles were destroyed, but the struggle between them went on, at which the devil, the enemy of mankind, rejoiced to see so many souls lost.

Manco Capac founded the city of Cuzco and gave it laws which he put into effect, and he and his descendants were called Incas, which means or signifies kings or great lords. They became so powerful that they conquered and ruled from Pasto to Chile, and to the south the Maule River saw their banners, and to the north, the Angasmayo, and these rivers were the boundaries of their empire, which was so large that the distance between these two limits was more than 1,200 leagues. And they built great fortresses and strongholds, and stationed captains and governors in all the provinces. They did great things, and governed so well that few in the world excel them. They were very keen of understanding, and kept careful accounts without writing, for none has been found in these parts of the Indies. They instilled good customs in all their subjects, and ordered them to clothe themselves and to go shod in *ojotas* [*usutas*], which is a kind of sandal. They gave much importance to the immortality of the soul and other secrets of nature. They believed that there was a Creator of all things, and the sun was their sovereign god, to whom they erected great temples. Led astray by the devil, they worshiped trees and stones, like the Gentiles. In the principal temples they had a great number of beautiful virgins, like those in Rome in the temple of Vesta, and these were ruled by almost the same statutes. For their armies they selected brave captains, and the most loyal they could find. They were very astute at converting their enemies into friends without war, and those who revolted were punished with great severity and no little cruelty.

PART III

The Early Modern Period, 1450–1750

BEGINNING IN THE MID–FIFTEENTH century, several new themes began to shape the larger patterns of world history, compelling all major civilizations to come to terms with some unexpected forces. The world did not become more homogeneous as a result, because different regions reacted quite differently to the common themes. But every society was altered in the process, even though some simply chose to become more isolated than ever before in hopes of insulating themselves from unwanted contact.

The key developments were intertwined. In the first place Western Europe began to take a larger role in world history, developing from a rather backward area, dependent on other regions for technological advance, into a growing power in its own right. Europeans tried to use expansion to compensate for key problems: they lacked good contacts with Asia that did not involve using Muslims as intermediaries, yet they feared the Muslims and craved Asian luxury products. They lacked obvious goods to exchange for Asian spices and silks, so sought gold in order to correct what in modern decades would be called a balance-of-payment deficiency. Europeans had, however, won access to crucial new technologies, such as explosive powder and the compass, thanks to contacts with leading Asian societies. And they added their own inventions: guns, which they could produce because they possessed good supplies of metals and advanced technologies that had been devised for the casting of great church bells, and superior sailing ships. Internal rivalries prompted individual European states to seek particular advantages in exploration and trade, fueling an aggressive European commerce and a zeal for colonies.

The rise of Western power soon brought Europe into contact with the Americas. Exploitation of American resources and the establishment of colonies propelled the Americas into international contacts for the first time since the arrival of people from Asia many millennia before. European control and also European diseases and animals now came to the Americas; and American crops such as corn and potatoes were taken to many other parts of the world, encouraging rapid population growth from China to Europe itself. American trade stimulated world commerce. Europe, particularly, began to increase its manufacturing sector, while relying on fairly traditional technologies and home-and shop-based production. It traded these finished goods for raw materials, precious metals, and spices from other parts of the world. Europe also managed to dominate most ocean-going trade, setting up huge commercial companies that provided another source of profits.

The intensifying commercial contacts around the world created a new set of international inequalities. Some areas, such as Latin America, produced cheap materials for export, depending on forced labor and lacking a large merchant class. They became heavily dependent on European trade initiatives. Africa, though not colonized like Latin America, was brought into this system through the slave trade; millions of Africans were conscripted by African merchants and government agents and sold to Europeans for transport to the Americas. Asian societies, less heavily involved in these trading patterns, found their relative commercial position declining. Indonesia was drawn in, however, through trade for spices and then because of Dutch-run colonies and estate agriculture. India became open to growing European penetration by the eighteenth century.

European gains, the inclusion of the Americas, and the formation of a more intensive international economy were not the only themes of the period. A new set of land-based empires formed, aided to a degree by the use of gunpowder and cannons. In the most dramatic change, the Turkish-led Ottoman Empire covered a large part of the Middle East, Egypt, and southeastern Europe; it replaced the loosening Arab political control and pushed back Christianity in the northern part of the region. The fall of Constantinople in 1453 essentially completed the conquest of the Christian Byzantine Empire. India experienced a new, Muslim-led Mughal Empire that dominated the Hindu majority during the sixteenth and seventeenth centuries. The Russian Empire began its expansion into central and eastern Asia and further into Eastern Europe. Some of these empires, along with the more traditional Chinese Empire, began to weaken somewhat toward the end of the early modern period, but their power, political hold, and internal cultural impact shaped the regions involved for several centuries. This was also a period of dramatic innovation in Japan, under the Tokugawa shogunate, a kind of feudal monarchy.

The early modern period saw no sweeping cultural changes of international scope. Islamic gains continued in parts of Asia. Christianity advanced particularly in the Americas, on the heels of European conquest. Confucianism gained ground in Japan, along with an extensive educational system. In Western Europe, a more scientific outlook accompanied massive discoveries in physics and biology; only in the eighteenth century, however, was this new intellectual framework exported, haltingly, to places like Russia and the British colonies of North America.

Though the early modern period offers no general cultural change of the type associated with the spread of world religions during the postclassical period, there were vital new cultural contacts. Growing trade and some Catholic missionary activity required reactions from leaders in various parts of Asia. African slaves learned to understand Western masters in the most adverse circumstances.

The great themes of the era, however, involve commerce and international contact, undergirded by new transportation techniques and military devices. In part through reacting to these patterns, various societies introduced important internal changes, and although the internal change theme was particularly important in the West, it also applied to the several new empires of Asia.

Developments in the early modern period have shaped world history ever since, despite the many changes that have occurred since 1750. The increasing contact among civilizations and the expansion of Western influence and interference still define major issues and opportunities. Societies that had particular difficulties in dealing with the key developments of the early modern period still echo their experience. The Latin American economy, for example, though far different from what it was during the imposition of colonial controls, faces problems in the treatment of labor inherited in part from early modern systems. China's isolation, though successful in the early modern period itself, led to a relative decline whose consequences still affect this proud civilization.

Comparative analysis unquestionably helps focus key issues in understanding world history in the early modern period. The chapters that follow illustrate several different kinds of comparative themes. First, and most basic to any comparative approach at the world history level, is the juxtaposition of developments in two different civilizations, responding to some broadly similar concerns but without mutual interaction or imitation. Most of the civilizations by the fifteenth century had a long history and a clear identity. They were capable of change, but they would usually continue to reflect earlier, largely separate traditions.

Comparisons with the West form a particularly important subset of this kind of juxtaposition, since the West itself was changing rapidly and the positions of other societies would soon depend in part on how their own patterns related to those of the West. A key chapter thus compares Asian and Russian reactions to the West, indicating the range of possibilities available and the potential results of different orientations.

Another comparative chapter deals with two Asian societies, both having extensive empires. This topic serves as a vital reminder that not every development in the early modern period has a Western twist. The consolidation of empire in China built on firmly established traditions; the Ottoman Empire was a newer construct, but it too developed an extensive and successful bureaucracy. Political strength allowed both of these societies to stand apart from the expansion of the West for a long time and increased their involvement in international trade. The political legacy would influence future reactions as well, in both China and the Middle East.

The rapid acceleration of international contacts, particularly in trade, defines a second major type of comparison, where two or more societies react to a similar cross-civilizational force. In the postclassical period, before 1450, international forces included the spread of world religions, the rise of trade and travel, and even the experience of plagues that could now pass rapidly from one area to another because of frequent human contacts. The various societies reacted differently to each of these common international influences.

In the early modern period, when contacts intensified, reactions diversified further. Societies such as China and Japan opted to become more isolated than before. The Americas were exposed to growing international intrusions because their people were powerless to resist. Societies such as Russia fell somewhere in between: they were strong enough to control contacts with the West but proved eager to imitate some Western developments and to participate a bit more fully in international trade.

Three chapters organize comparisons around common experiences in the early modern period. The mutual reactions of Europeans and American Indians to their first contacts form an obvious but complicated comparative case—complicated because the societies and their power bases were initially so different, and also because the availability of sources raises problems of interpretation. Mutual reactions of Europeans and Africans to the Western-dominated slave trade form another comparative set, again dealing with a new kind of contact of vital importance for all the societies bordering the Atlantic and for millions of enslaved individuals.

Efforts to participate in new export opportunities, or compulsions by foreigners or landlords to participate, created or encouraged new labor systems in several regions, even aside from the spread of slavery among imported Africans in the New World. Coercion of labor increased in several societies as a result, with important long-term impacts. Both Russia and Latin America built new forms of serfdom on their agricultural estates. Comparison of the two systems highlights some of the unexpected connections or kinships emerging in this period of international trade.

In sum, comparisons in this chapter focus on four basic developments in the early modern period: First, contacts among peoples that had known each other little if at all previously, as global relationships were shaken up particularly by the new European sea power. Second, the installation of new or vastly intensified labor systems to deal with problems of controlling workers and producing goods often central to the growing world trade. Third, the expansion of land empires (which involved much continuity in China but important new developments in the Ottoman Empire and Russia). And finally, outright interaction with Western Europe, both by peoples now part of European colonies and by societies independent but exposed to new or potential influences.

CHAPTER 14

EUROPEANS AND AMERICAN INDIANS

Explorers, Conquerors, and Aztec Reactions

The encounter between European explorers and settlers and Native Americans was one of the most fascinating, and from the Indian standpoint tragic, in world history. Europeans came with technologies, animals, diseases, and religious views for which the Indians had no prior preparation. Some Indians proved quite adaptable to the context that European arrival established, gaining skill with horses, learning new political forms, and so on. Overall, however, Europeans brought superior force, devastating diseases, and an attitude of superiority that would combine to severely restrict Indian life.

Early European arrivals, such as Columbus himself, often focused on the naïveté and timidity of the Indians they encountered, wondering at their nakedness and lack of metals and weapons but confident that they could proceed in friendship. Columbus's report on the 1492 voyage to the Caribbean islands shows this early openness, but also the menace that underlay it: "I have also established the greatest friendship with the king of that country, so much so that he took pride in calling me his brother, and treating me as such. Even should these people change their intentions towards us and become hostile, they do not know what arms are, but, as I have said, go naked, and are the most timid people in the world; so that the men I have left could, alone, destroy the whole country."

Later accounts changed, and terms like *deceitful* and *lazy,* as well as *pagan,* began to be applied to Indians. The following European accounts come from Diego Alvarez Chanca, a surgeon on Columbus's 1493 return to the Caribbean, who later published a somewhat "ethnographic," if hostile, account in his hometown of Seville, Spain; from Hernando Cortés, in letters to the Spanish government as he began the conquest of Mexico in 1519; and from the French explorer Champlain, in a diary kept as he traveled the coasts of Maine and Cape Code in the early seventeenth century.

The nature of the sources varies. Champlain and Chanca wrote accounts for general interest; Cortés was reporting to the Spanish royalty. Which kind of account is more accurate, less likely to exaggerate?

What of the Indian views implied in the European accounts? Why does their outlook toward different Europeans differ—or does it? Why did Europeans pick up different signals about their reactions to the first presentations of Christianity? There are few direct accounts of initial Indian responses, so it is important to speculate on the basis of European descriptions of varying behaviors. Also, is there any sign of a distinction, in dealing with Europeans, between the Indians of New England or the Caribbean islands, who combined agriculture and hunting, and the Indians in that part of Mexico long embraced in the elaborate civilizations of the Mayans, whom Cortés first encountered?

Finally, there is the Indian reaction directly. The Aztec Empire, founded in the fourteenth century and building on earlier civilizations in the region, was the key political power in Mexico and much of Central America. A set of Aztec accounts provides an unusual insight into initial contacts from the Indian side— interestingly, the comments refer to the same first encounters that the Cortés account deals with. The ruler of the vast Aztec empire, Montezuma (Motecuhzoma in the Aztec account), sent a mission to contact Cortés, and the results are documented in this passage, along with later observations about some of the biological impact of the Spanish arrival. Aztec response reflected among other things an old belief in a beneficent civilizer-god, Quetzalcoatl, who would return from the east in a particular type of year in the Aztec calendar, which 1519 happened to be. With this document, one set of Indian perceptions of Europeans can be directly compared with European reactions to the Indians—along with a complex mix of factors that explain why the Indian response combined resistance with various kinds of accommodation.

Questions

1. What were the dominant attitudes of the Europeans? Why did they feel justified in killing Indians? Were there also "good" Indians, and how were they defined?

2. Why do the accounts of Cortés and Chanca differ? Who were their audiences, and how might this factor have affected their emphases?

3. Which of the three European accounts was most optimistic about possibilities of dealing with the Indians, and why?

4. What did the Europeans believe Indian reactions to their arrival were?

5. Which looms larger in the European accounts: religious motivations or greed? Do the European accounts suggest an early form of racism?

6. How did Cortés treat Indians in Mexico? What were his basic assumptions?

7. Why did some Indians fight and others not? Why did the Aztecs not simply resist European intrusion in every possible way?

8. What suggestions does the Aztec account offer of why Spanish conquest succeeded?

9. How do the Aztec account and the comments of Cortés compare? How do the two groups evaluate the religious factor? Which side was more aggressive? Which side had more deeply rooted assumptions of superiority, and why?

For Further Discussion

1. Why were small numbers of Europeans able to conquer the numerous, often well-organized American peoples?
2. Were European incursions into the Americas one of the great tragedies of world history?
3. Why might hunting-and-gathering Indians be harder for Europeans to deal with than those in the civilizations of the Aztecs and the Incas?

SPANISH REACTIONS: CHANCA AND CORTÉS

Dr. Chanca's comments on Indians come from his experience with the second Columbus expedition of 1493, which visited various Caribbean islands. Dr. Chanca was interested in titillating his Spanish readership. Hernando Cortés (1485–1547) reported to the Spanish royal government from 1519 onward. He had been assigned an official expedition to Mexico and was able to converse with Indian representatives through his two interpreters, one a Spaniard previously abandoned in the Yucatan, one an Indian woman. Cortés used a combination of alliances with dissident Indian groups and outright fighting to defeat the Aztecs by 1521.

• • •

DR. DIEGO ALVAREZ CHANCA ON THE CARIBE INDIANS

The way of life of these *caribe* people is bestial. There are three islands, this one is called *Turuqueira*, the other, which we saw first, is called *Ceyre*, and the third is called *Ayai*. They are all agreed, as if they were of one lineage, doing no harm to each other. All together they make war on all the other neighbouring islands, going 150 leagues by sea to make raids in the many canoes which they have, which are small 'fustas' made of a single piece of wood. Their arms are arrows rather than iron weapons, because they do not possess any iron: they fix on points made of tortoise-shell, others from another island fix on fish bones which are jagged, being like that naturally, like very strong saws, a thing which, for an unarmed people, as they all are, can kill and do great injury, but for people of our nation are not arms greatly to be feared.

From Peter Hulme and Noel Whitehead, eds., *Wild Majesty: Encounters with Caribes from Columbia to the Present Day* (Oxford: Clarendon Press, 1953), 13–14.

These people raid the other islands and carry off the women whom they can take, especially the young and beautiful ones, whom they keep to serve them and have them as concubines, and they carry off so many that in fifty houses nobody was found, and of the captives more than twenty were young girls. These women also say that they are treated with a cruelty which seems incredible, for sons whom they have from them are eaten and they only rear those whom they have from their native women. The men whom they are able to take, those who are alive they bring to their houses to butcher for meat, and those who are dead are eaten there and then. They say that men's flesh is so good that there is nothing like it in the world, and it certainly seems so for the bones which we found in these houses had been gnawed of everything they could gnaw, so that nothing was left on them except what was much too tough to be eaten. In one house there a man's neck was found cooking in a pot. They cut off the male member of the boys they take prisoner and make use of them until they are men, and then when they want to make a feast, they kill and eat them, for they say that the flesh of boys and of women is not good to eat. Of these boys, three came fleeing to us, and all three had had their members cut off.

CORTÉS IN MEXICO

H. Cortés accordingly left Cuba and began his voyage with ten ships and four hundred fighting men, among whom were many knights and gentlemen, seventeen being mounted. The first land they touched was the Island of Cozumel, now called Santa Cruz, as we mentioned, and on landing at the part of San Juan de Portalatina the town was found entirely deserted, as if it had never been inhabited. Cortés wishing to know the cause of such a flight ordered the men to disembark and took up his abode in the town. It was not long before he learnt from three Indians captured in a canoe as they were making for the mainland of Yucatán that the chiefs of the Island at the sight of the Spanish ships approaching had left the town and retired with all the Indians to the woods and hills, being very afraid of the Spaniards as not knowing what their intentions might be. Cortés, replying by means of the native interpreter whom he had with him, informed them he was going to do them no harm but admonish them and bring them to the knowledge of our Holy Catholic Faith, that they might become vassals of your Majesty and serve and obey him, as had all the Indians and peoples of those parts which are already peopled with Spanish subjects of your Majesties. On the Captain reassuring them in this manner they lost much of their former fear, and replied that they would willingly inform

From Hernando Cortés, *Five Letters of Cortes to the Emperor*, trans. J. Bayard Morris (New York: Norton, 1991), 50–52, 92–94. Translation copyright © 1969 by J. Bayard Morris. Reprinted by permission of W. W. Norton & Company, Inc.

their chieftains who had taken refuge in the hills. The Captain thereupon gave them a letter by which the chiefs might approach in safety and they departed with it promising to return within the space of five days. After waiting for the reply some three or four days longer than the allotted time and seeing that they had not reappeared Cortés decided to search out the coast on either side of him, in order that the Island should not remain entirely deserted, and accordingly sent out two captains each with a hundred men, ordering them to proceed to either extremity of the Island and to hold conversations with any Indians they might meet, telling them that he was awaiting them in the port of San Juan de Portalatina in order to speak with them on behalf of your Majesty; such Indians they were to beg and urge as best they could to come to the said port but were to be careful not to do any harm to them, in their persons, their houses or their goods, lest the natives should be rendered more timid and deceitful than they were already. The two captains departed as they were commanded and returning within four days reported that all the towns which they had come across were desolate. They brought with them, however, ten or a dozen people whom they had managed to persuade, among whom was an Indian chieftain to whom Cortés spoke by means of his interpreter bidding him go and inform the chiefs that he would in no wise depart from the Island without seeing and speaking to them. The chieftain agreeing left with the second letter for the chiefs and two days later returned with the head chief to inform Cortés that he was the ruler of the Island and was come to see what he wanted. The Captain informed him that he wished them no harm, but that they should come to the knowledge of the true faith, and should know that we acknowledged as lords the greatest princes of the earth and that these in their turn obeyed a greater prince than he, wherefore what he desired of them was not otherwise than that the chiefs and Indians of that Island should likewise obey your Majesties, and that doing so they would be favoured, no-one being able to do them harm. The chief replied that he was content so to do and sent for all the other chieftains of the Island, who coming rejoiced greatly at all that the Captain Hernando Cortés had spoken to their chief, and were reassured in such manner that within a very few days the towns were as full of people as before, and the Indians went about among us with as little fear as if they had already had dealings with us for many years. . . .

Accordingly, as the Captain Hernando Cortés saw that stores were already beginning to run short and that the men would suffer much from hunger should he delay there any longer, and the true object of his voyage rest unattained, he decided, his men agreeing, to depart; and so hoisting sail they left that Island of Cozumel, now Santa Cruz, very peaceably inclined, so much so that if it were proposed to found a colony there the natives would be ready without coercion to serve their Spanish masters. The chiefs in particular were left very contented and at ease with what the Captain had told them on behalf of your Majesties and with the numerous articles of finery which he had given them for their own persons. I think there can

be no doubt that all Spaniards who may happen to come to this Island in the future
will be as well received as if they were arriving in a land which had been long time
colonized. The Island of Cozumel is small, without so much as a single river or
stream; all the water that the Indians drink is from wells. The soil is composed solely
of rocks and stones, a certain portion of it being woody. The Indians' only produce
is that obtained from bee-keeping, and our procurators are sending to your Majesties
samples both of the land and of the honey for your Majesties' inspection.

Your Majesties must know that when the Captain told the chiefs in his first
interview with them that they must live no longer in the pagan faith which they
held they begged him to acquaint them with the law under which they were henceforth to live. The Captain accordingly informed them to the best of his ability in
the Catholic Faith, leaving them a cross of wood which was fixed on a high building
and an image of Our Lady the Virgin Mary, and gave them to understand very fully
what they must do to be good Christians, all of which they manifestly received with
very good will, and so we left them very happy and contented. . . .

On arriving at the first town we found the Indians in boats drawn up on the
shore near the water. The Captain proceeded to speak to them both by means of
the native interpreter whom we carried with us and of Gerónimo de Aguilar who
spoke and understood perfectly the language of the country, telling them that he
came to do no harm but only to speak to them on behalf of your Majesties, and
accordingly requested them that they would see fit to allow us to land, since we had
no place to sleep that night save on the brigs and smaller boats in the middle of the
river and in these there was not even room enough for us to stand; as for returning
to our ships it was too late, since they had been left outside in the open sea. The
Indians on hearing this, replied that from where he was he might parley with them
as he would, but that neither he nor his men were to land on their shore and that
they would repel any attempt to do so. Immediately after this their bowmen began
to draw up in line so as to be prepared to shoot at us, at the same time threatening
us and bidding us depart. The day being much advanced (for the sun was on the
point of setting) the Captain decided to retire to the sandy beach which lay in front
of the town on the other side of the river, and there we landed and slept that night.
Early next morning a few Indians approached us in a canoe bringing several chickens
and enough maize to make a meal for a few men and bidding us accept these and
depart from their land. The Captain however spoke to them through the interpreters
giving them to understand that in no wise would he depart from that land before
he had found out the secret of it in order to be able to send your Majesties a true
account, and again begged them not to be offended at his project nor to deny him
entrance for they also were subjects of your Majesties. However they still forbade us
to make a landing and urged us to depart. On their return to the town the Captain
decided to move, and ordered one of his captains to go with two hundred men by a
path which had been discovered during the preceding night to lead to the village.

He himself embarked with some eighty men on the brigs and boats and took up his position in front of the town ready to land if they would permit him to do so: even as he approached he found the Indians in war paint and armed with bows and arrows, lances and small round shields, yelling that if we would not leave their land and wanted war it should begin at once, for they were men to defend their own homes. Cortés attempted to speak with them four times (your Majesties' notary who accompanied him witnessed to the same to the effect that he did not desire war) but seeing that it was the determined will of the Indians to resist his landing and that they were beginning to shoot their arrows against us, ordered the guns which we carried to be fired and an attack to be made. Immediately after the discharge of our guns and in the landing which followed a few of our men were wounded, but finally the fury of our onslaught and the sudden attack of our comrades who had come up in the rear of the enemy forced them to fly and abandon the village, which we accordingly took and settled ourselves in what appeared to be the strongest part of it. In the evening of the following day two Indians arrived from their chiefs bringing a few very inferior gold ornaments of small value and told the Captain that they offered him these in order that in exchange he might leave the land as it was before and do them no hurt. Cortés replied saying that as to doing them no hurt it pleased him well, but as to leaving the land they should know that from henceforward they must acknowledge as lords the greatest princes of the earth and must be their subjects and serve them; by doing which they would obtain many favours from your Majesties who would help them and defend them from their enemies. On this they replied that they were content to do this, but nevertheless still begged him to leave their land, and so we arrived at friendly terms.

Having patched up this friendship the Captain pointed out that the Spanish troops who were with him in the village had nothing to eat and had brought nothing from their ships. He therefore asked them to bring us sufficient food so long as we remained on land, which they promised to do on the following day, and so departed. But the next day and another passed without any food arriving so that we were faced with extreme shortness of provisions, and on the third day a few Spanish soldiers asked leave of the Captain to visit some of the near-lying farms and see if they could obtain some food. The Captain, seeing that the Indians were not coming as had been agreed, sent out four officers with more than two hundred men to search the neighbourhood for any provisions, and on their way they fell in with large numbers of Indians who shot at them with arrows so furiously that more than twenty Spaniards were wounded; and had not Cortés been quickly apprised of their danger and rescued them, as he succeeded in doing, there is little doubt that more than half the Spaniards would have been killed. In such wise we regained our camp, those that were wounded were attended to, and those weary with fighting were refreshed. Cortés perceiving the wrong the Indians had done him in pursuing the war instead of bringing provisions as they had promised, ordered ten horses and mules to be landed from among those which had been brought in the ships and everyone to keep a sharp look out, since he suspected that the Indians heartened by the success of the day before would advance to attack our camp with intent to do us harm. Everyone was thus on the alert and on the following day he sent other officers with three hundred men to where the battle had taken place to see if the Indians were still there or what had become of them: and very shortly afterwards he sent forward two more officers with the rearguard of a hundred men, he himself taking his way privily on horseback with ten mounted men to one side of the main path. Proceeding in this order the vanguard came upon a large body of Indians who were advancing to attack our camp, so that had we not gone out to meet them that day it is very possible we should have been hard put to it. And again the captain of artillery made certain representations (as your notary can bear witness) to the Indians whom he met in full war paint, crying to them by means of the native heralds and interpreters that we wanted not war but peace with them: their only answer was given not in words but in arrows which began to fall very thickly. The leading party was thus already engaged with the Indians when the two officers in command of the rearguard came up, and it was not until two hours later that Cortés arrived in a part of the wood where the Indians were beginning to encircle the Spaniards in the rear, and there he continued fighting against the Indians for about an hour; moreover such was their number that neither those among the Spaniards who were fighting on foot perceived those on horseback nor knew in what part of the field they were, nor could those on horseback so much as perceive one another as they surged hither and thither among the Indians. However, as soon as the Spaniards perceived the horsemen they attacked still more briskly and almost immediately the Indians were put to flight, the pursuit lasting half a league; whereupon Cortés seeing that the Indians were routed and that there was no more to be done (his men moreover being very wearied) gave orders that all should gather together in some farmhouses nearby, and on assembling there it was found that twenty men were wounded not one of whom, however, died nor of those wounded on the previous day. And so having attended to the wounded and laid them upon stretchers, we regained our camp taking with us two Indians who were captured there. These Cortés ordered to be loosed, and sent them with letters to the chieftains telling them that if they were willing to come to where he was he would pardon them the evil they had done and would be their friend. Accordingly the very same evening two Indians who purported to be chieftains arrived, declaring that they were very grieved at what had occurred and that the chieftains as a body begged him to pardon them and not punish them further for what was passed nor kill any more of their people, for over two hundred and twenty Indians had fallen; the past was past and henceforward they were willing to be subjects of that prince of whom he had spoken, and such they already held themselves to be, and bound themselves to do him service whenever anything in your Majesties' name should be desired of them.

In this wise they sat down and peace was made. The Captain then enquired of them by the interpreter what people it was who had fought in that battle, and they replied that tribes from eight provinces had joined together in that place and that according to the reckoning and lists which they possessed they would be about forty thousand men, for they could well reckon up to such a number. Thus your Majesties may truly believe that this battle was won rather by the will of God than by our own strength, for of what avail are four hundred (and we were no more) against forty thousand warriors?

FRENCH REACTIONS: CHAMPLAIN

Samuel de Champlain (1567–1635), was the chief French explorer in North America and a key founder of New France, in Canada. He made his first fur-trading expedition to the region in 1603 and subsequently participated in a number of other expeditions, sometimes joining in attacks on the Iroquois Indians by the Huron tribe. He wrote accounts of his travels in several editions, with a definitive edition completed in exile (during a period when the English had conquered New France) in 1632. In his later years, both before and after the English disruption, he served as virtual governor of New France, and he was buried in Quebec.

• • •

FRENCH ENCOUNTERS IN NORTH AMERICA

Now I will drop this discussion to return to the savages who had conducted me to the falls of the river Norumbegue, who went to notify Bessabez, their chief, and other savages, who in turn proceeded to another little river to inform their own, named Cabahis, and give him notice of our arrival.

The 16th of the month there came to us some thirty savages on assurances given them by those who had served us as guides. There came also to us the same day the above-named Bessabez with six canoes. As soon as the savages who were on land saw him coming, they all began to sing, dance, and jump, until he had landed. After-wards, they all seated themselves in a circle on the ground, as is their custom, when they wish to celebrate a festivity, or an harangue is to be made. Cabahis, the other chief, arrived also a little later with twenty or thirty of his companions, who with-drew to one side and greatly enjoyed seeing us, as it was the first time they had seen Christians. A little while after, I went on shore with two of my companions and two of our savages who served as interpreters. I directed the men in our barque to

From *Voyages of Samuel de Champlain, 1604–1618*, ed. W. L. Grant (New York: Charles Scribner's, 1907), 49–50, 71–74, 97–100.

approach near the savages, and hold their arms in readiness to do their duty in case they noticed any movement of these people against us. Bessabez, seeing us on land, bade us sit down, and began to smoke with his companions, as they usually do before an address. They presented us with venison and game.

I directed our interpreter to say to our savages that they should cause Bessabez, Cabahis, and their companions to understand that Sieur de Monts had sent me to them to see them, and also their country, and that he desired to preserve friendship with them and to reconcile them with their enemies, the Souriquois and Canadians, and moreover that he desired to inhabit their country and show them how to cultivate it, in order that they might not continue to lead so miserable a life as they were doing, and some other words on the same subject. This our savages interpreted to them, at which they signified their great satisfaction, saying that no greater good could come to them than to have our friendship, and that they desired to live in peace with their enemies, and that we should dwell in their land, in order that they might in future more than ever before engage in hunting beavers, and give us a part of them in return for our providing them with things which they wanted. After he had finished his discourse, I presented them with hatchets, paternosters, caps, knives, and other little knickknacks, when we separated from each other. All the rest of this day and the following night, until break of day, they did nothing but dance, sing, and make merry, after which we traded for a certain number of beavers. Then each party returned, Bessabez with his companions on the one side, and we on the other, highly pleased at having made the acquaintance of this people. . . .

The next day, the 21st of the month, Sieur de Monts determined to go and see their habitation. Nine or ten of us accompanied him with our arms; the rest remained to guard the barque. We went about a league along the coast. Before reaching their cabins, we entered a field planted with Indian corn in the manner before described. The corn was in flower, and five and a half feet high. There was some less advanced, which they plant later. We saw many Brazilian beans, and many squashes of various sizes, very good for eating; some tobacco, and roots which they cultivate, the latter having the taste of an artichoke. The woods are filled with oaks, nut-trees, and beautiful cypresses [read cedars], which are of a reddish color and have a very pleasant odor. There were also several fields entirely uncultivated, the land being allowed to remain fallow. When they wish to plant it, they set fire to the weeds, and then work it over with their wooden spades. Their cabins are round, and covered with heavy thatch made of reeds. In the roof there is an opening of about a foot and a half, whence the smoke from the fire passes out. We asked them if they had their permanent abode in this place, and whether there was much snow. But we were unable to ascertain this fully from them, not understanding their language, although they made an attempt to inform us by signs, by taking some sand in their hands, spreading it out over the ground, and indicating that it was of the color of our collars, and that it reached the depth of a foot. Others made signs that there was less, and gave us to understand also that the harbor never froze; but we were unable to ascertain whether the snow lasted long. I conclude, however, that this region is of moderate temperature, and the winter not severe. While we were there, there was a north-east storm, which lasted four days; the sky being so overcast that the sun hardly shone at all. It was very cold, and we were obliged to put on our greatcoats, which we had entirely left off. Yet I think the cold was accidental, as it is often experienced elsewhere out of season.

On the 23d of July, four or five seamen having gone on shore with some kettles to get fresh water, which was to be found in one of the sand-banks a short distance from our barque, some of the savages, coveting them, watched the time when our men went to the spring, and then seized one out of the hands of a sailor, who was the first to dip, and who had no weapons. One of his companions, starting to run after him, soon returned, as he could not catch him, since he ran much faster than himself. The other savages, of whom there were a large number, seeing our sailors running to our barque, and at the same time shouting to us to fire at them, took to flight. At the time there were some of them in our barque, who threw themselves into the sea, only one of whom we were able to seize. Those on the land who had taken to flight, seeing them swimming, returned straight to the sailor from whom they had taken away the kettle, hurled several arrows at him from behind, and brought him down. Seeing this, they ran at once to him, and despatched him with their knives. Meanwhile, haste was made to go on shore, and muskets were fired from our barque: mine, bursting in my hands, came near killing me. The savages, hearing this discharge of fire-arms, took to flight, and with redoubled speed when they saw that we had landed, for they were afraid when they saw us running after them. There was no likelihood of our catching them, for they are as swift as horses. We brought in the murdered man, and he was buried some hours later. Meanwhile, we kept the prisoner bound by the feet and hands on board of our barque, fearing that he might escape. But Sieur de Monts resolved to let him go, being persuaded that he was not to blame, and that he had no previous knowledge of what had transpired, as also those who, at the time, were in and about our barque. Some hours later there came some savages to us, to excuse themselves, indicating by signs and demonstrations that it was not they who had committed this malicious act, but others farther off in the interior. We did not wish to harm them, although it was in our power to avenge ourselves.

All these savages from the Island Cape wear neither robes nor furs, except very rarely: moreover, their robes are made of grasses and hemp, scarcely covering the body, and coming down only to their thighs. They have only the sexual parts concealed with a small piece of leather; so likewise the women, with whom it comes down a little lower behind than with the men, all the rest of the body being naked. Whenever the women came to see us, they wore robes which were open in front. The men cut off the hair on the top of the head like those at the river Choüacoet. I saw, among other things, a girl with her hair very neatly dressed, with a skin colored red, and bordered on the upper part with little shellbeads. A part of her hair hung down behind, the rest being braided in various ways. These people paint the face red, black, and yellow. They have scarcely any beard, and tear it out as fast as it grows. Their bodies are well-proportioned. I cannot tell what government they have, but I think that in this respect they resemble their neighbors, who have none at all. They know not how to worship or pray; yet, like the other savages, they have some superstitions, which I shall describe in their place. As for weapons, they have only pikes, clubs, bows and arrows. It would seem from their appearance that they have a good disposition, better than those of the north, but they are all in fact of no great worth. Even a slight intercourse with them gives you at once a knowledge of them. They are great thieves and, if they cannot lay hold of any thing with their hands, they try to do so with their feet, as we have oftentimes learned by experience. I am of opinion that, if they had any thing to exchange with us, they would not give themselves to thieving. They bartered away to us their bows, arrows, and quivers, for pins and buttons; and if they had had any thing else better they would have done the same with it. It is necessary to be on one's guard against this people, and live in a state of distrust of them, yet without letting them perceive it. They gave us a large quantity of tobacco, which they dry and then reduce to powder. When they eat Indian corn, they boil it in earthen pots, which they make in a way different from ours. They bray it also in wooden mortars and reduce it to flour, of which they then make cakes, like the Indians of Peru. . . .

Some eight or nine days after, while Sieur de Poutrincourt was walking out, as he had previously done, we observed the savages taking down their cabins and sending their women, children, provisions, and other necessaries of life into the woods. This made us suspect some evil intention, and that they purposed to attack those of our company who were working on shore, where they stayed at night in order to guard that which could not be embarked at evening except with much trouble. This proved to be true; for they determined among themselves, after all their effects had been put in a place of security, to come and surprise those on land, taking advantage of them as much as possible, and to carry off all they had. But, if by chance they should find them on their guard, they resolved to come with signs of friendship, as they were wont to do, leaving behind their bows and arrows.

Now, in view of what Sieur de Poutrincourt had seen, and the order which it had been told him they observed when they wished to play some bad trick, when we passed by some cabins, where there was a large number of women, we gave them some bracelets and rings to keep them quiet and free from fear, and to most of the old and distinguished men hatchets, knives, and other things which they desired. This pleased them greatly, and they repaid it all in dances, gambols, and harangues, which we did not understand at all. We went wherever we chose without their having the assurance to say anything to us. It pleased us greatly to see them show themselves so simple in appearance.

We returned very quietly to our barque, accompanied by some of the savages. On the way, we met several small troops of them, who gradually gathered together with their arms, and were greatly astonished to see us so far in the interior, and did not suppose that we had just made a circuit of nearly four or five leagues about their territory. Passing near us, they trembled with fear, lest harm should be done them, as it was in our power to do. But we did them none, although we knew their evil intentions. Having arrived where our men were working, Sieur de Poutrincourt inquired if everything was in readiness to resist the designs of this rabble.

He ordered everything on shore to be embarked. This was done, except that he who was making the bread stayed to finish a baking, and two others with him. They were told that the savages had some evil intent, and that they should make haste to embark the coming evening, since they carried their plans into execution only at night, or at daybreak, which in their plots is generally the hour for making a surprise.

Evening having come, Sieur de Poutrincourt gave orders that the shallop should be sent ashore to get the men who remained. This was done as soon as the tide would permit, and those on shore were told that they must embark for the reason assigned. This they refused in spite of the remonstrances that were made setting forth the risks they ran and the disobedience to their chief. They paid no attention to it, with the exception of a servant of Sieur de Poutrincourt, who embarked. Two others disembarked from the shallop and went to the three on shore, who had stayed to eat some cakes made at the same time with the bread.

But, as they were unwilling to do as they were told, the shallop returned to the vessel. It was not mentioned to Sieur de Poutrincourt, who had retired, thinking that all were on board.

The next day, in the morning, the 15th of October, the savages did not fail to come and see in what condition our men were, whom they found asleep, except one, who was near the fire. When they saw them in this condition, they came, to the number of four hundred, softly over a little hill, and sent them such a volley of arrows that to rise up was death. Fleeing the best they could towards our barque, shouting, "Help! they are killing us!" a part fell dead in the water; the others were all pierced with arrows, and one died in consequence a short time after. The savages made a desperate noise with roarings, which it was terrible to hear.

Upon the occurrence of this noise and that of our men, the sentinel, on our vessel, exclaimed, "To arms! They are killing our men!" Consequently, each one immediately seized his arms; and we embarked in the shallop, some fifteen or sixteen of us, in order to go ashore. But, being unable to get there on account of a sand-bank between us and the land, we threw ourselves into the water, and waded from this bank to the shore, the distance of a musket-shot. As soon as we were there, the savages, seeing us within arrow range, fled into the interior. To pursue them was fruitless, for they are marvellously swift. All that we could do was to carry away the dead bodies and bury them near a cross, which had been set up the day before, and then to go here and there to see if we could get sight of any of them. But it was time wasted, therefore we came back. Three hours afterwards, they returned to us on the sea-shore. We discharged at them several shots from our little brass cannon; and, when they heard the noise, they crouched down on the ground to avoid the fire. In mockery of us, they beat down the cross and disinterred the dead, which displeased us greatly, and caused us to go for them a second time; but they fled, as they had done before. We set up again the cross, and reinterred the dead, whom they had thrown here and there amid the heath, where they kindled a fire to burn them. We returned without any result, as we had done before, well aware that there was scarcely hope of avenging ourselves this time, and that we should have to renew the undertaking when it should please God.

AZTEC REACTIONS: *THE BROKEN SPEARS*

The Broken Spears **is a compilation of a number of Aztec and other Indian records from the sixteenth century, assembled in the 1960s by a Spanish scholar. The materials include codices originally written in the Nahuat language (one of the Aztec-stem languages) that escaped the general Spanish destruction of native-language documents, plus later recollections written by Indians in Spanish. The reassembly of the materials in rough chronological order, by the book's editor, permits unique insight into one whole side of this fateful encounter.**

• • •

Then Motecuhzoma gave the messengers his final orders. He said to them: "Go now, without delay. Do reverence to our lord the god. Say to him: 'Your deputy, Motecuhzoma, has sent us to you. Here are the presents with which he welcomes you home to Mexico.' " . . .

One by one they did reverence to Cortes by touching the ground before him with their lips. They said to him: "If the god will deign to hear us, your deputy Motecuhzoma has sent us to render you homage. He has the City of Mexico in his care. He says: 'The god is weary.' "

Then they arrayed the Captain in the finery they had brought him as presents. With great care they fastened the turquoise mask in place, the mask of the god with its crossband of quetzal feathers. A golden earring hung down on either side of this mask. They dressed him in the decorated vest and the collar woven in the petatillo style—the collar of *chalchihuites,* with a disk of gold in the center.

Next they fastened the mirror to his hips, dressed him in the cloak known as "the ringing bell" and adorned his feet . . . In his hand they placed the shield with

From *The Broken Spears* by Miguel Leon-Portilla. Expanded and Updated Edition © 1992 by Miguel Leon-Portilla. Reprinted by permission of Beacon Press, Boston.

its fringe and pendant of quetzal feathers, its ornaments of gold and mother-of-pearl. Finally they set before him the pair of black sandals. As for the other objects of divine finery, they only laid them out for him to see.

The Captain asked them: "And is this all? Is this your gift of welcome? Is this how you greet people?"

They replied: "This is all, our lord. This is what we have brought you."

Then the Captain gave orders, and the messengers were chained by the feet and by the neck. When this had been done, the great cannon was fired off. The messengers lost their senses and fainted away. They fell down side by side and lay where they had fallen. But the Spaniards quickly revived them: they lifted them up, gave them wine to drink and then offered them food.

The Captain said to them: "I have heard that the Mexicans are very great warriors, very brave and terrible. If a Mexican is fighting alone, he knows how to retreat, turn back, rush forward and conquer, even if his opponents are ten or even twenty. But my heart is not convinced. I want to see it for myself. I want to find out if you are truly that strong and brave."

Then he gave them swords, spears and leather shields. He said: "It will take place very early, at daybreak. We are going to fight each other in pairs, and in this way we will learn the truth. We will see who falls to the ground!"

They said to the Captain: "Our lord, we were not sent here for this by your deputy Motecuhzoma! We have come on an exclusive mission, to offer you rest and repose and to bring you presents. What the lord desires is not within our warrant. If we were to do this, it might anger Motecuhzoma, and he would surely put us to death." . . .

Then they left in great haste and continued to the City of Mexico. They entered the city at night, in the middle of the night.

The messengers went to the House of the Serpent, and Motecuhzoma arrived. The two captives were then sacrificed before his eyes: their breasts were torn open, and the messengers were sprinkled with their blood. This was done because the messengers had completed a difficult mission: they had seen the gods, their eyes had looked on their faces. They had even conversed with the gods!

When the sacrifice was finished, the messengers reported to the king. They told him how they had made the journey, and what they had seen, and what food the strangers ate. Motecuhzoma was astonished and terrified by their report, and the description of the strangers' food astonished him above all else.

He was also terrified to learn how the cannon roared, how its noise resounded, how it caused one to faint and grow deaf. The messengers told him: "A thing like a ball of stone comes out of its entrails: it comes out shooting sparks and raining fire. The smoke that comes out with it has a pestilent odor, like that of rotten mud. This odor penetrates even to the brain and causes the greatest discomfort. If the cannon is aimed against a mountain, the mountain splits and cracks open. If it is aimed against a tree, it shatters the tree into splinters. This is a most unnatural sight, as if the tree had exploded from within."

The messengers also said: "Their trappings and arms are all made of iron. They dress in iron and wear iron casques on their heads. Their swords are iron; their bows are iron; their shields are iron; their spears are iron. Their deer carry them on their backs wherever they wish to go. These deer, our lord, are as tall as the roof of a house.

"The strangers' bodies are completely covered, so that only their faces can be seen. Their skin is white, as if it were made of lime. They have yellow hair, though some of them have black. Their beards are long and yellow, and their moustaches are also yellow. Their hair is curly, with very fine strands.

"As for their food, it is like human food. It is large and white, and not heavy. It is something like straw, but with the taste of a cornstalk, of the pith of a cornstalk. It is a little sweet, as if it were flavored with honey; it tastes of honey, it is sweet-tasting food. . . .

When Motecuhzoma heard this report, he was filled with terror. It was as if his heart had fainted, as if it had shriveled. It was as if he were conquered by despair.

While the Spaniards were in Tlaxcala, a great plague broke out here in Tenochtitlan [the Aztec capital, now Mexico City]. It began to spread during the thirteenth month and lasted for seventy days, striking everywhere in the city and killing a vast number of our people. Sores erupted on our faces, our breasts, our bellies; we were covered with agonizing sores from head to foot.

The illness was so dreadful that no one could walk or move. The sick were so utterly helpless that they could only lie on their beds like corpses, unable to move their limbs or even their heads. They could not lie face down or roll from one side to the other. If they did move their bodies, they screamed with pain.

A great many died from this plague, and many others died of hunger. They could not get up to search for food, and everyone else was too sick to care for them, so they starved to death in their beds.

Some people came down with a milder form of the disease; they suffered less than the others and made a good recovery. But they could not escape entirely. Their looks were ravaged, for wherever a sore broke out, it gouged an ugly pockmark in the skin. And a few of the survivors were left completely blind.

CHAPTER 15

THE SPREAD OF SLAVERY AND THE ATLANTIC SLAVE TRADE

This chapter deals with the unprecedented transatlantic trade in African slaves, which began in the sixteenth century and continued for three hundred years. This trade had a host of impacts in world history and in the development of all the regions involved. It represented one of the chief examples of the widening range of international contact, as the commercial motives of one society and the labor needs of another reached deep into the personal lives of many people in yet a third civilization.

The capture and purchase of millions of Africans, who were sent as slaves to South and North America and the Caribbean by European slave traders from the sixteenth century until the early nineteenth, mainly for plantation work, constitute one of the key episodes of early modern world history. The result weakened internal trade balance and population size in West Africa, though individual merchants, rulers, and whole states might have benefited. The profits helped fuel Europe's commercial economy. The spread of slavery and the impact of diverse African cultures left durable marks on the Americas.

Slavery was an old institution. Most river valley civilizations had held slaves, often captives in war. Greek and Roman societies had depended heavily on slaves, who provided domestic service but also did vital, brutal work in mines and on agricultural estates. Roman use of slaves for agricultural labor indeed provided the clearest prior precedent for the new slavery of the early modern period. Although some civilizations largely eliminated slavery—it had become rare in China, India, and even Western Europe—others continued the practice. The Arab civilization relied extensively on slaves either captured or purchased from various areas, including Europe and Africa; a regular trade in African slaves from the east coast of Africa to the Middle East developed before the early modern period and continued beyond it, involving millions of people though over an extended period of time. Slavery also existed within Africa, again involving captures in war and the ensuing hereditary status of their descendants. Though the numbers of slaves were relatively small, Africa obviously contained a preestablished group of slave merchants.

Nevertheless, the volume, speed, and displacement of the new transatlantic slave trade had no precedent. Europeans began capturing African slaves, indeed, even in the fifteenth century for use on sugar plantations established in the islands they had just seized in the Atlantic, including the Azores and the Canaries. This prefigured the larger system introduced into the Americas. Europeans in the Americans hoped to find gold and other easy wealth. In fact, they discovered the profitability of some mining and also export agricultural production. Yet local labor was scarce, in large part because the majority of the American Indian population died off in contact with European diseases. Africa, newly explored by European voyagers, seemed to provide the answer, in a context where Europeans now ruled the seas.

Here, clearly, was a radical new international contact, which affected Europe, Africa, and the Americas. On the one hand, the impact on Africa has been much debated. Population loss and diversion of trade away from the Muslim world, as transatlantic commerce replaced trans-Saharan, definitely made a difference. On the other hand, strong governments persisted in Africa as did older cultural forms such as polytheism and expressive art. The huge transformation of Africa, resulting from European imperialism, came later. Europe was most obviously affected by the money its merchants made, which increased wealth and capital—helping to fuel further economic change, including ultimately the industrial revolution. More subtly, European views of Africans, though not yet as thoroughly racist as they would become in the nineteenth century, became hardened in ways that may be affecting world history still. The Americas received a massive new labor force at a time when Native American populations were decreasing because of disease. This enhanced the American ability to generate exports such as sugar for the world economy. Latin America and the Caribbean, particularly, where three quarter of the slaves were sent, were profoundly altered by this economy. In addition to their labor, Africans brought their cultures and their experience of the slave voyage and slavery itself, which would contribute vital ingredients to the history of the Americas from this time onward.

Finally, of course, there was the impact on the slaves themselves, for whom this was an unquestionably dreadful experience. Deaths and mistreatment on the slave ships were compounded by harsh treatment in the Americas—though there were different levels of awfulness. The fear and indignity of the experience affected surviving slaves more perhaps than the physical torment. Here, too, were important ingredients of early modern world history that would have ongoing impacts on the large African American minorities in the Caribbean and on both American continents.

The new slave trade and resultant American slavery raise a host of comparative questions. Scholars have assessed this slave system in light of earlier precedents, showing the important new features involved. Latin American and North American slavery can usefully be compared: Latin America harbored more slaves, generally in worse conditions, but with a less racist culture developing. A crucial initial comparison more simply involves perspectives on the African slave trade itself. In the following selections, a European slave trader presents his observations, indirectly highlighting some of the attitudes that would allow him to accept his active commercial role. Then, from a hundred years later, in the eighteenth century, an African former slave presents his view of the same process. We are able to juxtapose two different vantage points, that of the actors and that of the acted upon, to determine how they evaluated the same basic historical process and what larger consequences their perspectives suggest.

European accounts of the trade tended to be matter-of-fact, a bit sanctimonious. It was revealing that European intellectuals did not write much on the topic, unlike earlier authors such as Aristotle, who openly defended slavery. What explains European willingness to participate in this trade in people? How could the traders justify their calling to themselves? African accounts, though rare, present a very different picture. Is there any overlap with the ways Europeans explained the trade? What are the main disagreements between merchants and slaves over the treatment involved?

The slave trade constitutes one of those common events with at least two radically different sides, the winners and the losers. Comparison can help sort out what really happened, while sharpening the analysis of the experience of both parties.

Questions

1. What did Europeans offer Africans in the slave trade? How were slaves obtained from the African interior? Do Barbot and Equiano agree on the methods used?
2. Do the methods help explain why European traders were so nonchalant about their own involvement?
3. What impact did Europeans think they were having on Africa itself, including African states and rulers?
4. How did Christianity interact with the slave trade? Does Barbot reflect Christian criteria in his slave trader account?
5. Were the European traders aware of slaves as humans? Could they distinguish good from bad treatment? How did they understand and deal with the reactions of slaves themselves to the experience of capture and trade?
6. Are there any similarities between European and African descriptions of the trade? How did Africans react to European technology and material culture? What was the role of beliefs in magic? Did Africans have the fears of Europeans that the slave traders claimed? What motives did they ascribe to Europeans?
7. Slave traders and slaves both were potentially partisan. Does either of the following accounts seem exaggerated? Does Barbot show any signs of distorting

his descriptions to make himself look good, or does he not believe he has to bother? Does Equiano exaggerate problems or ignore benefits?

For Further Discussion

1. Which account most helps you to understand the slave trade and the experiences involved? Which is more informative? Which provides the better basis for assessing the effects of the slave trade?

2. Judging by Barbot's discussion, were slave traders racist? Scholars debate whether Western racism helped cause the European treatment of slaves or was a result of it. What does Barbot's account suggest? Is this a useful question for the early modern period?

3. What impact would the trade and the passage across the Atlantic have in the later lives of the slaves and their descendants? Does either of the accounts in this chapter suggest probable impacts?

THE SLAVE TRADER'S VIEW: JOHN BARBOT

John Barbot was an employee of a French slave trading company. He made several trips to West Africa in the 1670s and 1680s. His account is unusually detailed, suggesting an active intellect, whatever his other attributes were. And he clearly harbored some internal ambivalence about the treatment he saw and participated in—though it's possible to argue that he did almost nothing about his qualms.

• • •

Goods for Trade

. . . the French import common red, blue, and scarlet cloth, silver and brass rings, or bracelets, chains, little bells, false crystal, ordinary and coarse hats; Dutch pointed knives, pewter dishes, silk sashes, with false gold and silver fringes; blue serges, French paper, steels to strike fire . . . brass kettles, yellow amber, maccatons, that is, beads of two sorts, pieces of eight of the old stamp, some silver pieces of 28 sols value, either plain or gilt, Dutch cutlaces, strait and bow'd, clouts, galet, martosdes, two other sorts of beads, of which the Blacks make necklaces for women, white sugar, musket balls, iron nails, shot, white and red frize, looking-glasses in gilt and plain frames, cloves, cinnamon, scissors, needles, coarse thread of sundry colours, but chiefly red, yellow, and white . . . Particularly at Goeree, the company imports

From Elysbeth Doman, ed., *Documents Illustrative of the History of the Slave Trade to America* (Washington, D.C.: Carnegie Institute, 1930), 282–85, 286–90, 293, 294–95.

ten thousand or more every year, of those which are made in the province of Brittany, all short and thin, which is called in London narrow flat iron, or half flat iron of Sweden; but each bar shortened, or cut off at one end to about 16 or 18 inches, so that about eighty of these bars weigh a ton, or twenty hundred weight English. It is to be observ'd, that such voyage-iron, as called in London, is the only sort and size used throughout all Nigritia, Guinea, and West-Ethiopia, in the way of trade. Lastly, a good quantity of Coignac brandy, both in hogsheads and rundlets, single and double, the double being eight, the single four gallons.

The principal goods the French have in return for these commodities from the Moors and Blacks, are slaves, gold-dust, elephants teeth, bees-wax, dry and green hides, gum-arabick, ostrich feathers, and several other odd things. . . .

These people no way differ from the Foules; and there the French have built a small fort, mounted with eight guns, at a place called Gallem, or Galama, 120 leagues higher up the country than the Terrier-rouge, of which I shall speak in its place. There they buy slaves in considerable numbers . . . which they convey down to their factory every year. . . .

On the rivers Morsil and des Maringuins, at Mambrin, on the north-side of the Senega, and at Lametor, or Brak, on the south-side of the same, the French purchase a considerable number of slaves . . . The country of little Brak affords them slaves. . . .

At the villages of Bozaert, or Bozar, and Caye, near the factory they have slaves. . . .

Slaves

Those sold by the Blacks are for the most part prisoners of war, taken either in fight, or pursuit, or in the incursions they make into their enemies' territories; others stolen away by their own countrymen; and some there are, who will sell their own children, kindred, or neighbours. This has been often seen, and to compass it, they desire the person they intend to sell, to help them in carrying something to the factory by way of trade, and when there, the person so deluded, not understanding the language, is sold and deliver'd up as a slave, notwithstanding all his resistance, and exclaiming against the treachery. I was told of one, who design'd to sell his own son, after that manner; but he understanding French, dissembled for a while, and then contriv'd it so cunningly as to persuade the French, that the old man was his slave, and not his father, by which means he deliver'd him up into captivity; and thus made good the Italian Proverb, *A furbo furbo e mezzo*; amounting to as much as, Set a thief to catch a thief, or Diamond cuts Diamond. However, it happened soon after, that the fellow was met by some of the principal Blacks of the country, as he was returning home from the factory, with the goods he had receiv'd for the sale of his father, all which they took away, and order'd him to be sold for a slave.

The kings are so absolute, that upon any slight pretence of offences committed by their subjects, they order them to be sold for slaves, without regard to rank, or possession. Thus a Marabout, or Priest, as I believe, was sold to me at Goeree, by the Alcaide of Rio Fresco, by special order of king Damel, for some misdemeanors. I took notice, that this Priest was above two months aboard the ship, before he would speak one word; but I shall say more of him in another place.

Abundance of little Blacks of both sexes are also stolen away by their neighbours, when found abroad on the roads, or in the woods; or else in the Cougans, or corn-fields, at the time of the year, when their parents keep them there all day, to scare away the devouring small birds, that come to feed on the millet, in swarms, as has been said above.

In times of dearth and famine, abundance of those people will sell themselves, for a maintenance, and to prevent starving. When I first arriv'd at Goeree, in December, 1681, I could have bought a great number, at very easy rates, if I could have found provisions to subsist them; so great was the dearth then, in that part of Nigritia.

To conclude, some slaves are also brought to these Blacks, from very remote inland countries, by way of trade, and sold for things of very inconsiderable value; but these slaves are generally poor and weak, by reason of the barbarous usage they have had in traveling so far, being continually beaten, and almost famish'd; so inhuman are the Blacks to one another. . . .

The great wealth of the Fantineans [Fantyn, a West African country] makes them so proud and haughty, that an European trading there must stand bare to them. . . . A good slave sells there, as at all other trading places on the Gold-Coast westward, at the rate of one Benda of gold, which is two ounces. . . .

In time of war, it [Accra] furnishes so great a number of slaves, that it amounts to, at least, as many as are sold all along the rest of the coast. This country is continually in war with some of the neighbouring nations, which are very populous, and from whom they take very many prisoners, most of whom, they sell to the Europeans. The slaves are commonly purchased for coesvelt linen, slyziger, lywat, sheets, sayes, perpetuanas, firelocks, powder, brandy, bugles, knives, top-sails, nican-nees, and other goods, according to the times. The natives carry those commodities to Abonee market, which is four leagues beyond Great Acra northward, for the Accanez people, who resort thither three times a week; as do other Blacks from the country of Abonee, Aquamboe, and Aquimera, who all buy those goods of the Acra men, at such rates as they think fit to put upon them, the king refusing to permit those strangers to go down themselves to the European warehouses on the coast; for which reason, those Blacks pay often double the value for what they buy. The king has there an overseer, who has the power to set the price on all goods, between buyer and seller. This general overseer is assisted by several officers to act for him, where he cannot be present himself. Those employments are much sought after there, as being both honourable and advantageous; because, both the king's and their perquisites are very considerable. . . .

The king and chief Blacks of Acra were, in my time, very rich in slaves and gold, through the vast trade the natives drove with the Europeans on the coast, and the neighbouring nations up the country. . . .

The trade of slaves is in a more peculiar manner the business of kings, rich men, and prime merchants, exclusive of the inferior sort of Blacks.

These slaves are severely and barbarously treated by their masters, who subsist them poorly, and beat them inhumanly, as may be seen by the scabs and wounds on the bodies of many of them when sold to us. They scarce allow them the least rag to cover their nakedness, which they also take off from them when sold to Europeans; and they always go bare-headed. The wives and children of slaves, are also slaves to the master under whom they are married; and when dead, they never bury them, but cast out the bodies into some by place, to be devoured by birds, or beasts of prey.

This barbarous usage of those unfortunate wretches, makes it appear, that the fate of such as are bought, and transported from the coast to America, or other parts of the world, by Europeans, is less deplorable, than that of those who end their days in their native country; for aboard ships all possible care is taken to preserve and subsist them for the interest of the owners, and when sold in America, the same motive ought to prevail with their masters to use them well, that they may live the longer, and do them more service. Not to mention the inestimable advantage they may reap, of becoming christians, and saving their souls, if they make a true use of their condition. . . .

I also remember, that I once, among my several runs along that coast, happened to have aboard a whole family, man, wife, three young boys, and a girl, bought one after another, at several places; and cannot but observe here, what mighty satisfaction those poor creatures expressed to be so come together again, tho' in bondage. For several days successively they could not forbear shedding tears of joy, and continually embracing and caressing one another; which moving me to compassion, I ordered they should be better treated aboard than commonly we can afford to do it, where there are four or five hundred in a ship; and at Martinico, I sold them all together to a considerable planter, at a cheaper rate than I might have expected, had they been disposed of severally; being informed of that gentleman's good-nature, and having taken his word, that he would use that family as well as their circumstances would permit, and settle them in some part by themselves.

I have elsewhere spoke of the manner of valuing and rating the slaves among the Blacks, and shall conclude this chapter, which proves to be one of the longest, with an odd remark; which is, That many of those slaves we transport from Guinea to America are prepossessed with the opinion, that they are carried like sheep to the slaughter, and that the Europeans are fond of their flesh; which notion so far prevails with some, as to make them fall into a deep melancholy and despair, and to refuse all sustenance, tho' never so much compelled and even beaten to oblige them to take some nourishment: notwithstanding all which, they will starve to death; whereof I have had several instances in my own slaves both aboard and at Guadalupe. And tho' I must say I am naturally compassionate, yet have I been necessitated sometimes to cause the teeth of those wretches to be broken, because they would not open their mouths, or be prevailed upon by any intreaties to feed themselves; and thus have forced some sustenance into their throats. . . .

. . . This regulation being agreed on by the king and factors, the goods are brought ashore, and carried on men's backs to the French house, whither the king himself repairs, or else sends his factors or agents. When he has chosen what he thinks fit, the nobility or prime persons pick out what they have occasion for, and after them every other Black; and then every buyer, king or subject, pays the factor the number of slaves, according to the amount of the goods each of them has so pitched upon.

As the slaves come down to Fida from the inland country, they are put into a booth, or prison, built for that purpose, near the beach, all of them together; and when the Europeans are to receive them, they are brought out into a large plain, where the surgeons examine every part of every one of them, to the smallest member, men and women being all stark naked. Such as are allowed good and sound, are set on one side, and the others by themselves; which slaves so rejected are there called Mackrons, being above thirty five years of age, or defective in their limbs, eyes or teeth; or grown grey, or that have the venereal disease, or any other imperfection. These being so set aside, each of the others, which have passed as good, is marked on the breast, with a red-hot iron, imprinting the mark of the French, English, or Dutch companies, that so each nation may distinguish their own, and to prevent their being chang'd by the natives for worse, as they are apt enough to do. In this particular, care is taken that the women, as tenderest, be not burnt too hard. . . .

If there happens to be no stock of slaves at Fida, the factor must trust the Blacks with his goods, to the value of a hundred and fifty, or two hundred slaves; which goods they carry up into the inland, to buy slaves, at all the markets, for above two hundred leagues up the country, where they are kept like cattle in Europe; the slaves sold there being generally prisoners of war, taken from their enemies, like other booty, and perhaps some few sold by their own countrymen, in extreme want, or upon a famine; as also some as a punishment of heinous crimes: tho' many Europeans believe that parents sell their own children, men their wives and relations, which, if it ever happens, is so seldom, that it cannot justly be charged upon a whole nation, as a custom and common practice. . . .

As to the slaves, and the trade of them, whereof I have before spoke at large, it will be proper to observe here, that commonly the slaves we purchase at Fida and Ardra, are brought down to the coast from several countries, two and three hundred leagues up the inland; where the inhabitants are lusty, strong, and very laborious people: thence it is, that tho' they are not so black and fine to look at as the North-Guinea and Gold-Coast Blacks, yet are they fitter for the American plantations, than any others; especially in the sugar islands, where they require more labour and strength than in the other colonies of Europeans, at which the Fida and Ardra slaves are found, by constant experience, to hold out much longer, and with less detriment to themselves, than the other slaves transported thither from the other above-mentioned parts of Guinea. One thing is to be taken notice of by sea-faring men, that these Fida and Ardra slaves are of all the others, the most apt to revolt aboard ships, by a conspiracy carried on amongst themselves; especially such as are brought down to Fida, from very remote inland countries, who easily draw others into their plot: for being used to see men's flesh eaten in their own country, and publick markets held for that purpose, they are very full of the notion, that we buy and transport them to the same purpose; and will therefore watch all opportunities to deliver themselves, by assaulting a ship's crew, and murdering them all, if possible: whereof, we have almost every year some instances, in one European ship or other, that is filled with slaves.

THE AFRICAN SLAVE EXPERIENCE: OLAUDAH EQUIANO

Most slaves, needless to say, had no opportunity to write about their experience. Olaudah Equiano's account is unusual because of its existence, but the experience reported is not necessarily unusual. Equiano was born in a Nigerian village, Isseke, in 1745. He was kidnapped and in 1756 taken to Barbados and then to Virginia. Finally able to buy his freedom from his Quaker master, he went to England in 1767. He became active in the antislavery movement, publishing his memoirs in 1788 as a protest against the whole institution of slavery. His writings were among the first antislavery books by an ex-slave.

• • •

My father, besides many slaves, had a numerous family, of which seven lived to grow up, including myself and sister, who was the only daughter. As I was the youngest of the sons, I became, of course, the greatest favorite with my mother, and was always with her; and she used to take particular pains to form my mind. I was trained up from my earliest years in the art of war: my daily exercise was shooting and throwing javelins, and my mother adorned me with emblems, after the manner

From *The Interesting Narrative of the Life of Olaudah Equiano*, ed., Robert J. Allison (Boston: Bedford Books, 1995), 46–58. (Follows the first American printing [New York, 1791]). Includes modernized spelling.

of our greatest warriors. In this way I grew up till I had turned the age of eleven, when an end was put to my happiness in the following manner: Generally, when the grown people in the neighborhood were gone far in the fields to labor, the children assembled together in some of the neighboring premises to play; and commonly some of us used to get up a tree to look out for any assailant, or kidnapper, that might come upon us—for they sometimes took those opportunities of our parents' absence, to attack and carry off as many as they could seize. One day as I was watching at the top of a tree in our yard, I saw one of those people come into the yard of our next neighbor but one, to kidnap, there being many stout young people in it. Immediately on this I gave the alarm of the rogue, and he was surrounded by the stoutest of them, who entangled him with cords, so that he could not escape, till some of the grown people came and secured him. But, alas! ere long it was my fate to be thus attacked, and to be carried off, when none of the grown people [was] nigh.

One day, when all our people were gone out to their works as usual, and only I and my dear sister were left to mind the house, two men and a woman got over our walls, and in a moment seized us both, and, without giving us time to cry out, or make resistance, they stopped our mouths, and ran off with us into the nearest wood. Here they tied our hands, and continued to carry us as far as they could, till night came on, when we reached a small house, where the robbers halted for refreshment, and spent the night. We were then unbound, but were unable to take any food; and, being quite overpowered by fatigue and grief, our only relief was some sleep, which allayed our misfortune for a short time. The next morning we left the house, and continued travelling all the day. For a long time we had kept the woods, but at last we came into a road which I believed I knew. I had now some hopes of being delivered; for we had advanced but a little way before I discovered some people at a distance, on which I began to cry out for their assistance; but my cries had no other effect than to make them tie me faster and stop my mouth, and then they put me into a large sack. They also stopped my sister's mouth, and tied her hands; and in this manner we proceeded till we were out of sight of these people. When we went to rest the following night, they offered us some victuals, but we refused it; and the only comfort we had was in being in one another's arms all that night, and bathing each other with our tears. But alas! we were soon deprived of even the small comfort of weeping together.

The next day proved a day of greater sorrow than I had yet experienced; for my sister and I were then separated, while we lay clasped in each other's arms. It was in vain that we besought them not to part us; she was torn from me, and immediately carried away, while I was left in a state of distraction not to be described.

From the time I left my own nation, I always found somebody that understood me till I came to the sea coast. The languages of different nations did not totally differ, nor were they so copious as those of the Europeans, particularly the English.

They were therefore easily learned; and, while I was journeying thus through Africa, I acquired two or three different tongues. In this manner I had been travelling for a considerable time, when, one evening, to my great surprise, whom should I see brought to the house where I was but my dear sister! As soon as she saw me, she gave a loud shriek, and ran into my arms—I was quite overpowered; neither of us could speak, but, for a considerable time, clung to each other in mutual embraces, unable to do anything but weep. Our meeting affected all who saw us; and, indeed, I must acknowledge, in honor of those sable destroyers of human rights, that I never met with any ill treatment, or saw any offered to their slaves, except tying them, when necessary, to keep them from running away.

When these people knew we were brother and sister, they indulged us to be together; and the man, to whom I supposed we belonged, lay with us, he in the middle, while she and I held one another by the hands across his breast all night; and thus for a while we forgot our misfortunes, in the joy of being together; but even this small comfort was soon to have an end; for scarcely had the fatal morning appeared when she was again torn from me forever! I was now more miserable, if possible, than before. The small relief which her presence gave me from pain, was gone, and the wretchedness of my situation was redoubled by my anxiety after her fate, and my apprehensions lest her sufferings should be greater than mine, when I could not be with her to alleviate them. . . .

The first object which saluted my eyes when I arrived on the coast, was the sea, and a slave ship, which was then riding at anchor, and waiting for its cargo. These filled me with astonishment, which was soon converted into terror, when I was carried on board. I was immediately handled, and tossed up to see if I were sound, by some of the crew; and I was now persuaded that I had gotten into a world of bad spirits, and that they were going to kill me. Their complexions, too, differing so much from ours, their long hair, and the language they spoke (which was very different from any I had ever heard), united to confirm me in this belief. Indeed, such were the horrors of my views and fears at the moment, that, if ten thousand worlds had been my own, I would have freely parted with them all to have ex- changed my condition with that of the meanest slave in my own country. When I looked round the ship too, and saw a large furnace of copper boiling, and a multi- tude of black people of every description chained together, every one of their coun- tenances expressing dejection and sorrow, I no longer doubted of my fate; and, quite overpowered with horror and anguish, I fell motionless on the deck and fainted. When I recovered a little, I found some black people about me, who I believed were some of those who had brought me on board, and had been receiving their pay; they talked to me in order to cheer me, but all in vain. I asked them if we were not to be eaten by those white men with horrible looks, red faces, and long hair. They told me I was not, and one of the crew brought me a small portion of spirituous liquor in a wine glass; but being afraid of him, I would not take it out of his hand.

One of the blacks therefore took it from him and gave it to me, and I took a little down my palate, which, instead of reviving me, as they thought it would, threw me into the greatest consternation at the strange feeling it produced, having never tasted any such liquor before. Soon after this, the blacks who brought me on board went off, and left me abandoned to despair.

I now saw myself deprived of all chance of returning to my native country, or even the least glimpse of hope of gaining the shore, which I now considered as friendly; and I even wished for my former slavery in preference to my present situation, which was filled with horrors of every kind, still heightened by my ignorance of what I was to undergo. I was not long suffered to indulge my grief; I was soon put down under the decks, and there I received such a salutation in my nostrils as I had never experienced in my life: so that, with the loathsomeness of the stench, and crying together, I became so sick and low that I was not able to eat, nor had I the least desire to taste anything. I now wished for the last friend, death, to relieve me; but soon, to my grief, two of the white men offered me eatables; and, on my refusing to eat, one of them held me fast by the hands, and laid me across, I think, the windlass, and tied my feet, while the other flogged me severely. I had never experienced anything of this kind before, and, although not being used to the water, I naturally feared that element the first time I saw it, yet, nevertheless, could I have got over the nettings, I would have jumped over the side, but I could not; and besides, the crew used to watch us very closely who were not chained down to the decks, lest we should leap into the water; and I have seen some of these poor African prisoners most severely cut, for attempting to do so, and hourly whipped for not eating. This indeed was often the case with myself.

In a little time after, amongst the poor chained men, I found some of my own nation, which in a small degree gave ease to my mind. I inquired of these what was to be done with us? They gave me to understand, we were to be carried to these white people's country to work for them. I then was a little revived, and thought, if it were no worse than working, my situation was not so desperate; but still I feared I should be put to death, the white people looked and acted, as I thought, in so savage a manner; for I had never seen among any people such instances of brutal cruelty; and this not only shown towards us blacks, but also to some of the whites themselves. One white man in particular I saw, when we were permitted to be on deck, flogged so unmercifully with a large rope near the foremast, that he died in consequence of it; and they tossed him over the side as they would have done a brute. This made me fear these people the more; and I expected nothing less than to be treated in the same manner. I could not help expressing my fears and apprehensions to some of my countrymen; I asked them if these people had no country, but lived in this hollow place (the ship)? They told me they did not, but came from a distant one. "Then," said I, "how comes it in all our country we never heard of them?" They told me because they lived so very far off. I then asked where were their women? had they any like themselves? I was told they had. "And why," said I, "do we not see them?" They answered, because they were left behind. I asked how the vessel could go? They told me they could not tell; but that there was cloth put upon the masts by the help of the ropes I saw, and then the vessel went on; and the white men had some spell or magic they put in the water when they liked, in order to stop the vessel. I was exceedingly amazed at this account, and really thought they were spirits. I therefore wished much to be from amongst them, for I expected they would sacrifice me; but my wishes were vain—for we were so quartered that it was impossible for any of us to make our escape.

While we stayed on the coast I was mostly on deck; and one day, to my great astonishment, I saw one of these vessels coming in with the sails up. As soon as the whites saw it, they gave a great shout, at which we were amazed; and the more so, as the vessel appeared larger by approaching nearer. At last, she came to an anchor in my sight, and when the anchor was let go, I and my countrymen who saw it, were lost in astonishment to observe the vessel stop—and were now convinced it was done by magic. Soon after this the other ship got her boats out, and they came on board of us, and the people of both ships seemed very glad to see each other. Several of the strangers also shook hands with us black people, and made motions with their hands, signifying I suppose, we were to go to their country, but we did not understand them.

At last, when the ship we were in, had got in all her cargo, they made ready with many fearful noises, and we were all put under deck, so that we could not see how they managed the vessel. But this disappointment was the least of my sorrow. The stench of the hold while we were on the coast was so intolerably loathsome, that it was dangerous to remain there for any time, and some of us had been permitted to stay on the deck for the fresh air; but now that the whole ship's cargo were confined together, it became absolutely pestilential. The closeness of the place, and the heat of the climate, added to the number in the ship, which was so crowded that each had scarcely room to turn himself, almost suffocated us. This produced copious perspirations, so that the air soon became unfit for respiration, from a variety of loathsome smells, and brought on a sickness among the slaves, of which many died—thus falling victims to the improvident avarice, as I may call it, of their purchasers. This wretched situation was again aggravated by the galling of the chains, now became insupportable, and the filth of the necessary tubs, into which the children often fell, and were almost suffocated. The shrieks of the women, and the groans of the dying, rendered the whole a scene of horror almost inconceivable. Happily perhaps, for myself, I was soon reduced so low here that it was thought necessary to keep me almost always on deck; and from my extreme youth I was not put in fetters. In this situation I expected every hour to share the fate of my companions, some of whom were almost daily brought upon deck at the point of death, which I began to hope would soon put an end to my miseries. Often did I think many of the inhabitants of the deep much more happy than myself. I envied them the freedom they enjoyed, and as often wished I could change my condition for theirs. Every circumstance I met with, served only to render my state more painful, and heightened my apprehensions, and my opinion of the cruelty of the whites.

One day they had taken a number of fishes; and when they had killed and satisfied themselves with as many as they thought fit, to our astonishment who were on deck, rather than give any of them to us to eat, as we expected, they tossed the remaining fish into the sea again, although we begged and prayed for some as well as we could, but in vain; and some of my countrymen, being pressed by hunger, took an opportunity, when they thought no one saw them, of trying to get a little privately; but they were discovered, and the attempt procured them some very severe floggings.

One day, when we had a smooth sea and moderate wind, two of my wearied countrymen who were chained together (I was near them at the time), preferring death to such a life of misery, somehow made through the nettings and jumped into the sea; immediately, another quite dejected fellow, who, on account of his illness, was suffered to be out of irons, also followed their example; and I believe many more would very soon have done the same, if they had not been prevented by the ship's crew, who were instantly alarmed. Those of us that were the most active, were in a moment put down under the deck; and there was such a noise and confusion amongst the people of the ship as I never heard before, to stop her, and get the boat out to go after the slaves. However, two of the wretches were drowned, but they got the other, and afterwards flogged him unmercifully, for thus attempting to prefer death to slavery. In this manner we continued to undergo more hardships than I can now relate, hardships which are inseparable from this accursed trade. Many a time we were near suffocation from the want of fresh air, which we were often without for whole days together. This, and the stench of the necessary tubs, carried off many. . . .

At last we came in sight of the island of Barbados, at which the whites on board gave a great shout, and made many signs of joy to us. We did not know what to think of this; but as the vessel drew nearer, we plainly saw the harbor, and other ships of different kinds of sizes, and we soon anchored amongst them, off Bridge-town. Many merchants and planters now came on board, though it was in the evening. They put us in separate parcels, and examined us attentively. They also made us jump, and pointed to the land, signifying we were to go there. We thought by this, we should be eaten by these ugly men, as they appeared to us; and, when soon after we were all put down under the deck again, there was much dread and trembling among us, and nothing but bitter cries to be heard all the night from these apprehensions, insomuch, that at last the white people got some old slaves from the land to pacify us. They told us we were not to be eaten, but to work, and were soon to go on land, where we should see many of our country people. This report eased us much. And sure enough, soon after we were landed, there came to us Africans of all languages.

We were conducted immediately to the merchant's yard, where we were all pent up together, like so many sheep in a fold, without regard to sex or age. As every object was new to me, everything I saw filled me with surprise. What struck me first, was, that the houses were built with bricks and stories, and in every other respect different from those I had seen in Africa; but I was still more astonished on seeing people on horseback. I did not know what this could mean; and, indeed, I thought these people were full of nothing but magical arts. While I was in this astonishment, one of my fellow prisoners spoke to a countryman of his, about the horses, who said they were the same kind they had in their country. I understood them, though they were from a distant part of Africa; and I thought it odd I had not seen any horses there; but afterwards, when I came to converse with different Africans, I found they had many horses amongst them, and much larger than those I then saw.

We were not many days in the merchant's custody, before we were sold after their usual manner, which is this: On a signal given (as the beat of a drum), the buyers rush at once into the yard where the slaves are confined, and make choice of that parcel they like best. The noise and clamor with which this is attended, and the eagerness visible in the countenances of the buyers, serve not a little to increase the apprehension of terrified Africans, who may well be supposed to consider them as the ministers of that destruction to which they think themselves devoted. In this manner, without scruple, are relations and friends separated, most of them never to see each other again.

I remember, in the vessel in which I was brought over, in the men's apartment, there were several brothers, who, in the sale, were sold in different lots; and it was very moving on this occasion, to see and hear their cries at parting. O, ye nominal Christians! might not an African ask you—Learned you this from your God, who says unto you, Do unto all men as you would men should do unto you? Is it not enough that we are torn from our country and friends, to toil for your luxury and lust of gain? Must every tender feeling be likewise sacrificed to your avarice? Are the dearest friends and relations, now rendered more dear by their separation from their kindred, still to be parted from each other, and thus prevented from cheering the gloom of slavery, with the small comfort of being together, and mingling their sufferings and sorrows? Why are parents to lose their children, brothers their sisters, or husbands their wives? Surely, this is a new refinement in cruelty, which, while it has no advantage to atone for it, thus aggravates distress, and adds fresh horrors even to the wretchedness of slavery.

CHAPTER 16

FORCED LABOR

Latin America and Russia

This chapter deals with the spread of forced labor systems in Latin America and Russia during the early modern period. The growth of slavery, of course, was one such system. But millions of people were also involved in compulsory labor arrangements that were different from slavery but almost as galling. The causes of these expanding systems had some relationship to the causes of transatlantic slavery, but there were other, local factors involved as well, making comparison both necessary and complex.

The expansion of forced labor began in many cases in the sixteenth century, and it continued well into the nineteenth. It lasted longer than the new slavery, on the whole, and important remnants exist in parts of the world even today. The basic idea of forced labor involved requiring work performance and sometimes a share of the proceeds of other work, while preventing freedom of movement of the workers.

Forms of forced labor other than slavery had flourished before. During the postclassical centuries, manorialism existed in Western Europe and Japan, and it developed in the Middle East. In this system serfs did most of the agricultural work. They turned over part of their produce to their landlords in return for protection and access to the land; they also did some work service on land the lords owned outright. The serfs were not slaves; they could not be bought or sold and, if they fulfilled their obligations, they and their heirs could not be removed from the land. But they also could not legally leave the land or sell it.

What happened in the early modern period was an extension of this serfdom pattern—even as it was declining in Western Europe—to new parts of the world, under harsher conditions and with more explicit attempts to generate greater production. Latin America and Russia were two key areas where forced labor spread. In Latin America the systems were novel because they were imposed by Europeans or Americans of European origin as part of larger colonial controls. In Russia, growing serfdom replaced a pattern of generally free peasant ownership and production that had prevailed in earlier centuries. Forced labor systems began to spread to other areas, such as India and Southeast Asia, by the end of the early modern period.

The basic cause of the expansion of forced labor in the early modern period was the growing impact of a form of capitalism and world market pressures. European merchants and local owners both sought to assure cheap production of minerals and foods, to increase chances for profit in the export trade. Forced labor in this sense was another result of growing international commercial contacts, inspiring new interests in pushing workers to produce more and trying to control them for maximum benefit to the owners of land and mines.

Importation of African slaves into the Americas was the most famous instance of this development. But the use of Indian labor in Latin America, both for mines and for agricultural estates, was also widespread. Estate systems such as the *encomienda* and the *hacienda* required work services from Indians for long periods of time, though there was no outright slavery. Spanish estate owners gained government grants or bought the power to compel labor; because formal colonial governments were weak, in effect the landlords faced few restraints in their treatment of workers save the very real possibility of escape. In a situation where the supply of labor was scant, because of the ravages of European diseases on the native population, forced labor seemed an essential basis for the production of goods designed for export and colonial profit (such as the silver mines of the Andes) and for the foods needed to supply commercial and colonial government centers.

Forced labor in Russia from the sixteenth century onward originated on quite different bases, for Russia was not explicitly a colonial territory; most of the workers pressed into service were themselves Russian. Nor did Russia feature a lively export economy. Rather, the growing power of landlords and, often, the growing misery of many ordinary peasants, generated a very strict system of some outright slavery and even more serfdom, in which serfs owed produce and labor to the lords (much as in the case of the Indians in Latin America) and could be punished by them for a variety of real or imagined crimes. It originated in the sixteenth century not because of export opportunities, but as a means of controlling a large land mass in the interests of the czar (who owned many serf estates) and the aristocracy. Russian aristocrats gave their loyalty and service to the czar in return for a free rein over the serfs.

Russian slavery declined in the seventeenth century and was outlawed in the early eighteenth. But serfdom became more widespread, and laws steadily expanded the power landlords had over serfs. In the eighteenth century, when Russia began to import more equipment and luxury items from Western Europe and needed to sell more grain to pay for them, serfdom began to serve export needs as well. By this time Russia's forced labor, despite its entirely separate origins, began to have contact with the growing system of international trade. Russian estate owners wanted to increase their grain production for export to Western Europe, to obtain the money needed for vital imports. Through this whole period, from the eighteenth century onward, the Russian czarist state claimed great power but in fact left control of the serfs on private estates in the hands of the landlords—which proved to be a good way of buying loyalty and service from the upper class.

General factors both in Russian and in Latin American estate systems thus involved relatively weak states (with often grandiose claims) that could not control local labor arrangements and depended on landlords to provide the governing structure, which would also help cement the landlords' own loyalty. They involved power hunger and greed on the part of the landlords, who typically scorned their serfs and workers. They involved the pressures and opportunities from the world economy, where there were profits to be made from spurring production and keeping labor costs low.

But particular circumstances played a role too. In Latin America, Spaniards' disdain for Indians, their belief that Indians were idolatrous and lazy, made it easier to impose harsh conditions (though some Catholic missionaries resisted, which helped prevent outright enslavement). Russian serfdom, in contrast, was perhaps the most onerous labor system ever imposed by elites on their own people. Its origins were political, though economics added a further motivation later on. Comparison of labor systems in two very different areas of the world thus provides an opportunity to assess the impact of one of the great international forces of the early modern period—the growing export trade. But the different individual causes and settings invite attention to contrasts and nuances as well.

Serfs, like slaves, rarely wrote accounts of their own lives. The description of the labor system in Latin America is taken from the account of a British traveler, Thomas Gage. The British at the time were hostile to Spain as an imperial rival, and to Catholicism; Gage, by the time he wrote, was an ardent Protestant. Russia's slavery and serfdom can be captured a bit more directly; contracts exist from the seventeenth century showing how poor people sold themselves as slaves, and government laws in principle described how serfs could be treated. But, as in Latin America, serfs themselves rarely offered any direct discussion of their conditions, and the views of outside observers provide vital information and insight. In the second document a Russian nobleman, Alexander Radishchev, writes about his investigations of peasant conditions as he traveled through the empire. Radishchev was a reformer, convinced that Russia should become more like the West; he felt that what he learned about serfs made it obvious that the whole system should be abolished in favor of peasant ownership of the land. His book was banned by the czarist government until 1905.

Though from different specific eras, both sources describe the widespread labor systems of two key early modern societies and both attempt to look at their systems objectively. Nonetheless, the use of sources requires care. The documents presented in this chapter come from hostile witnesses: an anti-Spanish English traveler and a Russian reformist, neither of them serfs. Both observers were hostile to the systems they described. Can their assessments nevertheless be used to describe basic features of Latin American and Russian labor and social structure? Is Gage's status as an outside observer helpful in getting to the heart of the colonial labor system? Is Radishchev an outsider to the same extent?

Questions

1. How did Gage explain the motives of Spanish treatment of Indian labor? How did Radishchev explain Russian landlord motivation? Which account more clearly suggests the reasons these labor systems developed?
2. How do both Gage and Radishchev describe the real feelings of the laborers and serfs?
3. What do Gage and Radishchev suggest about the role of Christianity in helping to consolidate the labor systems in Russia and Latin America?
4. What were the differences between serfdom in Latin America and Russia, and outright slavery? Was one system harsher than the other? How did Russian and Latin American estate owners keep their laborers in line?
5. What are the potential biases in Gage's and Radishchev's accounts? Does either account seem exaggerated? What other evidence would be desirable in assessing the labor systems?
6. What were the key differences between the two systems, given the fact that in Latin America Europeans imposed conditions on a native population, whereas in Russia the people involved shared the same race, language, and religion?
7. Which had more autonomy: peasant villages in Russia or Indian villages in Latin America?

For Further Discussion

1. Given the main differences between Latin America and Russia in the early modern period—one a colonial territory with its native population decimated by disease, the other an expanding military power—how can the remarkable similarities in labor systems be explained? Is it easier to understand the causes of forced labor in the Americas than in Russia?
2. Were the labor systems economically productive (and what do Gage and Radishchev think about this)? Why might the systems be kept even if they were not maximally productive?
3. What were the relative advantages to landlords of slavery and of harsh serfdom?
4. Why did the systems mostly gain ground in different places (more slavery in Brazil and the Caribbean, for example, more serfdom in the Andes and Mexico)?
5. Peasant rebellions occurred in both societies (Tupac Amaru in parts of Latin

America, 1780–81 and the Pugachev rising in Russia in 1775, both put down). Why was rebellion not even more common?

ESTATE LABOR IN LATIN AMERICA: THOMAS GAGE

Thomas Gage (1603–56) was a British traveler and businessman who was able to travel in Central America because he was for a time a Dominican monk. His account focuses on the period 1625–1637 in what is now Guatemala and in Mexico. Gage later converted back to Protestantism and expressed hatred of his former religion as well as disdain for Spanish colonial conditions.

• • •

The Spaniards that live about that country (especially the farmers of the Valley of Mixco, Pinola, Petapa, Amatitlán, and those of the Sacatepéquez) allege that all their trading and farming is for the good of the commonwealth, and therefore, whereas there are not Spaniards enough for so ample and large a country to do all their work, and all are not able to buy slaves and Blackamoors, they stand in need of the Indians' help to serve them for their pay and hire. Therefore, a partition of Indian laborers is made every Monday, or Sunday in the afternoon, to the Spaniards, according to the farms they occupy, or according to their several employments, calling, and trading with mules, or any other way. For such and such a district there is named an officer, who is called *juez repartidor,* who according to a list made of every farm, house, and person, is to give so many Indians by the week. And here is a door opened to the President of Guatemala, and to the judges, to provide well for their menial servants, whom they commonly appoint for this office, which is thus performed by them. They name the town and place of their meeting upon Sunday or Monday, to the which themselves and the Spaniards of that district do resort.

The Indians of the several towns are ordered to have in readiness so many laborers as the Court of Guatemala hath appointed to be weekly taken out of such a town. These are conducted by an Indian officer to the town of general meeting. They come thither with their tools, their spades, shovels, bills, or axes, with their provision of victuals for a week (which are commonly some dry cakes of maize, puddings of *frijoles,* or French beans, and a little chile or biting long pepper, or a bit of cold meat for the first day or two) and with beds on their backs (which is only a coarse woollen mantle to wrap about them when they lie on the bare ground). Then they are shut up in the town-house, some with blows, some with spurnings, some with boxes on the ear, if presently they go not in.

From *Thomas Gage's Travels in the New World*, ed. J. Eric Thompson (Norman: University of Oklahoma Press, 1958), 216–19, 230–32. Reprinted by permission of the publisher.

Now all being gathered together, and the house filled with them, the *juez repartidor,* or officer, calls by the order of the list such and such a Spaniard, and also calls out of the house so many Indians as by the Court are commanded to be given him (some are allowed three, some four, some ten, some fifteen, some twenty, according to their employments) and delivereth unto the Spaniard his Indians, and so to all the rest, till they be all served. When they receive their Indians, they take from them their tools or mantles, to make sure that they do not run away; and for every Indian delivered unto them, they give unto the *juez repartidor,* or officer, for his fees, half a real, which is threepence. Yearly this amounts to a great deal of money, for some officers make a partition or distribution of four hundred, some of two hundred, some of three hundred Indians every week, and carrieth home with him so many half hundred reals for one or half a day's work.

If complaint be made by any Spaniard that such and such an Indian ran away and served him not the week past, the Indian is brought and securely tied to a post by his hands in the market-place, and there is whipped upon his bare back. But if the poor Indian complain that the Spaniards cozened and cheated him of his shovel, axe, bill, mantle, or wages, no justice shall be executed against the cheating Spaniard, neither shall the Indian be righted, though it is true the order runs equally in favor of both Indian and Spaniard.

Thus the poor Indians are sold for threepence apiece for a whole week's slavery, and are not permitted to go home at nights unto their wives, though their work lie not above a mile from the town where they live. Nay, some are carried ten or twelve miles from their home, and they may not return till Saturday night late, and must that week do whatsoever their master pleaseth to command them. The wages appointed them will scarce find them meat and drink, for they are not allowed a real a day, which is but sixpence, but for six days' work and diet they are to have five reals, which is half a crown, and with that they are to find themselves. This same order is observed in the city of Guatemala, and towns of Spaniards, where every family that wants the service of an Indian or Indians, though it be but to fetch water and wood on their backs or to go on errands, is allowed the like service from the nearest Indian towns.

It would grieve a Christian's heart to see how some cruel Spaniards in that week's service wrong and abuse those poor wretches. Some visit their wives at home, whilst their poor husbands are digging and delving; others whip them for their slow working; others wound them with their swords, or break their heads for some reasonable and well-grounded answer in their own behalf; others steal from them their tools; others cheat them of half. Some even cheat them of all their wages, alleging their service cost them half a real, and yet their work is not well performed. I knew some who made a common practice of this, when their wheat was sown, and they had little for the Indians to do. They would have as many as were due unto their farm, and on Monday and Tuesday would make them cut and bring on their backs as much wood as they needed all that week. Then at noon, on Wednesday, knowing the great desire of the Indians to go home to their wives, for the which they would give anything, they would say unto them: "What will you give me now, if I let you go home to do your own work?" Whereunto the Indians would joyfully answer, some that they would give a real, others two reals. This the Spaniards would take and send them home, and so they would have much work done, wood to serve their house a week, and as much money as would buy them meat and cacao for chocolate for two weeks. Thus from the poor Indians do those unconscionable Spaniards practice a cheap and lazy way of living. Others will sell them away for that week unto a neighbor who needs laborers, demanding reals apiece for every Indian, which he that buyeth them will be sure to defray out of their wages.

Similarly, are they in a slavish bondage and readiness for all passengers and travellers, who in any town may demand as many Indians as he needs to go to the next town with his mules, or to carry on their backs a heavy burden as he shall need. Then at the journey's end he will pick some quarrel with them, and so send them back with blows and stripes without any pay at all. They will make those wretches carry on their backs a *petaca,* or leathern trunk, and chest of above a hundredweight a whole day, nay, some two or three days together. This they do by tying the chest on each side with ropes, having a broad leather in the middle which they cross over the forepart of their head, or over their forehead, hanging thus the weight upon their heads and brows. By the end of the journey this makes the blood stick in the foreheads of some, galling and pulling off the skin, and marking them in the fore-top of their heads. So these carriers, who are called *tamemes,* are easily known in a town by their baldness, that leather girt having worn off all their hair. Despite these hard usages, yet those poor people make shift to live amongst the Spaniards, but with anguish of heart they still cry out to God for justice, and for liberty.

Their only comfort is in their priests and friars, who many times do quiet them when they would rise up in mutiny, and for their own ends do often prevail over them with fair and cunning persuasions, to bear and suffer for God's sake, and for the good of the commonwealth, that hard task and service which is laid upon them. And though in all seasons, wet and dry, cold and hot, and in all ways, plain and mountainous, green and dirty, dusty and stony, they must perform this hard service to their commanding masters, their apparel and clothing is but such as may cover the nakedness of their body, nay, in some it is such torn rags as will not cover half their nakedness. . . .

Besides this civility of justice amongst them, the Indians live as in other civil and politic and well-governed commonwealths, for in most of their towns there are some that profess such trades as are practiced among Spaniards. There are amongst them smiths, tailors, carpenters, masons, shoemakers, and the like. It was my fortune to set upon a hard and difficult building in a church of Mixco, where I desired to make a very broad and capacious vault over the chapel, which was the harder to be finished in a round circumference, because it depended upon a triangle. Yet for this work I sought none but Indians, some of the town, some from other places, and they made it so complete that the best and skillfullest workmen among the Spaniards had enough to wonder at it. So are most of their churches vaulted on the top, and all by Indians.

In my time they build a new cloister in the town of Amatitlán, which they finished with many arches of stone both in the lower walks and in the upper galleries, with as much perfection as the best cloister of Guatemala built by the Spaniard. Were they more encouraged by the Spaniards and taught better principles both for soul and body, doubtless they would among themselves make a very good commonwealth. They are much inclined to painting, and most of the pictures and altars of the country towns are their workmanship. . . .

In addition, those who belong to the service of the priest's house are exempt from the Spaniards' service. The priest hath change of servants by the week, and they take their turns so that they may have a week or two to spare to do their own work. If it be a great town, he hath three cooks allowed him; if a small town, but two. The cooks are men who take turns in serving. For any occasion of feasting, all come. So likewise the priest hath two or three more (whom they call *chahal*) as butlers. They keep whatsoever provisions is in the house under lock and key, and give to the cook what the priest appointeth to be dressed for his dinner or supper. They keep the table-cloths, napkins, dishes, and trenchers, and lay the cloth, and take away, and wait at table. The priest hath besides three or four, and in great towns half a dozen, boys to do his errands, wait at table, and sleep in the house all the week by their turns. They and the cooks and butlers dine and sup constantly in the priest's house and at his charge. He hath also at dinner and supper times the attendance of some old women (who also take their turns) to oversee half a dozen young maids who meet next to the priest's house to make him and his family *tortillas* or cakes of maize, which the boys bring hot to the table by half a dozen at a time.

Besides these servants, if the priest has a garden, he is allowed two or three gardeners, and for his stable, at least half a dozen Indians, who morning and evening are to bring him *zacate* (as they call it) or herb and grass for his mules or horses. These do not diet in the house, but the grooms of the stable, who come at morning, noon, and evening (and therefore are three or four to change) or at any time that the priest will ride out, and the gardeners, when they are at work, dine and sup at the priest's charges. So sometimes in great towns the priest has above a dozen to feed and provide for. . . .

If there be any fishing place near the town, the priest also is allowed three or four, and in some places half a dozen, Indians to fish for him. Besides the offerings in the church, and many other offerings which they bring whensoever they come to speak to the priest or to confess with him, or for a saint's feast to be celebrated, and besides their tithes of everything, there is a monthly maintenance in money allowed the priest, and brought to him by the *alcaldes,* or mayors, and jurats. This he has to write a receipt for in a book of the town's expenses. This maintenance, although it be allowed by the Spanish magistrate and paid in the King's name for the preaching of the Gospel, yet it comes out of the poor Indians' purses and labor, and is either gathered about the town, or taken out of the tribute which they pay unto the King, or from a common plot of ground which with the help of all is sowed and the produce gathered in and sold for that purpose.

RUSSIAN SERFDOM: ALEXANDER RADISHCHEV

This description was written in the late eighteenth century, just beyond the end of the early modern period. It reflects the conditions and intensification of Russian serfdom during the century as a whole. It also reflects the powerful impact on Russia of contact until the West accelerated by Peter the Great earlier in the century with more conservative purposes in mind (see chapter 18) Radishchev (1749–1802) was a Russian nobleman. Like many in his class, he had traveled in the West. Unlike most, who defended serfdom if they thought about it at all, he viewed Western standards of free labor and greater legal equality as far preferable to those of Russia. He was one of the first Russian intellectuals to attack domestic conditions on the strength of Western standards—a tendency that would spread (see chapter 23). Radishchev used his travels to observe serfs' conditions firsthand, and he claims to report their behaviors and beliefs directly. His work ran counter to the increasingly repressive trends of the later part of Catherine the Great's regime, when Western ideas began to be regarded as subversive and when landlords gained even greater power to punish recalcitrant serfs directly.

• • •

I suppose it is all the same to you whether I traveled in winter or in summer. Maybe both in winter and in summer. It is not unusual for travelers to set out in sleighs and to return in carriages. In summer. The corduroy road tortured my body; I climbed out of the carriage and went on foot. While I had been lying back in the carriage, my thoughts had turned to the immeasurable vastness of the world. By spiritually leaving the earth I thought I might more easily bear the jolting of the carriage. But spiritual exercises do not always distract us from our physical selves; and so, to save my body, I got out and walked. A few steps from the road I saw a peasant ploughing a field. The weather was hot. I looked at my watch. It was twenty

Reprinted by permission of the publisher from *A Journey from St. Petersburg to Moscow* trans. Leo Wiener, ed. R. P. Thaler (Cambridge, Mass.: Harvard University Press, 1958), 58–60. Copyright © 1958 by the President and Fellows of Harvard College.

minutes before one. I had set out on Saturday. It was now Sunday. The ploughing peasant, of course, belonged to a landed proprietor, who would not let him pay a commutation tax [*obrok*]. The peasant was ploughing very carefully. The field, of course, was not part of his master's land. He turned the plough with astonishing ease.

"God help you," I said, walking up to the ploughman, who, without stopping, was finishing the furrow he had started. "God help you," I repeated.

"Thank you, sir," the ploughman said to me, shaking the earth off the plough-share and transferring it to a new furrow.

"You must be a Dissenter, since you plough on a Sunday."

"No, sir, I make the true sign of the cross," he said, showing me the three fingers together. "And God is merciful and does not bid us starve to death, so long as we have strength and a family."

"Have you no time to work during the week, then, and can you not have any rest on Sundays, in the hottest part of the day, at that?"

"In a week, sir, there are six days, and we go six times a week to work on the master's fields; in the evening, if the weather is good, we haul to the master's house the hay that is left in the woods; and on holidays the women and girl go walking in the woods, looking for mushrooms and berries. God grant," he continued, making the sign of the cross, "that it rains this evening. If you have peasants of your own, sir, they are praying to God for the same thing."

"My friend, I have no peasants, and so nobody curses me. Do you have a large family?"

"Three sons and three daughters. The eldest is nine years old."

"But how do you manage to get food enough, if you have only the holidays free?"

"Not only the holidays: the nights are ours, too. If a fellow isn't lazy, he won't starve to death. You see, one horse is resting; and when this one gets tired, I'll take the other; so the work gets done."

"Do you work the same way for your master?"

"No, Sir, it would be a sin to work the same way. On his fields there are a hundred hands for one mouth, while I have two for seven mouths: you can figure it out for yourself. No matter how hard you work for the master, no one will thank you for it. The master will not pay our head tax; but, though he doesn't pay it, he doesn't demand one sheep, one hen, or any linen or butter the less. The peasants are much better off where the landlord lets them pay a commutation tax without the interference of the steward. It is true that sometimes even good masters take more than three rubles a man; but even that's better than having to work on the master's fields. Nowadays it's getting to be the custom to let villages to tenants, as they call it. But we call it putting our heads in a noose. A landless tenant skins us peasants alive; even the best ones don't leave us any time for ourselves. In the winter he won't let us do any carting of goods and won't let us go into town to work; all our work has to be for him, because he pays our head tax. It is an invention of the Devil to turn your peasants over to work for a stranger. You can make a complaint against a bad steward, but to whom can you complain against a bad tenant?"

"My friend, you are mistaken; the laws forbid them to torture people."

"Torture? That's true; but all the same, sir, you would not want to be in my hide." Meanwhile the ploughman hitched up the other horse to the plough and bade me goodbye as he began a new furrow.

The words of this peasant awakened in me a multitude of thoughts. I thought especially of the inequality of treatment within the peasant class. I compared the crown peasants with the manorial peasants. They both live in villages; but the former pay a fixed sum, while the latter must be prepared to pay whatever their master demands. The former are judged by their equals; the latter are dead to the law, except, perhaps, in criminal cases. A member of society becomes known to the government protecting him, only when he breaks the social bonds, when he becomes a criminal! This thought made my blood boil.

Tremble, cruelhearted landlord! on the brow of each of your peasants I see your condemnation written. . . .

The story of a certain landed proprietor proves that man for the sake of his personal advantage forgets humanity towards his fellow man, and that to find an example of hard-heartedness we need not go to far-off countries nor seek miracles through thrice-nine lands; they take place before our eyes in our own country.

A certain man who, as they say in the vernacular, did not make his mark in the government service, or who did not wish to make it there, left the capital, acquired a small village of one or two hundred souls, and determined to make his living by agriculture. He did not apply himself to the plough but intended most vigorously to make all possible use of the natural strength of his peasants by applying them to the cultivation of the land. To this end he thought it the surest method to make his peasants resemble tools that have neither will nor impulse; and to a certain extent he actually made them like the soldiers of the present time who are commanded in a mass, who move to battle in a mass, and who count for nothing when acting singly. To attain his end he took away from his peasants the small allotment of plough land and the hay meadows which noblemen usually give them for their bare maintenance, as a recompense for all the forced labor which they demand from them. In a word, this nobleman forced all his peasants and their wives and children to work every day of the year for him. Lest they should starve, he doled out to them a definite quantity of bread, known by the name of monthly doles. Those who had no families received no doles, but dined according to the Lacedaemonian custom, together, at the manor, receiving thin cabbage soup on meat days, and on fast days bread and kvas, to fill their stomachs. If there was any real meat, it was only in Easter Week.

These serfs also received clothing befitting their condition. Their winter boots, that is, bast shoes, they made for themselves; leggings they received from their master; while in summer they went barefooted. Naturally these serfs had no cows, horses, ewes, or rams. Their master did not withhold from these serfs the permission, but the means to have them. Whoever was a little better off and ate sparingly, kept a few chickens, which the master sometimes took for himself, paying for them as he pleased.

With such an arrangement it is not surprising that agriculture in Mr. So-and-So's village was in a flourishing condition. Where the crops were a failure elsewhere, his grain showed a fourfold return; when others had a good crop, his grain had a tenfold return or better. In a short time he added to his two hundred souls another two hundred as victims of his greed, and, proceeding with them just as with the first, he increased his holdings year after year, thus multiplying the number of those groaning in his fields. Now he counts them by the thousand and is praised as a famous agriculturist.

Barbarian! You do not deserve to bear the name of citizen. What good does it do the country that every year a few thousand more bushels of grain are grown, if those who produce it are valued on a par with the ox whose job it is to break the heavy furrow? Or do we think our citizens happy because our granaries are full and their stomachs empty? Or because one man blesses the government, rather than thousands? The wealth of this bloodsucker does not belong to him. It has been acquired by robbery and deserves severe punishment according to law. Yet there are people who, looking at the rich fields of this hangman, cite him as an example of perfection in agriculture. And you wish to be called merciful, and you bear the name of guardians of the public good! Instead of encouraging such violence, which you regard as the source of the country's wealth, direct your humane vengeance against this enemy of society. Destroy the tools of his agriculture, burn his barns, silos, and granaries, and scatter their ashes over the fields where he practiced his tortures; stigmatize him as a robber of the people, so that everyone who sees him may not only despise him but shun his approach to avoid infection from his example.

CHAPTER 17

EMPIRES AND BUREAUCRACIES

The great innovations in Western Europe and the Atlantic economy, including vital changes in Africa and the Americas, did not monopolize world history in the early modern period. Independent developments were occurring in Asia as well, where the emergence or consolidation of vast, land-based empires and complex cities and economies operated without significant interaction with the West. Asian societies continued to differ, though, so comparison must elicit both the features common to the political operation of empires and the differences in procedures and beliefs that distinguished the major centers.

Formal government almost always involved at least limited bureaucracies, from the Mesopotamian states onward. Rulers had to have some functionaries to help carry out their orders, administer justice, and provide information about what was going on outside the palace. More elaborate states, obviously, had larger bureaucracies. During the early modern period, the establishment of a number of new empires created the need to form and regulate bureaucracies in a number of parts of the world. Ultimately, some of the most important innovations in bureaucratic development occurred in the kingdoms of Western Europe, where kings began to establish more specialized government units and recruit bureaucrats who owed their loyalty to the state rather than to some aristocratic family. During much of the period, however, it was the great Asian empires that continued to have the largest bureaucratic structures; that helps to explain why they could rule such vast territories and arrange for the provisioning of the world's largest cities, such as Constantinople.

Two leading bureaucratic empires were the Chinese and the Ottoman. China had pioneered in the establishment of careful bureaucracies, complete with formal training, the elaborate Confucian ethic of loyalty and service, and recruitment through testing. The basic Chinese system went back to the Han dynasty, in the classical period (see chapter 3). China rebuilt its empire under the Ming dynasty (1368–1644), after the period of Mongol control. Then when the Ming declined, as Chinese dynasties were wont to do, a new dynasty, the Qing, took over, displaying considerable initial vigor.

The Ottoman Empire was formed in the fourteenth–fifteenth centuries, as Turkish invaders penetrated the Middle East. It was consolidated after the Ottoman conquest of the Byzantine Empire, which was highlighted by the capture of Constantinople in 1453.

Ottoman bureaucracy was newer, but it was partly modeled on what had been learned from the Byzantine and Arab empires that had come before. It also relied on Islam to encourage religious loyalty to the sultan and utilized some older Islamic principles of potential leadership (see chapter 7).

Comparing the two systems is complex, in terms of the documents in this chapter, because the comments on seventeenth-century Chinese bureaucracy, during the period when the Ming dynasty was declining and about to give way to another imperial house, are critical, whereas the Ottoman document is prescriptive. Both authors were intimately involved with bureaucratic life, but from different vantage points of bitterness and aspiration. More generally, Confucian commentators easily found fault with what Chinese bureaucrats were doing; the Ottoman document, in contrast, is based on the hope that its positive principles could be carried out.

Despite the different tones of the documents, some patterns are clear. Criticism and self-serving recommendations both reflect basic goals and standards. Both systems had to worry about the loyalty of bureaucrats; they tried to deal with abuses of power, cruelty, and corruption. These are standard concerns in any bureaucratic structure. Many ideals were shared. But Chinese and Ottoman approaches differed subtly. With its long Confucian tradition, Chinese comment placed greater stress on education and regulation; the Ottomans relied more on the self-control of the powerful first ministers—the viziers. Did basic philosophy play a role here, with China relying more on personal ethical training and the Ottomans hoping for religious inspiration? Subtle differences in bureaucratic culture relate to actual variations in function and functioning. The Ottoman and Chinese states claimed different degrees of power, for example over the economy. They had different systems of recruitment and hierarchy.

Both systems provided bureaucrats with great power, for the emperor and the sultan claimed absolute authority and their chief ministers eagerly cloaked themselves in this mantle. Yet both systems claimed to keep the interests of the masses of people in mind. They can be interpreted in terms of how well they performed this function—in addition to how they defined and handled power itself.

Ottoman and Chinese bureaucracies both functioned well through much of the early modern period. There is no question, however, that control over the viziers and other principal officials began to falter in the Ottoman realm before the Chinese system systematically weakened (seventeenth versus late eighteenth century). The Ottoman Empire reached its height around 1600. Heavily dependent on conquests to reward key officials and also provide military troops, it began to encounter growing difficulties, particularly after a final attempt to push further into Western Europe failed in the 1680s. Thereafter, the empire, though still potent, clearly deteriorated, and one sign of the decline was the increasing corruption and autonomy of regional officials. By the nineteenth century the empire's political woes caused it to be labeled the "sick man" of Europe. China's empire was still operating effectively in the eighteenth century, when emperors still disdainfully brushed aside European pleas for trade access. It was true that, after about 1750, Chinese bureaucracy itself began to become more cumbersome and less effective. Paperwork piled up, inhibiting effective policy, and by the later nineteenth century members of the world's greatest bureaucratic tradition were receiving guidance from European officials on how to operate an efficient system.

These developments were in the future. Comparing Ottoman and Chinese bureaucracies should first focus on how they helped hold huge land masses and complex economies together, in two of the great political units of the early modern centuries. It is fair, however, to also seek in the documentation some clues as to why deterioration might set in, and why one system maintained its vigor longer than the other.

Questions

1. How would you assess the differences in the personal motives of the writers of the two passages below? Which one was more idealistic? Which source provides a better means of figuring out what the government and bureaucracy were really like?
2. How did Asian governments in the early modern period define bureaucracy?
3. How did Huang reflect Confucian beliefs? How did he define problems, and what remedies did he propose?
4. How did Mehmed Pasha reflect earlier Islamic political ideals?
5. How did Confucian and Muslim definitions of the purpose of the state compare?
6. What economic functions did the Ottoman government claim, and why?
7. How did each system recruit other bureaucrats? Which one depended more on careful training?
8. Which system was more open to internal plots? Which was better designed to preserve the subordination of officials to the ruler?
9. Which system was better suited to serve the interest of the masses of people?
10. How do both documents suggest reasons for the success and durability of the Ottoman and Chinese Empires?

For Further Discussion

1. Do you think the Chinese system had deteriorated as much as Huang claims?
2. Confucianism emphasized order and the state. Could it also be used as a basis

for protest? What circumstances would be required, and what would the protest goals be?

3. How had Muslim views of the state organization changed since the time of the early Arab caliphate?

4. Do the documents suggest any reasons that the Ottoman bureaucracy began to deteriorate before the Chinese bureaucracy did, in the seventeenth and the eighteenth centuries, respectively?

5. Which is a better source for understanding how a system works, one written by an embittered critic or one written by someone hoping to please the powers that be?

MINISTERS IN CHINA: HUANG TSUNG-HSI

Huang Tsung-hsi, 1610–95, lived during the waning phases of the Ming dynasty and the early stages of its successor, the Qing Empire. He was the son of a high Ming official who had been killed by enemies at court. A Confucian, he added his own views on the role of law, going beyond the tradition. Obviously, his family experience turned him toward criticism, though Confucianism itself provided principles by which many bureaucrats could be found wanting. His sense of deterioration from earlier times is undoubtedly sincere, but it does not have to be taken at face value. Using this document requires understanding of the author's point of view, but also reading between the lines to see how the bureaucratic structure itself was organized, because it continued to contain many features that had been successful from the Han dynasty onward.

• • •

The reason for ministership lies in the fact that the world is too big for one man to govern and that it is necessary to share the work with others. Therefore, when I come forth to serve, it is for the whole world and not for the prince; it is for all men and not for one family. . . .

But those who act as ministers today do not understand this concept. They say that a minister is created for the prince, that he rules only because the prince shares part of the world with him and delegates to him some leadership over the people. They look upon the world and its people as personal property in the prince's pouch. . . .

Whether there is peace or disorder in the world does not depend on the rise and fall of dynasties, but upon the happiness or distress of the people. . . .

From William Theodore de Bary, Wing-tsit Chan, and Burton Watson, eds., *Sources of Chinese Tradition* (New York: Columbia University Press, 1960), 589–90, 592–94. Reprinted by permission of the publisher.

If a minister ignores the plight of the people, then even if he succeeds in assisting his prince's rise to power or follows him to final ruin, it still can never be said that he has followed the [True] Way of the Minister. The governing of the world is like the hauling of great logs. The men in front call out, "Heave!" those behind, "Ho!" The prince and his ministers are log-haulers working together. If some of them, instead of holding tight to the ropes with feet firmly set on the ground, amuse themselves by cavorting around in front, the others behind will think it the thing to do and the business of hauling logs will be neglected. Alas, the insolent princes of later times indulge themselves [in the same way] and do not tend to the business of the world and its people. From among the men of the country they seek out only such as will be servile errand-boys. And if from the country those alone respond who are of the servile errand-boy type, then when they are protected from cold and hunger for a while, they feel eternally grateful for his majesty's kindness. Such men will not care whether they are treated by the prince with due respect, and will think it no more than proper to be relegated to a servant's status . . . because people's minds had been contaminated for so long by degenerate notions about what a minister was, taking it as the accepted standard. How could they be expected to know that princes and ministers differ in name only, and are in fact the same? . . .

The terms "prince" and "minister" derive their significance from service to mankind. If I have no sense of duty to mankind I am an alien to the prince. If I come to serve him without any consideration for the welfare of mankind, then I am merely the prince's menial servant. If, on the other hand, I have the people's interest at heart, then I am the prince's mentor and colleague. Only then may I really be called a minister. . . .

If it should be said that there are only men who govern well, not laws which govern well, my reply is that only if there are laws which govern well, will there later be men who govern well. Since "unlawful laws" fetter men hand and foot, even a man capable of governing well cannot overcome the handicaps of senseless restraint and suspicion. When there is something to be done, he does no more than his share, and since he contents himself with trifling accomplishments, there can be no outstanding achievements. If the law of the early kings were restored, there would be a spirit among men which went beyond the letter of the law. If men were of the right kind, the full intent of the law would be fulfilled; and even if they were of the wrong kind, it would be impossible for them to govern tyrannically and make the people suffer. Therefore I say we must first have laws which govern well and later we shall have men who govern well. . . .

. . . In ancient times the selection of officials was liberal, but the employment of them was strict. Today the selection of officials is strict, but the employment of them is liberal. Under the old system of "state recommendation and village selection," a man of ability did not have to fear that he would go unrecognized. Later on, in the T'ang and Sung [dynasties], several types of examination were instituted, and if a man did not succeed in one, he could turn around and take another. Thus the system of selection was liberal. . . .

But today this is not so. There is only one way to become an official: through the examination system. Even if there were scholars like the great men of old . . . they would have no other way than this to get chosen for office. Would not this system of selection be called too strict? However, should candidates one day succeed, the topmost are placed among the imperial attendants and the lowest given posts in the prefectures and districts. Even those who fail [the metropolitan examinations] and yet have been sent up from the provinces are given official posts without having to take examinations again the rest of their lives. Would not this system of employment be called too liberal? Because the system of selection is too confined, many great men live to old age and die in obscurity. Because the system of employment is too liberal, frequently the right man cannot be found among the many holding official rank.

The common man, seeing only that in the past two hundred years a few men of character and achievement have appeared among those chosen, concludes that the examination system is good enough and there is no need to look elsewhere. He does not realize that among the hundreds and thousands taken in by the examination system, some men of character and achievement would inevitably find their way in. This means that men of character and achievement may find their way through the examination system, but the examination system does not find them. If we had scholars draw lots and chose them according to the length of the lot drawn, in the course of several hundred years men of character and achievement would naturally appear among those so chosen. But would we call this a good way to choose officials?

After all, the men of today who have character and ability are a far cry from those of the Han and T'ang dynasties. Today we have only mediocre and shallow men cluttering up the world. But it is surely not because Heaven has ceased to produce men of talent, is it? The system of selection is wrong.

Therefore, I would broaden the system for selecting officials, and choose men [not only] through the regular examinations [but also] through special recommendations, through the Imperial Academy, through the appointment of high officials' sons, through [a merit system for] junior officials in prefectures and districts, through special appointments, through [the recognition of] unique scholarship, and through the presentation of [outstanding] memorials.

THE OTTOMAN CHIEF MINISTER: SARI MEHMED PASHA

Sari Mehmed Pasha, author of the *Book of Counsel for Viziers and Governors*, was treasurer at the Ottoman court by 1702. He was periodically thrown out of office during revolts and intrigues, which were endemic in Ottoman bureaucracies (and perhaps, to a degree, in bureaucracies anywhere, anytime). He wrote his treatise in hopes of becoming grand vizier himself, which helps to explain its upbeat, idealistic tone and its careful references both to religion and to the sultan. Like many somewhat sycophantic writers, Sari Mehmed Pasha failed in his purpose; the top bureaucratic office continued to elude him. But he left an interesting record of what it was polite to say about the goals of this great empire's bureaucracy and governmental functions.

• • •

Since the Lord without Equal, who showers down abundant gifts (may His Glory be exalted beyond the reach of imagination!), has made that firmly founded dynasty, the surpassing Ottoman Sultanate, to be the refuge of the rulers of the times, and has made their court, which pours out on every hand favors from the ocean of abundance, to be distributor of the sustenance decreed by Providence to the people of the world, it has consequently become a necessary responsibility . . . to fulfil the incumbent gratitude due for this Divine Grace in accordance with the precept "Every one of you is a shepherd and every one of you is responsible for his flock." [Therefore] he should make affluent the condition of the governed and establish good order in the affairs of the citizens and carry out the injunctions of the illustrious Holy Law and protect the boundaries of the territories and coasts [of the Moslems]. As he obeys and executes continuously this essential and indispensably important command by protecting good order according to the rule: "There is no state save with men of substance and no men of substance save with wealth," he must certainly show his brilliance through the management of fortunate vezirs and the assembling of armies experienced in wars of the Faith. In consequence of this, it is more manifest than the sun and more clear than yesterday, most necessary of needs for both country and government, among the most essential of essentials of the practice of the sultanate that he should appoint a religious and upright chief minister, [one] like Aristotle in sagacity, an unrestricted representative, one who will obtain the products of labor and lay up stores of provisions and wealth and make the state treasures as abundant as the sea, one who will strive for the protection and preservation of secure tranquillity and good order among the poor subjects entrusted to him by the Creator of Mankind, as well as for that of all the servants of God. The whole of the regulating and ordering of the affairs of the country and of the ameliorating of the condition of the subjects should be committed to his responsibility, in accordance with the maxim: "Give back the trust to its owner." He should be granted complete freedom in the business of the vezirate. . . . The unrestrained

From Sari Mehmed Pasha, *Ottoman Statecraft*, ed. W. L. Wright, Jr. (Westport, Conn.: Greenwood Press, 1935), 64–69, 73, 74, 76–79, 81, 85–86.

grand vezir must have the favor of his patron and must seek after the highest virtues. As partaker in the freshness of one who shares the harvest of both noble and peasant, let him make laudable efforts and abundant endeavors utterly to destroy illegal practices and injustice, to remove the weeds and thorns of tyranny and corruption, and to drive out the torments of oppression and obstinacy by the benefactions of justice and equity.

First among the obligations of lofty endeavor and essential measures of the sublime sultanate is the support [in affluence] of the inhabitants of the most honored cities and districts, the most blessed habitations and regions, Mekka the Noble and Medina the Illuminated (may God—exalted is He—glorify them until the Day of Judgment!), through the complete shipment from Cairo of their customary yearly rents in grain. Before all else the produce of their properties must be properly loaded on ships, in order that it may be kept clean and pure. And to the *vāli* [governor] of Egypt repeated orders must be sent to make him extremely vigilant and insistent upon gathering everyone together at the proper time and place. Reliable men must be appointed to protect the rights of the poor during the course of the journey.

Throughout their period of authority let them treat with equality the humble and the noble, the wealthy and the poor, the learned and the unlearned, the one from afar and the one from nearby, the visitor and the neighbor. Let them not make use of their power until the evidence is complete. In short, let them treat all alike in executing the holy law, making no distinction between great and small, rich and poor, subject and prince.

To the glorious pādishāh [sultan] let them speak the word of truth without veiling or concealment. And let them never conceal the truth, which is necessary to every one, nor neglect to speak it where it is needed. For the Prophet of God (on whom be the commendation and salutation of God) has said: "Words of truth are the best alms." . . .

Not only outsiders but also the other vezirs must be ignorant of secret matters and of the dealings of the grand vezir with the pādishāh. In the service of rulers it is a very important thing not to disclose secrets. And certainly it is a noble habit to respect the secrets of one's brethren. Let them not even disclose their own secrets to any one, for it has been said: "Keep thy secret even from thy button," and again: "Every secret which passes beyond two persons becomes public." A secret which passes between two lips most certainly becomes known to everyone. Extreme care in concealing secrets is to everyone the most necessary of needs.

The grand vezir and all mankind should pray for His Majesty the Pādishāh of Islām and not fail in blessing him. For the Prophet (on whom be the commendation and salutation of God) has said: "Curse not the sultan, for behold! he is the shadow of God on earth." Let everyone always and with sincere heart bless and praise the pādishāh of mankind and hold not to the contrary course, for God who is Great in Majesty has made him caliph. . . .

The grand vezir especially must not be a time-server, thinking of the benefits of money. Let him shun the hope of gathering wealth and treasure and spend his ability in preparing a remedy for the weakness and languidness which prevent the good health of the country. For his rejoicing and glorying in the simple service of the pādishāh's court will gain for him felicity in this world and that to come. Let him always expend without stint persistent endeavors, that his actions may be successful in the manner desired. And let him not employ the special costumes and effects of sultans, approaching the circle of partnership with them. Let him not fail in his duty to know his proper degree of modesty and humility when the pādishāh shows him honor and respect, granting him the favor of proximity. Nor let him become puffed up with his greatness and exhibit to the people an appearance of haughtiness and disdain . . . Let him not consider the service of the pādishāh merely as a means of gaining wealth, and let him not be covetous of the riches of the sovereign's private domain or of the public property of peasants and sipāhis. If the grand vezirs be contented with what is specially appointed to them, definite sums and gifts from several quarters will not be lacking. It has been said in the days of prosperity of the government that this amount of reward was sufficient . . .

The grand vezir should perform the five obligatory prayers in his dwelling together with the company there. His door should be open and consultation with him should be easy. It has been said: "If any person to whom a single affair of the believers is entrusted shut his door so that the oppressed and needy cannot reach him, to that man the Gate of Mercy will be closed in the time of his great need, and he will be deprived of the universal compassion and perfect kindness of the Exalted and Lofty God."

The purpose of government and dominion in this passing world is not the obtaining of pleasures nor the satisfying of desires. Per-adventure it is the laying up of a store in the world to come and the gaining through good deeds of an eternal good name and eternal good fame. It is not fitting that the important time of rulers should be spent in music and song and love of pleasure. When one has reached such a station, the essentials are calmness, piety, justice, and contentment with what one has. As far as he can, one should seek goodness for himself and strive for the betterment of the world . . . All rulers must strive to their utmost to act in accordance with justice, but to the pādishāh beyond all others is it most necessary and important. For justice brings saving to the treasury and increase in the subjects. Treasure comes through the abundance of subjects and the welfare of the land. Through justice the country is made prosperous. A country which is ruined must lack its due share of wealth and even its rich people must be without riches . . .

Special and trustworthy salaried agents, both secret and open, must be appointed for [providing] information about the condition of rulers and subjects and whatever events of the times there may be, both great and small. Free expenditure of care should be made for information regarding the condition of the country. For when care is not taken, the peasants forsake their homes and are scattered to other districts as a result of the tyranny of oppressors and the remissness of governors and the domineering of brigands. In addition to the very many places which are destitute of peasants and void of profit, and by reason also of the complete lack of security on the highways of that region and of the plundering of the property and subsistence of many persons carrying on communication by road, and because the killing of people and destruction [of property] are not lacking, it is certain that a deficiency in the receipts of the treasury will result . . .

And let not the matter of establishing market prices be passed over with the mere intrusting of it to judges and inspectors of weights and measures. It is essential at all times for every ruler to keep track of the small things relating to the general condition of the people. He must set the proper market prices. Every thing must be sold at the price it is worth. For in case the pādishāh and the vezirs say: "The fixing of market prices, though part of the public business, is insignificant," and are not diligent about it, the city judge alone cannot carry it out. Since he has no connection with matters of policy, he cannot enter upon that path. Under such circumstances every one buys and sells as he pleases. Through senseless avarice the venom of vipers is added to lawful goods. The most contemptible of the people, useless both for the service of the pādishāh and for warfare, become possessors of all the wealth. They are notables of the government and country, while the great men of the people who deserve respect, becoming poor and powerless, pursue the road of bankruptcy. . . .

. . . The fruiterers and merchants put a double price on provisions and supplies and reap [a harvest of] profits. They rob the people. It is apparent that neglect in this matter redounds to the harm of believers in time of trouble and to the benefit of fruiterers and merchants. Therefore it is necessary that the grand vezir and the rulers who are in townships and provinces, the *vālis*, and the military commanders take pains to see to the execution of this business in person. . . .

. . . It is fitting also not to be heedless of the weak and poor and to know that the investigation of their condition is a duty. For the requirement of gaining for one's self the affections of mankind is the means of obtaining the approval of the Creator. It is most fitting to treat every one with sympathy and not to view any one with contempt and insult. . . .

Also it is necessary for a person not to incline toward the carnal passions. It has been said that the Lawgiver will surely cause every one to perish who is subject to his own passions and slights or makes light of Divine Law. Furthermore, what has a person been before this life? And after death what must he become? On this it is fitting to ponder. One must always meditate upon death and take warning from those who have passed on. One must at all times know his duty and understand his condition and always prepare what is needful for his journey. For thou knowest not when thou wilt depart. Thou must remember and meditate upon that day when, if they call, thou wilt be able neither to speak nor to hear, neither to work nor to act.

Thou shouldst think on the place to which thou wilt go, for there the slaves and the free, the joyful in heart and the beggar, are equal. Thou shouldst bring this to mind and not be proud. If thou suffer trouble for more splendid felicity, endure it; for trouble passes and felicity remains. If for transitory pleasure thou sinnest, the pleasure passes; the sin endures. This lower world is the mansion of dissolution and affliction and trouble and temptation and trial. Its riches are adorned with satiety, its dissolution decorated with evil. Its happiness is overcome by vengeance and its pleasure by abasement. Surely the end of the world is regret and affliction, and the goal of all endeavor is the reckoning of thy lawful acts and the punishment of thy transgressions. Men of discernment and wisdom, masters of thought and sagacity should in this life always ponder the condition of this impermanent mansion of affliction and picture to themselves its fading and passing away.

CHAPTER 18

ASIAN AND RUSSIAN REACTIONS TO THE WEST

All major societies experienced new contacts with Western Europe during the early modern period. Documents in this chapter suggest three different reactions, from China, India, and Russia. They demonstrate quite varied degrees of openness to the West, but they also show that none of the societies welcomed Western ways across the board. Even Russia, which under Peter the Great embarked on an explicit imitation program, was highly selective.

The two Asian comments—one Chinese, from the seventeenth century, the other from an Indian Muslim who, most atypically, actually visited London at the end of the eighteenth century—come from authors who had far more contact with the West than most Asians did in this period and who were more attracted to aspects of the West than were most Asians who did have contact. They saw real merits in Western culture, of a sort that far more people would have to consider in the nineteenth century. What did these two writers particularly admire? How did their reservations—for both worried about some Western features—reflect distinctions between Chinese and Muslim values, as well as the different types of Western contact involved?

The documents in this chapter from Russia reflect actual reforms carried out by Peter the Great, around 1700. Peter had traveled in the West before becoming czar, or emperor, and he believed key economic, cultural, and political features of the West should be established in Russia. His reforms mark an important change in Russian history, though they also provoked criticisms, because other Russian leaders found their own values preferable and attacked Western-style reformers. What aspects of the West did Peter emphasize, and what did he ignore? how did his sense of Western strengths compare to that of the Asian observers?

Western interactions with Asia and Russia in the early modern period were complex. Western technology did not permit Westerners easily force their way into Asian societies, except for island areas like Indonesia or the Philippines, or into Eastern Europe. Asians had no need for Western goods, and Russia was also self-sufficient.

China, with a long tradition of cultural superiority and considerable isolation, largely ignored the West. It granted Portugal control over the port of Macao, believing that this would help limit Western pressure. Otherwise, it successfully resisted most Western requests for trade. The government allowed a few Catholic missionaries to enter, but they did not prove disruptive, partly because most of them converted extensively to Chinese ways both as a tactical ploy and because they were truly impressed with Chinese culture. (The modest Chinese tolerance for Christian missionaries was reversed in the early eighteenth century.) At the same time the West offered a few limited attractions—one of the ways missionaries such as Matteo Ricci won attention from urban elites involved their clockmaking skills, though the Chinese had fairly good clocks of their own. With this entry, a few Chinese defended these elements of Western culture. Nevertheless, no significant interaction occurred until the nineteenth century, when China's power had declined and that of the West had increased. Chinese ideas about the West in the early modern period consisted mainly of dismissing these outsiders as barbarians. The only change was the development of a handful of commentators with slightly more open views—the first time in world history that even a few Chinese had ever thought seriously about the West.

Indian's situation was somewhat different. That subcontinent was more open to international trade and historically more tolerant of outside ideas. Rulers of India's new Mughal Empire, in the sixteenth century, were interested in certain Western styles and concepts, though contacts were limited except for coastal trade. This situation changed after 1700. The Mughal Empire weakened rapidly. British and French commercial companies, backed by their governments, intervened increasingly. The two countries warred for control of much of India, each allying with regional princely governments. After 1763 Britain emerged as the leading power on the subcontinent, though local governments retained day-to-day power. Many Indians resented the West by this time. Among Hindus, contact with the outsiders was shunned. Sketchy political institutions the British established, such as some law courts, seemed to ignore Indian customs and needs. Some leaders criticized British exploitation, for the British actively discouraged traditional Indian manufacturing, throwing hundreds of thousands out of work, while levying an annual payment in gold.

Clearly, Indians or Chinese who found it either possible or worthwhile to comment elaborately on the West, except in terms of dismissing barbarians or condemning greedy outsiders, were unusual. Comments by unusual observers, however, can suggest more general issues. Obviously, they can highlight some comparative contrasts with the West itself; thus, the following selections show elements of Western presentation that even a sympathetic Chinese observer did not like, and the same holds true for the Indian traveler as he compared the West to his Indian and Muslim values. The observers can also suggest entry points, which could later draw more Asians to pay some attention to certain aspects of the West and to condemn other aspects found particularly deficient by Asian standards.

Russia differed from the Asian societies in being closer to Western Europe and sharing Christianity (though a different version). After the Mongols were expelled in the fifteenth century, Russian rulers had increased contacts with the West, bringing in artists and some merchants. Russian territorial expansion westward brought the country closer to the European military-diplomatic orbit. This was the context for Peter the Great's travels to Europe and his desire to use certain Western forms to strengthen Russia and also the power of the czar within Russia. Nothing like this westernization program would occur in Asia for almost two centuries. But Peter had no desire to make Russia Western: what he left alone was as important as what he tried to change.

Asian and Russian reactions in the early modern period thus suggest a several-sided comparison. Over time, it would become clear that many Indians, though disliking British rule, developed a bit of a love-hate relationship with their colonial masters. China long remained more hostile. Russia moved farthest toward embrace of the West, but aspects of Russian society were actually veering away from Western patterns (see chapter 16), and the country developed its own ambivalence about Western ways (see chapter 23). The origins of these differences can be traced in the documents in this chapter: one set from a very cautious observer, one from a selective westernizer, and a third from an observer who was critical but also open despite the fact that it was his society that was actually losing its independence to the West.

The specific settings for the reaction to the West differed. Hsü Kuang-chi was a convert of the great Jesuit missionary Matteo Ricci (1542–1610), writing in 1617. Ricci had adopted many Chinese habits and a real esteem for Chinese culture in order to gain contacts with members of the imperial court, and Hsü reflects this approach. A high official, he thought that Western ideas could help China, though he also conveys nervousness about growing official opposition. Even Hsü's cautious position did not gain wide favor.

Peter the Great ruled Russia as czar from 1682 to 1725. He brutally repressed protest and moved vigorously in war, setting up a new capital called Saint Petersburg in territory conquered in the Baltic region. His westernization effort focused on updating Russia's administration and those aspects of the economy relevant to military supplies. He also urged Western culture on the Russian elites, to make Russia seem less backward in European eyes and also to increase his own control over the aristocrats and make them more useful to the state. His reforms clearly indicated what his goals were and why he found certain Western patterns useful—and others irrelevant.

After failing to get a job in the colonial administration, Abu Taleb Khan traveled from India to England with a Scottish friend, gaining a great reception as a "Persian prince" by the aristocracy. He wrote up his travels upon his return to Calcutta. His comments are somewhat superficial, indicating a delight in London life, but they do reveal an ambivalent reaction to British habits and ideas—and also a critical stance toward his own culture, which he began to see as backward in key respects, viewed in a Western light. Some of his comparisons are unexpected, such as those on women; did he simply misjudge, or were British conditions then so strict? Abu Taleb Khan also issues some of the attacks on clumsy British administration within India itself that would later, by the 1870s, help found Indian nationalism.

Questions

1. What aspects of the West did Hsü Kuang-chi find interesting? Did he want basic Chinese institutions and values to change? Was he really advocating Christianity? What kind of message does Matteo Ricci seem to have conveyed about the nature of Europe and about the validity of Chinese values? Was this kind of cultural contact likely to change China very much?

2. What arguments did Hsü Kuang-chi have to refute, and what traditional Chinese values did these arguments reflect? How does the phrasing of his argument suggest why Chinese policy largely opposed Western contacts?

3. What aspects of the West did Peter emphasize? How, even in reforming administration, manufacturing, and culture, did his approach differ from Western patterns at the time? What were his goals?

4. What did Abu Taleb Khan like about Britain? What did he dislike? Why might a Muslim find conditions of British women stricter than those of his own country, even though women were less confined in certain respects? Is this a plausible judgment? (On earlier Muslim attitudes toward women, see chapter 9.)

5. How do Abu Taleb Khan's reactions, based on quite different knowledge and on Indian Muslim rather than Chinese standards, compare with those of Hsü? Did the two Asian observers share any common sense of dangers posed by Western values?

6. How do Peter the Great's reactions compare with those of Asian observers? Did he value some of the same features of the West that they did? Would he have agreed with them about Western deficiencies?

For Further Discussion

1. Why, by the late eighteenth century, was an Indian, rather than a Chinese, more likely to break with general patterns and visit Europe directly?

2. How do the Asian comments illustrate certain features of Western society that people in many non-Western societies would dislike? Would any of the comments—for example, about the faults of the British—be repeated by non-Western critics in the twentieth century?

3. How did Peter the Great's reforms relate to Russia's labor system (see chapter 16)? How did Radishchev (chapter 16) compare with Peter as a Russian westernizer?
4. What aspects of the early modern West did Peter *not* try to imitate?

PETER THE GREAT

The first of the following decrees from the czar involved the creation of a Governing Senate (council), which reflected some of the changes he sought in administration and state functions. A second decree, from 1714, established so-called compulsory education for the nobles (though this was not actually fully enforceable); a related "instruction" urged selective study abroad. A 1721 decree (number 4) was designed to encourage manufacturing, but through a very distinctive means. Finally, a 1724 decree set up an academy modeled on Western associations—such as the Royal Society in England, which had been established in the seventeenth century—to encourage discussion of science. Which reforms probably had the greatest impact? Which would be most likely to encounter resistance? What groups and activities were left untouched?

• • •

1. Senate Decree

This *ukaz* [decree] should be made known. We have decreed that during our absence administration of the country is to be [in the hands of] the Governing Senate [Peter then names its new members.]. . . .

Each *gubernia* [region] is to send two officials to advise the Senate on judicial and legislative matters. . . .

In our absence the Senate is charged by this *ukaz* with the following:

1. To establish a just court, to deprive unjust judges of their offices and of all their property, and to administer the same treatment to all slanderers.
2. To supervise governmental expenditures throughout the country and cancel unnecessary and, above all, useless things.
3. To collect as much money as possible because money is the artery of war.
4. To recruit young noblemen for officer training, especially those who try to evade it; also to select about 1000 educated boyars for the same purpose.
5. To reform letters of exchange and keep these in one place.
6. To take inventory of goods leased to offices or *gubernias*.

From Basil Dmytryshn, *Imperial Russia: A Sourcebook, 1700–1917* (New York: Holt, Rinehart and Winston, 1967), 18–19, 21–22.

7. To farm out the salt trade in an effort to receive some profit [for the state].

8. To organize a good company and assign to it the China trade.

9. To increase trade with Persia and by all possible means to attract in great numbers Armenians [to that trade]. To organize inspectors and inform them of their responsibilities.

2. Education Decree

Send to every *gubernia* [region] some persons from mathematical schools to teach the children of the nobility—except those of freeholders and government clerks—mathematics and geometry; as a penalty [for evasion] establish a rule that no one will be allowed to marry unless he learns these [subjects]. Inform all prelates to issue no marriage certificates to those who are ordered to go to schools. . . .

The Great Sovereign has decreed: in all *gubernias* children between the ages of ten and fifteen of the nobility, of government clerks, and of lesser officials, except those of freeholders, must be taught mathematics and some geometry. Toward that end, students should be sent from mathematical schools [as teachers], several into each *gubernia,* to prelates and to renowned monasteries to establish schools. During their instruction these teachers should be given food and financial remuneration of three *altyns* and two *dengas* per day from *gubernia* revenues set aside for that purpose by personal orders of His Imperial Majesty. No fees should be collected from students. When they have mastered the material, they should then be given certificates written in their own handwriting. When the students are released they ought to pay one ruble each for their training. Without these certificates they should not be allowed to marry nor receive marriage certificates.

3. Navigation Study Abroad

1. Learn [how to draw] plans and charts and how to use the compass and other naval indicators.

2. [Learn] how to navigate a vessel in battle as well as in a simple maneuver, and learn how to use all appropriate tools and instruments; namely, sails, ropes, and oars, and the like matters, on row boats and other vessels.

3. Discover as much as possible how to put ships to sea during a naval battle. Those who cannot succeed in this effort must diligently ascertain what action should be taken by the vessels that do and those that do not put to sea during such a situation [naval battle]. Obtain from [foreign] naval officers written statements, bearing their signatures and seals, of how adequately you [Russian students] are prepared for [naval] duties.

4. If, upon his return, anyone wishes to receive [from the Tsar] greater favors for

himself, he should learn, in addition to the above enumerated instructions, how to construct those vessels aboard which he would like to demonstrate his skills.

5. Upon his return to Moscow, every [foreign-trained Russian] should bring with him at his own expense, for which he will later be reimbursed, at least two experienced masters of naval science. They [the returnees] will be assigned soldiers, one soldier per returnee, to teach them [what they have learned abroad]. And if they do not wish to accept soldiers they may teach their acquaintances or their own people. The treasury will pay for transportation and maintenance of soldiers. And if anyone other than soldiers learns [the art of navigation] the treasury will pay 100 rubles for the maintenance of every such individual. . . .

4. Right of Factories to Buy Villages

Previous decrees have denied merchants the right to obtain villages. This prohibition was instituted because those people, outside their business, did not have any establishments that could be of any use to the state. Nowadays, thanks to Our decrees, as every one can see, many merchants have companies and many have succeeded in establishing new enterprises for the benefit of the state; namely: silver, copper, iron, coal and the like, as well as silk, linen, and woolen industries, many of which have begun operations. As a result, by this Our *ukaz* aimed at the increase of factories, We permit the nobility as well as merchants to freely purchase villages for these factories, with the sanction of the Mining and Manufacturing College, under one condition: that these villages be always integral parts of these factories. Consequently, neither the nobility nor merchants may sell or mortgage these villages without the factories . . . and should someone decide to sell these villages with the factories because of pressing needs, it must be done with the permission of the Mining and Manufacturing College. And whoever violates this procedure will have his possessions confiscated.

And should someone try to establish a small factory for the sake of appearance in order to purchase a village, such an entrepreneur should not be allowed to purchase anything. The Mining and Manufacturing College should adhere to this rule very strictly. Should such a thing happen, those responsible for it should be deprived of all their movable and immovable property.

5. Founding the Academy

His Imperial Majesty decreed the establishment of an academy, wherein languages as well as other sciences and important arts could be taught, and where books could be translated. On January 22, [1724], during his stay in the Winter Palace, His Majesty approved the project for the Academy, and with his own hand signed a decree that stipulates that the Academy's budget of 24,912 rubles annually should come from revenues from custom dues and export-import license fees collected in the following cities: Narva, Dorpat, Pernov and Arensburg. . . .

Usually two kinds of institutions are used in organizing arts and sciences. One is known as a University; the other as an Academy or society of arts and sciences.

1. A University is an association of learned individuals who teach the young people the development of such distinguished sciences as theology and jurisprudence (the legal skill), and medicine and philosophy. An Academy, on the other hand, is an association of learned and skilled people who not only know their subjects to the same degree [as their counterparts in the University] but who, in addition, improve and develop them through research and inventions. They have no obligation to teach others.

2. While the Academy consists of the same scientific disciplines and has the same members as the University, these two institutions, in other states, have no connection between themselves in training many other well-qualified people who could organize different societies. This is done to prevent interference into the activity of the Academy, whose sole task is to improve arts and sciences through theoretical research that would benefit professors as well as students of universities. Freed from the pressure of research, universities can concentrate on educating the young people.

3. Now that an institution aimed at the cultivation of arts and sciences is to be chartered in Russia, there is no need to follow the practice that is accepted in other states. It is essential to take into account the existing circumstances of this state [Russia], consider [the quality of Russian] teachers and students, and organize such an institution that would not only immediately increase the glory of this [Russian] state through the development of sciences, but would also, through teaching and dissemination [of knowledge], benefit the people [of Russia] in the future.

4. These two aims will not be realized if the Academy of Sciences alone is chartered, because while the Academy may try to promote and disseminate arts and sciences, these will not spread among the people. The establishment of a university will do even less, simply because there are no elementary schools, gymnasia or seminaries [in Russia] where young people could learn the fundamentals before studying more advanced subjects [at the University] to make themselves useful. It is therefore inconceivable that under these circumstances a university would be of some value [to Russia].

5. Consequently what is needed most [in Russia] is the establishment of an institution that would consist of the most learned people, who, in turn, would be willing: (a) to promote and perfect the sciences while at the same time, wherever possible, be willing (b) to give public instruction to young people (if they feel the latter are qualified) and (c) instruct some people individually so that they in turn could train young people [of Russia] in the fundamental principles of all sciences.

CHINESE REACTIONS: HSÜ KUANG-CHI

Hsü Kuang-chi wrote his *Memorial* in 1617, to expand on the work of the missionary Matteo Ricci (1542–1610), with whom he had worked as at least a partial convert. The presentation is complex, for Hsü Kuang-chi clearly realized he needed to be very careful in his phrasing if he was to gain any audience—maybe even to avoid drawing criticism down on himself. It is also not entirely clear how many Western ideas Hsü Kuang-chi himself embraced; he clearly hoped for an amalgam of a few Western innovations with lots of Chinese tradition.

• • •

HSÜ KUANG-CHI'S MEMORIAL

Sü Kwángkí, guardian and tutor of the sons of the Imperial house, and Chancellor of the National Institute, respectfully presents this memorial:

Knowing full well that the arts and sciences of the foreigners are in a high degree correct, your majesty's humble servant earnestly begs of his sacred Intelligence, the illustrious honor of issuing a manifesto in their behalf, so as to render his own felicity eternal, and give great tranquility to ten thousand generations. Your majesty's servant has seen, in the Governmental Gazette, the report of the Board of Rites, impeaching [Dzdace de] Pantoya [a Ricci successor] and others, your majesty's European courtiers. In that Report it is said, "Their doctrines are penetrating deep, and spreading wide, so that even men of eminence are believing in them;" and, "although their discourses about astronomy are absurd, yet even scholars are falling into their cloudy visions." By thus specifying "men of eminence" and "scholars," ministers of the Board seem to fear that trunk and branches are being alike involved. Still they have failed to give the names of individuals. Now your servant is one of the ministers of the Imperial Court, who has been accustomed to discourse with your majesty's courtiers on religious subjects; and he is one who believes in the many books they have published. With them also he has been accustomed to investigate the laws of mathematics; his earlier and later reports thereon have all been laid before the Imperial presence; and thus also your servant is among those who have "discoursed about astronomy." If, therefore, your majesty's courtiers are to be found guilty, how can your servant hope to be so fortunate as to escape uncondemned by the ministers of the Board?

As your servant for years past has been thus accustomed to engage in discussions and investigations with these courtiers, he has become well acquainted with them, and knows that they are not only in deportment and in heart wholly free from aught which can excite suspicion, but that they are indeed worthies and sages; that their

From *Chinese Repository* 9 (March 1850): 118–23, 126.

doctrines are most correct; their regimen most strict; their learning most extensive; their knowledge most refined; their hearts most true; their views most steady; and that among the people of their own nations, there is not one in a thousand so accomplished, or one in ten thousand so talented as these men. Now the reason of their coming thousands of miles eastward, is because hearing that the teachers, the sages and worthies of China, served Heaven by the cultivation of personal virtue, just as the teachers in their respective nations by the cultivation of personal virtue, served the Lord of Heaven, and knowing that there was this correspondence in principles, they desired, notwithstanding the difficulties and dangers by land and by sea, to give their seal to the truth, in order that men might become good, and so realize high Heaven's love to man.

According to their sayings, the service of the High Ruler is a prime duty; the protection of the body and the salvation of the soul are grand essentials; fidelity, filial piety, compassion, and love are to be universally exercised; the reformation of errors and the practice of virtue are initiatory steps; repentance and purification are the requisites for personal improvement; the true fecilicity of life celestial is the glorious reward of doing good; and the eternal misery of earth's prison is the bitter recompense of doing evil. All their commands and injunctions are in the highest degree compatible with the principles of Heaven and the feelings of men. Their laws can cause men to do good most truly, and to depart from evil most completely, for that which they say of the favor of the Lord of heaven's producing, nourishing and saving, and of his principles of rewarding the good and punishing the evil, is perfectly plain and most strictly true; sufficient to move the hearts of men and to excite in them the love and confidence, the fear and dread, which naturally spring from internal rectitude. . . . The proof of this is, that the nations of Europe which are contiguous to each other, and more than thirty in number, receiving and practicing this religion, during a thousand and some hundreds of years up to the present time, whether great or small, have alike been kind to each other; whether high or low, have alike enjoyed repose; their prescribed boundaries have required no guard; nor has their sovereignty been hereditary; throughout their whole domain, there have been no deceivers nor liars; the vices of lewdness and theft from of old have never existed; no one would venture to take up an article dropped upon the highway; and even gates and doors of cities and houses it was not necessary to have closed by night. As to revolt and anarchy, rebels and insurgents, not only were there no such things and no such persons, but even such terms and such names had no existence. Thus for a long time, have these nations enjoyed tranquillity, and their governments have been well regulated. All their inhabitants have been thus intensely watchful only lest they should, by falling into error, become guilty of sinning against the Lord of Heaven. Accordingly it is most clear and most manifest that their laws assuredly can cause men to do well.

Such is the religion and such are the manners and customs set forth by your majesty's courtiers; and having repeatedly, and in the most thorough manner, examined their discourses and investigated their books, your majesty's servant knows that they are all perfectly free from error. . . .

If his [majesty's] sacred Intelligence would deign graciously to receive our apology, grant a manifesto, and for a short space of time, and on perfect equality with the disciples of Budha and doctors of the Táu [Daoist] sect, allow these courtiers to remain [in the empire] to promulgate their doctrines and urge on their reformation, it is humbly conceived that, ere many years have elapsed, the hearts of men and the ways of the world, will be seen to have undergone a steady and gradual change, progressing till at length there shall be one grand reformation, and perfect virtue become universal. Then every law enacted shall go into effect, and no command given shall be opposed. No unfaithful minister will then be in the capital or in the provinces. The manners of all the people without exception will be such as to render them worthy of being employed in the imperial service. The glorious felicity enjoyed by your majesty's sacred person will be infinite, and the peace of your blessed empire perpetuated to a myriad generations! . . .

Let all the courtiers, whose names have been included in the memorials, be called to the capital; and let a selection be made of your majesty's ministers both in and out of the capital; let all these jointly translate the standard works that have been brought from the West; let subjects be taken up in detail—what is said on serving Heaven and loving man, what relates to natural and moral philosophy, to the systems of civil government, to astronomy, to mathematics, to physic and medicine, to agriculture and irrigation, to political economy, &c.;—and let a distinct treatise be prepared on each of these; and then let his majesty command the ministers of his own palace, in general assembly, to decide whether they are correct or erroneous. And if indeed they be subversive of the cardinal virtues and opposed to the classics, involving wicked doctrines and sinister means, then let the said courtiers be immediately dismissed and expelled; and your majesty's servant will willingly abide the punishment appointed for those who aid and abet the deceivers of his majesty. . . .

Your servant in rashly presuming to approach the Heavenly Majesty, is overwhelmed with infinite fear and dread, while he earnestly awaits the imperial mandate in reply to this memorial.

MUSLIM INDIAN REACTIONS: ABU TALEB KHAN'S TRAVELS

Abu Taleb Khan was of Turkish and Persian descent, like many residents of northwest India. Born in 1752, he was a bureaucrat who worked for Indian princes and then tried to get a job from the English colonial administration. It was after this that, aided by some British friends, he went to England. He was taken up as

a novelty by British high society, which surely colored his reactions to this strange nation, though they did not deprive him of critical capacity. He wrote about his travels in Persian when he returned to India, still hoping for official patronage.

• • •

Glory be to God, the Lord of all worlds, who has conferred innumerable blessings on mankind and accomplished all the laudable desires of his creatures. Praise be also to the Chosen of Mankind [Muhammad], the traveler over the whole expanse of the heavens, and benedictions without end on his descendants and companions.

The wanderer over the face of the earth, Abu Taleb, the son of Mohammed of Ispahan, begs leave to inform the curious in biography, that, owing to several adverse circumstances, finding it inconvenient to remain at home, he was compelled to undertake many tedious journeys, during which he associated with men of all nations and beheld various wonders, both by sea and by land.

It therefore occurred to him, that if he were to write all the circumstances of his journey through Europe, to describe the curiosities and wonders which he saw, and to give some account of the manner and customs of the various nations he visited, all of which are little known to Asiatics, it would afford a gratifying banquet to his countrymen.

He was also of opinion, that many of the customs, inventions, sciences, and ordinances of Europe, the good effects of which are apparent in those countries, might with great advantage be imitated by Mohammedans.

Impressed with these ideas, he, on his first setting out on his travels, commenced a journal, in which he daily inserted every event, and committed to writing such reflections as occurred to him at the moment: and on his return to Calcutta, in the [Muslim] year of the Hejira 1218 [1803 C.E.], having revised and abridged his notes, he arranged them in the present form.

[Here Abu Taleb changes from the third to the first person, and laments:] I have named this work . . . "The Travels of Taleb in the Regions of Europe"; but when I reflect on the want of energy and the indolent dispositions of my country-men, and the many erroneous customs which exist in all Mohammedan countries and among all ranks of Mussulmans, I am fearful that my exertions will be thrown away. The great and the rich, intoxicated with pride and luxury, and puffed up with the vanity of their possessions, consider universal science as comprehended in the circle of their own scanty acquirements and limited knowledge; while the poor and common people, from the want of leisure, and overpowered by the difficulty of procuring a livelihood, have not time to attend to their personal concerns, much less to form desires for the acquirement of information on new discoveries and inven-

From Charles Stewart, ed., *Travels of Mirza Abu Taleb Khan in Asia, Africa and Europe* (New Delhi: Sona Publications: 1814; reprint, 1977), xiv–xvi, 82, 128–29, 158–61, 168–70, 178–80.

tions; although such a passion has been implanted by nature in every human breast, as an honor and an ornament to the species. I therefore despair of their reaping any fruit from my labors, being convinced that they will consider this book of no greater value than the volumes of tales and romances which they peruse merely to pass away their time, or are attracted thereto by the easiness of the style. It may consequently be concluded, that as they will find no pleasure in reading a work which contains a number of foreign names, treats on uncommon subjects, and alludes to other matters which cannot be understood at the first glance, but require a little time for consideration, they will, under pretense of zeal for their religion, entirely abstain and refrain from perusing it. . . .

> Henceforward we will devote our lives to London, and its heart-
> alluring Damsels:
> Our hearts are satiated with viewing fields, gardens rivers, and
> palaces.
>
> We have no longing for the Toba, Sudreh, or other trees of
> Paradise:
> We are content to rest under the shade of these terrestrial
> Cypresses.
>
> If the Shaikh of Mecca is displeased at our conversion, who cares?
> May the Temple which has conferred such blessings on us, and its
> Priests, flourish!
>
> Fill the goblet with wine! If by this I am prevented from returning
> To my old religion, I care not; nay, I am the better pleased.
>
> If the prime of my life has been spent in the service of an Indian
> Cupid,
> It matters not: I am now rewarded by the smiles of the British
> Fair.
>
> Adorable creatures! whose flowing tresses, whether of flaxen or of
> jetty hue,
> Or auburn gay, delight my soul, and ravish all my senses!
>
> Whose ruby lips would animate the torpid clay, or marble statue!
> Had I a renewal of life, I would, with rapture, devote it to your
> service!
>
> These wounds of Cupid, on your heart, Taleba, are not accidental:
> They were engendered by Nature, like the streaks on the leaf of a
> tulip. . . .

The English legislators and philosophers have wisely determined, that the best mode of keeping women out of the way of temptation, and their minds from wandering after improper desires, is by giving them sufficient employment; therefore whatever business can be effected without any great exertion of mental abilities or corporeal strength, is assigned to the women. Thus they have all the internal management and care of the house, and washing the clothes. They are also employed to take care of shops, and, by their beauty and eloquence, often attract customers. This I can speak from my own experience; for I scarcely ever passed the pastry-cook's shop at the corner of Newman street in Oxford road, that I did not go in and spend money for the pleasure of talking to a beautiful young woman who kept it. To the men is assigned the business of waiting at table, taking care of the horses and cattle, and management of the garden, farm, etc. This division of labour is attended with much convenience, and prevents confusion.

Besides the above important regulation, the English lawgivers have placed the women under many salutary restraints, which prevent their making an improper use of the liberty they have, of mixing in company, and conversing with men. In the first place, strangers, or persons whose characters are not well known, are seldom introduced to them; secondly the women never visit any bachelor, except he be a near relation; thirdly, no woman of respectability ever walks out (in London), unless attended by her husband, a relation or a confidential servant. They are upon no account allowed to walk out after dark; and they never think of sleeping abroad, even at the house of their father or mother, unless the husband is with them. They therefore have seldom an opportunity of acting improperly. The father, mother, and whole family, also consider themselves disgraced by the bad conduct of a daughter or a sister. And as, by the laws of England, a man may beat his wife with a stick which will not endanger the breaking of a limb, or may confine her in a room, the woman dare not even give their tongues too much liberty.

If, notwithstanding all these restraints, a woman should be so far lost to all sense of shame as to commit a disgraceful action, she is for ever after shunned by all her relations, acquaintances, and every lady of the respectability. Her husband is also authorised by law to take away all her property and ornaments, to debar her from the sight of her children, and even to turn her out of the house; and if proof can be produced of her misconduct, he may obtain a divorce, by which she is entirely separated from him, and loses all her dower, and even her marriage portion. From what has been stated, it is evident that the English women, notwithstanding their apparent liberty, and the politeness and flattery with which they are addressed, are, by the wisdom of their lawgivers, confined in strict bondage; and that, on the contrary, the Mohammedan women, who are prohibited from mixing in society, and are kept concealed behind curtains, but are allowed to walk out in veils, and to go to the baths (in Turkey), and to visit their fathers and mothers and even female acquaintances, and to sleep abroad for several nights together, are much more mistresses of their own conduct and much more liable to fall into the paths of error. . . .

I cannot pass over this opportunity of freely expressing my sentiments with respect to the establishment of British courts of law in India; which, I contend, are converted to the very worst of purposes, and, unless an alteration takes place in the system, will some time or other produce the most sinister consequences.

In Calcutta, few months elapse that some respectable and wealthy man is not attacked by the harpies who swarm round the courts of judicature. Various are their modes of extorting money; and many of them have acquired such fortunes by these nefarious means, as to live in great splendour, and quite eclipse the ancient families . . . These circumstances are all very distressing to a native of India, unacquainted with the English laws and customs; and many of them, rather than have the trouble and run the risk, willingly pay a sum of money; but the person accused is a resolute man, who determines to go through the whole process, he is obliged to employ an attorney, who understands not a word of his language, and to intrust an important concern in the hands of a counsellor, whom he cannot understand but through the medium of an interpreter; and the attorney, not being paid by the year, month, or day, as is the custom of India, makes what charges he pleases, and postpones the trial till it suits his convenience. . . . But suppose the defendant unable to give security for so large a sum of money; he is detained, the first day, in the court-house, under charge of the constable; where, if he is a Hindoo, he cannot eat; and if a Mohammedan, he is precluded from performing the duties of his religion. The following day he is carried to the same prison in which the felons are confined; to the great disgrace of himself and family: there he is every night shut up in a dark and hot cell, where he lingers for months. Many are the respectable persons who die under such misfortunes, before the trial comes on. If the supposed debtor survive till the day of trial arrives, he is then conveyed, under a guard, to the court, where, probably, the plaintiff plays the same tricks as before described; and the only consolation the poor man receives, is, that the court are very sorry he should have suffered so much trouble. . . .

As it may not appear fair or candid to censure any system so freely without an endeavour to point out some remedy to correct its defects, I shall here take the liberty of suggesting a few hints, which, I think, might be usefully applied.

For many years after the establishment of the Mohammedan religion, every person pleaded his own cause; and the cazies, being then men of great learning and sanctity, gave their decisions gratuitously.

As the English judges are at present paid from the public funds, and therefore cannot benefit themselves by prolonging suits, I recommend, that the counsellors, attornies etc. shall be placed on a similar footing, and that they shall not receive any fee or bribe from the litigating parties under a severe penalty. In order to defray the expense of this establishment, either let a small additional tax be laid on the nation at large, or a duty of so much percent be levied on all litigated property. By this plan, I am convinced that the number and length of suits would be much curtailed, the time of the witnesses would be saved, the law would be purified from those imperfections which are now a reproach to it, and the courts purged of those pettifogging lawyers, who are a disgrace to their profession. . . .

. . . The first and greatest defect I observed in the English is their want of faith in religion, and their great inclination to philosophy [atheism]: The effect of these principles, or rather want of principle, is very conspicuous in the lower orders of people, who are totally devoid of honesty. They are, indeed, cautious how they transgress against the laws, from fear of punishment; but whenever an opportunity offers of purloining anything without the risk of detection, they never pass it by. They are also ever on the watch to appropriate to themselves the property of the rich, who, on this account, are obliged constantly to keep their doors shut, and never to permit an unknown person to enter them. At present, owing to the vigilance of the magistrates, the severity of the laws, and the honor of the superior classes of people, no very bad consequences are to be apprehended; but if ever such nefarious practices should become prevalent and should creep in among the higher classes, inevitable ruin must ensue.

The second defect most conspicuous in the English character is pride or insolence. Puffed up with their power and good fortune for the last fifty years, they are not apprehensive of adversity, and take no pains to avert it. Thus, when the people of London, some time ago, assembled in mobs on account of the great increase of taxes and high price of provisions, and were nearly in a state of insurrection—although the magistrates, by their vigilance in watching them, and by causing parties of soldiers to patrol the streets day and night, to disperse all persons whom they saw assembling together, succeeded in quieting the disturbance—yet no pains were afterwards taken to eradicate the evil. Some of the men in power said it had been merely a plan of the artificers to obtain higher wages (an attempt frequently made by the English tradesmen); others were of opinion that no remedy could be applied; therefore no further notice was taken of the affair. All this, I say, betrays a blind confidence, which, instead of meeting the danger and endeavoring to prevent it, waits till the misfortune arrives, and then attempts to remedy it. Such was the case with the late king of France, who took no step to oppose the Revolution till it was too late. This self-confidence is to be found, more or less, in every Englishman; it however differs much from the pride of Indians and Persians.

Their third defect is a passion for acquiring money and their attachment to worldly affairs. Although these bad qualities are not so reprehensible in them as in countries more subject to the vicissitudes of fortune, (because, in England, property is so well protected by the laws that every person reaps the fruits of his industry, and, in his old age, enjoys the earnings or economy of his youth,) yet sordid and illiberal habits are generally found to accompany avarice and parsimony, and, consequently, render the possessor of them contemptible; on the contrary, generosity, if it does not launch into prodigality, but is guided by the hand of prudence, will render a man respected and esteemed. . . .

. . . The English have very peculiar opinions on the subject of *perfection*. They insist that it is merely an ideal quality, and depends entirely upon comparison; that mankind have risen, by degrees, from the state of savages to the exalted dignity of the great philosopher Newton; but that, so far from having yet attained *perfection*, it is possible that, in future ages, philosophers will look with as much contempt on the acquirements of Newton as we now do on the rude state of the arts among savages. If this axiom of theirs be correct, man has yet much to learn, and all his boasted knowledge is but vanity.

Their twelfth defect is a contempt for the customs of other nations, and the preference they give to their own; although theirs, in fact, may be much inferior. I had a striking instance of this prejudice in the conduct of my fellow-passengers on board ship. Some of these, who were otherwise respectable characters, ridiculed the idea of my wearing trowsers, and a night-dress, when I went to bed; and contended, that they slept much more at their ease by going to bed nearly naked. I replied, that I slept very comfortably; that mine was certainly the most decent mode; and that, in the event of any sudden accident happening, I could run on deck instantly, and, if requisite, jump into the boat in a minute; whilst they must either lose some time in dressing, or come out of their cabins in a very immodest manner. In answer to this, they said, such sudden accidents seldom occurred, but that if it did happen, they would not hesitate to come on deck in their shirts only. This I give merely as a specimen of their obstinacy, and prejudice in favour of their own customs.

In London, I was frequently attacked on the apparent unreasonableness and childishness of some of the Mohammedan customs; but as, from my knowledge of the English character, I was convinced it would be folly to argue the point philo-sophically with them, I contented myself with parrying the subject. Thus, when they attempted to turn into ridicule the ceremonies used by the pilgrims on their arrival at Mecca, I asked them, why they supposed the ceremony of baptism, by a clergy-man, requisite for the salvation of a child, who could not possibly be sensible what he was about. When they reproached us for eating with our hands; I replied, "There is by this mode no danger of cutting yourself or your neighbours; and it is an old and a true proverb, 'The nearer the bone, the sweeter the meat:' but, exclusive of these advantages, a man's own hands are surely cleaner than the *feet of a baker's boy;* for it is well know, that half the bread in London is kneaded by the feet." By this mode of argument I, completely silenced all my adversaries, and frequently turned the laugh against them, when they expected to have refuted me and made me appear ridiculous.

PART IV

The Long Nineteenth Century

BEGINNING ABOUT 1750, CHANGES in Europe's economy and politics began to create the conditions for another reshaping of the framework of world history. Some elements of this reshaping—the rise of industry and new kinds of powered equipment, for example, or new ideals of democracy—still persist today. But the changes initially generated a surge of European power in the world that has not endured in full force. In this sense a world history period that begins with European revolutions in the eighteenth century and ends in 1914, on the eve of Europe's relative decline in world affairs, constitutes an obviously coherent unit. Many historians call this period the long nineteenth century.

During the late eighteenth century the industrial revolution developed in Britain. It featured the rise of factory industry and the use of the new powered machinery, with the invention of a usable steam engine the central technological innovation. Industrialization fairly quickly spread to other parts of Western Europe and to the United States. It allowed a massive increase in the production of goods, including new kinds of weaponry, plus more rapid systems of transportation and communication. During the same period were also launched a series of Western revolutions and wars of independence, stretching from the United States to Western Europe and back to Latin America. New ideas of democracy, defense of individual liberty, nationalism, and even social justice, generated and to some degree implemented in this revolutionary era, led to significant transformations in Western society and in Latin America and had wider international implications. It was the redefinition of beliefs, for example, along with the new demands of the international economy, that set the stage for the abolition of serfdom not only in Western Europe but soon in Russia and other parts of Eastern Europe, and for the abolition of the slave trade and of slavery in the Americas.

These changes helped set in motion a massive increase in the power of the West in the world at large. Technology and military power were crucial. Western armies could now defeat much larger landed forces; the naval advantage was enhanced as well. Western victories or successful intimidations in Ottoman territory (1798), in China (1839–42), in Japan (1853), and in Russia (1854–55) demonstrated the new international balance of power. Massive imperialist conquests in Africa, Southeast Asia, and the Pacific brought direct European control to new areas.

Even Latin America, though now technically independent, found itself more fully dominated by Western commercial interests than ever before.

Yet, other developments accompanied and complicated this apotheosis of the West. Concern about slavery helped motivate European intervention in Africa, where internal slavery had ironically increased to compensate for the loss of the slave trade abroad. Ideas of nationalism and democracy could fuel new imitations of Europe but also new resistance. Anti-imperialist nationalist movements began to take shape in most parts of the non-Western world in the second half of the nineteenth century, though they often urged a modification of regional traditions in favor of Western science and technology.

Massive changes in the West itself, accompanying the rise of an industrial society and the gradual emergence of political democracy, were matched, in world history, by the need to react both to Western power and to Western values. These reactions varied, which means that comparative issues in world history remain complicated. Japan quickly saw the need to reform (though not to become Western), while China lagged. India's changes, as a colony, obviously differed from those of the Ottoman Empire, which remained technically independent though increasingly beleaguered. Africa, seized late in the imperialist surge and then exploited vigorously, displayed distinctive patterns of its own. Important new areas of the world, including the United States, Canada, Australia, and New Zealand, formed societies in many ways Western in orientation but tempered by frontier conditions and an unusual mixture of races.

Varieties of conditions—colonial or technically independent, industrializing or confined to food and raw material production, eagerly reformist or more strictly traditional—remained in the world of 1900. Even nationalism varied in strength and content, as a new political and cultural force. Variety was shaped both by differences in the way European power and values were encountered and by the distinct traditions of each major society. The result is a surprisingly complex tapestry in a century that, superficially, seemed to be shaped simply by the whims and interests of the West. Attention to careful comparisons in vital in order to get at the new Western influence amid very diverse settings and reactions.

This section deals with several key issues of world history in the long nineteenth century in a number of comparative groupings. The new political ideas and revolutions that rocked the Atlantic regions from the late eighteenth century to 1848 launched the period. Comparing revolutionary ideas and some unexpected consequences, including the powerful modern force of nationalism, involves Europe and the Americas alike.

Growing European power and decidedly undemocratic attitudes toward other peoples spawned the new wave of imperialism. Europeans' forced entry into China, from 1839 onward, represented the imperialist thrust while marking a tremendous—and very difficult—transition in Chinese history. The Chinese were fully opened to the world for the first time, and at a great disadvantage. There is a clear opportunity here to compare European imperialist ideas with the reactions of a proud but weakened civilization.

New political ideas accompanied by complex economic changes produced important shifts in the conditions of women, leading to new ideas and new complaints. Changes in the West, accompanying imperialism, also caused shifts in colonial areas such as India, although westernization was incomplete where women were concerned.

The end of widespread slavery (save in a few important pockets) and harsh serfdom was one of the great events of nineteenth-century world history, extending from emancipations accompanying the revolutionary era up to the final decades of the century. Emancipations occurred in response to some of the same economic and cultural forces the world over, but the precise forms and consequences varied. Many dissatisfactions remained, as labor was incompletely freed despite great legal change and as existing upper classes and dominant races worked to retain key advantages. Again, comparison helps pinpoint the crucial issues.

Industrialization was largely a Western achievement during the long nineteenth century, though it had huge consequences worldwide, in imperialism and also in growing economic inequalities between the West and other areas. By the end of the century, however, Japan and Russia had both managed to launch significant industrialization, imitating Western patterns in part but supplying special ingredients from their own cultural and institutional frameworks. Differences between Japanese and Western economic styles, still operative toward the end of the twentieth century, can be traced to the long nineteenth century, even though Japan openly copied the West in many respects. Russia and Japan also generated notable resistance to Western values, using nationalism to defend certain traditions and "inventing" others that would help preserve distinctive identities amid change. Here was an important reminder that, even in a century of triumphant Western power, the world remained diverse and many societies sought the means to limit Western influence.

CHAPTER 19

THE "AGE OF ATLANTIC REVOLUTIONS" AND EARLY NATIONALISM

This chapter invites comparison of political ideas, and particularly the bases of nationalism in France, in areas of Europe surrounding France (especially Germany), and in Latin America, during the great age of revolution from 1789 into the nineteenth century.

The wave of independence wars and revolutions that surged from the 1770s onward was one of the great developments in world history during the long nineteenth century. The action focused on the Atlantic regions: North America, Western Europe, the Caribbean, and South America. But the principles and institutions that resulted would have wider international impact—indeed, world history is still sorting through these principles.

Two forces spurred this extraordinary revolutionary contagion. First, European and some American thinkers associated with the eighteenth-century Enlightenment generated new ideas about politics and society. They urged greater protection of liberty, including religious liberty; they urged greater social equality or at least the abolition of legal privileges such as those of the nobility; some suggested the importance of democracy and many talked more vaguely of the will of the people. Along with these ideas, widely disseminated because of the growing literacy, new social forces pushed for change. Population pressure led to land hunger among Europe's peasantry. New commercial practices antagonized traditional artisans, while business wealth prompted many middle-class people to seek a more active political voice.

One early result of such pressures was the American Revolution, which was triggered also by new British colonial rules widely resented by the colonists. The big moment, however, was the French Revolution of 1789. France was Europe's most populous and prestigious country, with a monarchy that had flaunted its power for three centuries. If revolution could happen there, it might happen anywhere. Furthermore, the revolution spread itself directly. Many neighboring kings feared the revolution and by 1791 began attacking France. France on the whole held its own and even began conquering other territories. This process continued when the revolutionary government yielded to the dictatorship of Napoleon, from 1799 to 1814. Napoleon rejected some of the liberal principles of the revolution, but he embraced other ideals and instituted major social and political changes in many of the areas he conquered.

The French Revolution went through many phases, which complicated its basic meanings. The first phase was largely liberal: it abolished the aristocracy, provided religious liberty and attacked the power of the church, allowed greater commercial freedom, and destroyed the manorial system. Thanks in part to foreign attack, the revolution became more radical between 1792 and 1794, urging democracy (for men), universal education, and mass military conscription, while hinting at social reforms. Some of these radical goals persisted even as the revolutionary leadership turned toward a process of defense and consolidation that ultimately led to Napoleon's rule.

Both the French Revolution and Napoleon's reign opened the way for a major extension of revolutionary ideas to Latin America. Already in 1798, Toussaint l'Ouverture led a successful slave rebellion in Haiti against France. By 1810 revolutionary ideas plus Napoleon's invasion of Spain set the stage for widespread independence wars in Spanish America, from Mexico to Argentina. Military fortunes seesawed for a decade, but by 1820 most of Spanish America consisted of independent republics (Mexico briefly debated having a king but decided against).

The following selections focus on the nature and impact of revolution and independence wars in Europe and Latin America. They also call attention to one other result of the tumultuous era: the effective origins of nationalism.

Nationalism was not a traditional loyalty. Most people, previously, had been loyal to kings, localities, and religions. Some nationalist ideas emerged from the Enlightenment, though most Enlightenment thinkers believed in human universality, the reverse of nationalism. Yet the revolutionary era helped trigger nationalism in three ways.

First, the people of France, as well as those of the new United States, began to reason that if governments now belonged "to the people," the people should be actively loyal, should be willing to serve in armies, and so on; nationalism—the idea that each people was distinctive and should have its own state—could both express and promote this approach. Small wonder that the world's first national anthem resulted from the French Revolution.

Second, as ideas of liberty helped motivate attacks on colonial governments—the colonists' war against Britain, the Latin American wars against Spain—it was easy to think in terms of a right to nationhood. Americans (North or Latin) were different from Englishmen or Spaniards, and they deserved their own states. Nationalism gained ground in the United States, and nationalism formed as important part of Latin Americans' motivation throughout the wars for independence.

Third, French attacks on neighboring countries stimulated huge resistance. People did not want to be ruled by foreigners, even if they were bringing revolution. Furthermore, French ideas themselves included nationalism. So popular wars against the French turned increasingly to nationalist sentiments that were new yet were designed in part to protect older boundaries. Napoleon, particularly, expedited this process by destroying many traditional small states in Germany and Italy; that caused people in those areas to think in terms of large nationalist goals.

Nationalism and revolution thus went hand in hand, and for decades nationalism was seen as a largely radical force. But nationalism could complicate other revolutionary ideals as well. Which was more important for a nationalist: a state that granted wide liberties and so invited criticism and disruption, or a strong state that could demonstrate the nation's might? Even during the revolutionary era, different leaders balanced nationalism and political and social reform in different ways. Ultimately, nationalism could be a conservative as well as a radical force (see chapter 23)—and this versatility helps explain why nationalism has been one of the most important movements in modern world history.

The following selections suggest, first, an assessment of what some of the basic French revolutionary ideals were. This was a social as well as a political revolution, bringing huge changes to peasants and workers as well as middle-class businessmen. Next, however, the assessment should extend to the ways the French Revolution presented itself to conquered territory, where a mixture of ideals and controls complicated reactions. Other leaders, including those who were basically conservatives, such as the King of Prussia, could use reactions against France and a dash of nationalism to try to arouse popular support. Finally, Latin American leaders like Simón Bolívar embraced revolutionary principles—at least, the political ideals; the social commitments were less clear in movements dominated by property-owning men of European stock. But those leaders also articulated a strong nationalism that might at points overwhelm the more liberal goals.

The age of Atlantic revolutions came to an inconclusive end. Napoleon was defeated in 1814 and again in 1815 by a coalition of European monarchs including the Prussian king. This led to an intensely conservative period. But revolutions broke out again in 1820, 1830, and 1848, few of them as successful as the great French Revolution but all leading to change. In Latin America, independent regimes settled down to the task of building new states, often in very difficult circumstances. Great political instability and frequent dictatorships were one result. As in Europe, however, a strong liberal movement was planted, often supplemented by nationalism, and it would continue to play a major political role. Formal revolution was over in the Atlantic world after 1848 (though a new wave of revolution would begin in parts of Latin America in the twentieth century). But the revolutionary ideals, including nationalism, continued to spread worldwide during the late nineteenth century and beyond.

In the long haul, the revolutionary era is noteworthy for spawning both liberalism—in its nineteenth-century sense of urging political and economic freedoms—and nationalism. The two movements sometimes went hand in hand.

Sometimes, however, they were bitter enemies. Elements of this complexity emerged in the revolutionary period itself.

Questions

1. What were the key political principles of the French Revolution, as suggested by the 1792 decree? What were the key social changes, and how would they affect the status of peasants?
2. How did French revolutionary principles stimulate nationalism within France? To what extent was the 1792 decree a French nationalist statement, and to what extent did it strive for a more universalist approach?
3. How might French revolutionary actions of the sort suggested by the decree stimulate nationalism against France?
4. What principles did Frederick William evoke in urging opposition to Napoleonic France? How did he reflect the impact of revolutionary ideas? In what ways, and why, did he suggest German nationalism?
5. How did the tentative nationalism of a Prussian ruler in crisis compare with revolutionary nationalism?
6. What were Bolívar's political ideals? What aspects of the French Revolution did he seem to embrace? What aspects did he ignore? Was he primarily a nationalist or a political-social revolutionary?
7. How did his 1813 appeal and his 1819 speech compare: which was more purely nationalistic, and why?
8. What differences does Bolívar note between Latin America and Western Europe? How might these differences affect political action and revolutionary social change?

For Further Discussion

1. In what ways did nineteenth-century Latin American civilization turn out to differ from Western civilization in the same period?
2. Where would the American (U.S.) Revolution fit in a spectrum that includes the French Revolution and the Latin American wars of independence?
3. In what sense was early nationalism a radical political ideology and movement? In what sense did it carry antiliberal, even conservative implications?

THE FRENCH REVOLUTION AND NATIONALISM: A 1792 DECREE

The following decree was issued by the National Convention in France, a legislature elected in 1792 by widespread manhood suffrage. That body was much more

radical than the legislatures in the earlier years of the revolution. It quickly abolished the monarchy and soon had the king executed. It also took a more active
role in fighting off foreign attack and expanding French borders; early in 1793, for
example, France declared war against Holland, Britain, and Spain and annexed
Belgium. The December 15, 1792, decree from which the following selection is
drawn was stimulated by Belgian resistance to annexation and represents a combination of idealistic revolutionary principles and hard-headed administrative and
financial control. The principles were quickly applied to much of the annexed
territory, helping both to spread revolutionary gains and to arouse the kind of
resistance that could intensify anti-French nationalism.

• • •

The National Convention, having heard the report of its combined Committees of
Finance, War, and Diplomacy; faithful to the principles of the sovereignty of the
people, which do not permit it to recognize any institutions detrimental thereto, and
wishing to establish the rules to be followed by the generals of the armies of the
Republic in territories where they bear arms, decrees:

1. In territories which are or may be occupied by the armies of the Republic,
the generals shall proclaim immediately, in the name of the French nation, the
sovereignty of the people, the suppression of all established authorities and of existing imposts or taxes, the [manorial] abolition of the tithe, of feudalism, of seigneurial
rights, . . . of nobility, and generally of all privileges.

2. They shall announce to the people that they bring it peace, aid, fraternity,
liberty, and equality, and they shall convoke it thereafter in primary or communal
assemblies, in order to create and organize a provisional administration and justice;
they shall supervise the security of persons and property; they shall have the present
decree and the proclamation annexed thereto printed in the language or idiom of
the territory and posted and executed without delay in every commune.

3. All agents and civil or military officials of the former government, as well as
individuals heretofore considered noble, or members of any corporation heretofore
privileged, shall be, for this time only, inadmissible to vote in the primary or communal assemblies, and they may not be elected to positions in the provisional administration or judiciary.

4. The generals shall place, consecutively, under the safeguard and protection
of the French Republic all real and personal property belonging to the public treasury, to the prince, his abettors, adherents, and voluntary satellites, to public establishments, and to lay and ecclesiastical bodies and communities; they shall have a
detailed statement thereof drafted promptly and dispatched to the Executive Coun-

From John Hall Stewart, ed., *A Documentary Survey of the French Revolution* (New York: Macmillan,
1951), 381–84. Reprinted by permission of Prentice-Hall, Inc., Upper Saddle River, NJ.

cil, and they shall take all measures within their power in order that such properties be respected.

5. The provisional administration, elected by the people, shall be responsible for the surveillance and administration of matters placed under the safeguard and protection of the French Republic; it shall supervise the security of persons and property; it shall have the laws now in force relative to the trial of civil and criminal suits, to the police, and to public security put into effect; it shall be in charge of regulating and paying local expenses and those necessary for the common defence; it may institute taxes, provided, however, that they are not borne by the indigent and hard-working portion of the population.

6. As soon as the provisional administration has been organized, the National Convention shall appoint commissioners from within its own body to go to fraternize with it.

7. The Executive Council also shall appoint national commissioners who shall go, consecutively, to the places, to consult the generals and the provisional administration elected by the people concerning measures to be taken for the common defence and concerning the means to be employed to procure the clothing and provisions necessary for the armies, and to pay their [i.e., the armies'] expenses during their sojourn on its territory.

8. The national commissioners appointed by the Executive Council shall render it a fortnightly account of their activities. The Executive Council shall approve, modify, or reject same, and, in turn, shall render account thereof to the Convention.

9. The provisional administration elected by the people, and the functions of the national commissioners shall terminate as soon as the inhabitants, after having declared the sovereignty and independence of the people, liberty, and equality, have organized a form of free and popular government.

10. A statement shall be made of the expenses which the French Republic has incurred for the common defence, and of the sums which it may have received, and the French nation shall make arrangements with the established government for whatever is due; and, in case the common interest requires the troops of the Republic to remain upon foreign territory beyond that time, it shall take suitable measures to provide for their maintenance.

11. The French nation declares that it will treat as an enemy of the people anyone who, refusing liberty and equality, or renouncing them, might wish to preserve, recall, or treat with the prince and the privileged castes; it promises and engages itself not to subscribe to any treaty, and not to lay down its arms until after the establishment of the sovereignty and independence of the people upon whose territory the troops of the Republic have entered, who shall have adopted the principles of equality and established a free and popular government.

12. The Executive Council shall dispatch the present decree by special messengers to all generals, and shall take the necessary measures for assuring its execution.

The French People to the _____ People.

Brothers and friends, we have gained liberty and we shall maintain it. We offer to help you enjoy this inestimable good which has always belonged to us, and of which our oppressors have not been able to deprive us without crime.

We have expelled your tyrants: show yourselves free men, and we will guarantee you from their vengeance, their designs, and their return.

Henceforth the French nation proclaims the sovereignty of the people, the suppression of all civil and military authorities which have governed you up to the present, and of all taxes which you sustain, in whatever form they exist; the abolition of the tithe, of feudalism, of seigneurial rights, . . . fixed or contingent, of *banalités,* of real and personal servitude, of hunting and fishing privileges, [labor service and all manorial taxes], and generally of every species of contributions with which you have been burdened by your usurpers; it proclaims also the abolition among you of every corporation, noble, sacerdotal, and others, of all prerogatives and privileges that are contrary to equality. You are henceforth, brothers and friends, all citizens, all equal in rights, and all equally summoned to govern, to serve, and to defend your *Patrie* [fatherland].

Assemble immediately in primary or communal assemblies, hasten to establish your provisional administrations and courts, conforming therein to the provisions of article 3 of the above decree. The agents of the French Republic will consult you in order to assure your welfare and the fraternity which is to exist henceforth between us.

Prussian Kings and German Nationalism: A Proclamation of 1813

Frederick William, king of Prussia, issued the following proclamation in 1813, as he prepared to join the alliance against Napoleon that ultimately defeated the French emperor. Prussia was the strongest single state in Germany, amid a welter of small states. It contained a variety of regional people, from Prussians to other eastern Germans to Lithuanians. It had been built up carefully by previous kings, including a founding ruler known as the Great Elector. During Napoleon's reign, Prussia had lost many battles and had frequently made its peace with France. Some internal reforms, imitating French revolutionary measures, had been designed to provide a more efficient and popular state, though politically and socially the country remained conservative. The king's proclamation shows an interesting balance between updated, nationalistic sentiments and a simple interest in protecting the monarchy from foreign interference—though the idea of appealing to the people was itself novel for European kings. Prussia would continue to play an

ambivalent role in German reforms and nationalism until finally, in the 1860s, it successfully took the lead in German unification.

• • •

The King of Prussia Rouses His People against Napoleon

There is no need of explaining to my loyal subjects, or to any German, the reasons for the war which is about to begin. They lie plainly before the eyes of awakened Europe. We succumbed to the superior force of France. The peace which followed deprived me of my people and, far from bringing us blessings, it inflicted upon us deeper wounds than the war itself, sucking out the very marrow of the country. Our principal fortresses remained in the hand of the enemy, and agriculture, as well as the highly developed industries of our towns, was crippled. The freedom of trade was hampered and thereby the sources of commerce and prosperity cut off. The country was left a prey to the ravages of destitution.

I hoped, by the punctilious fulfillment of the engagements I had entered into, to lighten the burdens of my people, and even to convince the French emperor that it would be to his own advantage to leave Prussia her independence. But the purest and best of intentions on my part were of no avail against insolence and faithlessness, and it became only too plain that the emperor's treaties would gradually ruin us even more surely than his wars. The moment is come when we can no longer harbor the slightest illusion as to our situation.

Brandenburgers, Prussians, Silesians, Pomeranians, Lithuanians! You know what you have borne for the past seven years; you know the sad fate that awaits you if we do not bring this war to an honorable end. Think of the times gone by,—of the Great Elector, the great Frederick! Remember the blessings for which your forefathers fought under their leadership and which they paid for with their blood,—freedom of conscience, national honor, independence, commerce, industry, learning. Look at the great example of our powerful allies, the Russians; look at the Spaniards, the Portuguese. For such objects as these even weaker peoples have gone forth against mightier enemies and returned in triumph. Witness the heroic Swiss and the people of the Netherlands.

Great sacrifices will be demanded from every class of the people, for our undertaking is a great one, and the number and resources of our enemies far from insignificant. But would you not rather make these sacrifices for the fatherland and for your own rightful king than for a foreign ruler, who, as he has shown by many examples, will use you and your sons and your uttermost farthing for ends which are nothing to you?

From James Harvey Robinson, ed., *Readings in European History,* vol. 2 (New York: Ginn, 1966), 522–23.

Faith in God, perseverance, and the powerful aid of our allies will bring us victory as the reward of our honest efforts. Whatever sacrifices may be required of us as individuals, they will be outweighed by the sacred rights for which we make them, and for which we must fight to a victorious end unless we are willing to cease to be Prussians or Germans. This is the final, the decisive struggle; upon it depends our independence, our prosperity, our existence. There are no other alternatives but an honorable peace or a heroic end. You would willingly face even the latter for honor's sake, for without honor no Prussian or German could live.

However, we may confidently await the outcome. God and our own firm purpose will bring victory to our cause and with it an assured and glorious peace and the return of happier times.

Frederick William.
Breslau, March 17, 1813.

POLITICAL IDEALS AND NATIONALISM IN LATIN AMERICA: SIMÓN BOLÍVAR

Simón Bolívar (1783–1830) was one of the principal leaders in Latin America's successful struggle for independence early in the nineteenth century. A creole— that is, American born but of European stock, Bolívar was keenly aware of the political ideas of the European Enlightenment and the French and American revolution. He led the battles against the Spaniards in Venezuela, Colombia, and the northern Andes region, hoping to form one great state. He was selected as the initial leader but was unable to maintain the political structure or the unity he had intended, as the region soon split into separate, smaller countries. The following selections come from a proclamation calling Venezuelans to arms in the fight against Spanish occupation, which occurred in 1813, and an address to the legislature in Venezuela soon after independence, in 1819.

• • •

THE 1813 PROCLAMATION

Venezuelans: An army of your brothers, sent by the Sovereign Congress of New Granada [present-day Colombia] has come to liberate you. Having expelled the oppressors from the provinces of Mérida and Trujillo, it is now among you.

We are sent to destroy the Spaniards, to protect the Americans, and to reëstablish the republican governments that once formed the Confederation of Venezuela. The states defended by our arms are again governed by their former constitutions

From Vicente Lecuna, ed., *Selected Writings of Bolívar* (New York: Colonial Press, 1951), 1: 31–32.

and tribunals, in full enjoyment of their liberty and independence, for our mission is designed only to break the chains of servitude which still shackle some of our towns, and not to impose laws or exercise acts of dominion to which the rules of war might entitle us.

Moved by your misfortunes, we have been unable to observe with indifference the afflictions you were forced to experience by the barbarous Spaniards, who have ravished you, plundered you, and brought you death and destruction. They have violated the sacred rights of nations. They have broken the most solemn agreements and treaties. In fact, they have committed every manner of crime, reducing the Republic of Venezuela to the most frightful desolation. Justice therefore demands vengeance, and necessity compels us to exact it. Let the monsters who infest Colombian soil, who have drenched it in blood, be cast out forever; may their punishment be equal to the enormity of their perfidy, so that we may eradicate the stain of our ignominy and demonstrate to the nations of the world that the sons of America cannot be offended with impunity.

Despite our just resentment toward the iniquitous Spaniards, our magnanimous heart still commands us to open to them for the last time a path to reconciliation and friendship; they are invited to live peacefully among us, if they will abjure their crimes, honestly change their ways, and coöperate with us in destroying the intruding Spanish government and in the reëstablishment of the Republic of Venezuela.

Any Spaniard who does not, by every active and effective means, work against tyranny in behalf of this just cause, will be considered an enemy and punished; as a traitor to the nation, he will inevitably be shot by a firing squad. On the other hand, a general and absolute amnesty is granted to those who come over to our army with or without their arms, as well as those who render aid to the good citizens who are endeavoring to throw off the yoke of tyranny. Army officers and civil magistrates who proclaim the government of Venezuela and join with us shall retain their posts and positions; in a word, those Spaniards who render outstanding service to the State shall be regarded and treated as Americans.

And you Americans who, by error or treachery, have been lured from the paths of justice, are informed that your brothers, deeply regretting the error of your ways, have pardoned you as we are profoundly convinced that you cannot be truly to blame, for only the blindness and ignorance in which you have been kept up to now by those responsible for your crimes could have induced you to commit them. Fear not the sword that comes to avenge you and to sever the ignoble ties with which your executioners have bound you to their own fate. You are hereby assured, with absolute impunity, of your honor, lives, and property. The single title, "Americans," shall be your safeguard and guarantee. Our arms have come to protect you, and they shall never be raised against a single one of you, our brothers.

This amnesty is extended even to the very traitors who most recently have committed felonious acts, and it shall be so religiously applied that no reason, cause, or pretext will be sufficient to oblige us to violate our offer, however extraordinary and extreme the occasion you may give to provoke our wrath.

Spaniards and Canary Islanders, you will die, though you be neutral, unless you actively espouse the cause of America's liberation. Americans, you will live, even if you have trespassed.

THE 1819 SPEECH

Gentlemen:

Fortunate is the citizen, who, under the emblem of his command, has convoked this assembly of the national sovereignty so that it may exercise its absolute will! I, therefore, place myself among those most favored by Divine Providence, for I have had the honor of uniting the representatives of the people of Venezuela in this august Congress, the source of legitimate authority, the custodian of the sovereign will, and the arbiter of the Nation's destiny.

In returning to the representatives of the people the Supreme Power which was entrusted to me, I gratify not only my own innermost desires but also those of my fellow-citizens and of future generations, who trust to your wisdom, rectitude, and prudence in all things. Upon the fulfillment of this grateful obligation, I shall be released from the immense authority with which I have been burdened and from the unlimited responsibility which has weighed so heavily upon my slender resources. Only the force of necessity, coupled with the imperious will of the people, compelled me to assume the fearful and dangerous post of *Dictator and Supreme Chief of the Republic.* But now I can breathe more freely, for I am returning to you this authority which I have succeeded in maintaining at the price of so much danger, hardship, and suffering, amidst the worst tribulations suffered by any society. . . .

Let us review the past to discover the base upon which the Republic of Venezuela is founded.

America, in separating from the Spanish monarchy, found herself in a situation similar to that of the Roman Empire when its enormous framework fell to pieces in the midst of the ancient world. Each Roman division then formed an independent nation in keeping with its location or interests; but this situation differed from America's in that those members proceeded to reëstablish their former associations. We, on the contrary, do not even retain the vestiges of our original being. We are not Europeans; we are not Indians; we are but a mixed species of aborigines and Spaniards. Americans by birth and Europeans by law, we find ourselves engaged in a dual conflict: we are disputing with the natives for titles of ownership, and at the same time we are struggling to maintain ourselves in the country that gave us birth

From Vicente Lecuna, ed, *Selected Writings of Bolívar* (New York: Colonial Press, 1951), 1: 173, 175, 176, 184, 191–92, 196.

against the opposition of the invaders. Thus our position is most extraordinary and complicated. But there is more. As our rôle has always been strictly passive and our political existence nil, we find that our quest for liberty is now even more difficult of accomplishment; for we, having been placed in a state lower than slavery, had been robbed not only of our freedom but also of the right to exercise an active domestic tyranny. . . .

Passing from ancient to modern times, we find England and France attracting the attention of all nations and affording them a variety of lessons in matters of government. The evolution [*revolución*] of these two great peoples, like a flaming meteor, has flooded the world with such a profusion of political enlightenment that today every thinking person is aware of the rights and duties of man and the nature of the virtues and vices of governments. All can now appreciate the intrinsic merit of the speculative theories of modern philosophers and legislators. In fact, this political star, in its illuminating career, has even fired the hearts of the apathetic Spaniards, who, having also been thrown into the political whirlpool, made ephemeral efforts to establish liberty; but, recognizing their incapacity for living under the sweet rule of law, they have returned to their immemorial practices of imprisonment and burnings at the stake.

Here, Legislators, is the place to repeat what the eloquent Volney says in the preface of his *Ruins of Palmyra:* "To the newborn peoples of the Spanish Indies, to the generous leaders who guide them toward freedom: may the mistakes and misfortunes of the Old World teach wisdom and happiness to the New." May the teachings of experience be not lost; and may the schools of Greece, Rome, France, England, and North America instruct us in the difficult science of creating and preserving nations through laws that are proper, just, legitimate, and, above all, useful. We must never forget that the excellence of a government lies not in its theories, not in its form or mechanism, but in its being suited to the nature and character of the nation for which it is instituted. . . .

The formation of a stable government requires as a foundation a national spirit, having as its objective a uniform concentration on two cardinal factors, namely, moderation of the popular will and limitation of public authority. The extremes, which these two factors theoretically establish, are difficult to define in practice; but it can well be conceived that the maxim that must guide them is mutual limitation and concentration of power, in order that there may be the least possible friction between the popular will and the constituted public authority. The science of achieving this balance is acquired almost imperceptibly, through practice and study. Progress in the practice of this science is hastened by progress in the enlightenment of the people, and integrity of mind and spirit speeds the progress of enlightenment.

Love of country, love of law, and respect for magistrates are the exalted emotions that must permeate the soul of a republic. The Venezuelans love their country, but they cannot love her laws, because these, being sources of evil, have been harmful;

neither can they respect their magistrates, as they have been unjust, while the new administrators are scarcely known in the calling which they have just entered. Unless there is a sacred reverence for country, laws, and authority, society becomes confused, an abyss—an endless conflict of man versus man, group versus group.

All our moral powers will not suffice to save our infant republic from this chaos unless we fuse the mass of the people, the government, the legislation, and the national spirit into a single united body. Unity, unity, unity must be our motto in all things. The blood of our citizens is varied: let it be mixed for the sake of unity. Our Constitution has divided the powers of government: let them be bound together to secure unity. Our laws are but a sad relic of ancient and modern despotism. Let this monstrous edifice crumble and fall; and, having removed even its ruins, let us erect a temple to Justice; and, guided by its sacred inspiration, let us write a code of Venezuelan laws. Should we wish to consult monuments of legislation, those of Great Britain, France, and the United States of North America afford us admirable models. . . .

. . . . Venezuela, convinced that she possesses sufficient strength to repel her oppressors, has announced, through her government, her absolute determination to fight unto the death in defense of her political existence, not only against Spain but against all men, were all men to degrade themselves by coming to the aid of a rapacious government whose only mobile weapons are the sword of extermination and the flames of the Inquisition—a government that today does not seek dominions, but deserts; not cities, but ruins; not vassals, but tombs. The Declaration of [Independence of] the Republic of Venezuela is a most glorious act, a most heroic act, one most worthy of a free people. It is the one act which, with the greatest satisfaction, I have the honor to submit to the congress, as it has been sanctioned by the unanimous expression of the free people of Venezuela.

CHAPTER 20

THE OPIUM WAR

Chinese and English Views

One of the key events in nineteenth-century history was the West's forcing open of China. Like the Crusades many centuries before (see chapter 10), when Europe attacked Islam, the confrontation of the West and China allows a comparison of two societies' reactions to a single event. Unlike the Crusades, however, this event involved a decisive Western victory and a lasting impact on China because that society on the losing end. The whole episode was a crucial stage in expanding Western imperialism.

Since the rise of the West in the world trade in the fifteenth century, China had adopted a cautious, largely isolationist policy. The nation had no need for Western goods, and it distrusted these aggressive barbarians (see chapter 18). Hence trade, though it occurred, was very limited. The previous modest cultural contacts had been virtually eliminated in attacks on Christian missionaries and converts early in the eighteenth century. British requests for access to Chinese markets were rudely declined as late as 1796: China could stand alone.

Two developments altered this situation by the 1830s. In the first place, China's government was weakening, its hold over its bureaucracy and its tax revenues both slipping. The desire to maintain a traditional policy of isolation and rebuff remained, but the ability to implement it had declined.

More important was the greater strength of Britain and the West, thanks to early industrialization. The West had more wealth, which created a greater appetite for Chinese luxury goods such as silk and porcelain. It engaged in more production, which aroused some interest in gaining access to Chinese markets. It had better technology and better and more abundant armaments, which meant it could now give the Chinese a run for their money if it came to battle.

It was still true that the West had little to offer China economically, for the great empire had its own, preindustrial manufacturing and elaborate internal trade. That is why the final ingredient to this unhappy puzzle involved pressure to sell opium. All these elements drew together in the first (of two) opium wars in the late 1830s. With a small military force, the British compelled the Chinese to back down; China began to be open to foreign trade, though a second war was needed to confirm these results. The Opium War, in turn, was not only pivotal in Chinese history, ushering in many decades of disarray and Western intervention. It also signaled the beginning of the massive nineteenth-century explosion of European imperialism virtually worldwide.

Between 1839 and 1842, British forces, supplemented by other Western troops, successfully battled Chinese coastal contingents over the right to import opium and more generally to trade freely in China. The war demonstrated that the West could easily capture coastal cities. Chinese opposition to Western demands was based on its long-standing suspicion of foreigners ("barbarians") and foreign trade plus a keen awareness of the effects of opium, which had not been widely used before the late eighteenth century. The imperial government attempted to assert its normal strong control over internal affairs. Britain was battling for access to lucrative Chinese products and markets, the old commercial goal that Western military superiority could not attain. Opium, produced in British holdings in India, was a desirable means of earning Chinese currency to exchange for eagerly sought silks and craft goods—for the Chinese were not wildly enthusiastic about what the West itself had for sale. The war began a process of growing Western interference and internal confusion as China was reluctantly dragged into new international involvements.

Views of the war varied. The first selections reflect the official policy, backed by centuries of imperial confidence and responsibility. But reports from officials on the spot show the nation's weakness in fact, which made the emperor's goals unrealizable. An English participant, J. Elliot Bingham, gives an English explanation, offering a much different view of the opium issue, the quality of Chinese society, and the benefits of Western power. It is a classic imperialist statement. How does it compare to the views about non-Westerners prevalent in the slave trade and the conquest of the Americas (chapters 14 and 15)? Finally, a reforming official, Wei Yuan, offers a plan in 1842 for reviving China and defeating the West. His views long remained unheeded.

Questions

1. What was official Chinese policy? How did it reflect traditional Confucian ideas about the role and legitimacy of government? How did the emperor evaluate the Europeans (called barbarians by the Chinese)?
2. What kind of concessions did the imperial commissioner urge in 1842? What were his motives?
3. How did a British official justify the use of force and the sale of opium to the Chinese? How did his view of the Chinese compare with the Chinese view of the Europeans?
4. On what bases did the British now find the Chinese inferior? What, according

to Bingham, might ultimately bring the Chinese up to civilized levels? What evidence does Bingham offer about why the British were now able to defeat the Chinese?

5. Is Bingham a characteristic European imperialist, in his motives and his arguments? Using his statements, how would you define the imperialist approach?

6. What were the key ingredients of Wei Yuan's Defense Plan? What elements of traditional Chinese policy does he propose to change? Would his reforms have gone far enough to make China capable of resisting further European intervention? How would Bingham react to Wei Yuan's plan?

For Further Discussion

1. What impact did the Opium War have on long-term Chinese attitudes toward the West? Would China (and the eventual Chinese-Western relations) have been better served if the West had simply taken the nation over as a colony, as was done with India, rather than exploiting it economically without taking full responsibility?

2. Was Wei Yuan proposing a "modernization" of China? Why did China not at least quickly move to accept this kind of strategy? Why was China slow to reform, at a time when the West and other neighboring societies were clearly changing so rapidly?

3. Did many Westerners really believe their own rationales for imperialism, or was this simply a naked power grab?

4. How would a British history and a Chinese history, using these documents around 1900 when imperialist assumptions still reigned in Europe, differ in their accounts of the Opium War?

CHINA: OFFICIAL STATEMENTS

The following two documents, both issued in 1842 after the war had begun, come respectively from the emperor himself, outlining an official policy of resistance, and from a regional commissioner reporting on the actual course of the fighting.

• • •

IMPERIAL EDICT TO THE GRAND SECRETARIAT, JUNE 5, 1842

On account of the widespread evil of opium in depraving the lives of our people, I issued edicts in a preceding year commanding the various provinces strictly to pro-

From P. C. Kuo, *A Critical Study of the First Anglo-Chinese War* (Shanghai: Commercial Press, 1935), 289–92, 293, 296, 298.

hibit the drug. The warning was repeated many times thereafter. And since Canton is the port where the outer barbarians come to trade, Lin Tsê-hsü was specially delegated to go there to examine the affairs. The barbarian merchants of all nations obeyed the restrictions imposed by the Commissioner. The English barbarian rebel Elliot alone started disturbances on the pretext that our government had destroyed their opium. . . .

Yet the rebellious barbarians were cunning and fickle. Their demands knew no bounds. They evidently knew that Kishen was bent upon peaceful diplomacy and that he was not backed by force. Hence they dared to start hostilities by suddenly attacking the forts at Taikok and Shakok, killing our officials and disturbing the inhabitants. It is thus apparent that the rebellious barbarians began hostilities on account of smuggling opium. Then, they pretended to request favors, while in the meantime they enfolded their dark schemes. Such sheer insincerity and ingratitude should arouse the wrath of both the gods and men. When I called forth our punitive expedition, it was prompted by this consideration.

Later, when Yishan and his colleagues arrived at Canton, the rebellious barbarians had invaded the inner river and were besieging the provincial city itself. The provincial authorities thereupon agreed that the rebels sought only material profit and wished the restoration of trade. They prayed that the Hong debts be paid back to them. As I always treated things with true generosity, I thought that this negligible sum hardly deserved much consideration and that it was certainly not worth while to find an enemy in these rotten people, if by the grant the barbarians would abstain from creating further troubles. Thus again, I made an unusual concession out of a love for the lives of our people.

But, contrary to my expectations, the barbarians cherished mischievous ideas, offending heaven and ignoring reason itself. For no sooner had they composed the quarrels at Canton than fresh troubles arose in Fukien and Chekiang. They invaded Tinghai for the second time and took other cities in succession. It led to the suicide of our Governor and the martyrdom of our generals. The guilt of their depredation upon the lives of our people was beyond the power of redemption.

Therefore, we dispatched Yikin and others to extirpate them with our troops. During the past few months, the enemy withdrew from Ningpo, but captured Chapu in its stead. Thus these rebels first begged our favors while in Canton and fled. Then, in Chekiang, they filled their stores by robbery or depredation. Judged by their rapacious conduct, their guilt has really amounted to the full measure. While it will certainly receive the punishment from the heaven, yet there is no reason why the people should suffer this wise.

When I deliberate upon this situation, I feel tormented by it. So long as the evil were not eradicated, there is no salvation for the sufferings of the people. I censure myself for the inadequacy of my virtue, and can scarcely rest in peace. The generals, secretaries, governors, and all other officials should understand my mind and strive to relieve the sufferings of the people. They should not procrastinate, lest they should spoil the situation at present. Nor should they hope to evade their duties, lest they should perpetuate ill repute in the future.

As to the officers and soldiers in the army, there is a current belief among them that the sturdy ships and fierce cannons of the barbarians are irresistible. Hence, they gave up fighting the moment they saw the enemies on the battlefields. But they should know that the cause of the invasion of the enemies was our concession at the beginning. Should every one go forth bravely and with the coöperation of the village braves, it must be obvious that not only there is great difference between us the hosts and them the strangers, but also there is no comparison between the numerical strength of the two parties. Fighting with the advantage of knowing our own geography, there is no difficulty for us to achieve success. Thus it is apparent that the violence of the rebellious barbarians is all attributable to the inefficiency of our own troops. . . .

I am the ruler of all the people. If I should be content with peace for the time being, and not seek for the great and the far, and let the evil of the opium go its way without any prohibition, that would mean that I am betraying my ancestors who intrusted to me the care of the empire, and that I am unable to afford due protection to the lives of my subjects. Thinking about these points, how can I rest without strictly prohibiting it, how dare I not strictly prohibit it?

Although the barbarians are becoming daily more violent and rapacious, you commanders and governors, occupying important posts of the government, should arouse your conscience and enforce the laws of prohibition with vigor. Those who exert their energy will certainly receive rewards. Those who procrastinate will likewise receive penalties. When things are conducted this wise, I see no reason what attack launched by us cannot achieve success, nor what defense made by us is not impregnable.

The previous officials, who had managed things without propriety, were punished, but they were also retained in order to give them a chance to redeem their past misdemeanor. The object of this measure is to stimulate them to endeavors, and compensate the previous misconduct. If they should still fail to take the advantage of the opportunities and continue to make the people suffer and let the barbarians indulge in their violence, they will no longer be exempted from the punishments prescribed by the law. . . .

In a word, the prohibition of opium has its object in the saving of the lives of the people, while the defense against the invaders has its object in the protection of the same. I am obsessed by these tasks all the time. You ministers of the state must alike give united support to the cause, encouraging the troops to fight with persistence. Certainly it will result in the extermination of the rebels, and the eradication of violence along the coast. By that time, all of us can share with the people a universal peace.

REPORTS BY KIYING, IMPERIAL COMMISSIONER, 1842

As I examined into the said principles, I found that they truly indicate, as your Majesty had said, their [Western] insistence upon material profit. I believed that it was a good occasion for us to get them under our control. . . .

. . . Should we still persist in resistance and should the city fall to the barbarians, the loss of our own lives is an insignificant matter. But we fear that once this city, the metropolis of three provinces, should be upset, not only would the route of Chinkiang be cut off, but the barbarians could easily sail direct to the capitals of Anhwei, Kiangsi, and Hupeh. Moreover, according to a report of the magistrate of Yangchow, Pang I-chu, the barbarians had declared that if they fight and lose, they will employ native traitors to instigate troubles from within. Should this be true, the disaster would be still more inconceivable.

We believe that, although the demands of the barbarians are indeed rapacious, yet they are little more than a desire for ports and for the privilege of trade. There are no dark schemes in them. Compared with war which will inevitably entail great disasters, we would rather see assent be given to their demands, and thus save the whole country south of the Yangtze. . . .

In settling the barbarian affairs this time, we are governed at every hand by the inevitable and we concede that the policy is the least commendable. What we have been doing is to choose between danger and safety, not between right and wrong. For instance, the barbarians asked for as many as 21,000,000 dollars, and five ports. Although we are ignorant, yet we realize that the public revenues of our government are limited, that the coastal frontiers are important, and that we should not give concessions easily. But the spirit of the invaders is running high. They occupy our important cities. The illness on the limbs is becoming one in the heart of a person. Should we fail to take advantage of the present occasion, and to ease the situation by soothing the barbarians, they will run over our country like beasts, doing anything they like.

Moreover, during the past two years, we assembled the troops of several provinces. No matter whether it was for extirpation or for defense, it was of no avail. At present, the additional warships of the barbarians have almost doubled the number they used to have before. If it should happen that Nanking falls, they can easily ascend the river. The waters are deep and the banks extended; while the spots of defense are scattered, the man power available at each point must necessarily be feeble. It would be hard to erect forts at one stroke. Judged by these circumstances, the possibilities of victory or defeat must be manifest. Should their force cut off our communication between the south and the north, it is still more difficult to foretell the disasters.

The ships of the barbarians are sturdy and their cannons fierce. Previously this was only hearsay. But now we have been on their ships and personally have seen their cannons. After this experience, we are the more convinced that we cannot control them by force. It is because of the inevitable that we asked, in our previous memorial, to grant large sums of money in order to save the country.

BRITAIN: A VIEW FROM A PARTICIPANT

J. Elliot Bingham was a navy officer and the son of a clergyman (the latter fact is particularly interesting in view of some of his moralizing statements and moral blind spots). Bingham wrote his account right after the war, seeking to glorify the British cause to an adoring public back home—though popular enthusiasm for imperialism was not yet at the pitch it would attain a few decades later.

• • •

Now it might be supposed from the foregoing extracts, that the Chinese have been very ill-used, and that the opium trade has been forced on them; but such was not at all the case. I must beg my readers to divest themselves of such an idea; for be it remembered, while the Chinese statesmen pencil their highly moral edicts and memorials with one hand against the admission of this poisonous drug, with the other they receive bribes and fees, levied for the secret admission of this baneful enchantment. Nay, they themselves, in secret, revel in all the luxury of the opium pipe; a luxury which, when once indulged in, it is almost impossible to shake off. . . .

To *suppress* this traffic is utterly impossible, until the whole character of the Chinese nation becomes altered. Opium they will have; and experience has proved that all the obstacles and difficulties thrown in the way of its introduction have only tended to increase it, and extend its use. It would be just as easy to put down beer and gin drinking in England. I much question whether there are not as many English gin sufferers as there are Chinese opium sufferers, for the opium is used by them in the least deleterious manner, viz., by smoking.

But, as I have before observed, it is not the question of health or morality with the Chinese. The fact is, our imports have given a great balance in our favour, as is shown in the following table:—

Our purchases for the year ending June 30, 1838, for teas, silk, and all £.
  other articles, amount to 3,147,481
Our sales of opium, metals, and cotton, to 5,637,052
                                                                  ─────────
Balance in favour of British 2,489,571

which was generally paid in sycee, the export of which, in 1837–8, amounted to nearly nine millions of dollars.

Thus we see what was the chief and true reason for attempting to stop the trade

From John Elliot Bingham, *Narrative of the Expedition to China from the Commencement of the War to Its Termination in 1842. . . .* (London: Henry Colburn, 1843), 22–23, 34–39, 363–66, 369–72.

in opium, and accordingly the edicts previously or subsequently to this year, enlarged more on the abstraction of the sycee than on the morals of the people. . . .

[An initial agreement opened several ports to trade plus a Chinese payment. Provisions included a] first instalment [of] 6,000,000 dollars, her Britannic Majesty's forces to retire from Nankin and the Grand Canal, and the military posts at Chinhai to be withdrawn, but the islands of Chusan and Ko-long-soo are to be held until the money payments and the arrangements for opening the ports be completed."

Active hostilities therefore ceased, and the Emperor's assent to the provisions of the treaty having been intimated by an imperial edict on the 29th, vessels were despatched to the different Chinese ports to remove the embargoes on their trade.

During the preliminary arrangements of peace the Chinese authorities visited the Cornwallis, where they were received in great state and shown round the ship. The formidable appointments of *the barbarian sanpan* somewhat astonished the mind of their excellencies, while bumpers of cherry brandy upset the equilibrium of several jolly members of their suite. The entertainment was duly returned, when shamsoo took the place of cherry brandy. . . .

Conclusion

The dispute with "the celestial empire" having been brought, by the energetic measures of our present Government, to a triumphant conclusion, and that, not so much by the mere destruction of junks and forts as by the consequent pressure on the trade of the country, nothing more remains for me to do, than to offer a few general remarks in concluding this narrative of events.

The military tactics of the Chinese must be regarded as far below mediocrity; and can it be otherwise with a people, among whom the recommendation of a general for employment is not his intimate acquaintance with the arts of war, but rather his acuteness to frame and his effrontery to utter the most unblushing falsehoods, in order to deceive his opponents? No deceit is too gross, no artifice too mean and dirty for a mandarin, whether soldier, magistrate, or statesman, to stoop to. The following Chinese maxim illustrates the justness of this stricture:—"When the territory of our sovereign is in difficulty we ought immediately to deliver it. What would be the use of adhering bigotedly to a little bit of good faith, thereby involving doubts and delays?"

That individuals possessing personal courage are to be found, both among Chinese and Tartars, many a single combat has shown. The latter, indeed, both at Chapoo and Tchang-kiang, when all retreat was cut off, fought with a determination that was not expected. However, upon giving the subject our consideration, we shall find that this originated not so much from the *esprit de corps* of soldiers, as from the desperation of men fighting for their wives and children, whom they fully expected would be treated by their conquerors with the same inhuman barbarity as they would have inflicted upon us, had we lost the day. Let us take the following speech of one of their commissioners by way of illustration:—"We have been like children gambling, but not understanding the game we were playing; *we* have lost and must pay: had *you* lost, we should have made *you* pay." And most assuredly they would have made us *pay*; for hundreds of English would have been chopped up at Pekin to evince the triumph of the empire over the rebel barbarians.

"The Chinese," says the late Doctor Morrison, who had ample opportunity of forming a correct opinion, "are specious, but insincere, jealous, envious, and distrustful to a high degree; they are generally selfish, coldblooded, and inhuman." Can we, I would add, accord to them a single virtue? We might allow them one, filial affection, if that virtue, great and redeeming as it would otherwise be, did not arise more from the force of education and habit, than from the outpouring of a generous and humane heart.

The losses of the enemy, to say nothing of the wounded (vast numbers of whom probably died), cannot have fallen much short of twenty thousand, exclusive of such as perished by disease. This must of course be regarded as a rough calculation, their habit of carrying off their killed and wounded whenever by any exertion they could do so, rendering it impossible in any one instance to discover the exact number of the slain. Much as we may lament the necessity of inflicting so severe a chastisement on a people whose rulers alone were in fault, these losses are but a mere drop in comparison of the resources of an empire which maintains at least one million of men for military service, whom it draws from one-third of the human race. . . . It may also behoove us to maintain for some time a commanding force in the China seas, not forgetting the perfidious character of a nation who, having despised us before as barbarians, now hate us as their conquerors. It will be long ere their pride will forgive us for the humiliating discipline we have applied to them.

It will be our wisdom, however, to maintain the vantage ground which, through the blessing of the Almighty upon our arms, we have acquired, as well as to embrace every opportunity of making them understand the real character of the great nation they have to deal with; and in order to do this, we must treat them with firmness combined with liberality. Let us hope that the way may thus be opened for enlightening their minds with the truths of that Christianity which is the real basis of Britain's glory.

Much opposed as the government of China has ever been to the Christian religion, I do not despair of the arrival of that day, when under the influence of the spirit of the Most High the disciples of Christ shall abound and be protected even in the cities of "the central flowery land." Why should not Japan too, ere long, under the results of similar operations, be induced to open her ports to the Christian trader, and respect that cross of Christ on which she now tramples?

One observation more and we have done. There is an old legend among the Chinese containing a prophecy that their country would at some day be vanquished by a female hand. We are not superstitious in such things: nevertheless, it is some-what remarkable, that the exploits recorded in this Narrative have been carried on under the auspices of OUR GRACIOUS QUEEN! and who will be bold enough to deny that China has been prostrate at her feet? who will venture to assert that, while our forces were hourly increasing, the grand canal under our command, and Nankin at our mercy, almost any terms might have been dictated had aggression been our object? Pekin itself compelled to capitulate and the Mantchow dynasty overthrown? For, her navy annihilated, her forts in ruins, her cities captured, Canton ransomed, her ancient capital under the muzzle of our guns, and the throne of the Mantchows trembling to its foundation, it is not too much to affirm that

CHINA HAS BEEN CONQUERED
BY A WOMAN.

WEI YUAN'S DEFENSE PLAN, 1842

Wei Yuan was a government official, trained in Confucianism, writing in the wake of China's defeat in the first Opium War. He proposed to the emperor a number of changes, both in diplomacy and in military policy. His ideas were far too imaginative for a conservative, weak government to accept. Nevertheless, some of his proposals contain some interesting mistakes, particularly in Russian and Indian geography; why was an otherwise alert official in China prone to mistakes of this sort?

• • •

India is on the southwest of the Onion Range, and adjacent to our further Tibet, the Gurkhas, and Burma. From the homeland of the British barbarians, India is several myriad *li*. The British barbarians used warships and occupied the three parts of India, in the east, the south, and center. The Russian troops then, from the space between the Black Sea and the Caspian Sea, attacked and subdued the various nomadic tribes and made connection with the two western and central parts of India. They were only separated by the Himalayas. Each side was guarded by heavy garrisons of troops. From Bengal to Malwa in East India and from Bombay to Madras in South India opium is prevalent. The British barbarians annually collect from opium taxes more than ten million (taels) silver, and the Russians are jealous. When the British barbarians mobilized Indian . . . troops and warships to invade China, they were greatly afraid that Russia might take advantage of their weakness to invade Hindustan. . . . Therefore, the British barbarians' fear of Russia lies not in her national capital but in India. This is one opportunity which might be used. . . .

From Ssu-yü Teng and John K. Fairbank, eds., *China's Response to the West* (Cambridge: Harvard University Press, 1954), 32–34.

There is no better method of attacking England by sea than to use France and America. France is very close to the English barbarians, being separated only by an arm of the sea. America and the English barbarians, on the other hand, are separated by a great ocean. Beginning from the period at the end of the Ming and the beginning of this dynasty, France colonized the northeast territory of America. Cities and towns were built, markets and ports were opened. The British barbarians suddenly attacked and seized them. Thereupon the French barbarians and the English barbarians became bitter enemies. . . .

Let us establish a shipyard and an arsenal at two spots, Chuenpi and Taikoktow outside of the Bogue in Kwangtung, and select one or two persons from among the foreign headmen who have come from France and America, respectively, to bring Western craftsmen to Canton to take charge of building ships and making arms. In addition, we should invite Western helmsmen to take charge of teaching the methods of navigating ships and of using cannon, following the precedent of the barbarian officials in the Imperial Board of Astronomy. We should select clever artisans and good soldiers from Fukien and Kwangtung to learn from them, the craftsmen to learn the casting of cannon and building of ships, and the good soldiers to learn their methods of navigating and attack. . . . In Kwangtung there should be ten thousand soldiers; in Fukien, ten thousand; in Chekiang, six thousand; and in Kiangsu, four thousand. In assigning soldiers to the ships we must rely on selection and training. . . . Eight out of ten should be taken from among the fishermen and smugglers along the sea coast. Two out of ten should be taken from the old encampments of the water forces. All the padded rations and extra rations of the water force should be . . . used for the recruiting and maintenance of good soldiers. We must make the water forces of China able to navigate large (lit., "storied") ships overseas, and able to fight against foreign barbarians on the high seas.

CHAPTER 21

THE EMANCIPATIONS AND THEIR CONSEQUENCES

Abolition of the most sweeping forms of coercive labor—slavery and serfdom—was a key development in nineteenth century world history. Latin American countries abolished slavery between 1810 and 1890, and the institution was also attacked in Africa. Serfdom ended in Europe. Forms of work and power that had existed virtually since the origin of civilization were opposed and put down.

Historians continue to debate the origins of the unprecedented movement to abolish the most blatant forms of coercive labor. New democratic and humanitarian ideals played a role. Christian humanitarians began agitating against the Atlantic slave trade in the late eighteenth century. Enlightenment political theorists joined in. The French Revolution ended serfdom in much of Western Europe, whereas later revolutions (such as the 1848 revolution in Germany) spread this facet of the emancipation movement. Russian intellectuals like Radishchev (see chapter 16) picked up these sentiments as well, urging fundamental reform in Russia; American abolitionists stepped up the attack on slavery in the United States by the 1820s (after many northern states had ended the institution in the wake of the American Revolution). But new ideas, sincerely held, were not the only motivation. Some historians also point to the importance of new forms of capitalist labor, which demonstrated that workers could be exploited as "free" wage labor, and that slavery might in fact not be efficient enough for the commercial needs of the nineteenth century. Antislavery campaigns might also distract industrial workers from their own plight, by pointing to miseries elsewhere.

Discussions of the complex causes of the emancipation current relate also the question of results. On paper, emancipation ended legal servitude. But even the humanitarians had not necessarily thought much about the real conditions that would prevail for former serfs and slaves. And powerful interested parties, such as the estate owners, had obvious reasons to try to limit the impact of change. Emancipation, though real, in this sense set up further problems. Comparative analysis of two leading cases helps to sort out the resulting complexities.

Russia and the United States in the nineteenth century invite comparison. Both were huge, expanding countries beginning to have a growing impact in world affairs. Both clearly had distinctive labor systems that demanded some new attention, and in some ways the two nations' reactions were similar. Both discovered, finally, that reforming the system could lead to a new set of problems and protests—and, it can be argued, neither society has found it easy to deal with the long aftermath. Russia's 1917 revolution transformed the peasant problem, but it did not end it in the twentieth century. The United States settled the issue of slavery but not the larger issue of racial justice, which is still one of the most debated strands of the national fabric.

Two major moves occurred almost simultaneously: Russia's Emancipation of the Serfs in 1861 and Lincoln's Emancipation Proclamation of 1863. Circumstances differed. Lincoln acted during civil war, to rally support for the Union cause. Russia hoped to reduce peasant discontent and also build a more flexible economy and labor force, as it lagged behind industrial Western Europe. Russia was spurred by its embarrassing loss to Britain and France in the Crimean War (1854–55), which seemed to prove that change was essential. But some similar humanitarian ideals were involved in each case, at least on the part of some reformers, plus a belief that "free" wage labor was economically more productive than its forced equivalent. What are the professed intentions behind the two emancipations, as reflected in the initial documents below? Are they part of a single movement in world history, in two rather different societies?

Emancipation was merely the first step in what turned out to be a complex process. Both Russia and the United States experienced continued disruption after these major reforms. Russian serfs immediately complained of mistreatment, and their protest continued for decades. As Southern whites regained political control in the 1870s after the Reconstruction period ended, African Americans in the region experienced a loss of economic opportunities and other rights. Why was reform incomplete in both countries?

The Russian peasant protest would ultimately contribute to revolutions in 1905 and 1917. Southern black protest, though real, was less sweeping. New racial laws in the South, plus violent intimidation, reduced the protest movement by the 1890s, though it would resume in various and often powerful forms in the twentieth century.

Questions

1. How do the two emancipations compare? How do their justifications differ? Which pays more attention to the conditions likely to result from emancipation? In what sense can both reform measures be judged to be rather limited, despite their role in ending long-standing institutions of labor?

2. Why did Russia's peasants begin immediately protesting the conditions of emancipation? What institution did they think could fix the problems? Why did the kinds of problems and expectations expressed in these protests ultimately—a half century later—help lead to revolution?

3. In what ways did black protest in the American South differ from that of the Russian peasants? What were some similar complaints?

4. What happened to the social structure (class or class and race) of the two societies after emancipation? How did postemancipation reactions of the Russian aristocracy and the Southern planter class compare? Was either more violent than the other—and if so, for what reasons?

For Further Discussion

1. What caused the emancipation movements? Were the causes basically the same in Russia and the United States?

2. Which political system was more open to protest, that of Russia or that of the United States? Why did the protests of former serfs in Russia ultimately lead to revolution, whereas protests by former slaves in the United States did not?

3. On balance, did reform fail or succeed in Russia? In the United States? In either case, can you think of ways reform could have been done more successfully, with better long-term results?

THE EMANCIPATION MANIFESTO, 1861

Russia's emancipation of the serfs had been debated off and on for almost a century, as a reform element developed in the Western-oriented aristocracy. The loss of the Crimean War, when the industrially sustained armies of Britain and France beat Russia on its own southern border, accelerated the discussion. A new, reform-minded czar, Alexander II, resolved to act. The measure was the first of many reforms over the next two decades. Nonetheless, the emancipation clearly took into account the vital position of the Russian nobility; it was not intended to be a social revolution.

• • •

By the Grace of God We, Alexander II, Emperor and Autocrat of All Russia, King of Poland, Grand Duke of Finland, etc., make known to all Our faithful subjects:

Called by Divine Providence and by the sacred right of inheritance to the throne of Our Russian ancestors, We vowed in Our heart to respond to the mission which is entrusted to Us and to surround with Our affection and Our Imperial solicitude all Our faithful subjects of every rank and condition, from the soldier who nobly

From Basil Dmytryshyn, *Imperial Russia: A Sourcebook, 1700–1917* (New York: Holt, Rinehart and Winston, 1967), 221–23, 225.

defends the country to the humble artisan who works in industry; from the career official of the state to the plowman who tills the soil.

Examining the condition of classes and professions comprising the state, We became convinced that the present state legislation favors the upper and middle classes, defines their obligations, rights, and privileges, but does not equally favor the serfs, so designated because in part from old laws and in part from custom they have been hereditarily subjected to the authority of landowners, who in turn were obligated to provide for their well being. Rights of nobles have been hitherto very broad and legally ill defined, because they stem from tradition, custom, and the good will of the noblemen. In most cases this has led to the establishment of good patriarchal relations based on the sincere, just concern and benevolence on the part of the nobles, and on affectionate submission on the part of the peasants. Because of the decline of the simplicity of morals, because of an increase in the diversity of relations, because of the weakening of the direct paternal attitude of nobles toward the peasants, and because noble rights fell sometimes into the hands of people exclusively concerned with their personal interests, good relations weakened. The way was opened for an arbitrariness burdensome for the peasants and detrimental to their welfare, causing them to be indifferent to the improvement of their own existence.

These facts had already attracted the attention of Our predecessors of glorious memory, and they had adopted measures aimed at improving the conditions of the peasants; but these measures were ineffective, partly because they depended on the free, generous action of nobles, and partly because they affected only some localities, by virtue of special circumstances or as an experiment. Thus Alexander I issued a decree on free agriculturists, and the late Emperor Nicholas, Our beloved father, promulgated one dealing with the serfs. In the Western *gubernias,* inventory regulations determine the peasant land allotments and their obligations. But decrees on free agriculturists and serfs have been carried out on a limited scale only.

We thus became convinced that the problem of improving the condition of serfs was a sacred inheritance bequeathed to Us by Our predecessors, a mission which, in the course of events, Divine Providence has called upon Us to fulfill.

We have begun this task by expressing Our confidence toward the Russian nobility, which has proven on so many occasions its devotion to the Throne, and its readiness to make sacrifices for the welfare of the country.

We have left to the nobles themselves, in accordance with their own wishes, the task of preparing proposals for the new organization of peasant life—proposals that would limit their rights over the peasants, and the realization of which would inflict on them [the nobles] some material losses. Our confidence was justified. Through members of the *gubernia* committees, who had the trust of the nobles' associations, the nobility voluntarily renounced its right to own serfs. These committees, after collecting the necessary data, have formulated proposals on a new arrangement for serfs and their relationship with the nobles.

These proposals were diverse, because of the nature of the problem. They have been compared, collated, systematized, rectified and finalized in the main committee instituted for that purpose; and these new arrangements dealing with the peasants and domestics of the nobility have been examined in the Governing Council.

Having invoked Divine assistance, We have resolved to execute this task.

On the basis of the above mentioned new arrangements, the serfs will receive in time the full rights of free rural inhabitants.

The nobles, while retaining their property rights on all the lands belonging to them, grant the peasants perpetual use of their domicile in return for a specified obligation; and, to assure their livelihood as well as to guarantee fulfillment of their obligations toward the government, [the nobles] grant them a portion of arable land fixed by the said arrangements, as well as other property.

While enjoying these land allotments, the peasants are obliged, in return, to fulfill obligations to the noblemen fixed by the same arrangements. In this state, which is temporary, the peasants are temporarily bound.

At the same time, they are granted the right to purchase their domicile, and, with the consent of the nobles, they may acquire in full ownership the arable lands and other properties which are allotted them for permanent use. Following such acquisition of full ownership of land, the peasants will be freed from their obligations to the nobles for the land thus purchased and will become free peasant landowners. . . .

We leave it to the nobles to reach a friendly understanding with the peasants and to reach agreements on the extent of the land allotment and the obligations stemming from it, observing, at the same time, the established rules to guarantee the inviolability of such agreements. . . .

What legally belongs to nobles cannot be taken away from them without adequate compensation, or through their voluntary concession; it would be contrary to all justice to use the land of the nobles without assuming responsibility for it.

And now We confidently expect that the freed serfs, on the eve of a new future which is opening to them, will appreciate and recognize the considerable sacrifices which the nobility has made on their behalf.

THE EMANCIPATION PROCLAMATION, 1862

Abraham Lincoln did not come easily to the decision to emancipate the slaves. He was opposed to slavery, but his opinions had wavered over his adult life. He believed in property, and he did not want to antagonize the South more than necessary. But in the second year of the Civil War, with northern abolitionists pressing for action, it became clear that emancipation might improve support for the war and also help raise black resistance in the South, thus weakening the secessionist war effort. Lincoln's proclamation differed from the czar's in many ways, reflecting a very different political and religious system. But it expressed some similar cautions. As in Russia, this reform was followed by others, when the North took over the South during the Reconstruction period. As in Russia also, the reform era ended by the late 1870s or the 1880s.

• • •

Whereas on the 22d day of September, A.D. 1862, a proclamation was issued by the President of the United States, containing, among other things, the following, to wit:

"That on the 1st day of January, A.D. 1863, all persons held as slaves within any State or designated part of a State the people whereof shall then be in rebellion against the United States shall be then, thenceforward, and forever free; and the executive government of the United States, including the military and naval authority thereof, will recognize and maintain the freedom of such persons and will do no act or acts to repress such persons, or any of them, in any efforts they may make for their actual freedom. . . .

And by virtue of the power and for the purpose aforesaid, I do order and declare that all persons held as slaves within said designated States and parts of States are, and henceforward shall be, free; and that the Executive Government of the United States, including the military and naval authorities thereof, will recognize and maintain the freedom of said persons.

And I hereby enjoin upon the people so declared to be free to abstain from all violence, unless in necessary self-defense; and I recommend to them that, in all cases when allowed, they labor faithfully for reasonable wages.

And I further declare and make known that such persons of suitable condition will be received into the armed service of the United States to garrison forts, positions, stations, and other places, and to man vessels of all sorts in said service.

And upon this act, sincerely believed to be an act of justice, warranted by the Constitution upon military necessity, I invoke the considerate judgment of mankind and the gracious favor of Almighty God.

RUSSIAN PEASANTS AFTER EMANCIPATION:
PEASANT PETITIONS

Discontent with the conditions of emancipation surfaced almost immediately in Russia. For a time, petitions rained in. Over a longer period, major peasant protests surged, in which remaining estates might be occupied, records of redemption

From "The Emancipation Proclamation," *Encyclopedia Americana*, vol. 10, Grolier, 1989, 269.

payments that peasants owed for the land they had received burned. The petitions require some care in interpretation. They include detail that needs to be sorted out to find the main points. They include some hyperbole, because the peasants hoped to win the czar's attention by elaborate expressions of trust and obedience. What were the main grievances? How did peasants decide they could best define the justice of their case?

• • •

PETITION FROM PEASANTS IN BALASHOV DISTRICT (SARATOV PROVINCE) TO GRAND DUKE KONSTANTIN NIKOLAEVICH, 25 JANUARY 1862

Your Imperial Excellency! Most gracious sire! Grand Duke Konstantin Nikolaevich!

Most magnanimous prince, given by God for the welfare of people in the Russian Empire! The countless acts of mercy and humanitarianism of Your Imperial Excellency toward the loyal subjects have emboldened us to fall to your feet and plead:

Show your steadfast and just protection of oppressed humanity! Following the example of our fathers, grandfathers and ancestors, we have always and without complaint obeyed the laws of Russian monarchs and the authority of its rulers. Hence, as peasants in the hamlet of Blagoveshchenskoe and three villages (Avdot'evka, Aleksandrovka and Uspenskaia) in Balashov District of Saratov province, we and our families, while under the authority of the squire, a retired colonel, Prince Vasil'chikov, have always enjoyed the blessings of the all-merciful God: fertile land.

The monarch's mercy—which has no precedent in the chronicles of all peoples in the universe—has now changed the attitude of our squire, who has reduced us 1,500 peasants to a pitiable condition. . . . [sic] After being informed of the Imperial manifesto on the emancipation of peasants from serfdom in 1861 (which was explained to us by the constable of township 2 of Balashov District), we received this [news] with jubilation, as a special gift from heaven, and expressed our willingness to obey the squire's will in every respect during the coming two-year [transition] period [and to remain] on the fertile land which we occupy, where we could realise our life. . . . [sic]

But from this moment, our squire ordered that the land be cut off from the entire township. But this is absolutely intolerable for us: it not only denies us profit, but threatens us with a catastrophic future. He began to hold repeated meetings and [tried to] force us to sign that we agreed to accept the above land allotment. But,

From Gregory L. Freeze, ed., *From Supplication to Revolution: A Documentary Social History of Imperial Russia* (New York: Oxford University Press, 1988), 171–79. Reprinted by permission of the publisher.

upon seeing so unexpected a change, and bearing in mind the gracious manifesto, we refused. Then Prince Vasil'chikov, with terrible threats, went to the city of Saratov, and soon afterwards the squires, Prince Prozorovskii, Golitsyn, Colonel Globbe, and the peace arbitrator Baishev came to our township office. After assembling the entire township, they tried to force us into making illegal signatures accepting the land cut-offs. But when they saw that this did not succeed, they had a company of soldiers sent in and said that they had been sent—by the Tsar!—to restore peace between us and the squires. We heard this and, despite the unsuitability of the land, we were ready to accept it—at first as 3 dessiatines [unit of laud] per soul, then later 4 dessiatines. But we did not give the demanded signatures, suspecting here a scheme by the squires' accomplices. Then [Col.] Globbe came from their midst, threatened us with exile to Siberia, and ordered the soldiers to strip the peasants and to punish seven people by flogging in the most inhuman manner. They still have not regained consciousness.

The inhuman acts and intolerable oppression have forced us to fall to the sacred feet of Your Imperial Excellency: 1,500 voices most humbly ask for just, most august defense, which can save weeping families from certain death, and [we ask] that You issue a decree [on our case].

PETITION FROM PEASANTS IN PODOSINOVKA (VORONEZH PROVINCE) TO ALEXANDER II, MAY 1863

The most merciful manifesto of Your Imperial Majesty from 19 February 1861, with the published rules, put a limit to the enslavement of the people in blessed Russia. But some former serfowners—who desire not to improve the peasants' life, but to oppress and ruin them—apportion land contrary to the laws, choose the best land from all the fields for themselves, and give the poor peasants (who are just emerging from their domination) the worst and least usable lands. To this group of squires must be counted our own, Anna Mikhailovna Raevskaia, [who acted thus] during the division of fields and resources, which the 600 peasants of the village of Podosinovka (Krasninskaia Township, Novokhopersk District, Voronezh Province) have used from time immemorial. Of our fields and resources, she chose the best places from amidst our strips and, like a cooking ring in a hearth, carved off 300 dessiatines for herself. Other places—characterized by sand, hills, knolls and ravines (with the sparsest amount of hayland)—were designated as the peasant allotment; altogether, including the household plots, we were given four dessiatines per soul and assessed a quitrent of 12 rubles per soul. But our community refused to accept so ruinous an allotment and requested that we be given an allotment in accordance with the local Statute [of emancipation], without injury, even if the quitrent must be increased. The peace arbitrator Iakubovich and the police chief of Novokhopersk District informed the governor of Voronezh of our refusal [to accept the inventory]; in their report they slandered us before the governor, alleging that we were rioting and that it is impossible for them to enter our village. The provincial governor believed this lie and sent 1,200 soldiers of the penal command to our village of Krasnoe to inflict ruin upon us innocent people; three days after sending the troops, the governor himself came to our village (with the peace arbitrator, the district police chief, and the township constable) and summoned our township head Epat Chergin, his aide Vasilii Kirsanov, the elder Khariton Iartanskii and other representatives of the peasants. Without any cause, our village priest Father Peter—rather than give an uplifting pastoral exhortation to stop the spilling of innocent blood—joined these reptiles, with the unanimous incitement of the authorities (including eleven ill-wishers). They summoned nine township heads and their aides from other townships (Bulaevo, Pekhovo, Sadovo, Aferovo, Zarazivskoe, etc.) In their presence, the provincial governor—without making any investigation and without interrogating a single person—ordered that the birch rods be brought and that the punishment commence, which was carried out with cruelty and mercilessness. They punished up to 200 men and women; 80 people were at four levels (with 500, 400, 300 and 200 blows); some received lesser punishment. The governor ordered the township constable to punish the women; using his superiors' authorization, the constable cruelly punished innocent women with 100 blows each and struck them in the cheek with his fist, so that the punished were left without consciousness and reason. Of the men punished, most had earlier fought for the faith, tsar and fatherland, and when the inhuman punishment of these innocent people had ended, the provincial governor said: "If you find the land unsuitable, I do not forbid you to file petitions wherever you please," and then left.

Having explained the inhuman acts of our local authorities and our final ruination through the oppressive allotment of unusable land in strips, we dare to implore you, Orthodox emperor and our merciful father, not to reject the petition of a community with 600 souls, including wives and children. Order with your tsarist word that our community be alloted land according to the statute for this area, which peasants used prior to the publication of the all-merciful manifesto, and not in strips, but as the law dictates (without selecting the best sections of fields and meadows, but in straight lines) for the quitrent payment as fixed in the local statutes. [Order that] the meadows and haylands along the river Elan be left to our community without any restriction; these will enable us to feed our cattle and smaller livestock, which are necessary for our existence.

Most august monarch! If our former owner Raevskaia uses all her means, in hopes of protection from local authorities (so as not to give us, in accordance with our wish and laws on apportionment, usable field land and hayland), if our allotment is so oppressive, we will not have the strength to pay such a quitrent or to feed our families. Then, Sovereign, give your blessing to those of us who wish to have land allotments that might be indicated by your wisdom. Merciful emperor, permit us to be called state peasants. Such monarchical mercy, you all-merciful father and liberator, will echo in our hearts with eternal gratitude, and our prayers (not only of the old and young, but of infants in their cribs) will profoundly rise to the heavenly creator for the health and long life of God's anointed, and for all the members of your imperial family. . . .

PETITION FROM PEASANTS IN BEREZINO (VLADIMIR PROVINCE) TO THE MINISTER OF INTERIOR, 31 OCTOBER 1862

A most humble petition to His Excellency, Minister of Interior and cavalier of various orders, from the temporarily-bound peasants of the village Berezino (Aleksandrov District, Vladimir Province).

Our most humble petition to His Imperial Majesty on 14 July of this year was given to Your Excellency for your disposition. We received notification from the Land Division of the Ministry on 25 August that our request does not require any action on the part of the ministry, because the governor of Vladimir province removed the military contingent from our village, and with respect to the average land allotment, he allegedly explained everything to us and eliminated all our perplexity. This report from the governor of the province is absolutely unjust; not only have we not obtained satisfaction, but constantly encounter pressure from our squire and all the district and provincial authorities. The reason is that our squire holds the rank of marshal of the nobility, and because of his wealth, he is a friend of the governor as well as all the other provincial authorities. In examining our case, the governor made a personal visit to our village, but limited himself to removing the military contingent which had been here to punish us (because of the squire's caprice and the authorities' desire to please him). But we have obtained no satisfaction with regard to our request: (1) The squire has not changed the land allotment and does not want to give us land in one place. (2) When the military command was here to inflict punishment, the constable, peace arbitrator and squire took away 23 cows and 33 rams, allegedly for [unpaid] quitrent, but we have never refused to pay quitrent; nor do we refuse now. But our livestock has not been returned. (3) Our gain has been inventoried (in shocks) and we have been forbidden to sell it; and we have also been forbidden to use it. (4) Seven innocent people from our village are incarcerated in the stockade at Aleksandrov; their suffering families and young children do not have a crust of bread and depend entirely upon us to take care of them. (5) The squire has totally ruined us, and the authorities (who do his bidding) have even forbidden us to leave the village. . . .

Under such calamitous, murderous conditions we have fallen into the most extreme poverty and despair. It is impossible for us to fight the squire, a marshal of the nobility who is a friend of all the government authorities. Our only escape from this situation is intervention by dispassionate, higher authorities. We fall to the feet of Your Excellency and weep not tears, but blood at your feet, most valiant dignitary of our merciful monarch! Put yourself in our place, send a trusted official to investigate our case—an official who is not inhibited by our squire's wealth and high station and who can conduct a humane, dispassionate investigation. Most valiant general, order that our fellow-villagers be freed from arrest in the stockade. Order that the livestock taken from us be returned. Release our grain and other property for our own direct use. And designate for us a land allotment in one place. 31 October 1862. Because of the illiteracy of the petitioners, at their personal request the townsman Fedor Timanov Makarov signs this petition on their behalf.

African Americans after Slavery: Petitions in the South

For a decade after emancipation, former slaves had some opportunities to take advantage of new freedoms, because Reconstruction governments allowed them voice. While most land remained in the hands of former plantation owners, blacks managed to purchase some. They also set up schools and other community institutions. But the end of Reconstruction showed how vulnerable the former slave population was. Petitions from the 1870s focused on particular incidents (as did the Russian peasant petitions) but also on more general issues. They targeted the federal government, which during Reconstruction had shown some interest in conditions of African Americans.

• • •

JOINT AFFIDAVIT FROM GEORGE UNDERWOOD, BEN HARRIS, AND ISIAH FULLER

Caddo Parish, La., August 3, 1875

We worked, or made a contract to work, and make a crop on shares on Mr. McMoring's place, and worked for one-third (⅓) of the crop, and he (McMoring) was to find us all of our provisions; and in July, 1875, we was working alone in the field, and Mr. McMoring and McBounton came to us and says, "Well, boys, you all got to get away from here; and that they had gone as far as they could go, and you all must live agreeable, or you shall take what follows"; and the two white men went and got sticks and guns, and told us that we must leave the place; and we told them that we would not leave it, because we don't want to give up our crop for nothing; and

From Herbert Aptheker, ed., *A Documentary History of the Negro People in the United States* (New York: Citadel Press, 1951), 586, 600–603.

they told us that we had better leave, or we would not get anything; and we wanted to have justice, but he would not let us have justice; and we told them that we would get judges to judge the crop, to say what it is worth; and the white men told us that no judge should come on his place; and we did not want to leave the place, but they beat Isiah Fuller, and whipped him, and then we got afraid, and we left the place, and we got about thirty acres in cotton, and the best cotton crop in that part of the parish; and we have about twenty-nine acres of corn, and about the best corn in the parish, and it is ripe, and the fodder ready to pull, and our cotton laid by; and runned us off from the place, and told us not to come back any more; and we were due McMoring the sum of one hundred and eighty dollars ($180) and they told us that if they ever heard of it any more that they would fix us; and all the time that we were living and working on the place they would not half feed us; and we had to pay for all, or half of our rashings, or what we had to eat, and that is all that was due them for; and we worked for them as though we were slaves, and then treated like dogs all the time.

Jackson. Miss—June 20, 1876.

MEMORIAL FROM ALABAMA NEGROES

To His Excellency the President of the United States, and the honorable the Congress of the United States:

The colored people of the State of Alabama, who by virtue of the three latest amendments to the Constitution of the United States became emancipated, and also became citizens of the United States, feeling anxiously and solemnly impressed by their past and present condition in the State of Alabama, and by the grave and menacing dangers that now surround and threaten them and their constitutional rights, have as a race and as a people assembled together in convention to consider their situation, and to take solemn counsel together as to what it becomes them to do for their self-preservation.

We, therefore, for your better information upon the subject, do humbly present for your consideration and action the following memorial:

That as a race, and as citizens, we never have enjoyed, except partially, imperfectly, and locally, our political and civil rights in this State. Our right to vote in elections has been, in a large portion of this State, denied, abridged, and rendered difficult and dangerous ever since we became voters. The means used by our political opponents to destroy or impair their right have been various; but have chiefly consisted of violence in the form of secret assassination, lynching, intimidation, malicious and frivolous prosecutions and arrests, and by depriving or threatening to deprive us of employment and the renting of lands, which many of us, in our poverty and distress, were unable to disregard. These acts of lawlessness have been repeated and continued since our first vote in 1868, and their effect has been such that from ten to fifteen thousand of the votes of our race have in each election been either repressed or been given under compulsion to our political opponents.

It is true that in some counties, and in parts of other counties, we have been exempt from these acts of lawlessness, but yet they have been committed to such an extent as greatly to diminish our votes, and once at least, in 1870, and probably on the third of November, A.D. 1874, was this lawlessness so great as to give (without the other frauds perpetrated) the election and all its fruits to our political opponents. . . . *

The investigation made in the years 1870'71 by a committee of Congress known as the Ku-Klux committee, developed and established the fact of the organized existence, in many parts of this State since the year 1868, of a secret, powerful, vindictive, and dangerous organization composed exclusively of white men belonging to the democratic party in this State, and whose objects were to control the labor and repress or control the votes of colored citizens of this State. That organization, or a substitute and successor to it, under a changed name and a somewhat changed wardrobe and personal manifestation, still exists in all its hideous and fearful proportions.

It is composed chiefly of ex-soldiers of the late confederate army accustomed to military movements and the use of arms, and it is, essentially a military organization. This organization we solemnly believe pervades all of the late rebellious States, and contains more than a hundred thousand arms-bearing men, most of whom are experienced and skilled in war. The definite political object of this organization is, by terror and violence, to make the citizenship and franchises of the colored race, as established by the Constitution of the U.S. practically and substantially a nullity. Nothing but fear restrains them from making open war upon the Government and the flag of the United States. We pray you not to be deceived by their professions, for they are "wise as serpents," and they profess respect for the United States and obedience to its laws, while in their secret conclaves they curse them.

They have only changed their tactics. Defeated in their scheme of secession, they have fallen back upon the old South Carolina plan of nullification. Being unable to defeat or nullify the constitutional amendments by their votes while the republican party is in power, or by open war, they have resolved to nullify them by secret war, violence and terror.

*Many detailed statistics follow to prove his assertion.

Nor have we fared better in our civil rights of life, liberty, and property which have come for adjudication before the State courts. It is true that republican judges have generally presided over the superior courts of this State, and have generally shown a disposition to do us justice, but even these have been to some extent, warped by local pressure. But the main reasons for this failure of justice are that the sheriffs, probate judges and clerks of courts have almost universally, throughout the State, in plain violation of State laws, failed or refused to put men of our race on grand and petit juries in most of the counties in Alabama, and it has followed, as a consequence, that the lives, liberties, and property of black men have been decided by grand and petit juries composed exclusively of white men who are their political opponents. In controversies between our race and white men, and in criminal trials where the accused or the injured is a black man, it is almost if not quite impossible for a black man to obtain justice. . . . Our lives, liberties, and properties are made to hang upon the capricious, perilous, and prejudiced judgments of juries composed of a hostile community of ex-slaveholders who disdain to recognize the colored race as their peers in anything, who look upon us as being *by nature an inferior race,* and by right their chattel property. . . .

For three or four months past especially, our lives, and the lives of nearly all republicans in this State, have had no protection except the fear of the authority and laws of the United States. But for the presence of United states troops, and civil officers of the United States, hundreds of the active and earnest republicans of this State would have been assassinated. But even with the protection of these agencies, many of our race were shot down and killed at the polls on the 3d day of November last only because they chose to exercise their right to vote, as in the cases of Mobile and Barbour Counties, where Norman Freeman, Bill Jackson, and William Kinney (in Mobile), and Alfred Butler, George Walker, W. C. Keils, white, and others (in Barbour) whose names are at present unknown, were killed, and a large number wounded. Many of the victims of the White League in Barbour County were found dead in the woods and partially eaten by vultures; and these crimes will go utterly unnoticed and unpunished by the State courts. . . .

The legislature, now in session, has in its procedures displayed toward the colored race a spirit of marked bitterness, injustice, and vindictiveness which justly adds to our apprehensions of the future. With every department of the State government hostile to us, how may we expect or hope for justice or even for mercy?

Pressed around with these wrongs, misfortunes, and dangers, and solemnly impressed with their gravity, no resource or hope suggests itself to us but an earnest, prayerful, and we hope not unavailing, appeal to the President and the Congress of the United States, who still have the power and the agencies that may, in some measure, right our wrongs and diminish our misfortunes.

The question which our case and condition presents to you is simply this: whether our constitutional rights as citizens are to be a reality or a mockery, a protection and a boon or a danger and a curse; whether we are to be freemen in fact or only in name; and whether the late amendments to the Constitution are to be practically enforced or to become a nullity and stand only "as dead letters on the statute-book."

CHAPTER 22

WOMEN AND EDUCATION IN THE NINETEENTH CENTURY

The spread of education was one of the key developments in nineteenth-century world history. It began in the West, which already had reasonably extensive literacy and schooling. New political ideas, associated with the revolutionary era, pushed leaders to think about greater access to education in order to create opportunities for the lower classes and to produce better-informed (or more loyal) citizens. Children were increasingly cherished, particularly in middle-class ideology, and this led to the belief that they deserved the chance to learn—perhaps to learn even more than their parents had. Industrialization prompted demands for a better-trained workforce, able to do some arithmetic and capable of reading factory rules and consumer advertisements. As factories became more complex, child labor became less useful—another reason to think about schooling.

The expansion of education took place on several levels. Primary schools were extended, particularly from the 1830s onward. France passed a law encouraging primary schools in 1833. Later in that decade American states, headed by Massachusetts, began to require education. Schools also spread at the secondary and university levels, to provide business and government needs for a larger, and in some cases more technically trained, elite.

Given the Western example, which seemed to demonstrate that modern, widespread education was crucial to the operation of effective states and to economic growth, many societies began to follow suit. Japan, with a large school system already, decreed mass education in 1872 and also began to replace pure Confucianism with science and technology in the higher schools. Russia expanded its schools, and reform regimes in Latin America began to do the same.

The expansion of education also involved women, despite the widespread belief that women were intellectually inferior to men. In Europe and the United States officials realized that women might have as much use for basic reading and arithmetic skills as men, if only to hold factory jobs (in the working class) or run a household (in all classes). Further, women's special roles might require an additional, special kind of education, stressing domestic skills, virtue, and graceful arts such as piano playing. As women gained more schooling, they began to read more, sometimes focusing on topics related to marriage and domestic concerns but sometimes moving on to new ideas.

Women began to catch up with men in literacy and basic skills, at the primary level, at least. They lagged in higher schooling, but here too, by the late nineteenth century, a growing minority of middle-class women began to press into American high schools or the sex-segregated secondary schools in France. A handful even entered universities; a few were admitted to professional schools in areas such as medicine. Women's educational gains outstripped the roles available to them and created tensions with the widespread belief that women should concentrate on domestic virtues. Again, some differences divided countries such as France and the United States. In the period before 1900, a larger trickle of women entered American universities, for example, and in lower grades coeducation was somewhat more common in the United States.

Greater differences can be seen, however, when some societies outside Europe and North America are considered, particularly where traditional religious or philosophical ideas about women's inferiority were deeply rooted and where economic change was less extensive.

It was true that the spread of Western imperialism carried certain Western ideas about women to other countries. But in many cases women were newly exploited, as colonial authorities sought cheap labor for export industries. Many colonial women seemed exotic and debased, because of the different costumes they wore; both sexual exploitation and moralistic preachments resulted, from Africa to Hawaii. But where Western influence was particularly pervasive, additional signals were sometimes conveyed.

India was an obvious case in point. Effective British economic and military dominance of much of the subcontinent was established in the eighteenth century. During the nineteenth century, the British imposed fuller political control. For the most part, the British were content to leave Indian culture alone, but inevitably some new ideas gained entrance. The British tried to outlaw the practice of suttee, wherein some Indian wives killed themselves after their husbands had died on grounds that there was nothing more to live for. The British also set up some new schools. Upper-caste Indians chafed under British rule, for they were mostly confined to lower-level jobs in the colonial administration. At the same time, however, they sought to imitate some aspects of British practice in order to better their position. Gradually, a sense of Indian nationalism would emerge from this combination of imitation and discontent (see chapter 25).

Other developments in India included efforts to set up new types of schooling including some for women. The third section that follows, a historian's assessment, deals with these changes. The focus is on the Hindu reform group Arya Samaj, founded in 1875 and, after 1900, a major force for Indian nationalism. During the 1880s and 1890s the movement concentrated on reforms for Hindus themselves, including upper-caste women. The result, as in Europe, was a confusing pattern. Real innovation did occur: women in the upper caste received an education that Indian women had never before enjoyed. Yet ideas about women's inferiority did not change, and in India the Western idealism about women's morality penetrated less deeply. Other traditional practices, such as arranged marriages (often set up among children, who did not necessarily know each other in advance), continued to differentiate upper-caste India from the West.

Where upper-caste women were concerned, India offered a classic case of genuine but limited westernization. The comparative issues follow from this: what was imitated from the West, and why; what older attitudes persisted; how did the resultant combination compare with the complex developments affecting women in the West? In India as in the West, nineteenth-century patterns raised a host of issues that would continue to be worked through in the twentieth century and that continue to affect social life to the present day.

Questions

1. How did Necker de Saussure define appropriate education for women? How fully did she accept the domesticity arguments? How did she manage to argue for additional educational goals?
2. What is the nature of Duffey's argument for women's education? How does it compare with that of Necker de Saussure? Does the comparison suggest any pattern of similarities and differences in nineteenth-century situations for women in France and the United States? Do the different ideas about education relate to different family ideals in France and the United States?
3. How does Stanton's educational experience demonstrate the special limitations on women? How does it also demonstrate new opportunities?
4. Stanton was obviously an unusual woman, from an unusual family: did she reflect the more standard assumptions and situations at all? How does her actual educational experience compare with Duffey's arguments about women's education?
5. How does Stanton's experience help explain her leadership in American feminism?
6. What changes occurred in Indian education for upper-caste women in the late nineteenth century? Why did the changes occur? What were the limitations on educational goals?
7. How did Indian educational change and constraint compare with patterns in women's educational goals and experiences in the West?
8. How did many nineteenth-century women in France, India, and the United States accept and even encourage ideas and institutions that other women, at that time and since, have found unjust? Why did these accommodations occur?

For Further Discussion

1. Why, given various prejudices against women, did women's education advance at all in the nineteenth century? How did educational gains relate to other changes and continuities in the lives of adult women—did education change more or less than other aspects of life?

2. Considering education and family trends, do France and the United States fall within a common Western pattern with regard to nineteenth-century women, or do the differences suggest that the United States was a distinctive civilization?

3. Is westernization a useful concept in describing educational changes for upper-caste women in India? Or were special Indian features still predominant even amid change?

4. How do educational changes and ideas about women's education help explain the rise of feminism in the nineteenth century? Why was feminism stronger in the United States than in France, and in the West generally than in India?

5. How have twentieth-century women's patterns in the West and in India altered nineteenth-century developments? To what extent do they still reflect nineteenth-century issues?

FRANCE

This selection was written in 1838 by Albertine-Adrienne Necker de Saussure. Necker de Saussure was a Protestant of Swiss origin, but she was widely known in France. She had earlier written on more general educational issues. Her later book, from which this passage is taken, argued for a domestic education, granting women's special roles in marriage while pushing for a wider educational range.

• • •

The same gospel which says "Women, submit yourselves to your own husbands," teaches [them] also that there is no inequality among human beings in the sight of God. "Ye are all the children of God by faith in Jesus Christ." "There is neither bond nor free, there is neither male nor female, for ye are all one in Christ Jesus."

But this part of our celestial nature which education should constantly seek to bring out, man has scarcely taken into account. He has had this life only in view, and has shut his eyes upon whatever limited his rights here. He has seen only the wife in the woman—in the young girl only the future wife. All the faculties, the

From Albertine-Adrienne Necker de Saussure, *The Study of the Life of Woman* (Philadelphia, 1844), 27–29, 71, 74–75.

qualities which have no immediate relation to his interests, have seemed to him worthless. Yet there are many of the gifts bestowed upon woman that have no relation to the state of a wife. This state, although natural, is not necessary—perhaps half the women who now exist, have not been, or are no longer, married. In the indigent classes, the girl who is able to maintain herself, quits her parents, and supports herself by her industry for a long time, perhaps for life, without requiring aid from man. No social arrangements oblige her to become dependent. It is therefore important, that education should unfold in the young girl the qualities which give the surest promise of wisdom, happiness, usefulness, and dignity, whatever may be her lot. . . .

We do not desire that her end should be within herself—we wish that women should devote their lives to produce the happiness of others, but we wish this also for man.

There is, in our opinion, neither perfection nor happiness in any human creature, without a self-sacrificing spirit; but the self-sacrifice imposed by those who profit by it, and imposed without their giving the example, we believe is neither so constant nor so sincere as to deserve the name: and if, in order to obtain sacrifices which morality or affection would render voluntary, we paralyze the intellectual, or wound the dignity of the sensitive being, I say that we do not do justice to God's work. . . .

If we would have the selfishness of men plainly exhibited, let us listen to Rousseau.

"All the education of women should bear a relation to men—to please, to be useful to them—to possess their love and esteem, to educate them in childhood, to nurse them when grown up, to counsel, to console, to make their lives pleasant and sweet; such are the duties of women and should be taught to them from infancy."

If Rousseau had said that the education of women should bear a relation to what surrounds them, to the beings with whom nature or love had entwined their fate, we would applaud this language. Why particularly designate men? Why teach young girls to consider their own sex as nothing? and why give to the necessity of loving the most dangerous tendency? . . .

It is then at the age of ten years that we begin the education of young girls: an age which still belongs to childhood sufficiently to represent it as a whole. And if some of our remarks seem to relate to an earlier period, mothers will readily carry them farther back. The defects to be prevented in the character of their daughters must hitherto have occupied them as much as the qualities to be formed: so injurious is the atmosphere which surrounds women from the very cradle, so much is the influence around them addressed to their most dangerous tendencies, and calculated to increase their force.

With respect to this fact, the course followed in our preceding work would have for real life some advantages. The sisters brought up with their brothers would be subject to the same rules and duties, justice and truth being the only means employed to guide them. In this common education, there must be more firmness, less flattery; the promises and menaces of opinion, to which boys are comparatively insensible, are rarely employed. The motives proposed to all the children are those of goodness, reason, and true moral philosophy, adapted to their comprehension.

Since the comparative weakness of girls is rarely manifested before the age of ten years, why should they be freed from the laws of natural equality? Why led to calculate upon accommodations and consideration from the other sex? Many sad disappointments are thus prepared for them. . . .

Obedience is so important an element in education, it is so truly the first duty of childhood, and the way to observe every other, that in this respect no difference can be made in the education of the two sexes. However, docility, that internal disposition which naturally leads to the fulfillment of this duty, may well be the object of peculiar cultivation in young girls. Whenever boys are placed under public instruction, they are rather governed by general rules than by the will of individuals. Women, on the contrary, are called to bear, very often, and perhaps throughout their lives, the yoke of personal obedience. Since such is their fate, it is well to accustom them to it; they must learn to yield without even an internal murmur. Their gayety, their health, their equality of temper, will all gain by a prompt and cordial docility. . . .

Hence we would exhort mothers always to exercise fearlessly the authority with which God has entrusted them, since this also is sacred authority. Even though they might obtain the accomplishment of their plans in some other way, it would be important to accustom their daughters to submission. We would suggest that long expositions of motives invite objections, and seem to show that resistance is expected. It is with little girls especially that it is important to prevent rejoinders, the habit of contradicting and of arguing on all occasions.

A man is less exposed to this defect; he has but to express his will, and all yields to it in his family. A woman, on the contrary, who decides on no subject independently, if she prolongs indefinitely an insignificant opposition, both vexes her husband and disturbs the peace of her own heart.

The sentiment of superior duty, the idea ever present to the mind, that we are obeying God in observing the laws that nature or a formal engagement have imposed, prohibits all rebellion, and preserves, to a woman, her dignity, in the very bosom of obedience. This is what designates in her the immortal being, whatever be her mission upon earth.

In cherishing this sentiment you will also cultivate in your daughter other qualities: you will endow her with patience, resignation, and all the gentle virtues that a woman is infallibly called to exercise. To the caprices of fortune will be added, for her discipline, those of mankind. A multitude of illusive hopes and disappointed expectations form a part of her fate. Her best plans will be overturned: her occupations interrupted, she will have to suffer in silence humiliations and distresses still more poignant. But when, gentle and patient, she shall have supported all such trials, a high degree of virtue will be developed within her.

[Here is Necker de Saussure's schedule for organizing the hours in a young girl's day.]

Religious duties: worship and various exercises, 1

Literary and scientific studies—intellectual cultivation: elements of calculation and physical science, languages, history and geography, exercises of memory, 4 [total]

Fine arts: music and drawing, 1.5

Material duties and occupations: physical exercise, 1.5; female work and domestic care, 1.5; liberty, meals, and family circle, 4.5

On looking over the above plan, we see at once that the larger portion of the time is appropriated to recreations or duties purely material, and the smaller portion to study. It seems to us, therefore, that we cannot be accused of requiring too much mental application from young girls. But we can never approve of any diminution of the time claimed for purely intellectual education. If, then, we wish to preserve intact the four previous hours employed to develop the magnificent gift of intelligence, it is essential to lose not a moment; long preparations, idle words, must be prohibited, and this alone would be a valuable habit. The power of promptly fixing the attention forms what is called presence of mind, and also gives nerve to the character.

Undoubtedly it would be chimerical to expect that mothers should carry through their administrations the same exactness which forms the principal merit of institutions. But it would be, we think, possible for them to establish a more regular order in the employment of time than they usually do. A mother of a family is called to perform a variety of duties, and is exposed to interruptions in her functions as a governess; but may she not often anticipate the interruption, substitute one employment for another, and have in reserve some occupation for her daughters during her absence? Translations, extracts, tables, or charts to copy, serve as a continuation to interrupted lessons. . . .

When good proportions in the disposal of the hours of the day have been observed, the interior equilibrium is easily preserved in the young girl. Then you may often see her return of her own accord to her religious reading, carry on some object of study, and yield with moderation to her recreations; but it sometimes happens that a state of preceding fatigue is discovered, by a desire to depart as much as possible from habits; and as what usually wearies young girls is the constraint imposed by education, they abandon themselves to an excessive vivacity—whatever is out of the line of their previous existence, appears a recreation. This symptom, and some others, indicate the necessity of changing the course, and perhaps of multiplying the periods of repose; but nothing should induce the mother to let go the reins of education. One kind of order may be bad, but order itself is indispensable.

THE UNITED STATES

The following two selections come from a proponent not only of women's education but of coeducation, Eliza Duffey (d. 1898), and from the reminiscences of the tireless nineteenth-century feminist Elizabeth Cady Stanton (1815–1902). Duffey, writing in 1874, argued vigorously against limitations on women. She promoted the idea, among others, that they should be physically active. The evolutionary theories of Charles Darwin were used to bolster her position. Her work was part of the growing movement for more rounded education, including higher education and exercise—a movement that produced a growing number of women's colleges; it also resulted in women's gradual entry into high schools and coeducational colleges. Stanton, who married and had several children, was one of the distinctive personalities of nineteenth-century American history and a person of tremendous energy and persistence. By the late nineteenth-century, along with a few other leaders, she helped shape the movement that would soon lead to the granting of the vote to women (in 1920; women's suffrage in France did not arrive until 1945). Stanton's memoirs describe not only the pressures and bitter prejudices that shaped her goals as a young person, but also the opportunities, sometimes provided by men, that opened new doors.

• • •

ELIZA DUFFEY

As infancy begins to give place to childhood, then the distinctive training commences in earnest. The boy is allowed to be natural, the girl is forced to be artificial. Some girls break through all restraints and romp, but they are not the model girls whom mothers delight in and visitors praise for being "lady-like." Boy and girl as they are, with the same life pulsing in their veins and drawing its sustenance in precisely the same manner, with the same physical and mental needs, nature calls imperatively for an equally active life for both. They both want the air and the sunshine. They need equally to be hardened by the storms, tanned by the winds and have limbs strengthened by unrestrained exercise. But instead of this equality, while boys have their liberty more or less freely granted them, girls must stay at home and sew and read, and play prettily and quietly, and take demure walks. I am not

From Eliza Duffey, *No Sex in Education; or an Equal Chance for Both Girls and Boys* (Philadelphia, 1874), 40, 43, 100, 101.

speaking of girls in a single stratum of society, but of girls everywhere, from the highest down almost to the lowest, wherever the word "lady" is sufficiently reverenced and misunderstood. . . .

Girls, whose energies are still the most powerful, have no opportunity for working off their surplus vitality in rude and boisterous ways, for the restraint is never lifted from them. So they enter with the whole force of their natures into their studies, and, as every teacher will bear testimony, soon far outstrip their brothers. To be at the head of their class, to receive the highest mark of merit, is their ruling ambition. Their minds are prematurely developed at the expense of their bodies. This does not result because they are educated as boys, but because *both* are educated wrongly, and the girl far more wrongly than the boy, inasmuch and just so far as her education in the general discipline of her life differs from that of the boy. . . .

When we still further admit that in matters of fresh air, exercise and dress girls almost invariably labor under disadvantages which boys do not feel, I think there has been sufficient admitted to account for all failures (supposing there to be any) of girls in keeping healthful as well as mental pace with boys. It is pernicious habits in these respects which need looking after and correcting—these and the further and to my mind still more important fact that at the close of her school-days is removed a girl's mental stimulus, and she is left to collapse. Set these things right, and let girls find a "career" open to them, and education will take care of itself.

If there is really a radical mental difference in men and women founded upon sex, you *cannot* educate them alike, however much you try. If women *cannot* study unremittingly, why then they *will* not, and you *cannot make them*. But because they do, because they choose so to do, because they will do so in spite of you, should be accepted as evidence that they can, and, all other things being equal, can with impunity. Instead of our race dying out through these women, they are the hope of the country—the women with broad chests, large limbs and full veins, perfect muscular and digestive systems and harmonious sexual organs, who will keep pace with men either in a foot or an intellectual race, who know perfectly their own powers and are not afraid to tax them to their utmost, knowing as they do that action generates force. These are the mothers of the coming race. . . . The result will be truly "the survival of the fittest."

ELIZABETH CADY STANTON

When I was eleven years old, two events occurred which changed considerably the current of my life. My only brother, who had just graduated from Union College, came home to die. A young man of great talent and promise, he was the pride of

From Elizabeth Cady Stanton, *Eighty Years and More: Reminiscence, 1815–1897* (Boston: Northeastern University Press, 1993), 10–23. Reprinted by permission of the publisher.

my father's heart. We early felt that this son filled a larger place in our father's affections and future plans than the five daughters together. Well do I remember how tenderly he watched my brother in his last illness, the sighs and tears he gave vent to as he slowly walked up and down the hall, and, when the last sad moment came, and we were all assembled to say farewell in the silent chamber of death, how broken were his utterances as he knelt and prayed for comfort and support. . . . As he took no notice of me, after standing a long while, I climbed upon his knee, when he mechanically put his arm about me and, with my head resting against his beating heart, we both sat in silence, he thinking of the wreck of all his hopes in the loss of a dear son, and I wondering what could be said or done to fill the void in his breast. At length he heaved a deep sigh and said: "Oh, my daughter, I wish you were a boy!" Throwing my arms about his neck, I replied: "I will try to be all my brother was."

Then and there I resolved that I would not give so much time as heretofore to play, but would study and strive to be at the head of all my classes and thus delight my father's heart. All that day and far into the night I pondered the problem of boyhood. I thought that the chief thing to be done in order to equal boys was to be learned and courageous. So I decided to study Greek and learn to manage a horse. Having formed this conclusion I fell asleep. My resolutions, unlike many such made at night, did not vanish with the coming light. I arose early and hastened to put them into execution. They were resolutions never to be forgotten—destined to mold my character anew. As soon as I was dressed I hastened to our good pastor, Rev. Simon Hosack, who was always early at work in his garden.

"Doctor," said I, "which do you like best, boys or girls?"

"Why, girls, to be sure; I would not give you for all the boys in Christendom."

"My father," I replied, "prefers boys; he wishes I was one, and I intend to be as near like one as possible. I am going to ride on horseback and study Greek. Will you give me a Greek lesson now, doctor? I want to begin at once."

"Yes, child," said he, throwing down his hoe, "come into my library and we will begin without delay."

He entered fully into the feeling of suffering and sorrow which took possession of me when I discovered that a girl weighed less in the scale of being than a boy, and he praised my determination to prove the contrary. The old grammar which he had studied in the University of Glasgow was soon in my hands, and the Greek article was learned before breakfast. . . .

During all this time I kept up my lessons at the parsonage and made rapid progress. I surprised even my teacher, who thought me capable of doing anything. I learned to drive, and to leap a fence and ditch on horseback. I taxed every power, hoping some day to hear my father say: "Well, a girl is as good as a boy, after all." But he never said it. When the doctor came over to spend the evening with us, I would whisper in his ear: "Tell my father how fast I get on," and he would tell him, and was lavish in his praises. But my father only paced the room, sighed, and showed that he wished I were a boy; and I, not knowing why he felt thus, would hide my tears of vexation on the doctor's shoulder.

Soon after this I began to study Latin, Greek, and mathematics with a class of boys in the Academy, many of whom were much older than I. For three years one boy kept his place at the head of the class, and I always stood next. Two prizes were offered in Greek. I strove for one and took the second. How well I remember my joy in receiving that prize. There was no sentiment of ambition, rivalry, or triumph over my companions, nor feeling of satisfaction in receiving this honor in the presence of those assembled on the day of the exhibition. One thought alone filled my mind. "Now," said I, "my father will be satisfied with me." So, as soon as we were dismissed, I ran down the hill, rushed breathless into his office, laid the new Greek Testament, which was my prize, on his table and exclaimed: "There, I got it!" He took up the book, asked me some questions about the class, the teachers, the spectators, and, evidently pleased, handed it back to me. Then, while I stood looking and waiting for him to say something which would show that he recognized the equality of the daughter with the son, he kissed me on the forehead and exclaimed, with a sigh, "Ah, you should have been a boy!"

INDIA

Indian historian Madhu Kishwar describes here a major reform movement in the Punjab region by Hindu leaders. Dayanand Saraswati was the chief intellectual mentor of the Arya Samaj movement that Kishwar evaluates. Saraswati urged a Hindu revival, based on the authority of the classical Vedas; he urged more humane treatment of women, while emphasizing their purely domestic roles. Yet, he did see the need for education, if only to help upper-caste women counter Christian missionary efforts and the educational roles of Western female teachers in India. The Samaj reform movement flourished in the late 1880s and 1890s. The views developed here should be compared to Western ideals in the same period, but also to later presentations by women in India (see chapter 29).

• • •

The Arya Samaj movement was, on the one hand, an attempt by the educated elite to reform Hinduism and, on the other, to defend itself from ideological onslaught by the colonial rulers. Through this movement, the elite tried to evolve new forms of organisation to promote its own interests.

The Arya Samaj was not meant as a radical challenge to the existing structures

From Madhu Kishwar, "The Daughters of Aryavarta," in *Women in Colonial India: Essays on Survival, Work, and the State,* ed. J. Krishnamurty (New York: Oxford University Press, 1989), 78–79, 95, 101–3, 112–13. Reprinted by permission of the *Indian Economic & Social History Review.*

of society. Even while it represented an assertion of indigenous culture, it picked up for reform precisely those issues which British rulers had pointed to as evidence of the degenerate state of Indian society. Operating within the parameters of the given social structure, the Arya Samaj sought to reform only those features which they thought acted as obstacles in the way of the economic and social advancement of the educated elite. Nowhere is this more evident than in its programme concerning caste discrimination and the low status of women—the twin foundations of Hindu society. . . .

The growing contradiction between the kind of education provided by government schools and their purported intention to produce educated housewives was time and again pointed out in the course of the debate on whether women's education should be secular or religious. The upper castes were averse to giving their daughters the same education as their sons. Miss Greenfield, in her evidence before the Education Commission, noted: 'The people ask, "Are our daughters to become Munshis and do 'naukari' that they should learn Urdu?"'

Upper caste opinion on the right kind of education for women was summed up by Khan Ahmed Shah, Extra Assistant Commissioner, Hoshiarpur:

> With the exception of a few books especially compiled for girls, the course of instruction is the same as that followed in primary schools. Such instruction is not liked by the people, and the existing schools are not popular among the respectable classes. . . . In fact, to render these schools really useful and popular, religious instruction is indispensible. Neither would it be so impracticable, as in the case of boys, as there are separate schools for Christian, Muhammadan and Hindu girls. . . . *

To the argument that women could not utilise education to take up jobs as men did, none of the sections of the Arya Samaj had any answer nor did they desire to pose the question seriously. This is because even the champions of higher education for women advocated it primarily as a means to bridge the mental gap between husbands and wives, mothers and sons. Moreover, they argued that ignorant women had a 'negative influence' as wives and mothers.

Female education was considered the most effective way of countering the subversive activity of the missionaries. A more practical point was that unless higher education was given to women, there would be no primary school teachers for girls. Conservative opinion regarded this problem as almost insoluble. They felt that girls should not have male teachers and that the government would not be able to induce respectable Hindu and Muslim women to study in female normal schools. In their view, with Christian women as teachers, girls' schools were likely to do more harm than good. Under such circumstances, they found it difficult to suggest the best

*The quotes are from the *Education Commission Report, Appendix* (New Delhi: 1884), 126, 229.

method of providing teachers for girls' schools. The Samajists discovered 'the best method' which would also solve another grave social problem:

> Few well-to-do, even easily circumstanced parents, guardians or husbands will care to allow their girls and wives to engage in service after their marriage; but there is a class of females—at present a pest on the society, *source* of untold suffering and crime all around—who can be nicely utilised for the purpose; I mean the Hindu widows (emphasis added). . . .

But the fear persisted that higher education would lead to a particularly condemnable phenomenon—'overculture'—among women, which would become not only 'the cause of domestic aberration' but also of the 'annihilation of the race itself' because the effect of education would be 'physical deterioration' among women.

The proponents of the women's cause admitted that higher education for girls was not an unmixed blessing, but they assured their opponents that nobody was 'seriously thinking of turning out ladies mistresses of arts.' They tried to convince their opponents that 'the character of girls' education should be different from that of boys in many essential respects. . . . The education we give our girls should not unsex them.

It is obvious from this debate that neither of the two sections of the Arya Samaj addressed itself to the task of emancipating women. On the contrary, women's roles within the family as wives, daughters and mothers were re-emphasised and extended to conform with the requirements of the family in a changing situation. Women had to be able to adjust to the new style of life being adopted by men, had to come out of seclusion and act as hostesses. They had to supervise the education of children in addition to feeding them. They had to be 'managers' of the family's internal existence, which was becoming increasingly complex with the changing tempo of life in large cities. Here, there was no difference between the different sections of reformers. Even those, like Lajpat Rai, who actively opposed any effort for women's higher education, could, in the same breath, declare that ' . . . the nature of the duties imposed on a wife and mother in the Hindu scriptures and books of law, makes a fairly good education an absolute necessity for a wife and a mother.' But

> With all the sorrow and pain that an educated Hindu feels for the present position of Indian womanhood, he would not have his daughter and sisters go out into the world in search of employment as the girls in Europe do, not to speak of other excesses to which they are all liable by virtue of their conditions of life.*

This unwillingness to question the legitimacy of certain institutional forms of women's oppression defined the narrow limits of Arya Samaj activity. They wanted

*These quotes are from letters to the Punjabi newspaper *Tribune*, in 1894.

women 'enlightened' but 'dependent'; they wanted to give them 'dignity' but not 'freedom.' The contradiction was not resolvable. They could not envisage any significant change in the social role of women although a number of outstanding women were appearing all over India as professionals. The names of Anandibai Joshi, Rukmabai, Pandita Ramabai, Cornelia Sorabjee, and their achievements, were well known among the educated in Punjab because contemporary newspapers gave frequent coverage to their activities. . . .

The Arya Samaj helped remove some of the prejudices against women's education among the urban middle classes. It also fought against the more blatant forms of women's exploitation. Women's status was somewhat altered within the family. While the Arya Samaj did not address itself to the question of the emancipation of women, it created certain preconditions for the alleviation of some aspects of their oppression. Yet why did it fail to develop further?

The life histories of the Samaj women clearly reveal that women were not passive recipients of reform. Right from the beginning, they took the initiative themselves and the women's organisations and institutions that sprang up in the period were a reflection of a certain activity and unrest amongst women. . . . it is very clear that the trend of women's thinking on the question of their own status does not reveal the development of an independent self-view. This is also true of the women's organisations and institutions that mushroomed in and around the Arya Samaj.

The Samaj movement was led and initiated by men, who kept the activity of women's institutions under strict control and tutelage. For instance, around 1889, when the Stri Samaj (women's Samaj) was being founded in Jullunder, it was decided that it would be allowed to come into existence only if it accepted the jurisdiction of the Purush Samaj (men's Samaj) over it.

Women, therefore, joined the movement as subordinate partners—an extension of the wifely role of helpmeet—and Stri Samajes tended to play a subsidiary role. In fact, the Arya Samaj women's movement was so well contained that no subversive woman could ever emerge out of it. Even when women were allowed to speak for themselves, they spoke the language of men and their thinking remained within the parameters carefully defined for them by the patriarchal world view. This is amply evidenced by . . . the short stories [written by women] *Julvid Sackha,* all of which are designed to inculcate [traditional] virtue; the woman who is unfaithful to her husband is usually depicted as dying an untimely death in the throes of remorse . . .

In some ways it can be said that the Arya Samaj movement was intended to 'reform' women rather than to reform the social conditions which oppressed them. Women were to be educated into becoming more suitable wives and mothers for the new, educated men. The conditions of seclusion under which these upper caste women lived meant that, for the most part, they lived in a world of their own. Since they had very limited contact even with their own husbands, in some ways, they had been pretty much left to themselves to devise their own inner forms of life within the repressive culture. . . . In the process, their thinking had become inaccessible to men. But now, this extreme form of seclusion was creating its own problems because the needs of men seemed to have suddenly changed, making it necessary for women to change their lives and attitudes to adapt to men's requirements.

CHAPTER 23

RUSSIAN AND JAPANESE CONSERVATISM

Conservatism is as old as human politics. Any political arrangement involves some people a bit more eager for change and others insistent that current arrangements should be preserved. These latter are conservatives. Some political cultures, because of an emphasis on order, are more dominated by conservatism than others— China before the twentieth century is an example frequently cited. But the general phenomenon is a common one in history.

Conservatism in the nineteenth century took on two new elements. First, so many changes were occurring, because of new political ideas (including ideas spread by the French Revolution), industrialization, and imperialism, that conservatives in many areas were inclined to become more explicit about their viewpoint and even to organize as a political movement. Formal conservatism, as opposed to more informal groupings of like-minded leaders, thus emerged in Europe during the French revolutionary era, around 1800. Second, outside Europe, pressures to import political and social ideas and institutions from the dynamic West prompted conservatives to worry about foreignness as well as about change in general. Many conservatives found themselves defending against Western corruption what they saw as vital elements of their own cultural and political traditions.

Because political changes and Western influence were particularly widespread in Japan from the Meiji era (beginning in 1868) onward and in Russia under Alexander II (1855–81), conservatism in these two countries gained unusual importance and complexity. Conservatives were forced to define what aspects of the contemporary West were particularly objectionable. But they might also indicate certain ingredients that, altered to preserve national essentials, could be accepted as change. In both countries conservatives wielded great influence, shaping much of the reform process in Japan and, in Russia, preventing certain kinds of reforms altogether.

Conservatism in the nineteenth century was rarely simple-minded. Many conservatives recognized the need for some change: they merely insisted that many older values and institutions should be essentially preserved and that change should not be blindly embraced. Many Russian conservatives after 1861, for example, clearly recognized that the emancipation of the serfs had been a desirable reform; they did not argue for a return to serfdom, though they rarely wanted many more concessions to the aggrieved peasantry. Russian conservatives also saw that their country should participate in the kinds of scientific research being spearheaded in Western Europe; there was danger in lagging behind here. Japanese conservatives were even more flexible: they granted that the old system of feudalism and the shogunate should not be restored (though they sometimes sought to maintain some of the older values, including military honor). Interpreting modern conservatism as it began to develop in response to the massive changes of the long nineteenth century thus requires some subtlety: what did conservatives insist on keeping intact, and where were they willing to bend?

Russia and Japan were particularly important battlegrounds for conservatives in the nineteenth century, because both countries did go through periods of major reform that could easily be judged excessive. Under Alexander II, Russia not only emancipated the serfs but began to sponsor industrial development, legal reforms including reduction of many traditionally harsh punishments, new local governments, and wider literacy. Japan's Meiji era reforms embraced a new political system, ultimately including a parliament and a constitution; rapid economic development; new commercial laws; a commitment to mass education that initially, in the 1870s, included largely Western-style curricula and a horde of teachers imported from the West.

In these contexts, conservatives in both countries enunciated a more cautious policy, which was significant in Russian and Japanese history. Russian conservatives were in the ascendancy after Alexander II was assassinated by terrorists in 1881. Although they did not oppose all change (industrialization continued), they definitely resisted any further alterations to the political and social structure. Their obstinacy helped developed an atmosphere of inflexibility and repression that led to the revolutions of 1905 and 1907. Japanese conservatives gained ground in the 1880s also, with the backing of the emperor, amid a widespread sense that disorder was spreading, for example in the schools.

Both Japanese and Russian conservatives embraced nationalism. This movement, born in Western Europe and associated with radical changes such as the French Revolution, proved invaluable to conservatives in existing nations. With nationalism, conservatives could easily appeal to loyalty to the traditions that made the nation distinctive and great. With nationalism, conservatives had a beacon capable of arousing popular emotions, which could give them backing even when the espoused policies were particularly designed to benefit the elite. Conservatives in many countries, including the United States and Western Europe, turned to this use of nationalism from the late nineteenth century onward. Nationalism remained a radical force in other settings as well, such as the colonies held by European imperialism.

Conservative nationalists outside the West inevitably articulated certain objections to Western values. Russian and Japanese leaders expressed sentiments that many other societies shared or would come to share. After all, Western values were disruptive and hence unpleasant to conservatives. Western values were foreign and hence also unpleasant to nationalists. Understanding why serious leaders might oppose Western values such as individualism is both difficult and essential; an analysis of nineteenth-century conservatism provides a good place to start. It is difficult because, as Westerners, most of us believe in our key values, and it takes some effort to understand why and how others might attack them. But the process is essential because leaders in so many societies, even some that are friendly to the West in certain respects, oppose some of those values; this was true a century ago and it is still true today. Even here, of course, some subtlety is needed. Anti-Western spokespeople may oppose the West down the line, but more commonly they consciously or unconsciously imitate certain Western ways—just as conservatives often grant the importance of some change. Analysis requires identification of the values considered preferable to those of the West, but also recognition of areas where the West was acknowledged as an appropriate model.

Comparing Russian and Japanese conservatism highlights these issues of evaluation. In both cases conservatives opposed many but not all changes; in both cases nationalist sentiment resisted westernization but opened the door to some imitation. But the two cases were not identical. Russia, with more experience dealing with the West, produced harsher brands of conservatism by the 1880s and 1890s. Russia's czarist autocracy and its aristocratic upper class were severely beleaguered. Nationalists defined a wide gulf between Russia's superior values and the delusions of the West. Other conservatives worked hard—though ultimately in vain—to save a fundamentally traditional society amid change, and they inevitably urged new kinds of repression in the process. A few individual Japanese leaders took a similar stance, but in the main Japanese conservatives were more flexible. The nation had already fundamentally altered its political and social system. It was not a democracy, but it admitted newcomers to its upper class along with former aristocrats, and it did have a parliament through which various opinions might be expressed. In defending this system and trying to reincorporate some older values, conservatives were not really defending unaltered traditionalism. And though Japanese authorities could be highly repressive—as in attacking socialists after 1900—systematic repression was less prominent in Japan than in Russia. Comparison, then invites attention to the differences in conservative tone and to the significant variations in context in the two countries.

Russian conservatism was not uniform, though all its leading spokesmen favored nationalism, czarist autocracy, and the Orthodox church. Some conservative nationalists praised the Russian people in the abstract while defining distinctive views of the state and progress. Leaders such as Nikolai Danilevsky, in the 1860s, bitterly opposed the West, but they could grant the need for some limited change. After the terrorist assassination of czar Alexander II in 1881, however, Russian conservatism became more defensive. Constantine Pobedonostsev became Russia's conservative leader. A lawyer, he gained positions both in the government and in the Orthodox church, spurring reactionary policies between 1881 and 1905. Pobedonostsev was outspoken in his hostility to key Western principles and institutions.

In Japan, Yamagata Arimoto was the most conservative of the leading statesmen of the Meiji era and was closely associated with the army. He, too, objected to many Western values, but he also saw how certain Western practices, such as universal military conscription, though radical in terms of Japanese tradition, could actually benefit a conservative Japanese state. Here, he tried to show how history set a Japanese precedent for a practice that was apparently new.

Comparing these two conservative currents requires the now-familiar balance between noting the important points they have in common—do Russian and Japanese leaders agree about Western political fallacies, for example?—and discerning the ways in which they differ in degree of openness to limited change.

Questions

1. How did Danilevsky define Russian superiority? what, in his view, were Russia's key strengths?

2. What did Danilevsky mean by freedom? What recent reform was he willing to defend? What few aspects of the West did he admire?

3. How do Danilevsky and Pobedonostsev compare as Russian nationalists and conservatives? Did they agree on the qualities of a strong state? How do their emphases differ?

4. Which version of Russian conservatism do Yamagata Arimoto's views most resemble: Danilevsky's or Pobedonostsev's?

5. Why and how did Russian conservatism change between the 1860s (Danilevsky, and the 1880s (Pobedonostsev)?

6. What aspects of Western politics did Yamagata Arimoto, Danilevsky, and Pobedonostsev all criticize? Did they agree in their reactions to the West?

7. How did Yamagata Arimoto and Pobedonostsev view voting and political parties and the remedies for divisiveness?

8. How did Yamagata Arimoto's Confucianism compare with Pobedonostsev's conservative ideals? Would Russian conservatives' advice to soldiers be different from Yamagata Arimoto's? What are the implications of these differences? By Russian conservative standards, is it accurate to call Yamagata Arimoto a conservative at all?

9. What kinds of differences in national setting did the two conservative movements suggest? In which country did conservatives have an easier time defending the status quo in the 1880s and 1890s?

For Further Discussion

1. What is conservative nationalism? How does it differ from liberal or radical nationalism?

2. Why did both Japanese and Russian conservatives emphasize the importance of an emperor and a strong state?

3. What aspects of the West were most likely to be criticized by foreign observers in the late nineteenth century? Are the same aspects still likely to be criticized today, or has the list changed?

4. Can Japan's greater success in combining change and stability be traced in the nature of its conservatism? How did Russia's version of conservatism play a role in the conditions that led to major revolution?

DANILEVSKY

The following selection was authored by an ardent Slavic nationalist, Nikolai Danilevsky, in a multiple-edition book called *Russia and Europe,* first issued in 1869. Danilevsky asserts the special virtues of the Slavic peoples as against other Europeans and the dominance of Russia among the Slavs. Elements of his argument might seem comical: he twists history, he glosses over ongoing problems such as peasant discontent after emancipation, and he ludicrously promises stability in a country almost foredoomed to revolution. But Danilevsky's views about Russian distinctiveness and Western evil were widely shared, even by people opposed to the existing czarist regime. The complexities of his outlook were widely shared also, as he argued on the one hand for Russian superiority and a special, deliberately non-Western definition of freedom while hoping on the other hand for future Russian ability to beat the West at its own game, science. Complexities of this sort outlived the czarist regime and flourished after the Communist revolution of 1917.

•   •   •

And now let us turn to the Slav world, and chiefly to Russia, its only independent representative, in order to examine the results and the promises of this world, a world still only at the beginning of its cultural-historical life. We must examine it from the viewpoint of the above four foci of reference: religion, culture, politics, and

From Nikolai Danilevsky, *Russia and Europe,* in *The Mind of Modern Russia,* ed. Hans Kohn (New Brunswick, N.J.: Rutgers University Press, 1955), 200–211. Copyright © 1955 by The Trustees of Rutgers College in New Jersey. Reprinted by permission.

socio-economic structure, in order to elucidate what we rightfully expect as well as hope from the Slav cultural-historical type.

Religion constituted the most essential element of ancient Russian life, and at the present time, the overwhelming spiritual interest of the ordinary Russian is also involved in it; in truth, one cannot but wonder at the ignorance and the impertinence of these people who could insist (to gratify their fantasies) on the religious indifference of the Russian people.

From an objective, factual viewpoint, the Russian and the majority of Slav peoples became, with the Greeks, the chief guardians of the living tradition of religious truth, Orthodoxy, and in this way they continued the high calling, which was the destiny of Israel and Byzantium: to be the chosen people. . . .

. . . The religious aspect of the cultural activity belongs to the Slav cultural type and to Russia in particular; it is its inalienable achievement, founded on the psychology of its people and on its guardianship of religious truth. . . .

Whatever the future may bring we are entitled, on the evidence of the past alone, to consider the Slavs among the most gifted families of the human race in political ability. Here we may turn our attention to the special character of this political ability and show how it manifested itself during the growth of the Russian state. The Russians do not send out colonists to create new political societies, as the Greeks did in antiquity or the English in modern times. Russia does not have colonial possessions, like Rome or like England. The Russian state from early Muscovite times on has been Russia herself, gradually, irresistibly spreading on all sides, settling neighboring nonsettled territories, and assimilating into herself and into her national boundaries foreign populations. This basic character of Russian expansion was misunderstood because of the distortion of the original Russian point of view through Europeanization, the origin of every evil in Russia. . . .

But the expansion of the state, its attainment of stability, strength, and power, constitutes only one aspect of political activity. It has still another one, consisting of the establishment of equal relationships between the citizens themselves and between them and the state, i.e., in the establishment of civil and political freedom. A people not endowed with this freedom cannot be said to possess a healthy political sense. Is the Russian people capable of freedom?

Naturally our "well-wishers" give a negative answer: some regard slavery as a natural element of the Russians, and others are afraid, or pretend to be afraid, that freedom in Russian hands must lead to all sorts of excesses and abuses. But on the basis of Russian history and with knowledge of the views and traits of the Russian people, one can only form an opinion diametrically opposed to this view—namely, that there hardly ever has existed or exists a people so capable of enduring such a large share of freedom as the Russians and so little inclined to abuse it, due to their ability and habit to obey, their respect and trust in the authorities, their lack of love for power, and their loathing of interference in matters where they do not consider themselves competent. If we look into the causes of all political troubles, we shall find their root not in the striving after freedom, but in the love for power and the vain cravings of human beings to interfere in affairs that are beyond their comprehension. . . .

This nature of the Russian people is the true reason why Russia is the only state which never had (and in all probability never will have) a political revolution, i.e., a revolution having as its aim the limitation of the power of the ruler. . . .

With legality in the succession of the throne secured . . . and finally with the liberation of the peasants, all the reasons which in former times had agitated the people disappeared; and even an ordinary rebellion, going beyond the limits of a regrettable misunderstanding, has become impossible in Russia so long as the moral character of the Russian people does not change. . . .

. . . Thus we may conclude that the Russian people, by their attitude towards the power of the state, by their ability to sacrifice to it their own personal interests, and by their attitude towards the use of political and civil freedom, are gifted with wonderful political sense.

In the socio-economic sphere, Russia is the only large state which has solid ground under its feet, in which there are no landless masses, and in which, consequently, the social edifice does not rest on the misery of the majority of the citizens and on the insecurity of their situation. In Russia only there cannot and does not exist any contradiction between political and economic ideals. This contradiction threatens disaster to European life, a life which has embarked on its historical voyage in the dangerous seas between the Charybdis of Caesarism or military despotism and the Scylla of social revolution. The factors that give such superiority to the Russian social structure over the European, and give it an unshakable stability, are the peasant's land and its common ownership. On this health of Russia's socio-economic structure we found our hope for the great socio-economic significance of the Slav cultural-historical type. This type has been able for the first time to create a just and normal system of human activity, which embraces not only human relations in the moral and political sphere, but also man's mastery of nature, which is a means of satisfying human needs and requirements. Thus it establishes not only formal equality in the relations between citizens, but a real and concrete equality.

However, as regards the prominent place of the Slav cultural-historical type in the field of culture proper, one must admit that so far the Russian and other Slav achievements in the sciences and in the arts are insignificant in comparison with the accomplishments of the two great cultural types, the Greek and the European. . . .

Scientific and artistic activity can thrive only under conditions of leisure, of an overflow of forces that remain free from daily toil. Could much leisure be left over among Russians and Slavs? . . . All these considerations fully answer, it seems to me, the question why until now Russia and the other Slav countries could not occupy a respected position in purely cultural activities. . . . But indications of these aptitudes, of these spiritual forces, which are necessary for brilliant achievements in the fields of science and art are now indisputably present among the Slav peoples in spite of all the unfavorable conditions of their life; and, consequently, we are justified in expecting that with a change in these conditions, these peoples will bring forth remarkable creations. . . .

The Slav cultural type has already produced enough examples of artistic and, to a lesser degree, scientific achievements to allow us to conclude that it has attained a significant degree of development in these fields. The relative youth of the race and the concentration of all its forces upon other, more urgent types of activity have not, until now, given the Slavs the opportunity of acquiring cultural significance, in the exact meaning of the phrase. This should not embarrass us; rather, it points to the right path in our development. As long as there is no strong foundation, we cannot and we must not think of the erection of a durable edifice; we can only set up temporary buildings, which cannot be expected to display the talents of the builder in every respect. The political independence of the race is the indispensable foundation of culture, and consequently all the Slav forces must be directed towards this goal. Independence is indispensable . . . [for] without the consciousness of Slav racial unity, as distinct from other races, an independent culture is impossible. . . .

The requisite preliminary achievement of political independence has still another importance in the cultural as well as in all other spheres: the struggle against the Germano-Roman world (without which Slav independence is impossible) will help to eradicate the cancer of imitativeness and the servile attitude towards the West, which through unfavorable conditions has eaten its way into the Slav body and soul.

POBEDONOSTSEV

Constantine Pobedonostsev (1827–1907) was a statesman and jurist, trained in the law. He tutored the future czar Alexander II, then served in the holy synod of the Russian Orthodox Church (1880–1905), where he became the leading spokesman of religious orthodoxy, nationalism, and autocracy. He had great influence over czar Alexander III and encouraged policies of rigorous censorship, persecution of religious minorities, and repression of all political opposition. He also supported an activist foreign policy designed to enhance Russia's national prestige. He wrote widely on Russian law and also authored a number of attacks on Western rationalism and liberalism.

• • •

What is this freedom by which so many minds are agitated, which inspires so many insensate actions, so many wild speeches, which leads the people so often to misfor-

From Konstantin P. Pobyedonostsev, *Reflections of a Russian Statesman*, trans. Robert Crozier Long (London: Grant Richard, 1898), 23–30, 32–46, 52–54, 62–74.

tune? In the democratic sense of the word, freedom is the right of political power, or, to express it otherwise, the right to participate in the government of the State. This universal aspiration for a share in the government has no constant limitations, and seeks no definite issue, but incessantly extends . . . Forever extending its base, the new Democracy now aspires to universal suffrage—a fatal error, and one of the most remarkable in the history of mankind. By this means, the political power so passionately demanded by Democracy would be shattered into a number of infinitesimal bits, of which each citizen acquires a single one. What will he do with it, then? How will he employ it? In the result it has undoubtedly been shown that in the attainment of this aim Democracy violates its sacred formula of "Freedom indissolubly joined with Equality." It is shown that this apparently equal distribution of "freedom" among all involves the total destruction of equality. Each vote, representing an inconsiderable fragment of power, by itself signifies nothing; an aggregation of votes alone has a relative value. The result may be likened to the general meetings of shareholders in public companies. By themselves individuals are ineffective, but he who controls a number of these fragmentary forces is master of all power, and directs all decisions and dispositions. We may well ask in what consists the superiority of Democracy. Everywhere the strongest man becomes master of the State; sometimes a fortunate and resolute general, sometimes a monarch or administrator with knowledge, dexterity, a clear plan of action, and a determined will; in a Democracy, the real rulers are the dexterous manipulators of votes, with their placemen, the mechanics who so skillfully operate the hidden springs which move the puppets in the arena of democratic elections. Men of this kind are ever ready with loud speeches lauding equality; in reality, they rule the people as any despot or military dictator might rule it. The extension of the right to participate in elections is regarded as progress and as the conquest of freedom by democratic theorists, who hold that the more numerous the participants in political rights, the greater is the probability that all will employ this right in the interests of the public welfare, and for the increase of the freedom of the people. Experience proves a very different thing. The history of mankind bears witness that the most necessary and fruitful reforms—the most durable measures—emanated from the supreme will of statesmen, or from a minority enlightened by lofty ideas and deep knowledge, and that, on the contrary, the extension of the representative principle is accompanied by an abasement of political ideas and the vulgarization of opinions in the mass of the electors. . . .

In what does the theory of Parliamentarism consist? It is supposed that the people in its assemblies make their own laws, and elect responsible officers to execute their will. Such is the ideal conception. Its immediate realization is impossible. The historical development of society necessitates that local communities increase in numbers and complexity; that separate races be assimilated, or, retaining their polities and languages, unite under a single flag, that territory extend indefinitely. Under such conditions direct government by the people is impracticable. The people must, therefore, delegate its right of power to its representatives, and invest them with administrative autonomy. These representatives in turn cannot govern immediately, but are compelled to elect a still smaller number of trustworthy persons—ministers— to whom they entrust the preparation and execution of the laws, the appointment and collection of taxes, the appointment of subordinate officials, and the disposition of the militant forces.

In the abstract this mechanism is quite symmetrical; for its proper operation many conditions are essential. The working of the political machine is based on impersonal forces constantly acting and completely balanced. It may act successfully only when the delegates of the people abdicate their personalities; when on the benches of Parliament sit mechanical fulfillers of the people's behests; when the ministers of State remain impersonal, absolute executors of the will of the majority; when the elected representatives of the people are capable of understanding precisely, and executing conscientiously the programme of activity, mathematically expressed, which has been delivered to them. Given such conditions the machine would work exactly, and would accomplish its purpose. The law would actually embody the will of the people; administrative measures would actually emanate from Parliament; the pillars of the State would rest actually on the elective assemblies, and each citizen would directly and consciously participate in the management of public affairs.

Such is the theory. Let us look at the practice. Even in the classic countries of Parliamentarism it would satisfy not one of the conditions enumerated. The elections in no way express the will of the electors. The popular representatives are in no way restricted by the opinions of their constituents, but are guided by their own views and considerations, modified by the tactics of their opponents. In reality, ministers are autocratic, and they rule, rather than are ruled by Parliament. They attain power, and lose power, not by virtue of the will of the people, but through immense influence . . . and they fear no censure while they enjoy the support in Parliament of a majority which they maintain by the distribution of bounties from the rich tables which the State has put at their disposal. In reality, the ministers are as irresponsible as the representatives of the people. Mistakes, abuse of power, and arbitrary acts, are of daily occurrence, yet how often do we hear of the grave responsibility of a minister? It may be once in fifty years a minister is tried for his crimes, with a result contemptible when compared with the celebrity gained by the solemn procedure. . . .

Such is the complicated mechanism of the Parliamentary farce; such is the great political lie which dominates our age. By the theory of Parliamentarism, the rational majority must rule; in practice, the party is ruled by five or six of its leaders who exercise all power. In theory, decisions are controlled by clear arguments in the course of Parliamentary debates; in practice, they in no wise depend from debates, but are determined by the wills of the leaders and the promptings of personal interest. In theory, the representatives of the people consider only the public welfare; in practice, their first consideration is their own advancement, and the interests of their friends. In theory, they must be the best citizens; in practice, they are the most ambitious and impudent. In theory, the elector gives his vote for his candidate because he knows him and trusts him; in practice the elector gives his vote for a man whom he seldom knows, but who has been forced on him by the speeches of an interested party. In theory, Parliamentary business is directed by experience, good sense, and unselfishness; in practice, the chief motive powers are a firm will, egoism, and eloquence.

Such is the Parliamentary institution, exalted as the summit and crown of the edifice of State. It is sad to think that even in Russia there are men who aspire to the establishment of this falsehood among us; that our professors glorify to their young pupils representative government as the ideal of political science; that our newspapers pursue it . . . , under the name of justice and order, without troubling to examine without prejudice the working of the parliamentary machine. Yet even where centuries have sanctified its existence, faith already decays; the Liberal intelligence exalts it, but the people groans under its despotism, and recognizes its falsehood. We may not see, but our children and grandchildren assuredly will see, the overthrow of this idol, which contemporary thought in its vanity continues still to worship. . . .

The prevalent doctrine of the perfection of Democracy and of democratic government stands on the same delusive foundation. This doctrine presupposes the capacity of the people to understand subtleties of political science which have a clear and substantial existence in the minds of its apostles only. Precision of knowledge is attainable only by the few minds which constitute the aristocracy of intellect; the mass, always and everywhere, is *vulgus,* and its conceptions of necessity are vulgar.

Democracy is the most complicated and the most burdensome system of government recorded in the history of humanity. For this reason it has never appeared save as a transitory manifestation, with few exceptions giving place before long to other systems. It is in no way surprising. The duty of the State is to act and to ordain: its dispositions are manifestations of a single will; without this, government is inconceivable. But how can a multitude of men, or a popular assembly act with a single will? . . . Such conditions inevitably lead to anarchy, from which society can be saved alone by dictatorship—that is, by the rehabilitation of autocracy in the government of the world.

YAMAGATA ARIMOTO

Yamagata Arimoto (1838–1922), was born a samurai but backed the Meiji side in the turmoil of 1860s. He studied military science in Europe and in the 1870s led

in the restructuring of the Japanese army, copying German organizational models. In the 1880s he concentrated more on domestic affairs, encouraging more Confucian elements in the schools and repressing political opposition. He also supported Japanese imperialism and a strong military influence in the government. Clearly opposed to the more westernizing reformers in Japan, Yamagata Arimoto has been the subject of some debate among historians of Japan, who argue about whether a "conservative" label is most appropriate for this formative leader in modern Japanese history.

• • •

On Military Conscription, 1872

In the system in effect in our country in the ancient past everyone was a soldier. In an emergency the emperor became the Marshal, mobilizing the able-bodied youth for military service and thereby suppressing rebellion. When the campaign was over the men returned to their homes and their occupations, whether that of farmer, artisan, or merchant. They differed from the soldiers of a later period who carried two swords and called themselves warriors, living presumptuously without working, and in extreme instances cutting down people in cold blood while officials turned their faces. . . .

. . . Following the Hōgen [1156–58] and Heiji [1159–60] eras, the court became lax, and military control passed into the hands of the warrior class. Feudal conditions spread throughout the country, and there appeared among the people a distinction between the farmer and the soldier. Still later, the distinction between the ruler and the ruled collapsed, giving rise to indescribable evils. Then came the great Restoration of the government [1868]. All feudatories returned their fiefs to the Throne, and in 1871 the old prefectural system was restored. On the one hand, warriors who lived without labor for generations have had their stipends reduced and have been stripped of their swords; on the other hand, the four classes of the people are about to receive their right to freedom. This is the way to restore the balance between the high and the low and to grant equal rights to all. It is, in short, the basis of uniting the farmer and the soldier into one. Thus, the soldier is not the soldier of former days. The people are not the people of former days. They are now equally the people of the empire, and there is no distinction between them in their obligations to the State.

No one in the world is exempt from taxation with which the state defrays its expenditures. In this way, everyone should endeavor to repay one's country. The Occidentals call military obligation "blood tax," for it is one's repayment in life-

From Ryusako Tsunoda, William Theodore de Bary, and Donald Keene, eds., *Sources of Japanese Tradition* (New York: Columbia University Press, 1958), 704–7, 709–10, 712–13. Reprinted by permission of the publisher.

blood to one's country. When the State suffers disaster, the people cannot escape being affected. Thus, the people can ward off disaster to themselves by striving to ward off disaster to the State. And where there is a state, there is military defense; and if there is military defense there must be military service. It follows, therefore, that the law providing for a militia is the law of nature and not an accidental, man-made law. As for the system itself, it should be made after a survey of the past and the present, and adapted to the time and circumstance. The Occidental countries established their military systems after several hundred years of study and experience. Thus, their regulations are exact and detailed. However, the difference in geography rules out their wholesale adoption here. We should now select only what is good in them, use them to supplement our traditional military system, establish an army and a navy, require all males who attain the age of twenty—irrespective of class—to register for military service, and have them in readiness for all emergencies. Heads of communities and chiefs of villages should keep this aim in mind and they should instruct the people so that they will understand the fundamental principle of national defense.

Precepts for Soldiers and Sailors, 1882

1. The soldier and sailor should consider loyalty their essential duty. Who that is born in this land can be wanting in the spirit of grateful service to it? No soldier or sailor, especially, can be considered efficient unless this spirit be strong within him. A soldier or a sailor in whom this spirit is not strong, however skilled in art or proficient in science, is a mere puppet; and a body of soldiers or sailors wanting in loyalty, however well ordered and disciplined it may be, is in an emergency no better than a rabble. Remember that, as the protection of the state and the maintenance of its power depend upon the strength of its arms, the growth or decline of this strength must affect the nation's destiny for good or for evil; therefore neither be led astray by current opinions nor meddle in politics, but with single heart fulfil your essential duty of loyalty, and bear in mind that duty is weightier than a mountain, while death is lighter than a feather. Never by failing in moral principle fall into disgrace and bring dishonor upon your name.

The second article concerns the respect due to superiors and consideration to be shown inferiors.

3. The soldier and the sailor should esteem valor. . . . To be incited by mere impetuosity to violent action cannot be called true valor. The soldier and the sailor should have sound discrimination of right and wrong, cultivate self-possession, and form their plans with deliberation. Never to despise an inferior enemy or fear a superior, but to do one's duty as soldier or sailor—this is true valor. Those who

thus appreciate true valor should in their daily intercourse set gentleness first and aim to win the love and esteem of others. If you affect valor and act with violence, the world will in the end detest you and look upon you as wild beasts. Of this you should take heed.

4. The soldier and the sailor should highly value faithfulness and righteousness. . . . Faithfulness implies the keeping of one's word, and righteousness the fulfilment of one's duty. If then you wish to be faithful and righteous in any thing, you must carefully consider at the outset whether you can accomplish it or not. If you thoughtlessly agree to do something that is vague in its nature and bind yourself to unwise obligations, and then try to prove yourself faithful and righteous, you may find yourself in great straits from which there is no escape. . . . Ever since ancient times there have been repeated instances of great men and heroes who, overwhelmed by misfortune, have perished and left a tarnished name to posterity, simply because in their effort to be faithful in small matters they failed to discern right and wrong with reference to fundamental principles, or because, losing sight of the true path of public duty, they kept faith in private relations. You should, then, take serious warning by these examples.

5. The soldier and sailor should make simplicity their aim. If you do not make simplicity your aim, you will become effeminate and frivolous and acquire fondness for luxurious and extravagant ways; you will finally grow selfish and sordid and sink to the last degree of baseness, so that neither loyalty nor valor will avail to save you from the contempt of the world.

On Local Government, 1890

. . . According to what I have heard, discord between political parties has gradually extended into every aspect of community life. Hardly a person in social, business, and economic relations, and in education, has remained untouched by this situation. . . . There are some people who abandon what they should be doing and expend both time and effort in unproductive political debate, and some who, losing their sense of purpose, even run afoul of the law. These evils are spreading their influence, morally, economically, and politically, throughout the country. They will impair the people's happiness and exert a harmful effect on the prosperity of the nation. In general, if a new government, in the course of its establishment, is abused for reasons of personal interests, the results could be extremely harmful. They could affect the strength and the cohesion of the entire people and become the cause of the decline of the nation. The history of our country and that of other countries provides many such examples in every age. The people, if they wish to prevent the growth of such evil influences, must regard at all times the unified endeavor of all as their highest aim. And the responsibility of those in a position to guide the people must be to apply themselves as administrators of the government to this ideal.

His Majesty the Emperor has granted the constitutional system to his ministers and subjects for the purpose of elevating their morals and of promoting their happiness. By virtue of this constitution ministers and subjects have been enabled to gain a higher degree of freedom and to improve their lot in life so that they can stand on an equal footing with peoples of other civilized nations. But if, unfortunately, we should err—however little—in putting this constitutional system into operation, we the people will have lost our position of honor. And thus, today, the duty of a loyal subject is to cultivate true constitutional liberty and to enjoy its benefits in peace.

If men lack self-respect and self-restraint, there cannot be freedom in its true sense. One who respects himself will of necessity respect others. One who wishes others to respect his own opinions must respect the views of others. There is no logic in the position that only one's own opinions are correct. Irrespective of place, diverse opinions are inevitable when the interests of people are not the same. Thus, we must make every effort to tolerate the views of others and to resolve differences mutually. If this is not done contention will not cease. The constitutional system is an instrument for the adjustment of diverse views: the use of force and violence will not only fail to eradicate differences in viewpoints but will also aggravate them.

Political problems do not encompass the entire field of human interests. The people who might entertain different political views very frequently hold mutually identical views in religious and moral matters, and in matters of personal and social relations. It is not the way of a loyal, trustworthy man to set aside his religious, moral, personal, and social relationships in the sole interest of politics. Thus, to promote party rivalry to extremes is a human misfortune. Nay, to resort to violence and to use obstructionist methods against an opponent to promote one's political position is to permit personal passions to enslave him. It is against the principle of the observance of the law. It is against the spirit of the constitutional system.

It is especially undesirable that one abandon his occupational pursuit for the sake of a political cause. It is against his own interest as well as that of society as a whole. The economic strength of a country is dependent mainly on productive labor. Thus, it is not the way of the good citizen to indulge in needless arguments to the neglect of his calling. Not only will he thus fail to add his bit to the national wealth but he will also fail to induce others to develop industrious habits of self-reliance.

On Political Parties, 1917 (Repeating an 1898 Essay)

The parties seem smugly unconcerned over the danger to our country of having to stand alone and without support in the future among the powers of the world. The evils of partisan politics are indeed deplorable. If this trend is permitted to develop unchecked, I fear that the spirit of the Meiji Restoration will die and the splendid achievements of the late emperor will soon come to naught. The actual situation with respect to political parties in our country today indicates that when one party is excessively strong in Parliament, that party becomes reckless and arbitrary. When two parties are evenly matched, the struggle between them becomes extremely violent. Thus, to eliminate arbitrary actions and violent political struggles, it would seem advisable to divide their strength and to have them restrain each other mutually. I have faith in a plan to establish a three-party system in the Diet which would eliminate excesses and help foster moderation. If the third party is organized by men who are impartial and moderate, and possessed of intelligence and a sincere concern for the well-being of the country, it is my belief that it can make a contribution to the state toward the achievement of constitutional government, and it will set an example to others. At present there are two parties—the Kensei-kai and the Seiyū-kai—which are evenly balanced. We must organize a group consisting of fair and intelligent men who will stand between the two existing parties and be partial to neither; who can check party excesses and irregularities; who can restrain the ambitions of those who seek to satisfy their avarice or their desire for political power through the instrument of the party; who can transcend the common run of politicians for whom politics is a means of livelihood; and who can go forward, resolutely and firmly, with but the one thought in mind of service to the state. Only by the conduct of a central core of such men who would not be corrupted by thoughts of personal gain or fame, and only by having as a nucleus in the Diet men who would not falter in their public devotion, can the secret of true constitutional government be achieved.

The greater the number of such representatives we can gather, the better it will be. However, the number of such men, both economically established and patriotically inclined, need not be numerous. Only a sufficient number capable of standing between the two large parties and of checking their excesses is necessary. The immediate need is to find someone who would take it upon himself to rally such people together. So long as he is a man of true devotion to the country, it matters not whether he is a farmer, craftsman, or merchant. There must be several million among our population of seventy million who have fixed property and are economically secure, and who therefore are above corruption. If such men come forward to organize a solid nucleus in the Diet, the empire will be on a firm and secure foundation, and there need be no anxiety in the country. The epoch-making task of establishing our sovereign and our country was accomplished by thousands of devoted and self-sacrificing patriots of the period prior to and after the Restoration. Today, fifty years since the Restoration, when our national fortunes continue to rise, are there no patriots who would step forward to save our country from the dangers which are imminent? It is my fervent hope that such men will brace themselves and rouse themselves to action.

CHAPTER 24

BUSINESS VALUES IN THE INDUSTRIAL REVOLUTION

Western Europe and Japan

This chapter explores the similarities and differences between the ideas and motivations of businessmen in two of the key industrial areas of the long nineteenth century: Western Europe and Japan.

The industrial revolution was one of the fundamental developments of modern world history, introducing powerful new technology to most branches of production, transportation, and communication, while propelling manufacturing ahead of agriculture as a source of jobs and wealth. Industrialization affected virtually every aspect of human life. Family life changed, as work moved outside the home. Governments gained new resources and military technology, while facing new social problems and potential unrest. The rhythm of traditional leisure, with its emphasis on frequent festivals, yielded to more commercial recreations, timed to accommodate the workday. The new working class emerged, tied to the rapid pace and frequent dangers of the new machinery.

Amid all the facets of industrialization, the role of the business community was a crucial ingredient and an important result. Industrialization everywhere depended on business initiatives in the nineteenth century, but it also depended on new business attitudes. More traditional merchants, in places like Western Europe and Japan, did not welcome the innovations that came with industrialization. They found industrial technology messy, industrial investment too risky. They viewed industrial entrepreneurs as grubby upstarts—at least until success brought great wealth.

Yet there were new values and motivations available. In Western Europe, the Enlightenment helped provide a new belief in the value of work and the validity of increasing wealth. The same ideas of progress that could inspire political or scientific revolution could justify new economic initiatives. In some cases, Enlightenment ideals combined with religious interests to produce businessmen eager to demonstrate God's grace through economic success. Rapid population growth was another spur, since population levels often doubled in the late eighteenth century. This huge change produced new markets and a new labor supply, but it also prodded businessmen to innovate to help support their own growing families.

In Western Europe the role of individual businessmen was clear. Key innovators in Britain underwrote the production of machines such as the steam engine and the introduction of revolutionary equipment into textiles, railroads, shipping, and heavy industry. Business never acted alone. The role of inventive workers and a growing mass of experienced factory labor was crucial. So was the active participation of government. Governments provided tariff protection and subsidized railway development; they supported industrialists against labor protest.

Nevertheless, the business initiatives were essential. Pioneering leaders were backed by hundreds of active imitators and disseminators. The mechanized textile industry, a crucial sector both in the West and in Japan, depended on hosts of initially small firms and the ambitious new owners who ran them. Furthermore, ongoing industrialization itself propelled a growing acceptance of business values in an expanding middle class of commercial and professional personnel. This middle class drew on the older class of merchants and professionals—called the bourgeoisie in preindustrial Europe—but its numbers and many of its precepts were new. The creation of an industrially oriented middle class was a key social result of the economic transformation, which came about ultimately in many parts of the world. Even societies such as the Soviet Union that furthered industrialization under state rather than business control ended up creating a managerial middle class.

The development of a new middle class and new values received great support in Western Europe throughout the long nineteenth century. In 1776 the British economist Adam Smith argued that individual profit motives, if unregulated, would spur entrepreneurs to innovate in ways that would benefit the whole economy. Most Western governments worked to remove barriers to profit-seeking and competition.

By the early nineteenth century many spokespeople proclaimed the virtues of social mobility and the acquisition of wealth. Self-help manuals urged hard work, thrift, and daring as the keys to legitimate business success. And businessmen themselves periodically wrote tracts or memoirs extolling similar values, which they viewed as fundamental to their own success and the good of society at large.

The role of business and the "entrepreneurial spirit" in Western industrialization did not go unopposed. Not only many workers, but also intellectuals, aristocrats, and religious leaders often objected to untrammeled greed and a lack of concern for social consequences. One businessman's quest for personal mobility might mean low wages and harsh work requirements for many employees.

The new attributes associated with business innovation were even more challenging to many societies outside the West. Japan was a case in point. Japanese markets were forced open by Western navies in 1853, and by 1868, the beginning of the Meiji (enlightened) era, Japanese leaders were poised for a set of reforms including initial industrial development. Feudalism was abolished, and though individual samurai maintained important roles in politics and business, opportunities for other commercial leaders increased. Meiji leaders were keenly aware of the roles business innovators had played and continued to play in Western industrialization. Western-minded reformers such as Fukuzawa urged a new individualism in this vein. Translations of Western self-help tracts, the books of Samuel Smiles for example, won an important audience.

But Japan had a distinctive context for the emergence of a new middle class. Though it had a substantial merchant tradition, there were fewer preindustrial businessmen and less business wealth than had existed in the West. Japan had not experienced the scientific revolution or the Enlightenment. During the seventeenth and eighteenth centuries the hold of Confucianism had increased.

In this setting Japan developed a complex combination of imitation and adaptation, which would allow industrial development to mesh with established values. Businessmen and Confucian leaders alike wrestled with the problems of defining appropriate goals, and on the whole outright westernization was rejected. Government played a greater direct role in Japan's industrialization than had been the case in countries like Britain and France. A Ministry of Industry, set up in 1881, sponsored technological innovation, directly subsidized individual business leaders, and ran many operations in heavy industry directly.

But Japan did experience a surge of new business leadership and social mobility. Talented former peasants generated most factory operations in textiles. A large middle-class sector developed around them.

All aspects of Western and Japanese industrialization invite comparison, for Japan was one of the first two societies outside the West to industrialize rapidly (Russia was the other). What Western countries had done between 1780 and 1850 Japan achieved between 1880 and 1920. The process involved (1) explicit imitation, not only of technology but also of ideas, (2) comparable experiences because of the nature of industrialization itself, and (3) crucial differences resulting from distinctive policies and contexts.

Business beliefs and motivations provide an obvious focus for comparison. The combination of shared beliefs and roles, as well as a concerted effort to define an appropriate Japanese approach, serves to organize the comparative effort. But business alone is not the point. Business attitudes related clearly to the nature and role of the industrial state, and here too Japan and the West both overlapped and differed in the early industrial period and beyond. And they generated important similarities and differences in the approach to labor. Assessment of businessmen's values, and the ideals put forth by proponents of business, invites additional comparison of several wider implications.

There is the question of causation as well. Explaining why individuals in the West were ready to define, and act upon, new middle-class values is a vital historical issue, crucial in explaining the origins of industrialization itself. Japan was not a middle-class pioneer in this sense, but an imitator; nevertheless, it did generate business innovation in ways few other areas of the world have matched even today. Comparison with the West contributes to our understanding of why Japan was poised for rapid economic change, why it could create its own version of an energetic business class.

Western and Japanese business continues to interact and to differ. Distinctive approaches to middle-class goals, emerging in the early industrial periods, continue to matter in the two leading regions of industrialization today.

The following selections are from the writings of a British publicist and a Japanese reformer and from the accounts of actual industrialists in France and Japan.

Questions

1. What did Samuel Smiles mean by self-help? How did he compare the roles of business and of education in preparing the individual? What attitudes did he imply toward workers who did not manage to rise?
2. What, according to Smiles, were the rewards for work?
3. Did Narcisse Faucheur—a businessman, not a writer—show the same values that Smiles preached so widely? What were his main motivations? How did he define success? What kinds of attitudes toward his workers and toward society at large did Faucheur seem to have?
4. What is the nature of the individualism preached and practiced by members of the Western middle class in the nineteenth century?
5. How did Fukuzawa define and defend individualism? How did Shibuzawa's goals differ from Fukuzawa's prescriptions?
6. How did Confucianism affect definitions of business entrepreneurship in late-nineteenth-century Japan?
7. How did nationalism help justify business in Meiji Japan? Did early Western industrialists invoke nationalism in the same way? What might account for differences here?
8. How did Faucheur and Shibuzawa describe their own work values?
9. How would Faucheur react to Shibuzawa's statement of motives? How would Shibuzawa critique Smiles's basic approach to success?
10. What were the most important similarities between the roles and ideas of Japanese and Western business leaders?

For Further Discussion

1. How could two different sets of business values work equally well in under-girding industrialization and the rise of a new middle class?

2. How might Western and Japanese middle-class values lead to different attitudes toward the role of government in industry? How might they lead to different attitudes toward workers and worker organizations? Would the attitudes produce different reactions to aggressive worker unions and strikes—and which business group would resist protest more fiercely?

3. Were Japanese business values and political conservatism (chapter 23) opposed to each other, or did they blend together in creating a distinctive approach to modern society?

4. Did Western and Japanese business styles relate at all to earlier definitions of feudalism, in which the two regions had also overlapped and yet diverged (see chapter 8)?

5. How do different traditions of business goals continue to distinguish Japanese economic organization and behavior from their Western counterparts? Why do some Western leaders argue that certain Japanese emphases should now be imitated elsewhere?

BUSINESS IDEALS IN BRITAIN: SAMUEL SMILES

Samuel Smiles was the leading spokesperson for middle-class values of work and mobility in mid–nineteenth-century Britain. A small-town doctor, Smiles early turned to writing as his main source of income. His books, notably the classic *Self-Help* (first published in 1859), went through many editions, until interest in this up-by-the-bootstraps approach declined as business organization became more complex after 1870. Many artisans and shopkeepers read Smiles, seeking clues that would improve their own fortune. We cannot know how many people agreed with Smiles's preachments, but the evidence suggests widespread interest. The values themselves were not totally clear-cut: Smiles hesitated about what to urge on ordinary workers, for excessive hope for mobility might lead to disappointment; yet a reference to one former worker who did become a successful manufacturer, Brotherton, shows a certain openness to change. Smiles also wavered on the value of education and on intellectual activities, which were part of the broader middle-class lexicon but which coexisted somewhat uneasily with the emphasis on business. Interpreting Smiles and the many similar authors throughout the early industrial West is not a totally straightforward task, for though the value system was not complex, it was new, a departure from more traditional Western social measurements.

• • •

All nations have been made what they are by the thinking and the working of many generations of men. Patient and persevering labourers in all ranks and conditions of life, cultivators of the soil and explorers of the mine, inventors and discoverers, manufacturers, mechanics and artisans, poets, philosophers, and politicians, all have contributed towards the grand result, one generation building upon another's labours, and carrying them forward to still higher stages. This constant succession of noble workers—the artisans of civilization—has served to create order out of chaos in industry, science, and art; and the living race has thus, in the course of nature, become the inheritor of the rich estate provided by the skill and industry of our forefathers, which is placed in our hands to cultivate, and to hand down, not only unimpaired but improved, to our successors.

The spirit of self-help, as exhibited in the energetic action of individuals, has in all times been a marked feature in the English character, and furnishes the true measure of our power as a nation. Rising above the heads of the mass there were always to be found a series of individuals distinguished beyond others, who commanded the public homage. But our progress has also been owing to multitudes of smaller and less known men. Though only the generals' names may be remembered in the history of any great campaign, it has been in a great measure through the individual valour and heroism of the privates that victories have been won. . . . Even the humblest person, who sets before his fellows an example of industry, sobriety, and upright honesty of purpose in life, has a present as well as a future influence upon the well-being of his country; for his life and character pass unconsciously into the lives of others, and propagate good example for all time to come.

Daily experience shows that it is energetic individualism which produces the most powerful effects upon the life and action of others, and really constitutes the best practical education. Schools, academies, and colleges, give but the merest beginnings of culture in comparison with it. Far more influential is the life-education daily given in our homes, in the streets, behind counters, in workshops, at the loom and the plough, in counting-houses and manufactories, and in the busy haunts of men. This is that finishing instruction as members of society, . . . —all that tends to discipline a man truly, and fit him for the proper performance of the duties and business of life,—a kind of education not to be learnt from books, or acquired by any amount of mere literary training. . . .

The instances of men, in this and other countries, who, by dint of persevering application and energy, have raised themselves from the humblest ranks of industry to eminent positions of usefulness and influence in society, are indeed so numerous that they have long ceased to be regarded as exceptional. Looking at some of the

From Samuel Smiles, *Self-Help* (London, 1859), 38–39, 47–48, 115–19, 281–84.

more remarkable, it might almost be said that early encounter with difficulty and adverse circumstances was the necessary and indispensable condition of success. The British House of Commons has always contained a number of such self-raised men— fitting representatives of the industrial character of the people; and it is to the credit of our Legislature that they have been welcomed and honoured there. When Joseph Brotherton, member for Salford, in the course of the discussion on the Ten Hours Bill, detailed with true pathos the hardships and fatigues to which he had been subjected when working as a factory boy in a cotton mill, and described the resolu- tion which he had then formed, that if ever it was in his power he would endeavour to ameliorate the condition of that class, Sir James Graham rose immediately after him, and declared, amidst the cheers of the House, that he did not before know that Mr. Brotherton's origin had been so humble, but that it rendered him more proud than he had ever before been of the House of Commons, to think that a person risen from that condition should be able to sit side by side, on equal terms, with the hereditary gentry of the land. . . .

Fortune has often been blamed for her blindness; but fortune is not so blind as men are. Those who look into practical life will find that fortune is usually on the side of the industrious, as the winds and waves are on the side of the best navigators. In the pursuit of even the highest branches of human inquiry the commoner qualities are found the most useful—such as common sense, attention, application, and perse- verance. Genius may not be necessary, though even genius of the highest sort does not disdain the use of these ordinary qualities. The very greatest men have been among the least believers in the power of genius, and as worldly wise and persevering as successful men of the commoner sort. Some have even defined genius to be only common sense intensified . . . owing their success in a great measure, to their inde- fatigable industry and application. . . .

Hence, a great point to be aimed at is to get the working quality well trained. When that is done, the race will be found comparatively easy. We must repeat and again repeat; facility will come with labour. Not even the simplest art can be accom- plished without it; and what difficulties it is found capable of achieving: It was by early discipline and repetition that the late Sir Robert Peel [British politician, son of a businessman] cultivated those remarkable, though still mediocre powers, which rendered him so illustrious an ornament of the British Senate. When a boy at Drayton Manor, his father was accustomed to set him up at table to practise speak- ing ex tempore; and he early accustomed him to repeat as much of the Sunday's sermon as he could remember. Little progress was made at first, but by steady perseverance the habit of attention became powerful, and the sermon was at length repeated almost verbatim. When afterwards replying in succession to the arguments of his parliamentary opponents—an art in which he was perhaps unrivalled—it was little surmised that the extraordinary power of accurate remembrance which he displayed on such occasions had been originally trained under the discipline of his father in the parish church of Drayton.

It is indeed marvellous what continuous application will effect in the commonest of things. . . .

To wait patiently, however, men must work cheerfully. Cheerfulness is an excellent working quality, imparting great elasticity to the character. As a bishop has said, 'Temper is nine-tenths of Christianity'; so are cheerfulness and diligence nine-tenths of practical wisdom. They are the life and soul of success, as well as of happiness: perhaps the very highest pleasure in life consisting in clear, brisk, conscious working; energy, confidence, and every other good quality mainly depending upon it. . . .

How a man uses money—makes it, saves it, and spends it—is perhaps one of the best tests of practical wisdom. Although money ought by no means to be regarded as a chief end of man's life, neither is it a trifling matter, to be held in philosophic contempt, representing as it does to so large an extent the means of physical comfort and social well-being. Indeed, some of the finest qualities of human nature are intimately related to the right use of money; such as generosity, honesty, justice, and self-sacrifice; as well as the practical virtues of economy and providence. On the other hand, there are their counterparts of avarice, fraud, injustice, and selfishness, as displayed by the inordinate lovers of gain; and the vices of thriftlessness, extravagance, and improvidence, on the part of those who misuse and abuse the means entrusted to them. . . .

Comfort in worldly circumstances is a condition which every man is justified in striving to attain by all worthy means. It secures that physical satisfaction which is necessary for the culture of the better part of his nature; and enables him to provide for those of his own household, without which, says the Apostle, a man is 'worse than an infidel.' Nor ought the duty to be any the less indifferent to us, that the respect which our fellow-men entertain for us in no slight degree depends upon the manner in which we exercise the opportunities which present themselves for our honourable advancement in life. The very effort required to be made to succeed in life with this object is of itself an education; stimulating a man's sense of self-respect, bringing out his practical qualities, and disciplining him in the exercise of patience, perseverance, and such like virtues. The provident and careful man must necessarily be a thoughtful man, for he lives not merely in the present, but with provident forecast makes arrangements for the future. He must also be a temperate man, and exercise the virtue of self-denial, than which nothing is so much calculated to give strength to the character. . . .

Hence the lesson of self-denial—the sacrificing of a present gratification for a future good—is one of the last that is learnt. Those classes which work the hardest might naturally be expected to value the most the money which they earn. Yet the readiness with which so many are accustomed to eat up and drink up their earnings as they go renders them to a great extent helpless and dependent upon the frugal. There are large numbers of persons among us who, though enjoying sufficient means of comfort and independence, are often found to be barely a day's march ahead of actual want when a time of pressure occurs; and hence a great cause of social helplessness and suffering. . . .

There is no reason why the condition of the average workman should not be a useful, honourable, respectable, and happy one. The whole body of the working classes might (with few exceptions) be as frugal, virtuous, well-informed, and well-conditioned as many individuals of the same class have already made themselves. What some men are, all without difficulty might be. Employ the same means, and the same results will follow. That there should be a class of men who live by their daily labour in every state is the ordinance of God, and doubtless is a wise and righteous one; but that this class should be otherwise than frugal, contented, intelligent, and happy is not the design of Providence, but springs solely from the weakness, self-indulgence, and perverseness of man himself. The healthy spirit of self-help created amongst working people would more than any other measure serve to raise them as a class, and this, not by pulling down others, but by levelling them up to a higher and still advancing standard of religion, intelligence, and virtue.

A FRENCH BUSINESSMAN: NARCISSE FAUCHEUR

Narcisse Faucheur set up a textile factory during the early decades of French industrialization. He was not an industrial giant but a fairly average industrialist— the sort that really helped industrial firms to spread after someone else took a lead. Faucheur notes his dependence on British technological innovations, for example, which he simply imported. Faucheur began his operations in the 1820s in northern France, after service in the French military. He was from a rather traditional small merchant family, whose habits he both utilized and transcended as he moved into the modern business context. He wrote an autobiography reviewing his career, printed in the 1880s in a limited edition for his children and grandchildren. His focus was business, venturing little comment on wider cultural and political interests. Narrowness of focus may have been one of the common attributes of Western businessmen, as they dealt with the issues of setting up new operations and worried relatively little about other concerns. His discussion of his activities and his self-elevation provide solid clues about his basic ideas and motivations, though he never spells these matters out directly.

• • •

The French army, which at first had withdrawn behind the Loire, was then disbanded [after Napoleon's death 1815]. Every day officers arrived who didn't know what to do. Some even left France and went to seek their fortunes in foreign lands. The idea of leaving for America again struck my fancy, but my parents were absolutely opposed to it. I yielded to their wishes rather than cause them the least unhappiness. . . . Finally, after a long and very arduous search, our friend announced that he had found a position for me with the most important wholesalers in Clermont. . . .

The friend whom I mentioned in the last chapter had found an opening for me in the firm of M. Cassan-Guyot, who was a wholesale dealer in the products of Roubaix, Lille, Amiens, Rouen, and the cloth trade of the Midi. This firm was, without doubt, the most important in Clermont. Unfortunately, I received a very meager salary, and because I was living with my parents I gave my mother all my earnings to help with the household expenses, which had risen sharply upon my arrival. I had rather quickly observed how poor my unfortunate parents were, so it was with real joy that at the end of each month I placed into my mother's hands the paltry sum I had earned. . . .

I soon saw, therefore, that it would be necessary for me to find another source of income in order to maintain a modest but always neat and proper wardrobe. . . .

When I became a travelling salesman for M. Delcros, I had the opportunity to talk with many other merchants and salesmen in Lille. They spoke of it as a city with a great commercial future and as an area full of opportunities for a young man such as I to establish himself by his own efforts. I was taken with the idea because I was already preoccupied with plans for the future. I wrote to my brother about it, and he encouraged me to transfer to Lille, not only because we would have the pleasure of seeing each other often, but also because it would be a step toward the realization of my goals.

Although I was well liked by my employer, the firm offered me no prospects of a partnership. It didn't have enough capital to expand its operations to the point that I might one day acquire a financial interest in it. I was condemned, therefore, to grow old as a salesman and to devote all my energies to [working for] other people. . . .

My lace business prospered for several years, but gradually a new product began to hurt it. I am speaking of tulle, which replaced lace and was much cheaper. The designs on the tulle, all of which was imported, were nearly all in very bad taste. I

From Narcisse Faucheur, *Mon histoire à mes chers enfants et petit enfants* (Paris, 1886), quoted in Peter N. Stearns, ed., *The Impact of the Industrial Revolution* (Englewood Cliffs, N.J.: Prentice-Hall, 1972), 105–12. Reprinted by permission of the author.

thought that if I embroidered on the tulle some attractive French designs, I could sell it easily and make a large profit.

I went to England to learn about this industry and to see if I could bring it into France. I took from England all the information I needed, but I decided against buying the looms used to make plain tulle, for they were too expensive and their purchase would have used funds which I needed in my other commercial ventures. Therefore, I concentrated on information dealing with embroidering tulle, an operation I hoped to start in France. I returned to Lille with some detailed designs and some patterns by which one could determine the number of stitches each design required. Since tulle embroidery work was paid according to the number of stitches in a design, these patterns made it easy for me to determine labor costs and set the final price.

In Saint-Armand I was in contact with two old spinsters who had two very intelligent nieces. The nieces were very good embroiderers but they didn't know how to work with tulle. I showed these ladies some samples of this embroidery and they assured me that if a woman skilled in the technique would give them some lessons, they could easily learn to do it themselves. They also claimed that they would be able to train many other young girls in Saint-Armand to be embroiderers, since there was no other occupation open to them in the region, no matter what their social class. We agreed that if I put my plan into practice my workshop would be in the home of the aunts, who would then be directors, and that the nieces would be foremen, all of them earning a reasonable salary.

When I was sure of being able to establish an embroidery workshop at Saint-Armand on advantageous terms, I left for Paris, where I had a good designer make a number of attractive patterns. I next arranged for an English woman from Nottingham who was very skilled in embroidery work to teach the two nieces of the ladies Dutordoir. . . .

From the start everything succeeded according to my wishes. In a short time I had a factory of more than three hundred embroiderers in the Dutordoir home. The first pieces I put up for sale gave me a profit all the more considerable since labor costs were very low. . . .

In every way possible I tried to speed up production. I was involved with every detail, for the newness of the designs determined their merit and price. But I was unable to rush production as much as I hoped and the scale of my business remained limited. . . .

. . . [My sales] trips varied from twenty-five to forty days, . . . But an ordinary salesman would have certainly doubled the time, for he would not have wanted to subject himself to all the strain that I endured. For several years I had to make two or three of these whirlwind trips, and God knows all the difficulty that they stirred up for me, no matter how necessary they were!

My yearly profits did not reflect all the work I put in, but over the long run my fortune grew slowly. The market was such that one had to make his decisions with courage. The competition was intense, the profits small, and one could lose all his customers if he set his prices higher than his competitors. . . .

In the preceding chapters I have told you of the hard work to which your mother and I diligently devoted ourselves to make our business prosper. It is now time to describe for you the order and thrift which guided our expenditures. Since our annual profits were not very large, our budget had to be rigorously kept within our income if our savings were to increase little by little. . . .

For several years, I carried on my trade in linen and overalls as described above. But at each inventory I found that my income didn't increase as quickly as my small family, and that my profits didn't reflect all the time and effort I put in.

For quite a while I used linen woven in Belgium from machine spun thread, for there were no weavers in Lille capable of imitating the linen made in Belgium.

This product returned a moderate profit, but presented some very severe difficulties. At the time, the English and Belgians sold their cloth according to the numbers of threads in the warp and woof. In order to buy advantageously I had to deal with many parties, and even then I was forced to buy various types of cloth in amounts which were not geared to my sales. I could have sold many articles manufactured with warp numbers of 20, 22, 25, 28, and 30 threads, but it was precisely those numbers that I had difficulty finding. For a number of years I searched for a solution to this problem and several others which I won't take the space to describe. On one of my numerous trips to Belgium I met a very intelligent young man, employed by the Lys spinning mill at Ghent. He was the son of one of my long-time Belgian linen buyers. His goal in life was to build a small spinning mill, but his father, who was fairly well off, was not at all inclined to help him. He hoped that I would be able to help put his plans into operation. We held several meetings and were joined by an English foreman. They supplied me with some information on manufacturing cost, technique, etc. With the aid of these figures and information obtained from other sources, I could compute the production costs of the types of cloth which I had difficulty buying in Belgium.

After studying the matter thoroughly, I concluded that Belgium was not the right place to build a spinning mill designed to supply a cloth mill in France. Thus I began looking for a way to start a small spinning mill in Lille. At the same time, of course, I continued my trade in linen.

To avoid building anything, I was looking for a factory with a suitable power source. My plans became known and one day my brother-in-law, Lepercq, came to see me and asked me, in a timid voice, if it was true that I intended to start a spinning mill. I replied that in fact I was considering it, but that I had not yet reached a decision. Lepercq then took advantage of his knowledge of thread, with which he had been involved for some time in a small business venture. He emphasized his thorough knowledge of flax, with which he had been working for his whole life. Then he proposed that we join in a partnership to start a spinning mill.

The purchase of flax was precisely my weak point. Knowing nothing about it myself, I recognized the importance of having someone make wise purchases. It was unfortunate that I had decided to work with my brother-in-law. Had I been alone, I would have spared myself much trouble and torment, and I would certainly have earned more money. His financial and industrial contribution was infinitely below what I had expected.

With the architect M. Desrousseaux acting as intermediary, M. Boyer offered to build for us, on some land he owned in Wazemmes, a spinning mill equipped with a steam engine and all the necessary power transmission belts. Our rent would be based on Boyer's construction costs. This proposition, which contained some strongly leonine terms, appealed to us as a way to avoid sinking a great deal of capital into construction, while allowing us to start a large number of spindles.

If I had had an associate sharing my views and my ardor for work, and one who was able to contribute capital equal to mine, the conditions imposed by Boyer, although largely favorable to him, would have allowed us to make huge profits. Though limited by the factors mentioned above, the profits exceeded those from my trade in linen and overalls to such a degree that I quickly saw that the spinning factory offered me a much better future than my old business.

PRAISING INDIVIDUALISM: FUKUZAWA YUKICHI

The following two passages were written by a tireless Meiji westernizer. Fukuzawa (1834–1901) visited the United States and Western Europe early, in 1860. Proud of Japan and sometimes capable of defending Confucianism when he was too hard-pressed by more conservative figures (see chapter 23), Fukuzawa on the whole stood for change in a Western direction. Much of his work was devoted to educational reform, where he urged a more individualistic approach, but he also wrote on business topics directly. His views helped stimulate debate among businessmen, most of whom sought to reintroduce a more Confucian element—as the next selection suggests.

• • •

ON EDUCATION

In my interpretation of education, I try to be guided by the laws of nature and I try to co-ordinate all the physical actions of human beings by the very simple laws of

From Eichi Kiyooka, trans., *The Autobiography of Yukichi Fukuzawa* (New York: Columbia University Press, 1980), 44–47. Reprinted by permission of the publisher.

"number and reason." In spiritual or moral training, I regard the human being as the most sacred and responsible of all orders, unable in reason to do anything base. Therefore, in self-respect, a man cannot change his sense of humanity, his justice, his loyalty or anything belonging to his manhood even when driven by circumstances to do so. In short, my creed is that a man should find his faith in independence and self-respect.

From my own observations in both Occidental and Oriental civilizations, I find that each has certain strong points and weak points bound up in its moral teachings and scientific theories. But when I compare the two in a general way as to wealth, armament, and the greatest happiness for the greatest number, I have to put the Orient below the Occident. Granted that a nation's destiny depends upon the education of its people, there must be some fundamental differences in the education of Western and Eastern peoples.

In the education of the East, so often saturated with Confucian teaching, I find two things lacking; that is to say, a lack of studies in number and reason in material culture, and a lack of the idea of independence in spiritual culture. But in the West I think I see why their statesmen are successful in managing their national affairs, and the businessmen in theirs, and the people generally ardent in their patriotism and happy in their family circles.

I regret that in our country I have to acknowledge that people are not formed on these two principles, though I believe no one can escape the laws of number and reason, nor can anyone depend on anything but the doctrine of independence as long as nations are to exist and mankind is to thrive. Japan could not assert herself among the great nations of the world without full recognition and practice of these two principles. And I reasoned that Chinese philosophy as the root of education was responsible for our obvious shortcomings.

With this as the fundamental theory of education, I began and, though it was impossible to institute specialized courses because of lack of funds, I did what I could in organizing the instructions on the principles of number and reason. And I took every opportunity in public speech, in writing, and in casual conversations, to advocate my doctrine of independence. Also I tried in many ways to demonstrate the theory in my actual life. During my endeavor I came to believe less than ever in the old Chinese teachings.

ON BUSINESS

In the primitive, uncivilized world men could not benefit themselves without injuring others; therefore those who were active in mind and body and accomplished

Yukichi Fukuzawa, "On Business," trans. Fukuo Hyakawa, in Byron K. Marshall, *Capitalism and Nationalism in Prewar Japan* (Stanford: Stanford University Press, 1967), 33. Reprinted by permission of the publisher. © 1987 by the Board of Trustees of the Leland Stanford Junior University.

things were always thieves. This is not so in the civilized world; those who gain riches and fame always benefit others by doing so . . .

Everyone in the country individually aims at increasing his own private wealth. . . . Desiring more and still more, they utilize all their secret skills in the competition for new things, and in this way new methods are evolved, land is reclaimed and developed, machines are invented, transportation and communications are improved, and the investment of capital is effected . . . Private zeal is the source of national wealth.

A Japanese Businessman's Views: Shibuzawa Eiichi

The following selections were written by a leading businessman of the Japanese reform (Meiji) era, as industrialization was getting under way. Shibuzawa Eiichi (1840–1931) ultimately presided over a hundred companies, after a period of service in government. He was from a prosperous peasant family. As an industrialist he concentrated particularly on factory textile production. He also participated actively in the growing debate over Western values as they applied to economic life.

• • •

FROM THE *AUTOBIOGRAPHY*

The business world around 1873, the year when I resigned my post at the Ministry of Finance, was one filled with inertia. That condition is hard to imagine from the standards we hold for the business world today [1927, when Shibuzawa dictated this autobiography]. There was a tradition of respecting officials and despising common people. All talented men looked to government services as the ultimate goal in their lives, and ordinary students followed the examples set by them. There was practically no one who was interested in business. When people met, they discussed only matters relating to the affairs of state and of the world. There was no such thing as practical business education.

It was said that the Meiji Restoration was to bring about equality among the four classes of people. In practice, however, those who engaged in commerce and industry were regarded as plain townspeople as before, and were despised and had to remain subservient to government officials. I knew conditions such as this should not be allowed to persist. A rigid class structure should not be tolerated. We should be able to treat each other with respect and make no differentiation between government officials and townspeople. This was essential to our national welfare, as we looked forward to strengthening the country which required wealth to back it up.

From *Shibuzawa Eiichi Jijoden* [Autobiography of Shiuzawa Eiichi], in *Japan: A Documentary History*, ed. David J. Lu (Armonk, NY: 1997) M. E. Sharpe, 354–56. Reprinted by permission of the publisher.

We needed commerce and industry to attain the goal of becoming a rich nation. Unworthy as I was, I thought of engaging in commerce and industry to help promote the prosperity of our nation. I might not have talent to become a good politician, but I was confident that I could make a difference in the fields of commerce and industry. . . .

As to the question of development of commerce and industry, I felt that to engage in an individually managed shop would be going against the tide of the times, and it was necessary for small business firms to join their forces together. In other words, they have to incorporate, and I decided to devote my energy to this endeavor. As to the laws governing incorporation, I thought about them while studying in France. After my return from France and before my entering into government service, I organized a chamber of commerce in Shizuoka to serve as a model for incorporation in this country. Since that time, I have consistently advocated the advantages of incorporation.

In organizing a company, the most important factor one ought to consider is to obtain the services of the right person to oversee its operation. In the early years of Meiji, the government also encouraged incorporation of companies and organized commercial firms and development companies. The government actively participated in these companies' affairs and saw to it that their various needs were met fully. However, most of these companies failed because their management was poor. To state it simply, the government failed to have the right men as their managers. I had no experience in commerce and industry, but I also prided myself on the fact that I had greater potential for success in these fields than most of the nongovernmental people at that time.

I also felt that it was necessary to raise the social standing of those who engaged in commerce and industry. By way of setting an example, I began studying and practicing the teachings of the *Analects of Confucius*. It contains teachings first enunciated more than twenty-four hundred years ago. Yet it supplies the ultimate in practical ethics for all of us to follow in our daily living. It has many golden rules for businessmen. For example, there is a saying: "Wealth and respect are what men desire, but unless a right way is followed, they cannot be obtained; poverty and lowly position are what men despise, but unless a right way is found, one cannot leave that status once reaching it." It shows very clearly how a businessman must act in this world. Thus, when I entered the business world, I engaged in commerce and industry in a way consistent with the teachings of the *Analects* and practiced the doctrine of unity of knowledge and action.

FROM "MY VIEW OF LIFE"

There are in the final analysis only two types: i.e., those who consider the existence of self objectively and those who consider it subjectively. The objective view regards society first and the self second. The ego is disregarded to the point where one sacrifices the self for the sake of society without hesitation. The subjective view, on the other hand, is selfishly aware of the existence of the ego in all situations and recognizes the existence of society only secondarily. To this extent it is willing even to sacrifice society for the sake of the self. . . .

We would end in a situation in which the appetites could only be satisfied by men looting from one another. If the human heart comes to that, then the ultimate result would be such indecent behavior as forgetting our benefactors, turning our backs on our friends, and abandoning our loved ones. . . .

FROM "INDEPENDENCE AND SELF-RELIANCE"

One must beware of the tendency of some to argue that it is through individualism or egoism [*jiko hon'i*] that the State and society can progress most rapidly. They claim that under individualism, each individual competes with the others, and progress results from this competition. But this is to see merely the advantages and ignore the disadvantages, and I cannot support such a theory. Society exists, and a State has been founded. Although people desire to rise to positions of wealth and honor, the social order and the tranquillity of the State will be disrupted if this is done egoistically. Men should not do battle in competition with their fellow men. Therefore, I believe that in order to get along together in society and serve the State, we must by all means abandon this idea of independence and self-reliance and reject egoism completely.

From Byron K. Marshall, *Capitalism and Nationalism in Prewar Japan* (Stanford: Stanford University Press, 1967) 34–35. Reprinted with the permission of the publisher. © 1987 by the Board of Trustees of the Leland Stanford Junior University.

PART V

The Twentieth Century

THE TWENTIETH CENTURY HAS been so rich in events that its status as the opening of a new world history period must seem assured. Two world wars followed by a long Cold War (followed by its end, in turn, in 1989); major revolutions in Russia, China, Mexico, and Iran and many smaller upheavals elsewhere; the advent of the nuclear age; unprecedented population growth, which, along with intensifying global industrialization, helped significantly to alter the environment; the advent of airplanes, television, computers—the list seems almost endless. Of course, many centuries seem more full of change at the time than they turn out to be in retrospect; but recent decades unquestionably claim a place at the top of any list. The problem is to sort out the main lines of development.

Three major themes defined the twentieth century, from World War I onward, as a new period in world history; each of the themes carries important challenges for comparative analysis.

First, a number of societies—most, in fact—had to reconsider established political, cultural, and social systems and replace them with new alternatives. Some societies indeed introduced a series of innovations. By the 1990s, few civilizations outside the West had the same political system that they had had in 1900. The end of colonialism and many revolutions required innovation. Population growth, particularly outside the industrialized centers, formed another new theme, requiring response and some novel policies. Older belief systems, ranging from adherence to one of the major religions to the deeply rooted polytheism of areas such as sub-Saharan Africa, faced new rivals in movements such as nationalism and Communism and in popular cultural exports from the West. Changes in the nature of war, with more awesome military technology capped by nuclear weaponry in 1945, constituted another shift with worldwide implications, to which each society had to respond.

Comparison category number one, then, involves juxtaposing the nature of change and innovation in two or more societies. Was the widespread movement toward authoritarian nationalism—called fascism in its most extreme form—the same in its major European centers of power and elsewhere? How much did the leading Communist regimes have in common? How did different societies handle new activities by religious missionaries plus strong influences from Western consumer culture? How did societies with different traditions about families and conditions for women respond to the huge surge in the population growth rate? The list of comparative responses to common processes, in a century of great innovation, is a long one.

Second, international contacts accelerated. This was not a brand new development, for the pattern had been installed at least a thousand years before. But new levels of communication and trade unquestionably produced a substantive change in the rates and impacts of exchange. By the end of the century over a quarter of the world's population was watching the same key sporting events on television, World Cup soccer heading the list. Meetings of scientists drew experts from every corner of the globe who shared common methods and assumptions, whatever their specific cultural backgrounds—another first in world history.

The broad question for comparison category number two is, How did different societies respond to the new levels of contact? How did the spread of certain ideas—including ideas promoted by popular film or television exports—and the operation of international organizations affect the expectations and conditions of women? Were there new and to some degree global trends in this area? What kind of international interaction was responsible for the striking spread of political democracy at the century's end? How, on the other hand, might some societies try to insulate themselves from too much challenging contact?

Third, the relative power of the West declined. This change reversed five centuries of Western ascendancy, but it showed clearly in the declining military superiority, political control, and world economic dominance of the West, even with the United States included. Yet—partly because of the growing role of the United States in world affairs—Western influence remained high, and its cultural impact on other parts of the world may have exceeded developments in previous centuries. Western countries could no longer retain their colonies, but they could distribute new styles of clothing, like blue jeans; new youth music; new kinds of restaurants, like McDonald's; new films and TV shows (*Baywatch* became the world's most widely viewed television series); scientific discoveries; and even "international" artistic styles.

For comparative category number three, we examine the complex balance between new opportunities for global diversity, as the West's power declined, and new signs of looking to the West for models. Nationalism spread widely around the world and allowed many countries to praise distinctive features of their traditions; but nationalism was Western in origin, and the desire for national strength and respectability could lead to further borrowings from the West. Along with all the new events of this busy century, the new-old patterns of interaction with the West constitute perhaps the most obvious sign of a time of transition to which different societies responded differently, with responses sometimes changing as the century wore on.

These three categories of developments can be examined in somewhat greater detail. The first basic feature of the twentieth century, certainly the most obvious, is widespread political, social, and cultural experimentation: societies rejected certain traditional staples and groped to find satisfactory modern alternatives. The spate of revolutions and decolonizations formed part of this pattern. Monarchy and empire, as political forms, were far less important at the end of the twentieth century than they had been at the beginning. The aristocracy was widely displaced as the dominant social class, from England through China. Thanks to improved education and some legal gains, concerns about women's customary inferiority were raised in many societies. No worldwide substitutes were developed. Democracy spread as a new political form in many areas, but so did Communist political systems and authoritarianism during much of the century. The decline of the aristocracy meant the rise of a middle class in some societies, but it resulted in the development of a bureaucratic elite in others, such as the Communist countries. The twentieth century experienced some general international issues about political and social structure, without generating fully uniform responses.

In culture, the worldwide rise of scientific training, the great attraction of consumer values, plus the growth of nationalism and Marxist ideologies posed new competitions for traditional religions. The century unquestionably witnessed significant cultural changes, including many "conversions" to new beliefs. But religious forces remained strong as well, including missionary Christianity and Islam in Africa, fundamentalist Christianity as a new force in Latin America, and the revival of strong religious movements in the Middle East (Islam) and India (Hinduism) in the late twentieth century. Here too, new issues were raised, with some important new patterns but no clearly dominant international reaction.

Intensification of international contacts formed the second key feature of the new world history period. New technologies played a major role, increasing the speed and quantity of international communication; so did rising levels of trade. Several societies attempted to isolate themselves at certain points, for example, the Soviet Union under Stalin and China during the Cultural Revolution period of the 1960s; but isolation in the long run was too costly in terms of lagging technology and economic performance. New contacts meant important cultural pressures, including Marxist revolutionary ideology but also Western consumer culture (through international corporations and films), and the spread of modern science and "international" artistic styles. New contacts meant also a certain susceptibility to "world opinion," a vague force defined particularly by Western governments and media. "World opinion" helped press South Africa to end the legal discrimination against blacks, though only after many decades. It helped prompt at least lip service in most societies to women's rights, including voting rights. International contacts, in other words, had organizational and cultural features as well as technological and commercial foundations.

The third and final defining feature of the century, as a new world history period, involved the slowing or reversal of some of the trends that shaped the previous era—a standard, inescapable criterion for periodization. The twentieth century saw a relative reduction in the power of Western Europe, even if the United States is added to that civilization to define a larger West. The West's decisive military edge, though still visible, was muted by the rise of major military powers in Japan (until 1945) and Russia, by effective countertactics such as guerrilla warfare that could partially neutralize advanced technology, and by the emergence of strong regional military powers in China, India, and elsewhere that made Western interference far more difficult. The West maintained a vibrant industrial economy, aside from the huge uncertainties associated with the 1930s depression, but it no longer claimed monopoly; Japan and other Pacific Rim states became its industrial equals. Western colonial controls began to recede in the 1930s, and massive decolonization after World War II, creating a host of new or newly independent nations, constituted one of the decisive features of the contemporary world history framework.

The "rise of the West," a theme of world history since 1450, now receded, though there were important residues still, particularly in cultural influence. A power rebalancing included the rise of East Asia and the important regional power of many decolonized centers such as Indonesia and India. It also included the growing ability of several societies to reduce their dependence on Western imports; Brazil, Mexico, India, Turkey, and China are examples of societies that had not yet industrialized fully but had developed a significant industrial segment. It was not clear that any single civilization center was poised to replace the West as the dominant world civilization. Perhaps, for a time at least, there might be none. It is important to remember that the twentieth century as the opening of a new period was just that, an opening; all sorts of clarifications might follow in subsequent decades, as has been the case in world history transitions previously. In the meantime, societies outside the West, aware of lingering Western power and the siren call of claims to cultural leadership, had to make their own adjustments to continuing, sometimes novel forms of Western influence.

For, as in earlier periods of world history, novel forces elicited somewhat different responses depending on the civilization. Some societies were more open to international contacts than others. Some responded to the need for political change with democracy—India is a case in point—while others, such as China, innovated while explicitly rejecting pluralist democracy. As in previous eras, world history continued to involve comparing reactions to some common trends and impulses. The relative decline of the West, intensifying international contacts, and the need to reconsider traditional political, social, and cultural patterns affected virtually all regions; but the results varied, because of particular twentieth-century settings and diverse prior traditions. Careful comparison remains essential, even among the societies that seemed most eagerly to embrace "international" trends.

The chapters that follow tackle issues of political change by discussing both new forms of authoritarian government and the rise of democracy in additional areas of the world. They deal with world power balance in discussing nationalism and the atomic bomb. They deal with cultural innovations through nationalism, changes in religious balance, and the pressure of consumer values. Shifts in women's expectations and related changes in population behaviors and policies form a vital third category. In all these areas, the mixture of innovation with defense of older identities, the pressure of new international contacts, and changes in world power balance along with the continuing prestige of the West shaped the framework in which particular societies developed particular patterns that can be highlighted through comparison.

CHAPTER 25

NATIONALISMS

Nationalism is a central modern political and cultural loyalty. It argues that nations should form around coherent traditional cultures (though these may in fact be arbitrarily defined) and should be free from outside control. Most nationalists claim that a nation should have its own strong state. Nationalism originated in Europe, with new loyalties provoked by developments such as the French Revolution and the Napoleonic Wars (see chapter 19). It caught on in the Americas as part of the wars against colonial control. And it began to spread to other parts of the world in the late nineteenth century, where it could serve as a rallying cry against European imperialism and an appeal simultaneously to pride and to a need for reform in the interest of strength.

The spread of nationalism had complex implications concerning one of the major themes of twentieth-century world history: the increasing interaction of civilizations. Separate nationalisms obviously conveyed profound feelings of differentiation among the world's people, and nationalist leaders often enhanced these feelings by preaching the distinctiveness of a given nation's culture and, sometimes, promoting a hatred for other nations. Nationalism certainly helped limit the West's influence in the wider world, by urging that Western values and political controls could be disputed, that other systems were valid, even superior. Yet nationalists were in their own way copying the West, for the nationalist belief system was Western in origin. And most nationalists actually recognized that their societies should imitate other elements of the West, in the interest of competitive strength. So nationalism was often anti-Western even while it displayed the ongoing power of the Western model. Similarly, the very fact that nationalism spread so widely was in itself an odd kind of international link. Except for the most fanatical nationalists, everyone could recognize a common commitment in nationalism—even if the specific commitment went to separate states. Various world forums, such as the Olympic Games, developed to let people express nationalist excitements in a context of international context and bounded rivalry.

The same slippery characteristics of nationalism make it a challenging comparative target. By definition, all nationalisms have some elements in common: a desire to praise the nation, usually to vaunt an independent national state. All nationalisms also seek national strength, and often they urge certain changes in the interest of achieving strength and unity; nationalism, even conservative nationalism, is rarely simply traditionalist (see chapter 23). Yet each nation has somewhat distinctive features that a nationalist will want to praise. A Japanese nationalist will often praise Japan's industrial achievement, along with some of the more traditional values. Key Indian nationalists (though not all of them) were more interested in urging customary Indian economic practices, rather than the materialism and exploitation of industrial society. Nationalism picks up some of the earlier features of any society and blends them into the nationalist statement. This means that every nationalism is somewhat distinctive. Nationalisms also arise in different contexts. Some nationalisms develop in regions that have no prior tradition of government associated with internal cultural units. This was true both in Africa and the Middle East, where national boundaries had virtually no relationship to cultural borders. Other nationalisms develop in regions that do have some claims to a shared cultural tradition, as in India, China, and Japan. Such nationalisms will inevitably differ, if only in their ease in identifying at least certain cherished traditions, from the nationalisms that have had to define a nation itself anew.

As they intensified and spread to larger groups in the twentieth century, nationalisms continued to vary greatly, even within the same country. Some were belligerent, even militaristic; others urged peace. Some were generous in their views of other nations; others asserted their superiority. Some largely shunned outside influences, including the West, and others combined a desire to imitate certain Western features with an appeal to local identity. In addition to sharing the movement's basic features, most nationalists had three other points in common: they insisted that certain traditions that impeded national power and unity should be changed, even as they praised the national past; they tended to invent certain aspects of history in order to make their nation look particularly good; and they had problems in figuring out how to define national unity while dealing with internal divisions and minorities.

The intensification of nationalism in the twentieth century followed from and encouraged growing impatience with Western dominance and colonial controls. World War I taught many people the power of nationalism in Europe. Soldiers from India and Africa, used by Britain and France during the war, experienced these lessons and took them home. Then the principles discussed in the Versailles peace conference emphasized the validity of each nation's determining its own government—but the principles were really applied only in Europe, leaving nationalism better defined but angrier elsewhere.

This chapter invites comparison of two nationalisms that clearly surged in the first half of the twentieth century. Indian nationalism had begun, rather sedately, in the late nineteenth century among upper-class bureaucrats who were exposed to British education but aware that British rule confined them to lowly positions.

At first they merely asked for better treatment, but gradually their demands escalated. By the early twentieth century, Indian nationalism prompted consistent protest against British control. Mohandas Gandhi became the principal leader of the nationalist movement, blending Hindu traditions with nationalist goals in a distinctive, nonviolent effort. But there were other voices as well, some less traditionalist, some more militant. Indian nationalism put increasing pressure on British rule, and after World War II independence was achieved, though the subcontinent split between areas of Muslim dominance (Pakistan) and areas in which Hinduism prevailed (India).

African nationalism arose later than Indian, in part because imperialism swallowed Africa only in the final decades of the nineteenth century. Nationalist voices began to be heard around 1900 among Africans exposed to European education. Increasingly, these voices replaced the more traditional bases for resistance to European rule. The movements expanded between the wars, both in a pan-African version, urging the importance of Africanness throughout the continent or at least south of the Sahara, and in more specific movements tailored to the artificial political units the Europeans had established as colonies.

The following two passages come from major Indian and East African nationalist leaders during the first half of the twentieth century. Vinayak Savarkar was a militant Indian poet, arrested by the British for violence early in the twentieth century. It was a disciple of Savarkar who assassinated Gandhi in 1948, protesting Gandhi's pleas for tolerant treatment of Muslims. Jomo Kenyatta was an East African nationalist educated extensively in London, who wrote his powerful study of a Kenyan tribe in 1938. After World War II Kenyatta assumed leadership of the nationalist movement in Kenya, against British opposition, and later became the nation's first president after independence.

Savarkar's passage raises key questions about nationalism, including the way national history is represented and the changes in established tradition that many nationalists sought. Savarkar's approach was subtle, nonetheless; traditions were praised, not frontally attacked. Kenyatta focuses centrally on the nationalist objections to imperialism. Writing in English (almost all African leaders wrote in English or French, because of their education and the lack of a widespread, written African language prior to European arrival), he also suggests connections with African cultural traditions. Both Kenyatta and Savarkar wrote in the attack phase of nationalism, before independence was achieved. They need to be assessed in terms of the methods of anti-imperialist agitation they suggest, but also for what they imply about the nature of a postindependence state. For nationalism not only varied from place to place, depending on contexts and prior traditions. It also changed as larger world forces shifted and depending on the demands of the local context. A nationalist in power inevitably would address different issues from those of a nationalist fighting for independence, even if the core values remained the same.

Questions

1. Judging by the passages from Savarkar and Kenyatta, what is the central definition of nationalism? What do the two theorists have in common?
2. How accurately does Savarkar represent Indian history? How does his use of history compare with that of Kenyatta?
3. What changes does Savarkar want in Indian traditions, in the interest of nationalist unity? How does he manage to suggest them without attacking the Hindu past? What would Savarkar's nationalism offer to an Indian Muslim?
4. What (again implicitly) is Savarkar's attitude toward violence as a means of achieving nationalist goals? How do Savarkar and Kenyatta compare in the methods they imply?
5. What is Kenyatta's overall attitude toward the West, and how does he demonstrate the superiority of key African values? Kenyatta is clearly anti-imperialist; is he also anti-Western?
6. How do the two writers see the values of their nations in relation to the rest of the world?
7. Do both authors have the same views about Western culture and the possibilities of imitation? Do both use religion and prior cultural tradition in the same ways?

For Further Discussion

1. How did the main religious issues confronting African and Indian nationalist leaders differ? Which nationalist movement was more likely to be secular, and why?
2. What were the main causes of differences between Indian and African nationalism?
3. Why was it impossible for a nationalist leader to be purely traditionalist? Which context allowed the fuller defense of prior cultural and political traditions, the Indian or the African?
4. Judging by the statements of Indian and African nationalism, which region would be more successful in limiting the impact of Western popular culture in the late twentieth century, after independence was achieved? What other factors would affect Western cultural imports such as films and sports?

INDIAN NATIONALISM: VINAYAK SAVARKAR

Born in 1883, Savarkar began a career as a militant Hindu nationalist early on, with vigorous efforts against the British and the Muslims. He founded a terrorist organization while studying in London and was exiled until 1924. At that point he took over leadership of an extremist Hindu group. He was implicated in the 1948 assassination of Gandhi but for lack of evidence was never brought to trial. There is no question that his approach to Indian nationalism differed notably from that of Gandhi as well as more secular leaders like India's first president, Jawaharlal Nehru.

• • •

So far we have not allowed any considerations of utility to prejudice our inquiry. But having come to its end it will not be out of place to see how far the attributes, which we found to be the essentials of *Hindutva,* contribute towards [the] strength, cohesion, and progress of our people. Do these essentials constitute a foundation so broad, so deep, so strong, that basing upon it the Hindu people can build a future which can face and repel the attacks of all the adverse winds that blow; or does the Hindu race stand on feet of clay? . . .

. . . But behold the ramparts of Nature! Have they not, these Himalayas, been standing there as one whose desires are satisfied—so they seemed to the Vedic bard— so they seem to us today. These are *our* ramparts that have converted this vast continent into a cosy castle.

You take up buckets and fill your trenches with water and call it [a] moat. Behold, Varuna [the god] himself, with his one hand pushing continents aside, fills the gap by pouring seas on seas with the other! This Indian ocean, with its bays and gulfs, is *our* moat.

These are our frontier lines bringing within our reach the advantages of an inland as well as an insular country.

She is the richly endowed daughter of God—this our Motherland. Her rivers are deep and perennial. Her land is yielding to the plow and her fields are loaded with golden harvests. Her necessaries of life are few and a genial nature yields them all almost for the asking. Rich in her fauna, rich in her flora, she knows she owes it all to the immediate source of light and heat—the sun. She covets not the icy lands; blessed be they and their frozen latitudes. If heat is at times "enervating" here, cold is at times benumbing there. If cold induces manual labor, heat removes much of its very necessity. She takes more delight in quenched thirst than in the parched throat. Those who have not, let them delight in exerting to have. But those who have—may be allowed to derive pleasure from the very fact of having. Father Thames is free to work at feverish speed, wrapped in his icy sheets. She loves to visit her ghats and watch her boats gliding down the Ganges, on her moonlit waters. With the plow, the peacocks, the lotus, the elephant, and the *Gītā*, she is willing to forego, if that must be, whatever advantage the colder latitudes enjoy. She knows

From William Theodore de Bary, ed., *Sources of Indian Tradition* (New York: Columbia University Press, 1964), 329–35. Reprinted by permission of the publisher.

she cannot have all her own way. Her gardens are green and shady, her granaries well stocked, her waters crystal, her flowers scented, her fruits juicy, and her herbs healing. . . .

Verily Hind [India] is the richly endowed daughter of God.

Neither the English nor the French—with the exception of [the] Chinese and perhaps the Americans, no people are gifted with a land that can equal in natural strength and richness [our] land. A country, a common home, is the first important essential of stable strong nationality; and as of all countries in the world our country can hardly be surpassed by any in its capacity to afford a soil so specially fitted for the growth of a great nation; we Hindus, whose very first article of faith is the love we bear to the common Fatherland, have in that love the strongest talismanic tie that can bind close and keep a nation firm and enthuse and enable it to accomplish things greater than ever.

The second essential of *Hindutva* puts the estimate of our latent powers of national cohesion and greatness yet higher. No country in the world, with the exception of China again, is peopled by a race so homogeneous, yet so ancient and yet so strong both numerically and vitally. The Americans too, whom we found equally fortunate with us so far as the gift of an excellent geographical basis of nationality is concerned, are decidedly left behind. Mohamedans are no race nor are the Christians. They are a religious unit, yet neither a racial nor a national one. But we Hindus, if possible, are all the three put together and live under our ancient and common roof. The numerical strength of our race is an asset that cannot be too highly prized.

And culture? The English and the Americans feel they are kith and kin because they possess a Shakespeare in common. But not only a Kalidas or a Bhas, but Oh Hindus! ye possess a Ramayan and a Mahabharat in common—and the Vedas! One of the national songs the American children are taught to sing attempts to rouse their sense of eternal self-importance by pointing out to the hundred years twice told that stand behind their history. The Hindu counts his years not by centuries but by cycles—the *Yug* and the *Kalpa* [the age and the eon]—and amazed asks: "O Lord of the line of Raghu [Rama], where has the kingdom of Ayodhya gone? O Lord of the line of Yadu [Krishna], where has Mathura gone!" He does not attempt to rouse the sense of self-importance so much as the sense of proportion, which is Truth. And that has perhaps made him last longer than Ramses and Nebuchadnezzar. If a people that had no past have no future, then a people that had produced an unending galaxy of heroes and heroworshipers and who are conscious of having faught [fought] with and vanquished the forces whose might struck Greece and Rome, the Pharaohs and the Incas, dead, have in their history a guarantee of their future greatness more assuring than any other people on earth yet possess.

But besides culture the tie of common holyland has at times proved stronger than the chains of a Motherland. Look at the Mohamedans. Mecca to them is a sterner reality than Delhi or Agra. Some of them do not make any secret of being bound to sacrifice all India if that be to the glory of Islam or [if it] could save the city of their prophet. Look at the Jews. Neither centuries of prosperity nor sense of gratitude for the shelter they found can make them more attached or even equally attached to the several countries they inhabit. Their love is, and must necessarily be, divided between the land of their birth and the land of their prophets. If the Zionists' dreams are ever realized—if Palestine becomes a Jewish state and it will gladden us almost as much as our Jewish friends—they, like the Mohamedans, would naturally set the interests of their holyland above those of their Motherlands in America and Europe, and, in case of war between their adopted country and the Jewish state, would naturally sympathize with the latter, if indeed they do not bodily go over to it. History is too full of examples of such desertions to cite particulars. The Crusades again, attest to the wonderful influence that a common holyland exercises over peoples widely separated in race, nationality, and language, to bind and hold them together.

The ideal conditions, therefore, under which a nation can attain perfect solidarity and cohesion would, other things being equal, be found in the case of those people who inhabit the land they adore, the land of whose forefathers is also the land of their Gods and Angels, of Seers and Prophets; the scenes of whose history are also the scenes of their mythology.

The Hindus are about the only people who are blessed with these ideal conditions that are at the same time incentive to national solidarity, cohesion, and greatness. Not even the Chinese are blessed thus. Only Arabia and Palestine—if ever the Jews can succeed in founding their state there—can be said to possess this unique advantage. But Arabia is incomparably poorer in the natural, cultural, historical, and numerical essentials of a great people; and even if the dreams of the Zionists are ever realized into a Palestine state still they too must be equally lacking in these.

England, France, Germany, Italy, Turkey proper, Persia, Japan, Afganistan, [the] Egypt of today (for the old descendants of "Punto" and their Egypt is dead long since)—and other African states, Mexico, Peru, Chilly [Chile] (not to mention states and nations lesser than all these)—though racially more or less homogeneous, are yet less advantageously situated than we are in geographical, cultural, historical, and numerical essentials, besides lacking the unique gift of a sanctified Motherland. Of the remaining nations Russia in Europe, and the United States in America, though geographically equally well-gifted with us, are yet poorer, in almost every other requisite of nationality. China alone of the present comity of nations is almost as richly gifted with the geographical, racial, cultural, and numerical essentials as the Hindus are. Only in the possession of a common, a sacred, and a perfect language, the Sanskrit, and a sanctified Motherland, we are so far [as] the essentials that contribute to national solidarity are concerned more fortunate.

Thus the actual essentials of *Hindutva* are, as this running sketch reveals, also the ideal essentials of nationality. If we would we can build on this foundation of *Hindutva,* a future greater than what any other people on earth can dream of— greater even than our own past; provided we are able to utilize our opportunities! For let our people remember that great combinations are the order of the day. The leagues of nations, the alliances of powers, Pan-Islamism, Pan-Slavism, Pan-Ethiopism—all little beings are seeking to get themselves incorporated into greater wholes, so as to be better fitted for the struggle for existence and power. Those who are not naturally and historically blessed with numerical or geographical or racial advantages are seeking to share them with others. Woe to those who have them already as their birthright and know them not; or worse, despise them! The nations of the world are desperately trying to find a place in this or that combination for aggression:—can any one of you, Oh Hindus! [whatever your sect] . . . afford to cut yourselves off or fall out and destroy the ancient, the natural, and the organic combination that already exists?—a combination that is bound not by any scraps of paper nor by the ties of exigencies alone, but by the ties of blood and birth and culture? Strengthen them if you can; pull down the barriers that have survived their utility, of castes and customs, of sects and sections. What of interdining? But inter-marriages between provinces and provinces, castes and castes, be encouraged where they do not exist. . . .

Let the minorities remember they would be cutting the very branch on which they stand. Strengthen every tie that binds you to the main organism, whether of blood or language or common festivals and feasts or culture love you bear to the common Motherland. Let this ancient and noble stream of Hindu blood flow from vein to vein . . . till at last the Hindu people get fused and welded into an indivisible whole, till our race gets consolidated and strong and sharp as steel.

Just cast a glance at the past, then at the present: Pan-Islamism in Asia, the political leagues in Europe, the Pan-Ethiopic movement in Africa and America—and then see, Oh Hindus, if your future is not entirely bound up with the future of India and the future of India is bound up, in the last resort, with Hindu strength. We are trying our best, as we ought to do, to develop the consciousness of and a sense of attachment to the greater whole, whereby Hindus, Mohamedans, Parsis, Christians, and Jews, would feel as Indians first and every other thing afterwards. But whatever progress India may have made to that goal one thing remains almost axiomatically true—not only in India but everywhere in the world—that a nation requires a foundation to stand upon and the essence of the life of a nation is the life of that portion of its citizens whose interests and history and aspirations are most closely bound up with the land and who thus provide the real foundation to the structure of their national state. . . .

. . . [This] constitute[s] the foundation, the bedrock, the reserved forces of the Indian state. Therefore even from the point of Indian nationality, must ye, Oh Hindus, consolidate and strengthen Hindu nationality: not to give wanton offense to any of our non-Hindu compatriots, in fact to any one in the world but in just and urgent self-defense of our race and land; to render it impossible for others to betray her or to subject her to unprovoked attacks by any of those "Pan-isms" that are struggling forth from continent to continent. As long as other communities in India or in the world are not respectively planning India first or Mankind first, but all are busy in organizing offensive and defensive alliances and combinations on entirely narrow racial or religious or national basis, so long, at least so long, Oh Hindus, strengthen if you can those subtle bonds that like nerve-threads bind you in One Organic Social Being. Those of you who in a suicidal fit try to cut off the most vital of those ties and dare to disown the name Hindu will find to their cost that in doing so they have cut themselves off from the very source of our racial life and strength. The presence of only a few of these essentials of nationality which we have found to constitute *Hindutva* enabled little nations like Spain or Portugal to get themselves lionized in the world. But when all of those ideal conditions obtain here what is there in the human world that the Hindus cannot accomplish? . . .

. . . [300 million] people, with India for their basis of operation, for their Fatherland and for their Holyland, with such a history behind them, bound together by ties of a common blood and common culture can dictate their terms to the whole world. A day will come when mankind will have to face the force.

Equally certain it is that whenever the Hindus come to hold such a position whence they could dictate terms to the whole world—those terms cannot be very different from the terms which [the] *Gītā* dictates or the Buddha lays down. . . . "My country? Oh brothers, the limits of the Universe—there the frontiers of my country lie."

AFRICAN NATIONALISM: JOMO KENYATTA

Born in 1893, Kenyatta early campaigned for land rights for his Kikuyu tribe in Kenya. He spent sixteen years in England, studying at the University of London and linking with other African leaders. In 1946 he and Kwame Nkrumah, later the first leader of independent Ghana, formed the Pan-African Federation. Kenyatta returned to Kenya in 1946 and was jailed for a role in a violent uprising against white settlers. Released in 1961, he negotiated independence arrangements with the British while also reconciling two main tribal factions in Kenya. Kenyatta stands as one of the earliest and most revered African nationalist leaders.

• • •

And the Europeans, having their feet firm on the soil, began to claim the absolute right to rule the country and to have the ownership of the lands under the title of

From Jomo Kenyatta, *Facing Mt. Kenya: The Tribal Life of the Gikuyu* (London: Sedser and Warburg, 1938), 47–52.

"Crown Lands," where the Gikuyu, who are the original owners, now live as "tenants at will of the Crown." The Gikuyu lost most of their lands through their magnanimity, for the Gikuyu country was never wholly conquered by force of arms, but the people were put under the ruthless domination of European imperialism through the insidious trickery of hypocritical treaties.

The relation between the Gikuyu and the Europeans can well be illustrated by a Gikuyu story which says: That once upon a time an elephant made a friendship with a man. One day a heavy thunderstorm broke out, the elephant went to his friend, who had a little hut at the edge of the forest, and said to him: "My dear good man, will you please let me put my trunk inside your hut to keep it out of this torrential rain?" The man, seeing what situation his friend was in, replied: "My dear good elephant, my hut is very small, but there is room for your trunk and myself. Please put your trunk in gently." The elephant thanked his friend, saying: "You have done me a good deed and one day I shall return your kindness." But what followed? As soon as the elephant put his trunk inside the hut, slowly he pushed his head inside, and finally flung the man out in the rain, and then lay down comfortably inside his friend's hut, saying: "My dear good friend, your skin is harder than mine, and as there is not enough room for both of us, you can afford to remain in the rain while I am protecting my delicate skin from the hailstorm."

The man, seeing what his friend had done to him, started to grumble, the animals in the nearby forest heard the noise and came to see what was the matter. All stood around listening to the heated argument between the man and his friend the elephant. In this turmoil the lion came along roaring, and said in a loud voice: "Don't you all know that I am the King of the Jungle! How dare anyone disturb the peace of my kingdom?" On hearing this the elephant, who was one of the high ministers in the jungle kingdom, replied in a soothing voice, and said: "My Lord, there is no disturbance of the peace in your kingdom. I have only been having a little discussion with my friend here as to the possession of this little hut which your lordship sees me occupying." The lion, who wanted to have "peace and tranquillity" in his kingdom, replied in a noble voice, saying: "I command my ministers to appoint a Commission of Enquiry to go thoroughly into this matter and report accordingly." He then turned to the man and said: "You have done well by establishing friendship with my people, especially with the elephant who is one of my honourable ministers of state. Do not grumble any more, your hut is not lost to you. Wait until the sitting of my Imperial Commission, and there you will be given plenty of opportunity to state your case. I am sure that you will be pleased with the findings of the Commission." The man was very pleased by these sweet words from the King of the Jungle, and innocently waited for his opportunity, in the belief, that naturally, the hut would be returned to him.

The elephant, obeying the command of his master, got busy with other ministers to appoint the Commission of Enquiry. The following elders of the jungle were appointed to sit in the Commission: (1) Mr. Rhinoceros; (2) Mr. Buffalo; (3) Mr.

Alligator; (4) The Rt. Hon. Mr. Fox to act as chairman; and (5) Mr. Leopard to act as Secretary to the Commission. On seeing the personnel, the man protested and asked if it was not necessary to include in this Commission a member from his side. But he was told that it was impossible, since no one from his side was well enough educated to understand the intricacy of jungle law. Further, that there was nothing to fear, for the members of the Commission were all men of repute for their impartiality in justice, and as they were gentlemen chosen by God to look after the interests of races less adequately endowed with teeth and claws, he might rest assured that they would investigate the matter with the greatest care and report impartially.

The Commission sat to take the evidence. The Rt. Hon. Mr. Elephant was first called. He came along with a superior air, brushing his tusks with a sapling which Mrs. Elephant had provided, and in an authoritative voice said: "Gentlemen of the Jungle, there is no need for me to waste your valuable time in relating a story which I am sure you all know. I have always regarded it as my duty to protect the interests of my friends, and this appears to have caused the misunderstanding between myself and my friend here. He invited me to save his hut from being blown away by a hurricane. As the hurricane had gained access owing to the unoccupied space in the hut, I considered it necessary, in my friend's own interests, to turn the undeveloped space to a more economic use by sitting in it myself; a duty which any of you would undoubtedly have performed with equal readiness in similar circumstances."

After hearing the Rt. Hon. Mr. Elephant's conclusive evidence, the Commission called Mr. Hyena and other elders of the jungle, who all supported what Mr. Elephant had said. They then called the man, who began to give his own account of the dispute. But the Commission cut him short, saying: "My good man, please confine yourself to relevant issues. We have already heard the circumstances from various unbiased sources; all we wish you to tell us is whether the undeveloped space in your hut was occupied by anyone else before Mr. Elephant assumed his position?" The man began to say: "No, but—" But at this point the Commission declared that they had heard sufficient evidence from both sides and retired to consider their decision. After enjoying a delicious meal at the expense of the Rt. Hon. Mr. Elephant, they reached their verdict, called the man, and declared as follows: "In our opinion this dispute has arisen through a regrettable misunderstanding due to the backwardness of your ideas. We consider that Mr. Elephant has fulfilled his sacred duty of protecting your interests. As it is clearly for your good that the space should be put to its most economic use, and as you yourself have not yet reached the stage of expansion which would enable you to fill it, we consider it necessary to arrange a compromise to suit both parties. Mr. Elephant shall continue his occupation of your hut, but we give you permission to look for a site where you can build another hut more suited to your needs, and we will see that you are well protected."

The man, having no alternative, and fearing that his refusal might expose him to the teeth and claws of members of the Commission, did as they suggested. But no sooner had he built another hut than Mr. Rhinoceros charged in with his horn lowered and ordered the man to quit. A Royal Commission was again appointed to look into the matter, and the same finding was given. This procedure was repeated until Mr. Buffalo, Mr. Leopard, Mr. Hyena and the rest were all accommodated with new huts. Then the man decided that he must adopt an effective method of protection, since Commissions of Enquiry did not seem to be of any use to him. He sat down and said: "*Ng'enda thi ndeagaga motegi*," which literally means "there is nothing that treads on the earth that cannot be trapped," or in other words, you can fool people for a time, but not for ever.

Early one morning, when the huts already occupied by the jungle lords were all beginning to decay and fall to pieces, he went out and built a bigger and better hut a little distance away. No sooner had Mr. Rhinoceros seen it than he came rushing in, only to find that Mr. Elephant was already inside, sound asleep. Mr. Leopard next came in at the window, Mr. Lion, Mr. Fox, and Mr. Buffalo entered the doors, while Mr. Hyena howled for a place in the shade and Mr. Alligator basked on the roof. Presently they all began disputing about their rights of penetration, and from disputing they came to fighting, and while they were all embroiled together the man set the hut on fire and burnt it to the ground, jungle lords and all. Then he went home, saying: "Peace is costly, but it's worth the expense," and lived happily ever after. . . .

There certainly are some progressive ideas among the Europeans. They include the ideas of material prosperity, of medicine, and hygiene, and literacy which enables people to take part in world culture. But so far the Europeans who visit Africa have not been conspicuously zealous in imparting these parts of their inheritance to the Africans, and seem to think that the only way to do it is by police discipline and armed force. They speak as if it was somehow beneficial to an African to work for them instead of for himself, and to make sure that he will receive this benefit they do their best to take away his land and leave him with no alternative. Along with his land they rob him of his government, condemn his religious idea, and ignore his fundamental conceptions of justice and morals, all in the name of civilisation and progress.

If Africans were left in peace on their own lands, Europeans would have to offer them the benefits of white civilisation in real earnest before they could obtain the African labour which they want so much. They would have to offer the African a way of life which was really superior to the one his fathers lived before him, and a share in the prosperity given them by their command of science. They would have to let the African choose what parts of European culture could be beneficially transplanted, and how they could be adapted. He would probably not choose the gas bomb or the armed police force, but he might ask for some other things of which he does not get so much today. As it is, by driving him off his ancestral lands, the Europeans have robbed him of the material foundations of his culture,

and reduced him to a state of serfdom incompatible with human happiness. The
African is conditioned, by the cultural and social institutions of centuries, to a freedom of which Europe has little conception, and it is not in his nature to accept
serfdom for ever. He realises that he must fight unceasingly for his own complete
emancipation, for without this he is doomed to remain the prey of rival imperial-
isms, which in every successive year will drive their fangs more deeply into his vitality and strength.

CHAPTER 26

ITALIAN FASCISM, GERMAN NAZISM, AND ARGENTINE PERONISM

A new kind of authoritarianism was born in Europe at the end of the nineteenth century. It built on strong nationalism but added a greater hostility to liberal ideas and institutions. Authoritarians resented the divisions and bickering of parliamentary systems. They disliked individualism and the consumer society, believing that people should find a higher purpose in the nation and its state. Most feared the rise of socialism, seeking to cure social ills by other, state-sponsored means. The background of some authoritarians was discontented intellectualism; others came from social groups that felt bypassed by the rise of industrial society—groups like artisans and small-scale shopkeepers. Many authoritarian movements were anti-Semitic. Authoritarianism was a noisy but also a small force in Europe until the huge disruptions of World War I. Then additional nationalist discontents, the fear of Communism in Russia, and sheer confusion gave the authoritarian movements additional support. First in Italy, then in other countries, the movements were able to gain power, usually by legal means, though none ever obtained an outright majority in any free election.

Authoritarianism also grew outside Europe. In Latin America many authoritarian dictators had flourished at times during the nineteenth century; they were called *caudillos,* the Spanish word for leader. Most authoritarians defended existing institutions—property owners, the army, the church. They gained power because of the difficulty of establishing stable governments after the independence wars earlier in the century. Some caudillos added a populist twist, wooing elements of the common people by programs of public works and state jobs. Authoritarianism continued in the twentieth century, off and on, and it picked up some of the trappings of European fascism, from grandiose principles of state power and nationalism to the uniformed movements, whose members were taught to march in military style, a tactic designed to whip up loyalty and discipline. Authoritarian leaders sprang up in Africa, the Middle East, and parts of Asia after World War II, again in part because some newly independent states found it hard to generate effective political institutions in any other way. Some of these leaders, too, took on certain fascist overtones.

A comparison of European fascism and a significant adaptation of authoritarianism in Latin America allows consideration of one of the vital political currents of the twentieth century. Authoritarian movements, after the fascist example, undoubtedly shared certain features, both because they faced some common imperatives simply to install an authoritarian state and because they actively imitated each other at least on the surface. But they were not all alike. Ideas varied, and contexts varied as well; a full Nazi-style state was possible only in an industrialized society, for example. Even in Europe, Italian fascism and German nationalism clearly differed, despite some shared causes and shared impulses.

The emergence of new kinds of authoritarian political movements, hostile both to Communism and to liberalism, was one of the most important developments of the twentieth century. Some of these movements were fascistic, after the model of Benito Mussolini's Italian fascism. Others—Peronism in Argentina may be an example—incorporated some fascist elements but require a more specific and flexible definition. The problem of deciding what fascism is or was, and what movements do or do not meet its criteria, is a vexing one in twentieth-century world history. The label is sometimes used, often derisively, to cover any repressive political current. But some historians prefer a more elaborate and precise definition.

The existence of Nazism (short for the name of Hitler's party, the National Socialists) complicates analysis. This was unquestionably the most important of all the authoritarian movements, if only because Germany was a great power. But Nazism was not just a fascist movement; it had its own special features, particularly in Hitler's virulent racism. So its characteristics complicate comparative analysis, just as they massively complicated the history of the twentieth-century world.

Mussolini's movement came first, among the modern versions of authoritarianism. A former socialist, Mussolini developed a fascist ideology amid the social strife and disappointed nationalism of post–World War I Italy. Italian liberal democracy was a rather new creation, and it was not functioning well. Socialist and Communist movements were gaining ground. Many nationalists had expected huge territorial gains from Italy's participation on the war on the side of Britain and France. This was the context in which Mussolini formulated an alternative movement—not liberal, not socialist, not conventionally conservative—and gradually gained enough support that he was called to power in 1923.

Hitler, an ardent nationalist and anti-Semite and a disgruntled war veteran, struggled through the 1920s. Many Germans deeply resented their loss in World War I and the harsh peace imposed on their country. Hitler felt he had the solution in a racist version of authoritarianism that would quickly mount an aggressive foreign policy. But he got his chance only when economic depression, in 1929, fueled the discontent. Nazism began to gain ground, and because Communism expanded also, new fears advanced the movement further. Hitler came to power in 1933.

Authoritarianism in Latin America was a separate current, born as we have seen in the nineteenth century as an alternative to a strong liberal movement and to frequent political instability. Many caudillos simply wanted to hold on to power. But by the late nineteenth century some were embellishing their dictatorships by working for greater economic development and reaching out for more active popular support. Juan Peron was in this newer tradition. When he came to power in 1946, he also had the example of European fascism before him—Argentina was one of the more Europeanized Latin American countries, with a large minority of Italian origin. Although Peron also had the example of fascist failure—both Mussolini and Hitler had died in the collapse of their movements at the end of World War II—there is no question that he found some aspects of the fascist precedent appealing.

Comparing versions of contemporary authoritarianism logically begins with a look at the similarities and differences between fascism and Nazism. Then the Peronist movement, the product of a separate though related society, can be brought into the mix.

A key analytical problem, as sources from fascism, Nazism, and Peronism readily attest, is that leaders of those movements were not interested in careful statements of principle or even in complete consistency. They talked of subordinating the individual to higher purposes, but they also praised human freedom. They were hostile to Marxism, but they often talked about social justice and sometimes (as with Peron) established themselves as friends of the working class in order to gain extensive working-class support.

Fascists, Nazis, and related authoritarians did share some common impulses. They stood for a strong state. They were hostile to competing political movements and often repressed them and the freedoms of press, speech, and assembly that go along with a more open political climate. They disliked the divisions, ineffectiveness, and selfishness of liberal, middle-class parliamentary systems. They resisted any idea of going back to a preliberal structure, however; they wanted a modern movement, capable of introducing great change.

Mussolini's version of fascism in principle—he did not always carry out all his political impulses—went beyond the common ingredients of twentieth-century authoritarianism, for example in his praise of war and his (vague) invocation of empire. Hitler's clear racism constituted an even greater innovation, unpalatable to genuine, traditional conservatives unless they swallowed their objections in hopes that Nazism would serve their ends.

Peronism was presented even less systematically than fascism or Nazism had been, in part perhaps because the defeat of European fascism undermined any extensive statement of principles. Peron's speeches contained a variety of political signals, not all of them consistent. He could invoke the great nineteenth-century liberal San Martín, or he could talk about the need for individual self-sacrifice in the interests of the state. In what ways, if any, does he reflect a fascist impulse (which his opponents at home and abroad frequently accused him of harboring)? How does his political approach, at least as offered in public speeches, differ from Mussolini's?

A final question must be applied to Mussolini, to Hitler, and to Peron alike: why did they gain so much popularity? Do their ideas help explain the appeal of authoritarian movements in many different countries from the 1920s onward?

Questions

1. Why was fascism opposed to socialism? to democracy? to liberalism? What was the fascist alternative according to Mussolini? What were the principles and goals of a fascist state?
2. How did the fascist state contrast with the liberal idea of the state? What was the fascist alternative to individualism?
3. What was Hitler's definition of a folkish state? How do Hitler's ideas show the bases of the launching of World War II and the Holocaust?
4. What ideas did Mussolini and Hitler share concerning methods for their movements? Did they have similar ideas about the state? Did Mussolini anticipate Hitler's ideas of a folkish state?
5. Why did Hitler, Mussolini, and Peron all claim to be revolutionary?
6. How do Mussolini, Hitler, and Peron suggest some of the political and social problems that gave rise to their movements?
7. How did Peron learn what not to say, from the fates and international reputations of Italian and German fascism?
8. How did Peron's ideas of the nation compare with Hitler's? How did his idea of individualism compare with the fascist approach? Judging by his stated goals, is it useful to think of Peron as a fascist? as a Nazi?
9. How did Peron distinguish himself from traditional Latin American caudillos?
10. If Peron should not be called a fascist, how are his political movement and beliefs best described?

For Further Discussion

1. Why might elements of European fascism prove attractive in the Latin American political context after World War II?
2. Why was it unlikely that a leader like Peron could set up a full Nazi state?
3. What was the relationship between fascistlike movements and nationalism? What kinds of nationalism avoided some kind of fascist outgrowth, and why?
4. Do conditions for fascism still exist in world history today? What societies, currently, would seem the most likely potential centers of serious fascist movements?

ITALIAN FASCISM: MUSSOLINI

Mussolini (1883–1945) came to power in 1923, following a famous "march on Rome" when armed bands (*Squadriste*), which had been violently disrupting democratic political meetings, mounted a largely peaceful, symbolic protest surge on the national capital. Mussolini spelled out his fascist doctrine (the name fascist came from the movement's symbol, a bundle or *fascio*) at various points in his career. The following selection comes from a 1932 article, "Doctrine of Fascism," written at a time when he was already well established as dictator but before he faced competition from Hitler, which moved him toward a somewhat more Nazi stance, for example in the area of anti-Semitism, and toward a more aggressive foreign policy. During the 1920s Mussolini had suppressed political opposition and had developed extensive public works projects, while dismantling the previous liberal state and turning parliament into a rubber stamp. Mussolini was toppled by the allied invasion of Italy during World War II and killed by resistance fighters.

• • •

Fascism was not the nursling of a doctrine worked out beforehand with detailed elaboration; it was born of the need for action and was itself from the beginning practical rather than theoretical; it was not merely another political party but, even in the first two years, in opposition to all political parties as such, and itself a living movement. The name which I then (1919) gave the organization fixed its character. And yet, if one were to re-read, in the now dusty columns of that date, the report of the meeting in which the *Fasci Italiani di combattimento* were constituted, one would there find no ordered expression of doctrine, but a series of aphorisms, anticipations and aspirations which, when refined by time from the original ore, were destined after some years to develop into an ordered series of doctrinal concepts, forming the Fascist political doctrine—different from all others either of the past or the present day. . . .

The years which preceded the march to Rome were years of great difficulty, during which the necessity for action did not permit of research or any complete elaboration of doctrine. The battle had to be fought in the towns and villages. There was much discussion, but—what was more important and more sacred—men died. They knew how to die. Doctrine, beautifully defined and carefully elucidated . . . might be lacking; but there was to take its place something more decisive—Faith. Even so, anyone . . . will find that the fundamentals of doctrine were cast during the years of conflict. It was precisely in those years that Fascist thought armed itself, was

From Benito Mussolini, *The Political and Social Doctrine of Fascism*, trans. Jane Soames (London: Hogarth Press, 1933), 8–14, 16–26.

refined, and began the great task of organization. The problem of the relation between the individual citizen and the State; the allied problems of authority and liberty; political and social problems as well as those specifically national—a solution was being sought for all these while at the same time the struggle against Liberalism, Democracy, Socialism and the Masonic bodies was being carried on. . . .

And above all, Fascism . . . believes neither in the possibility nor the utility of perpetual peace. It thus repudiates the doctrine of Pacifism—born of a renunciation of the struggle and an act of cowardice in the face of sacrifice. War alone brings up to its highest tension all human energy and puts the stamp of nobility upon the peoples who have the courage to meet it. . . . This anti-Pacifist spirit is carried by Fascism even into the life of the individual; the proud motto of the *Squadrista, "Me ne frego"* ["We don't give a damn"] . . . is an act of philosophy not only stoic, the summary of a doctrine not only political—it is the education to combat, the acceptation of the risks which combat implies, and a new way of life for Italy. Thus the Fascist accepts life and loves it, knowing nothing of and despising suicide: he rather conceives of life as a duty and struggle and conquest, life which should be high and full, lived for oneself, but above all for others. . . .

Such a conception of life makes Fascism the complete opposition of that doctrine, the base of so-called scientific and Marxian Socialism, the materialist conception of history; according to which the history of human civilization can be explained simply through the conflict of interests among the various social groups and by the change and development in the means and instruments of production. . . . Fascism, now and always, believes in holiness and in heroism; that is to say, in actions influenced by no economic motive, direct or indirect. . . . It follows that the existence of an unchangeable and unchanging class-war is also denied—the natural progeny of the economic conception of history. And above all Fascism denies that classwar can be the preponderant force in the transformation of society. These two fundamental concepts of Socialism being thus refuted, nothing is left of it but the sentimental aspiration . . . towards a social convention in which the sorrows and sufferings of the humblest shall be alleviated . . . Fascism denies the validity of the equation, well-being = happiness, which would reduce men to the level of animals, caring for one thing only—to be fat and well-fed—and would thus degrade humanity to a purely physical existence.

After Socialism, Fascism combats the whole complex system of democratic ideology, and repudiates it, whether in its theoretical premises or in its practical application. Fascism denies that the majority, by the simple fact that it is a majority, can direct human society; it denies that numbers alone can govern by means of a periodical consultation, and it affirms the immutable, beneficial and fruitful inequality of mankind, which can never be permanently leveled through the mere operation of a mechanical process such as universal suffrage. The democratic regime may be defined as from time to time giving the people the illusion of sovereignty, while the real effective sovereignty lies in the hands of other concealed and irresponsible forces. . . .

Fascism has taken up an attitude of complete opposition to the doctrines of Liberalism, both in the political field and the field of economics. . . . Liberalism only flourished for half a century. . . .

But the Fascist negation of Socialism, Democracy and Liberalism must not be taken to mean that Fascism desires to lead the world back to the state of affairs before 1789 . . . we do not desire to turn back. . . . Absolute monarchy has been and can never return, any more than blind acceptance of ecclesiastical authority. . . .

The foundation of Fascism is the conception of the State, its character, its duty, and its aim. Fascism conceives of the State as an absolute, in comparison with which all individuals or groups are relative, only to be conceived of in their relation to the State. The conception of the Liberal State is not that of a directing force, guiding the play and development, both material and spiritual, of a collective body, but merely a force limited to the function of recording results: on the other hand, the Fascist State is itself conscious, and has itself a will and a personality—thus it may be called the "ethic" State. In 1929 . . . I said:

"For us Fascists, the State is not merely a guardian . . . nor is it an organization with purely material aims. . . . Nor is it a purely political creation. . . . The State, as conceived of and as created by Fascism, is a spiritual and moral fact in itself, since its political, juridical and economic organization of the nation is a concrete thing; and such an organization must be in its origins and development a manifestation of the spirit. The State is the guarantor of security both internal and external, but it is also the custodian and transmitter of the spirit of the people, as it has grown up through the centuries in language, in customs and in faith. And the State is not only a living reality of the present, it is also linked with the past and above all with the future, and thus transcending the brief limits of individual life, it represents the immanent spirit of the nation. . . ."

From 1929 until today [1932], evolution, both political and economic, has everywhere gone to prove the validity of these doctrinal premises. Of such gigantic importance is the State. It is the force which alone can provide a solution to the dramatic contradictions of capitalism, and that state of affairs which we call the crisis can only be dealt with by the State, as between other States. . . . Yet the Fascist State is unique, and an original creation. It is not reactionary, but revolutionary, in that it anticipates the solution of the universal political problems which elsewhere have to be settled in the political field by the rivalry of parties, the excessive power of the Parliamentary regime and the irresponsibility of political assemblies; while it meets the problems of the economic field by a system of syndicalism* which is continually

*Mussolini meant this as an alternative to class based Unions. He installed state-dominated employer-worker boards, outlawing other unions and strikes.

increasing in importance, as much in the sphere of labour as of industry: and in the moral field enforces order, discipline, and obedience to that which is the determined moral code of the country. Fascism desires the State to be a strong and organic body, at the same time reposing upon broad and popular support. The Fascist State has drawn into itself even the economic activities of the nation, and, through the corporative social and educational institutions created by it, its influence reaches every aspect of the national life and includes, framed in their respective organizations, all the political, economic and spiritual forces of the nation. A State which reposes upon the support of millions of individuals who recognize its authority, are continually conscious of its power and are ready at once to serve it, is not the old tyrannical State. . . . The individual in the Fascist State is not annulled but rather multiplied, just in the same way that a soldier in a regiment is not diminished but rather increased by the number of his comrades. The Fascist State organizes the nation, but leaves a sufficient margin of liberty to the individual; the latter is deprived of all useless and possibly harmful freedom, but retains what is essential; the deciding power in the question cannot be the individual, but the State alone. . . .

According to Fascism, government is not so much a thing to be expressed in territorial or military terms as in terms of morality and the spirit. It must be thought of as an Empire—that is to say, a nation which directly or indirectly rules other nations, without the need for conquering a single square yard of territory. For Fascism, the growth of Empire, that is to say the expansion of the nation, is an essential manifestation of vitality, and its opposite a sign of decadence. Peoples which are rising, or rising again after a period of decadence, are always imperialist; any renunciation is a sign of decay and death. Fascism is the doctrine best adapted to represent the tendencies and the aspirations of a people, like the people of Italy, who are rising again after many centuries of abasement and foreign servitude. But Empire demands discipline, the co-ordination of all forces and a deeply-felt sense of duty and sacrifice: this fact explains . . . the necessarily severe measures which must be taken against those who would oppose this spontaneous and inevitable movement of Italy in the twentieth century.

GERMAN NAZISM: HITLER

The following passage comes from Hitler's *Mein Kampf,* which outlined his goals for a Nazi state with suprising frankness. Hitler wrote the book after he was jailed for an attempted revolt in a Munich beer hall in 1923. He was released in less than a year and resumed his propaganda activities, though his movement was foundering until the Depression hit Germany at the end of the decade. Then, votes for Nazism began to soar, reaching more than a third of the total in a 1932 election. Conservative leaders, hoping to manipulate Hitler, then installed the Nazis in power legally in 1933, and the leader (Fuehrer, as he styled himself) began to take complete command. As a blueprint, *Mein Kampf* offered some of the vagueness characteristic of fascist doctrine, for Hitler, too, detested intellectualism, but it clearly identifies several key points. The passage that follows highlights Hitler's racist beliefs, including his association of Germans with the ancient Aryan peoples and his condemnations of past nationalist policies that attempted to use a strong state to fuse various races, such as Poles and Jews, into a common constituency. Once he was in power, Hitler constructed a dictatorship; actively promoted economic development, particularly toward building up German armaments; attacked and ultimately killed most Jews in Germany and Europe (the Holocaust); and launched a series of aggressive moves that led to World War II, committing suicide in 1945 as Soviet armies invaded Berlin.

• • •

For the realization of philosophical ideals and of the demands derived from them no more occurs through men's pure feeling or inner will in themselves than the achievement of freedom through the general longing for it. No, only when the ideal urge for independence gets a fighting organization in the form of military instruments of power can the pressing desire of a people be transformed into glorious reality.

Every philosophy of life, even if it is a thousand times correct and of highest benefit to humanity, will remain without significance for the practical shaping of a people's life, as long as its principles have not become the banner of a fighting movement which for its part in turn will be a party as long as its activity has not found completion in the victory of its ideas and its party dogmas have not become the new state principles of a people's community. . . .

This transformation of a general, philosophical, ideal conception of the highest truth into a definitely delimited, tightly organized political community of faith and struggle, unified in spirit and will, is the most significant achievement, since on its happy solution alone the possibility of the victory of an idea depends. From the army of often millions of men, who as individuals more or less clearly and definitely sense these truths, and in part perhaps comprehend them, *one* man must step forward who with apodictic force will form granite principles from the wavering idea-world of the broad masses and take up the struggle for their sole correctness, until from the shifting waves of a free thought-world there will arise a brazen cliff of solid unity in faith and will.

The general right for such an activity is based on necessity, the personal right on success. . . .

What has been profitably Germanized in history is the soil which our ancestors acquired by the sword and settled with German peasants. In so far as they directed foreign blood

From Adolf Hitler, *Mein Kampf,* trans. Ralph Manheim (Boston: Houghton Mifflin, 1971), 380, 390–95. Reprinted by permission of the publisher.

into our national body in this process, they contributed to that catastrophic splintering of our inner being which is expressed in German super-individualism—a phenomenon, I am sorry to say, which is praised in many quarters . . .

. . . [T]he state must, therefore, in the light of reason, regard its highest task as the preservation and intensification of the race, this fundamental condition of all human cultural development.

It was the Jew, Karl Marx, who was able to draw the extreme inference from those false conceptions and views concerning the nature and purpose of a state: by detaching the state concept from racial obligations without being able to arrive at any other equally acknowledged formulation, the bourgeois world even paved the way for a doctrine which denies the state as such.

Even in this field, therefore, the struggle of the bourgeois world against the Marxist international must fail completely. It long since sacrificed the foundations which would have been indispensably necessary for the support of its own ideological world. Their shrewd foe recognized the weaknesses of their own structure and is now storming it with the weapons which they themselves, even if involuntarily, provided.

It is, therefore, the first obligation of a new movement, standing on the ground of a folkish world view, to make sure that its conception of the nature and purpose of the state attains a uniform and clear character.

Thus the basic realization is: *that the state represents no end, but a means. It is, to be sure, the premise for the formation of a higher human culture, but not its cause, which lies exclusively in the existence of a race capable of culture.* Hundreds of exemplary states might exist on earth, but if the Aryan culture-bearer died out, there would be no culture corresponding to the spiritual level of the highest peoples of today. We can go even farther and say that the fact of human state formation would not in the least exclude the possibility of the destruction of the human race, provided that superior intellectual ability and elasticity would be lost due to the absence of their racial bearers. . . .

The *state* in itself does not create a specific cultural level; it can only preserve the race which conditions this level. Otherwise the state as such may continue to exist unchanged for centuries while, in consequence of a racial mixture which it has not prevented, the cultural capacity of a people and the general aspect of its life conditioned by it have long since suffered a profound change. The present-day state, for example, may very well simulate its existence as a formal mechanism for a certain length of time, but the racial poisoning of our national body creates a cultural decline which even now is terrifyingly manifest.

Thus, the precondition for the existence of a higher humanity is not the state, but the nation possessing the necessary ability. . . .

The state is a means to an end. Its end lies in the preservation and advancement of a community of physically and psychically homogeneous creatures. This preservation itself comprises first of all existence as a race and thereby permits the free development of all the forces dormant in this race. Of them a part will always primarily serve the preservation of physical life, and only the remaining part the promotion of a further spiritual development. Actually the one always creates the precondition for the other.

States which do not serve this purpose are misbegotten, monstrosities in fact. The fact of their existence changes this no more than the success of a gang of bandits can justify robbery.

We National Socialists as champions of a new philosophy of life must never base ourselves on so-called 'accepted facts'—and false ones at that. If we did, we would not be the champions of a new great idea, but the coolies of the present-day lie. We must distinguish in the sharpest way between the state as a vessel and the race as its content. This vessel has meaning only if it can preserve and protect the content; otherwise it is useless.

Thus, the highest purpose of a folkish state is concern for the preservation of those original racial elements which bestow culture and create the beauty and dignity of a higher mankind. We, as Aryans, can conceive of the state only as the living organism of a nationality which not only assures the preservation of this nationality, but by the development of its spiritual and ideal abilities leads it to the highest freedom.

But what they try to palm off on us as a state today is usually nothing but a monstrosity born of deepest human error, with untold misery as a consequence.

We National Socialists know that with this conception we stand as revolutionaries in the world of today and are also branded as such. But our thoughts and actions must in no way be determined by the approval or disapproval of our time, but by the binding obligation to a truth which we have recognized. Then we may be convinced that the higher insight of posterity will not only understand our actions of today, but will also confirm their correctness and exalt them.

From this, we National Socialists derive a standard for the evaluation of a state. This value will be relative from the standpoint of the individual nationality, absolute from that of humanity as such. This means, in other words:

The quality of a state cannot be evaluated according to the cultural level or the power of this state in the frame of the outside world, but solely and exclusively by the degree of this institution's virtue for the nationality involved in each special case.

A state can be designated as exemplary if it is not only compatible with the living conditions of the nationality it is intended to represent, but if in practice it keeps this nationality alive by its own very existence—quite regardless of the importance of this state formation within the framework of the outside world. For the function of the state is not to create abilities, but only to open the road for those forces which are present. *Thus, conversely, a state can be designated as bad if, despite a high cultural level, it dooms the bearer of this culture in his racial composition.* For thus it destroys to all intents and purposes the premise for the survival of this culture

391

which it did not create, but which is the fruit of a culture-creating nationality safeguarded by a living integration through the state. The state does not represent the content, but a form. *A people's cultural level at any time does not, therefore, provide a standard for measuring the quality of the state* in which it lives. It is easily understandable that a people highly endowed with culture offers a more valuable picture than a Negro tribe; nevertheless, the state organism of the former, viewed according to its fulfillment of purpose, can be inferior to that of the Negro. Though the best state and the best state form are not able to extract from a people abilities which are simply lacking and never did exist, a bad state is assuredly able to kill originally existing abilities by permitting or even promoting the destruction of the racial culture-bearer.

Hence our judgment concerning the quality of a state can primarily be determined only by the relative utility it possesses for a definite nationality, and in no event by the intrinsic importance attributable to it in the world . . .

If, therefore, we speak of a higher mission of the state, we must not forget that the higher mission lies essentially in the nationality whose free development the state must merely make possible by the organic force of its being.

ARGENTINA: PERONISM

The following materials are excerpts from speeches given by the Argentine dictator between 1946 and 1949, when he was head of state. Peron (1896–1973) entered the Argentine government as a result of a coup in 1943 and became president in 1946. Developing an ardent following, particularly among urban workers, he launched extensive building projects and welfare programs. He was ousted in 1956, returning briefly thereafter, but a Peronist political movement remained an important force in Argentine politics for some time.

• • •

1. 1946

The Argentine Republic was born as a country of peace and work, endowed by nature with everything people may hope for to live happily and in peace; on this fact our international policy is based, we are inevitably heading for prosperity and greatness achieved partly by reason of our geographical situation and by our historical destiny.

There is nothing we can envy others, since God gave us whatever we may wish

From Juan Peron, *The Voice of Peron* (Buenos Aires: Argentine government, 1950), 22, 36–7, 59, 64, 69–70, 71, 94, 110–11.

for. Our policy is born of this aspect of our own natural greatness. We can never seek to take something from someone since we are surrounded on this earth by countries less fortunate than ours. For this reason, our international policy is a policy of peace, friendship, and the desire to trade honestly and freely, whenever we are offered the same freedom we grant, for in a world where absolute freedom of trade does not exist, it would be suicidal to profess this absolute liberty.

2. 1946

Social conscience has banished for ever the selfish individualism that looked only for personal advantages, to seek the welfare of all through the collective action of unions. Without that social conscience modern peoples are driven to struggle and despair dragging their country to misery, war and distress.

This magnificent spectacle of the awakening of a social conscience is condemned by men maintaining old standards, but they must not be blamed for they are the product of an unhappy era already surpassed by the Argentine Republic. They are the product of that individualistic and selfish age. They were born when gold was the only thing that mattered, when gold was handled without consulting the heart and therefore without understanding and realising that gold is not everything on this earth, that dividends are not of paramount importance.

3. 1946

The Five-Year Plan, as we have drawn it up, is simply the result of a careful study of all the Argentine problems, in the institutional order, in the field of national defence, and also in the field of national economy. We have considered each of these Argentine problems in detail, trying to discover their roots in order to find an adequate solution.

Only a plan of vast proportions is in keeping with a great nation such as the Argentine Republic. The mediocre, those who lack courage and faith, always prefer small plans. Great nations, such as our own, with lofty ambitions and aspirations, must also envisage great plans. Nothing valuable can be achieved by planning trivialities.

4. 1946

Nowadays policy has changed: each person is at his post, working for the common patrimony. When something is achieved, it must benefit everyone; when suffering awaits us, all must share the sorrow. But let us advise those who still uphold ideas of the old politicians that today, Argentine men and Argentine women are aware of the existence of a movement supported by the whole country; that we all work and struggle for this joint movement; therefore, that any personal or group policy will be destroyed by us and also that our policy originates in this movement of union.

5. 1947

Encouraged by an overwhelming spirit of patriotism and steadily following the principles and standards of conduct set by precedent, an officer must apply all his strength of character and bring into play all his stalwart personality so that whatever may be the circumstances in which they find themselves, the Armed Forces will never cease to be an orderly and disciplined institution at the exclusive service of the Nation. He must be sure that they are never transformed into a constant danger which undervalues and hampers the will of a sovereign people.

6. 1948

To guide the masses one must first instruct and educate them, which can be done at meetings or at lectures on politics, to be given in our centres, not to tell them to vote for us, or that they must do this or that so that Peter or James will be elected to represent them. No, we must speak to them of what are their obligations, because in our country there is much talk of rights and little of moral obligations. We must talk somewhat more about the obligations of each citizen towards his country and towards his fellow countrymen, and forget for a time their rights since we have mentioned them often enough.

7. 1949

The Peronistic doctrine has to go forward with its fundamental idea; to free the people to prepare them to make the right use of this freedom. Neither can any Argentine, and still less a Peronist, use unfairly the individual freedom which the Magna Charter of the Republic offers him as a man of honour and not as a criminal. A Peronist must be a slave to the law because that is the only way in which he can eventually obtain his freedom. But it is not enough for a Peronist to be a slave of the law. He must also observe the Peronist code of ethics, because those who break laws are not the only criminals, those who abuse their freedom and who break the community laws of the land they live in to the detriment of their fellow beings, are also guilty.

8. 1949

Liberal Democracy, flexible in matters of political or economic retrocession, or apparent discretion, was not equally flexible where social problems were concerned.

And the bourgeoisie after breaking their lines, have presented the spectacle of peoples who all rise at once so as to measure the might of their presence, the volume of their clamour, and the fairness of their claims. Popular expectation is followed by discontent. Hope placed in the power of law is transformed into resentment if these laws tolerate injustice. The State looks on impotently at a growing loss of prestige. Its institutions prevent it from taking adequate measures and there are signs of a divorce between its interpretation and that of the nation which it professes to represent. Having lost prestige it becomes ineffectual, and is threatened by rebellion, because if society does not find in the ruling powers the instrument with which to achieve its happiness it will devise in its unprotected state, the instrument with which to overthrow them.

9. 1949

The ambition for social progress has nothing to do with its noisy partisan exploitation, neither can it be achieved by reviling and lowering the different types of men. Mankind needs faith in his destiny and in what he is doing and to possess sufficient insight to realise that the transition from the "I" to the "we" does not take place in a flash as the extermination of the individual, but as a renewed avowal of the existence of the individual functioning in the community. In that way the phenomenon is orderly and takes place during the years in the form of a necessary evolution which is more in the nature of "coming of age" than that of a mutiny.

10. 1949

We are building cities, we are constructing gaspipe lines 1,800 kilometers long; we are building an aerodrome which may quite possibly be the largest and best-equipped in the world and we are acquiring a merchant fleet which is already beginning to take its place among the most important on the high seas.

By this I mean to point out that I was not just being vainglorious three years ago when I took over the Government and said that the Country was sick and tired of little things, and I wanted to make it sick and tired of big things.

11. 1949

The "caudillo" [name given to South American autocratic political leaders] improvises while the statesman makes plans and carries them out. The "caudillo" has no initiative, the statesman is creative. The "caudillo" is only concerned with measures which are applicable to the reigning circumstances whereas the statesman plans for all time; the deeds of the "caudillo" die with him, but the statesman lives on in his handiwork. For that reason the "caudillo" has no guiding principles or clear-cut plan while the statesman works methodically, defeating time and perpetuating himself in his own creations. "Caudillismo" is a trade, but statecraft is an art.

12. 1949

The politician of the old school made posts and favouritism a question of politics, because as he achieved nothing of general usefulness, he had at least to win the good will of those who would support him in the field of politics. The natural consequences of this nepotism were political cliques; one politician dominated one clique and another a different one. They fought among themselves until one of the cliques came out on top and from them emerged the general staff bent not on fulfilling their public office with self-denial and sacrifice, but on making the most of their position to use the Nation as a huge body at the service of their own interests and to throw away the wealth of the country with [no] sense of order and the fitness of things. . . .

13. 1949

The revolutionary idea would not have been able to materialise along constitutional lines if it had not been able to withstand the criticism, the violent attacks and even the strain on principles when they run up against the rocks which appear, every day in the path of a ruler. The principles of the revolution would not have been able to be upheld if they had not been the true reflection of Argentine sentiments.

The guiding principles of our movement must have made a very deep impression on the national conscience for the people in the last elections to have consecrated them by giving us full power to make reforms.

CHAPTER 27

DROPPING THE ATOMIC BOMB ON JAPAN

On August 6, 1945, the United States dropped an atomic bomb on Hiroshima, killing eighty thousand people and injuring and sickening many more; it was followed by another, on Nagasaki, three days later, which killed ninety thousand (including later deaths from radiation sickness). Japan surrendered the next day.

This chapter deals with issues surrounding the atomic bomb. Bombing Japan not only hastened the end of World War II. It also opened a new age of military technology, which would steadily escalate during the Cold War. The threats and fears associated with atomic weaponry have been part of world experience ever since 1945. In the selections that follow, two sets of comparisons are offered: first, a comparison of the tenor of the American decision to drop the bomb with Japanese reactions; second, a comparison of historical memory, of how groups in the United States and Japan still disputed the interpretation of what happened, fifty years after the event. The second comparison is based on a secondary account of a recent bitter dispute about historical presentation in the United States, at the national museum complex, the Smithsonian.

American scientists were not unanimous in recommending dropping the bomb: some urged a demonstration first to give Japan a chance to surrender. But there were few bombs available, and the decision to act directly reflected an eagerness to end the war, the desire to punish Japanese intransigence, and a new concern about Russian intervention in the area. The first two documents suggest American attitudes—first, those of President Truman, who made the decision, and second, those revealed in the description of the Hiroshima mission by the pilot of the decisive plane, the super fortress *Enola Gay*. What kinds of attitudes are suggested about the bomb itself and about the Japanese? How did these two Americans relate themselves to one of the great events of contemporary history? A third passage, by a doctor in Nagasaki, recounts the experience of being bombed. Needless to say, from a comparative standpoint, the three documents together show the huge differences in perspective between people who do the bombing and people on the receiving end of an unprecedented technological experience. (This comparison deserves consideration in terms of another event-based, two-sided comparison, the one that deals with the Opium War, in chapter 20.)

Following World War II, of course, the United States developed its nuclear weaponry further, as fears of the Soviet Union increased and several other powers joined the nuclear arms race. Japan, under American occupation but also profoundly affected by the war itself, abandoned significant military activity and did not participate in the weapons buildup.

The second set of comparative issues requires more subtle analysis. An article by an American scholar recounts the bitter divisions that arose in the United States in 1995 over a proposed Smithsonian Institution commemoration of the bomb's anniversary. The planned *Enola Gay* exhibit presented American historians' current understanding of the complexity of the event, in light of what was known by then about motives and alternatives. This complex rendering (with which the author of the article clearly agrees) aroused massive hostility from veterans' groups and a growing conservative-nationalist sentiment in Congress at the time. The exhibit was replaced with a simpler narrative, about the *Enola Gay* itself. Japan protested this version because it clashed with its own complex memories. Historical memory is an active ingredient in the life of any society, and it is almost always composed of a mixture of selected facts and myths. After World War II most Americans were eager to see former opponents confront their "real" war history. The Germans should teach about the evils of Nazism; the Japanese should teach about their wartime atrocities, including mistreatment of many prisoners. Neither nation moved as far along as some observers thought they should, because nationalist traditions and the task of rebuilding an undeniably different political structure made confronting too much pain too difficult. But some Japanese, even in official life, did acknowledge some of the wartime responsibilities. The United States has its own set of historical memory issues (not just concerning the war) as it teaches its national history. Is the dropping of the atomic bomb something Americans should probe more deeply, in order to understand themselves?

Questions

1. What were President Truman's motives in deciding to use the bomb? Did he understand its potential? How did Truman's note suggest he was justifying his decision to himself?
2. What kinds of attitudes does the Tibbets note suggest? What were Tibbets's feelings about his unprecedented mission and its results? Would he and Truman have agreed about the way to approach the use of the bomb? What are the best arguments today for defending Truman's policy and Tibbets's participation? What are the leading questions about the policy?
3. How do Tibbets's and Akizuki's descriptions of the bomb's impact compare? How do the two accounts prepare for the different (American and Japanese) historical memories John Dower describes?
4. Do you think the Smithsonian was right to withdraw the original exhibit?

5. What kind of historical memory did John Dower think we should have? Why did he feel that rosy memories about World War II remain so important in the United States?

6. What attitudes toward Japan were involved in dropping the bomb? Are any remnants of those feelings still active now in the United States?

7. What kind of historical memory of the bomb do most Japanese seek? Why did they protest the simpler Smithsonian exhibit that replaced the controversial display?

8. What are the main disputes over how to remember the bombing, within each country (United States and Japan) and between them?

For Further Discussion

1. Was dropping the bomb a "war crime"?
2. Did the atomic bomb change the nature of modern war and diplomacy?
3. Why did the bomb experience have such different impacts in the United States and Japan?
4. How do both the American and the Japanese versions of remembering the bomb seem so important to citizens of the two nations, so long after the fact?
5. What kind of bomb "memory" works for you, and why?

Dropping the Bomb: Truman, Tibbets, and Akizuki

The following three selections surround the immediate experience of the bomb, in 1945. Harry Truman was the thirty-third president of the United States, succeeding after the death of Franklin Roosevelt in April 1945. When he took office, Truman was immediately confronted with basic military and foreign policy issues as World War II drew to a close. Decisions about the bomb, developed after five years of crash research, were paramount among these issues. Truman here writes at the Potsdam Conference—the last conference among the allies, including Stalin of the Soviet Union and Churchill of Britain—which dealt with conditions of the postwar world. Tensions between Stalin and the Western powers ran high at Potsdam.

Col. Paul Tibbets was an experienced pilot in the U.S. Army Air Force (the Air Force had not yet become a separate military branch). He was twenty-nine when he piloted the *Enola Gay*. Later, he frequently defended his action and refuted rumors that he had suffered mental illness as a result of remorse. In 1995 he argued that he had never had any doubts about his action and that it had saved lives by hastening the end of the war. Earlier, in 1976, he had caused controversy by recreating the attack in a Texas airshow complete with mushroom cloud; Japanese bomb survivors protested this act as callous.

Dr. Tatsuichiro Akizuki practiced medicine in Nagasaki. He described his experiences after learning about the earlier bomb in Hiroshima and then after the second bomb was dropped on his own city. His recollections were extremely unusual because there were so few survivors, though the doctor himself lived a number of years after the attack.

• • •

HARRY TRUMAN

Diary: Potsdam 25 July 1945

We met at eleven today. That is Stalin, Churchill, and the US President. But I had a most important session with Lord Mountbatten and General Marshall before that. We have discovered the most terrible bomb in the history of the world. It may be the fire destruction prophesied in the Euphrates Valley Era, after Noah and his fabulous Ark.

Anyway we 'think' we have found the way to cause a disintegration of the atom. An experiment in the New Mexican desert was startling—to put it mildly. Thirteen pounds of the explosive caused the complete disintegration of a steel tower 60 feet high, created a crater 6 feet deep and 1,200 feet in diameter, knocked over a steel tower ½ mile away and knocked men down 10,000 yards away. The explosion was visible for more than 200 miles and audible for 40 miles and more.

This weapon is to be used against Japan between now and August 10th. I have told the Sec. of War, Mr Stimson, to use it so that military objectives and soldiers and sailors are the target and not women and children. Even if the Japs are savages, ruthless, merciless and fanatic, we as the leader of the world for the common welfare cannot drop this terrible bomb on the old capital or the new.

He and I are in accord. The target will be a purely military one and we will issue a warning statement asking the Japs to surrender and save lives. I'm sure they will not do that, but we will have given them the chance. It is certainly a good thing for the world that Hitler's crowd or Stalin's did not discover this atomic bomb. It seems to be the most terrible thing ever discovered, but it can be made the most useful.

[The following day, 26 July, the Allies called upon Japan to surrender. The alternative they said was 'prompt and utter destruction.' Japan did not surrender.]

From Harry S Truman, *Off the Record: The Private Papers of Harry S. Truman* (New York: Harper and Row, 1986), 55–56. Reprinted by permission of Ann Elmo Agency, Inc. West.

COL. PAUL TIBBETS, USAAF PILOT OF THE BOMB-CARRYING PLANE

Up to this point it was common practice in any theatre of war to fly straight ahead, fly level, drop your bombs, and keep right on going, because you could bomb several thousands of feet in the air and you could cross the top of the place that you had bombed with no concern whatsoever. But it was determined by the scientists that, in order to escape and maintain the integrity of the aircraft and the crew, that this aeroplane could not fly forward after it had dropped the bomb. It had to turn around and get away from that bomb as fast as it could. If you placed this aeroplane in a very steep angle of bank to make this turn, if you turned 158 degrees from the direction that you were going, you would then begin to place distance between yourself and that point of explosion as quickly as possible. You had to get away from the shock wave that would be coming back from the ground in the form of an ever expanding circle as it came upwards. It's necessary to make this turn to get yourself as far as possible from an expanding ring and 158 degrees happened to be the turn for that particular circle. It was difficult. It was something that was not done with a big bomber aeroplane. You didn't make this kind of a steep turn—you might almost call it an acrobatic manoeuvre—and the big aircraft didn't do these things. However, we refined it, we learned how to do it. It had been decided earlier that there was a possibility that an accident could occur on take-off, and so therefore we would not arm this weapon until we had left the runway and were out to sea. This of course meant that had there been an accident there would have been an explosion from normal powder charges but there would not have been a nuclear explosion. As I said this worried more people than it worried me because I had plenty of faith in my aeroplane. I knew my engines were good. We started our take-off on time which was somewhere about two-forty-five I think, and the aeroplane went on down the runway. It was loaded quite heavily but it responded exactly like I had anticipated it would. I had flown this aeroplane the same way before and there was no problem and there was nothing different this night in the way we went. We arrived over the initial point and started in on the bomb run which had about eleven minutes to go, rather a long type of run for a bomb but on the other hand we felt we needed this extra time in straight and level flight to stabilize the air speed of the aeroplane, to get everything right down to the last-minute detail. As I indicated earlier the problem after the release of the bomb is not to proceed forward but to turn away. As soon as the weight had left the aeroplane I immediately went into this steep turn and we tried then to place distance between ourselves and the point of impact. In this particular case that bomb took fifty-three seconds from the time it left the aeroplane until it exploded and this gave us adequate time of course to make the

From Mark Arnold Foster, *The World of War* (London: William Collins and Sons, Thomas Television Ltd. 1973), 348–49.

turn. We had just made the turn and rolled out on level flight when it seemed like somebody had grabbed a hold of my aeroplane and gave it a real hard shaking because this was the shock wave that had come up. Now after we had been hit by a second shock wave not quite so strong as the first one I decided we'll turn around and go back and take a look. The day was clear when we dropped that bomb, it was a clear sunshiny day and the visibility was unrestricted. As we came back around again facing the direction of Hiroshima we saw this cloud coming up. The cloud by this time, now two minutes old, was up at our altitude. We were 33,000 feet at this time and the cloud was up there and continuing to go right on up in a boiling fashion, as if it was rolling and boiling. The surface was nothing but a black boiling, like a barrel of tar. Where before there had been a city with distinctive houses, buildings and everything that you could see from our altitude, now you couldn't see anything except a black boiling debris down below.

DR. TATSUICHIRO AKIZUKI

During the morning Mr Yokota turned up to see his daughter, who was one of our in-patients. He lived at the foot of Motohara Hill, and was an engineer in the research department of the Mitsubishi Ordnance Factory, then one of the centres of armament manufacture in Japan. The torpedoes used in the attack on Pearl Harbor had been made there. Mr Yokota always had something interesting to say. He used to visit me now and again, often passing on some new piece of scientific information.

He said: 'I hear Hiroshima was very badly damaged on the sixth.'

Together we despaired over the destiny of Japan, he as an engineer, I as a doctor.

Then he said gloomily: 'I don't think the explosion was caused by any form of chemical energy.'

'What then?' I inquired, eager to know about the cause of the explosion, even though my patients were waiting for me.

He said: 'The power of the bomb dropped on Hiroshima is far stronger than any accumulation of chemical energy produced by the dissolution of a nitrogen compound, such as nitro-glycerine. It was an *atomic* bomb, produced by atomic fission.'

'Good heavens! At last we have atomic fission!' I said, though somewhat doubt-fully.

Just then the long continuous wail of a siren arose.

'Listen . . . Here comes the regular air-raid.'

'The first warning . . . The enemy are on their way.'

From Tatsuichiro Akizuki, *Nagasaki 1945*, trans. Keiichi Nagata (New York: Quartet Books, 1981), 23–24, 25, 26–27, 29–31, 33. © 1981 Tatsuichiro Akizuki & Keiichi Nagata. Reprinted by permission of the Peters Fraser and Dunlop Group Limited.

Mr Yokota hurried back down the hill to his factory and all at once I began to feel nervous. It was now about ten-thirty. When such a warning sounded we were supposed to make sure our patients took refuge in our basement air-raid shelter. We were meant to do likewise. But recently I had become so accustomed to air-raids that, even though it was somewhat foolhardy, I no longer bothered with every precaution. In any case, breakfast was about to begin. At the time our diet at the hospital consisted of two meals a day of unpolished rice. The patients were waiting for their breakfast to be served, and so remained on the second and third floor.

I went out of the building. It was very hot. The sky had clouded over a little but the familiar formation of B29 bombers was neither to be seen nor heard. I asked myself: 'What route will our dear enemies choose to take today?'

I went in again to warn my patients to stay away from the windows—they could be swept by machine-gun fire. Recently we had been shot up once or twice by fighter-planes from American aircraft carriers in neighbouring waters.

About thirty minutes later the all-clear sounded. I said to myself: In Nagasaki everything is still all right. *Im Westen Nichts Neues*—All quiet on the Western Front.

I went down to the consulting room, humming cheerfully. . . .

I stuck the pneumo-thorax needle into the side of the chest of the patient lying on the bed. It was just after eleven a.m.

I heard a low droning sound, like that of distant aeroplane engines.

'What's that?' I said. 'The all-clear has gone, hasn't it?'

At the same time the sound of the plane's engines, growing louder and louder, seemed to swoop down over the hospital.

I shouted: 'It's an enemy plane! Look out—take cover!'

As I said so, I pulled the needle out of the patient and threw myself beside the bed.

There was a blinding white flash of light, and the next moment—*Bang! Crack!* A huge impact like a gigantic blow smote down upon our bodies, our heads and our hospital. I lay flat—I didn't know whether or not of my own volition. Then down came piles of debris, slamming into my back.

The hospital has been hit, I thought. I grew dizzy, and my ears sang.

Some minutes or so must have passed before I staggered to my feet and looked around. The air was heavy with yellow smoke; white flakes of powder drifted about; it was strangely dark.

Thank God, I thought—I'm not hurt! But what about the patients? . . .

No one knew what had happened. A huge force had been released above our heads. What it was, nobody knew. Had it been several tons of bombs, or the suicidal destruction of a plane carrying a heavy bomb-load?

Dazed, I retreated into the consulting room, in which the only upright object on the rubbish-strewn floor was my desk. I went and sat on it and looked out of the window at the yard and the outside world. There was not a single pane of glass in the window, not even a frame—all had been completely blown away. Out in the yard dun-colored smoke or dust cleared little by little. I saw figures running. Then, looking to the south-west, I was stunned. The sky was as dark as pitch, covered with dense clouds of smoke; under that blackness, over the earth, hung a yellow-brown fog. Gradually the veiled ground became visible, and the view beyond rooted me to the spot with horror.

All the buildings I could see were on fire: large ones and small ones and those with straw-thatched roofs. Further off along the valley, Urakami Church, the largest Catholic church in the east, was ablaze. The technical school, a large two-storeyed wooden building, was on fire, as were many houses and the distant ordnance factory. Electricity poles were wrapped in flame like so many pieces of kindling. Trees on the nearby hills were smoking, as were the leaves of sweet potatoes in the fields. To say that everything burned is not enough. It seemed as if the earth itself emitted fire and smoke, flames that writhed up and erupted from underground. The sky was dark, the ground was scarlet, and in between hung clouds of yellowish smoke. Three kinds of colour—black, yellow and scarlet—loomed ominously over the people, who ran about like so many ants seeking to escape. What had happened? Urakami Hospital had not been bombed—I understood that much. But that ocean of fire, that sky of smoke! It seemed like the end of the world. . . .

About ten minutes after the explosion, a big man, half-naked, holding his head between his hands, came into the yard towards me, making sounds that seemed to be dragged from the pit of his stomach.

'Got hurt, sir,' he groaned; he shivered as if he were cold. 'I'm hurt.'

I stared at him, at the strange-looking man. Then I saw it was Mr Zenjiro Tsujimoto, a market-gardener and a friendly neighbour to me and the hospital. I wondered what had happened to the robust Zenjiro.

'What's the matter with you, Tsujimoto?' I asked him, holding him in my arms.

'In the pumpkin field over there—getting pumpkins for the patients—got hurt . . . ' he said, speaking brokenly and breathing feebly.

It was all he could do to keep standing. Yet it didn't occur to me that he had been seriously injured.

'Come along now,' I said. 'You are perfectly all right, I assure you. Where's your shirt? Lie down and rest somewhere where it's cool. I'll be with you in a moment.'

His head and his face were whitish; his hair was singed. It was because his eyelashes had been scorched away that he seemed so bleary-eyed. He was half-naked because his shirt had been burned from his back in a single flash. But I wasn't aware of such facts. I gazed at him as he reeled about with his head between his hands. What a change had come over this man who was stronger than a horse, whom I had last seen earlier that morning. It's as if he's been struck by lightning, I thought.

After Mr Tsujimoto came staggering up to me, another person who looked just like him wandered into the yard. Who he was and where he had come from I had no idea. 'Help me,' he said, groaning, half-naked, holding his head between his hands. He sat down, exhausted. 'Water . . . Water . . . ' he whispered.

'What's the trouble? What's wrong with you? What's become of your shirt?' I demanded.

'Hot-*hot* . . . Water . . . I'm burning.' They were the only words that were articulate.

As time passed, more and more people in a similar plight came up to the hospital—ten minutes, twenty minutes, an hour after the explosion. All were of the same appearance, sounded the same. 'I'm hurt, *hurt!* I'm burning! Water!' They all moaned the same lament. I shuddered. Half-naked or stark naked, they walked with strange, slow steps, groaning from deep inside themselves as if they had travelled from the depths of hell. They looked whitish; their faces were like masks. I felt as if I were dreaming, watching pallid ghosts processing slowly in one direction—as in a dream I had once dreamt in my childhood.

These ghosts came on foot uphill towards the hospital, from the direction of the burning city and from the more easterly ordnance factory. Worker or student, girl or man, they all walked slowly and had the same mask-like face. Each one groaned and cried for help. Their cries grew in strength as the people increased in number, sounding like something from the Buddhist scriptures, re-echoing everywhere, as if the earth itself were in pain.

One victim who managed to reach the hospital yard asked me, 'Is this a hospital?' before suddenly collapsing on the ground. There were those who lay stiffly where they fell by the roadside in front of the hospital; others lay in the sweet-potato fields. Many went down to the steep valley below the hospital where a stream ran down between the hill of Motohara and the next hill. 'Water, water,' they cried. They went instinctively down to the banks of the stream, because their bodies had been scorched and their throats were parched and inflamed; they were thirsty. I didn't realize then that these were the symptoms of 'flash-burn.' . . .

In the afternoon a change was noticeable in the appearance of the injured people who came up to the hospital. The crowd of ghosts which had looked whitish in the morning were now burned black. Their hair was burnt; their skin, which was charred and blackened, blistered and peeled. Such were those who now came toiling up to the hospital yard and fell there weakly.

'Are you a doctor? Please, if you wouldn't mind, could you examine me?' So said a young man.

'Cheer up!' I said. It was all I could say.

He died in the night. He must have been one of the many medical students who were injured down at the medical college. His politeness and then his poor blackened body lying dead on the concrete are things I shall never forget.

THE CONTROVERSY OVER MEMORY: JOHN DOWER

This account was written by a historian specializing in international relations and Japan. It describes the controversy that arose over the proposed Smithsonian commemoration of the fiftieth anniversary of the bomb in 1995. A host of groups, spearheaded by several veterans' organizations, attacked the original plans, which had been prepared by a variety of historians and other experts. The opposition, echoed in a Congress dominated by conservatives, prompted the museum to back down and offer a minimal display centered around the airplane *Enola Gay* itself. This decision brought another set of protests, including criticisms from Japanese authorities who felt that the United States was adopting a double standard: real confrontation with historical issues for others, congratulatory history for itself.

• • •

REMEMBERING THE BOMB

Fiftieth anniversaries are unlike other commemorative occasions, especially when they are anniversaries of war. Participants in the events of a half century ago are still alive to tell their emotional personal tales. Their oral histories confront the skepticism and detachment of younger generations who have no memories of the war. Historians with access to materials that were previously inaccessible (or simply ignored) develop new perspectives on the dynamics and significance of what took place. Politicians milk the still palpable human connection between past and present for every possible drop of ideological elixir. History, memory, scholarship, and politics become entangled in intricate ways . . .

It is a measure of the impoverishment of our present-day political climate in the United States that Americans have been denied a rate opportunity to use the fiftieth anniversary of Hiroshima and Nagasaki to reflect more deeply about these developments that changed our world forever. That opportunity was lost early this year when the Smithsonian Institution, bowing to political pressure (including unanimous condemnation by the United States Senate), agreed to scale back drastically a proposed major exhibition on the atomic bombs and the end of the war against Japan in its Air and Space Museum in Washington.

The exhibition initially envisioned by the Smithsonian's curators would have taken viewers through a succession of rooms that introduced, in turn, the ferocity of the last year of the war in Asia, the Manhattan Project and the unfolding imperatives behind the United States decision to use the bombs against Japan, the training and preparation of the *Enola Gay* mission that dropped the first bomb on Hiroshima

From John W. Dower, "Triumphal and Tragic Narratives of the War in Asia," *Journal of American History* (December 1995): 1124–34.

(with the fuselage of the *Enola Gay* as the centerpiece of the exhibition), the human consequences of the bombs in the two target cities, and the nuclear legacy to the postwar world. The draft script included occasional placards that concisely summarized the "historical controversies" that have emerged in scholarship and public discourse.

This ambitious proposal proved to be politically unacceptable. The Senate denounced the draft script as being "revisionist and offensive to many World War II veterans." Critics accused curators responsible for the draft of being "politically correct" leftists and rarely hesitated to brand as "anti-American" anyone who questioned the use of the bombs. Confronted by such criticism, and by a conservative Congress threatening to cut off federal funding to "liberal" projects in general, the Smithsonian—like Japan fifty years earlier—surrendered unconditionally. Visitors to the Air and Space Museum eventually were offered only a minimalist exhibition featuring the refurbished fuselage of the *Enola Gay* and a brief tape and text explaining that this was the plane that dropped the first atomic bomb, following which, nine days later, Japan surrendered. The artifact, supporters of this bare presentation declare, speaks for itself.

Artifacts do not in fact speak for themselves. Essentially the United States government has chosen to commemorate the end of World War II in Asia by affirming that only one orthodox view is politically permissible. This orthodoxy amounts to a "heroic" narrative, and its contours are simple: The war in Asia was a brutal struggle against a fanatic, expansionist foe (which is true, albeit cavalier about European and American colonial and neocolonial control in Asia up to 1941). That righteous war against Japanese aggression was ended by the dropping of the atomic bombs, which saved the enormous numbers of American lives that would have been sacrificed in invading Japan. As the Senate's condemnation of the Smithsonian's plans put it, the atomic bombs brought the war to a "merciful" end.

Other euphemisms convey essentially this same simple story line. The heroic or triumphal narrative coincides with the identification of World War II as the last "good war"—a perception reified in American consciousness by the horribly destructive and inconclusive subsequent conflicts in Korea and Indochina. As captured in the title of a well-known essay by the writer and World War II veteran Paul Fussell, who had been slated to participate in the invasion of Japan as a young soldier, the heroic version of the war's end in Asia also finds common expression as the "thank God for the atom bomb" narrative—a memorable incantation that simultaneously places God on the American side and reminds us *pari passu* that the Japanese are pagans. The triumphal American narrative offers an entirely understandable view of World War II—emphasizing the enormity of German and Japanese behavior, eulogizing American "valor and sacrificial service" (in the words of the Senate resolution), and applauding the bombs for forcing Japan's surrender and saving American lives.

But what does this heroic narrative leave out? What are the "historical controversies" the Smithsonian's curators thought worth making known to the public? What might we have learned from a truly serious commemorative engagement with the end of the war in Asia?

There are many answers. To begin, the argument that the bombs were used simply to end the war quickly and thereby save untold lives neglects complicating facts, converging motives and imperatives, and possible alternative policies for ending the war. Such considerations can do more than deepen our retrospective understanding of the decision to use the bombs. They also can help us better appreciate the complexities of crisis policy making in general.

If, moreover, we are willing to look beyond the usual end point in the conventional heroic narrative—beyond (or beneath) the sparkling *Enola Gay* and the almost abstract mushroom cloud—we can encounter the human face of World War II. Humanizing the civilians killed and injured by the bombs, and, indeed, humanizing the Japanese enemy generally, is difficult and distasteful for most Americans. If this is done honestly in the context of Hiroshima and Nagasaki, it becomes apparent that we confront something more than the human consequences of nuclear war. We are forced to ask painful questions about the morality of modern war itself —specifically, the transformation of moral consciousness that, well before the atomic bombs were dropped, had led *all* combatants to identify civilian men, women, and children as a legitimate target of "total war."

To engage the war at this level is to enter the realm of tragic, rather than triumphal, narratives. As the Smithsonian controversy revealed, however, even after the passage of a half century there is little tolerance of such reflection in the United States, and now virtually none at all at the level of public institutions. We have engaged in self-censorship and are the poorer for it.

. . . Critics of the Air and Space Museum's early scripts emphasized what was missing in them—most notably, a vivid sense of the fanaticism, ferocity, and atrocious war conduct of the Japanese enemy. This was a fair criticism. Using the same criteria, it also is fair to ask what the heroic American narrative of the end of the war neglects.

At the simplest level, the popular triumphal narrative tends to neglect events and developments that are deemed important in the scholarly literature on the bombs. The entry of the Soviet Union into the war against Japan on August 8, two days after the bombing of Hiroshima, for example, tends to be downplayed or entirely ignored—and with it the fact that the American leadership had solicited the Soviet entry from an early date, knew it was imminent, and knew the Japanese were terrified by the prospect. Why the haste to drop the bombs before the effect of the Soviet entry could be gauged?

The nuclear devastation of Nagasaki on August 9 is similarly marginalized in the orthodox narrative. What are we to make of this second bomb? Why was it dropped before Japan's high command had a chance to assess Hiroshima and the

Soviet entry? How should we respond to the position taken by some Japanese—namely, that the bombing of Hiroshima may have been necessary to crack the no-surrender policy of the militarists, but the bombing of Nagasaki was plainly and simply a war crime . . .

Shortly after the end of the war, United States intelligence experts themselves publicly concluded that Japan was already at the end of its tether when the bombs were dropped. A famous report by the United States Strategic Bombing Survey, issued in 1946, concluded that the material and psychological situation was such that Japan "certainly" would have been forced to capitulate by the end of 1945, and "in all probability" prior to November 1, "even if the atomic bombs had not been dropped, even if Russia had not entered the war, and even if no invasion had been planned or contemplated." This was an ex post facto observation, of course, but it raised (and still raises) pertinent questions about the nature and shortcoming of wartime Allied intelligence evaluations of the enemy.

It also became known after Japan's surrender that alternatives to using the bombs on civilian targets had been broached in American official circles. Navy planners believed that Japan could be brought to its knees by intensified economic strangulation (the country's merchant marine and most of its navy had been sunk by 1945). Within the Manhattan Project, the possibility of dropping the bomb on a noncombat "demonstration" target, with Japanese observers present, had been broached but rejected. Conservative officials such as Acting Secretary of State Joseph Grew, the former ambassador to Japan, argued that the Japanese could be persuaded to surrender if the United States abandoned its policy of "unconditional surrender" and guaranteed the future existence of the emperor system. Through their code-breaking operations, the Americans also were aware that, beginning in mid-June, the Japanese had made extremely vague overtures to the Soviet Union concerning negotiating an end to the war.

These developments complicate the simple story line of the heroic narrative. Greater complication, however, arises from the fact that declassification of the archival record has made historians aware of how many different considerations officials in Washington had in mind when they formulated nuclear policy in the summer of 1945. No one denies that these policy makers desired to hasten the war's end and to save American lives, but no serious historian regards those as the sole considerations driving the use of the bombs on Japanese cities.

Although the initial Anglo-American commitment to build nuclear weapons was motivated by fear that Nazi Germany might be engaged in such a project, it is now known that by 1943—long before it became clear that the Germans were not attempting to make an atomic bomb, before Germany's collapse was imminent, before the Manhattan Project was sure of success, and before the lethal Allied military advance on Japan was clearly underway—United States planners had identified Japan as the prime target for such a weapon. Pragmatic considerations may have accounted for this shift of targets, but the change was nonetheless a profound one. The original rationale for moving to an entirely new order of destructive weaponry had evaporated, and the weaponry itself had begun to create its own rationale.

Sheer visceral hatred abetted this early targeting of Japan for nuclear destruction. Although critics of the Smithsonian's original script took umbrage at a passing statement that called attention to the element of vengeance in the American haste to use the bombs, few historians (or honest participants) would discount this. "Remember Pearl Harbor—Keep 'em Dying" was a popular military slogan from the outset of the war, and among commentators and war correspondents at the time, it was a commonplace that the Japanese were vastly more despised than the Germans. As we know all too well from our vantage place fifty years later, race and ethnicity are hardly negligible factors in the killing game.

Apart from plain military and sociopsychological dynamics, the development and deployment of the bombs also became driven by almost irresistible technological and scientific imperatives. J. Robert Oppenheimer, the charismatic head of the Manhattan Project, confided that after Germany's surrender on May 8, 1945, he and his scientific colleagues intensified their efforts out of concern that the war might end before they could finish—a striking confession, but not atypical. Almost to a man, scientists who had joined the project because of their alarm that Germany might develop a nuclear weapon stayed with it after Germany was out of the war. In the evocative phrase of the scientific community, the project was "technically sweet."

Other political imperatives largely extraneous to the war against Japan also helped drive the decision to use the bombs. Documents declassified since the 1960s make unmistakably clear that from the spring of 1945, top-level United States policy makers saw the bomb as a valuable card to play against Joseph Stalin and the Soviet Union—one that would, they hoped, dissuade the Soviet Union from pursuing its ambitions in Eastern Europe and elsewhere. . . .

. . . In Japan, as might be expected, popular memory of the atomic bombs tends to begin where the American narrative leaves off. In the heroic narrative, one rides with the crew of the *Enola Gay*, cuts away from the scene the moment the Little Boy bomb is released, gazes back from a great distance (over eleven miles) at a towering, iridescent mushroom cloud. If by chance one does glance beneath the cloud, it is the bomb's awesome physical destructiveness that usually is emphasized. Rubble everywhere. A silent, shattered cityscape. In this regard, the heroic narrative differs little from a Hollywood script.

By contrast, conventional Japanese accounts begin with the solitary bomber and its two escort planes in the azure sky above Hiroshima, with the blinding flash (*pika*) and tremendous blast (*don*) of the nuclear explosion, with the great pillar of smoke— and then move directly to ground zero. They dwell with excruciating detail on the great and macabre human suffering the new weapon caused, which continues to the present day for some survivors.

This Japanese perception of the significance of Hiroshima and Nagasaki can become maudlin and nationalistic. The nuclear destruction of the two cities is easily turned into a "victimization" narrative, in which the bombs fall from the heavens without historical context—as if the war began on August 6, 1945, and innocent Japan bore the cross of bearing witness to the horrendous birth of the nuclear age. In this subjective narrative, the bombs become the symbolic stigmata of unique Japanese suffering.

It is virtually a mantra in the United States media that what the Japanese really suffer from is historical amnesia. They cannot honestly confront their World War II past, it is said, and there are indeed numerous concrete illustrations of this beyond fixation on the misery caused by the atomic bombs. These range from sanitized textbooks to virtually routinized public denials of Japanese aggression and atrocity by conservative politicians (usually associated with the Liberal Democratic party, the United States government's longtime protégé) to the government's failure, until very recently, to offer an unequivocal apology to Asian and Allied victims of imperial Japan's wartime conduct.

In actuality, however, popular Japanese discourse concerning both war responsibility and the experience of the atomic bomb is more diversified than usually is appreciated outside Japan. Since the early 1970s, when Japan belatedly established relations with the People's Republic of China, the Japanese media have devoted conspicuous attention not only to exposing Japanese war crimes in Asia but also to wrestling with the complex idea that victims (*bigaisha*) can simultaneously be victimizers (*kagaisha*).

This Japanese sense of contradictory identity is not to be confused with the more simplistic notion of righteous retribution that critics of Japan commonly endorse—the notion that the Japanese reaped what they sowed; that having tried to flourish by the sword, they deservedly perished by it. Rather, it is a more complex perception that innocence, guilt, and responsibility may coexist at both individual and collective levels. A well-known series, *Atomic Bomb Panels (Genbaku no Zu)*, painted collaboratively by the married artists Iri Maruki and Toshi Maruki, provides a concrete illustration. After producing twelve stunning large renderings of Japanese nuclear bomb victims between 1950 and 1969, the Marukis took as their next subject the torture and murder of Caucasian prisoners of war by enraged survivors of the destruction of Hiroshima. They followed this with a stark painting depicting the piled-up corpses of Korean atomic bomb victims, being pecked at by ravens. . . .

Other Japanese have introduced other moral considerations in attempting to come to grips with the meaning of Hiroshima and Nagasaki. Some see the bombs as a plain atrocity—an American war crime, as it were, that cancels out, or at least mitigates, the enormity of Japan's own wartime transgressions. More typically, however—and this was true even in the immediate aftermath of the bombings—anti-American sentiment per se is surprisingly muted. The focus instead has been on using the bomb experience to bring an antinuclear message to the world. As Professor Rinjirō Sodei has reminded us, Kenzaburō Ōe, the 1994 Nobel laureate in literature, emerged as a spokesman for this position in influential essays written in the early 1960s. In Ōe's rendering, the *hibakusha* were "moralists" because they had experienced "the cruelest days in human history" and never lost "the vision of a nation which will do its best to materialize a world without any nuclear weapons."

Moral reflections of this sort—by Japanese or by critics of the use of the bombs in general—usually are given short shrift by American upholders of the heroic narrative. In their view, war is hell, the Japanese brought the terrible denouement of the bombs upon themselves, and the only morality worth emphasizing is the moral superiority of the Allied cause in World War II. Indeed, one of the formulaic terms that emerged among critics of the Air and Space Museum's original plans (alongside the "merciful" nature of the use of the bombs) labeled the nuclear destruction of the two Japanese cities "morally unambiguous."

It was not, and it may well be that the most enduring legacy of the Smithsonian controversy will be its graphic exposure of the moral ambiguity of the use of the bombs—and of Allied strategic bombing policy more generally. Here is where the triumphal story line gives way to a tragic narrative. The "good war" against Axis aggression and atrocity was brought to an end by a policy that the United States, Great Britain, and the League of Nations all had condemned only a few years previous, when first practiced by Japan and Germany, as "barbarous" and "in violation of those standards of humane conduct which have been developed as an essential part of modern civilization." That policy was the identification of civilian men, women, and children as legitimate targets of aerial bombardment. The United States, President Franklin D. Roosevelt typically declared in 1940, could be proud that it "consistently has taken the lead in urging that this inhuman practice be prohibited." Five years later, well before Hiroshima and Nagasaki, this inhuman practice was standard United States operating procedure.

The proposed Smithsonian exhibition threatened to expose this moral ambiguity in the most vivid manner imaginable, by literally visualizing ground zero; and here, I submit, many proponents of the heroic narrative confronted an unanticipated and unexpectedly formidable challenge. For the triumphal story they cherished and the great icon that represented it—the huge, gleaming, refurbished *Enola Gay* Superfortress itself—were overwhelmed by humble artifacts from the ashes of Hiroshima and Nagasaki. It was not so much the numbers of photographs and artifacts that the curators planned to include in the room on "Ground Zero," unit 4 of the planned exhibition, that undermined the heroic narrative, although this was fiercely argued. Rather, it was the intimate nature of these latter items.

Nothing brought this to life more succinctly than the juxtaposition of the Superfortress and the lunch box.

Among artifacts the Smithsonian's curators proposed bringing to Washington from the Peace Memorial Museum in Hiroshima was a seventh-grade schoolgirl's charred lunch box, containing carbonized rice and peas, that had been recovered from the ashes. The girl herself had disappeared. In the Japanese milieu, this is a typical, intensely human atomic bomb icon; and to American visitors to an exhibition, it would be intensely human too. This pathetic artifact (and other items like it) obsessed and alarmed critics of the proposed exhibition, and for obvious reasons: for the little lunch box far outweighed the glistening Superfortress in the preceding room. It would linger longer in most visitors' memories. Inevitably, it would force them to try imagining an incinerated child. Museum visitors who could gaze on this plain, intimate item and still maintain that the use of the bombs was "morally unambiguous" would be a distinct minority.

This sense of the tragedy of the war, even of the "good war" against an atrocious Axis enemy, became lost in the polemics that engulfed the Smithsonian. Yet it is not an original perception, certainly not new to the more civilized discourse on the bombs that has taken place in previous years. Indeed, in oblique ways even President Harry S Truman, a hero of the triumphal narrative, showed himself sensitive to the tragic dimensions of his decision to use the bombs. The day after Nagasaki was bombed, he expressed qualms about killing "all those kids."

CHAPTER 28

ISSUES OF CULTURAL IDENTITY

Africa and Latin America

This chapter focuses on efforts by intellectuals to define the position of their cultures—one Nigerian, one Mexican—in a period of rapid cultural change. Both areas had witnessed important cultural impositions by other societies, including Western Europe and the United States. Both, however, retained prior cultural traditions and an active desire to assert a distinctive identity.

The twentieth century was a period of major cultural change, almost literally worldwide. No culture retained all of the key assumptions and values that had predominated in 1900. Yet the patterns of change were complex. In a number of societies, the strength of traditional religion weakened as it faced competition from new beliefs such as nationalism, consumer materialism, or Marxism. But in certain cases new religious enthusiasms spread. Thus, in sub-Saharan Africa there were many conversions to Islam and Christianity; where 80 percent of the population was committed to some form of polytheism in 1900, only 20 percent retained pure polytheistic beliefs by the 1990s; 40 percent were now Muslim, 40 percent Christian. Latin America, converted earlier to Catholicism (though often in combination with older American Indian or African beliefs), saw a wave of enthusiasm for fundamentalist Protestantism toward the end of the twentieth century. Several societies, finally, including Hindu-dominated India and the Islamic Middle East, experienced a surge of religious revival from the 1970s onward. Cultural change was the order of the day, but the overall directions were far from clear.

One issue loomed large, though it was handled differently depending on current beliefs and past traditions: the influence of Western culture was a formidable force for change. From the West many societies incorporated new political beliefs including aspects of representative democracy and, of course, nationalism (see chapter 25). But the most important pressures from the West involved the power of modern science and the seductions of material acquisition and individual advancement.

Latin America and Africa faced particular pressures from outside cultural forces. Many Latin Americans had long looked to Western Europe for cultural models, beginning with Catholicism. Africa had more recently undergone Western imperialism, leading to new systems of education, missionary activity, and the general force of consumerism. Neither society was culturally Western, because of the diverse cultural groups that remained active and because of powerful prior traditions; yet neither could easily rely on traditional values to define personal beliefs or larger identities.

Not surprisingly, intellectuals in twentieth-century Africa and Latin America worried extensively about identity, particularly in relationship to Europe and the United States. African writers, usually educated in Western schools and writing in English or French, tried to deal with the need for a definable culture that would be something more than derivative. Latin American thinkers, with a longer tradition of encountering Western influence but equally preoccupied with defining values that were both distinctive and appropriate to the modern world, used history and comparison to try to define the flavor of their cultures.

This chapter features selections from two novels by the leading Nigerian novelist, Chinua Achebe, where he discusses successive phases of Western influence on Africa, first Christian, then urban-consumer. Writing from the 1950s onward, Achebe was fascinated by the process of change, which he felt undermined a coherent traditional culture but brought some undeniable benefits. The titles of his novels, *Things Fall Apart* and *No Longer at Ease,* suggest the confusions he believed change had created, as Africans renounced older belief patterns without fully clear or valid substitutes. Achebe's characterizations should be considered along with African nationalist views (chapter 25) and the views of African women (chapter 29), to widen the picture of African culture in a century of varied change.

A second set of selections comes from an essay collection by the prize-winning Mexican novelist and essayist, Octtavio Paz, written initially in the 1950s and supplemented in a 1970s edition. Paz attempts to define essential features of Mexican culture, while comparing it with what he sees as the culture of the United States, Mexico's powerful neighbor, and the more general forces of modern economic life. His impressions of cultural change differ from those of Achebe, but he grapples with some of the same issues of distinctive identity.

The passages below flow from the pens of intellectuals. They do not necessarily represent popular cultural beliefs, though they try to fathom popular values. Interpreting the significance of the passages has to involve some thinking about the role of intellectuals in modern life, in civilizations generally, and in Africa and Latin America in particular. Are the concerns of intellectuals particularly significant or revealing?

Questions

1. What forces of change does Achebe deal with in his successive novelistic treatments of Nigeria? How do the shifts under Christian missionary influence,

around 1900, compare with those of urban Nigeria in the 1920s, still under British rule?

2. What kinds of people were most open to Western-inspired cultures? What kinds resisted most firmly? Does Achebe believe that a coherent new culture emerged?

3. Does Achebe believe that it would be better for Africa if traditional values could be restored?

4. Why does Paz argue that Mexicans seek a certain kind of solitude? How does he define the major strengths of Mexican culture?

5. Does Paz believe that Mexican culture can accommodate to modern economic and political life? On what basis does he criticize Western values?

6. Do Paz and Achebe define Western values in similar ways?

7. What kinds of history have shaped Mexico, according to Paz? Does he have the same view of historical disruptions that Achebe highlights? Is his sense of the problem of modern identity the same?

8. Which author, Paz or Achebe, is more hostile to Western values? Which believes that Western values are more threatening to established cultural traditions?

9. How does Paz's characterization of modern worker culture, in its relationship to prior Mexican values, compare with Achebe's description of urban standards in relation to earlier village beliefs?

For Further Discussion

1. Is Achebe an African nationalist, by the standards suggested by leaders such as Jomo Kenyatta (see chapter 25)? How might Mexican nationalists disagree with Paz?

2. Did intellectuals such as Achebe and Paz represent widespread popular concerns in their respective societies? Did their views relate at all to the concerns expressed by African and Mexican women (see chapter 29)?

3. Why were many twentieth-century African and Latin American intellectuals particularly preoccupied with issues of cultural identity?

4. Will Latin American and African cultures become increasingly westernized in the next few decades (and how do you define cultural westernization)?

NIGERIA: CHINUA ACHEBE

Chinua Achebe, born in 1930, wrote a series of novels on the impact of the West on his native Nigeria, titling the first one *Things Fall Apart* (1958). This novel was set in the Ibo section of Nigeria around 1900, when Western missionary activity was increasing under the protection of British colonial rule. The passage describes the various reasons different Africans were drawn to Christianity; it also tells of the resistance to Christianity and the costs of accepting it, in terms of cultural identity. The selection ends with an account of a resistance meeting, centered around the strong traditionalist figure of Okonkwo (whose son had converted) and the arrival and death of a messenger sent by the English administration to prevent disorder. Achebe is fascinated by the divisions among Africans in response to Western values and colonial controls.

The second selection comes from Achebe's novel *No Longer at Ease;* one of the characters is a descendant of the same Okonkwo family, from the same village, who had moved to Lagos (Nigeria's capital) in the 1920s. Here the impact of Western-style urban culture is explored, as it further jeopardized traditional values and behaviors. Urbanization was beginning to accelerate in Africa at this time, and it inevitably challenged village values. Obi Okonkwo was the first village member to have received higher education in British-run schools, and he later obtained a civil-service job. Achebe describes the cultural attractions and shocks that a consumer culture provided and the ways it affected Obi Okonkwo's response to family ties. Cultural challenge, along with political and economic upheavals, clearly marked the twentieth century as a major watershed in African history.

• • •

THINGS FALL APART

The missionaries spent their first four or five nights in the marketplace, and went into the village in the morning to preach the gospel. They asked who the king of the village was, but the villagers told them that there was no king. "We have men of high title and the chief priests and the elders," they said.

It was not very easy getting the men of high title and the elders together after the excitement of the first day. But the missionaries persevered, and in the end they were received by the rulers of Mbanta. They asked for a plot of land to build their church.

Every clan and village had its "evil forest." In it were buried all those who died of the really evil diseases, like leprosy and smallpox. It was also the dumping ground for the potent fetishes of great medicine men when they died. An "evil forest" was, therefore, alive with sinister forces and powers of darkness. It was such a forest that the rulers of Mbanta gave to the missionaries. They did not really want them in their clan, and so they made them that offer which nobody in his right sense would accept.

"They want a piece of land to build their shrine," said Uchendu to his peers

From Chinua Achebe, *Things Fall Apart* (London: William Heinemann, 1959), 138–41, 162, 163, 166–67, 186–88. Copyright © 1959 by Chinua Achebe. Reprinted by permission of William Heinemann Limited.

when they consulted among themselves. "We shall give them a piece of land." He paused, and there was a murmur of surprise and disagreement. "Let us give them a portion of the Evil Forest. They boast about victory over death. Let us give them a real battlefield in which to show their victory." They laughed and agreed, and sent for the missionaries, whom they had asked to leave them for a while so that they might "whisper together." They offered them as much as the Evil Forest as they cared to take. And to their greatest amazement the missionaries thanked them and burst into song.

"They do not understand," said some of the elders. "But they will understand when they go to their plot of land tomorrow morning." And they dispersed.

The next morning the crazy men actually began to clear a part of the forest and to build their house. The inhabitants of Mbanta expected them all to be dead within four days. The first day passed and the second and third and fourth, and none of them died. Everyone was puzzled. And then it became known that the white man's fetish had unbelievable power. It was said that he wore glasses on his eyes so that he could see and talk to evil spirits. Not long after, he won his first three converts.

Although Nwoye had been attacted to the new faith from the very first day, he kept it secret. He dared not go too near the missionaries for fear of his father. But whenever they came to preach in the open marketplace or the village playground, Nwoye was there. And he was already beginning to know some of the simple stories they told.

"We have now built a church," said Mr. Kiaga, the interpreter, who was now in charge of the infant congregation. The white man had gone back to Umuofia, where he built his headquarters and from where he paid regular visits to Mr. Kiaga's congregation at Mbanta.

"We have now built a church," said Mr. Kiaga, "and we want you all to come in every seventh day to worship the true God."

On the following Sunday, Nwoye passed and repassed the little red-earth and thatch building without summoning enough courage to enter. He heard the voice of singing and although it came from a handful of men it was loud and confident. Their church stood on a circular clearing that looked like the open mouth of the Evil Forest. Was it waiting to snap its teeth together? After passing and re-passing by the church, Nwoye returned home.

It was well known among the people of Mbanta that their gods and ancestors were sometimes long-suffering and would deliberately allow a man to go on defying them. But even in such cases they set their limit at seven market weeks or twenty-eight days. Beyond that limit no man was suffered to go. And so excitement mounted in the village as the seventh week approached since the impudent mission-aries built their church in the Evil Forest. The villagers were so certain about the doom that awaited these men that one or two converts thought it wise to suspend their allegiance to the new faith.

At last the day came by which all the missionaries should have died. But they were still alive, building a new red-earth and thatch house for their teacher, Mr. Kiaga. That week they won a handful more converts. And for the first time they had a woman. Her name was Nneka, the wife of Amadi, who was a prosperous farmer. She was very heavy with child.

Nneka had had four previous pregnancies and childbirths. But each time she had borne twins, and they had been immediately thrown away. Her husband and his family were already becoming highly critical of such a woman and were not unduly perturbed when they found she had fled to join the Christians. It was a good riddance. . . .

"Does the white man understand our custom about land?"

"How can he when he does not even speak our tongue? But he says that our customs are bad; and our own brothers who have taken up his religion also say that our customs are bad. How do you think we can fight when our own brothers have turned against us? The white man is very clever. He came quietly and peaceably with his religion. We were amused at his foolishness and allowed him to stay. Now he has won our brothers, and our clan can no longer act like one. He has put a knife on the things that held us together and we have fallen apart." . . .

There were many men and women in Umuofia who did not feel as strongly as Okonkwo about the new dispensation. The white man had indeed brought a lunatic religion, but he had also built a trading store and for the first time palm-oil and kernel became things of great price, and much money flowed into Umuofia. . . .

Mr. Brown [the missionary to the Ibo village] learned a good deal about the religion of the clan and he came to the conclusion that a frontal attack on it would not succeed. And so he built a school and a little hospital in Umuofia. He went from family to family begging people to send their children to his school. But at first they only sent their slaves or sometimes their lazy children. Mr. Brown begged and argued and prophesied. He said that the leaders of the land in the future would be men and women who had learned to read and write. If Umuofia failed to send her children to the school, strangers would come from other places to rule them. They could already see that happening in the Native Court, where the D.C. was surrounded by strangers who spoke his tongue. Most of these strangers came from the distant town of Umuru on the bank of the Great River where the white man first went.

In the end Mr. Brown's arguments began to have an effect. More people came to learn in his school, and he encouraged them with gifts of singlets and towels. They were not all young, these people who came to learn. Some of them were thirty years old or more. They worked on their farms in the morning and went to school in the afternoon. And it was not long before the people began to say that the white man's medicine was quick in working. Mr. Brown's school produced quick results. A few months in it were enough to make one a court messenger or even a court clerk. Those who stayed longer became teachers; and from Umuofia laborers went forth into the Lord's vineyard. New churches were established in the surrounding villages and a few schools with them. From the very beginning religion and education went hand in hand. . . .

"You all know why we are here, when we ought to be building our barns or mending our huts, when we should be putting our compounds in order. My father used to say to me: 'Whenever you see a toad jumping in broad daylight, then know that something is after its life.' When I saw you all pouring into this meeting from all the quarters of our clan so early in the morning, I knew that something was after our life." He paused for a brief moment and then began again:

"All our gods are weeping. Idemili is weeping, Ogwugwu is weeping, Agbala is weeping, and all the others. Our dead fathers are weeping because of the shameful sacrilege they are suffering and the abomination we have all seen with our eyes." He stopped again to steady his trembling voice.

"This is a great gathering. No clan can boast of greater numbers or greater valor. But are we all here? I ask you: Are all the sons of Umuofia with us here?" A deep murmur swept through the crowd.

"They are not," he said. "They have broken the clan and gone their several ways. We who are here this morning have remained true to our fathers, but our brothers have deserted us and joined a stranger to soil their fatherland. If we fight the stranger we shall hit our brothers and perhaps shed the blood of a clansman. But we must do it. Our fathers never dreamed of such a thing, they never killed their brothers. But a white man never came to them. So we must do what our fathers would never have done. Eneke the bird was asked why he was always on the wing and he replied: 'Men have learned to shoot without missing their mark and I have learned to fly without perching on a twig.' We must root out this evil. And if our brothers take the side of evil we must root them out too. And we must do it *now*. We must bale this water now that it is only ankle-deep. . . ."

At this point there was a sudden stir in the crowd and every eye was turned in one direction. There was a sharp bend in the road that led from the marketplace to the white man's court, and to the stream beyond it. And so no one had seen the approach of the five court messengers until they had come round the bend, a few paces from the edge of the crowd. Okonkwo was sitting at the edge. . . .

"What do you want here?"

"The white man whose power you know too well has ordered this meeting to stop."

In a flash Okonkwo drew his machete. The messenger crouched to avoid the blow. It was useless. Okonkwo's machete descended twice and the man's head lay beside his uniformed body.

The waiting backcloth jumped into tumultuous life and the meeting was stopped. Okonkwo stood looking at the dead man. He knew that Umuofia would not go to war. He knew because they had let the other messengers escape. They had broken into tumult instead of action. He discerned fright in that tumult. He heard voices asking: "Why did he do it?"

He wiped his machete on the sand and went away.

NO LONGER AT EASE

As a boy in the village of Umuofia he had heard his first stories about Lagos from a soldier home on leave from the war. Those soldiers were heroes who had seen the great world. They spoke of Abyssinia, Egypt, Palestine, Burma and so on. Some of them had been village ne'er-do-wells, but now they were heroes. They had bags and bags of money, and the villagers sat at their feet to listen to their stories. One of them went regularly to a market in the neighboring village and helped himself to whatever he liked. He went in full uniform, breaking the earth with his boots, and no one dared touch him. It was said that if you touched a soldier, Government would deal with you. Besides, soldiers were as strong as lions because of the injections they were given in the army. It was from one of these soldiers that Obi had his first picture of Lagos.

"There is no darkness there," he told his admiring listeners, "because at night the electric shines like the sun, and people are always walking about, that is, those who want to walk. If you don't want to walk you only have to wave your hand and a pleasure car stops for you." His audience made sounds of wonderment. Then by way of digression he said: "If you see a white man, take off your hat for him. The only thing he cannot do is mold a human being."

For many years afterwards, Lagos was always associated with electric lights and motorcars in Obi's mind. Even after he had at last visited the city and spent a few days there before flying to the United Kingdom his views did not change very much. Of course, he did not really see much of Lagos then. His mind was, as it were, on higher things. He spent the few days with his "countryman," Joseph Okeke, a clerk in the Survey Department. Obi and Joseph had been classmates at the Umuofia C.M.S. Central School. But Joseph had not gone on to a secondary school because he was too old and his parents were poor. He had joined the Education Corps of the 82nd Division and, when the war ended, the clerical service of the Nigerian Government.

Joseph was at Lagos Motor Park to meet his lucky friend who was passing through Lagos to the United Kingdom. He took him to his lodgings in Obalende. It was only one room. A curtain of light-blue cloth ran the full breadth of the room separating the Holy of Holies (as he called his double spring bed) from the sitting area. His cooking utensils, boxes, and other personal effects were hidden away under the Holy of Holies. The sitting area was taken up with two armchairs, a settee (otherwise called "me and my girl"), and a round table on which he displayed his photo album. At night, his houseboy moved away the round table and spread his mat on the floor.

Joseph had so much to tell Obi on his first night in Lagos that it was past three when they slept. He told him about the cinema and the dance halls and about political meetings.

"Dancing is very important nowadays. No girl will look at you if you can't dance. I first met Joy at the dancing school." "Who is Joy?" asked Obi, who was fascinated by what he was learning of this strange and sinful new world. "She was my girl friend for—let's see . . ."—he counted off his fingers—". . . March, April, May, June, July—for five months. She made these pillowcases for me."

Obi raised himself instinctively to look at the pillow he was lying on. He had taken particular notice of it earlier in the day. It had the strange word *osculate* sewn on it, each letter in a different color.

"She was a nice girl but sometimes very foolish. Sometimes, though, I wish we hadn't broken up. She was simply mad about me; and she was a virgin when I met her, which is very rare here."

Joseph talked and talked and finally became less and less coherent. Then without any pause at all his talk was transformed into a deep snore, which continued until the morning.

The very next day Obi found himself taking a compulsory walk down Lewis Street. Joseph had brought a woman home and it was quite clear that Obi's presence in the room was not desirable; so he went out to have a look round. The girl was one of Joseph's new finds, as he told him later. She was dark and tall with an enormous pneumatic bosom under a tight-fitting red and yellow dress. Her lips and long fingernails were a brilliant red, and her eyebrows were fine black lines. She looked not unlike those wooden masks made in Ikot Ekpene. Altogether she left a nasty taste in Obi's mouth, like the multicolored word *osculate* on the pillowcase. . . .

On top of it all came his mother's death. He sent all he could find for her funeral, but it was already being said to his eternal shame that a woman who had borne so many children, one of whom was in a European post, deserved a better funeral than she got. One Umuofia man who had been on leave at home when she died brought the news to Lagos to the meeting of the Umuofia Progressive Union.

"It was a thing of shame," he said. Someone else wanted to know, by the way, why that beast (meaning Obi) had not obtained permission to go home. "That is what Lagos can do to a young man. He runs after sweet things, dances breast to breast with women and forgets his home and his people. Do you know what medicine that *osu* woman may have put into his soup to turn his eyes and ears away from his people?" . . .

"Everything you have said is true. But there is one thing I want you to learn. Whatever happens in this world has a meaning. As our people say: 'Wherever something stands, another thing stands beside it.' You see this thing called blood. There is nothing like it. That is why when you plant a yam it produces another yam, and if you plant an orange it bears oranges. I have seen many things in my life, but I have never yet seen a banana tree yield a coco yam. Why do I say this? You young men here, I want you to listen because it is from listening to old men that you learn wisdom. I know that when I return to Umuofia I cannot claim to be an old man. But here in this Lagos I am an old man to the rest of you." He paused for effect. "This boy that we are all talking about, what has he done? He was told that his mother died and he did not care. It is a strange and surprising thing."

MEXICO: OCTAVIO PAZ

Octavio Paz was born in 1914 in Mexico City. He enjoyed an outstanding career in poetry and criticism, founding a number of literary reviews. He served in the Mexican diplomatic corps, though he often protested government repression of political dissent. Paz frequently taught in the United States and wrote in English as well as Spanish; he also developed extensive contacts with intellectual circles in Europe. *Labyrinth of Solitude,* his most famous single work (published in 1962), is an exploration of Mexican character as it was shaped historically and as it compares to the characteristics of other nations in Latin America and the West. Paz won the Nobel Prize in literature in 1990. He died in 1998.

• • •

THE LABYRINTH OF SOLITUDE

Our [Mexican] sense of inferiority—real or imagined—might be explained at least partly by the reserve with which the Mexican faces other people and the unpredictable violence with which his repressed emotions break through his mask of impassivity. But his solitude is vaster and profounder than his sense of inferiority. It is impossible to equate these two attitudes: when you sense that you are alone, it does not mean that you feel inferior, but rather that you feel you are different. Also, a sense of inferiority may sometimes be an illusion, but solitude is a hard fact. We are truly different. And we are truly alone. . . .

Man is alone everywhere. But the solitude of the Mexican, under the great stone night of the high plateau that is still inhabited by insatiable gods, is very different

From Octavio Paz, *The Labyrinth of Solitude, and Other Essays,* trans. Lysander Kemp, Yara Milos, and R. P. Belash (New York: Grove Press, 1985), 19, 20, 29–30, 37, 66–67, 362, 372–73, 374. Reprinted by permission of the publisher.

from that of the North American, who wanders in an abstract world of machines, fellow citizens and moral precepts. In the Valley of Mexico man feels himself suspended between heaven and earth, and he oscillates between contrary powers and forces, and petrified eyes, and devouring mouths. Reality—that is, the world that surrounds us—exists by itself here, has a life of its own, and was not invented by man as it was in the United States. The Mexican feels himself to have been torn from the womb of this reality, which is both creative and destructive, both Mother and Tomb. He has forgotten the word that ties him to all those forces through which life manifests itself. Therefore he shouts or keeps silent, stabs or prays, or falls asleep for a hundred years.

The history of Mexico is the history of a man seeking his parentage, his origins. He has been influenced at one time or another by France, Spain, the United States and the militant indigenists of his own country, and he crosses history like a jade comet, now and then giving off flashes of lightning. What is he pursuing in his eccentric course? He wants to go back beyond the catastrophe he suffered: he wants to be a sun again, to return to the center of that life from which he was separated one day. (Was that day the Conquest? Independence?) Our solitude has the same roots as religious feelings. It is a form of orphanhood, an obscure awareness that we have been torn from the All, and an ardent search: a flight and a return, an effort to re-establish the bonds that unite us with the universe. . . .

. . . The Mexican is always remote, from the world and from other people. And also from himself.

The speech of our people reflects the extent to which we protect ourselves from the outside world: the ideal of manliness is never to "crack," never to back down. Those who "open themselves up" are cowards. Unlike other people, we believe that opening oneself up is a weakness or a betrayal. The Mexican can bend, can bow humbly, can even stoop, but he cannot back down, that is, he cannot allow the outside world to penetrate his privacy. The man who backs down is not to be trusted, is a traitor or a person of doubtful loyalty; he babbles secrets and is incapable of confronting a dangerous situation. Women are inferior beings because, in submitting, they open themselves up. Their inferiority is constitutional and resides in their sex, their submissiveness, which is a wound that never heals.

Hermeticism is one of the several recourses of our suspicion and distrust. It shows that we instinctively regard the world around us to be dangerous. This reaction is justifiable if one considers what our history has been and the kind of society we have created. The harshness and hostility of our environment and the hidden, indefinable threat that is always afloat in the air, oblige us to close ourselves in, like those plants that survive by storing up liquid within their spiny exteriors. . . .

. . . . The Mexican, heir to the great pre-Columbian religions based on nature, is a good deal more pagan than the Spaniard, and does not condemn the natural world. Sexual love is not tinged with grief and horror in Mexico as it is in Spain.

Instincts themselves are not dangerous; the danger lies in any personal, individual expression of them. . . . It is noteworthy that our images of the working class are not colored with similar feelings, even though the worker also lives apart from the center of society, physically as well as otherwise, in districts and special communities. When a contemporary novelist introduces a character who symbolizes health or destruction, fertility or death, he rarely chooses a worker, despite the fact that the worker represents the death of an old society and the birth of a new. . . .

The modern worker lacks individuality. The class is stronger than the individual and his personality dissolves in the generic. That is the first and gravest mutilation a man suffers when he transforms himself into an industrial wage earner. Capitalism deprives him of his human nature (this does not happen to the servant) by reducing him to an element in the work process, *i.e.,* to an object. And like any object in the business world, he can be bought and sold. Because of his social condition he quickly loses any concrete and human relationship to the world. The machines he operates are not his and neither are the things he produces. Actually he is not a worker at all, because he does not create individual works or is so occupied with one aspect of production that he is not conscious of those he does create. He is a laborer, which is an abstract noun designating a mere function rather than a specific job. . . .

. . . Not only the popular religion of Mexico but the Mexicans' entire life is steeped in Indian culture—the family, love, friendship, attitudes toward one's father and mother, popular legends, the forms of civility and life in common, the image of authority and political power, the vision of death and sex, work and festivity. Mexico is the most Spanish country in Latin America; at the same time it is the most Indian. Mesoamerican civilization died a violent death, but Mexico is Mexico thanks to the Indian presence. Though the language and religion, the political institutions and the culture of the country are Western, there is one aspect of Mexico that faces in another direction—the Indian direction. Mexico is a nation between two civilizations and two pasts.

Above and beyond success and failure, Mexico is still asking itself the question that has occurred to most clear-thinking Mexicans since the end of the eighteenth century: the question about modernization. In the nineteenth century, it was believed that to adopt the new democratic and liberal principles was enough. Today, after almost two centuries of setbacks, we have realized that countries change very slowly, and that if such changes are to be fruitful they must be in harmony with the past and the traditions of each nation. And so Mexico has to find its own road to modernity. Our past must not be an obstacle but a starting point. This is extremely difficult, given the nature of our traditions—difficult but not impossible. To avoid new disasters, we Mexicans must reconcile ourselves with our past: only in this way shall we succeed in finding a route to modernity. The search for our own model of modernization is a theme directly linked with another: today we know that modernity, both the capitalist and the pseudo-socialist versions of the totalitarian bureaucracies, is mortally wounded in its very core—the idea of continuous, unlimited progress. The nations that inspired our nineteenth-century liberals—England, France, and especially the United States—are doubting, vacillating, and cannot find their way. They have ceased to be universal examples. The Mexicans of the nineteenth century turned their eyes toward the great Western democracies; we have nowhere to turn ours. . . . The sickness of the West is moral rather than social and economic. . . . But the real, most profound discord lies in the soul. The future has become the realm of horror, and the present has turned into a desert. The liberal societies spin tirelessly, not forward but round and round. If they change, they are not transfigured. The hedonism of the West is the other face of desperation; its skepticism is not wisdom but renunciation; . . .

CHAPTER 29

WOMEN IN THE THIRD WORLD

This chapter deals with complex changes in the conditions of women in societies not yet fully industrialized, in the decades after World War II. For many women, a mixture of forces worked both to maintain and to alter traditional patterns. Influence from some internationally disseminated doctrines, not only feminism but also Communism, often pressed for improvements in status. But economic conditions frequently stagnated or even worsened. Legal rights might improve, at least on paper, but many cultures, sometimes reinforced by religious revivals, pressed for strong differentiation between men and women. Finally, conditions also varied by social level; what happened to the poorest classes differed from developments among middle-and upper-class women in the same society.

The focus is on several societies partly outside the industrial world—societies often called Third World. Third World is a term coined after World War II, initially to designate newly independent societies, not industrialized, that were not fully aligned either with the West or the Soviet bloc in the Cold War. Increasingly it came to mean more simply societies that had yet to industrialize fully, where average standards of living and health and educational levels were relatively low; most of the world's population currently lives in countries that, by these broad criteria, can be called Third World. Most people in Third World societies are still peasants or live in families that have moved to cities fairly recently, within the past two or three generations. Third World is a fairly loose category, however, and many analysts find it simplistic and misleading. It includes countries like Mexico that now have an urban majority, where well over half the population is literate, and where advancing industry has created a large middle class; as well as areas like much of sub-Saharan Africa, where population growth rates are higher, the urban percentage smaller though growing rapidly, and education and industry much less developed. The Third World category raises another set of issues for Western students and observers: the societies involved not only differ from each other, but also from the West—in ways that go beyond levels of economic development. They have distinctive traditions and values, which makes interpreting gender conditions very challenging: Western categories of evaluation may miss the mark.

The materials in this chapter are organized in two sets: first, conditions of poor women in Mexico and Kenya are studied, through interviews conducted by a Western anthropologist. Second, comments by educated, middle-class women in India and Nigeria provide another vantage point, in which Western priorities concerning women and non-Western traditions are challenged.

Conditions for poor women in Third World countries are alike in some ways, but there are important differences. The differences show why patriarchal civilizations in this category need to be compared, not simply lumped under a single heading. Women in Mexico and in Kenya, where the interview excerpts below were recorded, exist amid widespread poverty. Changes have in some ways increased the gap between them and the men they live with, or at least it seems that way to the women. This is an important point to consider, lest we think of our century as a time of inevitable women's progress, varying only in pace and extent. In some instances men have acquired greater familiarity with urban ways than women have and have gained new economic advantages in the process. In other cases men, themselves confused by change, seem to become rougher with women in compensation. In both Kenya and Mexico (and in other parts of the world) it is not easy to figure out what problems in the relations between men and women are simply part of the human condition and what problems result from recent social change. It is also important to remember that in Third World countries, as elsewhere, situations vary greatly by personality; abuse predominates in some families but not in others, where on the surface conditions seem fairly similar. And in both Kenya and Mexico, women have become aware of certain kinds of changes that might benefit them; the importance of education, either already acquired or hoped for, is an obvious case in point. Change, then, is a mixed quantity for many Third World women; an African great-grandmother, for example, notes that fewer babies die but says that as a result there is "more" death (by which she probably means that more people die as adults, since they survived infancy).

In both Kenya and Mexico, technically educated personnel, such as doctors and trained midwives, encounter rural women. The educated outsiders, whether male or female, bring suggestions for change but also important criticisms of rural culture. What impact would this approach have on the village women involved? How many solutions can "outsiders" provide?

Though the interviewer who spoke with various women in Kenya and in Mexico during the 1970s quite properly encouraged discussion of several similar topics—such as birth control, education, work and poverty, and treatment by men—and elicited a number of similar reactions and statements of problems, she also implicitly uncovered some important variations as well. Mexico and Kenya differ in many ways. Family customs differ, as references to polygamy suggest; Christian missionary work has had an impact in Kenya, but African culture is more varied religiously than that of Mexico. Although family relations can be an issue in both countries, Africa has been more affected by the departure (voluntary or forced) of men to seek work in the cities, leaving women back in the villages.

Women's cooperative efforts may as a result be distinctive in Kenya, even as their desire to restore traditional family security remains more intense. Women in both countries evince a mixture of customary and novel goals, but the combinations may differ.

An obvious comparison involves birth control. As a matter of fact, birth control advanced rapidly in Mexico by the 1960s, when a real demographic transition took place, with radically reduced birthrates. Africa has yet to experience this transition. Even so, African and Mexican women refer to similar tensions concerning their husbands and traditional values where birth control is concerned. Yet the levels being discussed and the specific goals involved are quite different. How is this distinction expressed? What causes might help account for it?

A series of short interviews by a skilled Western analyst provides only limited evidence about women's beliefs and conditions. Granting this, do you emerge with a sense of a common Third World female experience, or of a need to look at specific settings case by case in order to judge patterns of change and continuity among women? And in either case, how would you compare being a woman in late-twentieth-century Mexico or Kenya with being a woman in a country like the United States?

In the late twentieth century, important statements by women in a number of Third World societies began to challenge the common view that urged Western standards as the measurement of women's conditions. Scholars and journalists began to regard prior traditions as superior to Western ways, even though they did not measure up to criteria such as monogamy or individual rights. Defenders of this complex reaction to Western feminism were mainly middle-and upper-class. In the selections that follow, in the second set of documents, a Nigerian scholar, a university-educated woman whose father had been a chief and whose mother encouraged unusual education, writes about what she sees as Western misunderstandings of West African traditions. Another scholar, writing in a middle-class women's magazine in India (published in English), talks about a more specific set of issues surrounding marriage standards.

The two passages share a critique of assumptions about the superiority of Western feminist ideas. They do not oppose all change, though they differ on this point. They do argue that traditions should be maintained or revived to sustain a good life for women in their societies. Their views should be compared with the attitudes of the poor women whom Perdita Huston interviewed. What concerns do upper-class and village women share in contemporary Third World societies? Would they have the same appreciation of tradition? What kinds of class divisions, in terms of economic situation, customs, and educational level, make a difference in women's lives in late-twentieth-century societies?

Questions

1. What features of peasant life do educated personnel in Kenya and Mexico most criticize?

2. According to peasant women's own statements, what aspects of village life and expectations have been changing most rapidly for them? What aspects have changed least?

3. What kinds of traditional values do women continue to express, even amid change?

4. What are the main differences, according to interview evidence, between the situations and attitudes of Mexican and of African women? Are there differences in relations with men in the two societies?

5. What are the problems surrounding birth control as an issue in rural society? Were conditions in this regard significantly different in Africa and Mexico during the 1970s?

6. Why does Madhu Kishwar praise arranged marriages?

7. What Nigerian traditions does Ifi Amadiume identify as particularly hard for Western scholars to understand? What are her criteria for judging women's conditions?

8. Do Amadiume and Kishwar agree on some aspects of women's goals in the West that they find objectionable?

9. Do Amadiume and Kishwar agree on the directions of recent change? Which one seems to have more confidence that things are still going well for women?

10. Do Amadiume and Kishwar share any attitudes with village women in Third World societies? Which one suggests a clearer affiliation with upper-class status? Which one emphasizes recent changes that might harm lower-class women?

For Further Discussion

1. Judging by evidence from Mexico and Africa in the 1970s, have conditions for women on the whole been improving or deteriorating? Is there a similar process of "modernization" at work? How would a Western feminist judge the women's attitudes?

2. What are the advantages and limitations of interviewing as a source of evidence for contemporary history? Are interviewees likely to slant their remarks at all? What other evidence would help form a picture of women's views and conditions in late-twentieth-century Kenya and Mexico?

3. The evidence in Huston's interviews comes from the 1970s. How much change would you expect to have occurred, and in what directions, a quarter-century later? Would you expect the same kinds of change in Mexico and in Kenya?

4. Would Amadiume criticize Huston's approach as an example of Western bias about the Third World?
5. Why might upper-class Indian and African women differ about the directions of change in their societies in the twentieth century?
6. What is your evaluation of the relevance of Western feminist ideals to societies like India or Africa?

VILLAGE WOMEN

INTERVIEWS WITH MEXICAN PEASANT WOMEN IN THE 1970s

These interviews were conducted by an American anthropologist, Perdita Huston. Huston was trained in ethnographic interview techniques, though in several cases she had to rely on interpreters. She was also inspired by a feminist concern for women's issues, including cases of clear mistreatment. Sympathetic to her subjects, she was clearly interested in exploring cases in which traditional attitudes seemed to be holding back change. This helps account for her use of discussions with other, urban observers of village life, as well as with women themselves. The women who speak out here are from southern Mexico, many of them Indians. Their statements are supplemented by the views of a rural doctor.

• • •

Interview with a Zapotec Indian

Maria Luisa spoke to me about [Anna's] her sister's life:

"She is in the process of breaking up with her husband. They have four children, but they didn't get married until the third child was born. Then the priest said. 'If you don't get married. I'm not baptizing your children.'

"Anna's husband wants to live like the old men used to live—having women right under his thumb—not the way it is today. Even our family is against it. They say, 'He has such old-fashioned ideas.' The woman has to be in the house. She has to confess everything to him. She can't have a thought of her own. Even that's okay. You can be jealous. You can even be a tyrant. *But you have to do your share.* You have to bring in money. The reason the family is so down on him is not because he's a tyrant, but because he doesn't fulfill his part of the marriage. She has to go out and look for food while he's gallivanting around. That's what doesn't make sense. You know—rules are rules.

"Now he's beating her even more than before because his mother is constantly

From Perdita Huston, *Third World Women Speak Out* (New York: Praeger Publishers, 1979), 41–42, 78–79, 82–83.

filling his head with ideas. 'Anna doesn't cook good food,' she says—and things like that. He beats her up; she is black and blue on the thighs or on the back or wherever. He says he has the right to rule. You know, the male doesn't want to be made a fool of. He accuses other men of being weak. He says. 'I'm not like those men. I don't let women give orders in my house.'

"But Anna is a good wife. She works hard, and if he would let her out of the house, their family would have more money. She works hard in the field, but he doesn't even give her money for food. Granted, he doesn't really earn that much himself, but he *could*. He could take crops into town and sell them and bring back the money, but he doesn't. He feels she shouldn't have money. He works in the field, but he doesn't look for other work. So he gets very little. He doesn't want to sell much, and there is not enough money to feed the family, so Anna has to sell things or borrow five pesos here and there. Then he gets enraged and blames her for not managing. And this is where the mother-in-law comes in. The old woman thinks Anna can make do with even less. But if there's no money, you can't buy food. If there's no money, you can't buy tomatoes. And our new generation knows that children have to have their food."

"[Anna's] so nervous all the time; she needs a rest. But she's going to leave her husband and leave the children with him and take the baby. She wants to go someplace else. She's not going to go back to him. She said, 'I don't have to. I can't bear this. Who else would put up with him as long as I have?' " . . .

[On education, asked what she would have wanted to learn at school]: "I don't know *what* exactly, but it would have been something that would earn money. We are very backward here and we don't know anything. . . . the problem is that we don't know how to *earn money*."

Interviews at a Birth Control Clinic

"They say terrible things about women who want to [practice birth control]. Some say, 'The only reason you want birth control is so you can go with other men.' Once the radio said. 'Father of the family, if you want to give your children a good upbringing, take care of them well and remember that small families live better.' Well, my brother just laughed. You see, some people are very ignorant."

"The only thing I *don't* do is go to confession, because then I would have to confess that I take the pill, and the priest would say, 'Leave the church.' I could still go to mass, but he wouldn't give me holy communion if I told about the pill." . . .

"I went to school for a while, but the teacher didn't come to school very often, so we didn't learn much. I guess I taught myself to read.

"I have been married for four years. I have only these two children. The first is three, the other almost a year." . . .

"The main thing that makes the times different, I think, is the control women have over the number of children in a family. A family can be planned now; it can live a better life. Women have more facilities for everything because of this. I began to take contraceptives when this last child was eight months old. I take the pill.

"My husband wants a boy because these children are both girls; he doesn't know that I am taking the pill. He wants a boy and says that when I have one, then I can use contraceptives. I want to wait at least two years so that this little girl is older. Then I will try for the boy."

". . . My husband has a sister who is using a contraceptive method. She asked me if I was interested in using one, and I said 'no' because I didn't want her to tell my husband. He might find out that I already use them. I just want to wait a few years and rest. When I wanted the pills, I came here to the health center. I keep them in the kitchen. When I'm cooking dinner, I take a pill and he doesn't notice. Either that or I take one while he is sleeping. But all this is very dangerous, you know, because my husband went to school; he is smart. He knows about such things. One time he did find them and I was terribly frightened. I had hidden them in a closet, under some clothes. He found them and asked. 'What are these pills?' I just said that my baby daughter had found them and brought them into the house. I told him I took them away from her because she was going to eat them. My husband told me, 'You know, these pills are very dangerous because they are for not having children. If I find out that you are taking them, you will see what I will do to you!' He threatened to hit me. For me, family planning is very important because my husband does not earn big wages. For the moment, we just can't afford more than two children. . . .

"I told you we were very poor when I was a child. We were six children, and my father didn't earn much. That is why I want just two or three children. I don't want my children to grow up like me—without an education. I feel very ashamed and bad about not having any education. I want my children to go to school and learn many, many things. I don't want them to live by the rumors of the street. I want them to learn for themselves. I want them to be independent and proud of themselves."

Comment by a Male Doctor at a Rural Hospital

"The question of women going to a male doctor is a cultural problem. From childbirth on, a woman is accustomed to being treated by a midwife. If getting help means she is going to be in the care of a man, she will not want the help. A man would see her body and strange things inside her. . . . It is a problem for me, as a man, to treat women patients here."

"The major problems are malnutrition and infectious diseases. Both are derived from poverty. Ninety-five per cent of the population here has nutritional deficiencies. Anemia in women is extremely high. I don't really understand how they keep going."

INTERVIEWS WITH AFRICAN PEASANT WOMEN IN THE 1970S

In these selections, village women from Kenya provide most of the statements, discussing their goals in the context of changes and continuities they saw around them. Again, their statements can be compared with the judgments about rural life by Kenyan professionals such as a doctor and a social worker.

• • •

A Great-Grandmother

I don't really know my age, but I remember that I was married during the great war [World War I]. In those days we lived all right—happily. Things were quite different from what they are now. We got these clothes only recently. We used to wear something from banana fibers just to cover our lower parts. It was scratchy, but we were used to it. I think all the changes came when the churches came. We got our clothing, and then we said we should cover our bodies and go to school—maybe go to church.

"We had cows, goats, sheep, and hens. . . . Even the chickens didn't get sick in those days. These days, more people die than used to. We had no hospitals; we were just sick, and if you knew any medicines, any herbs, you used them. There were malaria, stomachaches, and backaches. But not many used to die. They lived to be very old men and women. When you heard so-and-so was dead, everyone used to go, because that was the only funeral in a long time.

"In those days, we also used to have old women who knew herbs and helped women in childbirth and with their babies' health. In the old days, even if you had ten children you could care for them. You were happy because you had many little girls and boys to be married, as well as many grandchildren. I had nine children; three died as babies. They had diarrhea and just died. I don't know why. Now children don't die as much any more because we have doctors and hospitals nearby." . . .

"What we need in this village is teachers to teach women handicrafts and sewing and agricultural skills. We have organized a women's group. I am one of the leaders. We are saving up for a building to meet in. All women are trying to earn money, and we want to have a building for our meetings. It will be called the 'adult education building'—with rooms for handicrafts, literacy, and other things.

From Perdita Huston, *Third World Women Speak Out* (New York: Praeger Publishers, 1979), 12–13, 42–43, 72–73, 79–80.

"We also want our children to be educated—so we can have good leaders to keep our country good. I think now it is best to have only four children—so you can take care of them.

"It is better to educate a girl than a boy, although one should educate both. Girls are better. They help a lot. See this house? My daughters built it for me. If you don't have any daughters, who will build for you? The boys will marry and take care of their wives—that's all. They don't care about mothers. For example, if my son gets married, the daughter-in-law will say, 'Let's take our mothers to live with us.' The son will say, 'No, we will just have our own family and do our own things.' So you are left alone. What do you do?". . . .

"These days there is no trust. Men have defeated us. They don't listen: they have big heads. Before, we mixed with each other—men and women. There were no differences between us. We trusted one another, but now men are not straight-forward. These are the changes taking place."

A Nineteen-Year-Old Student

"My mother has eleven children. She is my father's only wife. She works in the fields and grows the food we eat. She plants cabbage, spinach, and corn. She works very hard, but with so many children it is difficult to get enough food or money. All of my sisters and brothers go to school. One is already a teacher, and that is why I am trying to learn a profession. If I can get enough schooling, I can serve the country and my own family. I can also manage to have a life for myself. That is why I came to this school. We have a big family, and I have to help.

"My life is very different from my mother's. She just stayed in the family until she married. Life is much more difficult now because everybody is dependent on money. Long ago, money was unheard of. No one needed money. But now you can't even get food without cash. Times are very difficult. That is why the towns are creating day-care centers—so women can work and have their own lives. I have to work, for without it I will not have enough money for today's life.

"These are the problems I face and try to think about. How shall I manage to pick up this life so that I can live a better one? You know, we people of Kenya like to serve our parents when they are still alive—to help the family. But first, women have to get an education. Then if you get a large family and don't know how to feed it—if you don't have enough money for food—you can find work and get some cash. That's what I will teach my children: 'Get an education first.' " . . .

"If I had a chance to go to the university, I would learn more about health education. I could help women that way. If I were in a position of authority, I would really try to educate women. Right now, girls are left behind in education. It costs money, and parents think it is more important to educate boys. But I think that if people are intelligent, there is no difference. Girls and boys should be educated the same. I would make rules and teach women who are not educated and who have never been to school. They, too, must understand what today's problems are. If I have any spare time, I want to learn new things. I would like to learn how to manage my life, my future life, and have enough say in things so that my husband and I could understand each other and share life with our family. And I would change the laws so that men would understand women and their needs and not beat them as they do.

"I only hope that I will have a mature husband who will understand and discuss things with me."

A Leader of a Women's Cooperative

"Most women don't rely on their husbands now. If they get some money, well and good; and if they don't, they just try to get money for themselves—selling vegetables or making and selling handicrafts.

"Life is very difficult these days, and men are paying less attention to their wives. You see, men have wrongly just taken advantage of having more money. Instead of using money properly, to improve the lives of their families, they spend it on all the 'facilities' available at hotels. Instead of spending nights in their own homes, they fight at home and seek women outside—in the hotels. Many men cheat on their wives now because they are employed and have money. A husband can say, 'I have been sent as a driver to Nairobi' (or elsewhere), when he actually spends the money on girls.

"So women are fed up. They think now that relying on a man can be a problem. They say, 'We should try to do something ourselves. Then, whether we get something from our men or not, we still will be able to raise our children properly.' The problem that many women face is that they must become self-supporting. They either have no support from their husbands at all, or very little. And there is no law to protect them.

"But women *are* trying to do something for themselves, and if they had the capital they could establish businesses to help them make money. The main problem here is the money problem. Many women are alone. They need to earn for their families." . . .

"Women feel very hurt because they think their men don't recognize them as human beings. They are unhappy because of this inequality. I am lucky; my husband is good. He never took another wife. We are still together." . . .

Leader of a Village Women's Group

"We started with a missionary from England in 1966. Up to 1970, he taught the mothers about nutrition, and he tried to teach sewing also. We don't have a sewing machine. We just use a needle. Now the missionary has gone, so we are alone and we are trying to do the job. But we don't know if we can manage it. We are trying our best, but we don't know whether we are doing well or not."

Miss Janet explained that a medical field worker visits the village twice a week and that on Monday, Wednesday, and Friday, foodstuffs are distributed to the mothers of children under five years of age.

"The food comes from a missionary group in America. The mothers pay 3 shillings [U.S. $.42] per child, and with that money we pay for the transportation of the food from the coast. We give them five pounds in all—some wheat, some cereals, some cornmeal. We mix this together and teach them how to cook it. The mothers learn how to sew and cook at the same time. We teach them many things when they come here. They all want to learn how to sew and how to use a sewing machine—if only one were available. They want to make their own dresses and their husbands' shirts and to be able to mend everything. They would be happy if we could teach them those things.

"Now we are also trying to find money so we can pay someone to plough for us so that we can plant maize. If we succeed, we will teach the women—by demonstration—how to better care for their vegetable gardens. We must teach them these simple things. They want to learn more about agriculture and how to sew." . . .

"This woman says she has two [children]; three died in infancy. This woman has three alive, three dead. This woman: three died, five are alive. This woman: two alive, three dead. And this other woman: one died, one is alive. Children here often die from measles. This woman says her children were stillborn. And this young woman's baby stayed in her womb for ten months; it was dead. One child died of malaria when he was one and a half, and another died at age six. We have medicine for malaria, but we send the children to the health center for innoculations first. We also give medicine through a health assistant who visits us from time to time." . . .

"Some feel they can't answer that because they think perhaps this child or that will die. Some say, 'If some die, I will have at least a few remaining.' This mother, for example, thinks that four children is a good number to look after, educate, and feed. That woman thinks that if you have three children, if God helps, you'll be able to feed them. That one says four is a good number; she could look after them and educate them. She only has two, but she says that when she has four, she will join family planning."

Illiterate Village Woman

"I would like my children to get enough education. Women, you know, have more talents for doing things than men. It's only that men's talents are better recognized because they only concentrate on a few things. Women have got so many things to do that nobody ever looks at how many things they do. If I had a chance to learn something. I would like to learn how to help people. I would like to be a nurse."

Urban Family Planning Worker

"We get referrals from other workers. A nutritionist, for example, will come and tell us that she visited a home and feels that the home needs advice on family planning. So we go to the family and talk with them. We also go the child welfare clinic and talk with mothers there. We find that some do not feel free to talk about their problems there, so we go to their own homes and have further discussions. The woman might say, "I'm willing to practice family planning, but my husband is against it. I've tried to persuade him, but he has refused. So I don't know whether there is anything you can do for me.' " . . .

"Some say that they are able to care for their children—so they don't see why they should participate in family planning. Others say they don't see why they should plan their families, since the idea is not an African tradition but has been brought in by Westerners. Also, some men fear that when a woman starts using family planning, she is in that way exposed to the world and can go with any other man, since she knows she won't get pregnant. They don't trust their wives." . . .

. . . "Women fear medicines and they fear their husbands. There are a lot of fears, and it will take much time to catch on." . . .

"The men don't understand that family planning is good because it gives the woman time to rest between pregnancies. They don't care much about that, or about the condition of their children. You'll never see a man going to a family planning clinic. The men here believe: Let a woman be free of childbearing and she will go everywhere. They want a woman to have a child every year until she becomes old, while they are free to go gadding about. So if a woman doesn't keep on having children, her husband will get angry and take another wife."

A Male Doctor

"We have tetanus, measles, and—in the young ones—whooping cough. They also may have worms; when the children start growing, they crawl around and eat some sand and get worms. These are the things we deal with daily. We show women how to treat the children, and we encourage them to attend a health clinic. There is not too much anemia here, however. And kwashiorkor [acute protein deficiency] is not prevalent because some mothers understand what it is; they understand what they must feed their children to prevent it.

"This area is densely populated, and most of the women give birth at home, they know that if they come here we may not have a bed for them. At home, they are attended by local midwives—self-made midwives. They don't use sterile instruments. Sometimes the child is delivered outside, under a banana tree. There is not proper care—no cleanliness. That's why we get all this tetanus.

"We also have problems with the young wives. When they get married, they do not understand where to go for health care. They are ignorant of that. Then when they get pregnant, they do not know that we have what we call 'antenatal clinics.' It follows that when they have children, those children may not receive sufficient care. They may not come for vaccinations that prevent disease."

"We should have more field educators. Then, I feel, we could serve rural women. Another problem is transportation. We need vehicles and money for gasoline. But first of all, we need field workers."

A Female Midwife

The poor health here is not a poverty problem. There is plenty of land. The problem is the lack of knowledge about nutrition. That's one thing that has to be learned. If people knew how to utilize foods and what to plant to feed the children, it would be better. For example, here they plant groundnuts. They take these nutritious groundnuts to markets and sell them in order to obtain needed cash: then they buy bread, for example, from which they get less nutritional value. It doesn't make any sense. What we need here is health-nutrition education.

"Before, we had many nutritional field workers, but now our clinic is training those field workers to be nurses as well. They will be going out to teach both health and nutrition in the villages.

"We also have malaria here. In fact, most of our patients—adults and children— first come in to our clinic for malaria treatment. For the eight months I have served here. I have been encouraging mothers to come in not only for that, but also to bring their children to our healthcare class. Nutritional problems contribute to the mortality rate. Many children die from just measles. A child who suffers from measles and has not been well fed just wears down completely.

"The nutritional problem is also due to some of the superstitions and taboos. There are still many areas where people believe children should not eat eggs because, they say, the children will never talk. You just have to keep persuading people. When mothers realize that children who eat eggs *do* talk, they will convince other mothers that their children will not be harmed by eggs. But you can't *force* them to suddenly change what they do. First I ask them to try other things that give the same food nutrients as eggs. Women are not supposed to eat chicken either— although the men do. It's not fair.

UPPER-CLASS AND SCHOLARLY VIEWS

INDIA: MADHU KISHWAR ON LOVE AND MARRIAGE

Madhu Kishwar is an Indian scholar who has written widely on family issues; the next selection is from a magazine article by her on Indian and Western views of marriage. She reflects the influence of Western ideas, from her own education and

from channels such as Hollywood films. But she relies more heavily on polling data and the evaluation of traditional practices, which she juxtaposes with Western models.

• • •

The recent Eye-witness-MARG opinion poll conducted with 1,715 adults in the five metropolitan cities reported in SUNDAY magazine's 9–15 January 1994 issue that 74 percent of women and an almost equal proportion of men believe that arranged marriages are more likely to succeed than love marriages. Almost 80 percent of respondents felt that a young recently married couple—if they had a choice—should live with their parents. That these opinions are not a mindless hangover of "tradition" becomes evident as they report that over 90 percent of the same respondents believed that men should help with household chores, and eighty percent believed that, if they had one daughter and one son, they would leave an equal amount to each in any Will that they made. These poll results are supportive of some of my impressions gathered from talking to numerous young women, including my own students, as to why most young women are not very enamoured with "love" marriages.

Feminists, socialists and other radicals often project the system of arranged marriages as one of the key factors leading to women's oppression in India. This view derives from the West, which recognizes two supposedly polar opposite forms of marriage—"love marriage" versus arranged marriage. "Love marriages" are assumed to be superior because they are supposedly based on romance, understanding, and mutual love—they are said to facilitate compatibility. In "love marriages" the persons concerned are supposed to have married out of idealistic considerations while arranged marriages are assumed to be based on materialistic considerations, where parents and family dominate and deny individual choice to the young people. Consequently, family arranged marriages are believed to be lacklustre and loveless. It is assumed that in arranged marriages compatibility rarely exists because the couple are denied the opportunity to discover areas of common interests and base their life together on mutual understanding. Moving away from family arranged marriages towards love marriages is seen as an essential step towards building a better life for women. To it the social reformers add another favourite *mantra*—dowryless marriages as proof that money and status considerations play no role in determining the choice of one's life partner. The two together—that is, a dowryless love marriage—is projected as the route to a happy married life . . .

From Madhu Kishwar, "Love and Marriage," *Manushi: A Journal about Women and Society* 80 (1994): 11, 13–14, 18. Reprinted by permission of the author.

Self-Arranged Marriages

Critics of the family arranged marriage system in India have rightly focused on how prospective brides are humiliated by being endlessly displayed for approval when marriages are being negotiated by families. The ritual of *ladki dikhana,* with the inevitable rejections women (now even men) often undergo before being selected [is part of this process]. . . .

However, women do not really escape the pressures of displaying and parading themselves in cultures where they are expected to have self arranged marriages. Witness the amount of effort a young woman in western societies has to put in to look attractive enough to hook eligible young men. One gets the feeling they are on constant self display as opposed to the periodic displays in family arranged marriages. Western women have to diet to stay trim since it is not fashionable nowadays to be fat, get artificial padding for their breasts (1.5 million American women are reported to have gone through silicon surgery to get their breasts reshaped or enlarged), try to get their complexion to glow, if not with real health, at least with a cosmetic blush. They must also learn how to be viewed as "attractive" and seductive to men, how to be a witty conversationalist as well as an ego booster—in short, to become the kind of appendage a man would feel proud to have around him. Needless to say, not all women manage to do all the above, though most drive themselves crazy trying. Western women have to compete hard with each other in order to hook a partner. And once having found him, they have to be alert to prevent other women from snatching him. . . .

The humiliations western women have to go through, having first to grab a man, and then to devise strategies to keep other women off him, is in many ways much worse than what a woman in parent arranged marriages has to go through. She does not have to chase and hook men all by herself. Her father, her brother, her uncles and aunts and the entire *kunba* join together to hunt for a man. In that sense the woman concerned does not have to carry the burden of finding a husband all alone. And given the relative stability of marriage among communities where families take a lot of interest in keeping the marriage going, a woman is not so paranoid about her husband abandoning her in favour of a more attractive woman. Consequently, Indian women are not as desperate as their western counterparts to look for ever youthful, trim and sexually attractive marriage partners. . . .

In family arranged marriages, few parents are interested in marrying their young daughter to a divorced man, unless he is willing to marry a woman from a much poorer family (so that the family escapes having to pay dowry) or marry a divorced woman or widow. In India, relatively few men resort to divorce even when they are unhappy in marriage. The stigma attached to divorce for men, if not as great as for women, is at least substantial enough to get them to try somewhat to control themselves. They know that they cannot get away with having a series of divorces, as they do in the West, and yet find a young, beautiful bride 30 years their junior. But this is only true for marriage within tight knit communities where the two families have effective ways of checking on each other's background.

NIGERIA: IFI AMADIUME

Ifi Amadiume, a Nigerian scholar here studying a village in the Ibo (Igbo) territory—the same part of Nigeria referred to by Chinua Achebe (ch. 28)—has published widely on African gender and family traditions. From a locally promi-nent family, she spent time as a student in the West, and from that experience she feels she gained knowledge that she can apply to comparisons with Africa.

• • •

When the 1960s and 1970s female academics and Western feminists began to attack social anthropology, riding on the crest of the new wave of women's studies, the issues they took on were androcentrism and sexism . . . The methods they adopted indicated to Black women that White feminists were no less racist than the patri-archs of social anthropology whom they were busy condemning for male bias. They fantasized a measure of superiority over African and other Third World women. Black women's critique could not therefore be restricted to the male bias of social anthropology and not challenge White women. Drawing their data from the Third World, especially Africa, works on women produced in Europe and America have shown White women's unquestioning acceptance of anthropology's racist division of the world. In the debates in the West, the Third World supplied the 'raw data' for random sampling, citation and illustration of points. It baffles African women that Western academics and feminists feel no apprehension or disrespectful trivialization in taking on all of Africa or, indeed, all the Third World in one book. It is revealing that most such works have not been written by women from Third World nations; they, instead, tend to write about their particular ethnic group, their country or surrounding region. . . .

Igbo women were clearly unlike European women. . . . In their system, male attributes and male status referred to the biologically male sex—man—as female attributes and female status referred to the biologically female sex—woman. To break this rigid gender construction carried a stigma. Consequently, it was not usual to separate sex from gender, as there was no status ambiguity in relation to gender.

The flexibility of Igbo gender construction meant that gender was separate from biological sex. Daughters could become sons and consequently male. Daughters and

From Ifi Amadiume, *Male Daughters, Female Husbands. Gender and Sex in an African Society* (London: Zed Books, 1987), 3–4, 15, 89–90, 91, 132, 141. Reprinted by permission of the publisher.

women in general could be husbands to wives and consequently males in relation to their wives, etc. . . .

An insight into this remarkable gender system is crucial to the understanding and appreciation of the political status women had in traditional Igbo societies and the political choices open to them. . . .

It can, therefore, be claimed that the Igbo language, in comparison with English for example, has not built up rigid associations between certain adjectives or attributes and gender subjects, nor certain objects and gender possessive pronouns. The genderless word *mmadu,* humankind, applies to both sexes. There is no usage, as there is in English, of the word 'man' to represent both sexes, neither is there the cumbersome option of saying 'he or she,' 'his or her,' 'him or her.' In Igbo, *O* stands for he, she and even it, *a* stands for the impersonal one, and *nya* for the imperative, let him or her.

This linguistic system of few gender distinctions makes it possible to conceptualize certain social roles as separate from sex and gender, hence the possibility for either sex to fill the role. This, of course, does not rule out competition between the sexes, and situations in which a particular sex tends to monopolize roles and positions, and generates and stresses anti-opposite sex gender ideologies in order to maintain its own interests.

The two examples of situations in which women played roles ideally or normally occupied by men—what I have called male roles—in indigenous Nnobi society . . . were as 'male daughters' and 'female husbands'; in either role, women acted as family head. The Igbo word for family head is the genderless expression *di-bu-no.* The genderless *di* is a prefix word which means specialist in, or expert at, or master of something. Therefore, *di-bu-no* means one in a master relationship to a family and household, and a person, woman or man, in this position is simply referred to as *di-bu-no.* In indigenous Nnobi society and culture, there was one head or master of a family at a time, and 'male daughters' and 'female husbands' were called by the same term, which translated into English would be 'master.' Some women were therefore masters to other people, both men and women.

The reverse applied to those in a wife relationship to others. The Igbo word for wife, *onye be,* is a genderless expression meaning a person who belongs to the home of the master of the home. The other words for wife, *nwunye* or *nwanyi,* female or woman, also denote one in a subordinate, service or domestic relationship to one in a master position. It was therefore possible for some men to be addressed by the term 'wife,' as they were in service or domestic relationship to a master . . . There is a series of contradictions here, . . . there were, for example, women in master or husband roles and men in wifely or domestic roles. . . .

The use of these weapons of war must be understood in the context of polygynous marriage and compound structure. Of course it was possible for a man to turn to another wife when one wife refused to have sexual relations with him. The important point here is that women lived separately. The fact that a wife did not spend the night with her husband made it possible for her to use sexual refusal as a weapon of war without running the risk of marital rape. This is not the case for women in monogamous marriages who cling to the Christian idea of the sanctity and sexual exclusiveness of their matrimonial beds. Western feminists are still finding it difficult to have rape in marriage recognized as a legal offence.

Refusal of sexual compliance by a wife still proved effective even when a man had sexual access to other wives. Such refusal implied defiance and denial of rights, and was ultimately a challenge to a husband's authority over his wife. The customary solution was not for the man to take the law into his own hands; he had the option of calling in other members of the family or appealing to the formal patrilineage organizations. . . . Obviously the weapon of sexual denial was most effective when used collectively, either by all the wives of a man, all the wives of a patrilineage, or better still, all the women of Nnobi.

Indeed the earliest recorded mass protest movement by Igbo women was the Nwaobiala—the dancing women's movement of 1925. The basic demand of the movement, which was dominated by elderly women, was the rejection of Christianity and a return to traditional customs. Nnobi is mentioned as one of the three towns where a military escort was sent to restore order, as women there burnt the market, blocked the main road and piled refuse in the court house. Children were withdrawn from school and the market was boycotted. . . .

This resistance to conversion has been sustained by a few people in Nnobi. Eze Agba, the present priest of Idemili, does not go to church, nor does Nwajiuba, the 'male daughter,' who is head of the first and most senior *obi* in Nnobi. Together with a few other elderly people, they practise the indigenous religion—the worship of the goddess. The Christians refer to them as 'pagans' or 'heathens,' but they call themselves *ndi odinani,* the custodians of the indigenous culture. The youngest of them are middle-aged. All their children and grandchildren are Christians. Ironically, a new resistance against Christianity now springs from the Western-educated élite, who were in fact brought up in the church and educated in mission schools. They are now strong supporters and admirers of the indigenous religionists and preach the doctrine of cultural revival while condemning aspects of Western culture and dominance. . . .

Overwhelming evidence shows that women in Nnobi and in Igboland in general were neither more comfortable nor more advantaged from an economic point of view under colonialism. They had lost their grip on the control of liquid cash; men had invaded the general market, and women were becoming helpless in their personal relations with husbands. But, most important of all, pro-female institutions were being eroded both by the church and the colonial administration. . . .

. . . [W]omen's centrality in the production and sale of palm-oil and kernels in traditional Nnobi society gave them a considerable advantage over their husbands.

The introduction of pioneer oil mills mechanized the whole process of extracting the palm-oil and cracking the kernels. This, of course, meant a much higher oil yield which necessitated bulk buying by the agents of the mills and the channelling of most of the village's palm fruit to the mills. The main centre of production was therefore shifted from the family to the mills. At the same time, wives lost the near monopoly they enjoyed in the traditional method of production and the independent income they derived from it. . . . Instead of wives selling the palm-oil and keeping some of the profits, husbands now sold direct to the oil mills or their agents, and collected the money.

CHAPTER 30

REACTING TO THE POPULATION EXPLOSION

The population of the world, growing fairly rapidly since the seventeenth century, exploded from about 1900 onward. Improved sanitation measures reduced the incidence of many childhood diseases, allowing more people to live to adulthood and have children of their won. Public health operations, including attacks on disease-bearing insects and better disposal of human wastes, had striking results. Improved food supplies (despite widespread hunger and even famines in some areas) and medical care contributed to the same trend. Many governments had long favored population growth, which added to their labor force and armies—this had been a traditional goal in many societies. All these forces combined to generate a global population surge of several billions of people. Many population and environmental experts believe that stopping this surge is the most vital issue in the world today.

Western society had moved toward much lower birthrates by the early twentieth century; slow population growth was the result. This "demographic transition" was the product of new family decisions about the expense of rearing children, particularly as child labor opportunities declined, and about the amount of care children required in relation to other family goals. Improved artificial birth control, though not causing the demographic transition, contributed to it. Better methods of manufacturing rubber products, including condoms and diaphragms, provided key items in this process. By the 1960s many Western societies also eased prohibitions on abortion, despite some bitter, continuing disputes, particularly in the United States; even before this, illegal abortions had served as one common method of birth control. After World War II, Russia and Japan also dramatically reduced birthrates, relying considerably on abortions.

Expert opinion in the West, and in other countries such as India, largely came to view the world's twentieth-century population explosion as dangerous. Most economists and demographers argued that the new billions of people threatened resources and environmental quality for everyone and that the costs of sustaining such huge populations made rapid economic growth difficult in many Third World countries, where industrialization and living standards lagged.

Yet there was dispute over these issues and how to deal with them. The main issue was cultural: population control efforts and the dominance of economic goals ran afoul of a number of value systems. Religious groups, such as the Catholic Church and many Muslims, argued against artificial birth control and abortion, urging that taking human life was immoral and that nothing should encourage recreational or promiscuous sexuality. Gender issues were also involved. Birth control decisions often gave new power to women, allowing them greater control over their bodies and their family roles, and these implications could offend various traditional cultures. (On issues surrounding the complex interaction of cultural traditions and birthrates, see also chapter 29.) Even within Western countries, where birth control was widely practiced, there was no agreement on policy. Republicans in the United States attacked population control efforts by international agencies, because many Christian constituents in the country objected.

A 1994 United Nations population conference in Cairo, Egypt, dealt with these issues and these divisions. Expert opinion, urging population control through overt family planning and greater empowerment for women, was well represented. Western in origin and orientation, it commanded support from leaders in many parts of the world. Opposing views, including those from within Western society, were also represented, taking exception to elements of the final document.

Comparison, in this vital area, involves determining the nature of dominant "international" views and expertise, including the prominence given to education for women; what value systems are involved? Comparison also, of course, involves defining the reasons for objections from important groups. Finally, it involves identifying divisions within societies, including the Middle East as well as the West, over the role of religion in society, the conditions of women, and sexual morality. What leadership segments in the Middle East supported the United Nations document, for example, and why? More generally: in a clearly international forum, why did a pro–birth control, pro-woman document gain so much favor?

The 1994 conference was surprisingly harmonious, after several previous United Nations meetings had ended in bitter dispute. Although several groups took exception to key passages of the final statement, most were at pains to indicate their agreement with several goals of the conference as well. Why might the "international community" be moving toward somewhat greater concord on these issues, despite obvious religious and other divisions in the world at large?

The following documents are presented in two sections. First, basic differences of opinion are explored in comments addressed to and about the Cairo meeting. A speech by Gro Harlem Brundtland, the Norwegian prime minister, lays out the issues from the standpoint of secular Western expertise. This is followed by the views of a deputy public health minister from the vigorously Muslim government of Iran. The second section addresses the final report itself. A portion of the report indicates some of the principal recommendations about family planning goals and how to achieve them; to what extent did the document offer compromises over major areas of disagreement? Then, various national comments indicate some of the dissent even a careful document provoked, along with divisions within regions such as the Middle East; for example, Syria carefully stood apart from Iran.

Birthrates were falling in most of the world's regions by the 1990s, though much more rapidly in some areas (for example, Latin America) than in others. Population, of course, continues to gain, for it takes a long time for birth control to stabilize population size. Many billions of people will be added to the world before the middle to late twenty-first century, when the situation may stabilize. This huge growth raises important issues both for environmental quality and for world poverty.

Questions

1. What are the main disagreements over world population policy?
2. What societies particularly favor more vigorous birth control measures? How do they believe this goal can be achieved? Why is so much emphasis placed on women's education?
3. What groups particularly object to artificial birth control, and why?
4. In what sense was the Iranian objection to the United Nations majority especially sweeping? In what ways were Middle Eastern leaders divided over these policy issues? What kinds of leaders, from what Middle Eastern countries, supported the UN position?
5. What compromises permitted a successful conference report? How did most dissenters agree with some of the overall goals? What concessions did the pro–birth control groups accept in the final document?
6. Why, in an international forum, were pro–birth control, pro-woman views so dominant? Why, aside from some United States factions, is most of Western society eager for world population control?
7. Given actual cultural and gender divisions in the contemporary world, how rapidly, in your judgment, will new birth control measures gain ground in the world at large?

For Further Discussion

1. Ten years from now, what regions in the world will probably have the highest birthrates?
2. How does the population debate reflect the nature and importance of "world public opinion" in the late twentieth century?
3. Should more aggressive cultural efforts be undertaken to control world population? Would such measures have any chance of success where leaders and the

general public are not already convinced of the need for change? Is it in the interest of the United States to assist world birth control as actively as possible?

General Positions: Brundtland and Malekafzali

Gro Harlem Brundtland was the prime minister of Norway, a country where population control has been well established for more than a century and where environmental concerns run high. Norway has an active welfare state and contributes heavily, for a small country, in international aid. Hossein Malekafzali, interviewed for international television, was a deputy minister in the Public Health Ministry of Iran. His government, revolutionized in 1979 by a fundamentalist Shiite Muslim regime, represents traditional Muslim concerns that governments carry out the basic precepts of the religion. Religious beliefs, including hostility to artificial birth control and strong views about the roles of women, have kept birthrates relatively high in most Muslim regions, regardless of government policy.

• • •

THE NORWEGIAN PRIME MINISTER

This Conference is really about the future of democracy, how we widen and deepen its forces and scope. Unless we empower our people, educate them, care for their health, allow them to enter economic life, on an equal basis and rich in opportunity, poverty will persist, ignorance will be pandemic and people's needs will suffocate under their numbers. The items and issues of this Conference are therefore not merely items and issues, but building blocks in our global democracy.

It is entirely proper to address the future of civilization here in the cradle of civilization. We owe a great debt to [Egyptian] President Mubarak and to the people of Egypt for inviting us to the banks of the Nile, where the relationship between people and resources is so visible and where the contrast between permanence and change is so evident. . . .

Ten years of experience as a physician and 20 as a politician have taught me that improved life conditions, a greater range of choice, access to unbiased information and true international solidarity are the sources of human progress.

We now possess a rich library of analysis of the relationship between population growth, poverty, the status of women, wasteful lifestyles, and consumption patterns, of policies that work and policies that don't and of the environmental degradation that is accelerating at this very moment.

From United Nations, *Report of the International Conference on Population and Development*, Cairo, September 5–13, 1994, Addendum, 18–22. Reprinted by permission of the publisher.

We are not here to repeat it all, but to make a pledge. We make a pledge to change policies. When we adopt the Programme of Action, we sign a promise—a promise to allocate more resources next year than we did this year to health-care systems, to education, family planning and the struggle against AIDS. We promise to make men and women equal before the law, but also to rectify disparities, and to promote women's needs more actively than men's until we can safely say that equality has been reached.

We need to use our combined resources more efficiently through a reformed and better-coordinated United Nations system. This is essential to counteract the crisis threatening international cooperation today.

In many countries, where population growth is higher than economic growth, the problems are exacerbated each year. The costs of future social needs will soar. The punishment of inaction will be severe, a nightmare for ministers of finance and a legacy which future generations do not deserve.

But the benefits of policy change are so great that we cannot afford not to make them. We must measure the benefits of successful population policies in savings— on public expenditure on infrastructure, social services, housing, sewage treatment, health services and education.

Egyptian calculations show that every pound invested in family planning saves 30 pounds in future expenditures on food subsidies, education, water, sewage, housing and health.

Experience has taught us what works and what does not.

With 95 per cent of the population increase taking place in developing countries, the communities that bear the burden of rising numbers are those least equipped to do so. They are the ecologically fragile areas where current numbers already reflect an appalling disequilibrium between people and earth.

The preponderance of young people in many of our societies means that there will be an absolute increase in the population figures for many years ahead, whatever strategy we adopt here in Cairo. But the Cairo Conference may significantly determine, by its outcome, whether global population can be stabilized early enough and at a level that humankind and the global environment can survive.

It is encouraging that there is already so much common ground between us. The final Programme of Action must embody irreversible commitments towards strengthening the role and status of women. We must all be prepared to be held accountable. That is how democracy works.

It must promise access to education and basic reproductive health services, including family planning, as a universal human right for all.

Women will not become more empowered merely because we want them to be, but through change of legislation, increased information and by redirecting resources. It would be fatal to overlook the urgency of this issue.

For too long, women have had difficult access to democracy. It cannot be repeated often enough that there are few investments that bring greater rewards than investment in women. But still they are being patronized and discriminated against in terms of access to education, productive assets, credit, income and services, decision-making, working conditions and pay. For too many women in too many countries, real development has only been an illusion.

Women's education is the single most important path to higher productivity, lower infant mortality and lower fertility. The economic returns on investment in women's education are generally comparable to those for men, but the social returns in terms of health and fertility by far exceed what we gain from men's education. So let us pledge to watch over the numbers of school-enrolment for girls. Let us also watch the numbers of girls who complete their education and ask why, if the numbers differ, because the girl who receives her diploma will have fewer babies than her sister who does not.

I am pleased by the emerging consensus that everyone should have access to the whole range of family-planning services at an affordable price. Sometimes religion is a major obstacle. This happens when family planning is made a moral issue. But morality cannot only be a question of controlling sexuality and protecting unborn life. Morality is also a question of giving individuals the opportunity of choice, of suppressing coercion of all kinds and abolishing the criminalization of individual tragedy. Morality becomes hypocrisy if it means accepting mothers' suffering or dying in connection with unwanted pregnancies and illegal abortions, and unwanted children living in misery.

None of us can disregard that abortions occur, and that where they are illegal, or heavily restricted, the life and health of the woman is often at risk. Decriminalizing abortions should therefore be a minimal response to this reality, and a necessary means of protecting the life and health of women.

Traditional religious and cultural obstacles can be overcome by economic and social development, with the focus on enhancement of human resources. For example, Buddhist Thailand, Moslem Indonesia and Catholic Italy demonstrate that relatively sharp reductions in fertility can be achieved in an amazingly short time. . . .

In a forward-looking programme of action, it therefore seems sensible to combine health concerns that deal with human sexuality under the heading "reproductive health care." I have tried, in vain, to understand how that term can possibly be read as promoting abortion or qualifying abortion as a means of family planning. Rarely, if ever, have so many misrepresentations been used to imply meaning that was never there in the first place.

I am pleased to say that the total number of abortions in Norway stayed the same after abortion was legalized, while illegal abortions sank to zero. Our experience is similar to that of other countries, namely, that the law has an impact on the decision-making process and on the safety of abortion—but not on the numbers. Our abortion rate is one of the lowest in the world.

Unsafe abortion is a major public health problem in most corners of the globe. We know full well, all of us, that wealthy people often manage to pay their way to safe abortion regardless of the law.

A conference of this status and importance should not accept attempts to distort facts or neglect the agony of millions of women who are risking their lives and health. I simply refuse to believe that the stalemate reached over this crucial question will be allowed to block a serious and forward-looking outcome of the Cairo Conference—hopefully, based on full consensus and adopted in good faith.

Reproductive health services not only deal with problems that have been neglected, they also cater to clients who have previously been overlooked. Young people and single persons have received too little help, and continue to do so, as family-planning clinics seldom meet their needs. Fear of promoting promiscuity is often said to be the reason for restricting family-planning services to married couples. But we know that lack of education and services does not deter adolescents and unmarried persons from sexual activity. On the contrary, there is increasing evidence from many countries, including my own, that sex education promotes responsible sexual behavior, and even abstinence. Lack of reproductive health services makes sexual activity more risky for both sexes, but particularly for women.

As young people stand at the threshold of adulthood, their emerging sexuality is too often met with suspicion or plainly ignored. At this vulnerable time in life adolescents need both guidance and independence, they need education as well as opportunity to explore life for themselves. This requires tact and a delicately balanced approach from parents and from society. It is my sincere hope that this Conference will contribute to increased understanding and greater commitment to the reproductive health needs of young people, including the provision of confidential health services for them. . . .

Population growth is one of the most serious obstacles to world prosperity and sustainable development. We may soon be facing new famine, mass migration, destabilization and even armed struggle as peoples compete for ever more scarce land and water resources.

AN IRANIAN MINISTER IN INTERVIEW

CHRISTIANE AMANPOUR, Anchor: In Cairo, Sufis celebrate the feast day of one of their saints—a woman, by the way. Sufism is a sect of Islam, a mystical moderate sect that has often been the target of extremists, and it's precisely the emphasis put on giving women equal rights that's sending some of the Moslem nations into a frenzy. Some of those countries have boycotted this event, but Iran—one of the

From *CNN Specials,* transcript 380, interview of September 6, 1994. Reprinted by permission of the publisher.

nations with the fastest-growing populations—has urged Islamic countries not to boycott if they want their voices heard, and they do want changes made in the document. We spoke to Iran's Deputy Minister for Public Health, Dr. Hossein Malekafzali.

DR. HOSSEIN MALEKAFZALI, Iranian Dep. Minister for Public Health: First of all, is the abortion. We do not accept abortion as it is in the text, as a family planning tool, but also we think that we should have a good services, a good quality of services for family planning. Do not take the abortion, so abortion is not permitted, except in very few cases, when the life of the mother, for example, is in danger, and that time's OK, and also, the second point is the child education, or adults and education, regarding the sex education. This also is not permitted in Islamic countries like Iran, but when the men and women are in the age of marriage, then it is OK. We can have the sex education for those people who are ready to get marriage. This is the second point, and the third point is the importance of the family because the thing [is] that the family is the basic unit of the society, and the family is very clear. We don't need some vague words like 'union.' We don't know what is the meaning of the 'union.' We think about the family, the women and the men that have legally married, so we don't accept any other meaning or conception of the family, for example, men to men or women to women or to be together as a union. So these are not acceptable for us, and we hope during this discussion, we get to the good result, and we should have a good news for our people and our country.

AMANPOUR: *[interviewing]* Iran asked Islamic countries not to boycott this session, although some have boycotted. Why did you tell people not to boycott it?

DR. MALEKAFZALI: Because we think we will go and discuss about the matters. It is not good to boycott it. If to boycott, you are not ready to discuss about subject and the matter to change the sentences and the words. The way is to be here and to discuss, and to talk about that one, and they shall have to change it.

AMANPOUR: Some people, some Iranians, some newspaper articles, and indeed, some personalities in Iran, and in other Islamic countries, have suggested that this conference is a plot by the West to try to keep the Moslem population under control. Do you believe that that's what's going on here?

DR. MALEKAFZALI: I don't feel [so] now. It's really just [my] feeling that I hope it should not be . . . for the rest of the days that I am in the workshop or in seminar, and I hope that finally all the people, especially the Moslem people, will be happy for this conference.

FINAL DECISIONS AND DISSENTS: THE UN REPORT
AND VARIOUS NATIONAL REACTIONS

The following selections include basic recommendations from the United Nations report. These should be compared with the positions outlined in the first section: how close did the United Nations come to the recommendations of Western leaders? It is followed by some position statements from the Vatican (the Roman Catholic papacy) and various Muslim states including Iran, Syria, and the smaller nations of Yemen and the United Arab Emirates (this last is an oil-rich region linked with the West but with conservative chiefs, or emirs, in leadership positions). How did different Middle Eastern countries, all with Muslim majorities but some (like Syria) with secular governments, align themselves? How many objected outright to key UN provisions? How do rigorous Muslim and rigorous Catholic positions compare?

• • •

THE UN REPORT

The aim of family-planning programmes must be to enable couples and individuals to decide freely and responsibly the number and spacing of their children and to have the information and means to do so and to ensure informed choices and make available a full range of safe and effective methods. The success of population education and family-planning programmes in a variety of settings demonstrates that informed individuals everywhere can and will act responsibly in the light of their own needs and those of their families and communities. The principle of informed free choice is essential to the long-term success of family-planning programmes. Any form of coercion has no part to play. In every society there are many social and economic incentives and disincentives that affect individual decisions about child-bearing and family size. Over the past century, many Governments have experimented with such schemes, including specific incentives and disincentives, in order to lower or raise fertility. Most such schemes have had only marginal impact on fertility and in some cases have been counterproductive. Governmental goals for family planning should be defined in terms of unmet needs for information and services. Demographic goals, while legitimately the subject of government development strategies, should not be imposed on family-planning providers in the form of targets or quotas for the recruitment of clients.

Over the past three decades, the increasing availability of safer methods of modern contraception, although still in some respects inadequate, has permitted

From United Nations, *Report of the International Conference on Population and Development*, Cairo September 5–13, 1994, 46–49. Reprinted by permission of the publisher.

greater opportunities for individual choice and responsible decision-making in matters of reproduction throughout much of the world. Currently, about 55 per cent of couples in developing regions use some method of family planning. This figure represents nearly a fivefold increase since the 1960s. Family-planning programmes have contributed considerably to the decline in average fertility rates for developing countries, from about six to seven children per woman in the 1960s to about three to four children at present. However, the full range of modern family-planning methods still remains unavailable to at least 350 million couples world wide, many of whom say they want to space or prevent another pregnancy. Survey data suggest that approximately 120 million additional women world wide would be currently using a modern family-planning method if more accurate information and affordable services were easily available, and if partners, extended families and the community were more supportive. These numbers do not include the substantial and growing numbers of sexually active unmarried individuals wanting and in need of information and services. During the decade of the 1990s, the number of couples of reproductive age will grow by about 18 million per annum. To meet their needs and close the existing large gaps in services, family planning and contraceptive supplies will need to expand very rapidly over the next several years. The quality of family-planning programmes is often directly related to the level and continuity of contraceptive use and to the growth in demand for services. Family-planning programmes work best when they are part of or linked to broader reproductive health programmes that address closely related health needs and when women are fully involved in the design, provision, management and evaluation of services.

Objectives

The objectives are:

(a) To help couples and individuals meet their reproductive goals in a framework that promotes optimum health, responsibility and family well-being, and respects the dignity of all persons and their right to choose the number, spacing and timing of the birth of their children;

(b) To prevent unwanted pregnancies and reduce the incidence of high-risk pregnancies and morbidity and mortality;

(c) To make quality family-planning services affordable, acceptable and accessible to all who need and want them, while maintaining confidentiality;

(d) To improve the quality of family-planning advice, information, education, communication, counselling and services;

(e) To increase the participation and sharing of responsibility of men in the actual practice of family planning;

(f) To promote breast-feeding to enhance birth spacing.

Actions

Governments and the international community should use the full means at their disposal to support the principle of voluntary choice in family planning.

All countries should, over the next several years, assess the extent of national unmet need for good-quality family-planning services and its integration in the reproductive health context, paying particular attention to the most vulnerable and underserved groups in the population. All countries should take steps to meet the family-planning needs of their populations as soon as possible and should, in all cases by the year 2015, seek to provide universal access to a full range of safe and reliable family-planning methods and to related reproductive health services which are not against the law. The aim should be to assist couples and individuals to achieve their reproductive goals and give them the full opportunity to exercise the right to have children by choice. . . .

As part of the effort to meet unmet needs, all countries should seek to identify and remove all the major remaining barriers to the utilization of family-planning services. Some of those barriers are related to the inadequacy, poor quality and cost of existing family-planning services. It should be the goal of public, private and non-governmental family-planning organizations to remove all programme-related barriers to family-planning use by the year 2005 through the redesign or expansion of information and services and other ways to increase the ability of couples and individuals to make free and informed decisions about the number, spacing and timing of births and protect themselves from sexually transmitted diseases. . . .

In the coming years, all family-planning programmes must make significant efforts to improve quality of care. Among other measures, programmes should:

(a) Recognize that appropriate methods for couples and individuals vary according to their age, parity, family-size preference and other factors, and ensure that women and men have information and access to the widest possible range of safe and effective family-planning methods in order to enable them to exercise free and informed choice. . . .

Governments should take appropriate steps to help women avoid abortion, which in no case should be promoted as a method of family planning, and in all cases provide for the humane treatment and counselling of women who have had recourse to abortion.

In order to meet the substantial increase in demand for contraceptives over the next decade and beyond, the international community should move, on an immediate basis, to establish an efficient coordination system and global, regional and subregional facilities for the procurement of contraceptives and other commodities essential to reproductive health programmes of developing countries and countries with economies in transition. The international community should also consider such measures as the transfer of technology to developing countries to enable them to produce and distribute high-quality contraceptives and other commodities essential to reproductive health services, in order to strengthen the self-reliance of those countries. At the request of the countries concerned, the World Health Organization should continue to provide advice on the quality, safety and efficacy of family-planning methods.

VARIOUS NATIONAL VIEWS

17. The representative of the Syrian Arab Republic stated the following:

I should like to put on record that the Syrian Arab Republic will deal with and address the concepts contained in the Programme of Action . . . in full accordance with the ethical, cultural and religious concepts and convictions of our society in order to serve the unit of the family, which is the nucleus of society, and in order to enhance prosperity in our societies.

18. The representative of the United Arab Emirates stated the following:

The delegation of the United Arab Emirates believes in protecting man and promoting his welfare and in enhancing his role in the family and in the State and at the international level. We consider also that man is the central object and the means for attaining sustainable development. We do not consider abortion as a means of family planning, and we adhere to the principles of Islamic law also in matters of inheritance.

We wish to express reservations on everything that contravenes the principles and precepts of our religion Islam, a tolerant religion, and our laws. We would like the secretariat of the Conference to put on record the position we have expressed among the reservations that have been mentioned by other States on the final document.

19. The representative of Yemen stated the following:

The delegation of Yemen believes that chapter VII includes certain terminology that is in contradiction with Islamic Sharia [law code]. Consequently, Yemen expresses reservations on every term and all terminology that is in contradiction with Islamic Sharia. . . .

27. The representative of the Holy See [Vatican] submitted the following written statement. . . .

But there are other aspects of the final document which the Holy See cannot support. Together with so many people around the world, the Holy See affirms that human life begins at the moment of conception. That life must be defended and protected. The Holy See can therefore never condone abortion or policies which favour abortion. The final document, as opposed to the earlier

From United Nations, *Report of the International Conference on Population and Development,* Cairo, September, 5–13, 1994, Addendum, 141, 146–49. Reprinted by permission of the publisher.

documents of the Bucharest and Mexico City Conferences, recognizes abortion as a dimension of population policy and, indeed of primary health care, even though it does stress that abortion should not be promoted as means of family planning and urges nations to find alternatives to abortion. The preamble implies that the document does not contain the affirmation of a new internationally recognized right to abortion. . . .

. . . The intense negotiations of these days have resulted in the presentation of a text which all recognize as improved, but about which the Holy See still has grave concerns. At the moment of their adoption by consensus by the Main Committee, my delegation already noted its concerns about the question of abortion. The chapters also contain references which could be seen as accepting extramarital sexual activity, especially among adolescents. They would seem to assert that abortion services belong within primary health care as a method of choice. . . .

The intention therefore of my delegation is to associate itself with this consensus in a partial manner compatible with its own position, without hindering the consensus among other nations, but also without prejudicing its own position with regard to some sections. . . .

2. With reference to the terms "contraception," "family planning," "sexual and reproductive health," "sexual and reproductive rights," and "women's ability to control their own fertility," "widest range of family-planning services" and any other terms regarding family-planning services and regulation of fertility concepts in the document, the Holy See's joining the consensus should in no way be interpreted as constituting a change in its well-known position concerning those family-planning methods which the Catholic Church considers morally unacceptable or on family-planning services which do not respect the liberty of the spouses, human dignity and the human rights of those concerned. . . .

28. The representative of the Islamic Republic of Iran submitted the following written statement:

The programme of Action, although it has some positive elements, does not take into account the role of religion and religious systems in the mobilization of development capabilities. It suffices for us to know that Islam, for example, makes it the duty of every Muslim to satisfy the essential needs of the community and also imposes the duty of showing gratitude for benefits by utilizing them in the best possible way, as well as the duties of justice and balance.

We therefore believe that the United Nations should convene symposiums to study this matter.

There are some expressions that could be interpreted as applying to sexual relations outside the framework of marriage, and this is totally unacceptable. The use of the expression "individuals and couples" and the contents of principle 8 demonstrate this point. We have reservations regarding all such references in the document.

We believe that sexual education for adolescents can only be productive if the material is appropriate and if such education is provided by the parents and aimed at preventing moral deviation and physiological diseases.

CHAPTER 31

THE SPREAD OF DEMOCRACY AT THE END OF THE CENTURY

China, Africa, and the Middle East

During the decades after World War II, political systems in the world seemed divided among multiparty democracies (the West, India, Japan), Communist systems, and authoritarian regimes (see chapter 26). Many new nations, in Africa and elsewhere, initially tried democracy but then turned to military or one-man rule, if only because of huge internal divisions within their countries. Democratic ideals remained lively in areas such as Latin America and Africa, but the prospects often seemed bleak.

Beginning in the late 1970s, democracy began to spread. Western encouragement combined with a sense that democracy might be the best system to foster economic growth, an alternative to heavy-handed state planning. Democratic systems gained throughout Latin America and then in the former Communist zone of Eastern Europe. The Soviet Union sponsored more open political activity in 1985, and the collapse of the Soviet empire after 1989 brought democratic systems to most of the East European states plus Russia itself. In several noncommunist Asian states, such as South Korea and the Philippines, authoritarian regimes were replaced by more democratic governments. By the early 1990s democratic reforms were spreading in Africa, though still as a minority current. The establishment of democracy in South Africa, where the black majority had previously been excluded from voting as part of the racist apartheid system, was a huge achievement. In 1994 Nelson Mandela became that nation's first democratically elected president.

The late-twentieth-century spread of democracy thus involved both situations in which the majority of the people obtained the vote for the first time—the South African case—and situations where free elections, with open political discussion and choices among parties, replaced controlled voting systems—the more common ex-authoritarian or ex-Communist case.

Comparing democratic movements in areas where full democracy had not previously prevailed raises a number of analytical issues. The first involves causation: why, in places otherwise so different, did democracy begin to provide a more popular, acceptable political vocabulary? Do statements about democracy help get at the general, global conditions that gave this particular political system an edge in the final decades of the century?

Comparison also involves the usual, essential task of close analysis. Not all democratic movements were necessarily the same. Some doubtless reflected different contexts and traditions. Some may have been primarily for show, to win Western approval and support without real commitment.

Comparison is even more obviously essential in dealing with global exceptions to the democratic current. Democratic sentiment increased in China during this period, but the regime vowed to maintain a single-party, politically Communist system. China and the other Asian Communist nations of Vietnam and North Korea stood out as one of the main areas of resistance to the democratic current. Yet there was a democratic undercurrent, which raised important questions about the political future of these increasingly important societies.

The Middle East was another region where the surge toward democracy was halting. Israel was a well-established democracy, though with a long history of repressing the large Palestinian (Arab) minority. Turkey and a few other Muslim nations were democratic or made new gestures toward democracy, but in general Islam and democracy did not readily coincide at this point. Royal, military, or one-party rule was more common. Yet there were reasons for some new bows to democracy in this context, given the larger global patterns. The collapse of European Communism and the end of the Cold War made the West a more important player in Middle Eastern affairs, a fact that could generate more democratic influence.

The selections in this chapter come from three specific cases, all involving advances of democratic sentiment. Two of the cases—China and the Middle East—also involve some of the more resistant contexts. Comparison can thus highlight (1) assessment of the democratic phenomenon in general at this time period, (2) the search for general factors of causation, and (3) a juxtaposition of cases in which democracy surged forward (South Africa), gained ground amid inconclusive results (the Middle East), or had to yield, at least for a time, to overwhelming repression (China).

China had no deep democratic tradition. Confucianism, its dominant political culture, was strongly hierarchical. The Communist system that triumphed in the 1940s rejected Confucianism, though elements survived, but replaced it with a one-party dictatorship. In between, to be sure, from the 1890s to the 1930s, China did experience strong Western influence. A variety of reformers studied in the West and valued aspects of the West's political structure. The Chinese revolution of 1911 was led by Western-style reformers who hoped to install a democratic system, though their own movement, pressed by internal disarray and Japanese attack, turned increasingly authoritarian. Chinese Communists themselves moved to reform in 1978, but only in the economic sphere. Strict state controls were loosened, foreign enterprise was welcomed, and more market-driven economic activities sprang up. In this atmosphere, which included growing international contacts, a new democratic current arose, particularly among students. Many democrats believed that reform could not be complete without political change, and they bitterly resented the repressive, sometimes corrupt bureaucracy of the Communist state. The democratic surge crested in 1989 with a series of demonstrations in major cities including the capital, Beijing. The state cracked down, dispersing the demonstrators and arresting or exiling key leaders.

The Organization of African Unity backed democratic principles against the South African system of apartheid in a 1989 declaration issued in Harare, Ethiopia. African nationalists had long supported considerable unity among the African peoples, arguing that African cultures, though differing on specifics, had valuable common elements that deserved celebration and independence. This Pan-African sentiment provided some of the impetus to attacks on European colonialism, from the early twentieth century onward. As individual sub-Saharan African nations gained independence, beginning in the 1950s, they sought to institutionalize these ideas without abandoning individual governments in the former colonies. The Organization of African Unity was formed in 1963 to provide a loose format for mutual discussions. A key topic, inevitably, was South Africa, where a minority of white settlers had segregated and oppressed the black population for most of the twentieth century. The OAU attacked this apartheid (separation) system, as did many other nations in the world. By the late 1980s international opposition to the South African regime was growing, as was internal resistance, punctuated by periodic riots and other acts of disobedience. Government repression stiffened in the 1980s, with many arrests, but in 1990 a new white leadership began to offer concessions and, finally, democracy itself. Nelson Mandela, who headed negotiations for the black majority, had himself been a political prisoner for many years.

Israel gained independence as a Jewish state in 1948. For decades Jewish settlers, many of them nationalists, had been entering this historic territory, which was dominated by Arab settlers and held as a mandate territory (essentially, a colony) by Britain. The Jewish influx greatly accelerated in the aftermath of World War II. The British withdrew in 1948, amid bitter fighting among Jews and Arabs. Fighting continued, but the Jews had the upper hand; about seven hundred thousand Arabs fled, many of them abandoning property. Arab guerrilla action continued in subsequent years, amid Arabs who remained in Israel as well as those in neighboring states. In 1964 the dissident Arabs formed the Palestinian Liberation Organization. The PLO continually vowed to destroy Israel and emphasized terrorist attacks. But there were other tactics as well, and in the late 1980s efforts to appeal to world opinion helped prompt PLO leaders to de-emphasize terrorism in favor of broader political claims—including attacks on the Israeli state as fascist. Yet the organization remained illegal and partly terrorist, which might complicate democratic political claims. Apart from the special circumstances of the PLO, some observers believe that Islamic political ideals and democracy do not mesh well, because Islam emphasizes a religious state and does not encourage mass political interest. These judgments, however, are disputed, and of course traditions can change.

By the mid-1990s negotiations with Israel, strongly backed by the United States and West European powers, led to some compromise. Autonomous (but not independent) Palestinian territories were established within Israel, and the PLO took over their government with a pledge to set up a democracy. Disputes continued; Israeli anxieties about this new system included a belief that the PLO was not forming a democracy but was rather exercising authoritarian controls. Renewed tensions with Israel and accusations of PLO mistreatment of political opponents complicated the situation by 1997. It was not clear how much democracy would emerge.

Questions

1. What were the main arguments of the Chinese democrats? Why did some advocates anticipate difficulties in meshing democracy with Chinese traditions and current conditions?
2. Why did democracy provide a useful vocabulary in Organization of African Unity attacks on South Africa's racist regime? Why would member governments, most of them not themselves democratic in the 1980s, support these principles?
3. Do the African and Chinese statements display the same basic definition of democracy?
4. Is the PLO declaration democratic? Are there signs of undemocratic impulses—for example in the treatment of Arabs who had agreed to take office under Israeli rule? What factors might explain some PLO hesitation about untrammeled commitment to democracy? Are actual democratic procedures suggested?
5. What causes for increased global interest in democracy do the selections collectively suggest?
6. What differences were there in the definition and precision of democratic commitment among the Chinese students, the OAU, and the PLO?
7. What different world patterns favored or prevented democracy at the end of the twentieth century?

For Further Discussion

1. Is democracy an easy system to establish in areas that lack explicit democratic precedents? What kinds of conditions in the late twentieth century most favor the installation of new democracies?

2. Why, by the late 1980s and the 1990s, was Africa more friendly to the installation of new democracies than China or the Middle East?
3. Did Palestinian ideas about democracy reflect Muslim political traditions (see chapter 7), or was this a more purely secular movement?
4. Do you think democracy will spread further—for example to China?

CHINESE DEMOCRATIC DISSIDENTS: HAN MINZHU

The following passage was written by an anonymous dissident who used the Chinese words for "Han democracy" as his pseudonym (Han being China's dominant ethnic group). After the government crackdown, writing prodemocratic materials was extremely dangerous, though there was a postrepression flurry of such writings; some activists, including dissidents now in exile, have continued such efforts.

• • •

From a 1989 Poster at the People's University

. . . The government is facing bankruptcy. It has no money for education, no money for national defense, no money for energy, no money for transportation. It does not even have enough money to keep the living standard of ordinary state employees up to previous levels. Where has all the money gone? It has gone into the pockets of the corrupt officials, into the banking accounts of those big and small leaders who enjoy authority. The small amount of capital people have toiled to create has turned into Mercedes Benzes and Cadillacs—cars on the streets—and into hotels and restaurants [where these big and small leaders dine, stay, and entertain their relatives and friends for free]. . . .

Political corruption is the key problem [facing China]. The only weapon for smashing dictatorship and autocracy and ending all types of corruption that plague China is democracy. The power [presently] concentrated in individuals and a small portion of the people must be restricted; there must be some mechanism of checks and balances. The most basic meaning of democracy is that people themselves administer matters. In modern countries, direct democracy is not easy to implement; therefore, it is transformed into indirect democracy, that is, people entrust part of their power to others, and these people so entrusted are selected by the people. Since people are concerned that the people entrusted by them may abuse their power, they establish several institutions that counterbalance each other, and each institution is independently responsible to the people. This is the basic principle of democracy.

From Han Minzhu, ed., *Cries for Democracy: Writings and Speeches from the 1989 Chinese Democracy Movement* (Princeton: N.J. Princeton University Press 1989), 33–35, 72, 291–93. Reprinted by permission of the publisher.

What does China have? Nothing. On hearing [calls] for democracy, the government says that the level of the people is too low for the implementation of democracy. But they have forgotten that when Chiang Kai-shek [the head of the Nationalist Party] ran the country under a dictatorship, one of his rationales was that the people were unenlightened and that they needed "instructive politics." When the Communist Party was fighting Chiang Kai-shek and the Nationalist Party, the Party was eager to demand democracy. How can it be that the Chinese people are, after forty years of communist leadership, still in the same ignorant condition as they were under Chiang Kai-shek's regime? If some old people over the age of fifty are unenlightened, this can be blamed on Chiang Kai-shek. But people under the age of fifty were all born "under the red flag and raised under the red flag"! How can it be that forty years of communist rule have produced a citizenship that is not even fit for a democratic society? Is this self-contradictory? On the one hand, the party boasts in its propaganda of forty years of achievements. On the other hand, it denies those achievements [by denying that the people are ready for democracy]. What kind of logic is this? There is no way out for China if we do not have democracy now.

Of course, we do not expect to achieve a perfect and beautiful democratic society at once; after all, the Chinese people have not had a single day of a free life. The dictatorship of thousands of years, particularly that of the last several decades, has made most people unable to adjust quickly to a democratic society. But this is no excuse for not having a democracy. Certainly, at least urban citizens, intellectuals, and Communist Party members are as ready for democracy as any of the citizens who already live in democratic societies. Thus, we should at least implement complete democracy within the Communist Party and within the urban areas. Furthermore, during the process of urbanization, we should see that people in those [rapidly developing] rural areas become acquainted with democracy. . . .

. . . Chinese intellectuals still possess aristocratic airs: even in the revolutions for freedom and equality, they always give the impression of belonging to a class superior to others. Everyone is born equal; this issue was resolved during the Enlightenment. People's level of education may be high or low, and their contributions to society large or small, but they are all born as people and deserve the same respect. They all have the same right to pursue a good life. Intellectuals should not separate themselves from other classes and cannot claim special rights and interests. Intellectuals should be the spokesmen for the entire nation and the vanguard of social justice. The achievements of this movement that has been initiated by intellectuals will in the end be measured by the influence it has on the people. We should put our efforts into thinking about the future of the Chinese people. We should only be responsible to the people. Democracy and equality are like Siamese twins; one cannot have one without the other.

China's future rests on the shoulders of her one billion people. Only if we implement widespread democracy and more flexible economic policies will China have a way out. Democracy will check the hereditary system [that breeds corruption]; limited privatization will accelerate the development of the economy; freedom of speech and freedom of the press will provide effective supervision over the government; and equality will unite people into a greater force. But none of this will come to us: we must reach out and struggle for it.

From a 1989 Poster

—The unified slogans of the Provisional Students' Federation are:

1. Support the Communist Party and socialism! Support reform!
2. Long live democracy!
3. Oppose corruption in government; oppose special privileges!
4. Pledge to defend the Constitution to the death!
5. Patriotism is not a crime!
6. The press must speak the truth—oppose slander!
7. Long live the people!
8. Stabilize prices!
9. Every person is responsible for the fate of the nation!
10. The people's army protects the people!
11. Oppose violence! No persecution!
12. Demand dialogue!
13. Reform, patriotism, enterprise, progress!

Essay on a Banner in Tiananmen Square, Beijing, 1989

. . . We have never cast off the specter of authoritarianism which, either in the form of naked tyranny or in the cloak of idealism, never ceases to hover above our heads, sucking away the vitality of our nation and leaving our creativity sucked dry. Under the authoritarian system, the leaden weights of totalitarian politics and an unfree economy have suppressed the talents and wisdom of this most gifted people in the world. Mired in this stagnation, our nation becomes poorer and more backward with each passing day. China can be saved only if our political system is fundamentally transformed. Only democracy can save China. Our ancestors missed many opportunities for cultural regeneration. We cannot afford to miss another such opportunity. . . .

"There is never such a thing as a Savior." Let those who think themselves intelligent for advocating "old" authoritarianism or "new" authoritarianism [realize the impotence of their schemes] in the face of the people's immense power, and crawl off to console themselves. The realization of democracy cannot be dependent upon the benevolence of any person, as no dictator has ever shown a benevolent heart. Receiving alms while sitting locked in a cage is not democracy. Democracy can only be obtained by the struggle of the people themselves. It's nonsense to say that "the people would not know how to exercise democratic rights" or "democracy is not suited to the national conditions." Democracy has always been given to the government by the people, and *not* the other way round.

Democracy is not a mystical concept; it is a concrete way of conducting your life. It means that you can choose your own path in life. It means that you have the right to improve your government, the right to express your thoughts freely, and the right to write books and spread your beliefs. It means that every single person must abide by the law, while at the same time each may use your intelligence to the fullest to have a [bad] law rescinded. Under democracy, you can be free from the terror of a government which acts without the least regard for human life. In other words, if democracy is trampled upon, then the dark shadows of authoritarianism will be cast into the life of every individual. In China, it has always been the case that the officials are allowed to get away with arson while the people may not even light their lamps. In China, no one has ever valued the individual—"a human life isn't worth a cent." In China, no one has ever heeded the groans of the common people. It's about time, my fellow Chinese! We do not want to live our lives in this manner any more! . . .

It's about time, my fellow Chinese. Let us break our chains and become free human beings. Let us rise and free our country from the vicious cycle of its history.

With the blood of our devotion let us light the torch of truth, and let it illuminate this dark wilderness at this last moment before daybreak. The power of democracy is like a spring tide bursting through a tiny opening—once it starts coming there is no way to counter its force. This is where the hearts of the people lie. This is the march of history. How then can we let this hope be stifled?

SOUTH AFRICA: THE ORGANIZATION OF AFRICAN UNITY: HARARE DECLARATION, 1989

This declaration, issued from the meeting in Harare, Ethiopia, was designed to bolster democratic agitation in South Africa and to appeal to the growing crest of world opinion. It occurred at the time democracy was spreading in Russia and Eastern Europe, and doubtless it sincerely reflected this vital moment while also recognizing the new advantages these developments implied in the struggle against white racism in Africa.

• • •

1. Preamble

1.0 The people of Africa, singly, collectively and acting though the OAU, are engaged in serious efforts to establish peace throughout the continent by ending all conflicts through negotiations based on the principle of justice and peace for all.

2.0 We reaffirm our conviction, which history confirms, that where colonial, racial and apartheid domination exist, there can neither be peace nor justice.

3.0 Accordingly, we reiterate that while the apartheid system in South Africa persists, the peoples of our continent as a whole cannot achieve the fundamental objectives of justice, human dignity and peace which are both crucial in themselves and fundamental to the stability and development of Africa. . . .

5.0 We recognise the reality that permanent peace and stability in Southern Africa can only be achieved when the system of apartheid in South Africa has been liquidated and South Africa transformed into a united, democratic and nonracial country. We therefore reiterate that all the necessary measures should be adopted now, to bring a speedy end to the apartheid system, in the interest of all the people of Southern Africa, our continent and the world at large. . . .

7.0 We reaffirm our recognition of the right of all peoples, including those of South Africa, to determine their own destiny, and to work out for themselves the institutions and the system of government under which they will, by general consent, live and work together to build a harmonious society. The Organisation of African Unity remains committed to do everything possible and necessary, to assist the people of South Africa, in such ways as the representatives of the oppressed may determine, to achieve this objective. We are certain that, arising from its duty to help end the criminal apartheid system, the rest of the world community is ready to extend similar assistance to the people of South Africa.

8.0 We make these commitments because we believe that all people are equal and have equal rights to human dignity and respect, regardless of colour, race, sex or creed. We believe that all men and women have the right and duty to participate in their own government, as equal members of society. No individual or group of individuals has any right to govern others without their consent. The apartheid system violates all these fundamental and universal principles. Correctly characterised as a crime against humanity, it is responsible for the death of countless numbers of people in South Africa. It has sought to dehumanise entire peoples. It has imposed a brutal war on the whole region of Southern Africa, resulting in untold loss of life, destruction of property and

From John Pampallis, *Foundations of the New South Africa* (Atlantic Highlands, N.J.: Zed Books, 1991), 32–34.

massive displacement of innocent men, women and children. This scourge and affront to humanity must be fought and eradicated in its totality.

9.0 We have therefore supported and continue to support all those in South Africa who pursue this noble objective through political, armed and other forms of struggle. We believe this to be our duty, carried out in the interests of all humanity.

10.0 While extending this support to those who strive for a non-racial and democratic society in South Africa, a point on which no compromise is possible, we have repeatedly expressed our preference for a solution arrived at by peaceful means. We know that the majority of the people of South Africa and their liberation movement, who have been compelled to take up arms, have also upheld this position for many decades and continue to do so. . . .

13.0 In keeping with this solemn resolve, and responding directly to the wishes of the representatives of the majority of the people of South Africa, we publicly pledge ourselves to the positions contained hereunder. We are convinced that their implementation will lead to a speedy end of the apartheid system and therefore the opening of a new dawn of peace for all the peoples of Africa, in which racism, colonial domination and white minority rule on our continent would be abolished forever. . . .

15.0 We would therefore encourage the people of South Africa, as part of their overall struggle, to get together to negotiate an end to the apartheid system and agree on all the measures that are necessary to transform their country into a non-racial democracy. We support the position held by the majority of the people of South Africa that these objectives, and not the amendment or reform of the apartheid system, should be the aims of the negotiations.

16.0 We are at one with them that the outcome of such a process should be a new constitutional order based on the following principles, among others:

16.1 South Africa shall become a united, democratic and non-racial state.

16.2 All its people shall enjoy common and equal citizenship and nationality, regardless of race, colour, sex or creed.

16.3 All its people shall have the right to participate in the government and administration of the country on the basis of a universal suffrage, exercised through one person one vote, under a common voters' roll.

16.4 All shall have the right to form and join any political party of their choice, provided that this is not in furtherance of racism.

16.5 All shall enjoy universally recognised human rights, freedoms and civil liberties, protected under an entrenched Bill of Rights.

16.6 South Africa shall have a new legal system which shall guarantee equality of all before the law.

16.7 South Africa shall have an independent and non-racial judiciary.

16.8 There shall be created an economic order which shall promote and advance the well-being of all South Africans.

16.9 A democratic South Africa shall respect the rights, sovereignty and territorial integrity of all countries and pursue a policy of peace, friendship, and mutually beneficial co-operation with all peoples.

17.0 We believe that agreement on the above principles shall constitute the foundation for an internationally acceptable solution which shall enable South Africa to take its rightful place as an equal partner among the African and world community of nations.

THE PALESTINE LIBERATION ORGANIZATION: PROCLAMATION, 1988

The 1988 declaration was part of an internal reshuffling within this organization, operating from headquarters in exile. Using democratic language, PLO leaders hailed negotiations with leading (authoritarian) Arab states like Syria and also insisted on purging certain leaders assigned to regional responsibilities in the Gaza area (one of the areas heavily populated by Palestinians that is now part of the Palestinian autonomy territory). The PLO also refers to renewed agitation against Israel in its United National Command and seeks to raise support among ordinary Palestinians.

• • •

O masses of our people

Forty years have passed since the expulsion of our people from its homeland and the attempt to liquidate its existence and its national existence, but our valiant people is stronger than the expulsion and the efforts to suppress its identity. Its national revolution has succeeded, through the continuous processions of martyrs and victims, in thwarting those attempts and in gaining international recognition for its legitimate national rights [and] for its exclusive representation by the PLO. In the forefront of these rights is the right of return, self-determination, and the establishment of an independent national state under the leadership of the PLO.

The achievements of the Palestinian revolution, the glory of the magnificent uprising which is entering its sixth month, are continuing tirelessly and relentlessly. When our people declared the uprising, it understood the

From Shaul Mishal and Reuben Aharoni, *Speaking Stones: Communiqués from the Intifada Underground* (Syracuse, N.Y.: Syracuse University Press, 1994), 93–95. Reprinted by permission of the publisher.

scale of the sacrifices that would be required for liberation and independence.

Our people, who declared the uprising, is aware of the dimensions of the sacrifice that will be demanded of it on the road to national liberation. The people consciously pay the price for its aspirations in the form of victims, wounded, detainees, and deportees. [It] grasps the nature of the enemy with whom it is locked in struggle, his barbarism and the actions of his fascist forces, such as the use of poison gas, bullets, house demolitions, and a criminal war of starvation. Despite this, our people has chosen the road of struggle and sacrifice as the only road through which to achieve its national rights.

Just as our people grasps the essence of the enemy, so it is also aware of the character of the war it is waging. Our war is a lengthy one. It is a war of attrition in which each passing day raises the economic and political price paid by the occupier, intensifies his international isolation, exposes the ugly truth about the occupation, and shatters the illusion of coexistence that the enemy has tried to foster. Moreover, it reinforces our legitimate national rights.

The glorious December uprising was launched to demonstrate the solid strength of the fighting array and to raise the [people's] struggle and its national cause to a new level of which the axis is the continuation of the struggle and the resistance and escalation of the confrontation toward civil disobedience.

The United National Command of the Uprising, as it pursues the struggle with you and through you, under the banners of our sole legitimate representative, the PLO, reaffirms our people's readiness for great sacrifices and devotion, to move toward civil disobedience, meaning primarily the liberation of our masses from the occupation and all that this entails: sacrifices and belt-tightening, storing basic foodstuffs, storing medicines, suffering for the sake of the homeland, and relentless and tireless forbearance and determination. The United Command stresses the determination of the uprising masses to remove all the obstacles on the road to civil disobedience, involving especially the resignation of all [the personnel in] the mechanisms of the occupation such as the tax apparatus, the police, and the appointed municipalities.

O our glorious masses,

The United National Command welcomes the removal of the obstacles on the road to normalization of Palestinian-Syrian relations and on the road to perfection of Palestinian national unity through a constructive democratic dialogue. Marginal disputes must not be encouraged. We must turn to democratic dialogue as the only means for settling internal disputes. [The

United Command] condemns those who deviate from the unity of our people and are splitting its ranks, . . .

2. The immediate resignation must be effected of department directors in the Civil Administration in Gaza, especially Kheyri Abu Ramadan in the health department and Muhammad al-Jiddi in the education department. Let there be no mistake: the masses of the uprising and the shock squads will punish those who deviate from the will of the people and the decisions of its Command when they see fit.

3. Establishment of the popular committees and their dispersal in all areas must be completed. There must be no delay in executing this struggle mission. The other functional popular committees have the task of organizing the inhabitants' lives and ensuring proper services—food supplies, medicine, education, and security. For the popular committees are the government of the people and the uprising, a substitute for the collapsing occupation mechanisms, and a political tool for introducing civil disobedience and making it succeed.

4. Beat vigorously policemen, collaborators, and members of appointed municipal councils who, by not resigning from the service of the enemy, deviate from the national consensus.

ABOUT THE EDITOR

PETER N. STEARNS is Heinz Professor of History and Dean of the College of Humanities and Social Sciences at Carnegie Mellon University. He introduced a world history course into the General Education program at Carnegie Mellon in the mid-1980s, and has taught it every semester since. He has written a number of texts and essays in world history, and has contributed to world history projects for the College Board and other agencies. He is an active member of the World History Association.

He is also past Vice President of the American Historical Association and its Teaching Division. A social historian by training, he has written over fifty books on topics in U.S. and European social history as well as world history. At Carnegie Mellon, he has won the university's major teaching prize and has been active in various aspects of curriculum planning. He is also increasingly interested in approaches to training students in the skills of historical analysis, including comparison, and has participated in a number of innovative exercises and assessments.

medieval